The word 'quisling' is used all over the world as a synonym for traitor or treachery. The original Quisling – the man behind the word – was a Norwegian army officer of exemplary merits who earned notoriety when he collaborated with the German enemy on the first day of Norway's entry into the Second World War. Quisling's *coup d'état* in Oslo on 9 April 1940 was immediately denounced by the BBC and condemned as an act of arch-treason by the British press, who within days launched the general concept of 'quisling' and 'quislingism' to warn the world against collaborators. Even Churchill spoke of 'the vile race of quislings'.

This first Quisling – what was he like, and with what justification does he carry the heavy burden of his fame?

This biography is able to draw extensively on the 'missing' Quisling archives, discovered in Oslo a decade ago, and on the complete Quisling papers finally made available after the death of Quisling's wife. The picture that emerges is of a remarkable career, spanning from Quisling's pioneering work for the League of Nations in the Ukraine after 1918, to his diplomatic ventures in Moscow in the 1920s, and to his attempts to adopt fascist political ideas – Italian at first, then German – in Norway during the 1930s. During the Second World War, as Hitler's ally, he acquired a more decisive hand in the ruling of the country than any other of the Führer's vassals. Accordingly most Norwegians hated him, and after the liberation in 1945 he was tried and executed for high treason.

Quisling's ideas – a blend of Christian fundamentalism, scientific insights and Hegelian dialectics blended in a home-grown philosophical system called 'Universism' – failed to attract even his followers. His policy of siding with National Socialism, in what he thought was a stage towards World 'Universism', proved disastrous, and before his death he bitterly accused Hitler of betraying the idea of Europe for the sake of German imperialism. Quisling's career thus seemed absolutely futile; yet his name has continued to live until this day. This book, abridged from a two-volume study in Norwegian, is unique in drawing on such a comprehensive body of source material from Nordic, German, Italian and Russian archives, and from family archives now in the United States.

HANS FREDRIK DAHL was born in Oslo in 1939, and was educated as an historian at the University of Oslo where he received his doctorate in 1976 and where he is currently Professor of Media and Communication.

Quisling

A study in treachery

HANS FREDRIK DAHL

Translated by Anne-Marie Stanton-Ife

CAMBRIDGE
UNIVERSITY PRESS

PUBLISHED BY THE PRESS SYNDICATE OF THE UNIVERSITY OF CAMBRIDGE
The Pitt Building, Trumpington Street, Cambridge CB2 1RP, United Kingdom

CAMBRIDGE UNIVERSITY PRESS
The Edinburgh Building, Cambridge, CB2 2RU, UK   http://www.cup.cam.ac.uk
40 West 20th Street, New York, NY 10011–4211, USA   http://www.cup.org
10 Stamford Road, Oakleigh, Melbourne 3166, Australia

First published 1999

Printed in the United Kingdom at the University Press, Cambridge

Typeset in Minion 10.5/13.5pt   [CE]

A catalogue record for this book is available from the British Library

Library of Congress Cataloguing in Publication data
Dahl, Hans Fredrik.
[Vidkun Quisling. English]
Quisling: a study in treachery / Hans Fredrik Dahl: translated by Anne-Marie Stanton-Ife.
p.   cm.
'... abridged from a two-volume study in Norwegian ...' – Pref.
Included bibliographical references and index.
ISBN 0 521 49697 7 (hb)
1. Quisling, Vidkun, 1887–1945.   2. Fascists – Norway – Biography.
3. Politicians – Norway – Biography.   4. Norway – Politics and government – 1905–   I. Title.
DL529.Q5D3413   1999
948.104′1′092 – dc21   [B]   98–35102   CIP

ISBN 0 521 49697 7 hardback

Contents

Illustrations

Acknowledgements

The international archival research behind this book has been made possible by the support from the Ruhrgas Foundation, the American-Scandinavian Foundation, and the Norwegian Non-Fiction Writers' Association. The English-language edition, condensed from the original Norwegian two-volume edition by Nils Johan Ringdal, has been revised and updated by the author before being published with the aid of grants from the following institutions: The Norwegian Research Foundation, MUNIN (Marketing Unit for Norwegian International Non-Fiction) and Fritt Ord. To all the institutions involved I extend my warm appreciation.

HFD
Oslo, October 1998

Abbreviations

AA Auswärtiges Amt. The German Foreign Ministry, Berlin

ADAP Akten zur deutschen auswärtigen Politik, Series D and E. Documents from the German Foreign Ministry

APA Aussenpolitisches Amt der DNSAP. The Foreign Bureau of the German Nazi Party, headed by Alfred Rosenberg

AT Arbeidstjenesten, the NS Labour Service, a scheme for mobilising the youth for the work-force in Norway 1940–5

DNSAP Deutsche Nationalsozialistische Arbeiterpartei, the German Nazi Party

DRZW Das deutsche Reich und der Zweite Weltkrieg, the official German history of the Second World War (see bibliography under Kroener, Hans et al.)

FF Fritt Folk, the NS newspaper, published in 1936 and 1940–5

HT Historisk Tidsskrift, Norwegian journal of history

GS Generalstaben, the Norwegian General Staff

ICRR International Commission for Russian Relief, a League of Nations institution headed by Fridtjof Nansen

KTB Kriegstagebuch, war diary of the German High Command

NA Universitetsbiblioteket i Oslo, Norske avdeling, the National Division of the University Library of Oslo

NBL Norsk biografisk Leksikon, the Norwegian national biographical dictionary in 19 vols. Oslo 1923–83

ND Nuremberg Documents, published evidence from the Nuremberg Trials

NNT Nytt Norsk Tidsskrift, a Norwegian quarterly of history and politics

NS and *NS* Nasjonal Samling, National Union, Quisling's party and paper 1933–45

NSDAP National-socialistische deutsche Arbeiterpartei, the German Nazi Party

NSM Nasjonal Samling Meddelelser, NS announcements

NSPM Nasjonal Samling Propagandameddelelser, NS propaganda announcements

OKW Oberkommando der Wehrmacht, the German High Command

Ot.prp., Ot.forh. Odelstingstidende, forhandlinger – Norwegian parliamentary papers

ProMi Reichspropagandaministerium, Berlin, the Nazi Ministry of Propaganda headed by Goebbels

RFSS Reichsführer SS, Heinrich Himmler

RK Reichskommissariat, Reichskommissar, the title of the German official in an occupied country

RKVB Verordnungsblatt des Reichskommissars, the official gazette of the Reichskommissar

RSHA Reichssicherheitshauptamt, headquarters of the German State and Secret Police, Berlin

Rt. Norsk rettstidende, the official court register of Norway

SD Sicherheitsdienst, the German secret police

SKL, Sk. Seekriegsleitung, the German Admiralty

SS Schutzstaffel, originally the security guard of the German Nazi Party, after 1933 the central state police and security organisation of Germany

St.forh., St.med., St.prp. Stortingsforhandlinger, Norwegian parliamentary papers

Straffesak Straffesak mot V. A. L. J. Quisling, verbatim court proceedings of the Quisling trial in 1945, published in Oslo 1946

TFAH Tidsskrift for arbeiderbevegelsens historie, a Norwegian journal of labour history

TT Tidens Tegn, an Oslo daily newspaper 1911–41

UiB, UiO Universitetet i Bergen, Universitetet i Oslo (University of Bergen, University of Oslo)

UK Undersøkelseskommisjonen av 1945. The official Norwegian war investigation commission, established 1945

UKI Innstillling fra Undersøkelseskommisjonen, recommendations of the Investigation Commission, published in 5 vols., Oslo 1946–7

VG Verdens Gang, a newspaper

* indicates private archives of which the author holds photocopies of all material cited.

A list of archive sources can be found on pp. 419–21.

Innocent?

'I am innocent!' On the fortress rampart, these words were barely audible in the night wind. Vidkun Quisling had been fetched from his cell at 2 o'clock in the morning and was standing up against a wall inside the open wooden enclosure which had been erected against the gun tower of Akershus fortress. Wearing plus-fours and a grey woollen sweater, the condemned man was blindfolded and his arms tied to the planks behind him. A piece of white paper had been pinned to his heart so that the ten marksmen could get a better aim. Everything happened very quickly. Beyond the command to open fire, nothing was heard during the execution, nothing except Quisling's protestations of innocence.

The innocence Quisling felt at this point was something more than his usual protest that the legal system had misconstrued his motives and had misunderstood his mission. Indeed, he had protested his innocence both to the High Court in August and in the Supreme Court in the second week of October 1945. He tirelessly maintained that his coup of 9 April 1940, his leadership of the Norwegian Nazi party Nasjonal Samling – National Union – and his functioning as Minister President for German-occupied Norway had all been in the best interests of the nation.

But with the death sentence, which had been delivered unanimously in both the higher courts, there rose in him the sense of another, higher kind of innocence. What was about to happen was not simply the conclusion of an unjust sentence: 'There must be some deeper meaning to this,' he wrote to his brother from prison. 'In fact I am dying a martyr's death.' The agony he had suffered during the days leading up to his death became a necessary part of his martyrdom in bringing the Kingdom of Heaven to earth in the fulfilment of a divine plan. He had, of course, made mistakes, even expensive ones. He had believed in German National Socialism as a world power in the service of God and had made common cause with it for five difficult years. In his prison cell, he had to admit that National Socialism was clearly flawed in respect of its teachings on race among other things. For Quisling it was nevertheless a force that would, when the time came, prepare the way for God's kingdom on earth. He was to be punished by death for his convictions, but he was by no means the first: Christ himself and, in Norway, Olav Haraldsson in 1030 had both died for the same cause. Jesus, St Olav, Quisling. As a link in such a chain, his execution acquired meaning.

High-flown prison meditations such as these stood in sharp contrast to the unassuming and modest manner which had always, even during the last few days of his life, been his way. In fact, both modesty and megalomania were traits in Quisling's public character. He was a religious politician, and a party leader who prided himself on a historical consciousness which enabled him to judge when to stand on the sidelines of events, when to intervene, and when to let things be. This hubris prevailed in what he said and wrote in confinement in his cell, but had also coloured his entire leadership: he felt that he had been chosen. His inner convictions in this respect were strong, despite being manifested in shy, hesitant, even clumsy outward behaviour. Certainly he was not like other political leaders. For his followers, the outstanding spiritual strength underlying Quisling's shy and inward character compensated for his lack of such conventional political qualities as adaptability, shrewdness or cynicism.

His political influence, however, owed more to an extraordinary series of coincidences than anything else. As a party leader in the 1930s, he was an obvious failure. But sheer chance led him to Hitler's study in Berlin on 14 and 18 December 1939, fifteen weeks after the outbreak of the Second World War. What followed from the conversations here drew him into the maelstrom of world history.

Was he a traitor? In the eyes of the world, clearly he was. In his own view, being branded a traitor was the price he had to pay for his insight into the ways of God. It amazed him that so few Norwegians had taken his insights seriously, and now on the fortress rampart it was as though the majority of the population was lining up to execute him.

Nine bullets penetrated the white paper pinned to his heart.

After the lieutenant in charge of the platoon had pulled the trigger and delivered the *coup de grâce* to the temple of the prostrate figure, the police coroner certified Quisling dead at 2.40 on the morning of 24 October 1945.[1]

---

[1] Account based on the official police report and on interviews with several participants and witnesses to the execution, 24 October 1945; interview with Kjell Juell in the daily *VG* 29 September 1978; 'Jeg skjøt Quisling': interview with members of the platoon, *Dagbladet* 12 March 1988; report from Copenhagen chief of police Aage Seidenfaden, autumn 1945, *Dagbladet* 23 October 1985; various prison letters from Quisling to his family in UBO MS fol. 3920.

Back in Norway

I think that things in Norway seem extremely difficult with regard to
the general situation ... we shall not emerge from this business without
some kind of major upheaval. At such times a Norwegian ought to be in
Norway.   *Quisling, Moscow, November 1926*[1]

A few days before Christmas 1929, a tall, well-built man in a fur coat and a
Russian hat got off the Stockholm train at Oslo's East Station with his wife.
The large number of suitcases, baskets, trunks and boxes piled up on the
platform indicated that former legation secretary and General Staff officer
Captain Vidkun Quisling had returned to Norway for good.[2]

Nearly twelve years had passed since he had first left. He had lived abroad
for nine years: five and a half in Moscow; nearly two and a half in Finland;
one in the Balkans, Armenia and Paris, as well as short stays in London,
Geneva and Berlin. He had crossed the Soviet border twelve times on
various missions: on behalf of the Norwegian Ministries of Defence and of
Foreign Affairs, the League of Nations, Fridtjof Nansen's High Commission
for Refugees and also for a Russian–Norwegian timber company. By
contemporary standards it was a rare cosmopolitan who was now returning
to Norway.

The Quislings brought with them a large collection of paintings and
antiques which they had bought in Moscow. Vidkun Quisling also carried
with him schemes for a new organisation and plans for political action in
Norway. While he had been abroad, he had also spent time on serious
studies in the natural sciences, philosophy and history, and in compiling
copious notes for a self-made philosophical system which he called 'Universism'. The system had not been completely worked out, however. Over the
previous few years its author had been increasingly plagued by the feeling
that now was the time to act, not to interpret the world but to change it. He
had, however, been delayed in Moscow for two years before he was able to
wind up his affairs. When he eventually did so, it was with a feeling of

---

[1] Quisling in a letter to his parents 25 November 1926, UBO MS fol. 4096 I, 29.
[2] The Quislings left Moscow on 14 December and arrived in Oslo on 19 December 1929. He
gave his first interview to the Norwegian press in *Tidens Tegn* (*TT*) on 20 December 1929.

intense homesickness and an ambitious 'and perhaps even all-consuming interest in politics'.[3]

His ideas were based solely on theory. On his arrival, Quisling had no experience whatsoever of public life. He had never belonged to any political party, scarcely set foot in any organisation apart from officers' clubs, and was completely unknown to the Norwegian public. Still, he considered himself qualified to intervene in the domestic situation. This was due not only to the political ideas that he had developed but also to the understanding of organisation and social systems which he had acquired as a General Staff officer. It was a soldier who was coming home, a soldier with a head full of politics.

THE OFFICER

It was no ordinary programme the budding politician had returned with. The plans for Norwegian Action (Norsk Aktion) were laid out on a large, military-style campaign map with national, regional and local units sketched on it in columns and rows like an army. The lowest unit in the organisation was to recruit members according to the model of the Soviet Communist Party. Apart from this, Norsk Aktion was clearly inspired by l'Action Française, the militant wing of the French right and a core organisation of French fascism. Its purpose was, like the French model, to bring about a fundamental change in the Constitution. Quisling planned to transform the Norwegian parliament, the Storting, into a bicameral organisation, whereby the existing parliament would constitute one chamber, while the other would consist of corporate elected representatives from the working population – just like the Soviet councils.[4]

Many Norwegians at that time were attracted by the idea of strengthening the government and reducing the influence of the parliament so as to get rid of the ceaseless and unpleasant cabinet crises of the day. The idea of using a Soviet model in this context was, however, quite original. Quisling always maintained that his main political ideas had taken shape during his first year in Russia; the papers he brought back with him in 1929, however, show that most of his work on plans for both the Constitution and the new party had been carried out between 1925 and 1927, that is, in the latter part of his stay

---

[3] Quisling, in *Studentene fra 1905* (1930).
[4] The main sources are notebook III, UBO MS fol. 3920 VII, 28–43, and various undated MS pages on parliamentary reforms, author's archives.*

in Russia. However, of greater interest than this is the conceptual structure of Quisling's first comprehensive political plans.

The plans were thought out in a clear, military way. It is the orderliness and the mentality of a staff officer which characterises them, rather than the practical experience of a soldier of the line. To understand them, one has to take into account the entire career of their author.

Quisling always used to say that he had become an officer on the crest of the national euphoria of 1905, which was the year of his matriculation and also the summer of Norway's secession from the hundred-year-long union with Sweden. Becoming an officer was, moreover, the career move that afforded him the best opportunity to develop his interests, as the gifted young student from Skien in Telemark had a talent both for the humanities and for the natural sciences but no clear idea of how these talents could be channelled in any one academic direction. The generalist nature of military education at that time made the career of an officer a natural choice.

His first step was to enrol as a cadet in the War College (Krigsskolen) in Kristiania (later Oslo). In those days, competition was stiff and excellent grades were essential. His examination marks were the highest of the 250 candidates. His cadetship coincided with the national crisis of 1905. The plebiscite on 13 August gave overwhelming support for secession, but the subsequent negotiations between Norway and Sweden over the dissolution of the Union revealed that the King and government in Stockholm were not going to accept Norway's exit on her own terms. Tensions rose from week to week. The cadets therefore felt that there was a chance that they would be needed in a regular war with Sweden, as is shown by the young Quisling's letters to his parents that summer. 'People shouted Hurrah in wild excitement.'[5] But the crisis blew over. His remaining time at the Academy was uneventful. In the late autumn of 1905 he stood guard when the new royal family – the Danish prince Carl and his wife Maud, daughter of Edward VII, together with their two-year-old son Alexander – were cheered into the town as King Haakon, Queen Maud and Crown Prince Olaf. 'The new royal family gives a very favourable impression and will certainly win us all over in love and affection,' he told his parents. The young prince in particular 'has already waved his hand and stolen the hearts of all ladies and probably the men's too'.[6] In the summer of 1906, the cadets went their

---

[5] Quisling, letter to his parents 18 September 1905, in Collection Jon Qvisling.*

[6] Letter to his parents 27 November 1905, ibid. His first impression of King Haakon was very favourable. Later, when he met the King during his visits to the Military Academy, he

separate ways. Quisling chose to pursue his career in the army and joined the most senior training level at the Military Academy (Den militære Høyskole), which took two years to complete. Instruction took place on the Academy's premises at the Akershus fortress. In the final examination, Quisling averaged 1.18 – the Academy's best result since its establishment in 1817. To mark the occasion, he was given an audience with the King.[7]

On 1 November 1911 he was assigned to the General Staff as a junior member (aspirant) aged twenty-four. There, he had to serve in all the various divisions, eventually arriving in Intelligence. With his talents and his diligence, in the normal course of events Quisling would have risen steadily through the ranks of the military hierarchy and certainly have been made a general during the 1940s.

His way of thinking was greatly influenced by the operational methods of the Staff. Throughout his life, he believed that anything was possible provided there was a good plan that had been elaborated in a Staff headquarters. With a good plan, a Staff plan, a plan based on a military model, even political missions could be carried out successfully. His experiences from the Soviet Union no doubt reinforced his martial view of politics. Even though Quisling was critical of Bolshevik policies, he held their organisational skills in the highest regard, regularly cutting out articles, pictures and maps from the Soviet press showing how the Bolsheviks dealt with various challenges, and pasting them into his bulging notebooks.

Consequently, he planned to build his party, Norwegian Action, along the lines of a state-run organisation, complete with military codes and designations and led by a central staff with the various services organised in stellar formation around the leadership.[8]

Other baggage that Quisling brought with him from Russia confirms that his skills were organisational and staff-bound rather than executive and creative and that his talents lay more in planning than they did in practical matters. This is particularly the case with the manuscript of his great philosophical project, Universism.

---

modified his enthusiasm. Still, he found the monarch 'very kind indeed'. Letter 4 April 1906, ibid.

[7] Various testimonies in UBO MS fol. 3920 I. Letter to his parents 1909, in Collection Jon Qvisling.* Memoirs of fellow cadet Kahrs Budde in FF 18 July 1942; J. Schiøtz, Den militære Høiskole 1817–1917 (1917) pp. 208f; Militærkalender for den Norske armé og marinen 1909–1920. Also Odd Melsom, Boken om Quisling (1941) pp. 32ff; Straffesak p. 329.

[8] UBO MS fol. 3920 VIII.

UNIVERSISM

Presumably, there are more people than we imagine who spend their spare time trying to explain the world according to some system. Just how many of Quisling's generation or class did so is a matter of conjecture. What was special about his system was that it aimed at an explanation of the entire universe, based on a fusion of Christianity (which he considered to be the most highly developed religion so far) and the most recent discoveries in the natural sciences, especially in the field of physics.

Quisling was extremely well-read and studied both ancient and more modern philosophers in great detail: Spinoza and Kant were of particular interest to him, as was Hegel. Among religious thinkers, Swedenborg was one of his favourites. Of the more modern philosophers, he particularly admired Schopenhauer. Quisling seems to have been attracted to aphoristic writers and adopted the mode himself in his own writings, not without a measure of success, though Kierkegaard and Nietzsche were less attractive to him than the heavier and sterner Schopenhauer. But with the great German thinkers of the nineteenth century his interest seems to have stopped. His library suggests that he had no philosophical interests in any professional sense. Nor did he follow the main currents of twentieth-century thought: Wittgenstein, Russell, Heidegger, Husserl. What was new in contemporary philosophy simply passed him by.

Quisling had developed the rudiments of his 'philosophy' while he was still at school. In the course of his studies it grew into a planned lifework. When he was thirty, his manuscript was said to be two thousand pages long, but it was later revised and shortened. However, it was by no means a finished work: only scattered passages are in any sense complete. The 700-page version we know today in fact dates from the end of the 1920s.[9]

But if his interest in philosophy was strictly speaking that of the layman, he did have a certain talent for the natural sciences and kept up with developments in the field of quantum physics. In the spring of 1929 he brought himself up to date with Niels Bohr and the theory of complementarity. He was also familiar with Einstein and the general theory of relativity. In fact, his philosophising impulse took contemporary physics as its starting point and it was this that led him to the idea of a universal explanation. In a passage about Einstein, Quisling wrote that 'the Universistic theory follows

---

[9] UBO MS fol. 3920 IV, in which the typed pages are organised into and paginated in three series A, B and C. As for the history of the script, see Frederik Prytz in *TT* 24 June 1936 and *FF* 25 June 1936.

from the universal theory of relativity, of which the specific and general theories of relativity are special instances'. The term 'Universism' was borrowed from a textbook by De Groot on Chinese philosophy which argued that the three strands of Chinese thought from Tao, Confucius and Buddha, were all branches of the same Universism, 'the world religion'.

Quisling's *magnum opus* was to be divided into four parts, the first of which was intended to introduce the basic concepts of Universism with the title 'On Consciousness as a Starting Point for the Elucidation of Existence'. After a series of subsidiary chapters on the organising principle of his method – contrast, individuality, space, time, matter, 'the number' and development – would follow the second part, entitled 'The Universe'. Here Quisling wanted to prove that the history of the universe can be seen as a development of consciousness of an ever higher order: the individual consciousness first develops through the family to the clan, the race and the nation. A collective consciousness is the next stage, even though this can be primitive: the masses have no real intelligence, only an instinct for self-preservation, but on the other hand, this can be developed if intelligence assumes higher forms and embraces a consciousness of the whole world.

In the third part of the work, entitled 'Mankind', he envisaged chapters on the character of human life, immortality, man and woman, the will and the law. The fourth and final part was to be called 'The World' and was to consist of chapters on science, art, politics, history, race and religion. For the conclusion he had in mind an overview, 'The World's Organic Classification and Organisation'.

It is certainly fortunate for Quisling that this project remained unfinished: as a philosopher he would never have won recognition. A recent study of the unfinished drafts writes him off completely in this respect.[10] He himself took his speculations so seriously that he painstakingly wrote down and filed away all his fantasies, where others consign such stuff to the wastepaper basket. In his political schemes for Norwegian Action he not only talked of establishing Norway as the homeland of the Nordic race, but also of making the country the centre of Universism, 'the new world religion'. Indeed, the party's domestic goals ranged from 'the restoration of authority and discipline' to 'the introduction of Universism as the official state religion'. High priest, metropolitan, archbishop – Quisling wanted to be at the helm of something which can best be described as a combination of the United Nations and the Catholic Church.

---

[10] Else M. Barth, *'Gud, det er meg'. Vidkun Quisling som politisk filosof* (1996).

Was this madness or merely innocent fantasy? With hindsight, the psychiatrist Professor Gabriel Langfeldt, in 1969, was unequivocal in his conclusion that the idea of providing a 'unified explanation of existence' which 'would completely satisfy the demands of human thinking' in itself fitted the classic psychiatric description of the paranoid megalomaniac more exactly than any other case he had ever encountered.[11] What little of his manuscript Quisling did publish is, however, much more tentative and modest than the notes he left lying in his drawers. 'The positing of such a system depends on the progress of science; and science still has a long way to go ... Neither can one man alone master all its results,' reads one of his published manuscripts. This might go some way towards modifying Langfeldt's diagnosis.[12]

Independently of how one views Quisling's project, what is clear is that his cosmological speculations, his dream of organising the world and his urge to redeem humankind were all manifest in the private papers contained in the large suitcases that he carried from the train that December day in 1929, complete with a political vision of a new Norwegian constitution and plans for a complete overhaul of the political organisation of the country. Indeed, Quisling had come home. From now on, action was to take precedence over thought.

THE ART COLLECTOR

As soon as he settled in his flat, Quisling paid a visit to the Foreign Ministry in Victoria Terrasse. Ingeborg Flood, who was then an administrative assistant, recalled how he came storming into the office in his tall Russian fur hat, left a parcel with the diplomatic courier post on the table and disappeared without saying a word.[13]

Then he set off to see his old friend and colleague Frederik Prytz. Prytz's wife Caroline later wrote of the episode in the notes she kept for her grandchildren: 'On 22 December 1929 he came to see us. With a shy smile he handed me a parcel, and told Grandpa with perhaps an even more bashful smile, "I'm back, and now we can resume the work we began in Leningrad in 1918."' The two gentlemen shut themselves up in the study immediately. Mrs Prytz opened the parcel: it was a large box of

---

[11] G. Langfeldt, *Gåten Vidkun Quisling* (1969).
[12] Foreword to 'Universism', as printed in *Straffesak* p. 280.   [13] Ingeborg Flood, 1986.

caviar. From the study she could hear the sounds of intense political discussion.[14]

Prytz, who was nine years Quisling's senior, immediately filled his friend in on the domestic situation, which at the time was relatively stable. Prime Minister Mowinckel's Liberal (Venstre) government would presumably be safe until the general election the following autumn. Since the krone had been pushed up to par in 1926, the country had been enjoying a time of prosperity. Over the previous few years, a good many enterprises had been started up. But the Wall Street crash two months earlier was certainly ominous for Norway too; the businessman Prytz, with his good international contacts, gave his friend a realistic assessment of the situation, which showed that there was as yet no immediate cause for concern. Political tendencies within the Labour movement were, however, frightening. There were clear signs of unrest. Class hatred seemed to be increasing and the Labour Party had actually prepared a new revolutionary programme. Quite a number of Moscow-style Communists had now returned to the Labour Party, with the lawyer Emil Stang at their helm; the Labour Party might well become communist once more, just as it had been when it was a section of the Comintern in the years 1919–23. Prytz and Quisling had met some of the revolutionary academics in Moscow and Petrograd and were well aware of their commitment to Bolshevism and their unshakeable enthusiasm for the Soviet state. In Prytz's estimation, there was every reason for sticking to Quisling's plans for some action that would attempt to put an end to the destructive class struggle in the country.

But it was Christmas and Quisling had things to attend to before launching himself on the political scene. His apartment in Erling Skjalgssonsgate in the west end of Oslo was transformed in the space of a few days into a furniture and picture warehouse. Luggage arriving from Moscow piled up in the five rooms. Maria and he used the time between Christmas and the new year to unpack the things they were going to live off: a vast collection of antiques and works of art that they had acquired cheaply in Russia with a view to selling off gradually back at home and making a handsome profit so as to be able to live for politics.[15]

Like many foreigners in post-revolutionary Russia, they had been on big antiques buying sprees, for the simple reason that there was nothing else to buy. Ten years after the Revolution the remnants of aristocratic and

---

[14] Caroline Prytz's unpublished memoirs, hereafter Erindringer I–II.*
[15] Quisling's notes on his paintings in UBO MS fol. 4096 X, 6.

bourgeois splendour were all that was available for sale in Russia, and at prices well below the going rate in western Europe. That section of the tsarist aristocracy which had survived in Russia was, from sheer need, forced to put the last pieces of family treasures onto the semi-official antiques market in Moscow. Among professional dealers and collectors in western Europe, Russian antiques were not highly prized, because there was often doubt over their provenance; in fact, many of the paintings by the Old Masters which the aristocracy had surrounded themselves with were mere copies. The gentry in particular, when visiting western Europe, had been easy prey for unscrupulous dealers who were quick to notice and exploit the Russian nobility's desire to be European, and would fob them off with copies and imitations.

Quisling had made his first purchase in the Ukraine in 1922. After he had established himself in the Soviet capital in 1926, he took over an entire suite of furniture from the British ambassador, said to have belonged to Prince Stolypin, the great reformer under Nicholas II. But it was only towards the end of his stay that it occurred to him that what he had earned and had put aside in Moscow could profitably be invested in the systematic purchase of antiques which would enable him to set up a business on his return to Norway. As he was going to be unemployed on his return, he decided to make his living out of art, proceeding with his customary meticulousness by studying the history of art, particularly the Flemish Masters and eighteenth-century English painting. He carefully wrote the names of Vermeer, Boucher and Courbet down in his diary, copying their signatures from the pictures he was offered for sale. Murillo, Rubens, Rembrandt, Jan Steen – the offers were numerous, and Quisling bought and bought. All his spare money, plus what he had inherited from his mother, daughter of a wealthy ship owner from the south of Norway, went into the venture, as did Maria's inheritance from her father, which may also have helped finance a few pieces, although her mother was at that time completely dependent on them for regular maintenance.

Altogether, the Quislings packed up more than two hundred paintings to send to Oslo – an impressive private collection which included five Bouchers, three Poussins, two Monets, three Potters, together with work by Sisley, Cézanne, Goya, Van Dyck, Rubens and a whole host of other Masters. The two gems of the collection were a painting on wood by Rembrandt entitled *The Old Man* or *The Rabbi* and Frans Hals's masterpiece *The Dutch Family* or *Family in a Landscape*. It would have been a veritable treasure – had it been genuine. In Oslo, Quisling had the paintings insured for almost

300,000 kroner and deposited his most valuable pieces in the vaults of the Oslo Savings Bank.

Gradually the apartment, which had stood empty for a year, was transformed beyond recognition by all the paintings plus the French wall hangings, chandeliers, cloisonné eggs and heavy carpets. The Quislings' guests never failed to compliment them on their beautiful home.

At first, their socialising was limited to Vidkun's younger brother Jørgen and his wife Ingerid, who lived only a few streets away and were, like Vidkun and Maria, childless. Jørgen Quisling was a doctor at Ullevål hospital, Ingerid a painter and a housewife. They were all approximately the same age, and had shared many happy holidays and walking tours in the past. In 1929 they spent most of Christmas together and talked a great deal about the future: Vidkun explained to them that, as soon as the unpacking was over, the paintings deposited, and he had reached an agreement with the National Gallery over their restoration, he intended to go abroad to begin the task of valuing and selling off his treasures. He considered the Norwegian market too small and would have to go to the Continent, in the first instance to Berlin and Paris. His art business, then, was bound to involve a lot of travelling, which he had to accomplish before being able to devote himself entirely to politics.

But before that happened, news arrived from the county of Telemark. His father, the parson Jon Qvisling, had been taken ill at the end of January. Vidkun, his eldest son, rushed home.

THE PASTOR AND HIS SONS

Quisling's father, Jon Qvisling (who spelt the family name with a 'v'), was a kind and learned man, a spiritual role model for his children – three boys and a girl – who regarded him as the natural source of strength in the family. He was born in 1844, the son of a sheriff (*lensmann*) from Fyresdal, and was descended from the industrious and much respected Bakkas of Telemark. His paternal grandfather was well known for his great strength, his father for his strict orderliness. It was he who adopted the Danish name Quisling from his mother's side.[16]

Nine children grew up in the sheriff's house: of the six sons, one – Jon –

[16] The genealogy of the Quisling family is explained by Stian H. Finne-Grønn in *Norsk Slektshistorisk Tidskrift* 11 (1948) pp. 45–60; A. T. Glørsen, *Slekten Meidell* (1903) p. 100n; Dr Nils Quisling's notes in UBO MS fol. 3920 XI; various letters from Quisling's parents and siblings 1903–12, UBO MS fol. 4096 III, 2 and Collection Jon Qvisling.*

entered the Church, one joined the army and two became doctors; the others either settled as farmers or married into farming families in the village, or emigrated to America. The Quisling family was thus well established in Norway, despite its partly Danish roots as descendants of Laurits Ibsøn Quislinus, whose name was a Latinised variant of Kvislemark in Jutland. Laurits Quislinus had come to Norway as royal chaplain at the Akershus Castle church at the end of the 1600s; his descendants, a mixture of civil servants and farmers, established themselves both socially and geographically in Telemark, the heart of Norway, during the course of the 1800s.

During his schooldays in Skien in the mid-1850s the young Jon Qvisling encountered the strange Lammers Movement, a local charismatic revival led by the parish priest, G. A. Lammers, who, with pietistic fervour, led his followers out of the state church to set up the country's first meeting house of the Inner Mission (Indre Misjon), in direct defiance of the established church. Jon Qvisling was in church 'that unforgettable fifth Sunday after Trinity' in 1856, when Lammers with his characteristic eloquence, resigned his office and left the state church – later he became the model for Ibsen's Brand. The militancy of the movement held no appeal at all for Jon Qvisling, who was by nature a cautious and conservative man. As a theologian he became strict to the point of being dogmatic and was unequivocally in the conservative camp during the controversies of the 1890s, addressing his congregation in fervent, sometimes even learned, sermons, many of which were published. One bishop on an official visit to his parish of Fyresdal in 1890 remarked that the intricacy of Qvisling's sermons reminded him of work 'wrought in filigree', and later noted that his preaching was cherished by the congregation for its 'extraordinary inner mysticism'.[17]

Jon Qvisling's theological writings were also recognisable for the pietistic bent of their intellectualism. Between 1890 and 1897, he published his main work of theology, *The Souls of Angels* in three volumes. The first volume, *On the Angels*, gave a general introduction to and classification of all the biblical information on the angels, followed by more detailed studies of *The Holy Angels* and *The Devil's Angels*.[18] The work, doubtless intended as a doctoral

---

[17] Jon Qvisling, *Fra mine unge aar* (Skien 1912) pp. 144f. *Norsk Kirkehistorie* II (1987) pp. 219, 253, 269. Bishop Johan Chr. Heuch, *Visitatsberetninger 1889–1902* (Oslo 1965) pp. 37, 114.

[18] See the reviews in *Luthersk Kirketidende* 1890 II, p. 223 (*Om Aanderne eller Englerne*), 1897 II (*Djævelen og hans Engle*), 1899 II (*Jesu lidelse og død*); Jon Qvisling *Gjerpen* I (Kristiania 1917) pp. 114–17, and various articles by him in *Luthersk Kirketidende* 1892–1900.

thesis, has later been taken by the majority of Quisling biographers as proof of his father's eccentricity. But this is a misinterpretation. Jon Qvisling's work clearly belongs to the tradition of mainstream orthodox research. In fact, he had embarked upon his project during his final examinations at the University in 1869 with his essay, 'The Christian Teaching on the Devil', which earned him a distinction. It was not until the turn of the century, when theology changed course, that such research became less topical and rarely came up in academic debate. Qvisling was by then reputed to be 'Norway's foremost authority on the Devil'.[19]

Apart from his pietistic scholarship, Jon Qvisling retained a strong sense of the supernatural and its explanation through so-called psychic research. When the first wave of spiritualism reached Norway in the 1890s, Jon Qvisling was one of its more active proponents. In a European context, spiritualism is usually regarded as a religious movement that was a reaction to the shock of Darwinism and the implications of natural sciences for traditional religiosity, and in particular for the belief in man as immortal. Contact with the dead, just like clairvoyance and dream-fulfilment, served as evidence that the old belief in the soul's independence from time and space, and faith in human beings as immortal, had withstood the test of the sciences and their materialism. However, several strands of spiritualism were in direct conflict with Church doctrine and, moreover, constituted a challenge to ecclesiastical authority. Nevertheless, it attracted many clergymen during the decade around the turn of the century, among them Jon Qvisling.[20]

The intellectual tension between orthodoxy and spiritualism remained with him throughout his life. Neither was, however, taken to excess. In the same sense that Qvisling the theologian is most precisely definable as a traditionalist, Qvisling the spiritualist can only be described as sober and critical. Without exception, his books on the supernatural consist of carefully documented accounts of clairvoyance and other parapsychological phenomena, collected and written down after much painstaking scouring of the Norwegian and the foreign presses. 'Refero relata' – 'I write only what I have heard' – was his motto for these works, which can be read today as a unique collection of popular perceptions of inexplicable events and phenomena.

---

[19] Terje Christensen, *Gjerpen bygds historie* II (1978).

[20] Janet Oppenheim, *The Other World. Spiritualism and Psychical Research in England 1850–1914* (1985). *Luthersk Kirketidende* 1893 pp. 297ff; *Kirke og kultur* 1894 pp. 11ff, 65ff; 1900 pp. 457ff; 1912 pp. 388ff; 1919 pp. 11ff; 1920 pp. 30ff.

His sons were always amused by their father's taste for old ghost stories. They used to compare it with his brother, Uncle Rasmus's tireless attempts to invent machine and weapon technology. For the Quisling boys – Vidkun, Jørgen and Arne, the youngest – this was no more than a source of family entertainment, their father's book like their uncle's fantastic inventions, the result of amateur dabbling.

In the boys' opinion, other elements in their father's work were of much greater importance. The parson was also a local historian who wrote chronicles and compiled catalogues of priests, and had even won the admiration of the distinguished professor of history, Halvdan Koht, for his work.[21] In his youth he had published poems in the Telemark dialect and had also written an account of the 1864 Dano-German war. In short, the boys admired their father as a learned humanist. He was the natural head of the extended Quisling family, to which he lent a certain kudos as one of the country's best known clergymen, mentioned even as a candidate (though never elected) for vacant bishoprics. All his life he gave guidance to his brothers and sisters on various issues, interpreted the family's documents, chose suitable names for all their children, and was, for his twenty nieces and nephews both in Telemark and in Oslo, a mentor they naturally turned to.

FAMILY LIFE

A studious atmosphere prevailed at the Qvisling rectory. Visitors sometimes found it oppressive – and Jon's wife often complained about it.[22] Anna Karoline (née Bang) was much more socially active than her husband. Sixteen years his junior, she came from southern Norway and was the daughter of one of the district's best known figures, the Grimstad shipowner and businessman Jørgen Bang. She and Jon Qvisling had met while she was a pupil and he a teacher at a village school in Grimstad, where he taught to fill in the time while waiting to be assigned a parish. When he left Grimstad in 1876 for his appointment as chaplain at Sandsvær, Anna Karoline was only sixteen years old, but they kept up their relationship by letter and ten years later they married. He had in the meantime become the parish priest

---

[21] Review by H. Koht in the journal *Varden*, quoted on the cover of Qvisling's *Gjerpen. En Bygdebok* II (1919).
[22] Visitors quoted in Pål Repstad, *Mannen som ville åpne kirken* (1989) p. 335; Sverre Hartmann, *Fører uten folk* (1959) p. 58.

in his native village, Fyresdal, and from 1885 onwards he was also parson for Øvre Telemark.

The newly-weds moved into the Moland Rectory at Fyresdal in the spring of 1886. Their first child, Vidkun, was born in the blue room on the second floor, on 18 July 1887. Jørgen was born on 18 December the following year. Like most eldest children, Vidkun had a rather stricter upbringing than his siblings. Jørgen was certainly much more sociable and fun-loving than Vidkun, and the resident entertainer at the rectory. The five or six years that the family spent at Moland Rectory made a lasting impression on the children. They enjoyed the big white house with its large halls and attic, and the large garden that sloped down towards the sparkling Fyresdal lake. 'The parish of Fyresdal constitutes some of the most beautiful landscape in Telemark. *Breathtaking* is the only word to describe it,' their father wrote in his history of the village.

The boys were brought up to feel a sense of ownership over the rectory, for historical reasons. Their father's research into family history revealed that five, if not seven, of his direct ancestors had been parish priests there before him. The neighbourhood contained a rune stone and many other archaeological features, possibly dating from even more remote times.[23] Their father taught them that the local valleys had been among the last to offer resistance to assimilation into Harald Hårfarge's ancient kingdom, and that the local population had fought at the battle of Hafrsfjord and later sided with the impostor Sverre's men. A national romance was thus spun for the boys, a version of Norwegian history that drew them directly to the tales of the ancient sagas. Vidkun had always felt a particular sense of pride at having been born on the very day of the battle of Hafrsfjord – even though this date had been chosen for purely practical reasons in 1872 when it was decided to hold the millennium celebrations of Norwegian unification.

Promotion in the ecclesiastical hierarchy, however, meant that the family had to move on as early as 1893. It has been alleged that it was the Inner Mission movement from 1889 onwards which took the joy out of Jon Qvisling's calling, as the villagers were deserting the Church in droves.[24] But revivals were something that Jon took philosophically; they were part of 'the new time religion' which he had already experienced in Skien. Even so, he had his battles with the adherents of the Free Churches. In his capacity as the

---

[23] Taraldlien, *Fyresdal* (1910) pp. 2f, 52; J. Qvisling, *Fra mine unger aar*, p. 47.

[24] Thus Benjamin Vogt, *Mennesket Vidkun og forræderen Quisling* (1965) p. 24. Christensen, *Gjerpen bygds*, p. 822. Taraldlien, *Fyresdal*, however, dates the revival to the later 1890s, that is, after Jon Qvisling had left.

head of the school council he had to refuse them permission to hold private communions in the schoolhouse. In 1893, he was appointed chaplain to the parish of Strømsøe in Drammen, which laid the ground for future promotions. The family left enchanting Moland behind them and settled in at the Chaplaincy, a simple two-storey town house in Drammen's Strandgaten.[25]

For their mother, the move must have been difficult. She was heavily pregnant and soon after the move gave birth to her only daughter, Esther. Vidkun and Jørgen were also unhappy in their new environment. Vidkun, who went straight into the second form of the Latin School in Drammen that autumn, was teased about his singsong dialect and branded an ignorant country bumpkin as he had learnt only a small part of the Catechism at home, and was both innumerate and illiterate. But he soon got even with the other boys, and in the only way the Quisling children knew how. By dint of sheer hard work and willpower, Vidkun not only caught up with the others but raced ahead to the top of the class. School and homework were now taken more seriously in Jon and Anna Qvisling's home, and enormous pressure was exerted on all the children to excel at school.[26]

In 1898, while the family was living in Drammen, the fourth child was born – Arne. The two older brothers grew up in a home in which care of the little ones was an important part of everyday life. Letters and cards from the Quisling children's early childhood show the four children close and protective of each other. The two older boys, right from their earliest years, encouraged the younger ones to work hard and to make progress at school. Only 'A' grades were acceptable, and, like their father before them, 'A's were what the children delivered in almost all their examinations.

Later in life Vidkun said that during the Drammen years the mere smell of manure or a simple cockcrow in the morning could make him feel violently homesick for Telemark.[27] Around the turn of the century, Drammen was, however, still so little urbanised that hens and horses formed part of the daily childhood world. In winter the children went skating on the river. At twelve years old, Vidkun risked his life to save ten-year-old Johanne Jørgensen by hauling her out of an open channel in the ice and carrying her home.[28] Even so, his homesickness was real enough. An exercise book from

---

[25] The following account of the Quisling family is based on oral evidence from Arne Quisling, Signe Quisling, Aasne née Quisling and other family members, supported by the letters in Collection Jon Qvisling.*

[26] E. Østvedt, *Skien Gymnas gjennom halvannet sekel* (1972) pp. 236, 266.

[27] *Straffesak* p. 328.

[28] The local magazine *Rundtom Drammen* 1984 no. 4.

his last years in Drammen is worth quoting for what he wrote, as a twelve-year-old, about his native county in answer to the composition title 'What do you know from personal experience of the world outside your present home?'

Anyone who has ever seen the natural magnificence of Telemark, and has felt its power, never lives to forget it: he never forgets the people, never forgets the freedom on top of the mountains, the healthy openness, never forgets the mixture of peace and wildness which characterises everything. If, one beautiful summer's day, you stand on one of the viewpoints up there you will have a view before you such as will make your blood course through your veins. Telemark lies before you in all its unique and captivating splendour. Mountain after mountain, as far as the eye can see, an unending sea of hardened rock, but between the blue, snow-covered summits, among the shining peaks and the darkening mountain passes, lies the green-gold valley, and up in the mountains your eye meets a never-ending glistening mass of gleaming black water and silver-green lakes. Down in the valley are farms and fields, separated by graceful groves whose white-trunked birches with their fresh and abundant foliage relieve the sombre, deep green of the spruce forests; but through the clearings in the forest you can catch a good glimpse of a river, which wends its way, now strong and rebellious, now deep and silent, out towards the great lake.[29]

In the summer of 1900, the family moved back to Telemark. Their father, who was now fifty-six years old, took up his last post as parish priest in Gjerpen and parson in Skien. The Gjerpen parsonage was a lovely empire-style building set in an enormous garden. In order to keep up the house and the grounds, the Qvislings needed two domestic servants and a gardener. The years spent here were the family's happiest, with the house always full of the boys' school friends and the little ones' playmates.

Big brother Vidkun was precocious and intellectually gifted, and the most difficult one for the parents to understand. He was perhaps the least musical of the four, but he did love singing in his loud, clear voice. Their mother often played the piano, as did Jørgen, if he was not playing the violin or the accordion. Jørgen was extraordinarily good with his hands, building, among other things, his own instruments. Esther was perhaps the most artistic member of the family, and soon wanted to become an artist, preferably a painter.

The priest himself was constantly busy with all his various commitments – chairman of the school council, board member of the savings bank, an

---

[29] Copy made available by Jostein Nærbøvik.

ebullient lecturer at meetings and at clubs, as well as a regular contributor to the local paper, *Varden*. There was not much of a social life to be had, not in the usual sense at least, but family life was all the richer for it. Every summer Jon's brothers came over from the capital. Rasmus Quisling was childless; Nils and his daughters were particularly welcome guests.

Nils Andreas Quisling, an obstetrician in private practice, was ten years younger than his brother the parson. His four daughters were about the same age as Esther and Arne, and were in awe of their older cousins Vidkun and Jørgen. Cousins Signe, Eli and Andrea, nicknamed 'Konken', became and were to remain close to the brothers and especially to Vidkun for the rest of their lives. Konken later married Conrad Langaard, a tobacco manufacturer, one of Oslo's wealthiest men. One reason why the cousins became so important to the boys could have been that they missed their sister. Esther had died in the summer of 1914, when she was only twenty-one, after a particularly virulent attack of influenza which developed into tuberculosis. Their youngest cousin, Vivi, died of the same illness ten years later.

Every Sunday, the whole family attended church, but apart from that grace was not said at table nor was there any kind of organised evening prayers with the children. They subscribed to the conservative daily *Morgenbladet,* voted Conservative (Høire) and followed the development of the conflict with Sweden with a certain degree of uneasiness, before the sway of national unity took hold in that wonderful summer of 1905. On referendum day itself, Sunday 13 August, the priest made so bold as to liken the union with Sweden to a rotting tree 'that must be chopped down and thrown onto the fire'. Later in the autumn, before the second referendum on the issue of republic or monarchy, he warned his community urgently to vote for the latter. Such commitments were, however, slightly out of character, as the family did not generally pay much attention to politics.[30]

SCHOOL-DAYS

Vidkun and Jørgen's school-days in Skien were filled with hard work among a lively circle of friends. For such studious children, there was little opportunity for sport, but otherwise their interests were the usual ones for boys of their age, except for Vidkun's passion for mathematics. Work,

---

[30] Christensen, *Gjerpen bygds*, p. 655; letters to Jon Qvisling November 1905 in Collection Jon Qvisling.*

explained the precocious sixth-former, is essentially the only thing that brings satisfaction; everything else is meaningless. His mathematics teacher at the Skien Latin School took a great interest in his gifted pupil. The young Quisling had obvious talent, and amongst other things had produced his own proof of why the root of a number greater than 1 tends towards 1 when the power of the root grows towards infinity. For this he was acknowledged and quoted in a footnote in his teacher's algebra book. But it was not only Vidkun who did well at school. All the children shone, and one after the other they left Skien Latin School with straight 'A' grades – something unique in the history of the school.[31]

Vidkun's closest friends all went on to read engineering. They formed a group of four or five boys who kept in contact with each other until well into the 1930s.[32] All the others considered Vidkun to be a genius but were pleased that he wanted to be friends with them nevertheless. He was shy and quiet but also loyal and helpful, always friendly, occasionally breaking into a warm smile. Apart from his remarkable talents, his friends did not find anything unusual about him, except perhaps that he was extremely idealistic. He never took the floor at school society debates, although he did at least once make a speech, a talk entitled 'Culture'. At dances, he was something of an onlooker. All through his youth, he considered dancing exceptionally silly.[33] This did not, however, mean that he did not know how to talk to girls. His classmate Cecilie Blom was particularly close to him. She was the eldest daughter of the Latin teacher and headmaster, Christopher Blom, who was also a very distant relative of the Quislings. Cecilie and her sisters were very fond of their relatives from the rectory, and enjoyed their frequent visits.

Three years after they had left school, Vidkun and Cecilie worked together as supply teachers at their old school for a few months. Cecilie was tall, dark and striking, and was often seen in the company of the distinguished-looking cadet that winter; both families were expecting that something would come of their friendship. In vain – Cecilie and Vidkun never became sweethearts. As adults, they continued to be close, their relationship extending into politics. The same went for the youngest of the Blom sisters, Maggen, who married one of Germany's leading racist theorists and settled in Dresden. Hans Friedrich Günther was prominent both as an academic

---

[31] A. G. Eliassen, *Algebraisk kurs for gymnaset* (1912) p. 149. Østvedt, *Skien Gymnas*, pp. 212f.

[32] Dr Viggo Ullmann's account, 1986.

[33] Various letters to his parents 1905–11, Collection Jon Qvisling;* Skien Gymnassamfunns protokoll, copy provided by Stein Ørnhøi.

and in Hitler's party. Cecilie married an Englishman, and by the 1930s was keen to introduce her childhood friend to the British National Movement.[34]

Friends from school later recalled how Vidkun's interest in history seemed to absorb him nearly as much as mathematics had done. The young Quisling seems to have drawn inspiration from the great historian of the Romantic period, 'the Norwegian Herodotus', P. A. Munch. Munch had been brought up at Gjerpen Rectory sixty years earlier, and had also attended Skien Latin School. As a schoolboy Quisling found this coincidence significant, in exactly the same way as he undoubtedly found meaning in the fact that he grew up in the same town as Henrik Ibsen, the poet whom, as an adult, Quisling came to regard as the prophet and the soothsayer of his people. Born on National Unification Day; brought up in a house where important discoveries about Norway's historical line and connections had been made; a pupil at the same school as the poet-prophet: all this fuelled the imagination of a boy who, in his youthful daydreams, would try to work out his own significance and speculate on what his own place in history would be.

When Jon Qvisling came to the end of his time at Gjerpen, in 1918, he and Anna moved back to Fyresdal, where three of Jon's sisters also lived. There they built a villa, Jonsborg, on the site of the Quisling family estate Lunden, which had long since been divided between two of Jon's brothers. Jon's eldest, Vidkun, was also the oldest of the numerous cousins. 'Vidkun was a Jesus figure for us,' one of his cousins recorded; 'he was morality itself, and used to say to his mother "I want to become a doctor, but on Sundays I want to be a priest!" '[35] Instead, this young and exceptionally gifted man became an officer. His teacher is said to have been saddened by this choice. When the officer later became a politician, some members of the family were behind him. His authority was rooted in the family's traditions: their expectation that Vidkun would achieve great things in adult life was very much a part of the emotional baggage that he carried with him from his childhood.

STUDENT YEARS

When the children from the rectory at Gjerpen gradually started coming to Oslo to take up their studies, the family members looked after them. Vidkun

---

[34] Correspondence Quisling–Cecilie Blom Dahl, UBO MS fol. 4096 V. Accounts by Ellert Dahl 1987 and Ingerid Günther-Guzzoni 1989.
[35] Related by Signe Quisling 1988.

was met by Uncle Rasmus when he arrived in town as a cadet, and Nils
Quisling took young Jørgen under his wing when he went to study medicine
two years later.

During their student years, Vidkun and Jørgen more often than not
visited the family for Sunday lunch or excursions, and went to soirées or
dances with their younger cousins. The cousins' Oslo friends found these
country relatives interesting and quite different from each other: Vidkun
tall, well-built, always in uniform on Sundays, quiet and shyly serious, with
intense-blue eyes which invited contact despite his natural shyness; and
Jørgen, always smart and tastefully dressed – almost a dandy, so witty and
amusing that it was not always possible to tell whether he was serious about
anything or not. Everybody respected Vidkun for his erudition and strict
moral principles; everybody loved Jørgen for his sense of fun and his great
dexterity. But Uncle Nils regretted his nephew's interest in philosophy,
which had started to get in the way of his medical studies. Jørgen did not
qualify until 1921, and then with only mediocre grades, which it had taken
him fourteen years to achieve. On the other hand, he had managed to
publish a couple of books of which the aphoristic, short dissertation called
Sexual Studies dealt with the subject of men and women, desire and vice.
Nils Quisling, himself a specialist in gynaecology, must have been particularly astonished by his nephew's extremely liberal and daring arguments, of
the following type: 'since male sexual desire is more concentrated in the
phallus, and female desire radiates in many diffuse directions out from the
uterus, the male is more easily aroused by the female body. The male body is
nowhere near as exciting for the female as the female body is for the male.'[36]

Jørgen's work was subsequently to develop into a mixture of empirical
sexology of quite a pioneering nature, and a particularly homespun type of
speculative philosophy. The family was in no doubt that Jørgen had talent,
but the question was, for what? His broken engagement might have been
responsible for making him more reflective than scientifically oriented, but
in 1922 he met another woman, Ingerid Schølberg, whom he later married.
In 1931 he published an enormous tome entitled *Philosophy: The Anthropomorphic System* at his friend Frederik Somes's publishing house. This
peculiarly impenetrable book, in which categorical statements are joined
together without any paragraph divisions, explains how the whole world is
constructed, and how everything is mutually interdependent – all filtered
through the author's idiosyncratic way of seeing things. Among his con-

[36] Jørgen Quisling, *Seksualstudier* (1921) pp. 36f.

temporaries Jørgen was considered an original and perhaps even learned man. In hindsight both his and his own brother's writings seem to testify to a certain lack of a sense of reality within the family.[37]

However, there was one important difference between the two brothers. Jørgen's anthropomorphic musings stand remote from any intellectual discipline, giving no evidence of the premises on which he based his ideas. Vidkun was more self-critical and his work was at least in some ways related to the philosophical contributions of others. In fact, he worked hard to clarify his thoughts, with regular revisions of his manuscript. Such self-criticism was wholly alien to Jørgen, who, in order to reach a wider reading public, later translated his work into German, financed the printing and distributed a number of copies of his *Philosophy* to libraries in Norway and Germany. His was indeed an unusual diversion for someone who was a junior doctor at Ullevål Hospital and who from 1930 onwards owned and ran a private clinic in Oslo's Stortorvet.

Despite these differences, even on an intellectual level the relationship between Jørgen and Vidkun remained a close one. It was said that they competed in writing philosophy during their student days. When they were both adults, but before Jørgen had published his book, Vidkun talked about the two systems as a joint project: 'Universism, or the Anthropomorphic System'.[38]

Maria later said that Jørgen suffered from a sense of inferiority in relation to Vidkun, but it can hardly have been more serious than the rivalry that exists between most siblings.[39] As students, they were virtually inseparable: Vidkun tall, silent and shy, Jørgen dapper, cheerful and dominating the conversation. Politically, the Quisling brothers were at this time, if anything, conventional or conservatives in outlook, Vidkun with a tendency to moralise which sometimes appalled his relatives. He repeatedly attacked the 'materialistic' tendencies of the age, showed a strong distaste for ballrooms and operettas, and deplored the growing laxity of women's behaviour. 'Public whipping should be restored!' he exclaimed after having described to

---

[37] The book was favourably reviewed in *Dagbladet*, 24 October 1931, and *Bergens Tidende* 7 December 1931. Even one of the leading academics of the 1930s, professor of economics Wilhelm Keilhau, found Quisling's *Philosophy* an outstanding work. See *Det norske folks liv og historie* 11 (1938) p. 340.

[38] Quisling, 'Hvorfor Moses har horn', unpublished MS, probably *c.* 1930, INO. Arnold Ræsted, 'The Case Quisling' (1941), UBO MS fol. 154.

[39] Maria Quisling's account to Ralph Hewins, in Hewins, *Quisling, profet uten ære* (1966) p. 31.

his parents a particular deplorable scene in one of Oslo's restaurants.[40] As to their party commitment, Jørgen seemed quite indifferent. Vidkun, however, took a moral stand. The first time he witnessed a major May Day parade, in Oslo in 1906, he reacted with hostility, interpreting the red flags, the banners and the slogans as signs of sheer envy and childish protest. Later he became more sympathetic towards the socialists. On his sister's death in 1914 he emphatically committed himself 'to the struggle for the weak and the oppressed' so as to honour his beloved Esther, who had had a particular empathy with the more unfortunate in society. To his parents, Vidkun swore a solemn oath to continue her work 'to the benefit of mankind'. From that time he seemed to his family to be well disposed towards the workers. He always tried to understand rather than condemn the socialists' demands, his cousins noted.[41]

The family was naturally involved in the war in 1914, but on which side their sympathies lay is difficult to ascertain. In the main, perhaps, they were in favour of the Entente, but Aunt Margrethe Quisling was, at least by the end of 1917, pro-German, and the doctor's family fostered two German children after the war, while Jon and Anna, as far as their children and grandchildren could tell, supported England.[42]

Vidkun reacted as a professional soldier, showing that he both had insight into the situation and could be objective about it. Despite all his general idealism, he detested the modern 'peace' movement and reacted strongly against Bertha von Suttner's *Down with Arms* when he read the book as a cadet.[43] War, he thought, was something that could not be abolished. War, moreover, generally challenged the nations and gave them what they deserved – even if the price paid by individuals was too terrifying. On the fateful night of 31 July in 1914 he was on duty at the General Staff. 'I have just received the message that Germany has declared war on Russia,' he noted in a letter to his parents from the central telegraph desk. A few days later: 'My sympathy in the war is wholeheartedly on the German side ... I know what I owe to the German *Geist*.'[44] In the years that were to come, however, he seemed more relaxed and sometimes even gave the impression of being in favour of the Entente. At any rate his sense of ethical commitment to the country from which he had absorbed his philosophy seems to

---

[40] Quisling to his parents 4 February 1907, 24 March 1908, both in Collection Jon Qvisling.*
[41] Quisling to his parents 3 May 1906, 12 October 1914, ibid.
[42] Arne Quisling and Signe Quisling's account; family letters in Collection Jon Qvisling.*
[43] Quisling to his parents 11 December 1906, ibid.
[44] Quisling to his parents 1 August 1914, ibid.

have left him more or less totally. 'The more it seems that Germany's Junkers and Jewish businessmen will dominate not only their own country but the world, the more I turn against their cause.' By 1917, both he and his father had resumed their studies of the English language. Gradually, the horrors of the trenches dawned upon Quisling as far too high a price. But he grew increasingly pessimistic: 'I don't think this will be the last world war.'[45]

When Jon Qvisling caught pneumonia in the last days of January 1930, Vidkun must have realised that that was the end. Even though he had only just arrived back into the country, he dropped everything and left for Jonsborg. By 2 February his father had weakened considerably, and three days later, 'a quiet, fine day after several days of snowstorms', he died peacefully. The coffin was moved to Gjerpen for the funeral on 12 February. It was a family occasion which almost all the relatives attended to pay their respects. Vidkun, the son who had come home, was greeted as the new head of the family.[46]

A few weeks later, Vidkun left for Paris with a view to selling off his art treasures, and from there he made his way to Berlin in order to set up a contact at Rudolf Lepke's auction house in Potsdamer Strasse. On his return just over three weeks later, he was finally ready to enter politics.[47]

[45] Quisling to his parents 13 December 1914, 5 September 1915, letter to his father 1 September 1917, ibid.
[46] Notes in Quisling's Almanach, February 1930, in RA.
[47] Ibid.

2

The Russian dream

The neutral observer living in the midst of war and revolution was forced to recognise the universal nature of events in Russia. The problem was two-fold: how could a similar catastrophe be avoided in one's own country, and what was the real nature of this new order which the Russian Revolution heralded for the world, no more Marxist than its precursor the French Revolution was Jacobin?   *Quisling in 1937*[1]

In December 1929 the Norwegian Students' Association approached Fridtjof Nansen, asking him to recommend a lecturer who 'would be able to say something sensible about Russia' – 'preferably as hard-hitting as possible'. Nansen recommended Captain Quisling, who was due to return from Moscow any day: 'he knows Russia better than anyone I know'.[2]

All the evidence suggests that Quisling really was the Norwegian who knew most about the Soviet Union. His views were certainly 'hard-hitting', but they were based on first-hand experience as well as on careful reading of everything from statistics and timetables to learned dissertations written in and about the Soviet Union. Ideologically loaded as the issue remained, with diverse pros and cons according to political preferences, Quisling was indeed the one Norwegian at the time who was able to give a realistic account.

It was therefore a pity that his lecture never took place. The reason for this was that the Students' Association was beset with internal strife. When Quisling arrived to deliver his lecture on 3 May, a violent debate erupted. The radicals among the students strenuously objected to an 'arch-reactionary' like Quisling being given the floor (although it is unclear what this opinion was based on). The row took up the entire evening and the lecturer never got the chance to speak.[3]

Quisling reacted to the episode with equanimity. He was confident that his time would come. His engagement with Russia was a deep and long-standing one. When he was a junior member of the General Staff, the young lieutenants were each required to make detailed studies of a specific country.

---

[1] *FF* 13 May 1937.

[2] Nansen's *Brev* V, ed. S. Kjærheim (1978) pp. 181, 301.

[3] Quisling's Almanach 1930, in RA. Det Norske Studentersamfunds møteprotokoll UBO F 54. *Aftenposten* 5 May 1930.

Quisling's first choice was China, and he began collecting material on its history and culture, and taught himself some Chinese, but the 1911–12 revolution put a stop to everything and Quisling was assigned a new country: Russia. It seemed that a revolution might interrupt his studies again, but to Quisling the upheavals of 1917 appeared to be very different from those of 1912 in China. Rather than closing off the country to opportunity the Bolsheviks opened up the country again. By 1917 Quisling had been studying Russian for five years more or less continuously under the supervision of Professor Olaf Broch, the most prominent Slavist in Norway, and was ready to put his knowledge to practical use. In March 1918 he finally got the chance. He was appointed military attaché at the Norwegian legation in Petrograd.

PETROGRAD

Quisling, who at that time had never been outside Norway, made his first journey abroad through a central and eastern Europe at war. He was surprised at what a good, well-ordered life the Berliners, despite everything, seemed to be leading. Contrary to reports in the Norwegian press, there was not a single hollow-eyed hungry person to be seen.[4]

From Berlin the German train travelled north-east through former Poland to Byelorussia. East of Pskov the passengers were stopped at the frontier line of what was until the Brest-Litovsk Agreement of 1918 the German–Russian front. The passengers were transferred to shabby Russian wagons. While the western side of the tall, barbed-wire fence was closely guarded, on the other side there was hardly a soldier to be seen: 'just a handful ... on the entire stretch to Petrograd'. Russia, Quisling noted, was falling apart. The soldiers had deserted the front and revolution was sweeping through the towns while counter-revolution was taking hold in the rural areas.

When he arrived in Petrograd at the end of May 1918, Quisling found the supplies in chaos. Rations were scarce, old people died of hunger and horses were dropping dead in the streets. The first in a series of fifteen detailed reports home to the General Staff in Oslo gives a vivid description of the situation in the new revolutionary state. Quisling emphasised that the leaders of the Revolution had a very difficult task before them, but

---

[4] Quisling's official account of the journey is contained in his report to the General Staff of 1 June 1918, RA GS IV, box 86. The letters he sent to his family on 15 and 27 May 1918 contain much the same information. Collection Jon Qvisling.*

concluded positively: 'My preliminary impression is that the Bolsheviks have got an extraordinarily strong hold on Russian society.'

He drew attention to the methods Trotsky, the War Minister, had used to raise the Red Army. He had begun by mobilising volunteers but then enlisted age-group after age-group in the areas under the control of the revolutionary government. In this army the chaos of rebellion had been converted into a systematic striking force: 'there is just as much talk of iron discipline, order and endurance as there is of freedom and equality'. The new disciplined regiments were deployed on one front after another: against the Don Cossacks and the Tartars in the Crimea in the south; the Czechs and the Slovaks in the east; the interventionist forces in the north, and eventually against the Poles in the west. The Red Army was certainly short of both equipment and men, 'but even so there is a tremendous strength in such revolutionary masses, once mobilised'.

Later in the spring Quisling went to Moscow and met Trotsky himself, apparently ahead of a visit of foreign military attachés to the Kasan front. The encounter was a brief one. Neither of the two men touched upon the episode when Trotsky came to Norway seventeen years later.[5]

During his stay in Moscow he also visited the Winter Palace which had been converted into a museum of the revolution. In the Tsar's private apartment revolutionary wrath had left its mark: the slashes in the bed-clothes, ripped apart by furious masses when they stormed the palace a few months earlier; the bayonets which had been rammed through the eyes of the Tsarina's portrait. When he emerged from the palace and went down to Nevskij, Quisling spotted the newspaper billboards announcing the execution of the Tsar and his family in Ekaterinburg:

It became clear to me that what we are in the midst of is no world war, but the beginnings of a new era of enormous significance ... the symbol of a system which had lasted for almost two thousand years had now collapsed. The last of the Tsars was gone – the end of a line of Roman and Byzantine emperors ... two thousand years: this is the measure of the era we are caught up in today.[6]

By the time Quisling joined it, the Norwegian legation in Petrograd was a much reduced mission. The Norwegian and Russian governments barely acknowledged each other. The Minister himself was retained in Norway;

[5] Quisling to his parents 12 July 1918, ibid. Also *Straffesak* p. 329; Vogt, *Mennesket Vidkun*, pp. 39ff.
[6] Quisling's lecture at Ingeniørsalen, 18 January 1934, RA PANS 22; also reported in the letter of 12 July 1918, Collection Jon Qvisling.*

only the legation secretary remained as chargé d'affaires. But a few days after
Quisling's appearance a new colleague arrived: Captain Frederik Prytz, who
had been appointed temporary commercial counsellor on the initiative of a
group of Norwegian businessmen who felt their Russian investments to be
under threat. Quisling soon moved in with Prytz, who took over as chargé
d'affaires when the legation secretary was recalled to Norway that September.[7]

Quisling and Prytz had much in common, army officers and sons of
pastors both, but unlike his younger colleague Prytz was an extrovert with
an international outlook, having spent his childhood in Scotland and
attended a boarding school there. He too had joined the Military Academy,
but his interest in Russia had developed alongside his business interests. The
boom of the 1890s had opened the eyes of many Norwegians to Russia's
business potential.[8] In 1908, after attending language courses and making
study trips to Paris and Potsdam, Prytz arrived in Petrograd, in the first
instance to familiarise himself with the country and to learn the language.
Later he was assigned to a unit at the garrison at Novgorod. The following
year he returned to Petrograd, where he met a Norwegian timber merchant
and accompanied him to Archangel on the White Sea. Here, in the ensuing
years, Prytz amassed a modest fortune out of sawmills and timber export,
starting out with timber which was floated down the Dvina from the large
forests of north-west Russia. What made the area particularly attractive was
the abundance of raw material combined with local technical backwardness.
Russian timber was coarse and knot-free – first-class lumber which, despite
the enormous transport route round Kola, could compete on western
markets. Production was currently sluggish, but with competent management and the necessary technical support the sawmills round the White Sea
could be turned into a highly lucrative export business. Prytz started out as a
ship broker and a timber shipper, went on to become a buyer, and after a
while became a sawmill proprietor and timber merchant as well. His
company expanded and at the end of the war it owned three large sawmills,
several tugboats, tow-boats and barges and large tracts of forest. In the
meantime, Prytz had been appointed Norwegian vice-consul and had also
married. Every year he travelled between his family home and his business

---

[7] The following account of Prytz is based on Caroline Prytz, *Erindringer*, and Benjamin Vogt
in *NBL*, plus documents in RA PA Fr. Prytz, and documents supported by his family.* Also
Egil Danielsen, *Norge–Sovjetunionen* (1964), ch. 3, p. 3.

[8] Francis Sejersted, 'Veien mot øst', in S. Langholm and F. Sejersted (eds.), *Vandringer:
Festskrift til Ingrid Semmingsen* (1980) pp. 183ff.

on the White Sea. On his annual visits to the General Staff he had become acquainted with Quisling.

In the spring of 1917 Prytz, in alliance with the formidable Norwegian wood concern Union, founded a joint-stock venture, Russian Forest Industry Ltd, which was to buy up Prytz's assets and extend the operation considerably. Even the March Revolution, which erupted in the middle of the subscription stage, did not deter investors, as a certain amount of general modernising could only be beneficial for their new company. But in November the Bolsheviks struck, and one of the largest Norwegian ventures in Russia, the Dubrowka sawmill and pulp company on the Neva, was nationalised. Russian Forest Industry was temporarily spared as the front between the Reds and the Whites ran well to the south of Archangel. However, there was great concern that the new Bolshevik regime might eventually seize all foreign investments. In order to get a clearer picture of the situation, a number of Norwegian businessmen set up the Central Office for Norwegian Interests in Russia. With Prytz as the driving force, they successfully petitioned the Foreign Ministry in Oslo for representation in Russia, arguing that vast fortunes could be wiped out, with great losses to Norwegian industry. In May the Foreign Minister agreed to appoint Prytz temporary trade counsellor at the Petrograd legation.

DIPLOMACY AND TERROR

Diplomatic life in Petrograd in 1918 was not without its dangers. Violent conflicts between the Bolsheviks and other parties and factions raged in what was still the most important city in Russia, even though the capital had been transferred to Moscow that April. In the provinces civil war was intensifying, while western intervention was encroaching from the outer reaches of the country. All this contributed to a febrile atmosphere, dominated by mobilisation, assassinations, shootings and unrest. On 6 July the German ambassador was murdered by two radical social-revolutionaries. The following month the British military attaché was killed during a routine attack on the embassy. The Norwegian legation became the victim of a plot by an armed mob. Foreign legations closed down one after another and in the end only the Scandinavian legations remained.[9]

When Quisling went for his summer leave in Norway, his return journey

---

[9] E. H. Carr, *The Bolshevik Revolution* (1966) I, pp. 173, 175. Danielsen, *Norge–Sovjetunionen*, p. 66, and C. Prytz, *Erindringer* I, p. 75.

to Petrograd took a dramatic turn. On 4 September 1918, the boat from Stockholm to Åbo was rammed by a German ore ship and sank; the passengers were transported back to Stockholm in nothing but their night-clothes.[10] Quisling arrived in Petrograd twenty-four hours behind schedule as a result, only to find that the episode paled in comparison with what had been taking place in Soviet Russia in his absence: the proclamation of the terror.[11]

Both Prytz and Quisling had thitherto regarded the Bolshevik Revolution as understandable, if not downright reasonable in political terms. The tsarist oppression had been atrocious, both of the Jews and of the population in general. As for Kerensky's March government of 1918, it had sealed 'the downfall of its own regime' by introducing a wild and chaotic freedom which left everybody free to act and agitate against everybody else. The result was inevitable collapse and capitulation to the one party which had the weapons and the determination to take over – the Bolsheviks. Quisling and Prytz had both been outraged by the indifference displayed by the Russian aristocracy and intelligentsia during the summer of 1918. In a letter home, Quisling explained that the upper classes seemed to have given up com-pletely, a fact which 'could not fill me with deeper pity ... Why can't these people find anything useful to do?'[12]

The events of 30 August put an end to their indifference. On the same day as the local Bolshevik leader Uritskij was assassinated in Petrograd, Lenin himself fell victim of to gun attack in Moscow and was injured by two bullets. The two incidents were unconnected. Even so, the party leadership put them in the same category, and sounded the signal for terror on a grand scale in order to wipe out all opposition. A state of emergency was introduced on 2 September.[13]

Prytz and Quisling experienced the four months of terror at first hand. 'A couple of days ago a caretaker who lives upstairs from me was taken away in the middle of the night and shot because he had a son who was a counter-revolutionary. This is happening to hundreds of people,' Quisling wrote to his brother Arne. The number of executions ran to several thousands in Petrograd alone. The legations of the neutral countries protested. 'Thanks to

---

[10] As told by Quisling in a letter to his parents from Stockholm, dated 5 September 1918, Collection Jon Qvisling.* Also Arve Juritzen, *Privatmennesket Quisling og hans to kvinner* (1988) p. 37.

[11] Richard Pipes, *The Russian Revolution* (1990), ch. 18.

[12] Quisling in a letter home, quoted in *Berlingske Tidende* 30 September 1945.

[13] George Leggett, *The Cheka* (1981) p. 106. Also Frederik Prytz, in an undated manuscript.*

the intervention of neutral countries there has been a temporary lull in the mass-executions,' Quisling reported to the General Staff on 19 September. This was over-optimistic; immediately thereafter the terror only intensified. 'Here in Russia things are getting increasingly out of control,' he wrote home four weeks later, 'but you can only hear shooting in the evenings and at night. Otherwise it's quiet.'[14]

Yet out of the chaos and terror of revolution the two attachés saw a central government authority emerging, slowly developing in line with the Bolshevik struggle for absolute control. Their reports from the autumn of 1918 talk of internal consolidation in spite of the many confusing options which followed from the conclusion to the world war, not to mention the separatist movements in the Ukraine, Siberia and Byelorussia. Russia's situation in the autumn of 1918 was reminiscent of France's in the summer of 1793, Quisling reported. The Girondists had been crushed by the Jacobins, half of France was in turmoil and there were foreign foes on all frontiers. Yet Quisling cautioned against underestimating the importance of the Bolshevik Revolution, as so many in Norway did.[15]

His reports from Petrograd were read with keen interest back in Norway. At once objective, informative and well written, they were quickly picked up also by the Foreign Minister and thereafter sent on to the palace where they were read and signed by King Haakon in person. The King had asked Quisling to a special audience before he left, and now followed the reports from his remarkable staff officer with attention.[16]

As one country after another closed down its mission, Prytz and Quisling became increasingly involved in taking care of the affairs of other countries, in particular dealing with refugees. A British military mission was stuck in Moscow and had to be helped out of the country; Grand Duchess Helena, born Princess of Serbia, also received assistance in getting out of Russia. Both Prytz and Quisling went to Moscow in order to confer with the government and to obtain certain concessions on the restrictions imposed by the local revolutionary government. This task was not made any easier by the fact that the new People's commissariats were constantly being divided up, merged, moved and restaffed. Russian bureaucracy had survived the Revolution and in certain areas became even more impenetrable than it had

[14] Quisling's report 19 September 1918, RA GS IV, box 86. Also letter to Arne Quisling, 14 October 1918.* Prytz, letter to the Norwegian Foreign Office about the Red terror, in S. G. Holtmark (ed.), *Norge–Sovjetunionen 1917–1955* (1995) p. 38.

[15] Quisling's report 23 October 1918, RA GS IV, box 86; letter to Arne, 14 October 1918.*

[16] Nils Quisling to Jon Qvisling 13 May 1918, Collection Jon Qvisling.*

been under the tsars, due in part to the countless commissars appointed by
the Bolsheviks to oversee the administration.

In early December 1918 the Norwegian contingent was also forced to
leave. Quisling and Prytz were evacuated on a special train. The journey
home was dramatic, with Finnish border police forcing diplomatic bags
open with bayonets and badgering the legation staff. Finally, thirty-six hours
late according to the schedule, the staff reached Oslo.[17]

VISIONS

The seven months in Petrograd sealed a lifelong friendship between Prytz
and Quisling. Quisling visited Prytz's wife when he was back in Norway on
leave in August. The lively Caroline Prytz found it difficult to get through to
the shy captain, but the children loved him; in fact, Quisling was wonderful
with children and the Prytz daughters soon regarded him as a kind and
amusing uncle. Prytz himself was greatly impressed by Quisling's intellect,
and in particular his encyclopaedic knowledge of Russia. Later he referred to
himself as the first member of the NS. 'Ever since 1918 I have been working
with Quisling on the formulation of the ideology of our movement,' he
said.[18] The ideology he had in mind was what the two of them had been
conjuring up during the long nights in Petrograd when they were sharing
their thoughts about Russia. They agreed on the country's enormous
potential which in the long run would overshadow the danger represented
by the Bolshevik regime. The nature of this danger, though, was obvious
enough: it lay in the Bolshevik project of spreading revolution by organising
international proletarian solidarity abroad. The revolution in Germany in
October 1918 they felt was surely a sign of what Lenin had called 'the
ultimate revolution of the international proletariat'.[19] Their projected world
revolution was not, Quisling pointed out to Prytz, simply a pious wish on
the part of the Bolsheviks but integral to their international policy. Ever
since the Bolsheviks had been isolated by the international community as a
result of their confiscation of foreign capital, they had been compelled to
look for support from 'proletarian parties around the world', and even from
small, neutral countries like Norway, with which Russia traditionally had
had no quarrel. This danger came in addition to the old Russian desire to

---

[17] Reported by *Social-Demokraten*, 24 December 1918.
[18] Prytz, Draft for a lecture 22 October 1936;* C. Prytz, *Erindringer* I.
[19] Carr, *The Bolshevik Revolution* III, p. 102.

obtain ice-free harbours in the north to protect the Kola peninsula, from which further threats to Norway could be expected. Thus the Bolsheviks' promotion of international class war was a means of consolidating their own position at home. This was not obvious to the world in 1918. At that time, the idea of 'proletarian internationalism' sounded strange even to the pro-Russian Labour Party in Norway. Quisling's predecessor as attaché had criticised Bolshevik foreign policy on the grounds that it totally neglected Russia's position as a great power for the benefit of 'its own selfish class interests' – a complete misunderstanding of the Bolsheviks' aim.

In their nightly discussions, Quisling focused on what he considered was the real significance of proletarian internationalism, while Prytz was more concerned with Russian resources and how to exploit them in the future. However promising, in this respect Russia was faced with an inherent difficulty, 'the incompetence of the Russian race'.[20] The Slavs were a charming people, hospitable, cordial and at times profound, but their organisational and technical competence was pitifully backward. The measure of success enjoyed by the Russian economy had been achieved by the non-Slav population, the two Norwegians concluded. In the early Middle Ages the Nordic peoples had founded Russia, and later provided the aristocracy with the genetic material necessary for successful economic development. This Nordic colonisation was now reaching its dramatic conclusion through the Bolshevik revolution, which, by decimating the upper classes, saw to it that what was left of those genetic resources was liquidated. Prytz was able to underpin such theories with concrete examples from business operations, sawmills and economic transactions. The lower classes in Russia stood helpless before modern techniques for exploiting natural resources. Quisling was of course familiar with the theory that the Vikings had founded Russia; this was the prevailing wisdom of the Norwegian historical school of the 1800s. In their conversations the two men developed a biological schema which not only explained the past but also suggested a programme for the future: the fulfilment of a Nordic colonising mission in Russia. As the Bolsheviks were openly hostile to foreign capital and management, the mission presupposed the collapse of the Bolshevik regime, either through a war of foreign intervention, or through domestic upheaval once the revolutionary reign of terror had run its course.

The theory of the inferiority of the Slavs, an old notion in the West, had

---

[20] Prytz, undated *aide-mémoire* (autumn 1918).*

recently been underpinned by the growth of biological anthropology and the study of eugenics as a popular science. During the war, Norway's leading expert on eugenics, Jon Alfred Mjøen, had warned against the 'Mongolisation of Europe' which would follow from the victory of the Entente and of Russia, and which would threaten the Nordic genetic elements in eastern Europe and the Baltic.[21]

The revolution in Russia, furthermore, had racial consequences for the position of the Jews, Quisling pointed out. Among the Russian revolutionaries – Mensheviks, Bolsheviks and social revolutionaries – there was a conspicuous number of Jews. 'Nearly all the leading Bolsheviks are Jews,' Quisling noted. In fact, on the Central Committee just under half were Jews, in the Politbureau slightly more. The Jews had been 'pariahs under the Tsar', Quisling explained: at least a third of all the Tsar's pre-revolution political prisoners had been Jews, and thus it seemed as though the gruesome persecutions under the Tsar were being redressed. But there would come a turning of the tide: the Jews 'would almost certainly suffer from pogroms' as soon as the Bolsheviks were dethroned.[22] On the other hand, Quisling cautioned against believing that the majority of Russian Jews were Bolsheviks: 'On the contrary, the great majority of Jews are not Bolsheviks, and are treated accordingly, even by their fellow-Jews.' 'The Russian Revolution ... has fallen into the hands of the Jews and international revolutionaries,' he stated in another context.[23] His prediction that the Jews would at some point pay for this should not be taken as a sign of anti-Semitism at this stage. Anybody witnessing the events was bound to think along these lines. Nor did Prytz express any anti-Jewish sentiments. The eugenic perspective they both adopted focused exclusively on the Nordic–Slav tension.

Their ideas were not without wider implications, however. When Adolf Hitler wrote the second volume of *Mein Kampf* in 1925, he supported his argument for a German 'historic mission' in the East by maintaining that the Slavs had never been able to organise their own state, and that the Germans had had to do it for them. In the revolution of 1917, however, the Germanic elements in the population were 'completely wiped out and annihilated' and the role of the political élite passed to the Jews. But the Jews too, because of their destructive nature, were in the long run incapable of running a state. Therefore the Germans once again, after an interval of

[21] J. A. Mjøen, *Germanen oder Slaven? Die Mongolisierung Europas* (1917).
[22] Quisling in a letter to Arne 12 July 1918, Collection Jon Qvisling.*
[23] Lecture given at the Military Association, 17 February 1919, UBO MS fol. 3920 VI, 1. The last passage was deleted from the manuscript before the lecture was delivered.

hundreds of years, had to 'turn their eyes to the East ... to Russia and the Baltic states'.[24]

When the members of the legation finally arrived in Oslo shortly before Christmas 1918, they were greeted with some unexpected attention. The Labour movement raised a storm of protest over the government's decision to recall the legation. A protest meeting on 13 December called for a minimum four days' general strike. Insults were hurled at the Norwegian diplomats, who, in the opinion of the socialists, had fled Russia in cowardly terror.

Worse was to come when the Labourites attacked the legation staff for its supposed involvement in the swindling of the Soviet authorities. In the summer of 1918 a businessman of dubious reputation from the north of Norway received an advance of 3 million roubles for a consignment of fish which the Russian authorities never saw anything of. A court case followed, which to a certain extent compromised the integrity of the Norwegian legation when the businessman put about rumours that members of the legation had been indulging in black market activities and had seized various art treasures and antiques. These allegations were rife in the Labour press and resulted in a libel case. Even though the allegations were thrown out of court, the libeller imprisoned and honour restored to the legation, as in all libel cases some mud did stick. Quisling managed to keep out of the case, but the Labour press was highly suspicious of Prytz, considering him a capitalist and an anti-Soviet speculator whose wealth was ill-gotten.[25]

Prytz took up the question of claims for damages against Russia on behalf of Norwegian businesses. He succeeded in setting up both a public commission for Norwegian creditors and a Norwegian–Russian chamber of commerce, participating in the preparations for the 1921 trade agreement between the two countries. But agreement was slow in coming, and in the spring of 1920 the announcement came that Russian Forest's sawmill and all other foreign property in Archangel and Onega had been nationalised. Prytz took the news calmly. 'I would never have believed that anybody could take the news that most of his fortune had been wiped out so calmly,' said

---

[24] *Mein Kampf* (1934) II, p. 742.
[25] Danielsen, *Norge–Sovjetunionen*, p. 65 and C. Prytz, *Erindringer* I, p. 182.

someone who was present at the time. The truth was that Prytz had been expecting it, and was already planning a new eastern offensive.[26]

Quisling returned to the General Staff to become its acknowledged expert on Russia. Word of his reports had spread in officer circles and he was invited to lecture on his experiences to the Military Association. The lecture 'The Bolshevik Revolution in Russia', delivered on 17 February 1919, was a great success. Quisling gave a clear, balanced and elegant account of the aims and the results of the revolution. He also ventured to prophesy that 'perhaps, already in our time, a mighty Russian kingdom will rise up, a realm of unlimited possibilities, a new America ... this new land is a great opportunity for Norway and for Scandinavia. Exploited in the right way, it will lead us to power, glory and wealth.'[27]

To some of his listeners Quisling sounded dangerously pro-Bolshevik, but Professor Broch was delighted with his lecture and wanted it published in the prestigious magazine *Samtiden*. Quisling refused on the grounds that he had amassed the information in his official capacity at the legation and was therefore not at liberty to publish it.[28]

TO HELSINKI

Immediately after the meeting at the Military Association, Quisling was laid up for over a month with Spanish influenza. From his bed he followed the progress of the revolution: in March 1919 the Communist International was set up in Moscow, and in June the Norwegian Labour Party decided to join. It was a spring when it seemed that anything could happen. 'These are fateful times,' Quisling wrote to his brother Arne. 'We should expect anything. I have never followed events with such intense interest as I do now.'[29] The General Staff Office, filled with endless paperwork, seemed all too limiting. When the post of intelligence officer at the Norwegian legation in Helsinki became vacant that summer, Quisling applied and was appointed in preference to several more senior men. On 10 September 1919 he left Norway to take up his new post in the Finnish capital.[30]

Quisling's assignment in Helsinki in 1919–21 had obvious political

---

[26] C. Prytz, Erindringer I, p. 82.
[27] Lecture to the Military Association, 17 February 1919, UBO MS fol. 3920 VI, i.
[28] Quisling to Broch, 20 March 1919, UBO letter collection 337. In the lecture itself Quisling had warned against publicity. Nevertheless, *Morgenbladet*, *Dagbladet* and *Social-Demokraten* all gave (favourable) reports of the lecture the following day.
[29] Letter to Arne Quisling 5 April 1919.*   [30] Letter to Arne Quisling 12 August 1919.*

dimensions in addition to the diplomatic. The war and the ensuing floods of
refugees, together with the sudden radicalisation of the workers had created
an urgent need for political intelligence and tight surveillance in Norway, all
of which was co-ordinated by the General Staff Intelligence Office. The
London, Copenhagen and Stockholm legations were used as listening posts
for following the Labour movement world-wide and for gathering information on Norwegian revolutionaries abroad. Helsinki was regarded as 'being
of considerable importance ... as long as the revolutionary movement in
Europe gives cause for concern that it might spread into Norway too'. Soon
Quisling was involved in the compilation of a detailed list of all Norwegians
who had participated in the Finnish Civil War.[31]

The new intelligence officer had a balanced view of the Labour movement,
lamenting the unhappy class division in Finland. 'One can hardly speak of
one nation any more.'[32] In May 1920 he encountered the leading Norwegian
revolutionary Jacob Friis, on his way home from Moscow, and helped him
send an extensive interview with Lenin through the diplomatic post to Oslo.
Some months later there were rumours of a full-scale revolution in Norway.
Unfounded, as it turned out.[33]

Apart from the inevitable diplomatic parties, life in Helsinki was quiet.
Every free night Quisling sat down with his Universism papers, 'studying
and philosophising frenetically'.[34] One day he suffered a grave disappointment: picking up the first volume of Oswald Spengler's *Untergang des
Abendlandes* in the university bookshop, he was struck by the similarity
between his own thoughts and those of the German professor. 'All my work
– almost in vain,' he told his parents.[35] Soon, however, he was working at it
again, summarising the highlights of Chinese philosophy as well as ancient
history for his own, synthesising purpose. In the summer of 1920 he visited
Britain for a fortnight's stay in London and Oxford, apparently as a tourist
and primarily interested in bookshops. At least no trace of evidence for any
intelligence purpose for the trip has ever been found. The holiday in
England passed quietly.[36] Back in Helsinki, however, he was struck by a
most extraordinary event: he almost fell in love.

---

[31] Per Ole Johansen, in *TFAH* 1982/2.
[32] Letter to his parents 24 February 1920, Collection Jon Qvisling.*
[33] Friis, Memoirs. Typescript in AAB q 304 p. 66. Rumours: letter to Arne Quisling 7 August 1920.*
[34] Letter to Arne 7 March 1920.*
[35] Letter to his parents 6 May 1920, in Collection Jon Qvisling.*
[36] There is a slight mystery about his fourteen days in Britain in late September 1920. The

Ever since his schooldays Quisling had been handicapped by his extreme shyness. He never danced, blushed easily, and avoided close contact of any kind. Apart from his cousins, there was only one girl in his youth whom he seems to have had a genuine attachment to, his classmate Cecilie Blom. When his sister Esther died, he talked of never marrying. Jørgen, the sexologist, considered this excessive, but admitted that perhaps Vidkun's problem with girls was due to his understanding of Woman 'as a sister rather than a woman'.[37] When he arrived in Helsinki he was accordingly extremely inexperienced. At the legation there was only himself, the Minister and the office assistant. She was Anne Matina Bø, known as Nini, twenty-one years old. She was a clergyman's daughter from Arendal and her parents knew the Quislings. She was artistic and a little romantic and had been educated at the Oslo Academy of Arts and Crafts. She and Quisling were drawn to each other as single people in a strange town. The relationship developed. They used to go for long walks and have serious discussions about various subjects, including love. Nini was not only in love; she remained devoted to him for life, believing that his words amounted to promises of an engagement.

But when they separated, and Quisling left for Russia again, he returned a married man. Nini Bø never recovered from the heartbreak it caused her, but she bore Quisling no ill-will and went on worshipping him from afar. In 1940 she joined the NS, wrote enthusiastic articles about Quisling and took on a minor position in the party. When she was put on trial after the war, the court found reason to investigate the possibility that her treason in joining the NS was attributable to leader-worship, which had started as a fantasy love story in Helsinki. She was put under official psychiatric observation. The love theory was upheld but not given undue importance: she was sentenced to sixteen months' imprisonment.

Nini Bø never married. When she died in 1983 a large portrait of Quisling was found at the bottom of her safe-deposit box.[38]

---

only documentation is the stamp in his passport, apart from two tourist guides to London and Oxford from his bookshelves. No postcards or letters from the trip are mentioned in his father's otherwise comprehensive mail register in Collection Jon Qvisling.* Quisling never alluded to it later – apart from using it as the setting of the short story discussed below.

[37] Jørgen to his parents 27 October 1914, ibid.
[38] The story of Nini Bø is recorded in the court archives RA LD 3135; for her career during the war see *FF* 25 July 1940 and 24 December 1943. Additional information has been provided by her family, 1987.

NANSEN CALLS

During his time in Helsinki Quisling established the pattern he was to follow for many unsettled years to come: the life of a travelling hermit, always capable of absorbing himself in studies and writing in whatever hotel room he happened to find himself. His great project, Universism, was thought out and drafted in between twenty and thirty different towns, until he more or less settled in Moscow in 1926.

Travelling became a way of life, particularly after he was drawn into Fridtjof Nansen's small circle of 'international vagabonds', who in the years which followed were to tramp around administering international missions in many parts of Europe.[39]

Fridtjof Nansen was not only Norway's best-known explorer and scientist, he was also a first-class international diplomat who had organised the repatriation of political prisoners after the First World War. In the summer of 1921 he was appointed League of Nations High Commissioner for Russian Refugees. That autumn he was passing through Helsinki in search of a colleague for his new big project, international aid work in famine-hit Russia. He decided on Quisling, whom he had met the year before. His choice was to alter the course of Quisling's life and career completely.[40]

That summer the drought in the Volga Valley scorched all the crops. The consequences were likely to be even more catastrophic than the famine brought on by the 1891 drought. Nansen had agitated for the League of Nations' involvement, but in vain. Russian emigrants had convinced France of their view that it was not the job of the government to intervene. A larger number of private relief agencies, numbering among them several Red Cross units, joined forces to make Nansen the head of the private international effort that was needed – the International Committee for Russian Relief. Even though Nansen was a High Commissioner and used the apparatus of the High Commission for this task, the Russian relief was organised independently of the League of Nations.

Nansen's colleagues were carefully selected. The most important were Britons: Philip Noel-Baker, John Gorvin, T. F. Johnson and Thomas Lodge. Now the Norwegian Quisling was to join them as representative in the Ukraine. Nansen informed the Norwegian Foreign Minister of his choice.

---

[39] T. F. Johnson, *International Tramps* (1938) p. 167.

[40] Nansen met Quisling for the first time in Helsinki in the summer of 1920 and was assisted by him for a whole week, according to Quisling to his parents 27 July 1920, in Collection Jon Qvisling.*

Quisling had by then just returned to Norway to take up his post on the General Staff and had bought a flat in Oslo. Everything suggests that he was planning on a steady military career. He was more than adequately qualified to work for Nansen, however, both from his experience as staff officer and diplomat, and his knowledge of the Russian language. Nansen's offer was moreover tailor-made for someone with such high ideals and moral seriousness as Quisling.

Nansen treated Quisling as was his way with close colleagues, showing him the respect and admiration which characterised his particular form of leadership. He trusted them implicitly, allowing them extensive autonomy, which was repaid with unerring loyalty and devotion.

Providing relief for Russia's starving masses was no easy task in 1921. The general condemnation of the Bolsheviks led to a lukewarm, if not openly hostile, attitude to Nansen's project. Russian emigrants were not alone in wanting to see the regime blamed for, or even brought down by, social catastrophe. The chief Norwegian daily *Aftenposten* demonstrated its opposition by starting a collection for distressed fishermen in the north of Norway at exactly the same time as Nansen was initiating his campaign. In Britain, Lord Northcliffe's newspaper empire opposed outright the idea of sending the Bolsheviks food and medicine, arguing that there was no way of knowing whether the supplies would benefit the regime and thus result in further oppression of the Russian people.

Quisling saw things differently. He shared Nansen's view of a humanitarian duty which transcended politics. He received permission from the General Staff to leave Norway at the end of January 1922. In Moscow he visited John Gorvin, Nansen's local representative, who had already negotiated an agreement guaranteeing complete freedom of movement for the relief workers and securing free transport in the autonomous Soviet Republic of the Ukraine. Quisling arrived in the capital, Kharkov, in February 1922.

The Ukrainian wheat harvest had failed under at least five of the republic's governments; incidences of typhus, spotted fever and cholera were approaching a million.[41] Nevertheless, on his arrival in Kharkov Quisling found all kinds of foodstuffs available in shops and markets. The opera was putting on productions, the university was giving lectures. But on closer inspection the situation was not what it seemed. Food prices were extremely high. In the suburbs there were serious food shortages, and in the

---

[41] J. Sørensen, *Fridtjof Nansens saga* II (1940) p. 454.

surrounding villages famine. But there were no statistics to prove it. Only the Health Department had clear figures, showing an alarming spread of typhus and an increase in the number of fatalities. Quisling therefore started collating his own figures. 'The more I investigate the situation, the more desperate it seems,' was his first impression.[42] After a few days' work on the statistics, the figures began to take shape. Of the Ukraine's population of 26 million, around 8 million had to be defined as famine-stricken, if not then, certainly in the immediate future: 'I have seen villages where entire populations are dying, where there is no food, where there are no medicines. Cannibalism is on the increase.' Dogs and cats had long since been devoured; horses had practically disappeared from the region.

On 22 March he sent a lengthy report to Geneva, supported by maps and photographs, which was printed and distributed by Nansen's office. If judged according to the impact it made, this report is arguably Quisling's most important publication ever. It revealed that the authorities in Moscow were diverting wheat from the Ukraine to the Volga area even as late as January 1922. People thought that the country had enough food, as did the million refugees from the Volga region who were pouring into the Ukraine. The result was a catastrophe beyond imagination.

The famine, Quisling stated, had been brought about by a combination of civil war, government requisitioning, failed agricultural policies, the Allied blockade and the severe and enduring drought of the summer of 1921, which had reduced the crops to a fraction of the normal yield. The mortality rate was perhaps ten thousand a day, Quisling concluded. In certain areas the country was burnt to a cinder, with withered trees and bushes. Parents ate their children. Elsewhere the emaciated corpses of the dead were casually thrown on to heaps, without anyone even taking the trouble to close the eyes of the dead. In the cities, the Jewish population suffered particularly, Quisling reported, now being struck by famine after the string of pogroms during the years of turmoil of 1917–20.

In mid-May help arrived. Provisions and wheat trucks, parcels and medicines from Europe flooded into the coastal towns on the Black Sea and thereafter were sent on west by rail. A new phase in Quisling's work was beginning: the distribution of supplies, the setting up and management of

---

[42] Report of 18 February 1922, ICRR Info. no. 20. Ibid. no. 22, *Famine Situation in Ukraine.* Some of the original reports are preserved in Nansen's correspondence, UBO MS fol. 1988 RU3A B, with carbon copies in the mission's archives in Kharkov, now at the Central State Archive of the Supreme Power Institutions (CSASPI), Kiev, Ukraine, which have been examined for the author by Dr Alekseij Sottikov, Kiev.

kitchens, food stations and warehouses. The main difficulty was transportation, as the revolutionary rail authority was not renowned for its efficiency. But Quisling was a stubborn administrator and often got what he wanted by sheer persistence. His reputation among international relief organisations was higher than that of most other Nansen representatives in the field.[43]

Special committees distributed all sorts of food, from Danish sausages, Norwegian herring, Spanish wheat to Dutch cheese and Swedish children's clothes through Quakers, Baptists, students' committees, not to mention Jewish agencies. Altogether, it is possible that around a million Ukrainian lives were saved: of these, two hundred thousand under Quisling's administration, the rest mainly by the much more efficient and wealthy American Relief Administration of Herbert Hoover, who preferred to give less to many more of the victims than did the Nansen system.[44] The exact number of deaths is not known, but it is certain that it was significantly lower than both Nansen's and Hoover's reports supposed.[45]

The letters Quisling sent home to his family at this time present a picture of an unusually altruistic, efficient and tolerant aid worker, who could sympathise with the suffering of both individual families and the broader masses, as well as entire ethnic groups.[46] Far from being unfeeling, Quisling could be said to have been an easy touch. He found it difficult to turn people away and to say 'no' to their moving prayers. For this reason he was occasionally deceived into issuing rations which were not always justified. At the same time, the Ukrainians were reputed to have abused the aid system. Consignments often either disappeared on to the black market or were brought to Moscow for further sale.

Political criticism was not slow in coming and Quisling suddenly found himself involved in international arguments. A complaint from the Polish government demanded his resignation because there were allegations of mismanagement of the relief in favour of the Bolsheviks. 'An infamous lie!' he responded in injured rage. Such episodes did not spoil the satisfaction of working for the great man Nansen, however.[47]

---

[43] Roland Huntford, *Fridtjof Nansen* (1997) p. 516.

[44] Quisling to Jon Sørensen 2 December 1934, UBO MS fol. 4096.

[45] Huntford, *Nansen*, pp. 515ff; B. M. Weissman, *Herbert Hoover and Famine Relief* (1974) p. 6.

[46] Some ten letters to his family February–August 1922 are known from Collection Jon Qvisling* and other private collections.*

[47] Telegram from Quisling to Nansen 15 June 1922, Nansen Mission Archives, CSASPI, Fund 261 no. 108.

On the other hand Quisling did not see much of Nansen during this time. Their paths did not cross in the Ukraine, but Nansen's importance and his popularity in Russia were obvious everywhere. As early as the spring of 1920 an enormous portrait of him was hung next to Lenin's on the facade of the Comintern hotel Lux in Moscow.[48] Quisling later used to tell a story, probably from a later journey in the Caucasus, to illustrate the extent of Nansen's fame: 'During the night, while the train stopped at a small station, I woke up, and in this outpost of the world, heard a provincial soldier say to his fellow: "Did you know that Nansen is travelling through?"'[49]

TWO WOMEN

In August 1922 the Ukraine mission was drawing to a close. Food distribution was progressing well and transport problems had been sorted out. The supervision of the relief work could thus be handed on to the Moscow office according to the schedule.

Quisling left Kharkov a married man, and took his wife, the seventeen-year-old Alexandra Andrejevna Voronina, back to Norway with him. His colleagues in Kharkov were bewildered by this 'obvious mismatch', as one of them put it. They thought her wanton and considered her relationship with the mission leader to be most peculiar. Alexandra's mother was a simple pedlar and her daughter's 'behaviour and demeanour' were not thought to be appropriate for the wife of a morally upright man like Quisling.[50]

Alexandra, just like Nini Bø in Helsinki, was an assistant in Quisling's office, serving as switchboard operator at the Nansen mission. She later described her relationship with Quisling, eighteen years her senior, as an ordinary love story: she falling for his mature charm, he for her youthful appeal. They married on 21 August and he brought her home and proudly introduced her to his family and friends.[51]

From Quisling's point of view the relationship was of a somewhat different nature. Asja, as Quisling called her, was blonde, captivating and chic, reminding him of his cousins back home. Despite her naïveté there was something tragic about her which deeply moved him. Alexandra simply

---

[48] Friis, Memoirs, p. 66a.

[49] Sørensen, Fridtjof Nansens saga II, p. 399 (1931 edn, p. 278).

[50] H. Lannung, Min russiske ungdom 1917–19 og 1922–24 (1978) p. 163.

[51] Alexandra's version: as told to the magazine Alle Kvinner, August 1975, and recorded in Juritzen, Privatmennesket Quisling, ch. 4. The date of the marriage is given in a letter to his parents from Margrethe Quisling of 14 September 1922, in Collection Jon Qvisling.*

fulfilled his need to play the role of rescuer. He married her so that he could get her out of the Ukraine on a Norwegian passport and provide her with a good education, thus rescuing her from the dangerously unstable conditions of post-revolutionary Kharkov. Such at least is the impression given by his letters home and from remarks made over the years.[52]

The single most telling source of information about Quisling's feelings and intentions concerning Alexandra is hidden in a literary attempt of his, a short story or novella in three parts.[53] The stage is set in London in 1917, where an encounter takes place in a rainy street. The man in the story is a foreigner in the big city, an unhappy and lonely Russian count; the woman is a fallen angel, forced by illness and disability to walk the streets: 'Her eyes are beautiful, large and kind, but also sad and frightened.' Count Varian is easily recognisable as Quisling's fictional *alter ego*, bearing the same characteristics and sharing the same hopes and dreams. 'Let me come with you,' begs the fallen woman. The count refuses, insisting that he is not 'like that'. 'But all men are,' she protests. 'No, not all,' he answers gently, wrapping his raincoat around her shoulders and removing a wad of notes from his wallet which he discreetly hands to her.

Quisling consistently maintained that he had married Alexandra to keep her 'on the straight and narrow and to secure a good future for her'.[54] But he was misunderstood. His colleagues in Kharkov took his marriage as evidence that Quisling was a poor judge of character; some thought that he had not realised what sort of girl she was, and that he had taken her peroxide blonde hair as proof that she was of Nordic extraction, a descendant of the Vikings who had once settled in the Crimea.[55] But if Quisling had ever said anything of the sort, it must have been in jest, as his letters show that he was very well aware of his young wife's weakness for cosmetics.

Early in September 1922 the newly-weds arrived in Oslo and moved into his flat in Erling Skjalgssons gate. They slept in separate rooms; the maid's room was occupied by Quisling's youngest brother Arne that autumn. The cousins, who immediately took Alexandra under their wing and helped her to settle in Norway, noticed that their union was not quite a conventional one, and concluded that there was no sexual element in the marriage.[56]

[52] Letters to Arne Quisling 29 September and 18 November 1922,* and to his parents from Sofia 21 January 1924, INO, printed in *Folk og Land*, 9–10, 1985.

[53] UBO MS fol. 3920 III, 3; reprinted in Juritzen, *Privatmennesket Quisling*, ch. 6.

[54] Letter from Sofia 21 January 1924, INO, printed in *Folk og Land* 9–10, 1985.

[55] Lannung, *Min russiske ungdom*, pp. 162f.

[56] Signe Quisling's account; also Arne Quisling's account, 1988.

After seven months' absence Quisling resumed his work at the General
Staff. In October he lectured to the Military Association about the relief
work as an accomplished mission. However, as early as November, at a
meeting in Moscow, Nansen and Gorvin decided that the aid mission in the
Ukraine should be extended until autumn 1923. Nansen, who was awarded
the Nobel Prize for peace that autumn, let it be known at the General Staff
that Quisling was 'absolutely indispensable' in the Ukraine. At the end of
February 1923 he and Alexandra returned to the city where they had met the
previous year.[57]

But the Ukraine had changed 'beyond recognition'.[58] People were no
longer dying of hunger, as the famine was virtually over. Heavy rainfall
during the spring brought hope of a good wheat harvest, and it seemed that
the situation was about to turn from famine to surplus. The scope for aid
work was therefore greatly reduced, to about half of what it had been the
year before, and Quisling began to find the work routine and dull.

For Quisling the most significant event of the summer was that he met his
great love, Maria Vasiljevna Pasetsjnikova. She was Ukrainian, born in 1900,
and was completing her studies at the Institute of National Economy in
Kharkov, when in autumn 1922 she found employment at the local
secretariat for famine relief. Quisling met her at the office too; the last in a
series of three such encounters in four years, but this time it was serious.

Maria later described her early acquaintance with Quisling in detail: the
conversations they had; the walks they went on; his accounts of Norway,
Telemark, Fyresdal, his parents.[59] Everything indicates a blossoming love
affair in the summer of 1923. However, what she fails to address is the fact
that Quisling was already married when they met. Maria certainly knew
Alexandra, if not personally at least by name, and about the marriage, as
Quisling was a well-known and much admired figure in Kharkov, 'the man
the whole of the Ukraine is talking about'.

When Maria started to associate with this famous Norwegian, she must
have been told that his marriage to Alexandra was a temporary arrangement
designed to give the young girl a new start in life. At that time several
foreigners were entering into 'chivalrous relationships' in post-revolution
Russia in order to secure an exit, passport and citizenship for women who

---

[57] Nansen to Aavatsmark 30 October 1922, UBO MS fol. 1988 F6B.
[58] Letter to Arne Quisling, 27 May 1923* and to his parents, 1 June 1923, UBO letter
collection 1.
[59] Maria Quisling, *Dagbok* (1980) pp. 29–36; the original script is in UBO MS fol. 3920 X, 11.

wanted to get into western Europe. Maria must have accepted that this was the case also with Vidkun and Asja.[60]

During the months that followed, the situation became more complicated; in fact, it is difficult to establish the truth of what was going on in the Quisling–Maria–Asja triangle, as the two women's accounts are grossly at variance. On 10 September 1923, while Asja was in the Crimea, Vidkun and Maria married in Kharkov. It is not clear how they managed to sort out the technicalities of the marriage. It is also unclear whether Quisling at this point had actually divorced Alexandra as there is no record of either the marriage or the divorce. Among Quisling's otherwise complete personal papers, there is no marriage certificate pertaining to the second marriage, and no certificate has been found in the Kharkov municipal archives. There are two possibilities. Either both marriages were just agreements, or Quisling was only ever legally married to, and never divorced from, Asja. If his marriage to Maria was a formal one, from 1923 onwards he must be considered a bigamist.

Of the two possibilities, the former seems the more probable, bearing in mind Quisling's general formalism and the subsequent behaviour of all concerned. But the second possibility cannot be rejected out of hand. In the only contemporary reference made by Quisling himself, he expressly states that he and Asja had 'got married'.[61] His marriage to Maria is, on the other hand, curiously passed over in his letters to his parents. Suddenly she is there, and she is his *wife*, with Alexandra now described as his 'foster daughter'.[62]

If Quisling's first marriage was bona fide, it explains why no document attesting to his second marriage has ever appeared. Moreover, if his second marriage had been legal, it is surprising that Maria, at least, did not take care of the certificate. She was twenty-three years old, educated, and about to take up residence in a foreign country with a man she had known for only a few months. But no certificate has ever turned up, not even in 1945 when she went to court claiming a greater share in Quisling's estate and therefore had to provide documentary support for her claim. If Quisling had not divorced Alexandra, his relationship with Maria was technically concubi-

---

[60] Ibid., p. 18.

[61] Letter to Arne 29 September 1922:* 'I have got married, 21.8 [1922] – three days before Jørgen! I am sure you are surprised. There is nothing more to say except that I do believe you, in particular, will become good friends with her. You are so alike in many ways.' Alexandra added her greetings at the end of the letter.

[62] Letter to his parents 25 September 1923, in Collection Jon Qvisling.*

nage. This view is corroborated by the research carried out by the journalist Arve Juritzen in 1986–7, and is backed up by Jørgen Quisling's claim after the war that his brother had never been formally married, although his testimony does need to be seen in the context of the ongoing dispute over his brother's estate.

Whatever the facts, Maria and Vidkun always behaved like a married couple, and always celebrated their wedding anniversary on 10 September. It is therefore most likely that they did go through some kind of wedding ceremony, of whatever level of formality; they may have felt that formalities were unimportant as they were living in a period of revolution with upheavals in all areas of life. Their commitment to each other must have been enough for them, even if they had not been able to find a responsible authority to formalise it.

Getting Maria out of the country was no easy matter. Her name could not be put on to Quisling's passport since Alexandra's name had already been entered as his spouse. Nor could he obtain a Norwegian passport for her, if for no other reason than that the issuing of passports did not fall within the jurisdiction of the Norwegian trade mission in Moscow – the country's only diplomatic station in Soviet Russia. Instead Quisling furnished her with a document stating that she was employed by the Nansen mission. She left for Paris, where Quisling was to join her later.

The Nansen mission wound up on 12 September 1923. The Russian government had been exporting so much wheat that summer that Nansen found it difficult to make any convincing appeals to the world to send food to the Ukraine. The aid organisations were not co-operating fully either. Jewish organisations put themselves in a difficult position by openly reserving aid for their own people, while Nansen's organisation insisted on equal distribution.

After all the formalities at the mission had been sorted out, Vidkun and Asja left by train through Poland and Germany *en route* to Switzerland, where Quisling was due to make a report at Nansen's headquarters in Geneva. He was also planning to find a good boarding school for Asja and then go on to Paris to join Maria.

OUT OF THE GENERAL STAFF

From summer 1923 to summer 1924 Quisling lived in Paris. Maria had been largely responsible for his decision to spend this year studying in France. Quisling himself was no Francophile and had never felt it important to learn how to speak French, but saw this time in France as 'education' in a general sense. He considered that English was the great world language, and he thought that Russian would emerge as the language of the future. However, there were other factors involved in the decision. Quisling was unemployed as his time in the Forces was over. He took his leave from the General Staff in September 1923 – for one year in the first instance, but with the almost certain intention of never going back.

His departure had not been an easy one. The temporary leave he requested to go to the Ukraine in 1923 had only grudgingly been granted. Nansen had gained assurances on his behalf from the Minister of Defence that Quisling's work for the mission would stand his career in good stead, but these had been empty assurances, made only for Nansen's benefit. The General Staff saw the Russian mission as a dubious project and did not want any part in it. Quisling, for his part, remained loyal to Nansen. In the summer of 1923, when the second phase of the relief work overran the deadline of his leave, he was left with no choice but to apply for a discharge. The prospects for a later re-enlistment were meagre, as the defence budget was under tremendous pressure. Throughout the public administration, austerity measures were being introduced to save the state from bankruptcy. In the army, the number of positions was cut back massively, and in the space of only a few years the number of salaried officers shrank from 3,700 to 500–600. Moreover, Quisling was losing seniority despite the fact that he had been paying for his own replacement while he was away in the Ukraine, and thus was constantly passed over for the few positions that were available.

When Quisling took his leave and was discharged from the General Staff in the summer of 1923, he had effectively been excluded for good. As he began to realise his true situation, he grew increasingly bitter. Between 1925 and 1926 he spoke of the Staff in unfavourable terms, and was at times openly scornful, even though he did still harbour some sort of hope for re-entry. After four years he gave up waiting and took advantage of the offer from the Ministry of Defence of early retirement, a policy adopted to reduce the number of officers. He retained a reduced salary as captain in the reserve, and then from 1930 as major there. [63]

---

[63] The main sources for this account are: Quisling's letter to the King, 28 June 1923, UBO MS fol. 3920 I; to Arne Quisling 14 July 1923;* to Nansen 9 and 19 March 1925, and from Nansen 14 March 1925, UBO MS fol. 1988 A5A; to the King 1 November 1927, UBO MS fol. 3920 I; Juritzen, *Privatmennesket Quisling*, p. 127; Ræsted, 'The Case Quisling', UBO MS fol. 154, p. 20; C. Prytz's Erindringer II, p. 252. Emphasis has been laid on the earliest source, the letter to Arne Quisling of 14 July 1923:

If he had known at the time what the consequences would be, he would perhaps have acted otherwise. Nevertheless, in the summer of 1923 he had compelling personal reasons for taking a year off. Asja, his foster daughter, could be set up; Maria, his wife, wanted to see Europe; and he himself certainly needed some rest. An obstinate stomach pain had been plaguing him all winter, and he was still suffering from its after-effects in the summer. The year before, he had succumbed to the Ukraine malaria. He decided to leave for Paris and live on his share of his mother's inheritance from her father's fortune, which she had divided among her children. The money was in an account in the Gjerpen and Fyresdal Savings Bank and had fortunately survived the spring 1923 crash.

On their arrival in Paris, the three of them checked into the Hotel Studia in the Latin Quarter. Quisling spent most of his time working on Universism, but also devoted himself to reading politics and political theory, in particular Machiavelli. After several years of practical diplomatic and administrative work, he enjoyed browsing in the bookstalls along the Seine and in the spacious second-hand bookshops in the Latin Quarter.

Besides, his connection with Nansen provided him with a steady flow of new work. In Kharkov in January 1923 Nansen had decided to write a book about Russia, and depended on assistance from Quisling. When it was published that autumn, *Russia and Peace* was considered a rather naive little work. Its central thesis was that Russia was of greater importance to the

> I have applied to be released from the Staff from 1.8.[1923]. The truth is I finished my service there a year ago, and have simply been waiting for a position in the field artillery. But since none is vacant I have not been able to leave except as a supernumerary, which I have finally decided to do ... although ... this does mean giving up my career for the time being.

Since his application of 28 June 1923 was taken literally and granted (he was probably hoping that it might lead to extended leave instead), his relationship with the Staff became equivocal: see his statements made in the Storting on 7 April 1932: 'I left the General Staff and the army in the summer of 1923, and when I did so, I resolved never to return' (St.forh. 1932 b.7); compare this with 'when I ... was refused an extension to my leave, in order to finish off my work in Russia, much against my will, I had to resign from the General Staff, and with that from the army' (Quisling to the Storting special committee 17 June 1932, printed in St.forh., Innst. S. no. 184 1932). Quisling's inconsistency on this point has misled many of his biographers, in particular Vogt, *Mennesket Vidkun*, pp. 55ff, where Vogt, using Broch as his source, suggests that Nansen was not willing to intervene on Quisling's behalf with the authorities in order to help him back on to the Staff. However, Nansen's own letters prove that he went to great lengths on Quisling's behalf, and even took the matter up with the government (see T. Greve, *Fridtjof Nansen* (1974) p. 230, and Fridtjof Nansen, *Brev* V, p. 287).

West than was generally acknowledged, and that her importance lay primarily in her role as food producer for a dangerously over-industrialised Europe. Of Nansen's many international aides, only Quisling is mentioned by name.[64]

The plan was, further, that during the international launch of *Russia and Peace* Quisling should publish a longer, more political article in Norway, arguing for the necessity of reopening diplomatic channels with Russia. At last he was at liberty to let his voice be heard publicly. He wrote the article in Paris in September and took it with him when he went to Norway on holiday at the end of the month. On 2 October 1923 it went to press in the Oslo daily *Tidens Tegn* under the title 'The Recognition of Russia'. It was written in the spirit of Nansen, deliberately so, but its analysis of Soviet Russia was based on Quisling's independent insights. Politically, the demand for Russian recognition was still seen as so radical that *Tidens Tegn* was compelled to emphasise that the contribution was entirely the author's own.

In the article, while recognising the antipathy felt towards the revolutionary regime, Quisling argued that Norway should not allow emotions to interfere with politics, and added that the Soviet government was also unpopular in its own country for the way it had built up its power by force, and there was a chance that it might be overthrown. But, he stressed, the revolution, 'that gruesome necessity', had created a 'tremendous need for action' and had set an irreversible historical process in motion, making the return of the old social structure impossible, and thus even if the Bolsheviks were toppled, a new regime would still have to continue the work started by the revolution.

The publication of the article was extremely well timed, perhaps more so than Nansen and Quisling could have anticipated. The prominent Bolshevik politician Alexandra Kollontay, head of the Soviet trade delegation to Norway, paid a visit to the Foreign Minister in mid-December and explained that her government was under the impression that 'public opinion in Norway had recently swung strongly in favour of full recognition of Russia'.[65] On 15 February 1924 Norway's official recognition of the Soviet government 'as the only legitimate and sovereign' power in the Soviet Union was announced. Ambassadors were exchanged; Kollontay was posted to Oslo and Andreas Urbye to Moscow much to the satisfaction of Nansen and his assistant, who had been championing this cause for several years.

---

[64] Huntford, *Nansen*, pp. 541f.
[65] Danielsen, *Norge–Sovjetunionen*, p. 120.

Nansen was simultaneously involved in another matter. More than 2 million refugees had left Russia after the revolution, half of them had fled to eastern Europe and the Balkans and from there to the East. Nansen, in his capacity as the League of Nations High Commissioner for Russian Refugees, was responsible for the repatriation of all these people. In July 1923 a crisis in the relations between Moscow and Sofia put a halt to the repatriation of Russians from Bulgaria, and Nansen and his aides decided that they should send a delegate from the High Commission to organise the repatriation of all Russians in the Balkans. In view of his record in the Ukraine, which had earned him the respect of the Soviet authorities, Quisling seemed the most suitable choice for such a complex task. He received notification of his appointment while he was on an autumn holiday in Norway and accepted. He left for Geneva two weeks later to be briefed. Nansen had already informed the Soviet Foreign Minister, Tsjitsjerin, of the appointment.[66]

In Geneva Quisling received detailed instructions. He was to have no headquarters but was to travel around eastern Europe and the Balkans in order to persuade both the local refugee committees and the relevant governments to proceed with repatriation. On 15 November he went via Belgrade to Sofia and immediately contacted the government there. On 22 November 1923 he was able to cable that the Bulgarian government was ready to resume negotiations with the Russians. In the new year the first repatriations were in train.[67]

He met up with Maria in Vienna: she had arrived there after receiving money and instructions for the trip in Paris. She accompanied him for the next two months from town to town, hotel to hotel. They spent Christmas in Sofia, and went on from there to Constantinople and Athens. Quisling was struck by the poverty and miserable conditions in both the countryside and the towns in the Balkans. The complex questions of ethnicity also occupied him and he could not avoid noticing how Russian agents had mounted an intensive campaign of infiltration over the entire region, and in Bulgaria in particular.[68]

In January 1924 Maria returned to Paris to look after Asja and Quisling continued his travels alone. His mission was dragging on as the Russians

[66] Note outlining the functions of Capt. Quisling 30 November 1923, and Nansen to Tsjitsjerin 20 October 1923, in UNL LNA, Geneva C 1321.
[67] Gorvin to Eybye 22 November 1923, Johnson to Quisling 21 December 1923, both UNL LNA C 1322.
[68] See MS of his lecture to the Military Association, 29 November 1924, UBO MS fol. 3920 VI, 2, pp. 40f.

were less willing to take back their countrymen who had fled from the revolution than they had led Nansen to believe; many of the refugees were openly counter-revolutionary, and thus, instead of being sent back, they had to be helped to other countries. The High Commission took on the laborious task of negotiations with over fifty countries, issuing identity cards (later known as 'Nansen passports'), organising transport and the checking and stamping of documents. Soon the process gathered momentum: Quisling's mission organised six thousand repatriations from Bulgaria during this period. However, financial problems at the League put a damper on the whole project. When Quisling arrived in Paris at the end of February 1924, he had serious problems even trying to get his salary for that month.[69]

In Paris he resumed his reading and his extraordinary triangular relationship with Maria and Asja. Even in Montparnasse the fact that the Norwegian diplomat seemed to have two wives allegedly caused some raised eyebrows. They stayed in Paris until midsummer, when the threesome made its first appearance in Norway.

Quisling's family and friends received the two Russian women with astonishment. They had met Maria briefly the previous October; now she arrived in company with Alexandra, who had recently been Vidkun's wife but now seemed perfectly content to pose as his foster-daughter. Uncle Nils was amused, but Uncle Rasmus was scandalised and described the set-up as 'depraved'; the younger members of the family realised that the saintly Vidkun had been living in a fashion that was quite foreign to Norwegian bourgeois morality. What the pastor and his wife thought, they kept to themselves. Vidkun had written to his parents about his marriages, emphasising his motive for marrying and then becoming father to Asja: 'the only genuinely altruistic thing I have ever done'.[70]

Among his fellow officers eyebrows were raised over Quisling's marital situation. They speculated that one wife was the other's sister, or that the second wife had agreed to the marriage on the condition that he should first marry her friend (or sister) in order to get her out of the country. His colleagues were astonished that this gifted, serious man felt it appropriate to go around with two women and that he had the gall to expect people not only to accept his behaviour but also to praise his morals.

However, Maria got along with the family well. In contrast to Asja, she

[69] Note on the Rome Emigration Conference, May 1924; High Commission for Refugees; Budget for the Year 1924, both LNA C 1322; Johnson to Quisling 30 November 1923, LNA C 1321.
[70] Quisling to his parents, 21 January 1924, printed in *Folk og Land* 9–10 (1985).

quickly learnt to speak and write Norwegian and to function independently. Although her social background was similar to that of her new family (her husband insisted that she was the daughter of a Russian cabinet minister), she was very different from them in temperament, being warm, spontaneous and impulsive, and by Norwegian standards rather naive. Her relationship with Quisling was good, and improved greatly when Asja subsequently left to stay with an aunt in Nice. Alexandra never returned to Norway; Quisling's instructions, advice and financial support were all sent by mail. In 1929 she left Europe and settled first in the East, and eventually in America.

APPROACHING THE REDS

From summer 1924 to summer 1925 Quisling was living unemployed in Oslo: a depressing time, and an anti-climax after his eventful life abroad. One day he met his friend from Helsinki, Jacob Friis, who had recently been sacked from the Labour paper *Arbeiderbladet* and was in a similar predicament. Friis was a philologist and historian, four years Quisling's senior and not unlike him in character. Politically, however, they seemed worlds apart, as Friis's sympathies lay somewhere between the Labour and the Communist Parties, but they did share a passion for Russia, for the revolution and for Bolshevism. Friis had first-hand experience of both the Comintern and the executive committee and thus the two men had a great deal to talk about in their idle hours.

Friis was of the opinion that 'the wave of international revolution was over, and that the workers were being forced onto the defensive'. Quisling agreed: for the time being the Soviets could count on no support from the revolutionary masses in the West, and that was why they were stepping up their activities in the East. The movements in China seemed very promising for their cause. There was also ferment in India, not to mention Persia, Afghanistan and Arabia.[71]

When they were discussing the domestic scene, Friis talked of the danger of a fascist coup in Norway, and feared that the Labour movement might be suppressed, as it had been in Italy; thus the subject of arming the workers came up. The most significant event in the Norwegian Labour movement that year was the unsuccessful strike which the young Labourites had tried to initiate to paralyse the armed forces. The Labour youth movement called on all conscripts to stay at home and not turn up for the year's military

[71] Friis, Memoirs, AAB q 304, pp. 99f.

training 'in the bourgeois army'. The action was a total fiasco and the strike leaders were brought to court and sentenced for insurrection amid nation-wide condemnation. Friis and Quisling may well have seen the case as a testimony to the fact that the revolution was a spent force. But Quisling seems to have approached it from a more professional angle. He explained to Friis that the Labour movement, instead of demonstrating against conscription in this way, should draw up plans for supplementing national defence with a militia, a voluntary people's army in which the workers could play a major role, and at the same time receive the weapons training necessary to enable them to defend themselves against attacks from the extreme right. He went on to plan the form that such an organisation would take and discussed it in terms of a proper militia. Friis was fascinated by this line of thought, and suggested that Quisling talk his plans through with leading people from both the Labour and the Communist Parties. Quisling agreed and subsequently got involved in something that he would later come to regret deeply: his association with the revolutionary leaders of the Norwegian Labour movement.

This was not the first time that Quisling had offered to make a contribu-tion to the progress of the left.[72] In October 1924 he had sought out the parliamentary leader of the Labour Party, Alfred Madsen, who later became the leader of the Norwegian Federation of Trade Unions. The conversation took place at Labour Party headquarters and Madsen thought Quisling 'an appealing young man' with 'a fresh view of the Soviet Union and the struggle of the Russian Labour movement'.

On Friis's recommendation, Quisling now also called on Martin Tranmæl, the editor of *Arbeiderbladet*. A few years later Tranmæl claimed that Quisling approached him on 28 January 1925 with the offer of setting up defence organisations 'in the form of Red Guards for the party'. What

[72] Main sources for Quisling's meetings with the Labour movement 1924–5: Alfred Madsen in Storting 19 May 1931, St.forh. 1932 b. 7; Friis's Memoirs, AAB; Quisling's Almanach 1925 with entries for the various meetings; Friis's, Tranmæl's and Scheflo's almost identical statements to the Storting on 9 and 10 June 1932, in St.forh., Innst. S. no. 184, 1932; Vogt, *Mennesket Vidkun*, pp. 80ff. Chr. Hilt's statement of 25 May1931 with Furubotn's approval, printed in St.forh., Innst. S. no. 184, 1932; *Arbeideren* 5 June 1931; Furubotn's account in 1957 of conversations at Quisling's home in Hartmann, *Fører uten folk*, pp. 96f. (Both accounts wrongly date the meeting to 1926.) In Quisling's letter to the Storting Special Committee 17 June 1932, printed in St.forh., Innst. S. no. 184, 1932, the earliest and fullest source from Quisling's side, he maintained that it was Friis who had urged him to seek out Tranmæl and Scheflo, something which Friis's account of 1932 does not concur with, but nevertheless emerges in part from his memoirs.

Quisling had in mind was rather a people's militia, something similar to the Red Army in its early days, a 'home guard' in which the workers would feel welcome and which, in the event of a reactionary plot, could be used to protect both the Labour movement and others.

After his discussion with Tranmæl, Quisling headed straight for the offices of *Norges Kommunistblad*; he was actually watched from the windows of *Arbeiderbladet*. There he met the party secretary, and warned the Communists that they were subject to surveillance from the British legation in Oslo, among others. After Quisling left, the secretary informed the acting party chairman Peder Furubotn of his visit; they decided to contact Quisling to set up another meeting.

In the meantime Friis had arranged a meeting at his apartment between Quisling and Olav Scheflo, the editor of the Communist newspaper, whom Quisling knew both from Helsinki and from Moscow. Quisling asked whether the Communists were aware of just how systematically the General Staff was spying on the Labour movement, and whether they might be interested in his obtaining information on what the Staff did and did not know about revolutionary work in Norway.

So far the contents of the talks are fairly well documented. Quisling actually did intimate to the Communist leadership that he could disclose such military secrets. But both Friis and Scheflo later claimed that Quisling had offered to re-enter the Staff in order to secure more information for them. This is most doubtful and, as Quisling himself insisted a few years later when challenged, at that point he was neither willing nor able to return to the Staff and was therefore in no position to offer his services as a spy.

A week after the meeting with Scheflo, Quisling twice received the chairman and secretary of the Communist Party at his home in Erling Skjalgssons Street. He outlined his concept of a people's militia in military terms, with the help of maps and pointers. But he failed to inspire confidence. Tranmæl had already written him off and never mentioned his visit to anyone, so little importance did he attach to it, and now the Communists broke contact with him.

What was really behind these amateur overtures to the left? Quisling, unemployed and dispirited, was looking around for something new and absorbing. He was deeply resentful of the General Staff, and may have felt the urge to leak defamatory information out of revenge. In addition, he was in the process of becoming politically more radical. His ideas at this point were in fact very different from what they had been four or five years earlier.

In January 1925 the Fatherland League was founded.[73] The hall was packed when the main speaker, Fridtjof Nansen, cautioned the public that to strive for revolution and violent class struggle in a country with full civil liberties such as Norway was 'ridiculous nonsense'. Quisling was in total agreement with Nansen that neither violent class struggle nor communism would suit a technically and economically advanced society, but also with *Arbeiderbladet*, which distanced itself from this doubtless nationalistic and idealistic, but also unmistakably bourgeois, movement. The Fatherland League, whatever it claimed, was not for the workers.

At this time Quisling was developing his own views on nationalism as a social force, and did not follow the line of the League. 'There are two forms of nationalism in Norway: bourgeois nationalism which is calculated to curb communism, and a genuine sort of nationalism, which proceeds from the increasing strength of popular feeling,' he wrote in autumn 1924. It might be that his experiences in the Ukraine were influencing him, as he saw parallels between Ukrainian nationalism and the Nynorsk language movement in Norway. The two movements were actually quite similar in structure and scope: Ukrainian was as different from Russian as Nynorsk was from Danish, and both inspired a cultural movement of national liberation which invited many points of similarity. Quisling contributed an article on the issue in *Norges Kommunistblad*, 'The Language Struggle in the Ukraine', an elegant and learned introduction to the Bolshevik policy on nationality, besides showing sympathy with the Nynorsk movement in Norway.

Between 1924 and 1925 Quisling's political ideas seem to have revolved around the concept of a fusion of socialism and nationalism, based on the idea of the Russian Revolution as a three-tiered process of national liberation, radical democratic reforms and then finally an inevitable social upheaval. This led him to break with the right wing in Norway, which explains his peculiarly lukewarm interest in the newly founded Fatherland League.

At a lecture he gave at the Military Association shortly afterwards, Quisling impressed his audience as being strikingly sympathetic to the Bolsheviks. The Soviet regime was in the process of getting the economy back on its feet, without aid from abroad. He then went on to clarify the Soviet government's special two-edged foreign policy: on the one hand the ambition to become a great power, and on the other the goal of world-wide

---

[73] Andreas Norland, *Hårde tider* (1973) chs. 5 and 6; protocol of conference 10 October 1925, UBO MS fol. 2894; UBO Worm-Müller's archive.

social ferment and revolutionary internationalism.[74] The audience may well have registered that the lecturer, despite his emphasis on the revolution, also displayed a deep understanding of the long-standing Russian ambition to be a great power. If Quisling's behaviour in 1919 was interpreted as 'red' by his military colleagues, he must have seemed even redder now.

ARMENIA

Soon after Quisling had presented these ideas to his fellow officers, Nansen once again guided the direction of his life. The issue in question was a group of refugees who were to occupy Nansen for the rest of his life, a people who had suffered more than any other during the war and who had been persecuted and massacred, expelled and dispersed more than any other people: the Armenians. The Armenians had been promised a homeland by the great powers, but the promises had never materialised. At the League of Nations their cause was threatening to develop into a big international scandal when Nansen took it up in 1924. His motives were entirely humanitarian; during a visit to Siberia before the war he had met unhappy Armenians exiled because of their struggle for independence. Quisling added a whiff of ideology to the issue: the Christian Armenians, he stated a few years later, 'represent Europe's last outpost in the Muslim East and thus constitute the primary channel through which western ideals and western culture can penetrate Asia'.[75]

The journey Nansen and Quisling made to Armenia and the Caucasus in June 1925 was a promising, optimistic tour. Everywhere they were met by co-operative authorities. At last it seemed possible to do something for the Armenians. The idea was to help the Soviet Republic of Armenia repatriate as many as possible – perhaps some 50,000 – of the approximately 300,000 Armenians who were living in Turkey or as refugees in the Middle East. The republic itself made up a relatively small area and numbered just under 1 million inhabitants, with around 400,000 more Armenians living in other Soviet republics, particularly in the neighbouring republics of Georgia and Azerbaijan.[76]

---

[74] 'Enkelte hovedlinjer i Russlands nuværende utenrikspolitikk'. A two-part talk at the Military Association 22 November 1924 and 23 March 1925, script in UBO MS fol. 3920 VI, 2.

[75] Quisling, undated note on Armenia c. 1933.* Nansen in Gjennem Sibirien (1914).

[76] Quisling, Almanach, RA; Fridtjof Nansen, Gjennem Armenia (1927), Gjennem Kaukasus til Volga (1929), and the lengthy Nansen–Quisling correspondence of 1927 and 1928 in UBO MS fol. 3920 V.

A real effort was needed in order to make good the international promise of a homeland. One plan involved irrigation of the desert areas. British, French and Italian experts accompanied Nansen and Quisling on their trip. With Quisling as their secretary, the group collated a great deal of information, made extensive calculations and soon came to the conclusion that the plan to relocate 50,000 people to the desert was utopian. Instead, it was agreed to propose the setting up of three or four smaller agricultural projects.[77]

Their journey home took Quisling and Nansen through the Caucasus to Dagestan and then up the Volga by steamship. Everywhere on the 3,000- or 4,000-kilometre-long journey they would stop and visit companies, villages and fisheries, make assiduous notes and discuss their experiences in depth, usually with Nansen making observations and asking questions while Quisling took the notes and made comments based on his vast knowledge of geography, history and statistics.

In Moscow the government confirmed that as long as the local authorities agreed, they would approve the proposed agricultural projects. Quisling would return to Armenia on secondment from the more permanent settlement commission that had to be set up with the League if Geneva gave the go-ahead. And so it turned out. Even though there was little enthusiasm for the project amongst the western powers, still reluctant to participate in anything which might promote Soviet development, the League decided on an Armenian Refugee Settlement Commission in order to extend the work of the expert group. Quisling was invited to the first meeting in Paris and formally appointed to act as liaison between the Commission and the governments in Moscow and Armenia.

In November 1925 he presented himself at the Commissariat for Foreign Affairs in Moscow. The Soviet government promised to contribute to the project with a government guarantee via the Soviet National Bank. At that Quisling hurried on to the Caucasus to hear what the Armenians had to say. For three months he shuttled back and forth between Yerevan and Moscow, trying to guarantee the projects both economically and administratively. The bureaucracy was impenetrable and slow, but Quisling's reports to the League of Nations gave the impression that he had to a great extent mastered it. In mid-March 1926 he returned for the second meeting of the Commission in

---

[77] Report by Dr F. Nansen, 28 July 1925, printed in *League of Nations: Scheme for the Settlement of Armenian Refugees*, C.699.M.264. 1926. IV, Geneva 1927; Johnson, *International Tramps*, ch. 13; Greve, *Fridtjof Nansen*, ch. 19; Sørensen, *Fridtjof Nansens saga* II, ch. 'The Armenian Tragedy'; League of Nations Report C.328, 1926, II, UNL LNA Geneva.

Geneva, where the main cause for concern was the question of finance. There it seemed that the financial advisers considered the guarantees Quisling produced to be unreliable. Quisling then envisaged that the project be financed by an international loan; when asked who was to be responsible for guaranteeing such a loan, he explained that the Armenians would settle the debt with the help of projected agricultural surplus and guarantee it with an annual sum set aside from the republic's budget. The Commission was not satisfied. They wanted to know whether any reputable foreign banks were behind the Russian bank. Quisling was unable to answer, but tenaciously insisted that the guarantee was acceptable as Russia had huge assets abroad. The argument was dismissed. The Commission insisted that the western capitalists involved would ask for more, and decided to investigate the matter more closely. Quisling therefore returned to Moscow.

By the time the Armenia Commission met for the third time, the British technical expert, Michael McIntosh, had returned from Yerevan. The plan was now concentrated into two projects, but the financing remained unclear with regard to the guarantees. In its final report to the League, the Commission was forced to concede that it had not managed to come up with a financial solution.[78]

When the Assembly cancelled the budgets, the project was formally rejected. Quisling had believed in the Soviet government, argued its case, and defended its guarantees to the Commission – all in vain. The international financial and diplomatic communities were rejecting his proposals outright.

THE ROUBLE SCANDAL

Quisling spent two weeks in Paris with Maria before returning to Norway in 1926, where he was able to tell his family the good news that he had found a proper job and was to return to Moscow, this time to work for Frederik Prytz.

Since they had last been in touch, Prytz had succeeded in sorting out his claims against Russia. He had served as Norwegian delegate at the Geneva conference in 1922 and subsequently at The Hague conference, and had used these opportunities to work directly on the Russian Trade Minister. By

[78] Nansen, *League of Nations*; Armenian Commission, Report C.328.1926.II, UNL; Quisling to Rachel Crowdy 16 February 1926; Report by Captain Quisling 5 March 1926; minutes of meetings of 12 March 1926 and 14 May 1926 in UNL LNA 12/48295/46805, also printed in *League of Nations*.

this time, Prytz was regarded as something of an expert in international compensation.[79] And he was successful: when the NEP (New Economic Policy) was introduced in 1921, the need to attract foreign capital without harming the Soviet system resulted in the setting up of so-called concessions to foreign investors. Between 1921 and 1925, ninety concessions were given altogether, most of them to German and British capitalists, for trade, industry, mining, the lumber trade and even agriculture. Prytz won a 'mixed' concession which involved the previous owners of Onega Wood, plus two other Norwegian and Dutch companies, who reached an agreement with the Soviet authorities over a 50:50 ownership of a newly founded company, the Russian–Norwegian Onega Wood Co. ('Rus-Norvegoles'). The company obtained a concession to operate the sawmills in Onega and Archangel based on the forests around the White Sea. Its potential output was equal to the entire annual Norwegian timber output. Co-operation with the Russians certainly looked promising, as Prytz was met with general goodwill during his negotiations in Moscow and even managed to secure tax reductions for his venture. Quisling had had experience of negotiating concessions on his Armenia mission. Thus, when Prytz suggested his coming in on Onega, he was reasonably familiar with the conditions. He accepted the offer and met Prytz in Moscow in May 1926.[80]

Quisling had no direct business experience, and little aptitude for it either, but Prytz was confident that he would quickly learn the basics. Besides, he was not strictly speaking there in a business capacity, but rather to liaise with the Soviet authorities. This proved to be a laborious task which demanded both skill and patience, both of which Quisling possessed in quantity. Soon he was made responsible for Onega's Moscow office, and from then on spent most of his time waiting to be invited to conferences at the offices of the Commission for Concessions and the Department of Trade.

However, the authorities were increasingly interfering in the company. The party leadership was becoming disenchanted with the entire system of

---

[79] Jørgen Sehested to Prytz 11 December 1922, RAK private archive 6332; various correspondence therein attests to Prytz's role in arranging even the Danish and French settlement.

[80] Report to the General Meeting of Onega Wood Ltd, 29 May 1925 (Prytz archives);* C. Prytz, Erindringer I; Vogt, *Mennesket Vidkun*, pp. 63f, and his article on Prytz in *NBL* 11, p. 195; E. H. Carr, *Socialism in One Country* (1970) I, pp. 483ff. A similar 'mixed concession' arrangement was made with a Russian–British concern, Russ-Angloles, organised by Prytz's banking contact W. Schalit in London, according to an undated note in the Prytz archives.*

concessions, as it was attracting significantly less investment capital than projected, and yielded a lower annual profit than had been budgeted. The 14th Party Congress in December 1925 therefore adopted an entirely different approach: that of building up the country's industry unaided. Amidst a dramatic power struggle in the party, a resolution was passed to gamble on large-scale industrialisation, the implementation of which started in 1926. This was the death blow to foreign concessions. Early in January 1927 Prytz began the preparations for the winding up of Onega Wood.[81]

At the same time new prospects opened for Quisling. Following the severance of diplomatic relations between London and Moscow in the spring of 1927 – in fact a cover-up of the unsuccessful Arcos raid on the Russian trade legation in London – Norway was charged with taking care of British interests in Russia. Head of the Moscow legation Andreas Urbye consequently called in the man he needed most to equip his station: Quisling, his former subordinate from Helsinki, who was appointed temporary legation secretary to assist with British affairs.[82]

The Norwegian colony in Moscow at this point consisted of around fifteen people: five or six at the legation, a few businessmen and a few visiting academics, including Quisling's former tutor, Professor Olaf Broch, and the historian Halvdan Koht. Even Maria came along, after having stayed alone first in France and then for a whole year in Oslo. At last, in the autumn of 1928, she was reunited with her husband, and she and Vidkun set up their home in the empty house of the British legation.[83]

Vidkun and Maria got on well with the other Norwegians in Moscow, but he was perhaps a little too reserved and Maria a little too much of a foreigner for them to develop any close relationships. Quisling was the foremost expert on the Soviet Union at the legation, and Urbye tried to turn over most of the Norwegian concerns to him so as to leave the more routine British affairs to the second secretary. In this way he hoped to carve out a permanent position for the *ad hoc* secretary. The Foreign Office in Oslo,

[81] Prytz, Report 29 May 1925; Prytz to Sehested 27 April 1926 RAK private archive 6332; Vogt, *Mennesket Vidkun*, pp. 65f; C. Prytz, Erindringer II, pp. 212ff; Carr, *Socialism in One Country* I, chs. 6 and 8; Statement of 4 April 1928 and telegrams Prytz–Quisling 1927, both in the Prytz archives.*

[82] Oddvar Høidal, 'Quislings stilling ved den norske legasjon i Moskva 1927–29', *HT* 1974/2; see also Høidal, *Quisling. En studie i landssvik* (1988) pp. 31–6; Ole Ludvig Nymoen in *Bergens Tidende*, 24 April 1976.

[83] Quisling, Almanach 1927, RA; letter to his parents 16 May 1928, UBO MS fol. 3920 XII.

however, refused to establish a new post for budgetary reasons. Quisling's engagement remained a temporary one.[84]

Before the Rus-Norvegoles company finally closed down, an event took place which was to blacken Quisling's name for many years. Rumours about Prytz's company's involvement in a currency scandal were reaching the Norwegian Labour press. The story of what was dubbed the 'rouble scandal' of an illegal transfer of millions of roubles out of Russia intensified and the case soon took on enormous proportions, ending up with the allegation that Quisling had smuggled foreign banknotes through diplomatic channels and cultivated sinister connections with Turkish and Persian merchants to carry out illegal transactions to the tune of 3,000,000 roubles.[85]

Nearly all biographies of Quisling ever since have accepted 'the rouble affair' as a well-established fact, relying on the stories told by Quisling's contemporaries and repeated by the socialist press in Norway when he was appointed cabinet minister in 1931. Ever since, the story has been taken to be true, even in scholarly historical works, and seen as a sign of Quisling's dubious ethical standards if not of total moral bankruptcy.[86] There is, however, no proof of the story, and the opening up of the former Soviet archives makes it quite improbable that there ever was anything illegal or sinister in the conduct of the Prytz–Quisling business. At least no written account has ever appeared. The whole story seems to have developed in the following way.

When Labour MPs in 1931 broached the allegations of illegal transactions and of Quisling's being almost expelled 'with good reason' from the Soviet Union, they referred explicitly to what they had been told by Madame Kollontay or other members of the Soviet legation in Oslo. The Prime Minister in the late 1920s, Ivar Lykke, made a statement in the Storting that

[84] Høidal, *Quisling* and 'Quislings stilling'. Re the Norwegian colony in Moscow, see Quisling's letters to his parents, 1926, UBO MS fol. 4096 I, 10; G. Ræder, *De uunnværlige flinke* (1975) p. 164; Jonas Lied, *Over de høje fjelle* (1946), ch. 'Båksitt og vannkraft'; various letters from Lied to Quisling in the 1930s in UBO MS fol. 4096 V; Olaf Broch, *Arkivstudier i Russland mai–juni 1928* (1928), with a dedication to Quisling, INO; Quisling's letters to Broch 7 February and 14 March 1929, UBO letter collection 337.

[85] Main sources: Storting debate 19 May 1931; Nordahl Grieg, 'Hvordan en fører blir til' in *Veien Frem* 1936/2; Ræstad, 'The Case Quisling', MS 1941, UBO MS fol. 154; Benjamin Vogt, article on Prytz and Quisling, *NBL* XI (1952), and particularly *Mennesket Vidkun*. The only person to speak out against the allegations was Victor Mogens: 'it [is] not right, the claim that Quisling was involved in currency smuggling, and that he narrowly avoided punishment', in Victor Mogens, *Tyskerne, Quisling og vi andre* (1945) p. 43.

[86] Høidal, *Quisling*, p. 33.

neither he nor the government had received 'anything at all by way of complaint or grievance against Mr Quisling' from the Russians. Neither had Mr Urbye, the Norwegian Minister. True, in a conversation with the Foreign Commissar Litvinov in Moscow, Urbye once received a spoken complaint that Quisling had acted 'not loyally' in his conduct of the Rus-Norvegoles company. Urbye rebutted the allegations, insisting that, from his own thorough knowledge of the case, he was certain that Quisling could not be blamed, whereupon Litvinov dropped the case.[87] Nothing more was heard about it, not even during the Second World War, when the Soviets after 1941 had every possible motive to expose any scandal concerning Quisling to the world. Government archives in Moscow simply carried no proof of the matter. At least this was the case when they were inspected and scrutinised for all possible material on Norway in the 1990s.

It is in any case unlikely that any transaction could have been concluded in the manner suggested by the rumours. Half of the Rus-Norvegoles company was under Soviet state ownership. Accounting was done with the Russian directors jointly and inspected by Russian auditors. The possibility of large-scale black-market transactions with unauthorised cheques can therefore be dismissed. Moreover, there is nothing about Prytz's business conduct to suggest that he was likely to defraud the Soviet state. The concession question was so sensitive, with so much at stake, not least for the influential Norwegian shareholders, that it would have been hazardous to run the company according to anything other than normal business practice. Besides, Prytz had his reputation to think of, for an international businessman of his standing an indispensable asset. His business correspondence shows no sign of a loss in confidence after 1927–8; rather, he claimed a few years later that 'hardly any Norwegian was in a better position in the City [of London]' than he was. He never saw the concession settlement as a short-term arrangement; on the contrary, his wife's memoirs frequently refer to the disappointment he felt when he had to give up Onega Wood as early as 1927.[88]

Quisling's notes and surviving cheque books show that he deposited and withdrew large sums of money from the Onega account. Signs of irregular transactions are not among them. Neither Prytz's nor Quisling's files contain any trace of complaint by the Russians over irregularities. Moreover,

---

[87] Urbye, report from a conversation with Litvinov to the Foreign Office in Oslo 21 September 1932, reprinted in S. G. Holtsmark (ed.), *Norge–Sovjetunionen 1917–1955* (1995) pp. 195ff.

[88] C. Prytz, *Erindringer II.*

if investigations really had been started by Russians, it is surprising that
there are no contemporary sources which at least allude to irregularities.
That Quisling as Norwegian legation secretary should be summoned to a
hearing in Moscow, or even to the secret police, the GPU, as frequently
stated, without its resulting in a single piece of paper either in Oslo or
Moscow, is almost inconceivable.

Apparently the accusations were put into circulation after Prytz and
Quisling had left Russia – Prytz in December 1927 and Quisling two years
later. All things considered, there are grounds for interpreting the vicious
rumours as stemming from the internal conflicts over the question of
currency imports and of foreign influences during the post-NEP economy,
on a level with the other obstacles which the management of the companies
came up against after 1926. All foreign concessions were exposed to scrutiny,
and soon the entire concession apparatus was wound up. The Soviet
government needed some justification for why they were stopping the
concessions so much earlier than agreed, and allegations of suspected
profiteering circulated as rumours among their friends abroad provided a
convenient excuse.

It therefore seems that the rumours were planted in Norway by Soviet
representatives and then taken up first by the left wing as ammunition
against the right-wing government which Quisling joined in 1931, then by
various polemical authors, and finally by biographers and historians.

Quite apart from the termination of the concession and the Rus-
Norvegoles company, there were conflicts over the liquidation of Onega
Wood. Some of the senior employees of this company were called to
account before the Soviet authorities in the spring of 1928. Exactly what the
Russians were suspicious of is not clear, but they confronted Prytz and
maintained that some of the arrangements he had made were against Soviet
law. Prytz denied this.[89] During the same period Quisling was transferring
sums of about 100,000 roubles from the company's deposit account to its
cheque account each month. Nothing suggests that these transactions were
either irregular or had anything to do with currency exchange.[90]

The story of the rouble scandal was not the only rumour coming out of
Moscow at that time. Word went around in Oslo that Quisling was a British
Secret Service agent. The Norwegian Communists and their newspaper
Arbeideren were adamant on this point, and must have had some Soviet

---

[89] Prytz, Statement of 4 April 1928, Prytz archives.*
[90] Four cheque stubs dated 1926–9, UBO MS fol. 4096.

support for their view. What else could one expect from a former General Staff officer now living at the British legation in Moscow?[91]

FAREWELL TO MOSCOW

During his Moscow years Quisling kept in close touch with Nansen and made a point of visiting him every time he was in Oslo. He had promised to continue with the Armenia work, without payment for as long as he remained in Moscow. 'It is a great comfort for me to know that I have you,' Nansen asserted, as he continued his efforts to secure finance for the Armenian agricultural project, which included going to America on a fund-raising tour. In the meantime, it turned out that many Armenians could be helped in Syria, where a stable settlement of Armenian refugees was establishing itself around Aleppo. Still Nansen was determined to pursue the plans for repatriation.[92]

In autumn 1926 Armenia was hit by an earthquake. For Nansen this signalled that help was needed even more urgently. But the Soviet authorities refused to co-operate. Two years later, Nansen urged Quisling to go to Yerevan as representative of the High Commissioner to speed up the aid project. Quisling replied that the bottleneck was Moscow, not Armenia. Finally, on 1 June 1929 Quisling was sent for by the Armenian Prime Minister, who announced that the Soviet government had once and for all rejected the repatriation project.

The rejection came as a terrible blow to Nansen. Armenia had become a personal crusade for him, and his disappointment was not made any easier now that his opponents at the League of Nations were proved right in their view that the Soviet government was fundamentally opposed to humanitarian concerns. Nansen's naively positive impression of Russia had been built up during the liberal period of NEP and sealed while he was touring the Ukraine, the Volga Valley and Armenia and the Caucasus. But even at that time great changes had taken place. The process of compulsory collectivisation was already under way, and returning refugees were, like millions of others, forcibly deported and later executed under Stalin's brutal industrialisation policy. Many of the people Nansen had met on his Volga

---

[91] *Arbeideren* 15 and 22 May, 22 June 1931.

[92] Approximately fifty letters and telegrams were exchanged concerning Armenia, in UBO MS fol. 3920 V, some printed in Nansen's *Brev* V from the material in UBO MS fol. 1988 A5A–A7A.

and Caucasus tours had disappeared or been killed by the time that his sunny travelogues were published in Norway a few years later.

Quisling had originally shared Nansen's *naïveté*. He too had seen the refugee question as a purely humanitarian issue and had interpreted the great powers' scepticism as short-sighted egotism. He believed small countries were in a position to do more as their hands were clean and they had no vested interest. At the beginning of his time in Moscow he still approved of the way things were developing politically. 'Things here are such a mixture of good and bad,' he wrote home in the summer of 1926. The country was, as he put it, borrowing one of Machiavelli's maxims, 'a barbaric country on its way to civilisation and therefore full of contradictions'.[93]

But during the course of 1927 Quisling was to revise his opinions. Letters home started to take on a different tone, in tune with the great changes in the country. The intense strife over economic policy that followed the 15th Party Congress in the December of that year resulted in instability and violent clashes. The measures adopted by party secretary Joseph Stalin were becoming increasingly brutal, including large-scale purges and torture. In the following autumn, cereals were being collected by force from the villages. This, coupled with crop failure, led to a new famine in the Ukraine in the winter of 1928. Nansen announced that he was willing to start another international initiative for famine relief but the Soviet authorities declined his offer.[94] They did not want any foreign interference. It was becoming increasingly obvious that, in the case of both famine relief and refugees, the open door policy of Lenin's days was long gone. Quisling changed his views accordingly. His letters to Nansen in 1927 and 1928 aired his increasing distance from, even hostility to, Bolshevism, a shift of opinion with obvious consequences for his more general political views. The last contact Quisling had with Nansen from Moscow concerned a repatriation project in reverse – an attempt to get 40,000–50,000 Assyrian and Kurdish refugees *out of* Russia.[95]

The defeat over Armenia was nevertheless a hard blow, even to Quisling. He had shared Nansen's faith for the best part of seven years, which had cost him the goodwill of the General Staff, and indeed his military career. In the end the sceptics were vindicated: the Soviet government itself had called a halt to the humanitarian effort he had dedicated himself to for so many

---

[93] Letter to his parents 19 July 1926, UBO MS fol. 4096 I, 29; to Nansen 15 July and 12 August 1926, UBO MS fol. 1988 5A5.
[94] Nansen to Quisling 31 June 1928 and 9 January 1929, UBO MS fol. 3290 V.
[95] Quisling to Nansen 1 June 1929, UBO MS fol. 3920 V.

years. Besides, the regime became increasingly oppressive, as he said in his letters home.

While the process of compulsory collectivisation was being stepped up Quisling's time as a diplomat was drawing to a close. He had been feeling homesick for some time, and events in Norway in the latter half of the 1920s, with the severe debt crisis in the rural areas following deflation, the conflict between the Communists and the Tranmælites in the Labour movement and the notorious parliamentary instability all worried him deeply.

After the parliamentary elections in Great Britain in June 1929, it became clear that MacDonald's new Labour government wanted to resume diplomatic relations with Moscow. Quisling was therefore superfluous. Britain thanked the Norwegian legation for its help and awarded Quisling the CBE, one of many honours conferred on him for his work abroad. Others included the Romanian Crown Order for his Balkan initiative and the Yugoslav Order of Santa Sava for helping the Grand Duchess out of Petrograd.

While Quisling and Maria were preparing to leave Russia, collectivisation was sweeping the country. On 7 November, Revolution Day, Stalin proclaimed that the 'great breakthrough' had arrived. In December confirmation came that the kulaks (farmers with large holdings) were to be 'liquidated as a class'. Farming families by the hundred thousand were transported to Siberia. Those who refused to go were disposed of by other means. All told, collectivisation prompted 10 million forced deportations. When the Stockholm train brought the Quislings back to Norway on that December morning in 1929, they had left the greatest social upheaval in Russian history behind them for good. The Russian dream had become a Russian nightmare.

3

A reluctant leader

We were thus, much against our will, forced to found a new party, a movement independent of ordinary political parties. Quisling, in retrospect, 1940 [1]

In the spring of 1930 a circle of people who later referred to themselves as 'the club' started meeting at Frederik Prytz's house in Hafrsfjordsgaten in Oslo. Prytz himself was the focus of these meetings. Since his return from Russia he was running only a few businesses, mainly financial operations started up with the profits from his timber business. The dinner parties, meetings and conferences he was arranging at the time were all designed to build up political influence. Quisling, his talented friend from Moscow, was the ideologue of the circle.

Among those Prytz included in the circle was his friend Major Ragnvald Hvoslef, who ran the voluntary military organisation Samfundsvernet, which was the closest Norway came in the 1920s to a White Guard. This organisation recruited officers and volunteers for an armed guard against the strikers and revolutionary activists. Hvoslef was military attaché in Washington at the same time as Prytz was chargé d'affaires in Petrograd, and they were both involved in the timber business, as were other members of 'the club' most of them contemporaries of Prytz's or Quisling's from the War College.

Quisling had few nominations to make. Beyond his family and his old school friends from Skien, he did not really have any connections in Oslo apart from his colleagues from the General Staff, several of whom now attended 'the club', including Adolf Munthe, a distinguished staff officer, and Halvor Hansson, who had been at the Military Academy with Quisling.

Around this core of officers many others also found their way to Prytz's dinner parties: Thorvald Aadahl, the editor of the Agrarian Party newspaper, *Nationen*, was quick to join; two lawyers, Herman Harris Aall, a freelance legal philosopher, and the dynamic barrister Johan Bernhard Hjort, who often accompanied his father, the well-known marine biologist Professor Johan Hjort, to the meetings.

---

[1] *Quisling har sagt* I (1940) p. 32.

It has been said that the Prytz–Quisling circle fitted the textbook definition of a fascist initiative group.[2] It was certainly bourgeois and consisted mainly of business people of various kinds and of varying degrees of success. But what actually distinguished the group, and its core in particular, were all the middle-aged officers. This was a 'captains' movement', if ever there was one in Norway.

Although Quisling was Prytz's intellectual superior, Prytz was the more articulate of the two, and thus functioned as the mouthpiece for their commonly held perceptions and beliefs. Prytz's friends remarked on how he would always look eagerly at Quisling when he was speaking, and always expressed his admiration for him. It was obvious that Prytz had one main reason for hosting these gatherings, and that was to launch Quisling.

THE NANSEN INHERITANCE

On 13 May 1930 Fridtjof Nansen died of a heart attack at the age of sixty-eight. His death was a blow to Quisling, who lost both a hero and a very effective patron. Nansen's death came only a few months after Quisling had lost both his own father and then General Holdtfodt, his much loved Chief of Staff from his earlier years. At forty-three he was suddenly deprived of all his father figures, thus at the same time suffering personal loss and becoming free from the weight of the past.

In place of these figures other influential men emerged. Prytz was an acquaintance of Rolf Thommessen's, the editor of the daily *Tidens Tegn,* which had acted as Nansen's particular mouthpiece. Prytz managed to get Quisling a commission to write an analysis of what Nansen's death meant for Norway. The piece came out in the edition of Saturday 24 May and took up the whole of the front page: 'Political Thoughts on Fridtjof Nansen's Death. By Captain Vidkun Quisling'. Amidst the great rush of emotional outbursts filling the Norwegian press on the subject of Nansen's death, Quisling's was a sharp and most refreshing contribution.

Nansen did not consider his life's work would be complete without sweeping reforms in Norway, Quisling explained, and went on to show that, if Nansen's ideas were to be implemented in Norwegian politics, it would demand a complete reconstruction based on political unification around a ten-point programme, which Quisling formulated thus: total rejection of class strife and party politics, to be replaced by a 'strong and just

---

[2] H. D. Loock, *Quisling, Rosenberg und Terboven* (1970) pp. 69ff.

government, one that is not dependent on a capricious majority'; stimulation of industry through 'scientific organisation'; an increase in wages; a reduction in welfare benefits; stronger defence, improved public health, and greater emphasis on race and heredity. For this purpose what was needed was a 'new, tightly led and youthful national unification party which could take up the country's forsaken banner'. In launching this 'Nansen' programme, Quisling had to admit that Nansen had already embarked upon a unification organisation, the Fatherland League. Somewhat hesitantly, therefore, he added that the party question could 'perhaps' be resolved by the Fatherland League.

The chairman of the League, the young engineer Joakim Lehmkuhl, promptly responded by stating that the Fatherland League was not about to found a new party; what Norway needed was certainly not more parties but rather a mobilisation around the existing non-socialist parties in order to thwart Labour's revitalised revolutionary policy in the forthcoming autumn elections. Captain Quisling was indeed welcome to join in and make his contribution to this important task.

But Quisling had not abandoned his doubts as to what the Fatherland League could achieve. Together with Prytz, he set to work on his own national unification committee in Hafrsfjordsgaten, which started to take shape in the early autumn. At the same time he was busy developing the ideological concepts he had set out in the Nansen obituary into a grander scheme. Ever since his Moscow years he had been planning to write a book on Russia, and now the revolutionary turn of the Labour Party Congress in March 1930 prompted him to combine the two efforts: in one and the same presentation he would reveal the truth about the Soviet Union and raise the alarm against Marxism in Norway.

Thommessen, a bold and unconventional editor with an instinct for eye-catching headlines and grand projects, was anxious for more articles from Quisling. Hearing about the book, he commissioned a whole series for his paper. The first article in the series 'Russia and Ourselves' appeared in *Tidens Tegn* on 15 September 1930, and the series of thirteen long articles, most of which took up the entire front page, ran until early December, when they were published in book form.

'Russia and Ourselves' is a remarkable text, undoubtedly among the more interesting intellectual documents to come out of Norway in the inter-war years. Discussing Russia and the deplorable experiences the thirteen years of Bolshevik rule had brought with them, at the same time it highlights the risk that the Norwegian Labour leaders were exposing the country to in their desire to import a comparable political system into Norway. The chapter on farmers and the 'farming question' is particularly impressive, and it is hard to find a more knowledgeable introduction to the agricultural situation during the Revolution and in the Stalin years than Quisling's. In contrast to the liberals, who tended to defend Stalin's policies with rather naive arguments, Quisling fully understood the scale of the social and economic catastrophe taking place in the countryside in Russia.

Apart from its rich and informative documentation, *Russia and Ourselves* is also a ideological work. As such it shows that Quisling was going through a political transition away from national liberalism and towards National Socialism, but that the process was still far from complete. Committing himself to social biology and a wholly racist interpretation of world history, with the Nordic race at the helm throughout, he still continued to espouse liberal notions of the rule of law and social justice as against the repression, dictatorship and censorship that obtained in Russia. By and large it was Universism rather than racism which informed his political conclusions. 'How is the world to defend itself against Bolshevism?' he asked in the concluding chapter, offering the answer that, since Bolshevism was a 'conspiracy against western civilisation of the Nordic type', nothing less than a grand Northern Coalition of the peoples of Nordic blood would do – a coalition 'beginning with Scandinavia and Great Britain – and with the inclusion of Finland and Holland – which might attract Germany next, and possibly the British Dominions and America later on', designed to protect the Nordic genes now 'threatened by the devastating activities of inferior races'. 'This is not megalomania,' he asserted; it was the way things happened when one country after another faced the truth and started addressing the *race* issue instead of the obsolete class concept.[3]

Russia and Ourselves caused a stir among socialists. The sensational series of articles in *Tidens Tegn* was most unwelcome ahead of the general elections, since Labour had enough problems in defending their pro-Russia stance. *Arbeiderbladet* immediately set out to counter the effect, first by printing still more praise of Russia in the form of readers' letters, features and editorials, then by condemning the articles and their author as 'humbug'. The right, of course, was delighted: at last the truth about Russia was being given proper attention. In short, *Russia and Ourselves* was the book of the season.[4]

[3] Cited from the English translation of *Russia and Ourselves* (1931) pp. 274ff.
[4] *Arbeiderbladet,* editorial 29 September 1930, 'Sovjet Russland'; see also the articles 'Inntrykk

The book also made Quisling's name in Norway. He was invited to dinner
parties by some of the most influential people in the country and was in
demand as a speaker and a pamphleteer for right-wing parties during the
election campaign, despite the fact that he did not belong to any of them. In
the bitter post-mortem which followed the crushing defeat of the Labour
Party in the election, Tranmæl concluded that the right had frightened off
over 200,000 new votes as a result of its 'scare tactics' – among them the 'red
scare' raised by Quisling.[5]

The notoriety Quisling gained from the Russia articles also paved the way
for his entry into politics. Two weeks after publication of the book, he
accepted an invitation from the Fatherland League to join its Oslo board.
Christopher Borchgrevink, who sent the invitation, was full of admiration
for Quisling's book; he had himself fought in Finland on the side of the
Whites in 1918 and had published a book on the horrors of the Revolution
there. Quisling, who had rejected the League outright in 1925 and even as
late as his Nansen obituary in May 1930 had seemed reluctant to recognise
the Fatherland League, took up his seat on the executive committee of the
Oslo chapter together with J. B. Hjort and Professor of Medicine Johan
Holst. Soon he was also elected a member of the Norwegian Society (Den
Norske Selskab), the exclusive English-style gentlemen's club in Oslo. After
so many years abroad it must have been reassuring to receive such a
welcome from the social establishment.

But this was only the beginning. After election day in October 1930, Prytz
and Quisling, anxious to capitalise on Labour election losses, set in motion
their own plans to ward off the red danger by building up a 'comprehensive
guiding political system' under the slightly pompous name of the Nordic
Folk-Rising of Norway (Nordisk Folkereisning i Norge). The founding
meeting of this movement was attended by some thirty-four potential
members – a cross-section of the capital's well-known doctors, lawyers and
company directors as well as the core group from Prytz's parties. It gathered
to promote Quisling's ten-point programme, now condensed to five: to
overthrow Marxism; to enhance the race; to defeat Labour; to establish a
corporate state legislature and to pursue a foreign policy with a Nordic bias
– 'Nordic' in the strictly racial sense of the word. Prytz chaired the meeting.
He proposed various by-laws and principles, outlined by his co-founder in

fra Russland' 16 September, 'Nærmere sosialismen' 15 October, 'Russland, fremtidslandet'
(by Axel Sømme) 30 October 1930.
[5] Tranmæl in *Arbeiderbladet* 27 October 1930, 'Efter valget'.

two written treatises which were printed in advance and distributed around the table; Prytz urged that the assembly did not alter any of them. A certain amount of discussion did take place, but Prytz's proposals were passed more or less unmodified. The elections for the central committee also went smoothly. Prytz circulated a list of thirty-one names, which were voted in by acclamation. Most of the names were of well-known heavyweights: wealthy landowners, lawyers and several of the leaders of the Agrarian Party and the Fatherland League. Among the biggest names on the list were the well-known president of the Industrial League, Johan Throne Holst, and the rector of the University of Oslo. The assembly must have been surprised to hear that not all of the nominees for the central committee had been consulted beforehand, and that barely a third of them were present. There seemed no shortage of powerful names in the Folk-Rising, although the majority of those who turned up apparently did so out of sheer curiosity about Quisling. When the newly elected central committee met a few days later, Quisling was empowered to act as an interim executive committee on his own. The principle of having a *fører*, familiar to any rightist from Italian Fascism, was thus adopted for the first time in Norway. Quisling himself had never developed or even used the notion of *fører* in his political thought to date; moreover, Universism as a world religion recognised no *fører*, only a symbolic leadership on a par with the Pope. But he was ready to assume power, calling on the central committee to hold five meetings in spring 1931, with an average attendance of about one-third of the elected members.[6]

The tiny Folk-Rising was originally intended as a membership organisation, not as a system of private clubs. Quisling, however, returned to his original position regarding this issue, and soon argued for a postponement of the official launch of the movement, which would imply that anyone was welcome to become a member, in favour of expanding the organisation secretly through the private establishment of groups and cells, at least for a time.[7]

At the meeting of the central committee on 13 May 1931, however, the leader stepped down. Prytz was elected to the new one-man executive

---

[6] This account is based on the organisation's archives, in RA PANS 1 and 20. The earliest traces of the organisation are contained in a letter from Prytz to Balchen which was later lost. See Høidal, *Scandinavian Studies* 49/4, pp. 391, 409.

[7] Quisling's four-point programme for the Folk-Rising's military organisation was published in the weekly journal *Nå* no. 31, 1975.

committee on account of Quisling's recent appointment as Minister of
Defence in the new Agrarian government.

THE FASCIST IN THE MINISTRY OF DEFENCE

After Mowinckel's Liberal government was forced to stand down in the
spring of 1931, the Agrarian Party came to power with Peder Kolstad as the
new Prime Minister. Kolstad had several talented young officers in mind for
the post of Minister of Defence, including Otto Ruge and Carl Gustav
Fleischer, but eventually decided on Quisling, whom he did not even know
and who was not even a member of the Agrarian Party. He was persuaded to
do this by his friend Thorvald Aadahl, editor of the main Agrarian newspaper *Nationen*, who in his turn was influenced by his old acquaintance
Frederik Prytz. The reason, according to Prytz, was his book on Russia;
indeed, when asked why he had appointed this man at all, the Prime
Minister replied to a friend, 'He has written such a good book about Russia.'
In fact, there was little to distinguish the Prytz circle from Kolstad's
incoming cabinet. Besides Quisling, several ministers and people who had
been short-listed for ministerial posts were either existing or potential
members of the Folk-Rising.[8]

The new government took office at the moment when the country's ailing
inter-war economy was at its very weakest, and was forced to introduce
austerity measures and drastic cutbacks which resulted in the 1932 budget
being the tightest budget of the century.

The incoming government also had to face the serious labour unrest
which crippled Norwegian industry from March until September 1931,
when there was a general lockout on top of the economic slump that
followed the international crash of autumn 1929. The conflict between the
strikers and the strike-breakers was at the centre of the dispute, with the
rivalry between local Communists and the Labour Party adding fuel to the
fire. On 8 June a Communist-led demonstration of strikers and strike-
breakers stormed Norsk Hydro's Menstad plant in the Skien district of
Telemark. The angry demonstrators overwhelmed the considerable numbers
of police present, chasing after them hurling stones and pieces of iron

---

[8] B. Gabrielsen, *Menn og politikk* (1970) pp. 64ff, and Hartmann, *Fører uten folk*, ch. 'Quisling
blir forsvarsminister'; also A. Bjørneberg, *Parlamentarismens utväckling i Norge* (1939)
pp. 330ff; Prytz to Quisling 2 December 1934 (Prytz archives*); Ræsted, UBO MS fol. 147
p. 47.

piping. The episode, known as the 'battle of Menstad', represented a serious challenge to law and order.[9]

The government decided to send in troops, officially to protect the nearby weapon depots, but probably with the more political aim of preserving law and order in the district. Quisling, who seldom spoke at cabinet meetings, communicated the order of deployment to the Commander-in-Chief. The Royal Guards were duly dispatched to the Gråtenmoen base near Skien, where their tour of duty passed off without incident. The Labour press, however, blew this up into a major event, scolding 'the half-crazy Minister of Defence' for sending in troops and even calling for a general mobilisation against the workers. Quisling was made the scapegoat for the Menstad affair, partly because of the socialists' ignorance of military matters, but also through their eagerness to cash in on the political benefits arising from questioning Quisling's integrity as a cabinet minister: after all, it was only six years since the man had presented himself to both Labour and Communist Party officials with plans for a Soviet type of Red Guard, and now he had resurfaced as the minister responsible for this militaristic show of force at Menstad. It all smacked of political opportunism. The main attack was delivered by the Labour Party's parliamentary leader, Alfred Madsen, who reported the details of the 'Red Guard' talks to the Storting, while Jacob Friis simultaneously disclosed them in the Communist press. Quisling, in short, seemed to be a 'political philanderer' unworthy of his high office.

The Defence Minister had to answer these charges in what was to be his maiden speech in the Storting: 'After my return from Russia, I was accused of offering to start up a Red Guard, an offer which was allegedly refused,' he began, and went on to say little that actually refuted the accusations. On the other hand, he repeatedly stated that he had revised his opinions, both in regard to Russia and on the question of arming the working classes, insisting that he had learned from experience, and thereby, as the Labour MP Johan Nygaardsvold pointed out, conceding that the allegations made against him were true, namely that he *had* sympathised with the revolutionary workers' movement, and that his overtures in this respect *had* been sincere. Such a complete volte-face provided the basis for his role as the Menstad scapegoat.

On 19 June 1931 the guards returned to Oslo. A few days before, the government had got wind of the fact that Communist agitators in the

[9] A. Lindboe, *Fra de urolige tredveårene* (1965) ch. 'Menstadslaget'; P. O. Johansen, *Menstadskonflikten 1931* (1977) ch. 8; Nils Ivar Agøy, *Militæretaten og 'den indre fiende' fra 1905 til 1940* (1997) pp. 327ff; Quisling Almanach, RA, notes from 8–9 June 1931.

Menstad area were in direct contact with Comintern agents in Moscow. This was the first definite proof of such a Russian link, and it prompted Quisling to take a secret, pre-emptive initiative. He approached the Chief of the General Staff and the commanding general about preparing a new set of regulations to be implemented in the event of a coup. Later he also sat down to plan in detail in person the emergency measures required – plans for swift military action 'to prevent an impending revolutionary insurgence'.[10] Through the Staff Intelligence Office he also managed to draw up a list of the leadership of the Revolutionary Trade Union Opposition, which was supposed to have been involved in the Menstad uprising.[11] The police later arrested those who had been most active in the clashes, and twenty-eight men were brought to trial in Skien in December, charged with subversion and violence against the police. Several of them were on Quisling's list.

Menstad was not the only crisis confronting the incoming government. The quarrel with Denmark over the Greenland issue was exacerbated during the summer of 1931, as was the painful question of allowing foreign capital to establish itself in new fields of Norwegian industry. None of these issues involved the Minister of Defence, however. For his part Quisling ran his department quietly and efficiently, mainly implementing policies already in place. However, the following autumn he managed to increase the defence budget by 10 per cent.[12] A further area in which he made a significant contribution concerned the principle of government subsidies for a voluntary defence force to supplement the regular forces – the Leidang.

This was a sensitive issue in Norway. In the winter of 1932–3 the Leidang turned into an ideological issue which provoked much controversy, 'or rather hysteria', as one moderate member remarked. Government regulations for such an initiative had been in existence for a very long time, but there was no specific provision for a voluntary force, although elsewhere in Europe this was not uncommon: in Finland there was a mass movement of 100,000 members, the Skyddskåren, and in Sweden the Landstormen numbered 20,000. Very often these voluntary forces had a certain reactionary, if not fascist aura. In Norway, following the annual cutbacks in the budget, large numbers of junior officers passed into the reserve, and thus enthusiasm for developing the existing initiative into a permanent organisa-

[10] Agøy (1997) pp. 310f interprets the Quisling plan as a blueprint for a 'military *coup d'état*'.
[11] F. Fagertun, *Militærmakten og den indre fiende* (FHFS notat 1984 no. 7); Agøy, *Militær-etaten*, pp. 279ff.
[12] *Straffesak* pp. 197–201 and 237f; Lindboe, *Fra de urolige*, pp. 59–64; R. Godø, 'Forsvarets ledelse fra union til allianse', *Forsvarsstudier* 1989/1.

tion – a militia – increased. Now the idea became a reality thanks to Quisling. Quite possibly, he entertained a vision of something big in these plans, a national action starting from below, with a structure of clubs or committees in line with his Norwegian Action, and certainly with what he had proposed to the socialists in the mid-1920s. However, the Liberal Party dealt the death-blow to the project by voting in favour of the arrangement but at the same time offering considerably less financial support than Quisling had proposed to the Storting. Thus Quisling's special contribution to Norwegian defence turned out to be both modest and short-lived. In 1934 only seven Leidang units were established; a total of twelve altogether recruited no more than one thousand men, and the initiative died down.[13]

Politically, however, his name continued to hit the headlines and the Labour press sustained its attacks. In May 1931 a copy of the Folk-Rising programme that fell into the hands of *Arbeiderbladet* resulted in a sensational article about 'Defence Minister Quisling's New Society'. Attacks were directed more at what was conspiratorial and utopian in the programme than at the actual political contents; thus neither the revolutionary aims nor the racist principles of the Folk-Rising were touched upon, and references to 'fascism' were comparatively mild. Still, Prytz and his friends were alarmed and decided to take the bull by the horns and publish the full principles of the organisation as quickly as possible. The resulting press release stated that Quisling would remain outside the organisation for as long as he was in the cabinet. It explained that the initiative had come into being without 'any kind of model and independently of fascism or of German or any other brand of National Socialism'. The aim of the movement was quite simply to 'bring about the reconciliation of all classes'. The Agrarian *Nationen* carried a sympathetic discussion of the movement, but the radical *Dagbladet* printed a scathing leader entitled 'The Fascist in the Government'. After having quoted a few extracts from the programme on the racial qualities of the Norwegians, and the need for a new corporate assembly (Riksting) to supplement the Storting, the newspaper questioned the fitness of 'a man with such a predilection for methods outside existing systems of government, and with such an enormous lack of balance' for the position of Minister of Defence.

Quisling, then, had become a controversial figure almost immediately. He was the man who had changed his mind on the biggest question of the time,

---

[13] N. Ørvik, *Sikkerhetspolitikken* I (1960) pp. 118, 178f; Godø, 'Forsvarets ledelse', p. 25. B. V. Gabrielsen, 'Leidangen: en studie i frivillig norsk forsvar' (thesis) UiO 1967; St.forh., Innst. S. no. 2 1933 and St.prp. no. 6 1933.

the Russian Revolution; seen from the right this might have been an asset, but from the point of view of the left it could only be interpreted as opportunism *à la* Mussolini.

Quite a few people actually changed their views of the Revolution during the late 1920s, some ten years after Lenin's coup in Russia. Former Bolshevik supporters crossed the line and started to describe themselves as more or less fascist, just as Mussolini himself had done some years before, and as one of the most gifted Labour politicians of the inter-war period in Great Britain, Oswald Mosley, did by crossing the floor to the New Party, thereby embracing fascism.

But what was this new 'fascism' that Quisling and his Folk-Rising were supposed to represent? Few people in Norway had any idea what it meant, beyond vague notions that it represented everything the Communists were fighting against. Tranmæl called the Folk-Rising 'a swastika-organisation; a carbon copy of Hitler's fascist movement in Germany'. *Dagbladet* referred to Quisling as not only a fascist but also a National Socialist, comparing him with the Nazi ideologue Alfred Rosenberg – a man whom Quisling could only dimly have been aware of at that time. The allegations of 'fascism' surrounded the new Defence Minister with an aura of mystery: 'He is a man of darkness,' wrote the author and journalist Axel Kielland; he had his family ties to 'the counter-revolutionary circles in the Soviet Union', remarked a Labour politician in the Storting. One newspaper even speculated (wrongly) that the mysterious bearded foreigner observed at a Norwegian railway station in 1930 was the exiled Trotsky, on his way to seeking 'a formal audience with Captain Quisling'.[14]

THE PEPPER SCANDAL

Life as a cabinet minister involved a good deal of socialising for Maria and Vidkun, in contrast to the quiet life they had been accustomed to in Moscow. Dinner invitations from the legations of the great powers, from government colleagues, from old friends and new ones too kept pouring in. They were even received at the palace, where Maria danced with King Haakon and got on well with him, but Crown Princess Martha found her taciturn husband the dullest cabinet minister ever.[15]

---

[14] *Dagbladet*, 'Ukens portrett', 6 February 1932; F. Monsen in the Storting 29 June 1932, St.forh. b.7. p. 2522; *TT* 29 November 1930, 'Trotski i Oslo!'.

[15] Maria Quisling, *Dagbok*, p. 23; testimony of Lars Roar Langslet 1990.

Quisling had a large office on the second floor of the Ministry's beautiful building just outside Akershus Castle. He was a very disciplined worker who preferred actions to words, and soon earned a reputation for being an efficient administrator. It was also obvious that the country's officer class to a significant degree regarded Quisling as their man in the government.

On Tuesday 2 February 1932 Quisling received a dinner invitation from the architect Bredo Berntsen, a friend of Prytz's who was sympathetic to the Folk-Rising. The other guests gathered at 7.30, but neither Prytz nor Quisling arrived on time. Eventually Prytz did arrive, only to inform his host that Quisling had fallen down the stairs at the Ministry that afternoon and had to rest at home, at least until the following day, but it was nothing serious, and Quisling did not want anything to be made of it.[16]

But Prytz was troubled. It was not true that his friend had had a fall. He was at home, half-dead and exhausted after having been both stabbed and knocked unconscious in his own department office. Prytz had been alerted by Maria, and when he arrived at the apartment Quisling, who was in a very weak condition, only gradually managed to relate what had happened.

After lunch he had gone to the Defence Ministry to get some papers from the office. When he arrived he noticed that the door leading to the back room was open, which was unusual. When he went over to investigate he saw an unfamiliar suitcase on the floor by the entrance to the small room where the safe was kept. It was about 5 o'clock and dark. Suddenly someone brandishing a knife came rushing at him. Quisling sustained a few scratches but avoided being stabbed by swiftly parrying the blow. Then he felt a stinging sensation in his eyes, and must have received a blow to his head before he fell unconscious to the floor. When he came to, he was alone. He gathered up his things, left the office, and took a taxi home.

Prytz immediately thought of the police, but Quisling did not want any fuss. He wanted to sleep on the matter, and in the morning when he felt better try to find out who was responsible. He told Prytz to go on to the party and excuse him with the story that he had fallen down the stairs. But as the evening wore on Prytz became increasingly uneasy about the whole affair, and wondered whether he should not, after all, notify the police, and worried lest the cleaner remove any fingerprints in the morning. He

---

[16] All documents relating to the attack have disappeared from Oslo Politikammers Arkiv, Statsarkivet in Oslo. The following account is based on press reports 5–11 February 1932, and Quisling, Almanach.

discussed it with another guest, Captain Munthe, and slipped off to telephone Maria. At that moment dinner was about to be served. The hostess came and called Prytz and Munthe to table, and it was not until after midnight that they were able to act. Prytz telephoned the police and Munthe the Foreign Minister, Birger Braadland, who was also acting prime minister at the time.

When the police arrived at the scene of the crime they found traces of pepper on the floor, and concluded that the attacker had tried to blind his victim during the struggle. An investigation followed. Quisling arrived at the office as usual the next morning, despite feeling dizzy and generally weak. At the cabinet meeting the following day it was decided to make the incident public and to offer a reward of 5,000 kroner to anyone who could help the police in their enquiries.

On Friday 5 February the affair exploded in the press. Quisling attacked by an unknown intruder! The front pages carried a tale so full of mystery and so open to wild speculation that it became the story of the winter. Given the aura of mystery surrounding Quisling, this had to be expected. But neither the police nor the government could have foreseen what was to happen next: the Minister's explanation to the press was simply not believed.

The Labour press suspected that the entire incident had been staged by none other than the Minister of Defence himself. With *Nationen* and *Tidens Tegn* as the only active defenders of Quisling and the rest of the press in active opposition to him, an animated debate erupted over the veracity of the basic facts of the story. Rather than being viewed as an attack with grave implications for national security, or even as a serious police matter, the episode developed into a 'Quisling affair'.

With the case taking such a turn, the police decided to release more evidence and presented the entire expert medical report to prove that the scuffle had been very serious, and that the Minister's assailant had repeatedly tried to stab him in the chest and the throat, and that the blow to his head had been inflicted by a heavy cosh. However, this expert testimony helped Quisling little. To the delight of the press, the attacker was nowhere to be found. The Labour papers continued their provocation, declaring the attack to have been set up, Mussolini-style, so that the blame could be put on the Communists or the socialists. Among journalists the version preferred was that Quisling had been stealing a moment of passion with one of the cleaners that afternoon, only to be surprised by her jealous husband, a burly longshoreman who had come in to give the Minister a thrashing. Quisling himself consistently refused to give his opinion regarding the identity of his attacker, and was completely against the decision of the Chief of Police to make the case public, which suggests that he did have a shrewd idea of who was responsible. In the end he made a statement to *Nationen* to the effect that he was unable to comment on the case so long as he remained in office.

It was not until he appeared in the High Court in 1945 that he broke his silence on the matter and recounted how he had received a visit from a Swedish General Staff officer a couple of days before the attack, a Lieutenant Colonel Wilhelm Kleen, who had left some documents pertaining to military relations. Quisling regarded the attack as having been carried out by 'someone who was after those documents'.[17] The matter which Kleen had arrived in Oslo to discuss was quite sensitive as it concerned the extent to which Norway would be able to make her ports available for military transit to Sweden in the event of the Baltic's being turned into a theatre of war.[18] The background to the 'pepper affair', then, seems to have been that somebody with an interest in these plans of the Swedish General Staff found it easier to get hold of the Swedish documents in Oslo than in Stockholm, followed Kleen during his visit and discovered that he had left the material in the Ministry – and then entered the building at some point in the late afternoon when the offices were guarded only by unobservant conscripts. It was pure coincidence that the Minister himself had appeared.

The pepper riddle has never been solved. It is not even known what the Oslo police managed to uncover during their investigations as the case file disappeared from the archives and has never come to light. Quisling in any event did not consider the case to be of grave concern to Norway, and certainly not a covert Soviet operation. Had he entertained suspicions in that direction he would certainly have behaved differently. If, on the other hand, he had believed that German agents were active, he would hardly have remained so calm. It is therefore most likely that either agents from a lesser power were responsible – perhaps one of the Balkan states or Finland – or that the whole story of the Kleen papers was a cover for other and more political issues.

As it was, the controversy over the 'pepper affair' left a deep impression on the public. It polarised opinions on the subject of Quisling's trustworthiness between those who held that he had lied and should be exposed by every available means and those who saw in him an honest and brave man deserving of sympathy because such false accusations were hurled against him. Even after the case had died down, opinions continued to be divided

---

[17] *Straffesak* p. 335.   [18] Ørvik, *Sikkerhetspolitikken*, pp. 38f.

along these lines. During the 1933 elections, the chairman of the Labour youth movement declared that Quisling as Defence Minister had only concerned himself with 'women, parties and pepper'. While he was in custody at Akershus in the summer of 1945, Quisling was asked by a good-humoured guard whether that 'pepper affair' had not, after all, only been some 'woman trouble or other'. People wondered. But his cabinet and parliamentary colleagues were astonished by the fact that someone who seemed so sullen, charmless and wholly uninteresting had managed to stir up public opinion to such an extent.[19]

APPROBATION

On 5 March 1932, just after Quisling returned to work, Peder Kolstad died of coronary thrombosis. Jens Hundseid, Agrarian Party chairman and parliamentary leader, took over as Prime Minister. Quisling was retained as Defence Minister in the new cabinet.

As a result of this sequence of events, Quisling did not have to face the Storting in open debate until 7 April. By then he had had sufficient time to think out a suitable reply to his critics over the 'pepper affair'. It seemed to him that the role of the press in the wild speculations concerning the incident and his own part in it had become much more serious as the incident had been allowed to overshadow the actual threat to national security which Soviet infiltration represented. Moscow agents were operating quite openly in Norway, and many Labour politicians were co-operating with them, some out of *naïveté* but others from revolutionary motives. Quisling submitted documents to his cabinet colleagues concerning subversive activities which bore directly on the Menstad affair and which showed that Norwegian trade unions had received support from the Soviet Union, hundreds of thousands of kroner from the International Revolution leadership, partly in the form of strike contributions. The Soviets also gave financial support to the Communist press and Party activities. On 18 March 1932 the government paid 10,000 kroner into a secret account (approximately one good annual salary) to help the Minister of Defence in his investigations of foreign agents in Norway and to keep a check on illegal weapon imports. Quisling mentioned to his cabinet colleagues that he intended to question the motives of Tranmæl, Scheflo and Furubotn in his forthcoming speech in the Storting, exposing them as revolutionaries.

---

[19] *Arbeiderbladet* 13 September 1933; story related by a guard to the author in 1986.

When he was drafting his speech, Quisling carefully skirted around the word 'treason' by employing the expression 'enemies of our fatherland and our people'. Several members of the government later said that they had not known in advance that the Minister had intended to go so far in his attack, and few condoned it. However, the Prime Minister had urged Quisling at a number of cabinet meetings to make use of the information he possessed, and the inner circle of the Agrarians' leadership had also been apprised of the contents of his speech in advance.

On 8 April 1932 Quisling rose in the Storting to defend himself in an impassioned speech which turned into a cascade of attacks on Labour and the Communists. He spoke for almost half an hour, driving home his points with vigorous attacks, and insisting, by constantly patting his briefcase, that he had plenty of documentary evidence from military surveillance sources to substantiate his charges. The assembly was spellbound; what was to have been a self-defence against insulting allegations about women and the like turned out to be one of the most powerfully offensive speeches in the history of the Storting.

For Quisling personally the speech was a great success. *Nationen* and *Tidens Tegn* immediately rushed to his defence. Flowers and letters came streaming in, as did words of support from rifle clubs, forest owners' trade associations and patriotic groups from all over Norway. Letters and telegrams by the hundred brought greetings from fellow officers and admirers. 'I cannot hide my enthusiasm,' wrote the author Johan Bojer. Everywhere people said that Quisling was 'the only real man in the country'.[20]

To Prytz and his friends from Hafrsfjordsgate the speech gave the signal to start mobilising the political potential around Quisling. At the end of April the first draft of a call to support the courageous Defence Minister was circulated, and shortly afterwards the Fatherland League declared its support for the initiative. By early June a joint declaration was published in the shape of a flaming protest against 'the revolutionary parties' who were seeking to introduce class dictatorship and to make the country dependent on foreign powers: 'By the action which Minister Quisling has taken, the case has been brought to the attention of the government authorities. We demand that the authorities once and for all put a stop to revolutionary and treacherous activities in Norway.'[21] The names of 153 distinguished signatories were

---

[20] Approximately 150 letters and telegrams are contained in UBO MS fol. 4096 VI, 2.

[21] Cited in the Oslo press 3 June 1932. See also various documents in RA PA Prytz 4, and

added to the text, including those of two ex-prime ministers and several former cabinet ministers, a former chief of the Supreme Court, several leading generals, timber barons and ship owners: altogether a landslide in the popular opinion of the right.

In the Storting, however, the reaction to Quisling's speech was completely different. To the politically acute the speech was regarded as on a par with political suicide, since Quisling's accusations raised far greater political problems than they managed to clear up – and would ultimately backfire not only on the speaker himself but also on the government and the party. The problems started immediately, when the Labour parliamentary leader, Johan Nygaardsvold, demanded that the documents from the Minister's suitcase be handed over to the Storting to be investigated by a Special Committee. The crux of the matter was that, if Quisling – or the intelligence of the General Staff – really possessed documentary evidence of year-long illegal revolutionary activity, he ought to have submitted it earlier; in fact, the more serious the situation described in the documents was, the worse it was for the government, who had failed to take any action. The Prime Minister sensed the problem here. Mr Hundseid immediately distanced himself from Quisling in his introductory comments on the case. Both the leading Liberal politician Johan Ludvig Mowinckel and the Conservative C. J. Hambro, on behalf of their party groups, responded half-sympathetically to Quisling, acknowledging his need to defend himself, but stating that, nevertheless, to cause such serious alarm in order to serve that purpose was to mix personal matters with national ones in a way that could only in the end be to the detriment of the latter. To Quisling, such reactions demonstrated that the party politicians neither could nor would confront the reality of the situation, and would take to evasive actions at every turn.[22]

Worse was to come. Quisling's briefcase turned out to contain information compiled from several different sources – some anonymous, others insignificant, some consisting only of newspaper clippings. Instead of concentrating on a few well-documented substantial cases, Quisling chose to empty the files of the General Staff Intelligence Office, which turned out to be a serious miscalculation.

Police officials were summoned to the Special Committee to evaluate the substance of the documents from the Defence Ministry. Their official

---

H. F. Dahl, 'Quislings statskupp 9. april i forfatningshistorisk perspektiv', *HT* 1978 pp. 267f.

[22] Document no. 8, St.forh. 1932 b 5. Innst. S. 1932 no. 184 exhibit 1 and p. 473; for the debate in parliament see also Lindboe, *Fra de urolige*, pp. 45f.

relationship with Military Intelligence was, as always, strained, and now they had the pleasure of going through military information in fine detail and of showing that the intelligence officers had been relying on dubious sources, including well-known underground figures whom the police knew only too well to be unreliable persons.

Quisling had also claimed that he could prove that the Menstad uprising had been an attempt to carry out 'a planned agitation' orchestrated by Moscow. His main evidence was a telegram from a Norwegian Communist in Moscow to a Communist Party member in Oslo which an employee in the telegraph company had intercepted and handed over to the government on 15 June 1931. But the Committee concluded that by the time the Comintern first tried to intervene, the conflict was already dying out.

A group of Labour leaders, among them Martin Tranmæl, were interrogated about being on the Moscow–Comintern–Soviet payroll. All of them denied it, insisting that they had never received a penny from those quarters, and there was nothing to prove otherwise.

On 24 June 1932 the Special Committee was ready with its recommendations. The non-socialist majority cautiously closed ranks around Quisling, confirming that he did have grounds for the accusations he had made in his speech. Only Labour was unrestrained in its criticism of the Defence Minister and his staff sources. In reality, however, the case was buried, as the Committee recommended no further action be taken. The Storting refused to make Quisling's cause its own. The reality was that his suitcase had contained no really substantial proof of subversive activities other than what was known already, and nothing which could survive the crossfire of parliamentary enquiry – particularly as the Liberals were at pains not to distance themselves completely from the socialists.[23]

While the Special Committee concluded its work, Prytz's call for support to the cause of Quisling was circulated throughout the country. Tens of thousands of names were added to the declaration of protest issued by the 153 dignitaries. Even local actions were started: in Skien a group of citizens collected signatures for a printed tribute to honour Telemark's great son. In the rural press, the brave Defence Minister was now referred to as 'Norway's most talked-about man'. His extra-parliamentary reputation was clearly in the process of overshadowing his standing in parliament. Alf Mjøen, the

---

[23] Secret Soviet activities in Norway were in fact numerous, even if neither the General Staff nor the police managed to disclose them. See Tim Greve, *Spionjakt i Norge* (1982) pp. 114f, 124, 127; and Lars Borgersrud, *Nødvendig innsats* (1997) *passim*.

long-standing chairman of the Military Committee, approached Quisling in the Storting and said bluntly: 'There is strong feeling among the people for your cause, Minister.'[24]

The summer of 1932 was unusually hot and, for Quisling, hectic. There were naval visits from England, Germany and Sweden, involving the obligatory receptions and dinners. In July the Soviet representative in Norway registered an official protest on behalf of his government against Quisling's speech, announcing that his statements severely tested relations between the two countries. This diplomatic note would have caused a sensation had it reached the press, but fortunately for Quisling it did not. The Foreign Minister withheld it from both the Storting's Foreign Affairs Committee and the press. Perhaps he considered that Quisling had had enough trouble already.[25]

Quisling was in great demand as a speaker that summer. This was something completely new for him. Every weekend he would set off to address meetings and rallies called by the people who had supported the declaration. At the North Trøndelag Agrarian Party conference, Quisling was the main speaker and was received with great enthusiasm by the four thousand people who had turned up to hear him; his speech was followed by rapturous applause. The following Sunday he addressed the Fatherland League's Sørland convention at Tvedestrand. Again he was a success. 'Sørland farmers pay tribute to Quisling,' wrote *Nationen*. The following Sunday bands of curious people drove up to Hønefoss in order to cheer the Minister. Later on he gave the main speech at the Agrarian Telemark conference in Bø and delivered similar speeches at Kongsvinger and a fortnight later at Dokka. The turn-out on each occasion was in the thousands.[26]

Perhaps the most significant effect of the summer was the impression it made on Quisling himself. For him, the sound of approval, the applause of the public, was proof that he had the people with him, perhaps by the hundred thousand. For his audiences, on the other hand, it was obvious that the Minister, however courageous, was no great orator: the applause was

---

[24] Mjøen to Quisling 31 August 1932, UBO MS fol. 4096 VI. Also K. Gleditsch in *Mot Dag* 1932/11.

[25] The note of 20 July 1932 is printed in S. G. Holtsmark (ed.), *Norge-Sovjetunionen*, pp. 193ff. It was brought to public knowledge only the following year; see *TT* 21 March 1933.

[26] Press reports *Nationen* 18 July, 27 July, 15 August 1932; see also Quisling's Almanach 1932; various correspondence in UBO MS fol. 4096. Gabrielsen, *Menn og politikk*, pp. 108f.

usually louder before Quisling spoke than it was afterwards. But even so, people were very curious about him and tributes poured in in the form of resolutions from congresses and conferences whenever his name was brought up.

MAN OF THE YEAR

In the autumn of 1932 Quisling started to consolidate the exceptional position he had won in public opinion into political influence of an enduring kind. Two possible routes presented themselves. One was to build up his position inside the Agrarian Party and the cabinet, and to exploit public opinion as a base from which he could defeat the Prime Minister, the party and even the parliamentary majority from within. The alternative was to make direct use of popular feeling by founding a new party. In deciding which route to choose, he was forced to look beyond the Prytz group. His officer friends continued to be important to him, but new contacts were constantly being made in the ever-widening social circles he was moving in as a politician. That autumn he was introduced to a group a contemporary source referred to as the country's 'high finance'. He already knew Johan Throne Holst, and Conrad Landgaard was his half-cousin; now he was trying to forge closer links with important people from the financial and business sectors. His single most important contact, however, was the lawyer J. B. Hjort.

Hjort was thirty-seven years old, married to Anna Holst, a niece of Throne Holst's. He was a restless, energetic character who was also an exceptionally gifted lawyer. His insight into public finance was first-class and in the early 1930s he was investigating the problem of the agricultural deficit. His mother was German and two of his sisters were married to Germans who were prominent in Hitler's party. In the early 1930s he became a radical right-winger and left the Conservative Party to join the Folk-Rising and later the NS. In contrast to the Prytz circle, Hjort did have some political experience. In the Conservative Party he had occupied a number of posts, though he had been curiously inactive in the Fatherland League.[27]

On 13 May 1932 Quisling recorded their first meeting at the 'Polkom', the political committee, in his diary. This committee was identical with that

---

[27] Biography in *NS* 1934/25; see also *Statsøkonomisk tidsskrift* (1932) pp. 115f; Wanda Heger, *Hver fredag foran porten* (1984).

which from the spring of 1931 had organised the external work of the Nordic Folk-Rising. But the driving force behind these meetings was no longer the pleasant conversations at Prytz's home. Hjort was a realist, always looking for results, and the lightweight approach of the Folk-Rising had never suited him. It was when Quisling was appointed minister that his eyes were first opened to the possibility of political action, and he set to work. Hjort gradually directed the convivial group of captains away from Prytz and in the direction of more practical politics. As Hjort's importance to Quisling and his cause grew, Prytz withdrew. He put his money in a country estate at Fosna, in Trøndelag, where he settled with his family in the course of 1933. The change of partner proved to be decisive for Quisling.

Their first joint project was to draft a series of bills designed to bar revolutionary parties from putting up lists of candidates at elections and from receiving donations from abroad for political purposes; to revise the poor laws in order to suspend the voting rights of those in receipt of state benefits; and finally to clear up public finances and ease the burden of agricultural debt. The suggestions reflected the standard right-wing views of the early 1930s, and were not particularly extreme by contemporary standards. The interesting thing lay rather in the fact that Hjort and Quisling now imagined that this package of sensitive reforms could be pushed through and implemented quickly, and thereby create another 'Quisling case'.[28]

In the summer of 1932 much was achieved. Quisling mobilised considerable support and built up quite a reputation at the rallies around the country. When the autumn came and the political committee met for further discussions, the situation had undoubtedly improved for them. The first step in Hjort's plan was that Quisling should present his programme to the cabinet. The issue of the initiative against the revolutionaries was brought into sharper focus by a case coming up in the Ministry of Defence which Quisling pursued with a zeal far exceeding that of his colleagues. This was the so-called 'Kullmann affair', and concerned the naval officer Captain Olaf Kullmann, a revolutionary pacifist, who although on active duty would appear at pacifist rallies organised by the Labour movement in full uniform and urge all fighting men to lay down their weapons in the event of war. To the Minister this was the enemy within, a revolutionary threat from his own ranks which had to be crushed to show that he was serious on the question of the broader issues. The Ministry of Defence followed Kullmann's activities

---

[28] *Aide-mémoire* by Hjort 13 May 1932 in RA GS IV 1373 2, box 14.

closely, and when it was reported that he had urged fellow officers around the world to 'agitate against war' at an international rally, the time had come for action.[29]

Quisling and his staff set to work, determined that Kullmann be discharged and indicted for treasonous activity. 'This is about the conspiratorial international workers' revolutionary organisation,' Quisling stated, asserting that the case had now transcended the exploits of an eccentric officer. And indeed, leading Norwegian socialists spoke in defence of their fellow party member Olaf Kullmann. 'The Norwegian Labour Party is behind Captain Kullmann,' Tranmæl declared at party headquarters, and added, 'Should there be a war, it will be our duty to transform it into civil war.'[30]

Opinion was divided over Kullmann within the cabinet and outside it, however, and once more Quisling's intransigence served to polarise both public and parliamentary opinion. His allegations concerning the Soviet-backed peace movement seemed justified, even though they had been made in a somewhat dramatic manner. Nevertheless, it was considered too late to prosecute the Labour leadership for planning and producing anti-military propaganda as it had been going on openly for decades. Quisling's absolutist arguments often worked this way, forcing him to take up categorical positions; the basic political *modus operandi*, the interim compromise, was completely alien to him, and his intransigence thus prevented him from winning real political influence.

However, on this occasion, the Kullmann affair did seem to provide the perfect opportunity for a final confrontation with the Labour movement. But Prime Minister Hundseid, rather than exploit the case by finding a united course of action against the rebellious captain, distanced himself from Quisling's initiative, thereby compromising his own minister: he did not want to prosecute the Labour leadership at all, and took a firm line against the idea of legal prosecutions. Quisling, however, enjoyed the support not only of his own senior civil servants but also of a considerable number of the country's salaried officers, in addition to the backing of the armed forces in general. This led to a wider confrontation between the politicians of the Storting and the extra-parliamentary conservative opposi-

---

[29] Report from a pro-Soviet anti-war convention in Amsterdam, *Dagbladet* 5 September 1932.
[30] Ministry of Defence to Ministry of Justice 14 October 1932, document made available by Stein Ørnhøi.* Various press reports.

tion. In fact, the Kullmann affair was threatening to bring down the government.[31]

On Monday 21 November 1932 Quisling broke the silence he usually maintained at cabinet meetings. To the astonishment of his colleagues he delivered a lengthy and damning critique of the Prime Minister. Furthermore, with the help of Prytz and Aadahl at *Nationen*, he produced and mimeographed a devastating memorandum which he distributed in person to the Prime Minister and his cabinet colleagues the following Sunday. It was marked 'Strictly Confidential' and gave the signal of revolt to the Agrarian Party.[32]

After presenting his demands for economic reform, improved labour and industrial relations, and a more effective emergency policy for farmers, fishermen and the unemployed, the Quisling memorandum closed with this demand: 'I for my part have done my best, but find I can no longer accept the present leadership. I therefore request that the Prime Minister stand down.'

Quisling had done nothing to warn his cabinet colleagues of this bombshell. Whether or not the attack was aimed at the government or further afield – or perhaps both – one thing was clear: the Prime Minister and the Defence Minister were trying to oust each other. Quisling did not manage to secure the support of his colleagues, but neither did Hundseid get their endorsement for Quisling's removal. If such a popular figure as the Minister of Defence were forced out, all the divisions and conflicts in the cabinet would be exposed. Not until the government conference of 8 December was a coherent resolution drawn up. On the one hand Kullmann's commission was to be suspended and a civil case brought against him; but on the other hand the question of further prosecution of him and the others named in the Ministry of Defence's charges was to be 'subject to further investigation'. *Nationen* and *Tidens Tegn* interpreted the compromise as a great victory for Quisling. The radical press, on the other hand, highlighted the difference between this announcement and the bellicose manifesto that the press had received from the Ministry of Defence earlier, with its demand for full-scale prosecution. 'Quisling has humbled himself in order to save his cabinet position,' wrote *Dagbladet*; 'the treason charges have to be dropped.' On the other hand, it was clear that the Prime Minister no longer had a majority

---

[31] Hartmann, *Fører uten folk*, ch. 'Kullmannsaken'.
[32] Quisling's memorandum of 26 November 1932 is reprinted in Hartmann, *Fører uten folk*, pp. 278–86.

behind him in his own government.[33] With tensions mounting behind the government's locked doors, Quisling's star continued to rise among the public, to the extent that around Christmas he was widely referred to as this year's 'man of the year', a person from whom great things were expected in the forthcoming election of 1933.[34]

The popularity that Quisling had been gaining from his dramatic parliamentary speeches, from the summer conferences and from the Kullmann affair was a source of particular concern for the Conservatives. The party chairman, C. J. Hambro, went to Hundseid before Christmas, with Quisling's departure as a condition for his party's continued support for the Agrarian government.[35] The entire non-socialist party structure had the uneasy feeling that it was harbouring a viper in its bosom. Three days after the Hambro–Hundseid conversation *Tidens Tegn* gave a great deal of publicity to a provocative letter by Knut Hamsun which was clearly pro-Quisling and which poured sarcasm on the most prominent representative of the non-socialists, Mowinckel.[36]

But the real test for the non-socialists came early in December 1932 when rumours of a new party centred around Quisling first began to circulate. These rumours probably originated with the Independent Liberal Party (Frisinnede Folkepartiet) conference which opened in Oslo on 30 November. The delegates were troubled by certain doubts concerning the party's *raison d'être* following its humiliation at previous elections. *Tidens Tegn* fanned the flames of these doubts by suggesting the need for a new party with a broader base which could unite 'those scattered among the various parties and groups, who are essentially of one mind'. More than once the paper published an encomium on the Defence Minister and in the same breath delivered its exhortation to 'found a new party ... under the leadership of new, vigorous forces' which could take up the struggle in the elections and, together with the Agrarians, form a strong 'cross-party' national government.[37]

Still, however, the possibility of engineering a coup from within the cabinet was seriously considered by Quisling's circle of associates as an alternative to the party line. The Marxist journal *Mot Dag* had a shrewd idea of what was going on. A leading article, 'Pronunciamento', published on 23 December 1932, outlined with a higher degree of accuracy than the author

---

[33] *TT* 14 December 1932; *Dagbladet* 10 December 1942.
[34] Norland, *Hårde tider*, p. 198.   [35] Lindboe, *Fra de urolige*, pp. 188–90.
[36] *TT* 10 November 1932.   [37] *TT* 30 November and 2 December 1932.

could ever have guessed the possibility of a *coup d'état* in Norway – but eventually dismissed the possibility, concluding that 'Quisling cannot be as mad as that'. However, he was. Recent research in the innermost files at the Ministry of Defence suggests that his emergency plans for a counter-action in case of a (Red) coup, initiated in 1931, had at that time developed into a more offensive measure. Quisling himself commented with hindsight a few years later: 'For me the issue then was whether I should use force or not.'[38]

But the new year saw the door closing behind him. Quisling had to abandon the idea of a coup and to turn towards the electorate instead. In the second week of January 1933, as he was once again the focus of debate in the Storting, Nygaardsvold spoke at length on 'the new party which Mr Quisling is about to found', 'his new fascist party'. Hambro gave his conditional support to Quisling over the Kullmann affair, without touching on his feud with Hundseid. Spokesmen for the two smaller parties on the right displayed a strong interest in their potential rival at the ballot box, stating that 'the name Quisling implies … a political programme', a programme, that is, which would mobilise voters. From the negotiations which were going on simultaneously in the Finance Committee, it was leaked that the Liberals were planning to bring down the government at the first possible opportunity, at the finance debate scheduled for 23 February 1933.[39]

This sealed the fate of Quisling. When he gave his last speech in the Storting on 24 February, he made it clear that this was not his farewell to politics. He was looking ahead – to the parliamentary elections in October. No other path was now open than the party road to influence. When his article 'Clear Lines' appeared on the front page of *Nationen* the following Monday, he no longer wished to be considered a member of the Agrarian Party, but to act as an independent. On the other hand, his position with regard to the parliamentary system was, he claimed, one of complete loyalty; the point was simply that, in order to make the executive authority stronger and more autonomous, 'a concentration of power in a legal form' was needed. During a crisis such as the country was now facing, the National Assembly had to impose controls on itself and make way for a government which 'must stand over and above party politics'.

The following week he resumed the reconstruction of the Nordic Folk-

---

[38] Interview in *Berliner Börsenzeitung* 23 October 1940, quoted in Mogens, *Tyskerne*, p. 50. 'Pronunciamento': *Mot Dag* 1932/19 pp. 405–7. Recent research: Agøy, *Militæretaten*, pp. 310ff.

[39] St.forh. 1933 b.7 pp. 88f (Nygaardsvold), 99 (Hambro), 109 (Mowinckel), 114f (Greve), 118ff (Hundseid), 129f (Mjøen), 190–2 (Quisling).

Rising. With its original *fører* back in place, the organisation was turned into a political party. But just how closely it should co-operate with other parties was not yet clear, as Quisling continued to watch how the land lay in relation to the Agrarian Party. His feud with Hundseid was a definite obstacle. For a while it seemed that Hundseid would step down from the party leadership, in which case Quisling might perhaps be the man to be called in. Then Hundseid decided to resume his post, and Quisling moved on to envisage his own new party as a possible urban party complementary to the rural Agrarians. When the political committee met on 1 May, Quisling expressed his hope that an agreement of this kind was within reach. The following day, when he met with representatives from the Agrarians, together with Hjort and Prytz, the negotiations came to nothing. 'Quisling was not willing to co-operate,' Hundseid was told. Meanwhile, time was running out. Prytz and Hjort were both eager to let the new party enter the election campaign independent of any alliance. The impatient Hjort was particularly anxious not to waste time in lengthy negotiations with the Agrarians. He wanted to get the new party ready before the summer, and deal with the question of electoral pacts and sharing constituencies later. From May onwards, this was their tactic.[40]

THE NEW PARTY AND THE GENERAL ELECTION

With six parties already in the Storting, forming a seventh certainly felt something of an anti-climax to the father of Universism. Quisling had always proclaimed that there was only one party that he recognised – the Norwegian people's party, but circumstances now compelled him to establish something on a more modest scale. In many ways he saw the founding of the party as essentially a defeat; a party run along the lines of the other parties had no place in his philosophy. He regarded himself as the founder of a new religion, not a party leader; a Universist, not a pluralist, insisting that the Nasjonal Samling – National Union, NS – was no ordinary party but rather a movement designed to bring together and unite all through a common understanding. The new party's manifesto published that summer therefore contained the following statement: 'National Union will support those parliamentary candidates, both its own and others', who commit themselves in advance to the forming of a national bloc in the Storting ...

---

[40] Minutes in RA PAQ 11, *Hovedstyreprotokoll* 2 May 1933 and Quisling's letter of 4 May 1933 NBA.

our aim is to establish a strong and stable national government independent of ordinary party politics.'

Ordinary party work rather than lofty promises was what was needed to get the new party off the ground, which meant competition, struggle, practical obstacles, above all reliance on other, less outstanding party workers. In the spring and summer of 1933 Quisling had to face all this in full measure. When he decided to publicise a 'call for National Union' through the three big non-socialist newspapers on 16 May, the eve of Constitution Day, *Aftenposten* refused to publish it, and *Nationen* printed only excerpts. Still, the article provoked yet another outburst from Joakim Lehmkuhl, the chairman of the Fatherland League, who bitterly denounced the founding of a new party on the right. Indeed, NS was met with no general welcome, even among potential supporters.[41]

New supporters, however, kept appearing. A young and zealous advertising executive, Walter Fürst, turned out to be indispensable at the launch of the new party. Fürst was educated in Berlin and had been pressing Quisling to do this for months, eager to steal a march on a rival Norwegian National Socialist Party which was threatening to come forward, its leader appearing in what his followers took to be an SS uniform and calling for the immediate establishment of a Norwegian Hitler movement. Now Fürst urged the more reluctant Quisling to show his colours.[42] With his keen eye for visual effects he even supplied the NS with a regular logo – the Olav Cross, originally designed by Quisling himself for the use of the Folk-Rising – a banner, and a basic rally choreography of flags and national anthems. Fürst introduced the *fører* greeting – German-style upraised arm – and set out the basic rules for the leadership cult that was to bolster Quisling's position. Indeed, he arranged nearly everything, including an office suite in Prinsens Street in downtown Oslo, complete with a duplicator. Here the new party organisation took its first feeble steps. A stream of young people reported regularly to work for the new party. Fürst gave them leaflets and posters to distribute, and they soon covered the entire city by car and bicycle. Soon the party's symbol, the yellow St Olav's cross on a red background, was to be seen everywhere. In the course of only a few days it became evident that the party had found an effective propaganda officer.

[41] *ABC* 24 May 1933. See Loock, *Quisling*, pp. 106f. *Aftenposten*'s refusal, see Nesse to Quisling 15 May 1933: 'my main objection to the programme is that it has excessive faith in the ability of the *state* to take care of everything for us' (RA PAQ 2).

[42] Walter Fürst, *Min sti* (1981) pp. 20ff. (From the summer of 1940, Fürst spelled his name 'Fyrst'.) Also Hartmann, *Fører uten folk*, pp. 268ff, and John Sanness, *Mot Dag* 1934/16.

The first day of canvassing, Constitution Day, 17 May, a group of young law students campaigned for the new party in the main street, Karl Johan Street. It was claimed that fifty-eight people joined that day, most of whom remained loyal until 1945, among them Rolf Jørgen Fuglesang, soon to become the party's executive secretary and the single most loyal and competent of Quisling's closest men.

The pressing issue of finance was handled by Prytz, who managed to set up a finance committee of reputable men. Their first initiative was a large fund-raising party for potential benefactors. Just how successful the evening was is not known, but the NS soon gave the impression that 'big money' lay behind it. And indeed, the party that was soon called 'the captains' and lawyers' movement' won the sympathy of a considerable proportion of the Oslo upper classes.[43]

The appeal of the party extended even to the countryside. Among the groups now turning to Quisling was the organisation of indebted farmers, Rural Crisis Aid (Bygdefolkets Krisehjelp), roughly equivalent to the German and Austrian Landvolk movement. This group had been founded in 1931 and was concentrated in the Telemark–Buskerud–Oppland districts. Now it was on the verge of bankruptcy and looked to the NS, both with a view to winning political influence and to clearing its debts of 10,000 kroner, the price for its offer of an alliance with the NS. The co-operation was seen as a financial transaction and thus in the first instance administered by Prytz rather than Quisling or Hjort. Gradually it became clear that Crisis Aid was prepared to be absorbed into the NS. The agreement was made in secret, as the alliance provoked a great deal of comment and controversy even within the NS.[44]

However, much as the NS wanted a non-socialist coalition, it made no further progress beyond this agreement. It seemed that Quisling's reputation was too explosive for others to gamble on in an election. At least that was the attitude of the Conservatives. Their main paper, *Aftenposten*, hesitated to declare its sympathy for the Quisling party, even if the rank and file of its readers looked to the retired Defence Minister with respect and even admiration. In early August *Aftenposten* showed its true colours in its editorial 'The New Front', which denounced the NS altogether as a party that leaned too far in the direction of big government to earn support from

---

[43] Various notes in RA PA Prytz 4, in particular the report of 30 June 1933. *Telemark Arbeiderblad* 6 September 1933.

[44] Jostein Nerbøvik, *Bønder i kamp* (1991).

any true conservative. Later in the month the Conservative Central Committee stated that it could not under any circumstances enter into an electoral alliance with a party whose politics, 'in the understanding of the Conservative Party, is not feasible within the existing democratic and social framework'. The Conservatives in Bergen, who were in favour of setting up a joint list with the NS, were asked to withdraw from that venture but refused to follow the central committee. In the small Independent Party (a close ally of the Conservatives), opinion was divided. *Tidens Tegn*'s editorial sympathy for Quisling was well known; on the other hand, the Oslo party chairman, a well-known industrialist, agitated vociferously against any kind of alliance with a semi-socialist party such as the NS out of industrial concerns.

But even if officials from the other parties withheld their support in general, Quisling was able to hold out for local discussions, where the question of joint lists and electoral alliances could be negotiated. Scores of such negotiations took place in September. In certain key rural areas Quisling managed to gather a certain amount of support, whereas in all the urban areas outside Oslo and Bergen the NS was obliged to put up its own lists. This was most disappointing for a party which saw itself not so much as a party but as a unification movement. The Conservatives were proving to be their most formidable opponents. In his first open campaign meeting in Oslo on 12 September 1933, Quisling aired his disappointment with the Conservatives, accusing them of damaging the NS in the eyes of non-socialist opinion and scaring off potential voters.[45] He was in no doubt that it was Hambro who was making a *rapprochement* with the NS impossible. Hambro, after all, had conspired with Hundseid over Quisling's ouster from government, so it was not surprising that he should now be closing the door on a national unification movement. A counter-offensive against Hambro became a major theme in the party organ *Nasjonal Samling* in the weeks before the election.[46]

Faced with this opposition from the Conservatives, Quisling's original overriding struggle against the revolutionaries became less important. Only in one context did any real confrontation take place: the physical. His new party, like no other in the inter-war period, provoked fist fights and violence, a tendency which increased during the 1930s but which was discernible even in this first election campaign.

---

[45] *NS* 1933/3. *Aftenposten* 5 August 1933, and Quisling's reply 8 August 1933.
[46] On *Aftenposten*'s battle with the NS, see Tor Marius Løiten, 'Felles motstander – gjensidig mistenksomhet' (thesis) UiO 1989.

As the support for the movement was strongest in West Oslo and in the prosperous suburbs, Fürst started to organise rallies in East Oslo to woo the working classes. On one occasion he used a loudspeaker so powerful that the residents of the area could follow what was being said in the meeting hall. But the rally was disrupted by young Labour Party activists shouting 'Down with Quisling!', whereupon young socialists and Communists stormed the hall and tore down the microphone. The police were called, and according to the newspaper reports Quisling was driven off in a Black Maria. 'Public Goes Berserk at Quisling Meeting', the headlines ran. The same sort of thing was subsequently reported from other towns and cities as Quisling proceeded on his electoral round-trip. Such bad publicity served, if nothing else, to ensure that the party became well known. In contrast to other political débutants at the 1933 election, the electorate was indeed fully conscious of the existence of the NS.[47]

But the effectiveness of Quisling's personal performances was hotly disputed. He usually stood firm in the storms of shouting and yelling, carrying his message through by reading from his script. 'Mr Quisling is no orator,' commented one paper. 'Calm and controlled, without any kind of bravado, but serious and sincere,' wrote *Tidens Tegn* after the ninety-minute speech he delivered before two thousand enthusiasts in Oslo on 1 September.[48]

His lack of dynamism as a speaker was not Quisling 's worst handicap as the founder of a new party: more damaging was his reputation for causing scandals, the constant eruption of extraordinary situations which surrounded his person wherever he went. In this respect the support from the farmers' Crisis Aid lent his name a certain normality, a whiff of ordinary politics amidst the storms, which proved most useful during the important nomination process of his party before the election. Crisis Aid possessed local groups, well-trained officers and practical resources, and set up joint lists with the NS in a great many districts. Without these electoral pacts Quisling's party would not have been able to participate on a nation-wide basis in these elections.

The first joint list was that in Telemark, following a relatively peaceful nomination meeting in Bø. In south-western Norway nominations followed an initiative from Stavanger, where the new party had no fewer than three

[47] Fürst, *Min sti*, pp. 31–45; NS 1933/3; Gerhardsen to *Arbeiderbladet* 30 September 1933; *Arbeideren* 25 September 1933.
[48] *TT* 2 September 1933.

medical doctors as its driving force. In most districts nominations were made jointly with other parties and groups, sometimes with the greatest difficulty. When the deadline expired, seventeen lists had been submitted out of a possible twenty-nine. The party had put up 144 candidates altogether, including nine women. This was a more than satisfactory result: in fact, the rudiments of a national party organisation had been created in the space of a mere two months, thanks mainly to joint lists with Crisis Aid in rural areas and the attraction Quisling's name had for discontented non-socialist voters in the towns.

On the night of 17 October 1933 the results came through. In all, the NS pulled 27,850 votes, or 3.5 per cent of the total vote in the districts where it had entered candidates. However, neither the 5,500 votes in Oslo nor the 3,500 in Telemark were sufficient to secure a seat in the Storting. Quisling struck a positive note: 'Never before in this country has a party only a few months old received the endorsement of close to 30,000 convinced supporters, who, despite the lies, the slander, the swindling and the scare tactics, have stood by their belief in the movement.'[49] Some comfort was also to be derived from the fact that they had outperformed some established rivals such as the Independent People's Party and the Communist Party and had outdistanced the other two newcomers, the Social Party (Samfundspartiet) and the Christian People's Party. In fact, after the Labour Party, the Conservatives, the Liberals and the Agrarians, the NS might be considered as the country's largest party.

To improve on this result, new tactics, new skills and new ideas would be essential.

THE FØRER AND HIS FOLLOWERS

After the election defeat the most pressing task was to keep the brittle new movement united. In Quisling's pep talk to his activists ten days later, little remained of his principle of co-operation and support for other parties' candidates: instead, new battle lines were being drawn, above all the boundary between the NS and everybody else.[50]

Paradoxically, this phase of self-redefinition coincided with another initiative to unite the three small losers, the Independent Party, the Fatherland League and the NS, around the Agrarian Party in order to secure a new Agrarian government in the event of Mowinckel's fall. On 9 March 1934

---

[49] *NS* 1933/7.   [50] Quisling's speech 26 October 1933, RA NSRH 4.

representatives from the Agrarian Party and the three small organisations gathered at Hjort's home to discuss the prospects for a national bloc. Both Quisling's report and the minutes kept by Hjort demonstrate a growing interest in the idea. However, the government crisis passed, and the bloc negotiations with it.[51] After June 1934 the NS never again participated in any significant negotiations with the other parties. From then on the party wanted to be neither considered nor referred to as *borgerlig* – non-socialist in the bourgeois fashion. Instead, it went over to socialism – its own, national 'socialism'.

This step was taken as a new party manifesto was being worked out, a process in which the Fører naturally took the lead. During the autumn of 1933 he drafted several introductions to the new programme, most of them introduced by the formula that the present world crisis was due to the global confrontation between two 'systems', Marxism and liberalism, which were now fighting a self-defeating battle, and that a militant Marxism locked in confrontation with a weak and ailing liberalism made room for a host of negative cultural influences such as psychoanalysis, cultural relativism and decadence.

The party leader offered the great apocalyptic perspective: what we are dealing with is at the same time 'a social, a national and a spiritual crisis ... We are treading a narrow path with precipices on either side.' What was most urgently needed was 'first of all to save our society from the yoke of Marxism and to save our workers from Marxism'. Their main task was thus to address the workers – 'as the *borgerlige* will ensure their own demise we need not concern ourselves with them'.[52]

The 180 representatives of the party council who had come together from all over the country on 28 January 1934 for two days of debate and discussion were not formally invited to agree on the programme. This was a party structured around the *fører* principle and thus explicitly rejecting such institutions as discussion, parliamentarism, voting. Quisling presented the programme more or less as a *fait accompli*.[53] The great news was that the manifesto no longer described NS as *borgerlig* but as a socialist party. The NS represented the 'distinctively Norwegian aspect of the new view of life, a

---

[51] H. O. Brevig, *NS – fra parti til sekt 1933–1937* (1970) pp. 57–73; also Gabrielsen, *Menn og politikk*, pp. 156–63; Loock, *Quisling*, pp. 126–32; Norland, *Hårde tider*, pp. 237–51.

[52] UBO MS fol. 3920 VII p. 6; also 'Det Nasjonale samlingsprogram' (NSP) RA PAQ 10.

[53] NS Riks- og rådsmøteprotokoll 1934–1945;* Ragna Prag Magelsen to Quisling 30 January 1934, RA NSRH 2. See also Brevig, *NS – fra parti til sekt*, p. 70; Hans S. Jacobsen in *Ragnarok* (1937) p. 63.

new, true Norwegian socialism', as it came to be called in the final version of the manifesto. The businessman Hans S. Jacobsen later took the credit for that. He was a party member who had come under strong German influence during his student years at Kiel, where he had studied social economics and had worked as a ship broker, and was one of the few Norwegians of the day who had actually adopted National Socialism of the Hitler–Rosenberg type. The new socialism would, in Jacobsen's words, simultaneously 'free Norway from the Marxists, from party politics and from the plutocracy'.[54]

On 6 February the manifesto was read out at party associations all over the country. It was to remain unaltered until the party had put it into action and thus achieved its aim. The Oslo meeting was held in the great hall of the Lodge. The Fører was welcomed amid a sea of St Olav sun crosses and Norwegian flags. Quisling claimed that his party manifesto had a 'right to life', in contrast to the tenets of Marxism which had been scripted by 'a lonely Jew who did not know how to live life'. He rounded off his speech as he habitually did, with Ibsen's 'Norway is a realm; it shall become a people', and was saluted with a standing ovation and a forest of upraised arms.

In many ways the NS resembled a scout movement for adults in its youthful ardour, paramilitary marching, zeal and *naïveté*. The garrison pastor Kjeld Stub arranged the first NS song: 'Attention! Awake! This is not the time for sleep! Norway is calling on her men.' It was written and distributed just before the 1933 election, a resounding fanfare of military-chivalric metaphors. Another pastor, Knut Geelmuyden, contributed the movement's 'signature tune', which the party rules demanded be sung at the initiation ceremony of every party association at the raising of the NS flag – the yellow St Olav cross on a red background – while a strapping young member 'slowly unfurls the flag':

> The cross banner, the old flag
> Blazes forth in Norway's day
> To greet the people and the land ...
> Norway, our own country,
> Here we stand, man by man.
> Baptise us in holy fire
> To action once more.

The singing of the national anthem was compulsory, to which the more dedicated party members spread the habit of raising the right arm in a diagonal salute with outstretched palms, 'the old Norwegian salute, which

---

[54] Jacobsen in *Ragnarok* (1937) pp. 63, 57ff, 83ff.

was used in this country in earlier times, by St Olav and his men, among others'. Recent illustrations by Norwegian artists for the Snorri Sturlasson saga books were taken as proof of this assertion. 'Hail and good fortune!' (*Heil og sæl!*) was likewise adopted as the special written salutation in place of the bourgeois 'sincerely' or 'with kind regards'. The similarity with the German '*Sieg Heil*' was problematic. Quisling was very much opposed to importing the National Socialist movement into Norway; even the more German-oriented Hjort agreed that excessive use of NSDAP symbols might be off-putting for the uninitiated. Anne-Margrethe Hustad, a close friend of the Quislings and an otherwise committed party member, described how alarmed she was the first time she witnessed Pastor Stub from the rostrum raise his arm in salute before the assembly. It was a painful moment for the hesitant, and thoroughly disgusting for the sceptical.

Quite a few of the NS symbols belonged to the common heritage of the right. Collectively they must be seen as parallels to those used by the Labour movements and interpreted as part of the broader tendency to spectacular effects and stylised mass-movement behaviour which was gaining currency among the European parties in the 1930s. Advertising techniques were adopted and a certain militarising of political structuring became widespread in that period. But in Norway it was taken to greater extremes in the NS than in the other parties, as a necessary step to distinguishing itself and breaking away from the non-socialist *borgerlig* family of parties.

The desire to wear uniforms was a significant symptom of this. In 1932 the Labour Party Protective Force adopted blue shirts, red ties, bandoleers and caps, and the Fatherland League also introduced its own uniform in 1932: grey shirts, black ties and belts with shoulder straps. The fact that two sets of political opponents seemed to be mobilising themselves in this way, each in their own uniform, was more than the Mowinckel government was prepared to tolerate. Parallels with Nazi Germany were spreading fear in the Storting. In order to prevent 'clashes between uniformed members of the different units', a bill prohibiting political uniforms was pushed through parliament in record time before the summer recess of 1933.[55]

The uniform ban was enforced strictly, but could not prevent groups of people from wearing similar shirts. The most committed in the NS wore a special khaki 'party shirt' to meetings in place of the outlawed uniform. The

---

[55] Ot.prp. no. 89 1933; Ot.forh. 1933 pp. 908–16; 'On the Uniform Ban', memo of Odin Augdahl 14 February 1934, RA NSRH 1. On the Fatherland League uniform: see Norland, *Hårde tider*, pp. 216, 271.

propaganda officer Fürst and his fiancée even wore the shirts at their wedding in Oslo in 1934, at which Pastor Stub officiated wearing the NS badge on his cassock, and the bride carried a bouquet of yellow roses arranged into the shape of the sun cross on a red background.

The uniforms were sorely missed at the party's annual conventions, which were held in Trondheim in 1934, Stavanger in 1935 and Oslo in 1936, and on each occasion closed with open-air gatherings at historical sites – Stiklestad, Hafrsfjord and Akershus. Fürst organised the 1934 convention, having been present at the NSDAP Nuremberg rally the year before, and set the style for the decade: on closing the meeting, Quisling reminded those present of the historical significance of the place they had come to, incorporating into his speech a consideration of how the NS was continuing the work of Olav Haraldsson, Olav Tryggvasson and Harald Hardråde. At this 'a forest of hands' rose up in joyful salute. 'Lead us and we shall follow!,' shouted Hjort – and the crowd joined in with a rhythmic 'Heil og sæl!'

The party even formed a national assembly (Riksting) of its own. Quisling had been engaged in corporate issues 'ever since his days in Russia', where he was heavily influenced by the Soviet councils. The idea of a system of representation that was an alternative to parliamentarism was clearly attractive at the time, both to the right and the left wings. Quisling had launched the idea of a 'national congress' of trade unions in the programme outline for the new Fridtjof Nansen party in 1930. At the end of 1933 his thoughts took a new turn. He now envisaged a voluntary national assembly whose infrastructure would be spontaneously created by concerned citizens and developed through voluntary support. He may have got this idea from the lawyer and legal philosopher Herman Harris Aall, who in a long letter of December 1933 urged his Fører to set to work immediately on setting up the new institution. In the course of the spring the idea began to take shape. Quisling carefully studied a handbook of Italian *corporativismo* and other continental sources, among them the writings of the Austrian economist and polyhistor Othmar Spann.[56] In early July 1934 400 NS members and sympathisers were invited to participate in the founding of Norway's new corporate National Assembly in Trondheim. Barely 300 actually turned up that Saturday morning, and they were hardly aware of the scope of what was involved in the establishment of a corporate constitution in Norway. There

[56] Aall to Quisling 24 December 1933, UBO MS fol. 4096 V. The books he studied were O. Spann, *Der wahre Staat* (1921) and Walter Heinrich, *Der Faschismus* (1932). See Arnim Mohler, *Die konservative Revolution* (1989) and J. H. Pichler, *Othmar Spann oder die Welt als Ganzes* (1988).

is much to suggest that the party was somewhat bewildered by what the Fører had in mind. The idea of voluntarily setting up something which would later become a permanent constitutional body was not at all clear – and neither was the connection between the National Assembly as an NS body and the projected apolitical, anti-party character of the whole venture. The NS district leader in Trøndelag, Professor Ragnar Skancke, solemnly opened the meeting and proposed Hjort as chair; Hjort gave Quisling the floor. Quisling declared the assembly officially constituted, even though it was 'purely provisional'. Even so, there was at least enough interest in Quisling's ideas for *Tidens Tegn* to carry his outline for a corporate National Assembly as its main story on 13 July and to follow it up with a leading article a few days later. The leaders of the Agrarian Party and the Agrarian League were also sympathetic to Quisling's corporate views, whether they were of fascist or Bolshevik origins.[57]

Quisling continued to work on his plans through the autumn, but the practical problem of how someone who was not a member of the Storting could introduce a constitutional reform bill in the Storting persisted. Quisling finally put the motion before the Storting directly, and asked that it might be given consideration even so, arguing that, with a fair electoral procedure, the NS would have had 'at least three representatives'. According to established custom however the proposal was rejected.[58]

LEADER CULT AND FØRER AUTOCRACY

Early on Sunday morning 10 November 1935 the Hird – the NS vigilante guard – met for regular manoeuvres in Oslo. Led by Hjort, they marched under banners and flags from the suburb of Bærum west of the city and in towards the city's west end. The seventy participants marched a distance of nearly 30 kilometres, stopping for exercises, which were carried out with the utmost discipline. The party song was sung all the time, and with the NS banner heading the procession, they certainly drew attention to themselves. When they reached the Oslo district of Frogner, the column turned into Bygdøy allé towards Hafrsfjordsgaten, where it slackened pace, and 'the NS march sounded loud and harmoniously' outside Quisling's apartment.

---

[57] A record of the founding is printed in *NS* 1934/19, p. 6.
[58] Quisling to the Storting 6 June 1935, and the correspondence with Ræder, Stray and Hoff, RA PANS 28.

The chairman of the NS enjoyed a reputation far beyond that of any other party leader. Quisling was so much the focus of attention that he achieved cult status, something which ran contrary to the ethos and practice of every other political party. For the other parties, the party conference was always the ultimate authority, with the right to elect the party leadership, to agree on a new manifesto and to decide the platform on which to fight it. No such possibilities were available in the NS. Members did, of course, have the right to raise 'matters of importance' at the conference. But these were only matters pertaining to the party leadership. The party leadership consisted of the Fører and the party's national Executive Committee and Council, with the Fører in every sense the central figure. He selected the four members of the Executive Committee and supplemented them with his own chosen advisers. He also appointed the Council members. The Fører's authority was indisputable. Quisling had never been formally elected. He had formed the party, given it its name and manifesto, and without embarrassment described it as 'his own movement'. With such rules and practice supported by noisy enthusiasm for the Fører, it was hardly surprising that the new party was regarded by the others as a dictatorship movement, although this was energetically denied by all the NS spokesmen, and perhaps most vehemently by Quisling himself.[59]

However, Quisling was a peculiar leader. He had little sense of irony, no obvious sense of humour, and suffered from crippling shyness. He often looked embarrassed, trying to avoid eye-contact. His body language always seemed to indicate a desire to 'wriggle out of things'. It was therefore unlikely that his collaborators had allied themselves to the party out of a purely personal attachment to its Fører. Quisling lacked Frederik Prytz's natural ease with people, and as Prytz was temporarily out of the picture, both the party office and the meetings of the inner circle suffered from the lack of their former atmosphere of warmth and bonhomie. The Fører was on strictly formal terms with everybody. He behaved aloofly even in daily matters at the party headquarters. A friendly nod was all the secretary general of the party Rolf Jørgen Fuglesang and his people at the party headquarters got from the Fører when he arrived in the morning.

This aura of unapproachability naturally attracted comment among his followers. Stories about the Fører started to circulate: about his exceptional

[59] Quisling, 'Diktatur eller nasjonalt demokrati', *FF* 27 November 1937. 'His Own Movement': e.g. in *Hvem er hvem* (1934) p. 392.

talents, his long philosophical manuscript, his Russian weddings and about his impressive wealth of experience. His collaborators were able to testify to an unbelievably retentive memory and a razor-sharp mind. They would relate how their Fører always had all his arguments and facts at his fingertips, and was always sure of geographical details. Thus what Quisling was unable to inspire through natural sympathy and warmth was compensated for by the respect and admiration he earned.

His close collaborators and party members saw his remoteness as an expression of a thoroughly serious man on a busy and difficult mission. Camaraderie and carousing in hotels after meetings, an occasional affair – such familiar images of the politician on the move, so necessary for gaining acceptance and confidence – were completely alien to Quisling.

During the increasingly stormy meetings he always remained calm. Word got round that the Fører was fearless, that he strode right into the midst of agitated crowds, looked his opponents straight in the face, addressed his hecklers calmly, heedless of their threats of violence. On one occasion, when he was followed by shouting demonstrators down the street after a meeting in central Oslo, he stopped as though nothing was happening to study the window display of a nearby bookshop. But although Quisling seemed fearless, he was not invulnerable. On the contrary, there was a definite vulnerability about him which inspired a great deal of sympathy. With his introverted clumsiness he resembled a gifted child. Hounded and harangued in the wider political arena, he was all the more admired as a visionary by his own people.

This discrepancy between the public figure and his party image came to characterise both him and his following. The Fører was both a victim of persecution and a hero in the struggle to restore justice; the incarnation of the ambiguous figure of the sacrificial hero, the persecuted innocent, the man who was at once strong and vulnerable: St George fighting the dragon and at the same time St Stephen being stoned by the crowd. Not surprisingly, such a personality enjoyed a special power over women, inspiring particular admiration and unflinching loyalty among the women members of the movement. He received many letters from female admirers, many of which reflect a maternal concern for their vulnerable hero. The number of women who flocked around the NS certainly did not go unnoticed at the time. 'There is also a large number of women here,' reported *Dagbladet* from a typical election rally in 1933, 'between the ages of 39.5 and 39.7.' And as Hjort's conflicts with Quisling became more frequent, he complained of the 'many ladies and gentlemen' who rushed to the Fører's defence, hinting strongly that he considered the former to be alien to the political business of men.[60]

'HEADS WILL ROLL ...'

As usual, Vidkun and Maria spent the summer of 1935 at Jonsborg with his mother. Preparations had to be made for the national party meeting (*riksmøte*) in Stavanger, where he was to give four or five lectures. On 24 July he and Maria were picked up by the couple Peter and Halldis Neegaard Østbye; he was a manufacturer, she a skier and journalist, and both enjoyed prominent positions in the party's inner circle. The two couples left for the small town of Åmli, where the Fører was scheduled to speak that afternoon.[61]

But at about four o'clock in the afternoon, as the car was turning into the crowded meeting place at Åmli, Mrs Østbye started to feel uneasy. Hundreds of people were waiting for the speaker and they did not appear to be at all friendly; they were carrying placards with anti-Quisling slogans. The atmosphere was threatening, and worse: the Hird unit from Telemark, which had promised to be present to maintain order, had not yet arrived. There were only a few party organisers there. Even so, Quisling went in, took the floor, where a makeshift rostrum had been set up, and opened the meeting.

Hecklers shouted 'Out!' throughout his speech, as was to be expected. But Quisling continued his account of the horrors of communism, which only served to provoke further outbursts, and the atmosphere became more and more acrimonious. Halldis Østbye later wrote: 'There is no knowing what might have happened if the Telemark Hird had not eventually appeared.' About ten men lined up in front of the rostrum and Quisling was able to continue, with slightly fewer interruptions than before.

However, it was not this episode which distinguished Åmli from other meetings, but the sensational reporting it received in the Labour press in Arendal, first in the local paper, and shortly afterwards all over the country. The headline read, 'Quisling's Threats at Åmli: Heads Will Roll if the NS Comes to Power.'

Halldis Østbye always denied that Quisling had actually made this threat, but neither her nor Quisling's denials got further than the party circles in

---

[60] Hjort to Quisling 26 November 1936, RA NSRH; *Dagbladet* 16 September 1933. Various personal letters to Quisling in UBO MS fol. 4096 V.

[61] The following account is from H. N. Østbye, NS party history, MS RA PA H. N. Østbye 1.

which they were made. Whether or not he did actually speak the words, they became undeniably damaging for the party. All the newspapers carried the story. It was as though every suspicion that the party's idealistic facade concealed a subversive and objectionable, if not violent, character suddenly seemed justified. The episode was in fact becoming another in the series of 'Quisling scandals'.

The party activists noted an instant hardening of public opinion. Mrs Østbye wrote in her history of the party that no other single episode had damaged Quisling or the party prior to the 1936 elections as much as the 'Heads Will Roll' headline. News of it spread 'like wildfire through the country and provoked enormous indignation', and even contributed 'enormously to poisoning people's minds against Quisling and the NS'.

Membership statistics, in fact, seem to bear her out. The increase in the number of local NS parties, a reliable barometer of the party's popularity, stagnated in summer 1935. Growth had been steady through 1934 and had peaked with 127 local branches in August 1935. After that it dropped to 100, until the mobilisation ahead of the elections the following year, a tremendous effort which brought the number to only slightly more than it had been in 1935.

The year 1935 also witnessed the first exodus from the party. The painter Kai Fjell and his wife resigned, as did the well-known police lawyer and crime writer Jonas Lie and his family. Even Quisling's brother Jørgen and his Uncle Nils left. Nearly a third of the entire membership deserted the party between the summers of 1935 and 1936. New recruits never managed to compensate for this exodus. The Quisling moment in Norwegian public opinion seemed to have passed.

4

Mussolini or Hitler?

> We are not trying to adapt any foreign teachings to Norwegian conditions. What we are proposing is natural for us. We are aiming at a solution on specifically Nordic terms ... We want neither Fascism nor National Socialism. *Quisling in an election address, August 1933*[1]

There is little to suggest that Quisling's political thinking in the early 1930s found its inspiration in either Adolf Hitler or Benito Mussolini or any other fascist leader. When defining the precise nature of the NS, he would sooner find parallels in religious ideals than in foreign political movements. His audiences were often struck by his biblical references or his frequent exhortations to '[f]irst seek God's kingdom and His righteousness'.[2]

But even if the NS was 'divinely' inspired, this did not discourage overtures from secular organisations of a worldly order. The first serious initiative of this kind came from Fascist Italy. Count de Marsinach, the Italian minister in Oslo, had been following political developments in Norway closely ever since his arrival in autumn 1930. His reports to the Foreign Ministry in Rome made frequent references to Quisling, the '*uomo misterioso*', whose apocalyptic rhetoric had caused such a sensation among otherwise uniformly stolid Norwegian politicians; the Count even wondered whether Quisling might be a potential *duce* for Norway.[3]

Copies of his reports from Oslo were passed on to the Propaganda Minister and to a newly formed organisation for the promotion of Italian Fascism, the CAUR – Comitati d'Azione per la Universalità di Roma. Just like the empire of antiquity, as the CAUR statutes put it, the Fascist revolutionary regime had assumed the character of a higher civilisation which, if it spread from country to country, would acquire a 'universal character'. CAUR's objective was not simply to spread the cult of Il Duce; it was also to secure influence in like-minded European parties as a counter-movement to the ideological and political influence of Hitler and German National Socialism.[4]

---

[1] UBO MS fol. 3920 VII.   [2] *NS-Ungdommen* 1934 no. 14/15.

[3] MAE Roma, Affari Politici: Norvegia, 1–2, reports 6 February, 3 September and 27 September 1932; 6 February, 5 June, 5 July, 31 August, 21 October and 21 December 1933.

[4] The statutes and documents relating to the foundation of CAUR on 15 July 1933 are in ACS Roma, MCP 181. Re relations with the Propaganda Minister: from 1 August 1933 the

After Hitler established his government in January 1933, Mussolini was faced with a partner who, although acknowledging him as a role model and inspiration, constituted a rival for international influence, particularly in the Danube region and the old Habsburg domains. In political terms the power struggle turned on gaining influence over the nationalist parties in these countries and over corresponding parties in other areas of Europe: in Great Britain, other parts of western Europe and the Nordic countries. Moreover, the rivalry found a palpably ideological division in the debate on race: in contrast to Mussolini's universalist ideology stood Hitler's teachings on race as one of the fundamental principles of National Socialism.

FROM ROME TO GENEVA

For a long time Quisling kept his distance from the Italians, but when he was invited to the first CAUR conference in Montreux, Switzerland in September 1934, he accepted, explaining that he was eager to find out more about Italian Fascism 'which our Norwegian movement has so much to learn from'.[5] In December he set off on his first official tour abroad. It was five years since he had last travelled through Europe. After the breakthrough of National Socialism, there was reason to expect changes in Germany. And changes he found. He wrote to Maria on his arrival in Lausanne: 'When you think of the conditions in Russia one or two years after the Bolshevik Revolution – what a difference here! ... everything seems fine and orderly.'[6]

In Montreux he was introduced to delegates from most of the important European movements outside Germany: the Heimwehr in Austria; the Légion Nationale and the Ligue Nationale Corporative from Belgium; Denmark's Nationalsocialistiske Arbejderparti; Le Francisme from France; Ireland's Blueshirts; National Socialists from Lithuania and Greece; the Front Noir from Holland; the Romanian Iron Guard; fascist parties from Portugal and Switzerland and Sweden's Nationella Ungdomsförbundet – a diverse crowd which General Coselschi, who chaired the meeting, tried to

---

Propaganda Ministry was headed by Mussolini's son-in-law Count Ciano, first as Ufficio Stampa di Capo di Governo, from September 1934 Sottosegretario per la Stampa e Propaganda, and from June 1936 Ministero della Cultura Populare. Ciano left the department in June 1936 to become Foreign Minister.

[5] Quisling to Coselschi 22 September 1934, UBO MS fol. 3920 VIII, 3.
[6] Letter to Maria 14 February 1934, NHM 96 II.

bring together through a mixture of friendly appeals and high-sounding rhetoric.[7]

Quisling also took the floor at the conference. The *Berliner Tageblatt* described his contribution as a 'counter-speech' to Coselschi's, emphasising the rights of smaller nations in the Europe of the future. This conference, the Norwegian delegate maintained, showed that there were two main tendencies within the National Socialist or Fascist movement: the Latin and the Nordic. He did not ally himself with either position, but rather outlined the distinctive qualities of the two tendencies and insisted that they could more profitably complement than be hostile to each other. The Danish delegate, Frits Clausen, was impressed and thought that Quisling was a powerful man of courage and 'independent views'.[8]

Quisling and Clausen were jointly voted on to a co-ordination committee with the task of establishing the basis for a new, collective organisation – an 'Entente de Fascisme Universel', as the francophone conference literature called it.

As if to manifest the compromise between the two main tendencies in the international movement, the Norwegian delegate broke his return journey in Berlin, apparently in order to visit art dealers to explore the possibility of selling his paintings. The stay in Berlin nevertheless assumed a political character. By some extraordinary coincidence of events he ran into one of the leading figures of National Socialism – the chief ideologue of German Nazism and leader of the Hitler party's foreign policy unit, Alfred Rosenberg.[9]

The background for this meeting was rather complex. That summer, the head of the northern section of Rosenberg's foreign policy office, the romantic poet Thilo von Trotha, had made a trip to Norway and later reported at length on the NS and its Fører. Quisling, he told Rosenberg, was a man of great ability who, given the right circumstances, could one day become the Man in Norway.[10] That von Trotha was able to give such a

[7] Documents pertaining to the Montreux conference in UBO MS fol. 3920 VIII, 3; see also Carlo Lozzi, 'Appunti sur CAUR', memorandum (undated) 1935 in ACS MCP 181.

[8] *Berliner Tageblatt* 17 December 1934. See also the report on the conference by the German consulate in Geneva, in PAAA Bonn, Inland II A/B 25.1.

[9] The following account is based on: Quisling, Almanachs 1934 and 1935 RA; *Straffesak* pp. 33, 216, 342; Loock, *Quisling*, p. 188 n. 13; Hans-Jürgen Lutzhöft, *Der nordische Gedanke in Deutschland 1920–1940* (1971) p. 336; Seppo Kuusisto, *Alfred Rosenberg in der nationalsozialistischen Aussenpolitik 1933–1939* (1984) p. 340; Høidal, *Quisling*, p. 253.

[10] Von Trotha's account of his visit to Norway in Kuusisto, *Alfred Rosenberg*, p. 339. Original documents in Di6z Bundesarchiv, Abt. Potsdam.

detailed description of Quisling to his superior can be explained by the fact that he and Quisling had mutual friends in Berlin, in particular the Turkish specialist Gerhard von Mende, who was engaged to the Norwegian author Karo Espeseth, both of whom were connected with Rosenberg's office. Von Mende was working on a doctorate on non-Russian peoples in the Soviet Union and had heard about Quisling's work for Nansen from his Armenian friends as early as the 1920s. Karo Espeseth was herself a member of the NS and would certainly have talked to her fiancé about Quisling and his interest in Russia.[11]

There was also another Norwegian–German couple who may have contributed to setting up the contact with Rosenberg. Maggen Blom, the sister of Cecilie, had been corresponding with Quisling ever since her schooldays, and had frequently urged him to visit Germany. She and her husband Hans Friedrich Günther, the famous racist scholar, had strong connections with the National Socialist leadership, including Rosenberg.

Thanks to these two couples, then, Quisling and von Trotha came to meet each other ('by chance', as Quisling was to claim later) in Berlin when he travelled through on his way home from Geneva, and through that he was able to meet Rosenberg himself.[12]

Rosenberg was born in Riga and graduated in architecture in Moscow in 1918, the year Quisling arrived in Petrograd. The two men came to respect each other's knowledge of Russia, particularly as their views on the potential of the non-Russian peoples' nationalism as a lever against the Bolshevik regime coincided nicely.

During their meeting, Quisling tried to reassure Rosenberg about his engagement in the CAUR, obviously an unpopular organisation in Berlin.[13] Montreux had been unilaterally condemned in Rosenberg's newspaper *Völkischer Beobachter*, something which Quisling was very well aware of. CAUR publications on the other hand, were openly critical of the Rosenberg racist ideology, which they labelled 'dangerous' and 'arbitrary'.[14] However,

[11] Karo Espeseth [von Mende], *Livet gikk videre* (1983) pp. 110, 114f; Alexander Dallin, *German Rule in Russia 1941–1945* (1957) pp. 88f; *Straffesak* p. 342.

[12] Various correspondence between the Günthers and the von Trothas 1933–5 in BA Koblenz NS 8/103.

[13] Meeting discussed in *Straffesak* p. 33; also pp. 337, 342. Rosenberg's own diary makes no reference to it.

[14] Various newspaper cuttings from December 1934 in UBO MS fol. 3920 VIII, 3; Guido Botolotto, article on Rosenberg in *Roma Universa* 1933/3.

nothing significant came out of this meeting. Contact with the NS was taken care of by von Trotha until he was killed in a road accident in 1938.

During 1935 a series of new meetings was set up between Quisling and Marcello Roddolo, the new Italian representative in Oslo. Quisling attended two further meetings of the CAUR co-ordination committee in Paris in January and Amsterdam in March 1935. At the Amsterdam meeting, the delegates, after much pressure from Coselschi managed to agree on a statement which once more came out against the National Socialist policy on race: 'the concept of Universal Fascism must find its inspiration in the idea of a free and sincere co-operation of all the peoples and races which the nations embrace'.[15] This declaration, made in a spirit of tolerance, did not prevent Quisling, once outside the conference hotel, from noticing that there were 'an astonishing number of Jews' in the streets of Amsterdam. In a letter to Maria, he wrote that there were 'so many that they leave their mark on street life. They must make up between 5 and 10 per cent.' The stream of refugees from Germany had just started and was evident in Holland.[16]

With Italy's invasion of Ethiopia on 2 October 1935 and the League of Nations' subsequent blockade resolution, there was a swing in international opinion, with dramatic consequences for the CAUR's reputation. The new Roman Empire was moving into Africa with a shameless imperialist appetite. Rome's credibility sank ominously – more, it seemed, than Berlin's reputation had sunk the year before over the Roehm purge or the fiasco coup in Vienna.

In Norway there had been criticism of the CAUR even prior to Ethiopia. In September 1935 Hans S. Jacobsen made a comprehensive attack on Italian Fascism in general and on the CAUR in particular and Quisling's participation in that fascist organisation, in his newly launched journal *Ragnarok*.[17] The article sent shock waves through the NS. That their Fører participated in a Mussolini set-up was completely new to even his closest followers. In fact, the CAUR was almost unknown in NS circles. The more ideologically alert members of the party realised that Jacobsen's article was highly partisan, as the author obviously belonged to the rival organisation, the German Nordische Gesellschaft, which was run from Berlin and headed by Alfred Rosenberg, the man *Ragnarok* styled 'the modern-day Luther'. In any case, Jacobsen succeeded in bringing the feud between Mussolini and

---

[15] CAUR to Quisling 11 April 1935, Quisling's CAUR-file II, INO.
[16] Quisling to Maria 29 March 1935, NHM 96 II.
[17] *Ragnarok* 1935/6–7, pp. 141f.

Hitler into the Norwegian political arena. After the invasion of Ethiopia, the revelations in *Ragnarok* added more fuel to the fire.

Quisling defended himself by maintaining that he was not at all about to promote the Italian cause. On the contrary, he insisted, Norway must not be drawn into colonial conflicts. He stressed this view to the point that he even opposed the League of Nations' plans for sanctions against Italy, which is all the more remarkable as it signalled a dramatic break in Quisling's political views. In the 1920s he had not only worked for the League of Nations, but had faithfully pleaded its case in his lectures at the Military Association. However, from 1930 onwards the League's reputation suffered as the crises in the East and later in Europe intensified. Quisling's change of heart may be seen as part of a general shift in opinion in the early 1930s. For him personally to denounce the collective sanctions clause was, however, a wholly new departure. The fact that the Soviet Union joined in 1934 after Germany had left the League the year before seemed to indicate a remodelling of the League into a grouping of great powers in an anti-German alliance. The fact that the Bolshevik government was installed in Geneva, at France's invitation and with Britain's support, for him implied that Norway had become a member of an 'alliance, with fateful obligations both to defend and attack'.[18]

One consequence of the war in Ethiopia was that there were no more CAUR trips for Quisling, and his association with the movement petered out. In February 1936 he dutifully sent his promised draft for the proposed reorganisation of the new international to Rome – an enormous wall chart complete with boxes, arrows and lines in Quisling's best style. But the war in Africa and the indignant opinion in his own ranks made any further participation impossible. The same went for the other delegates, and thus the CAUR collapsed from within.[19]

The Italian envoy in Oslo nevertheless tried to maintain connections with Quisling for a little longer by making a personal contribution (though a relatively small sum) to the newspaper fund of the NS. In December 1935 he recommended that the Propaganda Ministry in Rome should contribute more, and suggested that the legation made a gift of a thousand kroner at the end of the year. In view of the NS's close links with Germany, he told the Ministry, a larger donation was out of the question.

---

[18] *NS* 1934/37.
[19] Quisling to Coselschi 11 January 1936; Coleschi's reply 15 February and 24 February 1936, Quisling's CAUR-file II, INO.

The 1,000 kroner at Christmas 1935 seems to mark the peak of Italian interest in Quisling. Neither the diplomatic material nor the party's own records of confidential donations reveal any more transfers to the NS. It was an insignificant sum compared to what the Italians usually paid for political support abroad. But, as now became increasingly obvious, the NS was 'closer to Berlin than to us'.[20]

BUILDING BRIDGES WITH GERMANY

In contrast to the Italians, Germany's official representatives in Norway were slow to pay attention to the Quisling movement. During his first years as a party leader, Quisling had hardly anything to do with the German legation in Oslo. Not until the summer of 1936 did he have a lengthy, confidential discussion with the German minister, who subsequently represented his views to Berlin.

Why were the Germans so much slower than the Italians to take an interest in Quisling and the NS? One reason was that the Italian contact was centralised through the legation in Oslo, from where the minister would report to both the Foreign and Propaganda Ministries in Rome. Diplomatic representation was thus openly used for political purposes. The German foreign service, conversely, continued long after 1933 to operate as a strictly diplomatic body.

Quisling himself, on the other hand, was from the outset neither particularly German nor Italian in sympathy. Culturally he was above all pro-British. During his time with the League of Nations he had learned to admire the British Civil Service, and like Nansen he spoke English better than any other foreign language, having taken German no further than school. He read *The Times* every day and had more English than German, French or Russian books on his shelves.

But after 1933 there was a discernible increase in his interest in Germany. The *Völkischer Beobachter* was delivered to the office daily and he soon started to cut out pieces from it as diligently as he did from *The Times*. Party associates coming back from visits to Germany brought greetings from people he knew there, above all from von Trotha and the Günthers. Such contacts as were gradually established owed, in fact, more to his own acquaintances than to official approaches.

Olaf Fermann, one of Quisling's Norwegian-German contacts, was a

---

[20] Roddolo to MCP 17 October and 26 December 1935, ACS Roma 387.

businessman in Hamburg and the most dedicated member of the local Norwegian NS group, which numbered twelve members in 1935. When Fermann was back in Norway, he would always visit Quisling. In spring 1934 he tried to forge links between his Norwegian party and German National Socialists, in the hope that a group of NS members would be able to attend the Führerschule in Germany.[21]

Among Quisling's closest collaborators was another German-oriented activist, Dr Herman Harris Aall, the renowned legal theorist. Dr Aall argued tirelessly for what he considered to be the solution to the party's most pressing needs, namely a daily paper. His main idea was to finance such a paper with the help of advertisements from German companies such as IG Farben, Siemens and Telefunken, which he thought would reach a market among the paper's nationalist and German-oriented readership. His research had shown that German companies spent 60 million marks annually on foreign advertising, and he felt that a share of that should come to Norway. Dr Aall, moreover, was very well connected. Ever since the First World War he had been a personal friend of the Secretary of State, Staatssekretär von Bülow, in the German Foreign Ministry, who had been glad to make use of the Norwegian lawyer for propaganda purposes for Germany.[22]

By and large, however, Quisling was much more influenced by ideas than by individuals. He would take up ideas and modify them to harmonise with his own philosophy. Thus, while fascism and National Socialism presented themselves as internationally rival doctrines, he preferred to regard them as objects of a possible synthesis, manifested in his own Norwegian movement. Over the years, however, he was showing an increasing tendency to respond to impulses from Germany, a tendency particularly traceable through his ideological acceptance of anti-Semitism in the course of 1935. In this case he learned positively from National Socialism, to the extent that when the NS went to the polls for the second time in 1936, he had in a sense become 'the Norwegian Hitler' which the Labour press had long claimed.

---

[21] Fermann to Quisling 20 and 28 April 1934, 20 February 1935, RA PANS 22 and 25; Loock, *Quisling*, p. 195.

[22] Aall's plans for an inter-Germanic paper to be published by the NS in Oslo, and correspondence with Helof Harstad in 1935–6, and Harstad's references to conversations in Berlin with Dietrich Hildisch, Krieg, Züchner, Fermann et al. November 1935, in RA PANS 28. See also von Bülow's note on Aall in PAAA Bonn, Inland II A/B 32/74.

'THE WORLD REPUBLIC OF JEWS'

Quisling made his decisive move to an anti-Semitic stance when he started to condemn both liberalism and Marxism as Jewish creations, and by extension interpreted the world's main contradiction as 'a duel between Jewish and Nordic principles', with the 'occult' or 'hidden' forces of Judaism underpinning the liberal democracies as well as the Bolshevik world movement. The word 'Jew' in this rhetoric could signify anything from an ethnic or religious description to a pseudo-political concept, and gradually – by the late 1930s – became the most damning label in Quisling's vocabulary. This was out of step with his customary intellectual rigour and his passion for facts, statistics and concrete data. None the less, he would indulge in vague and imprecise expressions, such as his insistence that a Jewish 'world league' had offshoots in Norway.

This intellectual lapse is all the more striking as his interest in Judaism had started as a serious intellectual engagement. As something like an expert on questions of nationalism, he had engaged with the Zionist problem; from 1917–18 he read whatever he could find about the Balfour Declaration and its outcome, Jewish immigration into the British-mandated Palestinian territory. From *The Times* he kept himself abreast of the inevitable conflict between the immigrants and the local Arab population and shared the general concern of the 1930s for a viable solution to the Jewish question.

The first sign of an overt anti-Semitic stance is to be found in a letter from 1935. In September 1935, during the Ethiopia crisis, he wrote to Dr Paul Wurm, who was on the staff of the extreme anti-Semitic NSDAP paper *Der Stürmer*, that his party's 'awareness of the Jewish question has now been sharpened': '[E]ven if the Jews are not particularly numerous in Norway, we can still appreciate – following the National Socialist movement in Germany's exposure of Jewish occultism – that Jewish power and Jewish morality aspire towards a decisive influence both on the development of the world and on the future of our country.'[23] There was more to this than its recipient Dr Wurm could imagine. In these lines Quisling revealed that the NS 'awareness' was a fairly recent development and that it had come about almost exclusively through German influence. In fact, groups within the NS had long been fighting on an anti-Semitic platform, including Hans S. Jacobsen and his *Ragnarok* circle who had been stoking the flames against 'Judah' in the manner of the National Socialists. Events in Germany after

---

[23] Quisling to Paul Wurm 21 September 1935, RA PANS 25.

1933 encouraged such behaviour and the NS registered a general protest against refugees, Jewish or otherwise, being allowed into Norway. This was in tune with a more general shift in public opinion towards more stringent immigration controls. The bitterness aroused by immigration may seem peculiar in view of the fact that at least until 1938, the number of refugees and immigrants to Norway from the Third Reich was minimal. Scarcely more than 300 to 400 persons arrived between 1933 and 1938, the majority of whom immediately left for other countries. The general hostility to immigration provided the NS with the base for action against particular Jews, among them Max Hodann and Wilhelm Reich.[24]

Hodann was a German Jewish doctor and sexologist who first visited Norway in 1931 when he gave a lecture at the Students' Association on sex education. He had been in prison in Germany for a few months in 1933, then fled to Switzerland and arrived in Norway in the autumn of 1934. There, a pamphlet he wrote about married life sparked off a long campaign on the part of the NS. A lecture which he gave was reported to the Ministry of Justice for showing 'a contempt for religion which defies all description ... He blatantly encourages young people to satisfy their sexual appetites through onanism and homosexuality.' The NS newspaper demanded Hodann's deportation and made a big issue of it. Later, the struggle against 'Hodannism' became a fixture in the party's cultural programme, conducted with the help of leaflets, meetings, demonstrations and polemics against radical doctors advocating such policies as sex education, legalised abortion and the establishment of family planning clinics. There followed almost automatically an increasing tendency to anti-Semitic diatribes against 'Jewish sexologists'. Wilhelm Reich, who had emigrated to Norway in autumn 1934, became the Jewish immigrant upon whose shoulders most of the responsibility for this so-called sexual Marxism fell.[25]

Such was the backdrop against which anti-Semitism first established itself in the vocabulary of the NS. The party organ took up the Jewish question with great zeal, explaining the concept of 'international Judaism' to its readers in a series of articles written by Mrs Østbye. Although the paper did not initially mention him by name, the leader of the Conservatives, C. J. Hambro, was branded for being 'of Jewish descent' and by extension 'devoid of patriotic sentiment'. In two speeches in September 1935 Quisling

---

[24] See Ivar Sagmo, 'Die Max Hodann Materialen in der Universitätsbibliothek Oslo' in Hans Uwe Petersen, *Hitlerflüchtlinge im Norden* (1991) pp. 183f.

[25] *NS* 1935/9 and 13 and Ø. Rottem, *Sigurd Hoel. Et Nærbilde* (1991) ch. 10 'Under Reichs svøpe'.

personally came out in public with an anti-Semitic account of international
politics in which his expression 'a world republic of Jews' appeared for the
first time.[26]

But the NS turned out to be divided on the Jewish question, and it soon
became a sensitive issue for the Fører. First of all there was the tension
between the Christian wing – the clergymen and the West Norwegian
branch – and the secular wing of the party. Then there was division between
the moderates and the activists in the party organisation, and then between
the German-oriented and the 'nationalist' tendencies within the rank and
file. In each case the Jewish question turned out to be divisive.[27]

The strong Christian contingent in the party's Vestland branch felt deeply
disturbed by any anti-Jewish agitation. Guldbrand Lunde, the party's chief
propaganda officer who was also the leader of the party's important
Stavanger branch, felt it his responsibility to tone down central office's anti-
Semitic rhetoric, and as propaganda leader he had the authority to do so.
During the autumn of 1935 he would frequently put the brakes on the anti-
Semitic offensive, while Quisling for the most part remained aloof, insisting
that he did not want to be troubled with 'trivial matters' and keeping out of
the heated arguments and conflicts. Others had to bear the brunt of the
friction. When indignant pastors and priests started to defect from the party
in protest against the 'heathen' tendencies of anti-Semitism, he read their
letters of resignation almost as personal insults.[28]

In Quisling's most intimate environment, Prytz and Munthe both kept
their distance from Germany. Prytz was never anti-Semitic. Hjort, on the
other hand, was caught up in the whole question, and advocated that the
original anti-Semitic clause of the Norwegian 1814 constitution be reinstated
– 'Jews are not to be permitted in the realm' – a clause which had been
abandoned since the 1850s. The growing tensions within the party on the
Jewish question demanded decisive action by a strong leader. Quisling was
put under pressure to speak out more decisively. Members wondered
whether the NS as such would adopt anti-Semitism as its policy.

The answer came on 28 December 1935, when Quisling appeared at the
NS Fører seminar to talk about the political situation. His message was now
clear: 'We will not be able to bypass this question, but we must not occupy

---

[26] *NS* 1935/37, 38, 42.
[27] Bruknap in R. Danielsen and S. U. Larsen (eds.), *Fra idé til dom* (1976) and Stein U. Larsen,
'Med korset mot hammeren', in I. Montgomery and S. Larsen (eds.), *Kirken, krisen og
krigen* (1982) pp. 279f. See also Bodil Wold-Johnsen, 'NS i Stavanger' (thesis) UiB 1972.
[28] Lunde to Østbye 22 October 1935, RA PANS 25.

ourselves with it unduly.' Even if the Jewish question could not be avoided, the struggle had to be conducted with a regard for certain rules. The necessary attacks would have to be carried out 'in a proper way and on an objective basis', without encouraging 'racial hatred on an individual basis'.[29]

Thus the NS declared that, while it was anti-Jewish, it was not against individual Jews. With this explanation the movement embarked on its decisive trial of strength: the election campaign of 1936.

TROTSKY IN NORWAY

The months leading up to the party's second election campaign were hectic. The NS installed itself in brand new premises in the centre of Oslo. After months of preparations the first issue of the party's new daily newspaper, *Fritt Folk*, was finally launched on 26 March. Simultaneously the election campaign began, and Quisling started touring more extensively than ever. According to his own records, he made over a hundred election addresses between March and October 1936, everywhere flanked by his loyal adherents. At the summer rally he was able to survey his ranks and jubilantly declare that they were the founders of the new Norwegian state, the new élite.[30]

If Quisling managed to speak relatively undisturbed on these tours, interrupted only by the by now customary heckling and the singing of 'The International', other NS arrangements were subject to more dramatic disruptions. Several places witnessed the throwing of stones and eggs in demonstrations by young workers. The worst incident took place during the 'Battle of the Market Place' in the inland town of Gjøvik on Ascension Day 1936. Hjort was talking from the roof of the propaganda car, surrounded by a Hird division bearing banners and flags. An audience of three thousand metamorphosed into a rioting mob, and a group of activists started to hurl stones at the car at the signal of a whistle. The police were apparently powerless to do anything. The propaganda car started its homeward journey followed by a shower of stones. The demonstrators chased the car all the way to Minnesund Bridge; in the small hours of the morning the expedition turned back to Oslo, exhausted and in shock. The Gjøvik incident caused a sensation, and although the NS had been the aggrieved party, the episode

---

[29] Minutes from NS *Førerkurs* 28 December 1935, RA PA Lunde.
[30] Quisling at the *riksmøte* 26 June 1936, recorded in *FF* 27 June 1936.

did not bode well for the future as nine people needed medical attention –
one policeman and eight NS members.[31]

The general opinion was that it was clearly German National Socialist
influence which was making its presence felt on the domestic political scene.
The NS was coming to resemble Hitler's movement in increasingly obvious
ways. During the course of the election campaign, even the eagle symbol
made its appearance with wings outstretched, superimposed on the sun
cross as a part of the party's emblem.

At the end of July a new NS sensation broke: the Trotsky affair. Leon
Trotsky had unexpectedly arrived in Norway on his remarkable odyssey, in
exile after Stalin had expelled him following his defeat in the leadership
elections in the 1920s. The new Labour government led by Johan
Nygaardsvold welcomed this famous asylum-seeker. The press, depending
on party allegiance, looked on him with a scepticism that ranged from
solidarity to terror mixed with curiosity; *Fritt Folk* assumed that the
'Marxist' government had definitely 'brought' Trotsky to the country as a
concession to its left, revolutionary wing.

A group of young Hird members from Oslo and Akershus came together
at the party offices to plan what to do. Trotsky had to be exposed, it was
decided; he was an international revolutionary agitator and the brains
behind the Fourth International; he represented a threat to Norway and
therefore did not qualify for refugee status in that he had broken the
condition of his residence which expressly forbade political activity. They
calculated that all they needed to do was put him under surveillance, and
then they would have all the proof they needed. Six Hird members duly left
for Hønefoss and established their quarters close to Trotsky's house. Hjort
(possibly in charge of the operation) was kept posted throughout. Quisling
was kept out of it.

During July 1936 the Hønefoss group managed to collect the evidence it
was looking for, partly by stealing documents from Trotsky and his secretary
after burgling the premises, partly by keeping watch on the movements of
those who entered and left the building ('mainly Jews'), and eventually by
tapping Trotsky's telephone.

The evening papers of Thursday 6 August reported the break-in, which
became the sensation of the summer. Hjort submitted a report on Trotsky,
supported by ample documentation. The culprits were arrested and taken to

---

[31] This account is based on reports in *FF* 22–25 May 1936, besides interviews with eye-
witnesses.

a hearing. Quisling conceded that the Hird's break-in was illegal, but argued that it was justified as it had averted 'a much graver misfortune' – Trotsky's continued subversive activities. When the case was brought before the magistrates' court the proceedings were interrupted by the sensational announcement from Moscow that 'terrorist Trotsky–Sinovjev groups' had been organising secret attacks on the state and the party for years, and that, among others, they were behind the murder of Leningrad's party leader Sergeij Kirov in 1934. The announcement went on to maintain that these groups were directed by Trotsky in exile. It was impossible to know what to believe. The Norwegian public was utterly perplexed. It took some time before the press realised that the Moscow trials of 19–20 August, which to the astonishment of the entire world were carried out completely openly, were no more than a staged farce, based on confessions obtained under torture. By a fantastic coincidence the Moscow trials opened at precisely the moment when the main culprit stood in the dock of a remote Norwegian magisterial court, defending himself against accusations brought by the Quisling party. But coincidence or not, the government decided to play safe with Moscow and intern Trotsky by placing him under 24-hour police surveillance.[32]

'NS Victorious in Trotsky Case! The Government Gives in to Stalin' ran the headline splashed over the front page of *Fritt Folk*. It was a guaranteed triumph: the government had interned its dangerous guest and at the same time had shown that it took orders from Moscow, exactly as the NS had claimed. The case afforded the party an opportunity to mobilise, which was an invaluable boost to its campaign. The propaganda office grasped the opportunity and organised nation-wide protest meetings.

Their victory in the Trotsky affair could not but increase the anti-Semitic agitation of the election campaign. The Jew Trotsky was the perfect symbol of everything the NS was now fighting against: Judaism, Marxist subversion, clandestine international organisations, and the Labour Party's pliability.

BEHIND THE SCENES

Despite the apparent progress during the election campaign, there was much to dampen the Fører's optimism in 1936. The recruitment drive in many areas produced no dramatic increase in members, only a slight compensa-

---

[32] Y. Ustvedt, *Verdensrevolusjonen på Hønefoss* (1974) pp. 88f, whose account is based on the trial material. Documents concerning the internment are in St.med. no. 19, 1937; see also Håkon Meyer, *Bak Moskvaprosessene* (1937), and Isaac Deutscher, *The Prophet Outcast. Trotsky 1929–40* (1963) ch. 'An Enemy of the People'.

tion for lost membership from the previous year. Membership stagnated at 8,500. Financing the daily *Fritt Folk* turned out to be a huge problem. Its budget was originally calculated on the basis of 4,000 subscribers – enough to give the paper a solid operating base. Moreover, the promoters reckoned that it would be a simple task to persuade more members to take out subscriptions. Neither assumption proved correct. After an initial daily run of 5,500 copies, *Fritt Folk* soon had to cut back when it became clear that party members were not coming forward. The small contribution the Italians made to the paper was one of several gifts of 1,000 kroner, some from party activists but most from wealthy people outside the party. The whole project of launching the daily would have failed but for a handsome contribution of 10,000 Reichsmarks from Germany. The gift was apparently arranged by a businessman, Ellef Ringnes. In February 1936 he had a meeting with Quisling and told him that the money had been raised by Norwegian businessmen in Germany. In fact it had come from the Propaganda Ministry in Berlin. Quite how Goebbels's department secured an export authorisation for 10,000 Reichsmarks, and how the money was transferred to Norway and paid into *Fritt Folk*'s account, has never been clearly documented. The fact remains that the paper actually came into being with secret German support.[33]

Soon, however, both the party and the paper ran into difficulties; new members did not turn up and the main contributors had grown weary of the struggle. Hjort decided to make an appeal for support in Germany and left for Berlin in the last week of May. There is no record of whether he returned with either money or concrete pledges; most probably he managed to secure neither and never told Quisling of his trip.[34]

Shortly thereafter, however, a new German envoy, Dr Heinrich Sahm, arrived at the Oslo legation: 'no involvement in domestic politics, particularly in election year' was his brief from Berlin. When the office manager of *Fritt Folk* paid him a visit in July, asking him to help keep the newspaper alive, Sahm promised to make enquiries in Berlin, although he thought it scarcely worth his while, and, indeed, no donation via the legation was forthcoming. All the same, the new German minister's arrival in Oslo signalled a great improvement in NS relations with Berlin, in that from that time the party and its Fører regularly appeared in the legation's political

---

[33] Quisling to Harry Høst 19 February 1937, RA NSP 3; information given by R. J. Fuglesang, Autobiographical MS, Fuglesang archives.*
[34] Memo, von Trotha 3 June 1936 on Hjort's visit in APA, BA Koblenz NS 43/54.

reports. Sahm declared in one of his earliest reports to Berlin that he thought the NS was 'under-estimated'. He drew this conclusion after having attended the national party meeting (riksmøte) at the Coliseum cinema in Oslo, where he followed Quisling's speech on foreign policy and the Nordic union particularly closely. He managed to acquire a text of the speech and three days later called on Quisling at home.[35]

This was the first time that a member of the legation had taken the trouble to pay him a visit, and Quisling took the opportunity to present his views on their respective countries. He explained to Dr Sahm that Norway was the 'key' country in Scandinavia, and while he was content with the rallying of support around the NS and considered that the party had additional potential support among the country's 120,000–150,000 unemployed, the difficulty lay in people's misconceptions about Germany, which had a negative influence on their attitude to the NS. Quisling sincerely believed that he *had* the potential support of some 100,000 voters – and their financial backing too. He gave Dr Sahm the impression of being a firm and confident believer in his own case.

The Italian legation seems to have been better informed. Roddolo had followed events closely from the newspaper which he had helped finance, and he could see very clearly where things were moving. In the summer of 1936 his time in Oslo came to an end. 'I admire the work you are doing for your fatherland,' he wrote in his farewell letter to Quisling, 'and I am confident that I will hear about your future success, if only from a distance.'[36]

While Roddolo was preparing to leave, about thirty participants from the Third International Nationalist Congress arrived at the Nobel Institute in Oslo to discuss the founding of 'a nationalist academy of international law'. In his report to the Foreign Ministry in Rome, Roddolo described the organisation as 'similar to the CAUR but in a German, Nazi direction, and expressly anti-Latin in its aims'.[37] He quite rightly suspected that the enterprise was financed by Germany. The Internationale Arbeitsgemeinschaft der Nationalisten was in fact set up and financed by the Propaganda Ministry in Berlin and led by the ambitious young international lawyer Dr Hans Keller, who managed to recruit such prominent Norwegians as the leading lawyer Professor Gjelsvik and the Agrarian leader Johan

---

[35] Heinrich Sprenger, *Heinrich Sahm: Kommunalpolitiker und Staatsmann* (1969) pp. 271f; *Vermerk* by Sahm 4 July 1936, PAAA Bonn Ges. Oslo 23/201.

[36] Roddolo to Quisling 28 July 1936, UBO MS fol. 4096 X.

[37] Report from Oslo 3 and 10 August 1936, MAE Roma, Affari Politici: Norvegia 3.

Mellbye. Professor Poul Heegaard presided over the meeting, and the Norwegian-American Charles Stangeland, at the time a professor in Berlin, was among those who attended. Keller had wanted Quisling to be there too, but the Fører was on holiday in Fyresdal. Several others from the party did attend, led by Dr Aall.[38]

The Italian legation was not slow to discover that, by this move, the NS had given its support to an anti-Italian undertaking, and that *Fritt Folk* was giving Keller's international organisation ample coverage. 'Nazi theories on the supremacy of the Germanic race are gaining influence over the nationalist movement in Norway,' the legation's report to Rome concluded. In February 1937, in a much fuller report reviewing 'Italian interests and Norway', the NS was expressly written off. This was the last time that any Italian report referred to Quisling's movement in Norway. The Germans, it seemed, had now taken over.[39]

SPLIT IN THE PARTY

The general election of 1936 turned out to be catastrophic for the NS, putting paid to any hope of establishing the party as a real parliamentary alternative. Not a single Storting seat had been won; worse, the party had actually lost ground since 1933. Lists had then been put up in at least half the districts, and the party had amassed 27,900 votes. This time, with lists in all districts, the total fell to 26,600, registering a net loss in the old districts, and an insignificant gain in the new ones. *Fritt Folk* closed down on 22 October, an indication of the hopelessness of the situation.[40]

In view of this, Quisling's opening of the meeting on the Sunday before All Saints' Day at the party headquarters was astonishingly optimistic. Facing his closest followers and party officials ten days after the defeat, he declared that, although the other parties considered the NS to be finished, this was merely wishful thinking on their part; in fact, the national break-through was unstoppable.

The meeting turned out to be very much divided over the question of what had been responsible for their humiliation at the polls. Some blamed

---

[38] Papers from the Oslo conference in MAE Roma, Affari Politici: Norvegia 3; a lengthy correspondence concerning Dr Keller in PAAA Bonn Inland II A/B 132/74 (25/1), also containing Sahm's report of 5 August 1936; report in *FF* 27 July 1936.

[39] Report 10 August 1936, MAE Roma, Affari Politici: Norvegia 3; Report 19 February 1937, ACS Roma, MCP 386.

[40] Election reports in *FF* 20–21 October 1936; Høidal, *Quisling*, pp. 183f.

the party's stance on the Jewish question, others the battle against socialism. The party's symbols and political style came under fire, and eventually doubt was raised over the suitability of a parliamentary strategy altogether. Quisling himself stressed this point. In the hour of defeat he stated bluntly that the party no longer necessarily needed to win parliamentary power, and even sharpened this message to his office holders in a circular which followed on from the meeting. Now was the time to build up the Corporate Assembly (Riksting) and the Guild Organisation necessary to fill it, rather than wait for the next elections. The task was urgent: 'The country and the people are heading towards calamitous times.'

Apparently the Fører believed in this wholly unrealistic strategy. He told Prytz in a letter after the meeting that he had been just as astonished by the election results as he had been by 'the stoicism with which the movement accepted them'. With that, the party showed that it was 'possibly stronger today than ever', and ready for new challenges.[41]

Before they reached that point, however, the inevitable happened: the party cracked under internal pressure from the election defeat. Quisling's closest collaborator Hjort broke away, taking others with him. The disagreements between the two leaders were exacerbated by a personality clash: Hjort was proud and bold, Quisling hesitant and vague. Where Quisling had vision, Hjort demanded results. There had also been tension between Hjort as district Fører in Akershus and the Quisling-dominated Oslo party, concerning the Hird and its campaign car. Hjort's people from Akershus mainly came from the west end and the fashionable suburbs, while in central Oslo there was a greater social spread, with inevitable tensions between the two. Slowly these trivial differences escalated into a full breach which ultimately divided loyalties within the party, in the sense that loyalty to Quisling was increasingly interpreted as a stand against Hjort and vice versa.[42]

To the realist Hjort, the election defeat clearly demonstrated that the NS now stood on the verge of collapse. He therefore demanded that the party leadership be restructured as there were far too many inferior people surrounding the Fører, who demanded his attention for minor matters. In place of the cumbersome executive committee which had developed into a large collection of Quisling's acolytes, handpicked by the Fører, a leaner and more effective council of competent people should be set up, and thereafter

---

[41] Quisling to Prytz 8 November 1936, Prytz archives.*
[42] Various party correspondence Hjort–Quisling 1935–6 in RA NSRH 1.

the organisation would have to be decentralised. For two months after the elections, Hjort bombarded Quisling with letters and memoranda concerning the need for a shake-up in the NS leadership.[43]

Hjort's own cell, the Hird, had been divided for a long time. The majority remained faithful to their old leader, and drank toasts to him at their Christmas party at the same time talking disrespectfully of Quisling. 'And Hjort like a torch through Akershus . . . ,' sang the youths at the tops of their voices, while the Fører came in for derision. News of the episode soon reached the leadership, and eventually Quisling himself. It was suspected that Hjort was trying to use the Hird to stage a coup.[44]

On New Year's Eve, Hjort received a message from Quisling to the effect that he was no longer a member of the executive committee. A month later he left the party. This was a heavy blow, as there was no other single individual apart from Quisling who represented the party more than he. In April 1937, leading party members petitioned Quisling for an extraordinary party convention, a *riksmøte*. Their letter was addressed: 'To the incumbent leadership of the National Union, care of Major Quisling', a boldly provocative gesture which suggested that the problems over Hjort might yet have serious consequences.[45]

The demand for a convention, or at least a major discussion meeting, was debated by the leadership and the opposition groups throughout the spring of 1937 until Quisling, with the endorsement of the executive committee, eventually excluded twenty-one of the individuals who had insisted on the meeting. The expulsions were communicated to the party organisation on 15 May. That day, the individuals in question had gathered together a couple of hundred other malcontents to make a stand against the threats of the Fører and close ranks around the party opposition. Altogether, no more than fifty people were either expelled from or left the party in the aftermath of Hjort's departure. The majority of them, however, were party officeholders and activists who demonstrably no longer wished to be involved in the movement. A great many more left the party quietly in the spring. And this was only the beginning. Thousands of members gradually drifted away by failing to renew their subscriptions, local groups were disbanded and district parties and organisations were wound up during the summer of 1937.

---

[43] Hjort to Quisling 17 and 31 October, 1, 5, 19 and 26 November 1936, RA NSRH 1.

[44] Songs and speeches from the Christmas party 21 December 1936, RA D 29 div. 3.

[45] Quisling's lengthy statement to party officers 15 May 1937 and his correspondence with Wiesener, RA NSP 3.

The devastating effects of all this were fully exposed during the nation-wide municipal elections in October 1937. Quisling put up his own lists of candidates but only where the organisation stood a good chance – in some twenty municipalities out of a total of several hundred. Progress was made in two of these relative to 1934. All the other municipalities registered a dramatic fall in votes, with Oslo giving the most disappointing result. Scarcely 800 votes were cast for the NS list, which was headed by the party general secretary, the lawyer Rolf Jørgen Fuglesang – as against 5,000 on the previous occasion. 'A great many of our erstwhile supporters must have deserted us,' remarked Quisling drily, and consoled his colleague with the words of Peter the Great: 'They will beat us until we learn how to beat them.'[46] Strangely enough, the party did not go completely under at this point, but the enormous new office space had to be vacated for more modest premises and activities shrunk to almost nil.

THE HAPLESS ART DEALER

During this time of disaster for the party, Quisling was also beset by personal tragedy. His sister-in-law Ingerid fell ill: a brain tumour had made her blind, which meant that she had had to give up painting. After two operations in Boston she died at home in 1938. Vidkun and Maria had been extremely fond of Ingerid and took her death very hard. Jørgen was all alone, and rapidly declined into a pitiful figure who greatly worried the family, even though he continued to run his medical clinic.

There was also bad news from his brother Arne who had emigrated to the United States and was living in Brooklyn. His wife had had a baby who had died at birth. Arne telegraphed Vidkun, asking him to 'break the news to Mother gently'. The ageing Mrs Quisling worried about her sons. In 1940 Arne and his wife had another child – a daughter who was to be Anna Quisling's only grandchild, and the only direct descendant of the provost. But Anna, Vidkun and Jørgen never met her.

Vidkun and Maria's marriage remained childless. There is no evidence of his feelings on the subject, except from a party in Oslo when a guest who was discussing the subject, turned to Maria and asked if she was planning to have any children. Quisling instantly interrupted, 'Not as long as it's up to me!'

It has been alleged that Maria had had a miscarriage in the 1930s and that

---

[46] *FF* 9, 16 and 23 October 1937. See also Ivo de Figueiredo, 'Ideologiens Primat', *HT* 1995/3.

she had a relationship with an accountant in Oslo to compensate for the warmth that her husband never showed her. But none of this seems very likely in view of the fact that the Quislings' private life occasioned so few rumours or comments despite his exceptionally high profile. In fact, most evidence suggests that the marriage was quite uneventful.

The fact that Quisling himself never showed signs of erotic inclinations does not necessarily mean that his marriage to Maria was not physical. But he was reserved, even with her, and work always came first. Maria was left on her own a lot. The Quislings once attended a houseparty together, arranged by the Oxford Movement, and one or two meetings at the Union of Russian Emigrants in Oslo. Otherwise they seldom went out and socialised with very few people outside their family or the inner circle of the party.

Only when Quisling was away did Maria invite her friends to the house. One day they were discussing their husbands, and one after the other related how their husbands constantly complained that their work kept them away from their families. Maria remarked quietly: 'My husband never says that.'[47]

The Quislings slowly began to encounter financial difficulties, particularly after the party split in 1937. As an unsalaried major after 1930, Quisling was forced to support his family from private sources, and he and Maria kept a rather expensive apartment, with domestic help, throughout the 1930s. To begin with he was able to live on what was left of his inheritance from his maternal grandparents, which his mother had shared out among her sons when Jørgen needed financial support to complete his long-delayed studies. But soon Quisling had to look for other sources of income.

After his return to Norway from Russia he had intended to earn money from writing. Between 1930 and 1932 he received a small sum from his book *Russia and Ourselves*; Dybwad's, his publishers, paid out 2,000 kroner in royalties. But sales were no greater than for any book with a social focus in the 1930s. In 1931 the London publishers Hodder and Stoughton took on the book for the British edition, in the author's translation, but it never received any notices in the British press and enjoyed only a limited circulation. The reason why they took on the book at all was doubtless the influence exercised by Quisling's friend in Kent, Cecilie Dahl, née Blom, who was a close friend of the publisher's wife, Mrs Hodder, another Norwegian woman married to an Englishman. A Spanish edition was

---

[47] This account is based on information obtained from members of the Quisling family, and from Johan Vogt, Stein Ørnhøi and Siren Zimmer.

similarly produced with the help of a pro-NS Norwegian–Spanish couple, but nothing much came of that either.[48]

The main source of both private income and support for Quisling's political career was the paintings he had brought from Russia. Ever since his return in 1929 he had devoted a great deal of time and attention to ensuring that he got a good price for his collection. Immediately after his return he had put up two of the lesser known works for sale with Oslo dealers. Two of the supposed masterpieces had been restored at the National Gallery. When subject to scrutiny, both turned out to be copies.[49]

His brother Arne took eleven pictures with him to New York in 1931, ten of which he hung on the walls of his Brooklyn home as they proved unsaleable. In the summer of 1933 he took thirty more, including some painted by the most famous artists in the collection: Rembrandt, Poussin, Van Dyck and Frans Hals. But an expert on 58th Street declared that these too were copies, worth between 25 and 100 dollars each. Only three turned out to be originals. 'So it seems that you risked your money without having sufficient knowledge to distinguish originals from copies,' concluded Arne in October 1933.

But one picture in the collection was apparently an original, and a valuable one at that – Frans Hals's *The Dutch Family*. Arne had it restored and valued at between 50,000 and 60,000 dollars. In autumn 1933, after the election defeat had made it clear that no MP's salary was waiting for him, Vidkun telegraphed Arne and told him to proceed with the sale. But the dealers, Furst, Lilienfeld and Brandt of Fifth Avenue, did not manage to secure a sale as the market was very slack because of the Depression.

The summer of 1934 brought another unpleasant surprise: 'Yesterday's message that the painting is not after all an original came like a bolt from the blue,' wrote Arne to his brother. Worcester Museum, which had been interested in the painting, had had it X-rayed, revealing brushstrokes which could not possibly have been Hals's. It seemed likely that the painting had been done by two slightly later artists. The museum offered 4,000 dollars for the copy and expected an answer within twenty-four hours. Quisling

---

[48] Documents related to *Russia and Ourselves* in UBO MS fol. 4096 IV, 2; the possibility of a Finnish edition was discussed by Quisling and Minister Elfving, Helsinki. The Hodder connection: Hewins, *Quisling*, p. 33.

[49] All information concerning Quisling's paintings is based on his various lists and letters, and his lengthy correspondence with his brother Arne on the subject: UBO MS fol. 4096 II, 2 and X, 6; Vidkun's letters in Collection Arne Quisling.* See also H. F. Dahl in *Dagbladet* 29 August 1984.

accepted, but even this offer threatened to evaporate. When Arne went to accept the offer Furst informed him that the museum had withdrawn the offer as more than twenty-four hours had elapsed. The dealer, however, was willing to equal the museum's offer, and Arne accepted at once.

Quisling thus became 3,000 dollars richer during the NS convention at Stiklestad, after Arne had taken his commission. It was enough to live on for a year or two, but no more. Another attempt to sell another 'Rembrandt' through Floriet in Paris similarly came to nothing. In London Christie's refused to put up for auction pictures offered first by Arne in 1934 and then by Cecilie Dahl in 1937 as the proceeds would scarcely cover the transport costs.

As a result Quisling had to live fairly frugally in 1935 and 1936 and asked that the party account refund in full all his expenses, down to the last postage stamp. Quisling himself kept detailed accounts. The party was being run on a tight budget and many creditors were kept waiting, but the Fører's expenses were reimbursed immediately. He was having to use up what was left of his inheritance. In 1935 he entered '0' as his net income on his income tax return; the following year the city treasurer had to take away a table from Erling Skjalgssonsgate as security for the municipal tax that he was unable to pay.[50]

The extent of the problem became known publicly in April 1937. During the liquidation of *Fritt Folk* it came to light that, the year before, Quisling had had to put 500 kroner of the money raised in his own pocket as an unofficial advance for his expenses, and that he had later submitted a claim for the same expenses. Legally, this was a mere detail, but on a personal level the matter was very painful for Quisling, whose financial straits were being laid bare before the entire party.[51] According to his own notes, the last of his inheritance ran out during 1937 and 1938. After that he began to take money out of his mother's account for basic necessities; she retained possession of the estate, and technically this was not eating into his brothers' share of the inheritance.

During these years the art collection became a source of increasing distress. In the spring of 1936 Arne Quisling came across an article in *The New York Times Magazine* about Dutch Masters in American possession, and found *The Dutch Family* listed – as an original! The painting now

---

[50] Vogt, *Mennesket Vidkun*, p. 182; Quisling, Almanachs 1935, 1936, RA.
[51] Quisling to Arne Wiese 6 April 1937, RA NSRH 3; *FF* 8 April 1937; Høidal, *Quisling*, p. 206.

belonged to the San Diego Fine Arts Gallery in California, and was valued at 100,000 dollars.[52] Arne immediately sought legal advice and after a while found out what had happened: Furst had, after paying 4,000 dollars for the painting, sold it on to a colleague, who in turn had sold it to an associate. The picture was subsequently bought by a German dealer, who sold it to the millionaire sisters Amy and Anne Putnam in Texas, who donated it to the Fine Arts Gallery. An art historian had examined the picture at an exhibition in Detroit in 1935 and declared it to be the original. Arne suspected a ring of conspiracy, involving art dealers who had let the picture pass through different hands in order to cover up their swindle, and then divided the profits afterwards.

With his brother's blessing and his lawyer's encouragement, Arne brought a lawsuit against Furst, Lilienfeld and Brandt. The case came before the court in January 1937 and reports in Norwegian-American newspapers meant that even the Oslo press got hold of the story. 'The case is sensational, and is awaited with great interest,' *Dagbladet* reported. This was certainly an exaggeration, but both the *Herald Tribune* and *The New York Sun* covered the final judgement in October 1938: the Quisling brothers were forced to drop the case, as they were unable to prove that any of the dealers implicated in the case had profited excessively from the sale of the painting.[53]

For Quisling this defeat was all the more bitter as the international art market in the meantime had recovered and prices had picked up. Not since 1929–30 had such prices been paid as in the summer of 1938, and Frans Hals was particularly sought after. An international Hals exhibition in Haarlem in Holland that summer was much discussed in the world press. Quisling cut out what the papers were saying and also took note of what Rosenberg's paper *Völkischer Beobachter* alleged: that the Haarlem exhibition had proved that there was an extensive 'Jewish swindle' operating with Hals copies. According to the NSDAP paper (which used the Dutch press as its source), Jewish dealers were speculating in copies and fakes. In fact the swindle had been going on since the 1600s, when a Jewish pupil of Hals's had started to circulate false signatures.[54] It is not difficult to imagine Quisling's reaction to these reports, and how he immediately connected his

---

[52] Also known as *Family Group in Landscape*. Information regarding this painting has been collected from international catalogues by Anne Schølberg. Today the painting is not regarded as an original Hals.

[53] *New York Sun* and *Herald Tribune* 16 November 1938, press cuttings in Collection Arne Quisling.* *Dagbladet* 8 February 1937.

[54] *Völkischer Beobachter* 1 September 1937; compare *The Times* 6 and 23 August 1937.

own 'tragedy' – that he had been cheated and swindled, deprived of the
means with which he could have built up the NS – to the larger scene. 'All
the people involved are Jews,' he said to Arne after the Hals affair. An
international ring of fraudulent Jews which had been operating secretly over
the centuries and across continents was exactly what he had been warning
his followers of politically. Now he himself had fallen victim to it financially.
A profit which ran to tens of thousands of dollars, sufficient to finance his
political activities for the rest of his life, had been snatched from under his
nose by a gang of unscrupulous Jews.[55]

The hapless art collector had other opponents to face too. A good fifty
paintings which Quisling had put up for sale over the years through the
dealer Warberg in Oslo had disappeared without the owner receiving any
payment. Eventually Quisling reported Warberg to the police. His tribula-
tions as an art collector were in danger of becoming a public soap opera,
alluded to even in variety songs broadcast on the Oslo radio. In August 1938
a public case was brought against the dealer. Quisling recorded how he had
left Warberg fifty-one paintings, two lithographs and a pencil drawing. The
dealer was found guilty of embezzlement, but Quisling was none the richer
for it.[56]

In the summer of 1939 Arne packed up and sent back most of the pictures
he had received from Vidkun. He offered to buy the remainder for 1,700
kroner, the same sum as he had already put into his failed attempt to sell the
paintings. And with that Quisling's role as an international art dealer came
to an end, thwarted, as he saw it, by dishonest people and sabotaged by
underground crime rings. A bitter conclusion indeed to his dream of a
financially independent life dedicated to the service of politics and ideas.

THINGS FALL APART

In Quisling's apocalyptic vision of the world two sets of events in 1938–9
pointed to the disintegration of the established order of society. At home the
party politicians of the Storting extended their period of office from three to
four years, a move which some people – and certainly Quisling – interpreted
as a constitutional *coup d'état* to be followed by further assaults on the
Constitution at any moment. On the international scene, the Czechoslovakia
crisis showed that the situation in eastern Europe would almost certainly

---

[55] Vidkun to Arne Quisling 4 March and 2 May 1938, Collection Arne Quisling.*
[56] *Aftenposten* 23 September 1938.

lead to war between the western powers, Russia and Germany, in which case Norway would become a battlefield for strategic reasons. In Quisling's mind, the two issues – the threat of war and a constitutional crisis – would combine to create an overall state of emergency in which his own party, however small, might play a leading role.

The background for the internal situation was as follows. In April 1938 the Storting amended Article 71 of the Constitution after a bill proposed in the previous session, to the effect that the term of office be extended from three to four years. The reform was overdue and had majority support in the Storting, but the implementation raised some doubts as to when it should be put into operation: immediately on being written into the Constitution, or from the following session. The presidency of the Storting, the ultimate authority on the matter, decided on the first option, but critics held the decision to be unwise since it could be said, with some justification, that parliament had prolonged its own term of office. The Liberal daily *Dagbladet* even spoke of a *coup d'état* on the part of the Storting. Nobody, however, interpreted the reform so dramatically as did Quisling and the NS, who mounted a violent campaign against the amendment. Quisling spoke of a 'criminal violation of the Norwegian Constitution', a 'lawless state which can have the most disastrous consequences', calling into question the legitimacy of the government and arguing that after 1 January 1940 the government of Norway would not be legitimate. In short, Quisling saw the amendment in terms of a usurpation of the executive power, promoted by the inherent self-interest of the party system, and certainly a chance for him to take the political initiative.[57]

Then in the spring of 1939 came the urgent task of securing the country's neutrality. Norway had to leave the League of Nations, Quisling argued, and to increase her armaments to a level comparable with those of her neighbours. He was certainly not alone in predicting world war as a distinct possibility from the middle 1930s, and as alarmingly imminent from 1936. The one single event which made this dreadful scenario inevitable was Austria's *Anschluss* in March 1938, which made war a question of months rather than years, and autumn 1939 the most probable time.[58]

---

[57] *FF* 26 November 1938, 18 December 1939; various documents in RA PAQ 8. *Dagbladet*, editorial 2 April 1938.

[58] See Quisling's comment in *FF* 19 March 1938, 'Samling av alle tyskere'. In his trial in 1945 Quisling told the court that *FF* editors had been so opposed to the article because of its conditional endorsement of Germany that it only appeared in a shortened, censored version; see *Straffesak* p. 339.

For Norway the situation seemed to be this: the west coast of Scandinavia
had for a long time lain within the domain of British naval hegemony.
Norway's neutrality in another war would, by virtue of this, be at least as
precarious as it had been during the previous war; in all probability it would
not be sustainable during a new conflict. Therefore, any attempt to have
Norwegian neutrality recognised within the framework of the League of
Nations' covenant was, in Quisling's view, naive. Moreover, a new threat
had presented itself in the form of the huge naval base in the Murmansk
area which the Russians had developed since the previous war, and which
made Norwegian waters a potential theatre of war between the Russian and
German navies.

Norway was thus ineluctably drawn into the war between the powers
from every side, east, south and west, and therefore her neutrality could not
be safeguarded by the great powers as it had been before, at least not with
the very low level of armaments that Norway maintained. Quisling frequently pointed out that Norway used less than half of what Sweden and
only a third of what Finland spent on defence per head of population. His
main aim for Norway was one he shared with everyone else – neutrality to
safeguard the nation's interests: non-involvement. But relying on British
naval supremacy would not be sufficient to obtain this, as both Russia and
Germany now had other strategic interests than those of 1914.

To his followers Quisling appeared more deep-thinking and clear-sighted
than others, because of the dramatic rhetoric he used. His reactions to the
Czechoslovakia crisis and the Munich Agreement of September 1938 were
typical: 'We are as close to the hell of war as we can be without its actually
breaking out.' After Munich, when things seemed to be easing up in eastern
Europe, the pressure on Scandinavia increased. In the event of a new crisis
between the great powers, Norway would be dragged into the war 'at most
two days after its outbreak', he declared.[59]

It might be asked to what extent he allowed his reasoning to be coloured
by political sympathy for Hitler during the lead-up to the war. As late as the
spring of 1939 Quisling was urging co-operation between Britain and
Germany based on a balancing out of British naval hegemony and German
continental ambitions.[60] That Quisling, despite such comments, was generally held by the public to be decidedly pro-German, is to some extent due to
his growing anti-Semitism, which certainly signalled an ideological sym-

[59] *FF* 8 and 15 October and 12 November 1938.
[60] Quisling to Aall 22 April 1939, RA PAQ 12; various articles in *FF* May 1939.

pathy with Hitler. The extent to which he embraced National Socialism in this respect had in fact revealed itself fully during the pogroms in Germany in November 1938.

Kristallnacht, 9 November 1938, proved to the world that the National Socialist Jewish policy was more radical than the apartheid system suggested by the Nuremberg laws. Synagogues were burnt down and Jews injured in a series of demonstrations directed by the Propaganda Minister Goebbels himself. Throughout Europe these ruthless pogroms were provoking indignant reactions, and even Quisling refused to justify Germany. He spoke of 'the tragic development of the Jewish question in Germany', and predicted that the situation would only get worse if the Jews were expelled from Germany and Austria. 'A new Jewish country' had to be established in one of the places which were featuring prominently in contemporary debates on the Jewish question – Brazil, Madagascar, New Guinea, Cyprus – 'and the task has to be taken seriously'. There is much to suggest that he personally considered Cyprus the best solution.[61]

In the NS, Mrs Østbye was given a free hand to express her detailed knowledge of Jewish networks, agents and conspiracies. In the summer and autumn of 1938 her book *The Jewish Problem and its Solution* was published in two editions, written under the pseudonym of Irene Sverd, perhaps because she feared that the Attorney General might be a little too interested in its contents. Within the party the anti-Jewish and anti-Masonic initiatives in the autumn and winter of 1938–9 were taking on an increasingly German and National Socialist hue, and this activism must be seen above all as an expression of the party's growing ideological sympathy for Germany's cause in the fast-intensifying conflict with the great powers.

Five months after *Kristallnacht* and only a few weeks after Germany's invasion of Czechoslovakia, Quisling sent Hitler greetings to mark his fiftieth birthday on 20 April 1939, including a carefully worded message of thanks for having 'saved Europe from Bolshevism and Jewish domination'.[62]

---

[61] Quisling spoke about the Jewish question in Bergen on 23 November, Oslo 1 and 5 December, Drammen 8 December 1938, Oslo 7 February, Gjøvik 13 February, Oslo 14 February and Trondheim 3 March 1939; Quisling, Almanachs 1938–9, RA. Odd Nansen, the son of Fridtjof Nansen, was present at one of the Oslo meetings and gives an account of it in *Langs veien* (1970).

[62] Text in *FF* 22 April 1939; also RA PAQ 12, RA PAQ 8. The draft of an earlier telegram to

This open approach to Germany was not the only foreign contact the party tried to establish. Links with fraternal groups in Scandinavia were now in the making, as Quisling started to speak, during the spring of 1939, in favour of making official contacts with like-minded groups in Sweden and Denmark.

It may seem remarkable that the contact between Nordic fascists and Nazis was not officially established until 1939, considering that NS counterparts had been active throughout the 1930s in Sweden and Denmark, and to some extent in Iceland too. Generally, however, a nationalist movement like the NS had to be sceptical about Nordic co-operation, Quisling pointed out to the other Nordic leaders when they met in 1939, as nationalism in Norway implied taking a firm stance against the former Danish and Swedish domination of the country.

The fact that co-operation between the Nordic parties was established at all in 1939 was due to the initiative of Frits Clausen. His Danish National Socialists had doubled their votes in the general election of spring 1939, a result that was noted with admiration by both the NS and the Swedish party the SSS – Svensk Social Samling. Thus when, from this new position of strength, Clausen invited Quisling and the SSS leader Sven-Olov Lindholm to the party's national convention in Kolding on 17–18 June 1939, they both accepted. The British leader Sir Oswald Mosley was invited too, but could not come to the meeting, which took place in a friendly, Nordic atmosphere.[63]

Quisling liked his colleague Frits Clausen. This friendly and slightly portly forty-five-year-old village doctor from South Jutland was not a powerful personality but nevertheless a lively and likeable man who was quite a good speaker. Moreover, he and Quisling had experiences in common from their time in Russia. During the First World War Clausen had served on the eastern front in the German army and had been taken prisoner at Masurien and held in a Russian prisoner-of-war camp from 1915 to 1918. He spoke some Russian and shared with Quisling the feeling of having lived through the Revolution 'and all that it brought with it'. After the Kolding meeting, Clausen and Quisling motored down to Dybdøl Skanse together, where Quisling was initiated into the history of South Jutland, which he knew little

---

Hitler and the NSDAP, written by Hjort and signed by Quisling in January 1934 was probably never sent. *Vi Menn* 1980/14.

[63] Quisling's speech at Kolding, reported in *FF* 1 July 1939. Documents pertaining to the meeting in RAK 52e. Wärenstam, *Fascismen och nazismen i Sverige 1920–40* (1970) ch. 'Nordiskt Samarbete', pp. 103f.

about. This was the first of several meetings of the Nordic leaders scheduled to take place in the following years.[64]

Quisling was in the middle of planning his trip to Kolding when he was unexpectedly summoned to the Nordic Association (Nordische Gesellschaft) annual summer convention in Lübeck. NS students and others from Quisling's circle had been invited to Lübeck before, to quite a prominent annual cultural event sponsored by Reichsminister Alfred Rosenberg. This was the first time that the Fører himself was to attend, and he certainly thought of it as some kind of rehabilitation after two years of shameful neglect of the NS by Germany's official representation in Oslo. And as if this were not enough, he suddenly received a third invitation, from Dr Aall in Berlin. He decided to accept, and planned his visits as a round trip: Oslo–Berlin–Kolding–Lübeck–Copenhagen–Oslo, a political summer circuit that promised well for a Norwegian Fører so badly hit by misfortunes at home.[65]

He found Berlin in June 1939 a city seething with nationalistic euphoria following the Czechoslovakian and Austrian triumphs. Quisling was thrown into a hectic round of meetings and conferences, where he was warmly received. Apart from Dr Aall, he was guided around by an NS party member from Dresden, the Bergen-born Albert Viljam Hagelin, who had made his fortune in Germany by a combination of business and marriages and who was now coming to his Fører's assistance. Quisling had met Hagelin on one previous occasion, in 1936, and was as impressed by his wealth as by his straightforward behaviour and energetic manners. For several days Quisling and Hagelin also met with the young, personable Hans Wilhelm Scheidt, a most enthusiastic official of Rosenberg's foreign policy office, who guided them round the corridors of power. Fermann from Hamburg also made himself available for driving them around in his car. Even his old friend

[64] For Clausen's biography see reports from his hearing in 1947 by Dr Max Schmidt 19 January 1947, LAK Køb. Pol. Clausen-Sagen pk 1. See also Frits Clausen, *Volk und Staat im Grenzland* (Internationaler Arbeitsgemeinschaft der Nationalisten), Zurich 1936. There is no Clausen biography available in any language.

[65] Aall to Maria Quisling 5 and 8 April 1952, and a statement 10 May 1951 UBO MS fol. 3920 X, 7. For earlier accounts of Quisling's trip to Germany in June 1939, see especially M. Skodvin, *Striden om okkupasjonsstyret* (1956), and also Hartmann, *Fører uten folk*; Loock, *Quisling*; P. M. Hayes, *The Career and Political Ideas of Vidkun Quisling 1887–1945* (1971); and Høidal, *Quisling*.

Maggen Günther busied herself over the visit, eager to introduce him to her most influential friends in the capital.

The Hagelin–Scheidt duo was a dynamic one, a more efficient driving force than any previous German contacts had been. Scheidt had for instance set up a meeting between Quisling and Rosenberg: this time Rosenberg had been fully briefed in advance and gave Quisling a full hour to expound his ideas on a Germanic union against the dangers from both east and west. The Rosenberg connection also paved the way to the permanent under-secretary Paul Körner in the Four-Year-Plan Ministry of Hermann Göring, where Hagelin supported Quisling's request for a 6.5 million mark subsidy for setting up a pro-German daily newspaper in Norway, complete with Sunday edition.

Dr Aall also had interesting contacts to offer. In the Foreign Ministry he introduced Quisling to two SS men who worked in a staff office directly responsible to Foreign Minister Ribbentrop himself. From there they left for a travel agency in Kurfürstendamm, where Aall introduced Quisling to Herr La Roche, a businessman with an ideological bent, who together with his colleague Prince von Hohenstein had decided to open an office in Scandinavia to promote a particular form of social philosophy, 'Social Individualism', which in many points resembled National Socialism. Now they asked Dr Aall and his friend for help, and Quisling agreed to act as an adviser for the project for a small fee. What neither Aall nor Quisling could have known was that the men's names were de la Porte and von Hippel respectively, and that they were involved in a large-scale espionage operation of Scandinavian infiltration. It is not known whether or not Quisling suspected anything; with his military background he should certainly have been on his guard.[66]

From Berlin Quisling went to Kolding to speak at the Clausen rally, and from there to Lübeck to attend the Nordische Gesellschaft meeting. Once more he met with Rosenberg, and on one occasion during the three days they spent together informed the Reichsleiter of the coming constitutional crisis in Norway and the prospects for the NS in this connection. Rosenberg looked quite worried, Scheidt noted.[67] He must have decided to monitor the situation in Norway: on the day of Quisling's return to Oslo, Scheidt arrived from Rosenberg's office in order to gauge the enthusiasm for National Socialism by means of a series of interviews and visits to various prominent

---

[66] Hartmann, *Fører uten folk*, pp. 25ff; Høidal, *Quisling*, pp. 255ff. Quisling, Almanach 1939, RA.

[67] Scheidt to Admiral Boehm, in a series of letters January–April 1955, BA-MA Freiburg N 172/14.

'national' Norwegians. He met Quisling in mid-July, and expressed his optimism with regard to possible support from Göring. Consequently, at the party conference on 11 August 1939 Quisling explained to his supporters that a daily party newspaper was once again a possibility, perhaps even to supplement the weekly paper rather than replace it. The visit to Berlin indeed seemed to have paid off nicely.[68]

The conference was to be one of the last occasions on which he addressed his supporters in peacetime. On the brink of war, his words rang out more alarmingly than usual: a terrible calamity awaited Europe, but at the same time things looked bright for the NS: 'After years of tireless struggle, with high points and low, we are now, at our seventh party conference, facing the possibility of events that could be decisive for this country too.' The task since 1936 had been to consolidate and to keep the party alive so that the NS could 'continue to be the kernel around which the national rising can crystallise when the time is right ... *This time seems to be upon us.*' The British and the Russians were busy negotiating in Moscow. Were the alliance between the western powers and the Kremlin to be made, the war which threatened would be inevitable, and 'we will be forced to prepare ourselves for the fact that Norway and the North will become a theatre of war'. If in this case neutrality had to be abandoned, Norway would have 'to go with Germany'. [69]

On 23 August, the Non-Aggression Pact between Hitler and Stalin was signed. Ever since 1935 Quisling had been warning of a *rapprochement* between Moscow and the West. The fact that, in order to relieve Soviet pressure in a situation where the conflict between the western powers over Poland was intensifying, Hitler managed to get Stalin to negotiate at the last minute could mean only the postponement of the inevitable. The antithesis between communism and National Socialism would sooner or later lead to a confrontation, and Germany would have to go east to liberate the national republics which the Bolsheviks had annexed, such as the Ukraine and Byelorussia. He collected newspaper cuttings from the international press on the Hitler–Stalin pact in a file, and wrote on the outside, as if it were a secret warning to Hitler: 'Nobody takes the Devil into his service without himself becoming the Devil's own hireling.'[70] But this did not mean that he was

---

[68] Scheidt's Aktennotiz für Stabsleiter Schickedanz 20 January 1939, Bundesarchiv Abt. Potsdam 62 Di/203 Alfred Rosenberg. NS Råds- og Riksmøteprotokoll 1934–45,* entry for 11 August 1939.

[69] Speech recorded in *FF* 19 August 1939, complete manuscript in INO. Italics added.

[70] File in UBO MS fol. 4096.

about to embark on a facile criticism of Germany. Germany needed to avert war on two fronts, which would in the short term mean the establishment of a 'Germano-Slavic world cultural fellowship'; in the long term, however, Germans and Slavs would unite under German leadership.

But at the same time the pact sent out new danger signals to the North. Russia had been given a free hand, both in the Baltic area and in Finland; in fact, the Soviet Union was coming closer to the North every day via the mounting conflict with Helsinki. Northern Norway would be at the mercy of the Soviet Union, while the other great powers would step up the pressure on southern Norway. For Norway there was, therefore, even greater reason to try to secure peace by turning to Berlin.

The Norwegian government, however, turned to the West. For the Foreign Minister Halvdan Koht in the Labour cabinet, as well as for Mowinckel and Hambro in the Storting, the obvious course for Norway to adopt was the same as in the previous war: to become 'the neutral ally' of Britain. Although this implied playing a double game in international politics, with all the risks involved, it was the only game that responsible Norwegian authorities could envisage in the crisis to come.[71]

CONTACTS WITH THE GERMAN LEGATION

On 3 September 1939 war broke out. In the course of three weeks the German army had overrun Poland. Surely the West could now see that Hitler's war machine was superior? NS members in Norway interpreted the events as the fulfilment of their Fører's prophecy of the long-awaited catastrophe, and the esteem in which he was held in the inner circle reached new heights. 'I have an instinctive feeling that your genius now alone can bring about the miracle the world is waiting for,' a party official from the Hedmark district wrote to tell him. A little later he received a similar message from a veterinary surgeon in Ryfylke: 'The great danger which Quisling had warned of is now upon us,' he said in Fritt Folk. At the same time, from his retirement in Trøndelag, Prytz urged him to endeavour to do what he could do better than most others: mediate between Chamberlain and Hitler.[72]

It may seem strange that well-educated people should have arrived at the

[71] N. Ørvik, Norsk sikkerhetspolitikk (1962) p. 93; Sikkerhetspolitikken II part II; O. K. Grimnes, Veien inn i krigen (1987) p. 23.
[72] Ørnulf Lundesgaard to Quisling 8 and 9 October 1939, RA NSRH 2; Steinar Klevar in FF 11 November 1939; Prytz to Quisling 5 October 1939, Prytz archives.*

view that the fifty-two-year-old reserve major, Vidkun Quisling, twice humiliated at the polls and now the leader of a peripheral party without any noticeable influence in any area of Norwegian politics, was the man the world was waiting for. But for a generation which had experienced the success of Fridtjof Nansen it did not seem at all unreasonable that it should be a Norwegian who settled the crisis between the great powers. In fact many Norwegians, Bishop Eivind Berggrav and the painter Henrik Sørensen among them, were actively involved in private peace initiatives. Then why not the NS Fører, with his wealth of experience in international aid organisations, diplomacy and the cabinet?

On 11 October Quisling telegraphed Chamberlain urging Great Britain to make peace with Germany. Prytz had suggested in his letters a currency and trade union between Britain, Germany and the other European states. Quisling took this idea further and argued for full European union. He told Chamberlain that the time was now ripe to create the European Commonwealth of Nations. The timing of his initiative may seem a little out of place, but Quisling sincerely believed that it was only now, on the brink of disaster, when war had been declared and destruction of untold proportions threatened, that the old dream of a federation which everybody desired but rendered impossible in normal times, had any chance of success. He signed his message 'Quisling CBE'.[73]

But one telegram was not enough to make peace. Prytz suggested that the two of them should offer their services actively as arbiters. Prytz on his side would use his influence in London via his friend Lord Swinton, one of Chamberlain's closest advisers, whom he knew from the Geneva Conference in 1918–19. Quisling, for his part, should go to the German legation to secure his entry to Berlin, Prytz urged.[74]

And this is exactly what they did. On 26 October Quisling visited the German chargé d'affaires, von Neuhaus. He passed on a copy of the telegram he had sent to Chamberlain and explained Prytz's planned visit to London. He stressed that Hambro, 'the half-Jew', was officially working on Norway's behalf against all true peace initiatives by gambling on Germany's purported internal collapse, for which reason something had to be done quickly.

Von Neuhaus listened to his guest. Two months earlier he had invited Quisling for dinner at the Hotel Bristol and actually offered him financial support for his newspaper. On that occasion Quisling had declined, but this

[73] Quisling to Chamberlain 11 October 1939; *Straffesak* p. 491.
[74] Prytz–Quisling correspondence October 1939, in UBO MS fol. 4096.

was probably a sham, for after the outbreak of war in September the Germans renewed the offer and thereafter made a regular monthly contribution of 1,000 kroner to *Fritt Folk*. The transfer from the Propagandaministerium was so thoroughly disguised that even Quisling never knew about it, even though it was quite a remarkable acknowledgement of his importance: no Danish or Swedish Nazi newspapers ever received such support.[75]

After his meeting with von Neuhaus in late October 1939, Quisling started to draw up plans for Germany's admission to the peace process, while Prytz began to prepare the first draft for the peace talks, which consisted of a recommendation for a cease-fire between Britain, France and Germany. This was to be followed up by peace negotiations in Oslo, once Germany had declared herself willing to renounce all colonial claims in order to secure her participation in a customs and currency union with the British. The idea was that this co-operation would eventually lead to a full economic union which all European countries would be invited to join. Prytz also suggested a renewal of the British–German naval discussions, and an agreement that Poland's status and borders would be decided by a referendum in the German-occupied areas. Quisling produced a comprehensive outline for the discussions, complete with a basis for negotiations among the three powers. The outline was reminiscent of his old dreams for the World Universist League: each state should negotiate admission to an 'international corporate organisation' to form a new league of nations with a view to establishing 'a universal peace league', after having secured peace through a 'Greater Nordic Peace Union'.

Together with these far-reaching aims came Prytz's list of proposals for reconciliation between the great powers: the abrogation of the Treaty of Versailles, the recognition of Poland and Czechoslovakia in their current German forms, together with the establishment of a German sphere of influence in eastern Europe in exchange for the recognition of Franco-British interests in the Mediterranean and the East. Prytz arrived in Oslo in order to hand over the final version of the proposal to Quisling personally.

The ambitions behind these schemes were truly megalomaniac. Quisling envisaged that the Greater Nordic Peace Union (Stornordiske Fredssamband) would consist of seven groups, ranging from the Scandinavian–Nordic to the 'Russian–Norman' group, with the German, the British, the

[75] Von Neuhaus to AA 26 October 1939 and AA to Ges. Oslo 19 December 1939, PAAA Ges. Oslo 23/193. See also Henning Poulsen, '*Fædrelandet*. Tysk understøttelse af danske dagblade 1939–45', *Historie* 7, Århus 1967, pp. 232–72; Åke Thulstrup, *Med lock och pock* (1962) pp. 182ff.

Dutch, the Franco-Norman and American groups in between. As groups eight, nine and ten he had Latin America, the Mediterranean and the Far East in mind. The problem was how 'to create the possibility for the expression of the world will, the people's will, world unity' at the same time as preserving a racial hierarchy. The solution seemed to be that the civilising influence of the North would prevail everywhere: 'Our Nordic (Aryan) language has conquered the world.' The Jews, however, were resistant to northern civilisation. Universism therefore had to be modified by certain racial limitations: world unity could only be brought together under the ægis of the Nordic people, by their taking up the struggle against the clandestine Jewish International.[76]

However, there was no reply from the German legation. And on 10 November Quisling left for Denmark to celebrate Clausen's birthday and to give a speech in Copenhagen. At this time the relevance of the peace plan had faded, as Soviet pressure on Finland was being stepped up. When at last he received a reply from the legation, it contained no reference to any negotiations in Berlin, but just passed on an invitation to the opening of the German book fair on 28 November and to a cultural evening the following day. An anticlimax, certainly, but still something to attend.[77]

In this way he came to meet the new German envoy to Norway, Curt Bräuer. He was a short, dark, lively man with whom Quisling exchanged a few words on the delicate subject of the Hitler–Stalin pact. Quisling stressed that he did not think the pact was in Germany's best interest, not even from a military point of view, considering how far behind Germany Russia was. Bräuer showed little interest in his views.[78] However, at the book fair he made another acquaintance, a reader in Nordic history at Greifswald University, Dr Ulrich Noack, who told him that he was there to help with the organisation of the fair, but who was also interested in the Norwegian estimation of the international situation. Noack made it clear that he was very well connected back in Germany; this pleasant if somewhat pushy academic was clearly some kind of information or intelligence officer, connected to the Foreign Ministry in Berlin. This gave Quisling the chance

---

[76] Prytz's draft 26 October 1939 and Quisling's 'Avtale om en våbenstillstand' 1 November 1939, with the heading 'Konferance nr 1 Torsdag 26. Oct kl 11 fm' RA PAQ; draft of 4 November 1939 in *Straffesak* pp. 492–7; Quisling draft telegram to Prytz 23 October 1939, UBO MS fol. 4096. The original of 'Utkast til avtale om våbenstillstand' has disappeared from RA PAQ. The most authentic version is that in *Straffesak*.

[77] PAAA Ges. Oslo 23/125; Quisling, Almanach 1939.

[78] Bräuer to AA 17 December 1939 *ADAP* D XI no. 466 pp. 429f.

to talk to a German without having to beg for an audience, and moreover one who would report what he heard without having to go through the usual diplomatic channels; this was precisely what he needed. He invited Noack to his home early in December and elaborated his peace plan to him. On his world map he pointed out Germany's 'natural continental sphere of influence' and sketched out the radius of the union of states – the European Commonwealth – which under German leadership would be able to replace the moribund League of Nations after peace had been declared.

But Noack showed little interest in peace plans. He had been involved with many idealistic Norwegian initiatives since the outbreak of war, including those of Bishop Berggrav, the group around the painter Henrik Sørensen, and the circle of the factory owner Johan H. Andresen. He had even had a hand in King Haakon's letter of appeal for peace to his uncle George VI, all while he was in touch with Foreign Minister Halvdan Koht, whom he had known since 1930. The only thing to come out of these discussions was that Noack was severely reprimanded by Bräuer for his *naïveté* and was asked to keep his distance from these kinds of peace initiatives in future.[79]

However, when Quisling got on to the subject of Russia, Noack began to pay more attention; here was a real expert speaking and, moreover, a trained military strategist. In the war between the Soviet Union and Finland which had just started, Quisling was of the astonishing opinion that the Finns would be able to hold out for quite some time, provided they received consignments of weapons from Sweden. He considered that the Red Army had been considerably weakened by Stalin's purges within the officer corps, and thus the Soviet fighting machine should not be overestimated, especially not by the Germans. But now, of course, Germany had made common cause with Russia through the unfortunate Non-Aggression pact. Quisling agreed with all Noack's other Norwegian informants that the Soviet invasion of Finland constituted a serious political problem for Hitler too. Besides, Quisling saw the pact as an error in relation to what in the final analysis was Germany's real mission in Europe: to liberate Russia and the eastern region, to establish free nation states and to create a unified technical and economic

---

[79] The meeting is described by Quisling in *Straffesak* p. 344, and discussed in Skodvin, *Striden*, pp. 41f, based on a later account by Ulrich Noack, *Norwegen zwischen Friedensvermittlung und Fremdherrschaft* (1952), based in turn on Noack's diaries. A different version of the meeting was given by Noack to Victor Mogens during the war and is contained in Mogens, *Tyskerne*, pp. 59ff. See also Noack, *Ein Leben aus freier Mitte. Festschrift zum 60. Geburtstag* (1961) pp. xv ff.

area under German influence which would extend from western Europe to the Urals.

Noack was fascinated by these views and wanted to hear more, so they arranged another meeting. Quisling presented his views on Russia with the help of maps and pointers. He explained that the country had incomparable natural resources, but the government was suppressing both its people and the country's development potentials. Germany, however, was in a position to put a stop to all this: if Germany attacked Russia, her motorised units would in the course of only a few weeks be able to accomplish what Napoleon had needed months to do. The Leningrad–Moscow line could be reached in the course of a fairly short campaign. It was therefore important that Germany abandon her current policy on Russia and instead start planning her offensive against the East.

The gains would be tremendous. The unpopular Soviet government would fall, and the one-party dictatorship would come to an end. People everywhere would rise up and re-establish their nation states, not only the Ukrainians and the Byelorussians but also the Russians, the Turks, the Uzbeks and scores of others. With German capital and organisation the newly liberated nation states in the East would flourish. He told Noack that a small group of Norwegians, with some basic organisation and a modest capital from Norwegian shareholders, had been sufficient to manage the enormous forest area around the Dvina with a good profit.[80]

Noack found Quisling's proposals so fascinating that he considered they should be presented at the highest level in Berlin without delay – to Ribbentrop, if not to Hitler himself. Quisling mentioned that he was intending to make a trip to Berlin anyway. He had just received another invitation from Dr Aall, who was still in contact with Prince von Hohenstein and Herr La Roche, and who perhaps had more than ideological projects on their agenda.[81] Now Aall's invitation was not in itself enough to make him embark on a journey, but with Noack promising that he would help him to get both his peace plan and his Russia plan heard by the most important people at the Foreign Ministry, he decided to go. He telegraphed Aall in Berlin and asked him to notify Hagelin in Dresden of his arrival.

It took a few days to get the visa, but on Saturday evening 9 December 1939 Quisling took the night train south. He told neither Prytz nor the party

---

[80] Noack, report to Informationsstelle des Auswärtigen Amtes 8 December 1939 and 10 December 1939, PAAA Ges. Oslo 23/125; Skodvin, *Striden*, pp. 41f. The meetings with Noack took place on 4 and 8 December 1939.

[81] Høidal, *Quisling*, pp. 262f.

office of the real purpose of his visit. Even Maria had no clear idea of his whereabouts.[82]

When Noack informed Bräuer the following morning that the Norwegian major was on his way to Berlin, he was astonished at Bräuer's insistence that he abandon the whole idea. The notion of a Russian campaign went against German policy in every way; the Russian–German pact could not, at least for the moment, be abandoned. But Noack stood his ground; Quisling was, after all, already on his way, and he himself intended to follow him the next day. Bräuer therefore had little option but to telegraph Noack's superiors in the Information Division of the Ribbentrop Ministry and warn them about the two collaborators who were *en route* to Berlin with their 'fantastic' plans.

THE THIRD MAN

On 10 December Quisling was met at Stettiner station by Aall and Hagelin. These two cannot have had a very pleasant time waiting for the train as they detested each other deeply. Hagelin saw Aall as an otherworldly theoretician, while the mild-mannered Aall considered Hagelin impetuous and pompous with his incessant talking and irritating gesticulations. Aall wanted his guest, as on his previous visit in June, to stay with him. Hagelin, however, had made other arrangements. Quisling was to be put up at the NSDAP's foreign policy office. When Quisling got off the train, he was immediately swept along by the officious Hagelin, who told him that they were to visit Rosenberg together the following morning. Aall and his contacts would have to wait; Quisling and Hagelin thereafter disappeared to the study centre at Rosenberg's office in Berlin-Dahlem, where he was to stay.[83]

---

[82] On the preparation see Hayes, *The Career*, pp. 158f. The delay was unlikely to have been caused by the legation's stalling as Høidal and Hayes suggest; see Bräuer to Altenburg 11 December 1939, PAAA Ges. Oslo 23/1251. Quisling's peace memorandum 'On the Necessity for a Greater Germanic League' (Noack's translation) has gone missing. The following account assumes that it was this document which Quisling took with him to Hitler on 14 December, an assumption supported by Quisling during his trial. According to Mogens (*Tyskerne*), two memoranda were mentioned, one emphasising a British–German alliance and the other written to secure the Arctic interests of Norway as against Denmark.

[83] Bräuer to Altenburg, telegram and letter 11 December 1939, PAAA Ges. Oslo 23/1251. See also Berit Nøkleby, 'Fra november til april. Sendemann Bräuers personlige politikk', in Helge Paulsen (ed.), *1940 – fra nøytral til okkupert* (1969) pp. 54f. See also Skodvin, *Striden*, pp. 29f, Hayes, *The Career*, pp. 160f, Høidal, *Quisling*, pp. 262ff, and statements from Aall's family* besides Aall's note of 10 May 1951, UBO MS fol. 3920 X, 7.

Dr Aall was not the only one Hagelin treated in this way. When Noack arrived a few days later and telephoned Quisling, then at Rosenberg's office, he received a cool reception. Quisling, who had been so enthusiastic in Oslo, was no longer interested in putting forward his plans to the Foreign Ministry as Hagelin had told him that breaking the pact with Russia was out of the question. Thus Noack had exceeded his brief with both Bräuer and his protégé. He had to inform his superiors of Quisling's change of heart, and they in turn wrote to Bräuer in Oslo telling him that the danger had been averted: Quisling had given up hope of seeing Ribbentrop and Hitler. This was only partly true:[84] the very day that the reassuring letter to Bräuer left Berlin, Quisling, by an extraordinary turn of events, did in fact manage to get an audience with Hitler and present his plans to him.

What happened was really the result of a series of coincidences. Quisling had arrived in Berlin at a time when Hitler happened to be there – he had spent at least a third of the autumn out of Berlin. When Quisling and Hagelin met Rosenberg on 11 December, Rosenberg suggested that they also went to see Grand Admiral Raeder, who was free later the same day. Raeder met Hitler the next day and talked to him about the Norwegian former Defence Minister in favourable terms, as did Rosenberg the same evening. On 13 December there was another meeting between Rosenberg and Hitler, and by 14 December Quisling's audience had been scheduled for the afternoon of 18 December. During the four days leading up to the meeting, a plan which would normally have required months of preparation had been worked out – if in fact such a meeting could ever have taken place under 'normal' circumstances.[85]

---

[84] Altenburg to Bräuer 14 December 1939, PAAA Ges. Oslo 23/125. Secretary of State von Weizsäcker advised against Quisling meeting Ribbentrop: Ernst von Weizsäcker, *Die Weizsäcker-Papiere 1933–50* (1974); Noack, *Norwegen*; Hagelin, Memo, APA BA NS 43; and also Mogens, *Tyskerne*, pp. 60f.

[85] The chronology of events leading up to Quisling's meeting with Hitler is given in detail in Loock, *Quisling*. The chronology is as follows:

10 December 1939: Quisling arrives in Berlin.

11 December: In the morning Quisling and Hagelin visit Rosenberg. This is followed by a visit to Raeder at noon at the Naval Command, also attended by his adjutant Schulte-Mönting (recorded in Naval Command protocol BA-MA RM 6). Rosenberg visits Hitler and tells him he should receive Quisling.

12 December: Raeder commends Quisling to Hitler; Hitler discusses Quisling again with Rosenberg.

13 December: Rosenberg writes to Raeder with extensive information on Quisling following another meeting with Quisling, Hagelin and Scheidt.

14 December: Raeder reads Rosenberg's memo in the morning, then goes to Rosenberg

It was Hagelin who had arranged everything, at least so it seemed to Quisling. In the course of the autumn, he had pulled enough strings to get as far as the Grand Admiral in the German Navy's High Command.[86] The fact that the old route through Rosenberg was now bolstered with an important contact in the navy proved decisive for the Quisling–Hagelin effort to gain support for the NS in Berlin. But at the same time it involved a radical revision of the arrangements for Quisling's visit. He was firmly advised (perhaps on arrival, but certainly during his visit to Rosenberg the following day) that both his peace plan and Noack's idea of arguing for a German offensive in the East would have to be set aside. The important opportunity now was to get the German Navy interested in the fate of the NS in Norway. The navy had for many years wanted to establish German bases along the Norwegian coast so as to open Atlantic waters fully to German sea power. The political prospect for such a strategic vision was, however, nil, unless some sort of political support from within Norway could be obtained. Quisling offered a way out of this dilemma, and Hagelin played shrewdly on the possibilities of paving the way to Hitler through the – normally unlikely – combination of Rosenberg and Raeder.

The British threat was their trump card, both with Raeder and the navy and later with Hitler himself. Britain's threat to use Norway as a transit country for her planned military assistance to the Finns was now being reported in the international press. Quisling was able to reinforce this message with a great deal of secret information – namely that a secret meeting between the Norwegians and the British was about to take place, thus compromising Norwegian neutrality; and further, that 'the Jew' Hambro's international network included close links with Britain's War

to discuss the possibility of Quisling meeting Hitler once more. They agree that Raeder should accompany Quisling to meet the Führer as Rosenberg had to rest his injured foot. At 3 p.m. Quisling and his companion are received by Hitler at the Chancellery. Raeder is not present.

16 December: Quisling and Hagelin meet Ambassador Hewel, Admiral von Puttkamer and General Tippelskirch.

18 December: Quisling and Hagelin meet Hewel again, and Hitler's adjutant Schmundt; a second meeting with Hitler at the Chancellery.

20 December: Final meeting and summation with Rosenberg.

21 December: Quisling leaves Berlin. Arrives in Oslo the following day.

[86] There is no clear account of how Hagelin managed to get to Raeder; that he did so via Raeder's Chief of Staff Schulte-Mönting is one possibility. The diary of the naval High Command makes no mention of a visit from Hagelin at this time, and thus contact must have been made on an informal basis.

Minister, and that British propaganda had a very strong hold on Norwegian opinion. Quisling and the NS could offer loyal collaborators in the Defence and Communications Departments, who would be able to counteract British interests. Moreover, Quisling claimed a legal base for seeking political power after the Storting opened on 10 January, inasmuch as the *coup d'état* of the previous year would then plunge the Norwegian state into a major crisis of legitimacy. The NS, which had very clear constitutional reform in its manifesto, might get a chance to take power and use it to prevent British violations of neutrality. Furthermore, the NS would have the opportunity to spread German influence through its newspaper, on condition that *Fritt Folk* got the subsidies it needed to become a truly effective daily paper.

This was the scenario that Hagelin and Quisling described in Berlin in December 1939. It was highly conspiratorial and would mean abandoning Norway to Germany if neutrality were no longer viable. Quisling, who preferred neutrality but did not think it possible, would act in Germany's interest so as to prevent Britain from establishing herself in the country. His aim was, as he put it, 'to save Norway from entering the war with Germany on the British side' and thus 'prevent Norway from falling into British hands'.[87]

The plan was surprisingly well received by the Germans. Raeder had for years been trying in vain to persuade Hitler on the question of naval bases in Norway, and thus had his own motives for recommending that Quisling was granted an audience with Hitler. Rosenberg envisaged the incorporation of Norway into the Greater German Reich for the promotion of his racist 'Nordic' foreign policy, while Hitler was thinking in geopolitical terms. Although the Führer entered into these discussions with the explicit aim of maintaining Norwegian neutrality at all costs, he emerged with a very clear second option, namely, that if the occupation of Norway proved necessary in order to pre-empt a British occupation, it would give Germany further advantages in the war against both the East and the West and, moreover, would serve to defend central Germany – a radical rethinking of his strategy indeed.

We do not know how much of this Quisling himself understood at the time. From the outset he seems to have been completely unaware of the strategic naval deliberations. Although he had been writing and talking about foreign and security questions for years, he had never entertained the possibility of a German naval action in Norway. Nothing suggests that he

---

[87] Quisling to Hitler 19 June 1941 (marked 'not sent'), RA UKA.

was acquainted with the writings of Admiral Wegener and the discussions within the German Navy which had been going on since the First World War about the need for bases on the west coast of Scandinavia that would secure German access to the Atlantic. What he saw was that the war in Finland quite obviously increased the possibility of an Allied engagement in Norwegian waters, which in its turn was bound to intensify Germany's interest in the region. His nightmare scenario was that Norway would suffer the same fate as Poland with the three powers of Britain, the Soviet Union and Germany each attacking from a different side. In his view, the Norwegian government was pursuing a dangerous, pro-British policy. A new government would be able to change that and turn to Germany if neutrality were violated. A unilateral German occupation of the country was scarcely an option that he considered.[88]

Hagelin, on the other hand, had in mind German military action in Norway. Ever since the outbreak of war in September he had been airing this possibility with his German contacts. He quickly manipulated people and used arguments which must have been difficult for Quisling, with his limited knowledge of German, to follow. Many of Hagelin's arguments certainly went over his head, even though he was loath to admit it. At any rate he allowed Hagelin to do all the talking and remained for the most part silent.

This proved disastrous, for Hagelin was inclined to exaggerate and dramatise almost everything Quisling told him. Whenever Quisling used the expression 'the Jew' or rather 'the half-Jew Hambro', Hagelin would translate it as 'the Jew and Freemason Hambro and his circle'. When Quisling mentioned that he had a great many reliable people in the armed forces, Hagelin turned this into 'everywhere in the post and telegraph services and the railways', which was absolutely untrue. When Quisling declared the number of his followers to be a maximum of 100,000 or so, Hagelin quickly doubled the figure – '200,000 at least'. Norway's pro-western attitude, or the Labour movement's sympathy for the Soviet Union, were painted in the most dramatic colours, which had only a tenuous relationship with reality. Quisling's message, while unrealistic, became distorted into grotesque proportions via Hagelin's exaggerations.[89] On one point at least this proved decisive: the discussion about the *coup d'état*.

A very hazy picture emerges from the documents concerning the

[88] Quisling in *FF* 23 September 1939, 'Kampen for nøitraliteten'. For Raeder's view, see his address to Hitler 12 January 1939, made in the presence of Keitel, Jodl and von Puttkamer, printed in *Straffesak* p. 38.

[89] Examples from Loock, *Quisling*, pp. 167f.

December meetings of just how wide-reaching this 'action' in Norway was to be in political terms, and when it was expected to take place. Hagelin spoke of a full, albeit vague, takeover of power (*Machtübernahme*) on the part of the NS: when the pro-Russian Labour government 'fell', all Quisling would have to do would be to 'move in'. Even the naval leader's notes talk unambiguously of a coup. Rosenberg, obviously influenced by his discussions with Hagelin, wrote in his diary that the next time they met 'Norway's Minister President would be called Quisling'. The first mention Scheidt made in his memoirs of a coup was in the summer of 1939. Hitler, on the other hand seems to have been more hesitant, if not completely opposed to the idea. Obviously so little was said that all concerned were able to draw their own conclusions. 'Action' and 'help' were often mentioned, but with no generally understood meaning. Quisling's role in these discussions must have been more than ambiguous.[90]

His basic point concerned the 'illegal' Storting from 10 January and the subsequent constitutional crisis. The initiative lay with the King – Quisling had the idea that the King would have a special and clearly autonomous role in such a situation. And the King would surely think of the NS, the party that had warned most emphatically about the crisis. How it was all to be resolved was, however, difficult to say. Perhaps the Marxist government would collapse when the Russians invaded Finnmark. The only thing certain about Quisling's ideas at this point is that the notion that he should take over, or at least be called in as cabinet minister, had occurred to him independently of any German invasion. He saw it as his moral right, which arose from a crisis which must certainly result in the King's using his constitutional prerogative to summon an expert cabinet to the table. And whether as prime minister, or in any other capacity the government's key man, he would have to pursue the foreign policy he considered best. In his diary earlier in the year he had made a note of whom he would want to serve alongside him in the government: the best men of the NS. The government list thus resembled the ones he had drafted before the elections of 1933 and 1936. It was his duty to compile it, as it was written into the party statutes that he, as leader, was 'responsible for choosing the party's parliamentary candidates and government ministers'. Now in 1939 he took steps to ensure that some of the candidates at least were ready. He asked Ragnvald Hvoslef if he would be willing to participate in his national government if he was

[90] *Straffesak* pp. 34, 40, 41, 59, 60, 73. The plans Quisling here suggested he made with Hitler and Raeder for a coup were all made on the understanding of a prior British invasion.

needed. Hvoslef at least did not decline. Quite probably Quisling said the same thing to other candidates.[91]

The idea of an NS cabinet then was not a direct outcome of the Berlin talks. Quisling thought in a complex way, and his German was poor. Thus it is not so surprising that his German contacts in Berlin were under the impression that he was planning a coup which would rely on a German invasion. The vague, complicated but also dangerous aspects of the Berlin talks all came to light when Quisling and his associates were summoned to Hitler's study on 14 December 1939.

WITH HITLER

It was just before 3 o'clock in the afternoon when Quisling, Hagelin and Scheidt arrived at the new Chancellery in Berlin. Hagelin was acting as interpreter, and Scheidt was representing Rosenberg, who had been taken ill. The most important person there was Quisling, whom Hitler, on Raeder's recommendation, had asked to see in person, 'to form my own impression' – a rare and much coveted honour.[92]

The surroundings served to reinforce the sense of occasion. The monumental building on the former Voss Strasse in the centre of Berlin, with its resplendent colonnades and galleries, had been specially designed to impress foreign visitors. Quisling and his two companions were led over the polished marble floors by Hitler's adjutant Brückner, first from the reception room to the mosaic-covered central hall and from there to the domed entrance to the 150-metre-long main gallery, where Hitler's study, a circular room decorated with National Socialist reliefs and sculptures, lay immediately on the left.

---

[91] Quisling to Prytz 3 August 1939, Prytz archives;* see also C. J. Hambro, *De første måneder* (1945). Cabinet list drafted in Quisling, Almanach 1939.

[92] Hitler to Raeder 12 December 1939, *Straffesak* pp. 53f. The dating of the two Hitler–Quisling meetings was long disputed, but finally established in Carl-Axel Gemzell, *Raeder, Hitler und Skandinavien* (1965) and Loock, *Quisling*, p. 223 n. 78. Main sources: Rosenberg's diary, printed in *Straffesak* p. 36 and Hans-Günther Seraphim (ed.), *Das politische Tagebuch Alfred Rosenbergs* (1956) p. 113; Hermann Boehm, *Norwegen zwischen England und Deutschland* (1956) pp. 49f, and François Kersaudy, *Kappløpet om Norge. Det allierte felttog i 1940* (1990) pp. 40f; Scheidt's memorandum 26 May 1940, in *Straffesak* p. 49; Quisling's written account of 21 June 1945 in *Straffesak* pp. 573f. Quisling's spoken account at the High Court 7 September 1945 contains several discrepancies probably due to exhaustion: among other things he claimed that it was Raeder who introduced him to Hitler, which is impossible as the admiral was not even present: *Straffesak* pp. 346f. A recent survey in H.-M. Ottmer, *'Weserübung'* (1994) pp. 24–6.

Hitler was waiting there with a silent man from the Foreign Ministry. The discussion between the five men was never officially recorded. There are three versions of what was said: the account that Quisling gave to Rosenberg that same evening (and which the Reichsleiter recorded in his diary a few days later); a fuller account from Scheidt, written up many years later with the help of records from 1940–1; and finally Quisling's concise and somewhat selective account in 1945. From these various accounts it is possible to make an approximate reconstruction of the two-hour meeting. Hitler opened with a twenty-minute monologue on Norway's role in the war. He took the stand that was customary at that time; that the North would best serve itself and Germany by remaining strictly neutral. However, if Britain threatened to establish bases along the coast, Germany would be forced to take action. Hitler was categorical: Norway must not on any account become a support to Britain. Germany would install six, ten, twelve or however many divisions were necessary to prevent this from happening.

Quisling presented his peace plan in writing, which stressed the necessity for a Greater Germanic Union. It is said that Hitler read the memorandum carefully and gave his guest to understand that he too had great respect for Britain, claiming to 'have always been an Anglophile'. But unfortunately Germany had been forced to go to war with Britain; this was a theme the Führer expanded on considerably. Quisling then took the floor to present his and the NS's policy orally. This was a long and detailed process according to Scheidt, who recalls that Hitler nevertheless followed Quisling with keen interest, but also with growing amusement as his Norwegian guest explained the 'illegal situation' in which the Norwegian state would find itself after 10 January. 'Believe me, Herr Major, we National Socialists are what you might call experts at revolution,' Hitler assured him, urging him to dismiss any thought of revolution on these terms. The meeting was concluded in such a positive atmosphere that there was talk of a second one.

And indeed, four days later Hitler resumed the discussion with Quisling, who in the meantime had been having meetings with representatives of General Jodl, the Chief of the General Staff in the High Command. Scheidt had been present when Quisling was shown staff documents concerning Norway and asked for his assessment. Perhaps this was a test to see whether Rosenberg's and Raeder's assurances to Hitler were correct, that the former Defence Minister really was willing to support a possible action against Norway. Quisling is reported to have shaken his head over the staff map: hopelessly dated and inadequate, he could not believe that this was all the

German High Command had at its disposal. Scheidt noted that Quisling was careful, however, not to go into detail.

At the second meeting with Hitler on 18 December the Führer summarised the position to date: Norway should in principle remain neutral. Failing that, a German action to pre-empt a British strike could be carried out, whether by invasion or at Norway's own invitation. Close surveillance would have to be kept on both Norwegian policy and the movements of the British. Quisling would receive financial support for 'intensive but legal' bolstering of the NS.[93] He said he would be prepared, after a change in government when he would himself seize power, to call on Germany to assist Norway against Britain. Hitler warned that in that case Britain would be sure to strike, thereby letting it be understood he would go ahead irrespective of Quisling's political influence. The Führer then reiterated (after being expressly asked to do so by Quisling) his promise of help for the NS; presumably he meant financial help.

The peace initiative was not discussed. But Quisling left behind a second memorandum for Hitler, this time on the old Norwegian possessions of Iceland, the Faeroe Islands and Greenland, for which he had drafted prolix plans in case Germany should occupy these islands for strategic reasons. It urged co-operation with a national government in Norway, which for its part would try to make a settlement with a National Socialist-governed Denmark over the two countries' conflicts in these areas. This document is perhaps most interesting as evidence of Quisling's need to distinguish between his own 'national' and his colleague Clausen's 'National Socialistic' movements. He also told Hitler explicitly that he did not consider himself to be a National Socialist.[94]

After the meeting Hitler asked Scheidt to stay behind for further discussion. Rosenberg's protégé was then given secret orders to travel to Norway as Hitler's personal representative to observe political developments and to gather information on British activity. He was instructed to keep his distance from Quisling and the NS, and to find a discreet method of transferring the subsidies. Quisling was to be kept out of things at all costs.

What sort of impression did Quisling make on Hitler? Clearly not a bad one. In general, Hitler did not like the National Socialist leaders from other countries, like Anton Adriaan Mussert from Holland and Oswald Mosley

---

[93] According to Scheidt, *Straffesak* p. 49. Other sources (Rosenberg's diary, Scheidt's and Hagelin's later letters and memorandum of January 1940) suggest that the coup rather than building up the NS was the main focus of discussion.

[94] Quisling, *Denkschrift* 18 December 1939, photocopy Alfa Bibliotek, Oslo.*

from Britain. They were in his view unoriginal men who simply parroted the NSDAP. On Quisling he never passed any direct judgement, positive or negative. Presumably he considered him to be less unattractive than his European counterparts. Honest but naive – this assessment seems to tally with the accounts, and was, moreover, the impression most sympathetic people formed of Quisling.

The Norwegian Fører's idea of a Greater Germanic Union was not perhaps urgent, but it did correspond with the Führer's own thinking, and it is possible that Hitler allowed himself to be flattered by this. In any case, he found Quisling worth listening to. Raeder had obviously been right in his judgement that Quisling 'gave the impression of being trustworthy'. The information that Quisling had given about the British menace and the pro-British climate in Norway reinforced the Admiral's fear that Norway would fall into Britain's hands, and thus from a naval point of view was a useful piece of information.

For Hitler as Commander-in-Chief, the most important consideration was clearly that of the progress of the war in general. The planned autumn invasion of France had been postponed continually, week after week, because of the particularly bad weather that season. The Luftwaffe needed at least five days of clear weather to carry out its part of the enormous operation, but cloud masses were covering Europe. With each delay, the possibility that the war would drag on increased, in which case the North would become increasingly important as a base for the type of warfare which would then be more likely: an economic war with a total blockade of Britain.

The visit from Norway was thus only one of many influences in the extremely complex network of factors determining Hitler's thinking during those days. But it was an influence which Germany's Commander-in-Chief devoted many hours and much attention to. Indeed, compared with his otherwise hasty and impromptu methods of conducting the war, it must be said that the Norwegian situation at this time was given quite thorough consideration.

On 14 December, immediately after his first conversation with Quisling, Hitler gave the order to make preliminary preparations for a possible invasion of Norway. The order is recorded in General Jodl's diary: 'At 17.15 the Führer ordered us to find out with as limited a number of staff as possible, how we can occupy Norway' – limited, that is, to maintain maximum security.[95]

---

[95] Quisling was with Hitler at 3 o'clock in the afternoon. At 5.15 Jodl received the order (Jodl's diary 14 December 1939, printed in Walter Hubatsch, *Weserübung* 1960). Both

For Quisling the ten days in Berlin were the high point of his political career to date. 'I realise that there is such a thing as Fate,' he said happily to Scheidt when they were back in Dahlem after their second meeting with Hitler. 'For a long time I have been presenting my ideas to various people but without any result. And now suddenly, at the decisive moment, we are getting the help we need.' In his diary he marked down 18 December as a great day, with three thick crosses and the word 'Dec[ision]'.[96]

And the decision immediately took effect in Germany, where different forces were involved in often intense and mutually antagonistic action. The General Staff's High Command began work on the plan, which soon took shape as a combined operation of the navy, army and airforce. On 18 December Jodl had the first draft ready. The navy was to conduct its own contribution in parallel. Grand Admiral Raeder was, at least as long as Britain seemed to be keeping quiet, inclined to rely on Norwegian neutrality in principle.[97] Rosenberg's office, on the other hand, showed no restraint at all. After the meeting with Hitler on 18 December, grandiose plans for a coup in Norway were set in motion. But Rosenberg's associates were neither diplomats nor legal experts – rather, political conspirators and propagandists with little understanding of formalities. It is therefore not surprising that Hagelin was popular in that circle. His bold talk of action, initiative and ways of transferring money to the NS soon got back to Rosenberg and his Chief of Staff, who produced many ill-considered documents on 'the action in Norway' in the months that followed.

Above all, the German foreign service was put to the test as a result of Quisling's visit. The need for information about what was really going on in Berlin became acute. As early as 23 December, Bräuer realised that something dramatic had taken place, as Scheidt turned up at the legation and handed a letter to him, saying: '*Amtsleiter* Scheidt is on a special mission for the Führer in Norway to negotiate with non-Norwegians. The mission and the nature of these negotiations are strictly confidential. Scheidt is under

---

Quisling and Rosenberg were unaware of the order (there is no mention of it in Rosenberg's diary). Moreover, there is no record of it in the war diaries of the naval High Command, which suggests that only a limited circle within the OKW were informed, as in other naval documents the connection between Quisling's visit and Hitler's order is clearly attested. See the naval High Command's war diaries 13 January 1940, 22 April 1940 (*Nachtrag zum KTB*), Raeder to Assmann 10 January 1944, *Straffesak* p. 51.

[96] Rosenberg's diary 19 December 1939; Quisling, Almanach 1939, RA.
[97] Kersaudy, *Norway 1940*, pp. 41f; Branner, *9 april 1940* (1987) ch. 2.2; Loock, *Quisling*, pp. 230f.

orders not to give information to anybody.' The letter was signed by Dr Lammers, the head of Hitler's Chancellery.[98]

Immediately afterwards, telegrams from Bräuer's superiors in Berlin came pouring in, asking if he would kindly pass on all his information on Quisling and Hagelin and whether he could find out from Scheidt what exactly Hitler and Quisling had discussed in Berlin. The latter request came directly from Ribbentrop. The Foreign Minister of the Reich was anxious to find out more of what had taken place between Hitler and Quisling. There was not much to report, however. Nobody in the legation had ever heard of Hagelin. He had been living in Germany since the First World War and was completely unknown in Norway. Quisling, on the other hand, was well known, but certainly of no significance at all in Norwegian politics. In his correspondence with Berlin, Bräuer adopted a polite but firm tone. Overall he gave the impression that the Norwegian National Socialists were people whom the legation did well to avoid.

However, the legation did not avoid them completely, as von Neumann saw to it that the *Fritt Folk* received its monthly subsidy from Germany, and that the legation carried a lot of the expenses of another small, sectarian newspaper the *Norsk Folkeblad*, a pro-German alternative to *Fritt Folk* and the Quisling movement. Thus Bräuer's office had indeed been involved for a long time both with the NS and with people further to the right.

Strange things suddenly began to happen to Bräuer during the winter of 1940. He received orders from Berlin that *Ragnarok* and those associated with its editor Hans S. Jacobsen should be monitored very closely, as this NS breakaway group was said to be taking an anti-German turn. Disturbing reports that the head of the Fatherland League, the editor Victor Mogens, was developing Anglophile tendencies were also reaching Berlin from Norway. Bräuer denied such rumours vehemently, insisting that both Jacobsen's and Mogens's loyalty to Germany was unquestionable, and that the legation had for many years been cultivating them in preference to Quisling and the NS. Perhaps he understood that Hitler's special envoy Scheidt was in the process of discrediting the legation's informers by spreading rumours in the relevant circles.

After a fairly intense correspondence with Berlin in January and February 1940 things quietened down at the legation, however, and nothing more was heard either directly or indirectly about Quisling.

---

[98] Lammers to Ges. Oslo 21 December 1939, BA NS 43. On Bräuer and Scheidt, see Nøkleby in Paulsen, *1940*, p. 57; Skodvin, *Striden*, pp. 40–51.

5

A time of crisis

If enough influential Norwegians had joined the NS in time, Norway's neutrality, defence and supplies would all be guaranteed today, and the Norwegian people would be able to face the future with confidence. But when the people stood at the crossroads, they chose Barabbas. *Quisling in* Fritt Folk, *9 March 1940*

Soon after new year 1940 Quisling started to experience strange pains in the chest and head. After a while, the pain became so intense that he was unable to go to his office. A fortnight later he developed a fever and was confined to bed. His doctor diagnosed serious pneumonia and recommended hospitalisation, but Quisling refused. For weeks his temperature had stabilised at around 40°C, with frequent crises in between. Maria nursed him.

After seventeen years of marriage they were closer than in their Moscow years. Socially they lived quietly, for although Maria spoke Norwegian quite well, she was and would always remain an immigrant. Vidkun's ageing mother was still alive and lived nearby, as did his brother Jørgen. But after the death of his wife, Jørgen could not really offer very much support, not even when his brother was sick.

After a series of re-examinations the doctor declared that his initial diagnosis had been wrong, and changed it to nephritis in both kidneys. But the diagnosis was unusually tentative, and in retrospect one can only wonder whether his illness was not psychosomatic in origin. After the Berlin discussions Quisling knew that something important was about to happen, but was in no position to know what. According to Hitler's orders he was kept in the absolute dark (uncompromised, as Scheidt understood the Führer's words) in order that the situation discussed in December might develop. His party heard practically nothing from him during his illness, and after mid-January he fell silent in even his most important channel of communication with his associates, the weekly editorial in *Fritt Folk*.

There was only one area in which Quisling seems to have exercised any influence over the party that winter, and that was the issue of Finland. Ever since the Soviet invasion on 30 November 1939 he had been remarkably cool towards young party members who wanted to volunteer against the

Bolshevik attack. Norwegian sympathy for its neighbour ran deep, and young NS men were among the first to consider leaving to join the Finnish struggle. But their Fører told them that they were needed at home. The most loyal among them accepted this decision, but the less committed (among them the *Ragnarok* circle) greeted his orders with unrestrained contempt.[1]

Many people thought it was Hitler's Non-Aggression Pact with Stalin which prompted Quisling to keep his men at home. However, his stance on this issue should be seen in the context of his general opposition to voluntary service abroad, and his previous reluctance concerning NS men going to fight in Spain on Franco's side. The person who had the greatest difficulty in accepting his position on Finland was Prytz. The two men, otherwise so like-minded, were seriously divided over the issue. Prytz openly supported Norwegian mobilisation to defend Finland's eastern border as an entrenchment against the Bolshevik advance. Quisling warned against this in the strongest possible terms from his sickbed, arguing that a joint war with Sweden against the Soviets would amount to making an opening for Swedish hegemony in Scandinavia. On the subject of the planned Allied rescue mission to Finland, Quisling insisted that this would lead to Norway allowing herself to be dragged into the war on the British side. The two old friends, who just before Christmas had collaborated to produce a peace plan, were now unable to agree on the nature of the current threat to Norway.[2]

While they were drifting apart, Quisling's new collaborator Albert Hagelin returned from Dresden to settle permanently in Norway. He and his wife checked into the Hotel Continental in Oslo, from where he liked to conduct his business in between his frequent trips to Germany. Hagelin arrived in Oslo on the same day as Scheidt, 23 December 1939. The two kept in constant contact after their 'joint invasion of Norway' as Hagelin came to refer to their arrival. The partnership otherwise went according to plan, in that only Hagelin was supposed to have contact with Quisling.[3]

Scheidt and Hagelin sorted out the new, massive transfer of funds to *Fritt Folk*. Scheidt, in real gangster style, brought a suitcase containing fifty thousand-pound notes from the German Foreign Ministry, all counterfeits from the Reichsbank. Hagelin spread them around several Oslo banks so as not to arouse suspicion. That month the paper doubled in size and started

---

[1] *FF* 9 December 1939; H. N. Østbye's MS NS history in RA PA H. N. Østbye 4; Hirdspeilet 28 February 1943; H. F. Knudsen, *Jeg var Quislings sekretær* (1951) p. 112; see also Kjell Fjørtoft, *Mot stupet. Norge inn i krigen* (1989) pp. 91ff.

[2] Quisling to Prytz 11 January 1940, Prytz archives;* Maria Quisling, *Dagbok*, pp. 84f.

[3] Hagelin to Scheidt ('Jano') end of 1940, BA NS 43/56.

to appear in editions of 20,000–30,000 copies. It also got a permanent editor. Party headquarters moved into elegant new premises in Rådhusgaten 17, one of Oslo's smartest office buildings. The staff increased, both in Oslo and nationally.[4]

Between his fever attacks Quisling would occasionally go for short walks in the city, usually to the kiosk to buy foreign newspapers. Occasionally he bumped into people he knew. Some of them were alarmed by how ill he looked. Two of his school friends found him almost delirious when he was holding forth on the lurking catastrophe which was waiting to pounce on the somnolent Norway. 'I think that Vidkun has gone stark raving mad,' reported one of them to his family afterwards. A more distant acquaintance of Quisling's came across him in a *pâtisserie* one day in February. Quisling was sitting on his own, and started to expound his apocalyptic views of the future, but nobody was able to make any sense of what he was saying.[5]

He remained ill for another four weeks. It was not until about 13 March, the day Finland surrendered to Russia and the Winter War was over, that he felt fit enough to go to his office. But he was by no means well. His fever came and went for many weeks, and his associates noticed that he was frequently pale and would often break out into a cold sweat. Press photographs taken that April show him with a very drawn face and large protruding eyes.

TURNING POINT

He was still bedridden when the British attacked the German merchant ship *Altmark* in Norwegian waters on 16 February 1940. Having successfully liberated two hundred prisoners of war, HMS *Cossack* disappeared down the fjord while the Germans were left counting their dead and their injured on deck. The entire episode took place in full view of the Norwegian Navy.

The incident extended the naval battle of the great powers into Norwegian territory from both the west and the south, while the Soviets posed a threat through a Finland that was on the point of capitulation. The race for Norway had begun in earnest, and the country was indeed in danger of sharing the fate of Poland. It looked as though the west coast of Scandinavia was going to be the next theatre of war. British and French planning strategy

---

[4] Loock, *Quisling*, pp. 228f; Scheidt to Boehm 1955, BA-MA N 172/14. An exact sum has never been established, but it seems to have been around NOK 70,000. RA LD 846 Hagelin.

[5] Viggo Ullmann's account, 1985;* Leiv Kreyberg, *Efter ordre – eller uten* (1976) p. 49.

vacillated between simpler invasion projects and an all-out Allied assault on main Norwegian coastal towns, while Hitler for his part decided to step up the *Weserübung* plan into a full-scale operation, to include the occupation of Denmark. He summoned Lieutenant General von Falkenhorst to make the preparations.

The *Altmark* incident was also a turning point for Scheidt and Hagelin. Suddenly it became clear to them that the Norwegian government had been holding preliminary discussions with London, and had given its assurances that the navy would not under any circumstances attack British warships. True neutrality, of the kind Hitler wanted for Norway, was obviously not being adhered to by the Norwegians. Everything Quisling had claimed in Berlin was turning out to be true. Scheidt was standing outside the offices of the Oslo daily *Morgenbladet* on Saturday 17 February when the day's headlines were posted up, and witnessed how the public accepted Churchill's propaganda to the extent that they were 'actually celebrating the British action'.[6] Scheidt and Hagelin, and Quisling from his sickbed, might easily conclude that Hitler would now put his second option into action: a pre-emptive strike to ensure that the Allies could not take control of the country. It was just a question of time before German troops would arrive in Oslo. What role they themselves were to play under those circumstances seemed quite vague.

Even at the Reich Chancellery in Berlin there was uncertainty as to what Hitler was planning for Oslo. When Rosenberg spoke to the Führer three days after the *Altmark* incident, they both seem to have discounted altogether the idea of a Quisling-led coup.[7] Two weeks later Rosenberg was back with Hitler, who spoke even more urgently against any kind of 'active political action' on Quisling's part, although the NS could count on 'substantial support' for its general activities. The reason was that Hitler found himself increasingly nervous about possible leaks.[8] Hitler must have realised that Rosenberg and his staff were making plans with Quisling and his people, and felt uneasy about the potential security risk. In the meantime, the Norwegian action had became very serious, so serious that the operation in the North was given priority over the campaign in the West. But in contrast to the western offensive the world was waiting for, the Scandinavian operation relied on absolute secrecy. The action Hitler and

[6] Scheidt to Boehm 1955, BA-MA N 172/14.
[7] Rosenberg's diary, 19 February, 3 March and 6 March 1940, quoted in *Straffesak* p. 37.
[8] Sverre Hartmann, *Spillet om Norge* (1958) pp. 106ff.

von Falkenhorst planned for was a fully-fledged strategic attack which demanded that Rosenberg's agents had to be kept in check. Hitler spoke directly to Scheidt and impressed on him the importance of discretion.

Hitler had good reason to be nervous. The notes from Hagelin and Scheidt which Rosenberg furnished him with aimed to demonstrate that Norway was not pursuing a line of neutrality but was conducting preliminary discussions with Britain, and that the NS was actively preparing for the impending action. Disturbing details such as the story of a secretary of Quisling's who fell in love with an officer from the French General Staff and had to be fired immediately, or rumours about the quality of Scheidt's agents, among them a German-born cabaret artist and a restaurateur of doubtful reputation as well as a German language teacher in Oslo known for his slippery tongue, scarcely stood up to the discretion demanded. Hitler had of course other, more reliable information at his disposal, and was thus rightly sceptical about Scheidt's reports. On one point, however, they stuck to the conditions previously agreed upon. There was no contact at all between Scheidt and Quisling from the Berlin meetings to 9 April, and only one conversation between Quisling and Hagelin before Quisling took to his bed in January. Thereafter, contact was broken until his recovery in March.[9]

Independently of all this, the Supreme Command's planning machinery rolled relentlessly forward. Rosenberg's office and its contacts played as insignificant a part as did Minister Bräuer's and the continued reassurances to the German Foreign Ministry that Norway, despite the *Altmark* episode, genuinely wanted to maintain her neutrality.[10] The logic of war, or more precisely the logic of war preparation, had taken over. Within this logic there was less and less room for political adventure, although during the navy's discussion of the situation on 5 March it was said that Quisling should perhaps be alerted in advance about the impending action.[11] At that time, however, Hitler had completely reversed his plans and decided to

---

[9] The Scheidt–Hagelin reports were: 5 January 1940, in *ADAP* D VII document no. 5.11; 1 February 1940, in BA NS 43; 21 February 1940, in *ADAP* D VII document no. 613; 23 February 1940, in ND PS-947; 5 March 1940, in BA NS 43; 26 March 1940, ibid. – Scheidt later said that he had about twenty people working for him 'for shorter or longer periods', see his interview with Bjørn Bjørnsen, *Dagbladet* 24 September 1977. Rumours: Rosenberg's diary 6 March 1940, in *Straffesak* p. 37. Kristine Arnesen of the NS office was involved with a man from the French legation, according to Rolf Jørgen Fuglesang in 1985. The episode is touched on by Quisling in *Straffesak* p. 350. See also Hitler to Scheel 13 April 1940, according to Hewel in *ADAP* D IX no. 107 p. 125.

[10] Bräuer's assurances: Nøkleby in Paulsen, *1940*.

[11] Loock, *Quisling*, p. 257, citing SKL KTB 5 March 1940.

pursue the operation through legal co-operation with the governments in both Denmark and Norway. He intended that the German occupation of both countries should be carried out as an *occupatio pacifica* on a friendly basis by arrangement with the national governments. He would thus need to secure the support of the Nygaardsvold government after the military *fait accompli*.[12]

In the meantime both de Laporte and other German intelligence agents had arrived in Norway. Abwehr was at this point trying to dissuade Hitler from making any moves against Denmark and Norway, and the agents were thus collecting information to serve this end. De Laporte even spoke to Quisling in person. Scheidt smelled a rat and followed de Laporte back to Berlin, in an attempt to tune down the effect of his reports.[13]

While Scheidt was trying to prevent this unwelcome intrusion, Hagelin was making contact with naval intelligence in Berlin. On Easter Tuesday he met Grand Admiral Raeder. Raeder was no great admirer of Hagelin's, yet he always made use of the information he provided in his arguments against those of his colleagues who were opposed to engaging the German Navy in a risky invasion of Norway. Hagelin now suggested that they obtain concrete military information from Quisling himself. Raeder took the idea to Hitler, who once more interfered in von Falkenhorst's planning. A colonel in Abwehr's Intelligence Department was summoned to the Chancellery and ordered to make direct contact with Quisling to prepare a meeting with him in Copenhagen. On Hagelin's suggestion the meeting was arranged at the Hotel d'Angleterre, where he himself was planning to spend the night *en route* to Oslo on 3 April.[14]

Quisling received his summons on Sunday 31 March, right in the middle of the preparations for launching *Fritt Folk* as a daily newspaper. The telegram from Berlin was short and peremptory: it was imperative that he be in Copenhagen on the following Wednesday. Quisling was obviously displeased with the message. In the first instance he told the middleman (we

---

[12] Directive to the OKW 6 March and 13 March 1940; see Kersaudy, *Norway 1940*, p. 47, containing phrases which also occur in Keitel's note to all 'Oberste Reichsbehörden' 9 April 1940, pkt 3, *ADAP* D IX no. 76, p. 91.

[13] Skodvin, *Striden*, pp. 76f; Hartmann, *Spillet om Norge*, pp. 154f; Hayes, *The Career*, pp. 205f; Hartmann in *Samtiden* 1956/5 citing Erwin von Lahousen's diary. Differing accounts are given by Scheidt, Hagelin, Lahousen and Aall. Scheidt's report of 28 March 1940 in BA NS 43/59, Aall's *Erklæring* of 18 April 1940, 12 December 1952 in Alfa Biblioteket, Oslo.

[14] Hartmann, *Spillet om Norge*, pp. 155f; von Bürchner 29 March 1940, BA-MA RM 6/72; Odd V. Aspheim in *Aftenposten* 17 July 1987, based on documents in BA-MA RM 11/40.

do not know who he was) that a meeting was difficult in general and that Copenhagen in particular was impossible. If absolutely necessary, he might be persuaded to make the journey to Stockholm. Late that evening his message left for Berlin, and a response via Hagelin was not slow to reach Quisling: 'Stockholm inconvenient. If at all possible: Copenhagen. Albert'.

It is not difficult to see why Quisling resisted Hagelin's pressure. Hagelin was far too indiscreet, and Quisling must have realised that his German contacts and his frequent trips were attracting the unwanted attention of both civil and military intelligence. On the other hand, he may have been aware of the fact that the Norwegian secret police was insufficiently staffed with either officers or assistants and therefore impotent against the vast network of contacts Scheidt worked with. Quisling himself was only intermittently under surveillance, whereas Hagelin and his German contacts were more visible.[15] The police received regular information on Hagelin's movements from the doorman at the Hotel Continental.[16] French and British intelligence agents were also active in Norway that winter, working on a much more ambitious scale. It was also impossible to tell what Danish intelligence knew about Quisling's co-operation with Frits Clausen. However, when Berlin insisted, Quisling gave in, deciding that the trip would after all be an opportunity to visit Clausen, whom he was going to see soon anyway.[17]

On Tuesday 2 April Quisling took the night train from Oslo to Copenhagen. *Fritt Folk* had made its second appearance as a daily that morning, its editorial discussing the British threat to Norway. On Wednesday morning he checked into the Hotel d'Angleterre in Kongens Nytorv.

The German intelligence officer Colonel Hans Piekenbrock met him there, but was disappointed with the result of their discussion: 'Quisling's answers to specific questions were generally elusive', mainly discussing the situation in general terms. When asked if the Norwegian coastal batteries would open fire on unidentified vessels – a crucial question for the German Navy – Quisling answered that he did not believe they would do so without

---

[15] The surveillance of Quisling in the spring of 1940 was severely limited by lack of police manpower. Of the secret police unit of altogether fifty persons only one man could be spared, and he had other duties too according to C. Christensen in *Adresseavisen* 8 March 1989. See also Trond Bergh and Knut E. Eriksen, *Den hemmelige Krigen* I (1998) pp. 42ff; Greve, *Spionjakt*, pp. 172ff, 195f; Egil Ulateig, *Raud krigar, raud spion* (1989) pp. 115f.

[16] Caspar Brochmann, *Mors hus* (1984) pp. 65f.

[17] DNSAP, invitation to Quisling 7 February 1940, initially declined 22 February 1940, UBO MS fol. 4096 X.

first receiving instructions from the Norwegian Military High Command or the Ministry of Defence. Apart from that he gave a few 'useful pieces of information' about the airports and reported that Oslo fjord was not mined.

Piekenbrock in turn feigned ignorance when Quisling asked him whether Germany had the capacity to occupy Narvik, feeling that he was not at liberty to discuss the subject 'and certainly not to disclose such vital information'. Neither did he reveal anything about the time when a possible German action might take place, leaving Quisling not much wiser. Raeder was directly informed of the outcome of the meeting and logged the results into his war journal, but none of this had any direct bearing on the plans or preparations as the first invasion ships had already set sail from the naval bases on the Baltic.[18]

That evening Hagelin arrived from Berlin, and he and Quisling had dinner in the hotel.[19] The following morning Hagelin left for Oslo, while Quisling stayed on in Copenhagen in order to look up Clausen and to bring himself up to date with the activities of the Danish movement. He telephoned the party offices, and it so happened that the leader, who otherwise stayed in South Jutland during the parliamentary recess, was in Copenhagen. Clausen came to the hotel, and they set off on a walk around the city.[20]

It was a peaceful walk on a lovely spring day. Nobody paid any attention to the two leaders as they strolled through the city. It was not until five years later that the Danish police started to take an interest in Quisling's visit to the capital. Clausen was repeatedly asked what they had discussed, and whether or not Quisling had information concerning German plans. But Clausen could tell no more than the truth: that they had not even touched on the subject of a German invasion (although he himself was under the impression that Quisling had stopped off in Copenhagen on his way home

---

[18] Piekenbrock to Sverre Hartmann 1956 in Hartmann, *Spillet om Norge*, pp. 155f. See also Piekenbrock to IfZ München 22 January 1958, IfZ ZS 1592. The clearest indication that the discussion was of slight importance is the fact that no 'Feindnachrichtenblatt' was subsequently issued by the intelligence unit of Group XXI after 3 April 1940.

[19] It is possible that Hagelin arrived at the hotel in the morning (he registered at approximately the same time as Quisling according to the copy of the hotel log in RA LD 29) and may even have been present during the discussion with Piekenbrock, as Aspheim suggests in *Aftenposten* 17 July 1987, although Piekenbrock clearly stated that he spoke to Quisling alone.

[20] Clausen's account of the meeting is taken from LAK Køb. Pol., Clausen-Sagen pk 18, interrogation report, and Kort Levnedsbeskrivelse pk 1, and RAK Rigsadv., Clausen-Sagen, CIC Rapport p. 44.

from Berlin). Clausen did notice, however, that Quisling believed that he would 'soon come to power', but thought little of it. One of his men also thought he heard Quisling say in passing that the warships that had been reported going north from German shores could have been intended for Denmark or Norway.[21]

After lunch Clausen telephoned the head of the Copenhagen section of the Danish party and asked him to come and entertain their Norwegian guest. Together, the three men drove down to one of Copenhagen's most recent attractions, the Grundtvig church. From there they went on to the Langelinie pavilion for afternoon coffee, from where they enjoyed a splendid view of the Little Mermaid. In between they made a visit to the party headquarters.

Early on Saturday 6 April Quisling left for Norway. The following day there was an NS Council meeting. Several district leaders and officials sent apologies, including Gulbrand Lunde from Stavanger, Prytz and Aall. But some thirty of the most loyal members gathered at the new offices. The Fører's report on the current situation was as usual hotly anticipated, but he gave no specific details about anything. The minutes read: 'The Fører gave an account of the general situation. He called attention to the most serious situation facing our country and movement, and to the fateful events we are to confront in the immediate future ... [He] closed with an urgent appeal to all the members of the Council for absolute commitment to the movement.' After a short discussion, the members of the Council went to Café Engebret. During the meal they talked about the storm clouds gathering over Norway, as there had been rumours in the press before the weekend of both Allied and German naval activity. Predictions of a British–French assault on the Norwegian coast which had been in circulation for a month were intensifying. There was great excitement surrounding Foreign Minister Koht's speech to the Storting the following day. Quisling stayed calm, as usual, and later in the evening joined in the birthday celebrations of a party member at the Hotel Astoria.[22]

When the party leadership met at the office on the morning of Monday 8 April, the Allies had brought the war on to Norwegian territory. Shortly

---

[21] Clausen to Jes Asmussen 14 April 1940, RAK BA 50a/12/15.

[22] NS Riks- og Rådsmøteprotokoll 1934–45. When Quisling was under investigation in 1945 and was suspected of having prior knowledge of the German occupation, several of the Council members were interrogated to collect evidence regarding the contents of his speech. See RA D 29. H. N. Østbye, NS history, RA PA H. N. Østbye 1. H. F. Knudsen, *Jeg var Quislings sekretær*, gives a less dramatic account of the speech.

before 6 o'clock that morning Koht had been wakened by the British envoy to be told that at dawn the western powers had laid mines to sabotage German merchant ships in Vestfjord as well as in the waters outside Stadt. The announcement went out on the radio news bulletin that morning. When Quisling arrived at the party offices he summoned his associates and solemnly explained the implications of this action. It meant that Norway had been brought into the war.[23]

CONSPIRACY AND COUP

Quisling believed the Germans were certain to respond to the British move, and with enemies attacking from the west, east and south the time had come for the NS to claim power in Norway. He sat down to draft a proclamation. He knew that his candidate members for the cabinet were at home, apart from Jonas Lie who was on a special mission for the secret police in Finnmark, and Ragnar Hvoslef who was in Finland to oversee the demobilisation of Norwegian volunteers. But how should he present his demands?

In the Storting that day confusion reigned, with meeting after meeting but no official statements. The government spent this critical day in closed conferences instead of keeping people informed and reassured. Quisling tried to follow the events from party headquarters. Mrs Østbye left the office to attend Koht's speech in the Storting. The gallery was packed. 'The hall shook with excitement.' Koht delivered the sensational piece of news that, three days earlier, the western powers had disregarded Norwegian neutrality in a diplomatic note which he had hitherto kept secret. But now the government considered itself entitled to dispose of the mines and otherwise to register its protest over the violation of its neutrality.

In the meantime Quisling's statement had been printed. The Hird was summoned and instructed to distribute the leaflets round the city. 'Norway must without delay acquire an effective national government,' it read, and went on to demand power for the NS. For most people there could scarcely have been a more inappropriate comment on the dreadful situation of the day. Quisling, however, was never more in earnest. He had been arguing for a strong national government independent of party politics for ten years in theoretical terms; now he was demanding concrete power.[24]

[23] H. N. Østbye, party history, RA PA H. N. Østbye 1.
[24] The proclamation is reproduced photographically in Dahl, *Dette er London*, p. 57. H. N. Østbye, party history, RA PA H. N. Østbye 1.

During the afternoon of 8 April word started to get round that the German counter-attack was about to begin. Fuglesang received a telephone call from Clausen's people informing him that a fleet was moving through the Danish straits.[25] Towards 6 o'clock news came that a German ship carrying troops had been torpedoed by an unidentified U-boat outside Kristiansand. At 7 o'clock the state broadcasting service, the NRK, reported that between fifty and a hundred German ships had been sighted heading north between Storebelt and the Kattegat.

After supper at home with Maria, Quisling returned as usual to the office, where he was visited by a young party member who related the latest news from the Storting – that the soldiers aboard the torpedoed German ship had said that they were *en route* to Bergen. Quisling was horrified. The same account was given on the state radio at 10 o'clock and in a special edition of *Dagbladet*.[26]

That evening Quisling's newly appointed secretary Harald Franklin Knudsen visited him at home to try to persuade him to leave his home that evening. Other party officials had also been on the telephone to Maria with the same advice, urging their Fører to think of his personal safety and not stay at his home address during such a crisis. After repeated pressure Quisling finally gave in, packed a small suitcase and left for the Hotel Continental. Knudsen had selected the hotel on the grounds that it had a bomb shelter and was, moreover, close to the underground which could also offer cover. The fact that Hagelin was staying there too was unlikely to have influenced his choice, as the secretary did not even know him.

At about 7.30 on the morning of 9 April there was a knock on Quisling's hotel room door. He had been lying awake for some time as there had been an air raid warning at 4.30 when German planes had flown over the city centre and the anti-aircraft struck up on the roof of the building opposite the hotel, after which it had been impossible to get back to sleep.

Scheidt was at the door. He too had had a restless night. Since the small hours he had been standing down at the harbour waiting for the cruiser ship *Blücher*, which was supposed to be transporting the German occupation forces to the quay at 4.30. At 4.30 precisely Koht was visited by Bräuer, who announced that Norway was about to be peacefully occupied by superior German forces, and warned that any resistance would be futile. The cabinet which, uneasy at the general situation, had met at Koht's office, rejected the

[25] Fuglesang in *FF* 9 April 1941.
[26] Sundberg's account, 1991; H. F. Dahl, *Dette er London* (1978) pp. 44f.

German ultimatum. 'This means war and nothing can save you now,' said Bräuer, to which Koht heroically replied, 'The battle has already started.'

But this was true only in part. The German flotilla which was to land the remaining occupation forces had turned round in the Drøbak Sound when the *Blücher* was sunk at Oscarsborg. The fortress had opened fire without having received orders to do so and launched the torpedo which was to alter the course of the Second World War.[27] Oslo was still unoccupied in the morning hours, although German soldiers were pouring in at other points along the Norwegian coast as far north as Narvik. It was 7 o'clock before Scheidt and his companion returned from the quay to the German legation, where confusion reigned. The invasion of Norway had not gone according to plan. Bräuer, whose brief was to persuade the government to co-operate and on no account to allow King Haakon to leave his palace, lacked any means to carry out his orders. The government had refused to co-operate and the King had already left the palace. The Foreign Ministry in Oslo announced to all the foreign legations that the King, the government and the Storting were planning to relocate to Hamar.

Scheidt then went down to the Continental, presumably to confer with Hagelin, and found both Quisling and Hagelin. After a few hours of intense deliberation they agreed to stage an immediate coup. The hotel was conveniently situated, with both the Storting and the NRK studios close by.[28]

It was clearly a high-risk operation. Bräuer and the German Foreign Ministry were certain to oppose it. Military planning had not anticipated a coup either, and thus it was not at all clear how the German military commander would react when he arrived in Oslo. As for the Norwegian government, it had fled after issuing the order for general mobilisation, leaving the capital in a political vacuum. If Quisling were to step in and set up an alternative government, and at the same time make himself instrumental to the German cause by cancelling the mobilisation, his government could be presented as a *fait accompli* to Bräuer and official German foreign policy. Germany would then have to choose whether she wanted to continue

---

[27] John Lukacs, *The Duel: Hitler vs. Churchill* (1990) pp. 33f.

[28] Details concerning the movements of the three conspirators on 9 April are given in Skodvin, *Striden*; Bjørn Bjørnsen, *Det utrolige døgnet* (1977) pp. 200ff; Knudsen, *Jeg var Quislings sekretær* and Dahl, *Dette er London*. Further references are not provided. It has never been established whether or not their meeting at the hotel that morning was coincidental. Scheidt maintains (letter to Boehm 1955) that it was Hagelin who took him to Quisling's room that morning. See Schreiber's report, 13 April 1940, BA-MA RM 7/92.

to deal with Nygaardsvold or to change over to Quisling. In this situation, Quisling would unquestionably be able to rely on Hitler's support as the situation in several respects had reverted to the conditions of the original Berlin talks of 14 and 18 December. Quisling could then form a government in Oslo which would negotiate with Germany and secure the legitimate arrival of German troops in Norway. Such was Quisling's line of thought on the morning of 9 April, and that was how the conspirators behaved over the following days, when the first Quisling government made the historic move of changing the direction of Norwegian foreign policy from west to south by co-operating with Germany instead of Britain.

Of the three, Scheidt's role was to secure some kind of co-operation from the legation. Without its help, the coup would be unsupported by any technical apparatus, and thus lack the authority it needed to build on as the emergent power in Norway: that of Germany and its official representatives. But Bräuer then had to be sidestepped. Quisling needed to mobilise his party and his close associates behind the new government and its call for a halt to the very military mobilisation his own party had been urging ever since the *Altmark* crisis and criticising the government for neglecting to initiate. He needed to talk the NS into a radical change of policy, and quickly. Hagelin, for his part, had to try to make use of his connections in Berlin and to keep these channels open despite the extreme difficulties of communication in wartime.

Quisling's task was perhaps the most awkward one. The natural response of the NS youth, like the majority of young Norwegians, was to report for duty with their units after the order went out for general mobilisation. The Germans or the British: the defence of the country rested on this choice. But on 9 April the situation in the NS, as in other organisations and institutions, was one of utter chaos. The radio did not bring any news from the government apart from a short, repeated announcement that it had relocated to Hamar. On the morning of 9 April, anxious party representatives, several of them on their way to their mobilisation units and trying to find out what was going on, gathered at party headquarters, but the Fører did not appear. Word soon got round that he had moved into the Continental, and anxious members had to seek him out there. Fuglesang was summoned and asked to book into the hotel.

During the afternoon the three conspirators conferred once more. Scheidt was particularly euphoric, reporting that he had contacted Berlin and had gained Hitler's personal approval for a Quisling government. The three must have discussed how such a government could be set up, and agreed to make use of the NRK broadcasting station. After the meeting Quisling sat down to write the final version of his declaration of power, complete with his list of cabinet members: 'Following England's violation of Norwegian neutrality by laying minefields in Norwegian territorial waters without meeting any resistance beyond the usual lame protests of the Nygaardsvold government, Germany has offered its friendly assistance, with promises of guaranteeing Norwegian freedom and independence ... In response the government raised armed resistance and promptly fled.' He declared that under these circumstances it was 'the duty and the right of the movement of National Union to take over governmental power' in order to safeguard national security and independence. The Nygaardsvold government 'has withdrawn', and 'the national government has taken over power'.

Did this constitute a coup? Clearly it did. The government had neither 'fled' nor 'withdrawn' as Quisling maintained; it had simply relocated 50 kilometres outside the capital to avoid falling into German hands. And from there it conducted its business in close contact with the King and the Storting, among other things by signalling to Bräuer in Oslo that it was prepared to negotiate a second time about a possible 'Danish' solution by accepting the German presence as an *occupatio pacifica*. The negotiations were scheduled for the next day, 10 April, and were indeed a triumph for Bräuer. At the same time, however, officials from his legation took part in Scheidt's preparations for a Quisling government. In this way Germany's official representation followed a two-track course – Nygaardsvold and Quisling at the same time.[29]

At 2.30 in the afternoon the capital was formally occupied as airborne German units marched into the town and down the main Karl Johan Street. Three hours later a small German patrol unit arrived at NRK headquarters and ordered that broadcasting cease. Music had been playing non-stop since the early morning, while the programme makers desperately searched for either the government or the General Staff to make some kind of address to the nation. At the German request silence now descended over the airwaves.

One hour later – at 6.30 in the evening – Quisling's secretary Knudsen presented himself to the German guard outside the building stating that Quisling wanted to make a proclamation to the Norwegian people. The German shook his head. Nobody was allowed to enter. It was not until

---

[29] The evidence for the legation's support for Quisling is: Report, 9 April 1940, signed Gelderblom, PAAA Ges. Oslo 245/18: Besatzung Norwegens; and Quisling's 'Aufruf an die Bevölkerung Norwegens'. Written on the legation's typewriter with handwritten insertions by von Neuhaus, signed and dated 9 April 1940, PAAA Ges. Oslo 245/19.

Scheidt appeared in an SA uniform that they were given access to the premises. Programme director Olav Midttun was called in to find out what Scheidt and Quisling's business was, and on whose authority Quisling was to make his proclamation. Scheidt explained that this was the decision of the German authorities, and showed him the letter from the chief of the Reich Chancellery, Lammers, which stated that he was 'im Sonderauftrag des Führers'. Midttun, who believed that the letter had been signed by Hitler himself, asked Scheidt whether he had come on behalf of the legation, and Scheidt told him that he had: Midttun was assured on this point, as Scheidt grasped a nearby telephone, dialled the number of the legation and asked for someone who actually confirmed to Midttun when he was handed the receiver that Herr Scheidt was certainly acting on behalf of the official German legation, absolutely.[30]

This bluff cleared the way for Quisling who arrived shortly after. He entered the studio and installed himself behind the microphone. At 7.25 p.m. the gramophone started playing Bruch's *Kol Nidrei*. Two minutes later Quisling began his address. 'Women and men of Norway . . .' His tense voice reflected the gravity of the situation. He explained that Nygaardsvold's government had fled and as only the NS movement could save Norway now, he had formed a government and thereby cancelled the 'criminal' order of mobilisation issued by his predecessor.[31]

After completing his broadcast, Quisling went down to the Ministry of Defence to try to contact the two officers on the General Staff who had special responsibility for mobilisation, but was unable to get any word to them. He did manage, however, to make a telephone call to an old friend and former colleague at Elverum and ask him to 'arrest the Marxist government', which was on its way there from Hamar. The colonel ignored the order, thus thwarting Quisling's first initiative as proclaimed head of government. His second initiative was no more successful than his first, as his order to the Oslo chief of police to present himself for immediate briefing was flatly ignored.[32]

At 10 o'clock Quisling returned to the broadcasting studio. In the mean-

---

[30] For the Germans' and Quisling's use of NRK see Dahl, *Dette er London*, ch. II, 2 and documents 2 and 3.

[31] The only known recording of Quisling's proclamation of 9 April is that made by the NRK on the occasion of Quisling's second address at 10 o'clock. The 7.30 p.m. speech was not recorded. Transcript in Dahl, *Dette er London*, p. 356. Quisling's manuscript in RA PAQ.

[32] Skodvin, *Striden*, pp. 99f. See also Loock, *Quisling*, who suggests a somewhat different chronology.

time the listeners had been informed that Quisling was again to make 'an important announcement'. Quisling repeated the proclamation he had made at 7.30 and read out the list of his cabinet again: himself as Prime Minister and Foreign Minister; Jonas Lie as Minister of Justice and Guldbrand Lunde, Ragnar Skancke, Frederik Prytz, Albert Hagelin – altogether nine ministers. He made it clear that civil servants and officers were to take orders exclusively from the new National Government, and issued the stern warning that any 'refusal to do so will henceforth involve the most serious consequences for the individuals concerned'.

In Berlin Hitler reacted exactly as they had hoped he would, by recognising Quisling's government immediately. During the intense excitement at the Chancellery as reports were coming in of the mixed fortunes of the enterprise – nearly the entire German Navy and the greater part of the Luftwaffe were at stake in this grandiose surprise attack – the news of Quisling's coup was immediately welcomed. 'Our middleman Quisling comes to the helm,' Goebbels noted after his conversation with the Führer that night. Hitler informed Bräuer over the telephone that the Nygaardsvold government could now be discounted, as the King would be forced to recognise a cabinet headed by Quisling. Rosenberg noted in his diary that Hitler had laughed when he heard that Quisling had formed a government, which suggests that the coup had come as a surprise to him. If this is true, Scheidt had not been telling the truth earlier in the day when he gave his assurance to Quisling and Hagelin that he had sought and obtained Hitler's approval in advance.

The government which Hitler recognised was the one which Quisling had outlined in Berlin in December, but which for reasons of security had been eliminated from the planning. But now, Hitler told Rosenberg on the night of 10 April, 'Quisling can form his government'.[33]

BRÄUER THE DIPLOMAT

However, after only a few days, Hitler went back on his word. The great victor in Berlin – congratulated by Mussolini for having achieved what Napoleon failed to do: the conquer two capitals within twenty-four hours – vacillated and changed plans. Quisling was removed from office, and his government made way for a government commission known to Norwegians

---

[33] Goebbels in his diary for 11 April 1940: *Die Tagebücher von Joseph Goebbels* (1987) p. 107. Rosenberg's diary, cited in *Straffesak* p. 37.

as the Administrative Council and to the Germans as the Governmental Commission (Regierungsausschuss). This came as such a volte face that all Hitler's assurances about Quisling as Germany's special friend were shown to be hollow.

Incredibly to Quisling, it was the German Reich's special envoy, Minister Bräuer, who was behind it all. True, Bräuer was not the only opponent around. During the few days of his coup government, friends and enemies, both German and Norwegian, all descended on him ferociously, united in their attempt to force him to back down. But at the centre of this united stand was Bräuer.

When Hitler insisted, in his telephone conversation with Bräuer at midnight on 9 April, that King Haakon appoint Quisling head of government, this was part of a 'legal approach', which, if successful, would secure the peaceful occupation of Norway. Quisling was indeed aiming at something of the sort. With his radio speech he had appointed himself as an act of revolutionary urgency, without securing the co-operation of the King, but he was confident that he would reach an understanding with the monarch later, as he knew King Haakon personally and could also benefit from the fact that some of his collaborators enjoyed close palace connections.

After Bräuer's visit to the King at Elverum on the afternoon of 10 April, however, it seemed extremely unlikely that such an understanding would be reached. The King had categorically refused to accept Quisling's government, declaring it out of the question that a man who had twice been rejected at the polls could be appointed head of government. With that, negotiations for a peaceful arrangement of the occupation broke down. The Nygaardsvold government then favoured continued resistance, and Hitler's plans for an *occupatio pacifica* with the co-operation of the constitutional authorities and a Quisling government appointed by the King, collapsed.[34]

Thus there were now two governments in the country: one legal, which was fighting the war supported by the Allies, and an alternative government seeking to call off the struggle. It might have seemed natural for Germany to ally itself with the latter, but this was not the case. Bräuer succeeded in manoeuvring Berlin away from any co-operation with Quisling. He had explained to Foreign Minister von Ribbentrop in several reports prior to 9 April that he was not only against Quisling personally, he regarded him as downright incompetent to carry out pro-German politics in the country.[35]

Instead, another possibility emerged: that of a legal government commis-

[34] Dahl, *Dette er London*, pp. 58f.   [35] Nøkleby in Paulsen, *1940*.

sion for the occupied area, one which did not need to define itself in relation to the King or the Nygaardsvold government, but which could gradually take over power after the Germans had gained control over the whole country. Such a commission could be established through the Supreme Court by the invocation of an obscure provision in the Constitution which accorded the court some sort of authority of this kind in case of extreme crisis. Bräuer welcomed the solution enthusiastically, as it would facilitate a peaceful occupation after all. However, if it were to succeed, Berlin would have to be persuaded that the midnight telephone call from Hitler had been unwise, and to let Quisling go.

Immediately on his return from Elverum on the evening of 10 April Bräuer found support for this line. The first people to appear at the legation to register their protest at the Quisling government were Germans resident in Oslo, led by Dr Noack, who kept insisting that Germany must not on any account attach itself to Quisling, quoting many Norwegians on the subject. Perhaps the most influential single communication on the matter came from Germany's faithful friend, Consul Dietrich Hildisch, whose letter ended with the salutation 'Heil Hitler!'. He informed Bräuer that there was a strong, 'even violent revulsion' towards the Quisling government among the Norwegian people.[36] Of the many protesters who approached the minister in person, the largest group consisted of people who had first-hand experience of Quisling as a leader – those who had left or been thrown out of the party in 1937, headed by J. B. Hjort and supported by the *Ragnarok* editor Hans S. Jacobsen and the chairman of the Fatherland League, Victor Mogens. Hjort also went straight to von Falkenhorst, with whom he had personal connections, as two of his sisters were married to sons of von Falkenhorst's former superior, General von der Goltz. Such things were important to the Germans. Hjort even tried to reach the King at Elverum in order to keep him informed. In fact, the legation was inundated with petitions to remove Quisling's government in the interests of good relations between Norway and Germany and soon began picking up signals which might persuade Berlin to change course.

Other groups continually sending communications were Norwegian industrialists, led by Fridtjof Heyerdal, the director of Siemens, and Gunnar

---

[36] The classic account of the events leading up to Quisling's removal is UK II, *Administrasjonsrådet*, ch. 'Opprettelsen', pp. 127–65. The legal solution is ascribed to J. Rivertz, son of Supreme Court judge Rivertz. For a more recent account of the opposition to Quisling 9–15 April, see Høidal, *Quisling*, pp. 306ff. Hildisch to Bräuer 10 April 1940, PAAA Ges. Oslo 245/19.

Schelderup, the director of Spigerverk, who above all wanted to see the intolerable economic situation brought to an end. The war had disrupted production to a considerable degree and people were fleeing Oslo in fear of British air raids. Production was threatening to come to a complete standstill, and Quisling was a most unwelcome irritant in this context. Schelderup also discussed the situation with his brother Ferdinand, who was a Supreme Court judge. Within the court discussions had already begun concerning the possibility of the judiciary providing the basis for a legal appointment of an alternative to Quisling. Thus Chief Justice Paal Berg suddenly became the centre of the Norwegian campaign to get rid of Quisling, supported by industrialists, leading civil servants, Bishop Eivind Berggrav and other prominent persons.[37]

For the Germans, the political developments were soon overshadowed by military concerns. After the triumph of the first twenty-four hours logistical difficulties as well as a growing irritation at Norwegian resistance hampered the Wehrmacht's progress. The chaos in the Norwegian decision-making apparatus aggravated the confusion, especially over whom people were supposed to be dealing with. The Nygaardsvold government was alternately addressed as the 'government' and the 'previous government', whereas Quisling was regarded as Prime Minister, head of government, Major, or simply 'Mr'. Some German authorities considered him their legitimate opposite number, while more senior men in the army saw him as a disturbing or even dangerous complication. Bräuer seems to have been the only one who knew exactly what he wanted: to get rid of him altogether. The reports he sent to Berlin, aiming at changing opinion in the Reich Chancellery, were masterpieces of diplomacy to this end.[38]

To Quisling and his government the lack of support from the official German legation was a heavy blow, but it was scarcely the most urgent problem of their first forty-eight hours in power. Rather, these days were fraught with difficulties created by conflicts with their own civil service. The Oslo chief of police was clearly trying to sabotage the new government, and Quisling's attempt to circumvent him by handing over his position to the chief of the Aker police failed. Government offices and ministries were to a large extent evacuated, and the people who remained seemed reluctant to

[37] RA LD 4152 Mogens, accounts of Mogens, Jacobsen, Frithjof Plathe; Mogens, *Tyskerne*, pp. 103f; also H. F. Dahl, 'Quislings staskupp i forfatningshistorisk lys', *HT* 1977/1 and Norland, *Hårde tider*, pp. 304ff.

[38] Particularly Lagebricht to AA 11 and 12 April 1940, PAAA Ges. Oslo 245/19, Besetzung Norwegens.

take orders from the new authority. Quisling fared a little better with representatives of industry. One meeting with the Shipping Brokers' Federation actually did take place. The Agrarian League was invited to send out an appeal against the mobilisation. The director of the Industrial Federation twice met Quisling and the Federation of Trade Unions (LO) sent representatives to a meeting with the new government. Quisling interpreted such events as signs of recognition and willingness to co-operate. A more realistic approach would perhaps have revealed that industry and commerce abhorred the situation as much as anybody else.[39]

The worst thing for Quisling was that discipline in the party had broken down, starting with the cabinet itself. The new Prime Minister had not received any word or message from his ministers outside Oslo. Central figures such as Prytz, Lunde and Jonas Lie kept silent. In fact, they all deserted the Fører at this time of crisis.

Guldbrand Lunde did not dare come out publicly and confess his opposition to the new government. He preferred to leave a written statement to that effect with the district governor, and stayed quietly at home in Stavanger. The party's long-standing propaganda chief's desertion at such a crucial time came as a terrible blow. But harder still to bear was Prytz's rejection. Prytz himself had not heard Quisling's proclamation of 9 April. That day there had been an air strike over the island in Trondheim Fjord where he lived; a British plane had been shot down and that was more than enough for Prytz to think about. He was told about Quisling's broadcast by one of his maids. Prytz was completely nonplussed by the news and on 11 April he caught the first boat to Trondheim, where he joined forces with Ragnar Skancke, another of Quisling's cabinet ministers, at the Hotel Britannia. Skancke was absolutely opposed to Quisling's government; Prytz was ambivalent. *Adresseavisen*, the local paper, carried a piece on them and on Jonas Lie, who had also turned down his appointment, headlined 'Quisling Government Mystery'. Even Hvoslef, who had been informed in advance, refused the appointment as soon as he heard about it.[40]

[39] UK II; Jan Debes, *Sentraladministrasjonens historie* V (1980) ch. 5; Sigmund Bråtveit, *Kornband og hakekors* (1990) p. 18; Tore Pryser, *Klassen og nasjonen* (1988) p. 256; Knut Aagesen, 'Fagopposisjonen av 1940', in Paulsen, *1940*, pp. 373ff.

[40] Re Lunde: Trygve Wyller, *Aprildagene 1940* (1959) p. 148; Prytz, Skanche: Else Astrup Prytz's account, 1987;* Einar Rustad, 'De stridens år' (undated MS*) p. 19; Lie: Sverre Rødder, *Min ære er troskap* (1990) p. 79. Hvoslef: Hewel, *Aufzeichnung* 13 April 1940, *ADAP* D IC no. 99 p. 117 and Hvoslef's own account in *Studentene fra 1890* (1942) p. 68; K. Fjørtoft, *Ulvetiden* (1990) pp. 215f, 319f.

The defection within the government was accompanied by a general desertion within the NS 'battle organisation', which consisted of the 700–800 active members who had sworn their allegiance to Quisling in writing, and whom the Fører in return considered to be his 'inner circle' which would, as he repeatedly said, stand firm when the rest of society collapsed. One estimate shows that as many as 10 per cent of the Oslo and Akershus membership officially left the party after 8 April. If unofficial defection from the party is taken into account, which was at least twice as high, then it appears that at least one in three of Quisling's dedicated followers abandoned him in early April 1940. In addition, a great number of the younger party members simply ignored his orders to break off mobilisation and to abandon resistance. Rather, they actively participated in the struggle in southern Norway well into May, in the same way as Ministers Hvoslef and Lie, who both responded to their dishonourable appointments by promptly reporting for duty with the armed forces. Other senior officers who had been prominent in the Folk-Rising or the NS, like Adolf Fr. Munthe, severed all connections with Quisling and went to war.[41]

At the time, the true scale of the defections from the party remained unknown. To Quisling at least, far more important than counting the losses was to try to make the new government work amidst the general chaos in Oslo. On 10 April he installed the government's official headquarters inside the Storting. It was ironic, perhaps, that the country's most anti-parliamentary party chose this of all places. However, the situation was that the government offices nearby were all immediately placed under German guard, and were soon visited by a special Wehrmacht division which was under orders to sort out all archive material that might be of interest to Germany and to forward it to Berlin. Quisling therefore had to make do with a building that the Germans ignored, and took over the presidential office in the Storting while his ministers were given space in the abandoned party offices. Fuglesang was appointed cabinet secretary and the lawyer Wilhelm Koren Christie functioned as government secretary. Scheidt, it appears from the only surviving document relating to the structure of the government, a telephone list, was number two in the hierarchy, referred to as 'Head of German Liaison Staff to the Norwegian Prime Minister'.[42]

[41] Compiled from membership lists of the Battle Organisation (Kamporganisasjonen), INO; also Fuglesang's account in NRK ho 57993.
[42] Skodvin, *Striden*, p. 169; Scheidt to Bräuer 13 April 1940, *ADAP* D IX no. 110 p. 129. Documents relating to the German sorting out of archive material in PAAA Ges. Oslo 245/ 25, Besetz. Norw. Verwaltung.

The new government's trump card in those first few days was its control of the state radio station, which had declared Quisling Prime Minister, and in whose broadcasts he still remained so.[43] In addition to this, Quisling secured another effective channel of communication through ordering *Fritt Folk* to be enclosed in all copies of the other Oslo newspapers every morning. This was an extraordinary injunction as it appeared to contradict German declarations to the press that they wanted to co-operate. As the Communist press had been banned and the Labour *Arbeiderbladet* had ceased publication, only non-socialist and apolitical papers remained to distribute free copies of *Fritt Folk*, but even so the NS paper certainly enjoyed an extended readership. The first issue included a long biographical article about the Fører and his long struggle, together with a reassuring piece about the task of the NS, which was surprisingly moderate. The party declared itself committed to introducing a corporate constitution in Norway, but emphasised its willingness to co-operate with any people or group of 'good will'.

There were not too many such groups, however. All the Prime Minister's time was taken up with inconclusive meetings, with interrupted discussions and improvised troubleshooting, leaving little opportunity to introduce new policies. These first days in office consisted almost entirely of quarrels: with the German legation; the German military; with the Norwegian civil service; and not least with the advancing circle of highly politicised top-level civil servants, the triumvirate of the Bishop of Oslo Eivind Berggrav, the Chief Justice Paal Berg and the district governor of Oslo and Akershus, Ingolf Christensen, who were now seizing the reins of power and steering a course which pointed in the direction of Bräuer's and not of Quisling's plans.

IN THE RESERVES

From their office in the Storting, Quisling, Hagelin and Scheidt could easily guess what was going on in the German legation. Particularly depressing was the fact that Bräuer seemed to rely on information from the Hjort circle. These people were 'worse than Bolsheviks', Quisling thought. In order to prevent their views from reaching Hitler via Bräuer and Ribbentrop, he decided to send Hagelin to Berlin. Hagelin managed to get a flight, and with Rosenberg's help he was received at the Reich Chancellery on 13 April.

---

[43] The complete radio proclamations of the Quisling government are collected as Document no. 3 in Dahl, *Dette er London.*

The records from Hitler's two lengthy conversations with Quisling's representative that Saturday show that the Führer was in an irritable and indecisive mood. He twice said that 'it is a matter of indifference to me who governs up there!' Hagelin's information did not reassure him, even though he put NS support at 15 per cent of the population as well as emphasising Quisling's close links with industry and shipping. Hitler did not even attempt to hide the fact that he did not believe him, and decided to send his own observer to report impartially on the situation.[44]

His choice of representative was Theodor Habicht, under-secretary in the German Foreign Ministry. Habicht was an Austrian with a longstanding association with National Socialism who, amongst other things, had been involved in the unsuccessful Vienna coup of 1934, when local National Socialists had struck against Chancellor Dollfuss, but were overpowered and humiliated by the fact that Hitler and their parent party in Germany lent no support at all.

On Sunday 14 April Habicht landed in Oslo and immediately sought out Berg, Berggrav and Christensen, as well as General von Falkenhorst and General Engelbrecht, who was in command of the forces in Oslo. Later in the evening he arranged a meeting with Quisling, Scheidt and Hagelin at the Hotel Continental, which was also being used as the quarters for Engelbrecht's staff. Quisling struck him as indecisive and incapable of producing any concrete plans. Moreover he was trapped in an impossible situation: earlier that day German military leaders had expressed bitterness at being identified with such a usurper, whom people all over the country believed they were trying to protect. The situation reminded Habicht of the ill-fated episode of the occupation of the Ruhr in 1923, and the general condemnation of the French puppet, Dr Dorten, when he tried to seize power.

Habicht soon identified Berg as the man who would be able to lead them out of the impasse. If he could select a legal government commission for the occupied areas which could remain loyal to the occupying forces and at the same time reassure industry and public opinion, this would put a stop to all opposition in the occupied areas. The commission, which would undoubtedly gain recognition from the King, could even put a stop to the resistance in regions that had not yet been occupied through broadcasts on the national radio.

---

[44] Hewel's account of the discussions at the Reich Chancellery in *ADAP* D IX no. 99 pp. 117ff; Rosenberg's account of his conversation with Hagelin in *Straffesak* p. 48 (the original is in BA NS 43). Hagelin's mission is described in Loock, *Quisling*, pp. 305f.

But Quisling rejected this option altogether. Article 46 of the Constitution referred to the role of the Supreme Court only in the event of the King's dying without leaving an heir, he pointed out to Habicht. With the support of Hagelin and Scheidt he presented a fierce defence of the political advantages of his own government, which he argued consisted of Germany's only true friends in Norway. 'Even in politics, there is such a thing as fidelity and friendship,' he said, in a veiled reference to the Berlin discussions. However, this was lost on both Habicht and Bräuer, who were unaware that any talks had taken place. In response to Quisling's appeal to friendship and fidelity, Habicht replied that unfortunately, in certain situations, concerns of a higher order had to prevail, and thus political friends sometimes had to go their separate ways. After this meeting, Quisling was so disturbed that he made another unsuccessful attempt to contact Hitler in person. But as usual at that time, Hitler was out of reach, at least for him.[45]

The following day, after more discussions in Oslo, Bräuer and Habicht gave their assessment of the situation to Ribbentrop. They rashly gave the impression that the commission in question was a 'government' by neglecting to contradict Ribbentrop's repeated use of the terms *Regierung*, *die kommende Regierung*, even though they themselves employed the more guarded term *Regierungsausschuss* (government committee). And of course they did not mention at all that the official Norwegian version was simply 'administrative council', a slightly misleading term which was chosen to avoid any confusion with the Nygaardsvold government.

From the discussions, it appeared that Hitler had decided to let Quisling go, but only on the express condition that Habicht should tell him that the Führer greatly appreciated his stance, a message that he would put in writing. In addition, Hitler wanted Quisling's departure to be effected with dignity, so that he would neither lose face nor be compromised, as the Führer wanted to see him as a reserve candidate for the future leadership in Norway. Thirdly, he was to be given a seat in the new government.

With that, the way was cleared for the two diplomats. Quisling was summoned and informed that Hitler had decided to appoint a government commission, but with the proviso that Quisling was kept on in reserve, and that Hitler would ensure both an honourable withdrawal and favourable conditions for expanding his organisation. Quisling was given reassurances

---

[45] Habicht's report in PAAA Ges. Bräuer. Quisling's account of the negotiations in *Straffesak* pp. 87f. The original German written by Scheidt is in *ADAP* D IX no. 18 pp. 137f. See also Loock, *Quisling*, p. 318.

that this government commission would not seek to limit the activities of the NS, or hinder its progress. That 'would not be tolerated', said Bräuer. His own seat on the commission was not mentioned, as the diplomats knew this would be impossible and had decided to substitute that with a special appointment of some kind. Quisling asked whether the ban on uniforms would be reinstated, and was told that it would not. He then expressed his desire that Scheidt remain in Norway as his adviser and liaison, and that Hagelin should take up residence in Berlin as his representative. It was half-past one in the morning before Quisling and his associates returned to the Hotel Continental having promised that they would take this proposed settlement 'into consideration'.[46]

But in Bräuer's view, there was nothing to 'consider'. All that remained was to establish the Administrative Council and to arrange its inauguration ceremony at the Norwegian Academy of Science and Letters next door to the legation the following afternoon. There was still a lot to be done. The list of the members of the Council had to be drawn up, as had Paal Berg's speech of thanks to Quisling, which was to ensure the dignified departure which Hitler was insisting on. Quisling also wanted to make a speech, but nobody knew what he was intending to say. The important thing now was to get the Council launched as soon as possible. That day the Lysaker bridge on the city's western approach was blown up in an act of sabotage, and the military became even more nervous.[47]

During the early afternoon of 15 April Quisling approached Bishop Berggrav, Berg and Christensen in a last attempt to frustrate the Council and to buy time. But his telephone conversations, in which he alternated between threats and entreaties, all came to nothing. The most obvious sign that he was up against formidable opposition came when he and his associates were thrown out of their hotel and had to move into the Grand. Even his attendance at the inauguration ceremony of the Council was considered unnecessary. The Supreme Court's announcement that it had established a 'temporary Administrative Council' for the occupied areas did not make any mention of the government of 9 April. The Supreme Court was acting independently, 'relying on the King's approval' of the appointments. But one way or another, Quisling had to resign. Bräuer and Berg had discussed the option of his doing so on the radio, as soon as the ceremony at

---

[46] PAAA Ges. Oslo 245/19, 'Ferngespräch des Unterstaatssekretärs Habicht und des Gesandten mit dem Reichsaussenminister am 14. april 1940 ab 21.40 Uhr', also in *ADAP* D IX no. 115 pp. 132ff.

[47] UK II, *Administrasjonsrådet*, ch. 'Opprettelsen', pp. 127–65.

the Academy was over. Berg had found it extremely difficult to word the message of thanks to Quisling in such a way that it would be acceptable to Bräuer. Bräuer wanted Berg first of all to explain that Quisling's government could not in the circumstances be considered illegitimate, but Berg refused. What he did agree to do was to convey his own opinion that he 'personally felt that Quisling had been acting in good faith – that he really did believe that what he had done he had done in the interest of his country'. Berg was under enormous pressure from his fellow judges who with the slimmest majority – seven to six – had agreed to the establishment of the Council at all, and thus an announcement giving thanks to Quisling was certain to outrage them. At the last minute he managed to arrive at a compromise between what Bräuer wanted and what would be acceptable to his colleagues. At 6 o'clock in the evening he met Quisling at the NRK, each man with his own script, the contents of which had been given Bräuer's prior approval.

The official ceremony now taking place on the radio was of an entirely different nature from the one which had just taken place at the Academy. In his speech, Quisling said that he was handing over his governmental power to the Administrative Council as the continued military mobilisation ordered by the Nygaardsvold government raised the danger of bloodshed for which he could take no responsibility. But since the Administrative Council was assuming this responsibility, it was time to 'transfer my office to it'. He closed with an appeal for calm.

Berg was astonished when he heard Quisling's address. It was not what he had been led to expect by Bräuer. He had made it sound as though the Supreme Court's initiative was to take over from Quisling's government only on the grounds of the prevailing circumstances. But there was no time to alter his script as he was already on the air. Berg therefore thanked Quisling while the nation listened:

Following the departure of the Nygaardsvold government [9 April 1940] there was no longer any representative of the executive power left in the capital. During this fateful time Mr Quisling has acted in order to prevent bloodshed in the occupied areas and to maintain calm and order. By stepping down at this point he has shown once more his sense of responsibility and his patriotism. I therefore, on behalf of the Supreme Court, extend my thanks to Mr Quisling for his announcement, which has made the establishment of the Administrative Council possible.

If this was not an outright acquittal, it certainly came very close to one. In any event, Berg's announcement appeared to be much more than a personal expression of belief in Quisling's good faith; the Chief Justice simply confirmed that he had acted patriotically. Quisling thus had good reason to believe that his government would not legally be considered treacherous in a later consideration of the events.

'The Moor has done his duty and can now go', was the BBC's verdict on his departure on 15 April: a tool of German interests, but also a traitor and a collaborator. Now his bitter defeat was being broadcast to the entire world.[48]

The catch was, of course, that nobody knew of his arrangement with Hitler to be in reserve, just as they knew nothing of the prior agreements of December 1939. These pieces of information were strictly confidential. In a letter to Hitler at the end of April Quisling outlined his feelings, and questioned the value of the 'reserve' arrangement as the press and public opinion in Norway so ruthlessly denounced him and his movement as treacherous and kept attacking him for unwarranted collaboration with the enemy.

'Why is Quisling so much hated?' asked the NS paper *Fritt Folk* in a survey of the injustice being heaped on their Fører. The answer, which could not be touched upon but which everybody could see for himself, was that he had simply fundamentally miscalculated both the public's feelings and its sense of morality. An officer and a party leader attacking his King and government from the rear during a national emergency was quite simply outrageous and unpalatable to most people. Quisling underrated both the extent of this outrage and the depth of the underlying feelings, and found himself denounced by the whole world. His name went out over the airwaves on 9 April and before long had replaced the name of Kuusinen as the synonym for a traitor. British journalists were quick to pick up on the phonetic advantage of the peculiar yet easily pronounced Norwegian name.[49] During the spring of 1940 Quisling became a byword for traitor in nearly all languages. In a speech to the leaders of the Dominions, Churchill characterised the new phenomenon in Shakespearean cadences: 'a vile race of Quislings – to use the new word, which will carry the scorn of mankind down the centuries – is hired to fawn upon the conqueror, to "collaborate" in his designs and to enforce his rule upon their fellow countrymen while grovelling low themselves'.[50] The name quickly gained currency from the BBC World Service. During the spring of 1940 Quisling became a byword for traitor in nearly every language. French newspapers were soon writing

---

[48] A quotation from Schiller, *Die Verschwörung des Fiesco*, 3, 4 (1783).

[49] *The Times* 19 April 1940, 'Quisling Is As Quisling Does'; *Daily Mail* 23 April 1940; Hewins, *Quisling*, pp. 11f.

[50] Quoted in Martin Gilbert, *Finest Hour: Winston S. Churchill 1939–41* (1989) p. 1108.

about 'les quislings' as the latest development in the wave of traitors.[51] The collaborator Laval was branded *un quisling* in 1941, and soon there were quislings everywhere. At the end of the war Quisling was sitting in the palace in Oslo reading reports from the international press about 'Japan's Quisling' and 'Russia's Quisling'.[52] The name was linguistically suitable as an international label, but it ran deeper than that – an archetypal traitor adapted to modern times, with the use of the airwaves and a 'fifth column' of organised associates to assist the advancing occupying forces.[53]

Even his sympathisers were alarmed by his example. When Dr Frits Clausen's party members were working for their leader to join a coalition government set up under the peaceful occupation of Denmark, Clausen refused. In an open reference to Quisling, he insisted that he 'did not want to ride on German bayonets like Quisling', and kept a determined distance from his Norwegian colleague.[54] For Mussert in Holland the Norwegian Fører, whom he knew from their work together on the CAUR, was an embarrassment. When Holland was invaded a month after Norway, Mussert felt seriously hampered by the discredit which Quisling had brought on all forms of co-operation with Germany, and was forced ask the German Foreign Ministry to clear his name from any suspicion of treason *à la* Quisling.[55]

Signs of the general loathing came even from his native Fyresdal, from where his Aunt Malene wrote to Jørgen in Oslo and advised the brothers not to come down in the summer as the atmosphere in the village was so full of hatred that she feared an arson attack. The kitchen window of her home had recently been smeared with tar, an expression of the utmost loathing. 'People feel sorry for those of us who carry the name Quisling, and there are those of us who would like to change name,' she wrote. The maid at the farm thought that *Fritt Folk* brought shame on them all. 'These are terrible times for Norway. May God be a help and comfort to us all,' the old lady closed.[56]

Quisling must have felt a certain satisfaction when Bräuer's and Habicht's

[51] Cuttings in BA 58-Zsg 117/1172; Jean Lacoutre, *De Gaulle: The Rebel* (1990) p. 405.
[52] RA FMK 14, e.g. *Svenska Dagbladet* 13 November 1944.
[53] Louis de Jong, *Die deutsche fünfte Kolonne im zweiten Weltkrieg* (1959).
[54] LAK Køb. Pol. Clausen-Sagen 18.
[55] Rudolf Likus, 'Aufzeichnung über mein Gespräch mit Herrn Mussert' 25 May 1940, PAAA Handakten Luther, Verschiedenes. Also G. Hirschfield, *Nazi Rule and Dutch Collaboration* (1988) pp. 265f.
[56] Malene Quisling to Jørgen Quisling 25 May 1940, UBO MS fol. 4096 III.

plans collapsed like a house of cards after only two days. On 17 April it became known that the King had dismissed the Administrative Council as having no constitutional basis in Norwegian law, and decreed the Nygaards-vold government to be the country's only legitimate government. The trick with the translation was uncovered, Hitler was furious and the two diplomats only managed to save their necks by instantly joining the army, from which, after a time, they disappeared – Habicht was killed and Bräuer ended up in a Russian prisoner-of-war camp. Their plan had secured neither a peaceful solution nor the King's return to the capital. On 18 April 1940 the first British forces landed in Åndalsnes and the government embarked on a joint campaign with the Allies, which gradually took it further and further away from Oslo. The King would never be won over, and it became clear that the Wehrmacht would have to secure its own peace.

Quisling's ouster and the attempt to replace him with a legal govern-mental commission seems in fact to have been doomed from the start. By 19 April Hitler had finally lost patience with the entire Norwegian govern-mental tangle, and decided to take action. On 24 April he appointed one of his most capable junior party administrators to Norway. Josef Terboven was district party leader in the Rhineland and now became supreme authority as Reichskommissar in occupied Norway, responsible only to Hitler himself.

The great western campaign was finally scheduled for 10 May. The evening before, the Führer left Berlin on his special train, the *Amerika*, to be nearer the front. His departure was smoke-screened by reports that he was on his way to Oslo to inspect yet another of the capitals in his fast-expanding empire, just as he had visited Warsaw immediately after the Polish campaign. But the *Amerika* turned west shortly after leaving Berlin. Hitler did not return to Berlin until the beginning of July – long after the invasion of France had been brought to its triumphant conclusion, and when the time had come for the next stage of the Blitzkrieg, the invasion of England. From May until July, therefore, Quisling had to manage on his own, under Terboven's firm leadership.

ROLL OVER TERBOVEN

Quisling and Terboven met for the first time at the Hotel Bristol on 23 April. Quisling immediately made a very bad impression on Terboven, who found him slow, hesitant and dull, 'not at all the right sort of personality to lead a National Socialist party'. Terboven was later to describe him as 'stupid to the nth degree'. Quisling had failed to be precise on such matters as party finances, membership numbers and local leadership. In Terboven's view, he needed to be replaced.[57]

Terboven's impression of Quisling was similar to that of Bräuer and Habicht, who had both found him most unprepossessing. Both Terboven and Habicht had passed judgement on Quisling after relatively short meetings and with the specific objective of securing his ouster. Even so, it is not difficult to see how they formed their impressions. Quisling's German was slow and halting; besides, he was suspicious of all the questions these Germans were asking, and reluctant to reveal details about his own movement. Part of his slowness was moreover the expression of a general Norwegian characteristic, which the German envoys could have familiarised themselves with from the army's own 'Guidelines for Personal Dealings with the Norwegian Population', which stated that the Norwegians were by nature reticent and withdrawn, 'rather like the Frisian peasants', and should be treated accordingly. But Terboven chose to ignore such tolerant guidelines, especially in view of the fact that he had already decided on the most desirable outcome, that is, a solution in Norway that was independent of both Quisling and the NS.

What or who had originally led Terboven to this conclusion is not clear, as during the days following his appointment, while he was making arrangements for his Kommissariat and constantly travelling between Oslo and Berlin, he must have come into contact with a great many people. It was rumoured within the NS leadership itself that Terboven was acquainted with Hans J. Jacobsen from his student days, and that it was the editor of *Ragnarok* who was poisoning his mind against Quisling. Others suspected Jonas Lie. Neither of these rumours had any basis in reality, as Terboven, prior to his arrival in Oslo, did not know any Norwegians. The fact that Quisling seemed to be Rosenberg's protégé was probably enough to prejudice him against the NS Fører. Moreover, it was certainly quite natural for him not to wish to be tied to a party leader with such a dismal international reputation as Quisling's when he was building up his own administration.[58]

More surprising is that he appears to have received no precise directives from Hitler as to how to handle Quisling. True, at a meeting a few days after their first encounter, Terboven gave assurances of German support for the

[57] Delbrügge, Testimony 1946;* Statement of Ministerialrat Berghold 5 July 1945, *Straffesak* p. 591; Boehm, *Norwegen*, p. 102.
[58] Rumours: Memo 18 July 1940, PAAA Ges. Oslo 245/19; Espeseth, *Livet gikk videre*.

NS, just as Bräuer and Habicht had done. But at the same time he warned Quisling that it would be imprudent to make himself completely reliant on German subsidies. He added that, were he the leader of the NS, he would for political reasons have avoided a situation in which he would be 'supported by the occupying forces and presented as a traitor to the Norwegian people', as this would make him a sitting target for his opponents. Financial support for the NS was duly kept to a cautious minimum.[59] While Hagelin had imagined a monthly loan of around 100,000 Reichsmarks, the actual amounts were much smaller. The party received around 20,000 in May, twice that in June but less again in July and August. Most of the money went on salaries for the rapidly expanding central offices. Only about 10 per cent was available for *Fritt Folk*.[60]

On the other hand, the party did receive help of another sort. In May 1940 three experts from the NSDAP in Germany were appointed to advise the NS on matters concerning propaganda, the Hird and party finances. How far they identified with the party, and to what extent they were trying to exercise influence on behalf of the Reichskommissariat and the occupants, was debatable. The party secretariat viewed the appointments as more of a nuisance than a help. Moreover, Terboven forced Scheidt to leave Norway on 19 May, leaving Quisling without any connections to the German authorities.[61]

Nevertheless, Terboven did in a sense keep his word. The ban on political uniforms was after a while lifted by the Administrative Council for the benefit of the NS. Hird parades quickly became a familiar sight in the larger towns, to the outrage of the majority of the local population, but perhaps with the effect that it did promote party recruitment within the more limited circles where the NS enjoyed a certain popularity.[62]

In the meantime, Terboven had come up with his own plans for a legal solution. On 10 June 1940 King Haakon and his cabinet left northern Norway and fled to London, whereupon the rump of the Norwegian forces capitulated to the Wehrmacht. With the whole country now under the jurisdiction of the Reichskommissar, Terboven decided that the Storting should meet in order to depose the King who was now in exile and set up a

---

[59] Loock, *Quisling*, pp. 339ff, 336f.

[60] Helge Paulsen, 'Rikskommissariat og *motytelsene* under riksrådsforhandlingene', in Paulsen, *1940*, pp. 320ff.

[61] Fuglesang's memorandum 26 June 1945, RA LD 1099 pp. 17ff; Knudsen, *Jeg var Quislings sekretær*, p. 157; Quisling to Terboven 17 June 1940, BA NS 43.

[62] Magne Skodvin, 'Det store fremstøt', in Sverre Steen (ed.), *Norges krig 1940–1945* II (1948).

new government, whereupon the Storting would be permanently dissolved. This new government would have to be co-operative, just as the Administrative Council had been, gradually assuming a more pro-German stance as new members were appointed. With this long-term objective, a political party was needed, a party which would be more effective than any of the old parties at promoting Germany's cause in Norway. With Quisling at its helm, the NS was far too compromised, but with a new leadership the party might stand a good chance of expanding, and some sections of it could perhaps even be incorporated directly into the NSDAP. If this could be accomplished, then Germany would have established a legal government in Norway, simultaneously ensuring that it was subject to political pressure to follow the desired course. In this way Norway would become an occupied yet self-governing territory just like Denmark, related to the Reich through the Foreign Office in Berlin, and the Reichskommissariat could be withdrawn.[63]

Terboven's plan involved multi-level negotiations. On 11 May he included Scheidt in his plans for removing Quisling in order to give the party the opportunity to win popular support. Later he made it clear that he had Jonas Lie in mind as a suitable replacement, and at the end of May he got the Administrative Council to appoint Lie as Chief of Police with a special 'political' mandate, obviously to prepare his way into politics. Terboven also approached Lie unofficially and made him promise to take up the leadership in the event of the party's reorganisation.

When the Norwegian campaign finished on 10 June, the 'renegade circle' of Hjort and Jacobsen, joined by Mogens of the Fatherland League, became active again. After his protests against Quisling in April, Hjort had acted as counsel for the defence at the German courts martial for Norwegians who had been mounting a more or less regular armed resistance to the occupying forces. Now he resumed his political activities, this time aiming to form a national bloc, a new party to replace those who were responsible for 9 April – a merger of various rightist groups such as the Fatherland League, the former NS and preferably the Agrarian Party too, with Mogens as figurehead, Hjort in control and the *Tidens Tegn* as the official organ. Walter Fürst also resurfaced, this time as an administrator in the Labour Service which

---

[63] The main work on the negotiations is Sverre Steen, *Riksrådsforhandlingene* (1947), reprinted in Paulsen, *1940*; greater reliance is placed on German sources by Skodvin, *Striden*; Sverre Hartmann, *Nytt lys over kritiske faser* (1965); and Loock, *Quisling*; see also Ellef Ringnes's memoirs in *Bak okkupasjonens kulisser* (1950).

the Administrative Council agreed to set up and in which the Germans showed a great deal of interest.

Hjort's initiative offered dangerous competition for the NS, and the fact that it was building itself up on German support was obvious. It was clearly the intention of the new bloc to force the NS out of the picture, or even finish the party altogether.[64] On 11 June Mogens went to the NRK and made an impassioned, Quisling-style speech against the old Nygaardsvold government. The government's resistance, he said, was 'the greatest madness in our history', 'the greatest crime ever committed against this tolerant and slow-witted nation'. Two weeks later he lectured on the state and the Constitution, announcing the victory 'of the German system' over 'the old parliamentary system'. *Tidens Tegn* followed the same course. Jacobsen, Hjort and Lie were also given access to the state radio, which was now under the control of the Reichskommissariat's radio department. In addition the NS leadership noted that the head of propaganda at the Kommissariat, Georg Wilhelm Müller, Terboven's second-in-command that summer, was on particularly friendly terms with Mogens, whereas Hjort was often seen in the company of the SS colonel in charge of German security. At the same time, there were clear connections between Hjort's circle and the top-level group with which the Reichskommissariat led official discussions about the new government-to-be in Norway – the presidency of the Storting and the circles round the Administrative Council. Hjort was in fact regularly seen in the company of the president of the Council, Christensen.[65]

On 17 June, the day of the fall of France, Christensen and the Norwegian negotiators agreed to depose the King and dismiss the Nygaardsvold cabinet in order to make way for a Storting-appointed government which would co-operate with the Reichskommissar. The Germans suggested one or two appointments from Quisling's associates, Axel Stang in particular, the rich landowner whose mother had once been lady-in-waiting to the late Queen Maud. Pushed in all directions, the Norwegian negotiators were forced to accept a certain NS presence in the government, but by no means Quisling himself – a condition to which Terboven actually bowed, but in his own particular way: on 25 June he summoned Quisling to his office and asked him to stand down as leader of the NS and to go to Germany in order to

---

[64] Quisling in *Straffesak* p. 90.
[65] Dahl, *Dette er London*, pp. 184, 394; Mogens, *Tyskerne*, pp. 145ff; Norland, *Hårde tider*, pp. 306ff.

take up the study of constitutional law, reassuring him that he could confidently leave the appointment of his successor to him, Terboven.[66]

At first Quisling was completely stunned and could not believe what he was hearing. He protested, arguing that it was absurd to suggest that he, who had done Germany so many services, was obstructing the solution. But Terboven brushed his objections aside by pointing to the consequences of his refusal to agree: a new political movement that would be set up in the space of two months and to which the NS would lose all the subsidies. Quisling had to give in, as the party had been waiting in vain for more generous support and was heavily in debt as it was. If Germany withdrew all financial support, the consequences would in fact be disastrous. However, he continued to argue that this could not possibly be what Hitler wanted, and once more used his argument of 'German loyalty'. Terboven told him that Hitler had hitherto always accepted his suggestions. And not only Hitler, it turned out: the following day, as Quisling reiterated these objections to some of Terboven's men, he discovered that plans were already being made for his imminent departure, which they insisted was in the best interests of the party, suggesting that Quisling become the president of Rosenberg's Nordische Gesellschaft, or perhaps take over the post of Norway's envoy in Rome as the minister there was reaching retirement age. On 29 June Terboven demanded Quisling's signature on a document stating that he agreed to take up temporary residence in Germany. In his absence, the party would be resurrected. He comforted Quisling by reminding him that Hitler too in his time had temporarily withdrawn from the leadership of the NSDAP, after the failed 1923 Munich coup. Before Quisling got a chance to say that he wanted Hagelin to take over in his absence, Terboven announced that he had already appointed Jonas Lie. Quisling protested once more, but gave in to the 'reality of power' when Terboven insisted. A police chief as party leader could only 'benefit the movement' as the Reichskommissar said slyly.

Throughout the entire discussion Hagelin had been waiting outside in the corridor, and was disappointed by Quisling's compliance. Hagelin was a very different character from Quisling. In his discussions with the Germans, he was quick to anger and slow to compromise, something which inspired admiration in the party. On the other hand, his reputation in the Kommis-

---

[66] Quisling's reference to his conversations with Terboven, Stahlecker and Müller in his letter to Hitler 8 July 1940, BA NS 43, also in *Straffesak* (dated 10 July 1940) pp. 66f; the conversation is also referred to in Rosenberg's memo after his discussion with Quisling on 6 July 1940, BA NS 43.

sariat suffered.[67] He clung to his position as Quisling's number two, and was constantly in touch with Rosenberg and Raeder, not to mention Scheidt, to whom he sometimes offered daily reports on events in the Norwegian capital. Unknown to Terboven, Hagelin had access to a telex machine at the legation. The news that Quisling had agreed to Lie's appointment was telegraphed to Berlin on 1 July, but by then Hagelin had already persuaded Quisling to renege on the whole compliance as his agreement had been extracted on the 'emphatic orders of the Reichskommissar'. This proved an intelligent move. Whether on advice from Berlin or not, Terboven took cognisance of Quisling's change of heart and dropped Lie in favour of Hagelin himself. Two days later, on official party notepaper, Hagelin signed himself 'Deputy Fører – Gauleiter von Gross-Oslo'. Together with the former prominent NS figures Herman Harris Aall and Tormod Hustad he managed to set up a front to resist further German demands during Quisling's absence.

WAITING FOR HITLER

On 5 July Quisling flew to Berlin in Terboven's plane, carrying an invitation from Goebbels. One of Terboven's men accompanied him on the flight, obviously under orders to keep an eye on him. After two days at the Hotel Kaiserhof, Scheidt took him to the study centre in Dahlem and found him lodgings there. From then on Rosenberg's office took over, offering him effective protection from Terboven's prying minions.

A certain mystery surrounds Quisling's stay in Germany in the summer of 1940. The forty-five days from 5 July to 20 August are among the least well-documented periods in his adult life. He made only a few entries in his diary and did not keep in touch with the party at home. The telex messages from Scheidt to Hagelin were later burnt for security reasons. Maria waited for news in vain, she recalls in her memoirs, and her anxiety was all the greater because she herself was unwell and had to have an operation.[68] The party

---

[67] Skodvin, *Striden*, pp. 280f; see also Herbeth Noot, statement to Sverre Hartmann 4 October 1954: 'Bei uns galt Hagelin als unehrlich, als ein verschlagener Politiker', INO. Noot belonged to SD and not RK, and did not arrive in Norway until May 1941, but his evaluation certainly reflected the general feeling among the German authorities.

[68] Main sources for Quisling's stay in Germany: Scheidt to Boehm 1955, BA-MA N 172/14, and Hagelin to Schickedanz 29 July 1940, BA NS 43. Rosenberg, Memo 7 July 1940 and Quisling's letter to Hitler 10 July 1940, *Straffesak* pp. 66f. Maria Quisling, *Dagbok*, pp. 124ff. She did not receive a letter until the beginning of August (via Hagelin and Schickedanz),

leadership agonised over what had become of the Fører, and soon the story started to circulate that Quisling was being forced to live incognito in Germany in order to escape contract killers. The story reached Maria, who felt sure that it was Terboven who was threatening her husband's life, which would explain his apparently constant changes of address, and the fact that he was unable to write home.[69]

The reality was somewhat less dramatic. Quisling waited for an audience with Hitler, but circumstances were such that he could not seek one openly without compromising his own position. Listening to the advice of Scheidt, with whom he was in almost daily contact, he remained in Dahlem to make it easier to be received by Hitler, as a meeting would be much harder to arrange from home, and all the more difficult, if not impossible, if Terboven wanted to stop him. It was not, therefore, Gestapo agents Quisling was hiding from but rather his own powerlessness, waiting uncertainly for the day when the issue of who should govern Norway could finally be resolved by being brought before Hitler.

Time passed, one day very like the last. There were few official invitations, but on one occasion he was taken to see the Maginot Line, France's fortress against the East. He was impressed by what he saw: a built-in fortress construction with concealed artillery and supply stores. Exactly how the Germans had managed to overcome it during the western offensive in May was almost a mystery, he explained to Maria later. On another occasion, the Propaganda Minister took him on a tour of the production site of the highly prioritised German film industry. He also visited the Frederick the Great exhibition in Potsdam, and received an invitation from Scheidt's SA regiment.

The most important event of his stay was the grandiose programme put on by Goebbels to celebrate the victory in France, soldiers marching decked in flowers through the Brandenburg Gate and Under den Linden with all Berlin's church bells ringing. Quisling was present in the Reichstag when Hitler gave his resounding 'Victory and Peace' address on 19 July, which contained his final and definitive proposal of peace to Churchill. The Führer talked for two and a half hours, surveying the progress of the war, from Versailles to Poland and the northern flank. He left Denmark out of his

Hagelin and Schickedanz 31 July and 6 August 1940, BA NS 43/26. The Goebbels Diary 4 and 6 July 1940, in *Die Tagebücher von Joseph Goebbels*, ed. Else Fröhlich (1987).

[69] Knudsen, *Jeg var Quislings sekretær*, pp. 157f; Hewins, *Quisling*: 'Quisling's stay in Germany was the most humiliating episode on his path to power and he maintained his well-known silence whenever he was asked about what had happened.'

résumé, but devoted ten minutes to Norway, referring to the Allied plan to attack and to the Norwegian government's compromised neutrality. 'The *Altmark* incident proved that the Norwegian government was not prepared to safeguard its neutrality,' Hitler stated. 'We could glean from our agents' reports that the leading figures in Norway's government had an understanding with the British, something which their reaction to the British mines later left us in no doubt over.' This was an acknowledgement, albeit not an open one, of Quisling's, Scheidt's and Hagelin's efforts at that time to open the eyes of Hitler to the British threat. Hitler went on to praise all the Germans involved in the Norwegian campaign, particularly the navy, and described the undertaking as 'the boldest ever in the history of warfare'.[70]

This was all Quisling had managed to see of Hitler up to that point. Behind the scenes, however, Rosenberg and Raeder were being very active on his behalf. Both the Reichsleiter and the Admiral still closely identified themselves with Quisling and his case as they made their repeated visits to Hitler to discuss the Norwegian problem.

The reasons why Rosenberg stuck to his Norwegian protégé were quite obvious. His foreign department of the NSDAP was constantly hampered by Ribbentrop's Foreign Ministry, by Himmler's SS, and increasingly frustrated by the military leadership too. In fact, after the campaign in the West he had no discernible regional influence at all. France and Belgium were under military rule, and there was no room for political influence. Holland had been subject to a Reichskommissariat directly under the orders of the Führer, and Denmark was officially an independent state under Ribbentrop's jurisdiction. Rosenberg had tried to exert influence in eastern Europe, but this had so far borne no fruit. Thus Norway remained his special area of concern, with Quisling as his main project. If Rosenberg wanted plausible influence in Norway he would have to remain committed to his man Scheidt's work, and could not, like Terboven, look around for alternatives.

Raeder's enduring faith in Quisling is harder to explain. While Rosenberg was caught up in various ideological arguments which lent a somewhat irrational colour to his conduct, Raeder was of an entirely different calibre, yet both he and his representative in Norway, General Admiral Hermann Boehm, stood firmly behind Quisling too. The reasons why remain to this day obscure. It has been suggested that their loyalty can be explained in the context of an ideology of 'naval National Socialism', to the right of

---

[70] M. Domarus, *Hitler* (1963) pp. 1539ff.

mainstream NSDAP, and close to Quisling's own ideology.[71] However, Raeder's support is more likely to have been strategically rather than ideologically informed: the navy saw Terboven as basically Göring's 'man', and Göring as head of the airforce was himself the navy's main rival in terms of armament priorities. He was, moreover, in charge of the four-year plan which would also ensure that the airforce's need for light metal and electrical power took priority over the navy's need for submarine bases and shipyards. To counteract the Terboven–Göring connection, Quisling became an asset – or rather a pawn – in the navy–airforce rivalry.

The news from Oslo that reached Rosenberg from Hagelin during July 1940 was clearly alarming: Terboven and his Kommissariat were now openly supporting the Hjort–Mogens–Jacobsen circle, trying to strangle the NS economically and to put all possible political obstacles in the way of Hagelin's leadership. The reports that simultaneously went from Boehm to Raeder suggested that Terboven, under cover of the law, wanted to pursue a tough line in Norway, something along the lines of making Norway a *gau* in a Greater Germany – very disturbing news indeed. Rosenberg and Raeder thus had several arguments at their disposal when they went to Hitler to warn him of Terboven's policy. Their main point was that Terboven's quasi-legal solution would immediately push the Anglophiles into the Norwegian government. Frustrating Quisling was not to Germany's advantage, and could indeed have disastrous consequences, they maintained. With each day that passed without the NS forming a government and winning over the Norwegian people to the idea of 'a voluntary solution', the greater was the hold the Anglophile circles were gaining on public opinion.

Terboven was fully aware of what Raeder and Rosenberg were up to and did his utmost to neutralise their influence. In July he made frequent visits to Berlin, sometimes for extended stays, with the same purpose as Quisling – to be ready for an audience with Hitler. By the end of July the Führer had at last arrived at some sort of decision, at least for the time being, and called for his Reichskommissar.[72] He preferred to stand by Quisling and ordered Terboven to work together with Rosenberg. Rosenberg and Terboven were unable to reach an understanding when they met on 20 July. Terboven still hoped that Hitler would be won over to his line. When, on the following day, he came back to Oslo, he informed his associates of the new directive

---

[71] Loock, *Quisling*, pp. 492–500.
[72] There is only an indirect source for this: see Helge Paulsen, 'Terboven i konflikt med Kriegsmarine' (1972) p. 71.

from Berlin, and of how Quisling was presumably to return as the leader of the NS, subsidised by Germany. He himself was to conclude the negotiations with the presidents of the Storting with a view to setting up a government along the lines of the June negotiations, which would mean deposing the King and removing the Nygaardsvold government from office, and installing a new government through the Storting.[73]

By early August rumours were running high in Norway. The NS suddenly became optimistic; its leading members started to prepare for cabinet careers. But Quisling's opponents were also on the alert. Victor Mogens acknowledged as a reality that a party to the right of the NS was no longer feasible and began calling meetings to discuss various forms of co-operation, to which he invited a young NS member, Tore Hamsun, the author Knut Hamsun's son. Hjort for his part was now convinced that the best way to thwart Quisling's comeback was to mobilise the old parties; he started to draft a manifesto for a united party, Rikspartiet, which would be made up of all the parliamentary parties. Alarmed by the rumours of Quisling's break-through with Hitler, representatives of the central committees of all four main parties actually met and set up a joint committee. So successful was Hjort's initiative that it was immediately torpedoed by Terboven, who had the participants summoned one by one and forced them to withdraw, as a united national front composed of all parties in a single organisation ran counter to the new signals from Berlin: getting the presidents of the Storting to accept a government solution that was in some way based on Quisling.[74]

In fact a time of most difficult manoeuvres started for the Reichskom-missar. On the one hand he had to carry out Hitler's wishes to stick to Quisling; on the other he had to find a solution acceptable to the Norwegian negotiators from the Storting; thirdly he had to take into account his own position and the future of the Reichskommissariat in the long term. His associates drafted several scenarios, varying the degrees of Quisling's influence, the legality of the Storting-based Norwegian independence, together with a greater or lesser degree of permanence for the Reichs-

---

[73] Hartmann, *Nytt lys*, p. 104; Loock, *Quisling*, pp. 489f.

[74] 14 August 1940 'Retningslinjer for Rikspartiet': meeting of Agrarian Party working committee 20 August in a letter from Dietrichson to Smitt Ingebretsen 22 August 1940, NBA; draft arrangement and manifesto, ibid.; Dietrichson to Moseid 27 August 1940, with reference to meetings with Dr Knab the previous day, ibid.; note from von Weizsäcker after a visit from Hjort in AA 5 August 1940, PAAA 12/169 Büro Staatssekretär, Nicht-Diplomatbesuche.

kommissariat. All these documents show that the situation was above all fluid and far from clear.[75]

On 16 August Quisling finally got his audience with Hitler. For months Rosenberg had been bombarding the Chancellery with file upon file of reports from Hagelin and Scheidt. Hitler had read some, although obviously not all, of this vast documentation, and now he wanted to hear Quisling's assessment of the situation.[76]

Quisling responded with a complaint about how badly he had been treated by Bräuer, Habicht and Terboven. Hitler agreed with him that the two diplomats were 'impossible'. Terboven, on the other hand, he said, should not be seen as an enemy, as he had at least spoken well of the NS to Hitler, and his mistakes could be put down to his unfamiliarity with the Norwegian situation. Hitler then asked Quisling which solution *he* would recommend, and Quisling replied unequivocally: an NS government independent of the Storting, even, if so desired, without his own participation. Quisling assured Hitler that he had no personal interest in gaining power. Then the Storting could be dissolved and the NS built up. He does not appear to have given his opinion of the Reichskommissariat, but told Hitler that, although he had no objections to it in principle, he would have preferred it to have a different title. Hitler agreed with him wholeheartedly and promised him the leadership in Norway.

For Quisling, this meeting was a tremendous relief, a source of encouragement in times to come. At last, after a month and a half of waiting, he had managed to win Hitler over. The Führer spoke to him warmly and respectfully, thanking him for his warnings about Britain during the December talks, giving him all the assurances he needed in order to resume his work in Norway.

News of the meeting reached the party even before Quisling touched down at Fornebu airport on 20 August. The Hird stood guard. Hagelin headed the reception committee. The Fører was returning in triumph. At the same time Terboven left for Berlin to be briefed by Hitler: they must have discussed the wider strategy, and reached an agreement on all essential points. On 4 September, after Terboven had been back to Norway and had sounded Quisling out, there was a further meeting between Hitler and

---

[75] Paulsen in Paulsen, *1940*, p. 310ff.

[76] The meeting is known through the account of Scheidt, who was present: 4 September 1940, BA NS 43, also printed in Seraphim, *Tagebuch Alfred Rosenbergs*.

Terboven, in which it was finally decided how Quisling should be supported as the future centre of power in Norway.

However, Hitler made it clear that there was no question of Terboven's removal. In August he had come to the conclusion that the presence of the occupying forces should remain as strong as possible both in Holland and in Norway. This decision led to a contingency plan for what Terboven should do in the event of his negotiations with the presidency failing: a Kommissariat-led government appointed by Terboven himself be replaced by a Quisling cabinet when the NS had gained sufficient strength.[77]

On 5 September Quisling was officially notified in person, flown down from Fornebu in the morning and received at the Chancellery for a brief but nevertheless crucial audience the same evening. Everything was confirmed. He was to acquire power in Norway, following a provisional solution which would give him time to build up his movement to a respectable strength.

LAST ROUND OF NEGOTIATIONS

Terboven soon ran into difficulties over trying to negotiate a solution that accorded with the Führer's orders concerning the three elements: the Reichskommissariat, the Storting and the NS all participating in the setting up of the new government.

Quisling accepted the Reichskommissariat, but rejected the Storting. To endue the presidents of the Norwegian parliament with the right to appoint the members of the new government at that time and in the case of future vacancies would be to act against Germany's interests, he maintained. Terboven read his words as an affirmation that on his own, without German support, Quisling was a nonentity as a political figure in Norway.

The presidents of the Storting for their part accepted the NS – but only to a certain degree. Instead of one NS member, as in June, they had to accept four at the final negotiations in September. But when Terboven came up with demands for a fifth NS member – the lawyer Herman Harris Aall – they refused. To fill the new cabinet with so many of Quisling's men was unacceptable, they told Terboven's negotiator.

The reason why Terboven increased his demands for NS participation was

---

[77] Telegram from Dr Walther Weber in the Reichskommissariat to the Commercial Policy Division, AA 29 August 1940, PAAA 34/96 Ha-Pol Wiehl, Norwegen 1932–42.

partly because of pressure from Quisling and Hagelin, now backed by considerable moral support from Berlin, and partly the need to counteract a growing feeling among the Norwegians that they should perhaps not denounce their King so completely as the presidents advised them to do. When the members of the Storting gathered in Oslo on 10 September to endorse the result of the negotiation, they voted 75–55 to remove the King so as to leave the way open for a government solution 'necessitated by the war'. A definite abdication was turned down, as the MPs hoped that the future peace treaty with Germany which the new government would ensure would allow for the King to be reinstated – or possibly his son or grandson, at least in the future. Growing demands on both sides, then, sealed the fate of the legal restructuring. The negotiators from the Storting refused to accept Mr Aall in the cabinet, not because the difference between four and five NS ministers mattered greatly, but from a feeling that each time they gave in to German pressure, new demands would be made; somewhere a line between the constitutionally acceptable and the revolutionary solutions had to be drawn. And they were right: the next move from Terboven would have been to extract declarations of loyalty to Quisling not only from the NS members of the cabinet but from an additional three or four of the remaining cabinet ministers, so as to secure Quisling's control over the government.[78]

To his fellow countrymen, Quisling during these negotiations played the role of a dark, evil outsider: never a formal part of the official discussions, never in dialogue with the Storting's presidents or the other Norwegian negotiators, but only with the Germans. With Terboven's men, Quisling and Hagelin drew up the new government in secrecy, discussing the composition of ministries, the ministers, the various cabinet functions. The Germans wanted to recast the cabinet structure according to their own model, so as to promote the *Aufsichtsverwaltung* – the government surveillance – from Berlin. Quisling and Hagelin accordingly advised them on what structural changes should be implemented: the setting up of a Ministry of the Interior, a Ministry of Propaganda, a Ministry for Labour Service, a separate Ministry for the Police and so forth: altogether thirteen ministries instead of the usual Norwegian eight.

Thus Quisling's role became a strange one in the official negotiations. He

---

[78] Quisling, *Almanach 1940*, RA; Quisling to Terboven 10 September 1940, IfZ MA 110; *Straffesak* p. 100.

was the trump that Terboven's negotiator threatened to throw on the table whenever the Norwegians hesitated to accept his demands. 'The alternative is Quisling,' the negotiator Dr Dellbrügge would say to intimidate his opposite numbers, and the Norwegians would swallow another humiliation. The 'dark outsider' himself seemed unaffected by the role. Quisling prepared for government, confident that the official negotiations would break down, well satisfied with the position he had at last won among the Germans. He had met with Hitler three times that summer: on 16 August, when the Führer declared that he was putting his faith in him, then again on 5 and 11 September when the details of the NS *Machtergreifung* were worked out in the presence of Dr Lammers and Martin Bormann, the NSDAP Party Minister: a transition government, either legal or commissarial, with a majority of NS or NS-loyal ministers, then after a period of heavy consolidation of the party with German support in the course of some six months, a proper Quisling government with the Fører as Prime Minister.

The talks at the Reich Chancellery in Berlin were, of course, most encouraging to him, overshadowing the humiliations of 15 April. Hitler in fact deplored his dismissal from government then, blaming the diplomats Bräuer and Habicht for having misinformed him altogether. The Reich Propaganda Minister Joseph Goebbels apparently was of the same opinion. Prior to the talks with Hitler, Goebbels received him, eager to see this 'mysterious Quisling' with his own eyes. Goebbels listened to Quisling's life story with sympathy and noted in his diary that Quisling had been treated 'unjustly' in April. 'He is no traitor to his country and certainly no idiot,' although 'more a professor than a politician, and scarcely a national leader,' the great propagandist said to himself. Goebbels indeed found no mystery about him at all: Quisling was 'a typical reddish Germanic blond, a little tired, a little absent-minded'.[79] Quisling felt that the hour-long conversation with Goebbels had been to his advantage. As for his relationship with Hitler, he had clearly fallen victim to the Führer's well-known charisma. Throughout their meetings in the summer of 1940 he felt he had been taken into Hitler's personal confidence, evident in the warmth of the handshake, the intense staring eyes, the special glow which seemed to promise so much and demanded such unquestioned loyalty. It was of course part of the daily reality in the Third Reich that the Führer bound his men to him by a

---

[79] The Goebbels Diary 4 and 6 July 1940.

certain hypnotism, as he himself put it, or blew them up like 'inflatable animals' in order to ensure their loyalty and commitment to the party and the cause. Even Goebbels and Speer attested time and again to the fact that nobody was completely immune to Hitler's spell.[80]

But to what extent was Hitler sincere in his assurances that there was a 'special relationship' between himself and Quisling? Hitler's decision to appoint him as his trustee and head of government in Norway was, Quisling thought, a fulfilment of the promises from December. But in fact the choice, seen from the perspective of the summer of 1940, implied at least two more important and separate decisions: the preference for a quasi-legal solution, and the decision to retain the Reichskommissar at all costs. The two decisions were made in completely different contexts, although it is not possible to determine what precisely had led Hitler to reach them.

Hitler had always favoured legal governments in occupied countries. At the beginning of September 1940 he took great care to avoid risks, as he was balancing the strategic advantages of going to war against Great Britain – Operation Seelöwe – with going to war against the Soviet Union (Operation Barbarossa).[81] The arguments in favour of an eastern offensive necessitated taking no risks in Norway. A legal solution would be preferable because in the short run it would cause minimal upheaval. Consequently Hitler preferred the Storting to vote in the new government.

The decision to retain the Reichskommissar was informed by quite other factors. During August Hitler decided to keep German troops in Norway for the winter and to bring in reinforcements in order to withstand a Soviet attack or, possibly, even to support an offensive against Petsamo. It was news of Russian movements in the North which set in train this series of events. A German administrative apparatus in Norway was therefore a logical undertaking. At the same time a corresponding move was made regarding the occupation regime in Holland: on 23 September Mussert was summoned by Hitler and assured that he would be given a more prominent role, at the same time as the Reichskommissariat was being strengthened as

---

[80] 'Inflatable animals': comment overheard by Terboven and related to Valentin Feuerstein, possibly made after 7–18 April 1943 when Hitler had received Mussolini, Horthy, Antonescu and Quisling at Schloss Klessheim: see Valentin Feuerstein, *Irrwege der Pflicht* (1963); another, less objective version is given by Ernst Züchner in 1945, *Straffesak* p. 602, in which he states that Hitler specifically referred to Quisling as an 'inflatable pig'.

[81] Jurgen Förster, 'Der historische Ort des Unternehmens "Barbarossa"', in Wolfgang Michalka (ed.), *Der Zweite Weltkrieg: Analysen, Grundzüge, Forschungsbilanz* (1989) pp. 626ff; Skodvin, *Striden*, p. 296; Loock, *Quisling*, pp. 510ff.

the main body of the occupation administration.[82] In both cases it was considerations of military preparations which led to these decisions. The alternative was to introduce direct military control as in France and Belgium, but this was thought to be too drastic and would create unnecessary alarm.

But Hitler's idea of a legal revolution in Norway failed. On 18 September, after repeated stalling on the German side, the negotiations in Oslo finally and conclusively broke down. Thus Terboven was left with Hitler's contingency plan, which in fact may have been his own preferred course all along – that is, a commissarial government in direct control of Norway until Quisling was considered strong enough to take over again

WHY QUISLING?

On 22 September 1940 Terboven gathered together the German civil and military commanders-in-chief at his residence at Skaugum. This was the first time that such a top-level meeting had been held since 30 June, when Terboven had declared Quisling 'stupid to the nth degree'. Now his task was to persuade his people to co-operate with him.

Terboven began by outlining the conditions he had found when he had first arrived in Norway, namely the limited competence of the Administrative Council and its complete lack of influence in the country as a whole: 'Chaos ruled everywhere.' The political parties were all Anglophile, except for Quisling's NS, which unfortunately lacked influence, and its members were 'everywhere derided as traitors'. But slowly Quisling had succeeded in reversing the image, having started out with only twelve party officials, and now employing 250. This improvement in his fortunes was most reassuring, as the channels of national communication were in process of being resumed and exploited to Germany's advantage.

'The Führer's stance with regard to Quisling is as follows,' announced Terboven. All present immediately understood that he was referring to Hitler's revised opinion, which now held Quisling to be 'the only Norwegian to have taken up Germany's cause'. Terboven had learned that Hitler on several occasions before the war was warned of the dangers of a British invasion of Norway, warnings which had slowly come to nothing: 'Then in

---

[82] Konrad Kweit, *Reichskommissariat Niederlande* (1968) pp. 92f; Hirschfeld, *Nazi Rule*, pp. 19ff; Loock, *Quisling*, p. 509.

December 1939 Quisling visited the Führer. His arguments were so compelling that the Führer was convinced of Britain's sinister intentions. From that
moment on the Führer started to make plans for his Norwegian initiative.
For this unquestionable service, Quisling is deserving of every help and
support from Germany.'[83] The concluding sentence was carefully underlined
in the notes which Admiral Boehm's secretary wrote up. Indeed, it expresses
the heart of the matter. Contrary to the situation in April, Terboven was
now aware of the fact that Hitler himself regarded the December conversations with Quisling as decisive for his determination to pre-empt the British
with his action in Norway.

But what precisely did Hitler mean by this? It was not as if Quisling's visit
in itself had led to the occupation. The decision to attack Norway had been
prompted, as Hitler himself stated in his speech to the Reichstag of 19 July,
by the *Altmark* episode of mid-February 1940. But the fact that the decision
to go north had been taken at all was a direct result of the December
warnings. Between December and February the military and naval leadership
had been carrying out a number of studies which provided the basis for
General von Falkenhorst's brief when he was called to Berlin and charged
with leading Operation Weserübung on 21 February. In fact, only a few days
after he had assumed command, von Falkenhorst received a comprehensive
report which provided the basis for further strategic planning. Von Falkenhorst's own work soon made it clear that the only possible time for the
execution of the offensive was at the first new moon in April. A new moon
was absolutely necessary for such a fully-fledged strategic attack as this one
would have to be. The March new moon was too soon for them to set off,
and May too late in terms of night darkness, which in the opinion of the
navy was essential for a successful operation. Weserday therefore had to be
scheduled for early April – or not at all. Hitler, who had the campaign in
western Europe preying on his mind, was aware of this. It was in this context

---

[83] Record of the meeting at Skaugum 22 October 1940 signed Weisshaupt, BA-MA RM 45/
Norwegen. Statement of 5 June 1945 from Finn Dahl, C. Erlandsen and J. F. Hansen in
Norsk Arbeidsgiverforening (Union of Norwegian Employers), about what Dr Kurt Gusko
told them of the contents of Terboven's speech just before he left the country in January
1941, RA LD 29 Q div. 7. Terboven was unaware of Quisling's December talks with Hitler
when he arrived in Norway. Scheidt tried to inform him, but the handwritten communication he wrote at the end of April 1940 and gave to Wegener (see Scheidt's report 22 May
1940, BA NS 43) does not seem to have reached Terboven. In fact, in July 1940 Rosenberg
attacked Terboven for his seeming ignorance of Quisling's role (Memo 22 July 1940,
printed in Steen, *Riksrådsforhandlingene*); on Terboven's lack of insight into Hitler's
promises, see also Dellbrügge's statement 1946.

that the help he received from the Norwegian Major had to be acknowledged. Without it, the planning would have started after the *Altmark*
incident in February – too late to be accomplished in time.[84]

Terboven's staff understood well that this dramatic information had to be
handled as top secret. Any leakage could easily make Quisling's reputation
even more shaky than it already was. But at least one of them could not keep
quiet. In January 1941 Dr Kurt Gusko, head of the social and labour
divisions at the Reichskommissariat, related in confidence to his Norwegian
counterparts in Norsk Arbeidsgiverforening (Union of Norwegian Employers) the story of Quisling's December 1939 meetings with Hitler, just
before he himself was about to leave the country. From there the information was later passed on to the leadership of the Home Front in Norway.
Still the secret remained almost unknown until it was brought out during
Quisling's trial in 1945.

In his talk, Terboven went on to outline some of the consequences of
Quisling's 'unquestionable service' to Germany. Two days later, he told his
staff, he planned to make a speech on the radio which would clarify the
political situation in Norway from the German side. The political parties
except for the NS would have to be liquidated and the lodges broken up, the
Norwegian Jews would come under the Nuremberg laws – and the NS
would be assured the full support of the authorities. A cabinet made up of
acting heads of government departments would be formed.

By Wednesday 25 September, the list was ready. With that, Terboven
announced that the 'commissary' phase of the country's history was about
to begin. Two days later the thirteen new department heads were summoned
to his Storting office in order to receive their official appointment as acting
ministers.

---

[84] The earliest and best account of the German plans for Norway is B. H. Liddell Hart, *The
Other Side of the Hill* (1951), ch. 'The Brauchitsch–Halder Era', based on interviews with
German General Staff officers.

6

Leader on probation

I am no prophet. But what I predicted has come to pass. And I tell you all now, that what Norway once was, she will once more become, despite all the difficulties. *Quisling in the Coliseum cinema, 12 March 1941*[1]

Quisling was not present when the new cabinet was appointed on 25 September, but immediately afterwards summoned the ministers. From then on, the NS members among them – ten of the thirteen – met every Thursday as if they were at ordinary cabinet meetings. Quisling would sit at one end of the table with Fuglesang, the cabinet secretary, at the other. In addition, weekly cabinet meetings were convened with all thirteen present and the most senior minister in the chair. In his capacity as NS Fører, Quisling was often present even at these occasions. Thus the new government really had two heads: Terboven off-stage, and Quisling as acting Prime Minister.[2]

However, the thirteen commissarial ministers appointed by Terboven did not technically constitute a cabinet. The Reichskommissar had the right under international law to make use of the Norwegian civil service. He gave each ministry a head, and each head was placed under the supervision of an administrative chief – *Berater* – from the Kommissariat. The Germans referred to this arrangement as an *Aufsichtsverwaltung,* a supervisory administration, soon to be introduced in Holland too. The Germans did not run the administration directly but made sure that the national civil service did so; the only administrative tasks they carried out themselves were to run their own police and censorship of the press.[3]

Nevertheless, the commissarial ministers did resemble a cabinet in as much as the majority of them, in addition to having been appointed by Terboven, were bound by a written pledge of loyalty to Quisling. It was he who had decided on both the structure of the ministries and the personnel, albeit in

---

[1] *FF* 13 March 1941.

[2] Helge Paulsen, 'Litt om forholdet mellom NS og Reichskommissariat', in Danielsen and Larsen, *Fra idé til dom,* pp. 200f.

[3] The term 'Aufsichtsverwaltung' was developed by the SS lawyer Werner Best (who later became Reich plenipotentiary in Denmark) in 1941. See Hirschfield, *Nazi Rule,* pp. 132f; Hans Umbreit, 'Auf dem Weg zur Kontinentalherrschaft', *DRZW* 5 (1988) pp. 97f.

conjunction with Terboven, but certainly with his own long-term interests in mind – building up the party and himself as future prime minister. Unlike the individual ministers, Quisling did not have a designated *Berater* over him, either in his capacity as party Fører or as shadow Prime Minister.[4]

THE NEW ORDER

Hagelin headed the new Ministry for the Interior, modelled on the Reichsinnenministerium and designed to take care of a great many political issues, among others the planning of a Riksting, the introduction of the *fører* principle into all areas of the administration, as well as the supervision of public servants. It was an extraordinary career for a former architecture student turned opera singer who had lived the whole of his adult life making money in Germany and never touched politics. The Department for Labour Service and Athletics was entrusted to the young Axel Stang. The Labour Service (Arbeidstjenesten or AT) was something close to the heart and the manifesto of the NS, although Quisling had never envisaged a separate department for it. However, if the AT was to function as a conscription centre for compulsory labour service for the country's youth, then it did merit its own department.

The Ministry of Churches and Schools was headed by Professor Ragnar Skancke, and the new Ministry of Culture and Public Information (in Quisling's drafts the Propaganda Department) by Guldbrand Lunde. Two of the dissenting ministers of 9 April were thus back in office; the third, Frederik Prytz, was made district governor in Sør-Trøndelag as Hagelin, in his intrigues with the Germans, had used every means possible to prevent Quisling's oldest friend from holding any cabinet post. The fourth, Jonas Lie, was forced on Quisling by Terboven. Quisling had no choice but to give in, but he remained distrustful of the 'renegade Lie' even though Lie's behaviour never indicated that he was working against either the party or its Fører. The gifted lawyer Sverre Riisnæs was assigned the Ministry of Justice. He was a public prosecutor and had previously acted in this role against the NS Trotsky gang in 1936; now he pledged 'to do his utmost on behalf of the party'. Hagelin's brother-in-law Kjeld Stub Irgens, a well-known captain in the merchant marine, was given a ministry tailor-made for him: the Ministry

---

[4] Debes, *Sentraladministrasjonens historie*, p. 86, and ch. 10 'Departmentsordningen under okkupasjonen'; *RKVB* 1940/7; various documents in Th. Dahl-Saken, RA LD 4088 Dahl; Laila Kristiansen, 'NS og nyordningen av arbeidslivet' (thesis) UiO 1972, ch. 1.

of Shipping, and one of Quisling's old classmates from the Drammen Latin School, the veterinary surgeon and forester Thorstein Fretheim, was appointed Minister of Agriculture.

Three ministries were given to independent experts: the Ministries of Supplies, Trade and Industry, and Finance. There are no records of any conflicts between these three independents and the NS Party, but the three did constitute a distinct group within the unofficial government in that they did not sign the declaration of loyalty to Quisling and did not attend his weekly meetings.

With these men, Quisling set out to lay the foundations of what was now commonly called 'the New Order' in Norway – by stamping out any trace of what he termed 'the destructive principles of the French Revolution: representation, dialogue and collegiality', above all the principles of party pluralism and parliamentary rule.[5]

The most important part of this undertaking was the reform of the local municipalities led by the young NS judge, Ole Vries Hassel, now one of Hagelin's department heads, who proved to have an exceptionally practical approach to constitutional reforms. Hassel transformed the existing mayors into real leaders by giving them *fører* power from above, while democratic or elected bodies disappeared altogether from the municipalities – their term expired by 1 January 1941 anyway. During the spring of 1941 one municipality after another was restructured, and in most cases the mayors – irrespective of which of the old parties they had been voted in by – went over to the NS. Where this did not happen, the mayor was replaced by somebody on the central municipal council who was either a party member or who had no objections to becoming one. By the end of 1941 the overwhelming majority of the hundreds of mayors were NS, and the old party system to all intents and purposes was wound up.[6]

Next in importance to the abolition of parliamentary democracy, the party manifesto called for the spiritual life of the nation to be guided. This was now the task of Guldbrand Lunde and his people in the new Ministry of Culture. The NS was the only party demanding substantial state subsidy for culture, albeit with definite demands that art and cultural institutions should 'promote the interests of the nation'. The budget for culture was

---

[5] Quisling's speech to leaders of municipalities 5 June 1941, in *FF* 6 June 1941.

[6] NS Personalkontor to Ministry of the Interior 27 October 1942, RA NSRG Personalavd. 1, and the NS statistic of January 1942, RA LD 4088 Th. Dahl. Quite a few of the NS mayors came from the Labour Party according to Tore Pryser, *Arbeiderbevegelsen og NS* (1991) pp. 100ff.

substantially increased and the existing cultural institutions overhauled with a view to complete restructuring. The first to be reshaped was the Norwegian News Bureau (NTB) and the Broadcasting Corporation (NRK). In the first directive issued by the commissarial government on 27 September 1940, the task of such institutions was defined as being 'to serve the interests of the Norwegian people'. The NTB was placed under a director who was given full authority while in broadcasting a 'state plenipotentiary' was appointed as the head of an expanded college of four directors with responsibilities for administration, technical matters, music and programmes – all of them NS members. In January 1941 the department took over control of the allocation of all arts grants in order to ensure that the distribution was 'impartial'. In February a directive was issued concerning the 'protection of Norwegian literature' which gave the department complete and indisputable permission to confiscate any book which was 'harmful to national and social progress'. Booksellers and libraries were instructed to clear their stocks and holdings of a long list of titles of blasphemous, psychoanalytic, Marxist and Jewish literature. The most important 'subversive' publishing houses were dealt with: the Labour Party press, Tiden, was closed, and the largest literary publisher, Gyldendal, of which Knut Hamsun was a major shareholder, was assigned the author's son Tore as its head, following the arrest of its director by the Germans. In this way, the limits of acceptable publishing were clearly defined for other publishers. [7]

Next came the offensive against the cinemas. Existing legislation concerning film censorship was duly extended, and from April 1941 it was not only the showing in public but also the importing, renting and production of films which was forbidden without the prior permission of the department. In this way, brakes could be put on what Quisling used to call the 'overwhelming mass of Hollywood films which has been thrust upon the Norwegian market'. A special film directorate was set up, followed by the reorganisation of the theatres: theatre directors had to be approved by the department and were held accountable for the content of their productions. [8]

---

[7] Helge Giverholt, *Nyhetsformidling i Norge*; Dahl, *Dette er London*; List of forbidden literature, and Lists 2 and 3, UBO Krigstrykksamlingen; A. Kildal, *Presse- og litteraturfronten* (1945) pp. 303ff; H. N. Østbye, *Jødenes krig* (Oslo 1943) pp. 40ff. Censorship of books came in more generally with the law on the publishing of printed matter 26 February 1942.

[8] Odd Melsom, *Fra kirke- og kulturkampen* (1980). Quisling's speech Frankfurt 28 March 1941, *Kampen mellem arier og jødemakt* (1941) p. 8; censorship in general: Kildal, *Presse-*; 'Norsk åndsliv på vegen heim', lecture series, NRK, winter 1941–2, Oslo 1942; T. C. Wyller, *Fra okkupasjonsårenes maktkamp* (1953) pp. 113f.

There are no similar directives to be found regarding the press in the minutes of cabinet meetings. The Norwegian press was to a great extent a party press and closely tied to parliamentary activities. But apart from the ordinance regarding the NTB there were no cabinet resolutions on the subject. Not until later was it prohibited to launch a new newspaper or to close down an old one, but there was never any general demand for licensing. The contents of newspapers were unofficially controlled through pressure, but never formally censored or vetted. The Ministry set up a Press Directorate which issued daily directives to the editors through a circular. These directives were considered binding even though the directorate itself did not have the authority to take disciplinary measures. It had to lean on the not inconsiderable authority of the Reichskommissariat's Press Division, which carried out censorship and also summoned the editors to daily briefings on what foreign news to publish and what not. A broad spectrum of disciplinary measures was available, ranging from German police action, raids and arrests to regulations concerning paper rationing which could threaten the very existence of the newspapers. All in all, the system worked both to the advantage of the occupying forces and to the NS's satisfaction, despite not being formalised in any particular law or ordinance. The Police Department was in addition given the authority to censor mail and telegrams for the purpose of 'maintaining public calm and order', and no doubt political order too.[9]

Concern for Nordic genetic material in the population and its capacity for quantitative reproduction played a significant role in Quisling's political thinking: 'Our aim is to make sure that the Norwegian people by the turn of the century number 10 million,' he declared in 1941. His calculation was based on the fact that there were 3 million Norwegians living in the country and a further 3 million abroad, mainly in the United States. If 1 million were to be persuaded to return to Norway and if there were a significant increase in the number of children, by the year 2000 the population might reach 10 million. Re-immigration would have to wait until after the war, but the battle against contraception, which had broken the bond between sex and procreation, could be started without delay: 'The race is being weakened in the cities, and we are in a sense a dying nation,' he reminded an assembly of agricultural representatives in February 1941.[10] In July that year a decree was issued

---

[9] Law prohibiting the publication of new newspapers without permission, no. 2, 11 February 1942; Kildal, *Presse-*, ch. 3; Guri Hjeltnes, *Avisoppgjøret etter 1945* (1990), ch. 'Aviser i okkupert land'; Gunnar T. Foss, *Den undertrykte presse* (1990).

[10] *FF* 19 February and 3 June 1941.

ordering the closure of all the family planning centres which had been opened in the inter-war years. This cleared the way for the establishment of new health centres for mothers and children, subsidised directly by the municipalities with a view to increasing the birth-rate. This was followed in December by another decree which severely restricted the sale of contraceptives.

The Ministry of the Interior, which was responsible for the nation's genetic heritage, was also given a Corporations Office, which was to take on the task Quisling had been championing for so long: the registration and control of the country's voluntary organisations in order to make them corporate members of the state. All sorts of organisations allowed themselves to be registered without protest during spring 1941, and far-reaching legal measures of registration and control, of compulsory mergers and even the closing down of unwarranted organisations were prepared by the Ministry. However, in the course of months the organisations became the centre of a new, non-politically motivated opposition to Quisling and the NS. Initiated by the cartel of public functionaries who feared the NS's intention of appointing only party members in the civil service, a protest in the form of an open letter to Terboven was signed by a number of national organisations expressing discontent with the commissarial ministers and the NS in general. From this point a national stand in the form of widespread civil disobedience and political opposition emerged.[11]

Quisling considered the letter to Terboven, the prelude to all this, as symptomatic of the old business and political élite's clinging to positions of power, in parallel with the struggle of the old professional politicians. At the NS Whitsun meeting of 1941 he explained the situation in this way:

There was a small clique in the country which used to call itself the representatives of the people's will – a few politicians and a few newspapers. Some of these people are terrorising the Norwegian people and the NS. There are also writers, artists, trade unionists and the very wealthy who also belong to certain small cliques. But I know ... that the NS in reality has the majority of the Norwegian people behind it, even though large groups among the population dare not join [the party] for fear of terrorisation of these cliques. I know this to be a fact ... By their letters to Reichskommissar Terboven these people have in fact signed their own death warrants.[12]

Thus half a year after its introduction, the new government order showed its determination to establish itself by force.

---

[11] The standard work on the resistance put up by organisations is T. C. Wyller, *Nyordning og motstand* (1958).

[12] Quisling's speech at Borre, *FF* 3 June 1941.

BUILDING THE PARTY

On 26 September 1940 the NS had become the only legal party in Norway as a result of Terboven's decree outlawing all other parties and ordering their dissolution. This kind of party monopoly followed the German Reich pattern from July 1933 onwards, when all parties, with the exception of the NSDAP, were explicitly outlawed.

There is nothing to indicate that Quisling remonstrated at the introduction of a similar regulation in Norway, although he had never himself seriously contemplated doing away with the other parties. In the 1930s when he and his associates were discussing outlawing the Labour parties, they did so in the context of these particular parties' revolutionary and subversive, and therefore illegal, organisations. It was more a non-party system than a one-party system that he had always envisaged – a return to the old élitist state preceding the introduction of parliamentary government in Norway in 1884.

The NS monopoly meant that a big coalition party had to be built up gradually in the vacuum left by the old parties. This happened quickly. Immediately after 25 September the old Labour Party's assets were made over to the NS through a decree from the Ministry of the Interior; the NS mouthpiece *Fritt Folk* was thus able to take over *Arbeiderbladet*'s offices and be printed free on the paper's press; the Labour-owned *Aktietrykkeri* was renamed *NS Press*; the Culture and Information Department moved into the party's central premises, with Lunde in the Labour Party leader's old office overlooking Youngstorget. The other parties were similarly dissolved within months and their assets turned over to the NS. The newly built Conservative Party headquarters in central Oslo was renamed Hird House and the Oslo branch of NS moved in too. The Fatherland League, which scarcely had any assets at all, was given permission to see to its own liquidation, while the Communist Party of Norway had already been liquidated by the German security police.

It was Hagelin's department which constituted the political bastion of the new state. The 265 civil servants in the Ministry of the Interior received strict instructions to support the NS and all its associated organisations 'actively in every sense' so that the movement could be expanded as quickly as possible.[13]

---

[13] Circular from Ministry of the Interior, signed by Hagelin 16 December 1940, AAB q 940.6.6481.

The Reichskommissariat's special branch, Einsatzstab Wegener, named after its leader Paul Wegener, was to assist by financing and advising the NS on the way to take over power. Wegener's advisers were installed in each of the various NS branches, where they soon displayed all their organisational skills at every level of the party organisation. Wegener himself was a high-ranking party official, a major general in the SS, deputy gauleiter in the important Mark Brandenburg district and an influential NSDAP politician. He set to work in Norway with great impartiality. The NS index of members was sorted through, and the old estimates of 'around 15,000 members' made way for more precise figures. The Einsatzstab came to the conclusion that the party had never had more than 8,542 adult members at its peak in 1935–6. In April 1940 the number was estimated at 1,500 – considerably lower than the figure which Quisling and Hagelin had reported in Berlin. From this point things could only get better.

And indeed membership was on the increase. In August 1940 the Einsatzstab counted 4,000 members, by October 14,000 and at the end of the year 25,000 NS members. The increase was so great that even Terboven's associates who had been dubious about Quisling now openly acknowledged their surprise. During the summer of 1941 the party membership rose to 30,000: at least as many as had voted for the NS in the 1930s election had joined. 'Our movement is now a strong political organisation with a membership of one per cent of the population,' Quisling stated at a meeting of district leaders in February 1941. 'That is sufficient to control a state, but we will go further.'[14]

He now had to convince Terboven that the party was actually capable of administering the state. In his discussions with Hitler in the summer of 1940, 1 March 1941 had been suggested as a possible date for his taking over power. But when the six months had come and gone without any further discussion, he decided to set himself an even higher target in order to prove what the movement was capable of. In the spring of 1941 Quisling launched the 'one hundred thousand plan' by which the membership needed to reach 100,000 so as to show that it was winning over the Norwegian people.[15]

It was later claimed that it was the Germans who had set this target for the party's expansion. The 100,000 member plan was, however, worked out in the party's membership office without any demonstrable influence from the

---

[14] From a meeting in Oslo 8–9 February 1941, recorded in NS Riks-og rådsmøteprotokoll 1934–45.*

[15] Reports on NS membership in RA FMK 58. See also Skodvin, 'Historisk innleiing' in *Om landssvikoppgjøret* (1962) pp. 18f.

1   Quisling, a photograph taken during his visit to Hitler at Schloss Klessheim on 19 April 1943.

2   The only known portrait of Jon and Anna Quisling and their family, 1896. The nine-year-old Vidkun stands between his parents, behind Esther aged three and Jørgen aged eight.

3 Quisling's wife Maria and his father Jon, photographed by Jørgen Quisling in the summer of 1926.

4 Quisling as countryman, photographed by his brother Jørgen around 1930.

5 Dramatic portrait cover of *Oslo Illustrerte*, 30 November 1932.

6 Quisling in Berlin, February 1942, with (*from left*) the Reichskommissar for
Norway, Josef Terboven, and Reichsminister Hans-Heinz Lammers.

7 Quisling (*left*) with the Norwegian Interior Minister, Hagelin, and Hitler in the
Chancellery, Berlin, February 1942.

8   Quisling and Hitler at Schloss Klessheim, 19 April 1943.

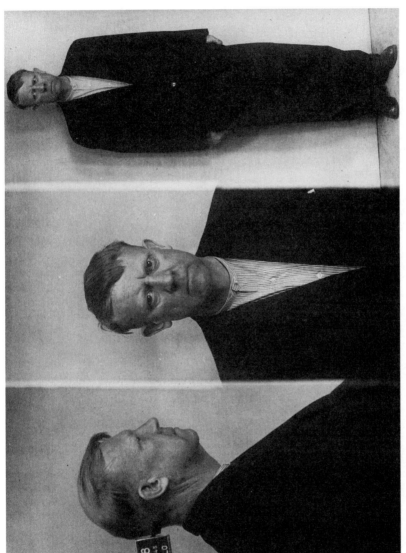

9 Quisling after his arrest, July 1945.

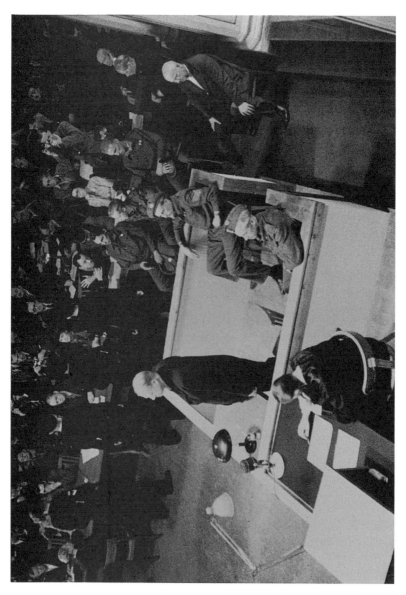

10 Quisling on trial.

Einsatzstab. This figure was a natural goal for the Fører himself as this was the number of supporters which Quisling had always claimed to have, and the figure he had often quoted in Berlin as representing the extent of his 'real' support. However, when the NS wanted to prove that it was capable of amassing this level of support, it proved a serious challenge. On the anniversary of the establishment of the commissarial government, 25 September 1941, membership numbers barely exceeded 30,000 and never reached more than the 40,000 mark.

The rise in membership which had seemed so promising in 1940–1 was in fact short-lived. NS membership stood at roughly the size of a 'normal' Norwegian party of the 1930s – the Liberals or the Conservatives, for example; only the Labour Party had reached 100,000 long before the war, and then on the basis of collective membership. Quisling was probably referring to the Liberal Party when he asserted that 1 per cent of the population was enough; the Liberal leaders had certainly managed to have their own people installed in every area of political influence during the inter-war period with a similar number of members.

In principle the NS party organisation was self-financing, relying on subscriptions and donations. In practice it relied entirely on German funding. Even before 25 September 1940 it had ceased being an idealistic voluntary organisation to become a vehicle of official political functions along the lines of the German Nazi Party. The transfer from Wegener amounted to approximately 6 million kroner annually, to be drawn from the Norwegian state budget directly from 1943.[16] With all this money the movement was also taking on a more obvious National Socialist identity, a fact which was most clearly discernible in its increasingly militaristic appearance.

War, Quisling was fond of remarking, inevitably leads to a 'concentration of power'. For a party which at that time was to supplant all other parties, it was unavoidable that it assumed a military organisation. Moreover, the party's recruitment policy resembled military conscription more than normal party membership drives. In these circumstances it was also natural that the party adopted military terminology. The NS departments had 'staff' instead of an office; the leaders had 'adjutants' instead of secretaries, and 'liaison officers' instead of messengers. Least surprising of all was the party's

[16] Apart from regular transfers, the NS even received German donations, such as the Reichskommissar gift of 250,000 Reichsmark in September 1940. Schickedanz to Lammers 5 March 1941, BA R 4311/673ᵃ. The real amount of German state transfers to the NS is given in the official documents printed in full in § 104: *Mere lys over rettsoppgjøret* (Oslo 1955) pp. 22–6, and in *Straffesak* p. 223.

wish to reintroduce uniforms, which had been banned in the summer of 1933.

The first section to adopt a uniform was the Hird. This marching and singing unit enjoyed a reputation as 'the political soldiers' of the Fører and the movement. The heyday of the Hird was, however, a thing of the past, of the tumultuous 1930s when NS speakers needed protection from the abuses and stones hurled at them from young Communists everywhere. An image from this time of struggle resurfaced during the autumn and winter of 1940 when the Hird came out on numerous occasions in defence of harangued NS members. In particular among students and schoolchildren, bitter clashes occurred whenever the party badge was spotted on a lapel. When the Hird came marching in to defend its own, bickering turned into fighting, and fist-fights sometimes escalated into veritable battle scenes. In Oslo in mid-December 1940, fighting threatened to turn into full-blown riots in the city centre. However, during the first months of 1941 these confrontations became less frequent. Badgering NS members became a more risky activity as the Hird was given the formal support of the police and of the new State Attorney.[17]

At that time the NS Youth were also given the right to wear a uniform – grey shirts with black ties and maritime caps. Quisling and the party leadership were by then uniformed as well. The first picture of the party leader in uniform after 25 September 1940 shows him in the Hird shirt and tie, but soon the need was felt for the leader to have his own uniform. This impulse had, of course, come from Germany; it was considered improper to go on a study trip to the NSDAP in civilian clothes or to receive important German guests in a hat and overcoat. A brown uniform was first suggested, but the party official who paraded a test uniform of this colour was soon nicknamed 'our chocolate boy' when he turned up at the party office. Even Quisling himself collapsed with laughter over his desk. The colour was thus modified to dark green, with a cap in the hunting style.[18]

But vanity follows its own rules. The party uniforms, which bore an unfortunate resemblance to those of bus drivers, despite their unambiguously military insignia representing the ten different ranks within the party, were never popular. The majority of party representatives preferred the uniforms of more prestigious organisations. In this respect, the Hird seems

[17] Skodvin, 'Det store fremstøt', pp. 624, 635ff. See also Hirdspeilet 1942/1; party ordinance 12 August 1943 on the Hird's relationship to the main organisation, RA FMK 12; membership statistics in RA FMK 58.

[18] Various circulars on uniforms in RA FMK 7. Information related by Tom B. Jensen.

to have had a clear advantage over the party. The same went for the Labour Service or AT. But the party, the Hird and the AT uniforms alike were all inferior to the prestigious uniforms of the units of Norwegian SS, not to mention the shiny black uniforms of the Allgemeine-SS, or the Waffen-SS field green. The unofficial hierarchy of uniforms thus followed the demands of war, reflecting the soldier's moral superiority over the functionary, irrespective of background.

Meanwhile, more people needed uniforms as the party administration expanded. In the autumn of 1941 there were over a hundred employees at the offices in Rådhusgata alone, including drivers and messengers. Quisling's secretariat on the top floor was staffed by eight people, Fuglesang's by ten, the Organisation Department and the propaganda section by thirty altogether. Ten people issued membership cards alone, as each month new members by the thousands kept pouring into the ranks of the party. In its first year of power the movement indeed seemed promising as the one authorised channel for Germany's cause in Norway. To the Fører this apparent success came as a great relief after the long period of waiting. Photographs of Quisling from the year 1941 show a relaxed, confident and sometimes even broadly smiling figure. After the lonely days of December 1939, when only Hagelin and Scheidt had witnessed the secret reversal in the fortunes of the NS, and even more after the strained negotiations of the summer 1940 when his role was confined to behind-the-scenes activities, it felt tremendously encouraging to be able to step forward and engage in some overt politics again: shaking hands openly, giving direct leadership both to the party and to the nation. At last he was in the position of contributing to changing the world and not only interpreting its course.

'IF GERMANY FALLS, NORWAY FALLS'

With the cabinet working on the restructuring programme, and the party increasing its membership with the help of Einsatzstab Wegener, Quisling directed most of his energies to trying to get the commissarial government wound up and replaced by an independent Norwegian government. This was a task which demanded extreme diplomacy, both with Skaugum and with Berlin.

He mapped out the objectives for the future national government in a comprehensive memorandum intended for Hitler in October 1940, which was written after discussions with the German Navy's High Command in Norway and with other dignitaries. The basic aim was the same as it had been during the December talks of the previous year: the Greater Germanic Union. But instead of taking in the entire vista of Europe, the memorandum restricted itself to the bilateral relationship between Norway and Germany, working on the express premise that 'Norway remains a free, indivisible and independent state, bound to the Greater German Reich in a Greater Nordic union. Norway's territorial integrity and freedom is guaranteed by the Greater German Reich.' Though not incompatible with the December plans of 1939, the bilateral perspective was somewhat twisted by an altered reality.[19]

The reality from Quisling's point of view was that Norway's status as a dependent and occupied territory placed an enormous burden on the party which had been chosen to lead the country, a burden that was preventing it from building up the necessary support among the population. Hagelin had said the same thing in a somewhat indiscreet letter to Rosenberg earlier in the autumn. The German presence was 'crippling', 'oppressive', indeed 'fatal' for the future national government because it was making it impossible for the NS to cultivate a warm relationship with Germany, Hagelin said. The Reichskommissar was attacked. Whether Hitler ever read these protest letters from the Norwegian Minister of the Interior is highly doubtful, but it is possible that their gist was communicated to him.[20]

Quisling handled the matter rather more diplomatically. He did not consider it appropriate to berate the occupying power in the way Hagelin did; nor did he think it defensible to stick principally and unswervingly to the point of view of a small nation as many of his advisers preferred to do. It was necessary to take into account the realities of power and build up long-term influence for Norway, bearing in mind the fact that German policy was not static, and might for example move to make Norway a protectorate, thereby placing the country under even closer control from Berlin. There were rumours in Oslo that Terboven was in fact thinking along such lines.[21] His memorandum of 25 October 1940 was the first in a long series of communications to Hitler, carefully outlining the mutual advantages to Germany and Norway of forming the nucleus of a future Greater Germanic

[19] Quisling's memorandum 25 October 1940, original in BA NS 43, complete German version in *ADAP* XI, 1 no. 233 pp. 337f, shortened version in *Straffesak* pp. 95f. Boehm, *Norwegen*, p. 121 indicates the navy's part in the preparation of this document.
[20] Hagelin to Schickedanz 2 October 1940, *ADAP* XI, 1 no. 144 pp. 204f, and 14 October 1940, BA NS 43, printed in Seraphim, *Tagebuch Alfred Rosenbergs*, and in Paulsen, 'Terboven i konflikt', pp. 74f.
[21] Ringnes, *Bak okkupasjonens kulisser*, pp. 267f.

Union, based on a common defence and foreign policy and a common currency, and free movement of goods, labour and capital. In this union Norway would have in some way to give up her claims to exercise full sovereignty to some extent, in recognition of existing German military supremacy. But with Reich protection the Greater Germanic Union would be a federation of independent states in line with the vision of *Russia and Ourselves* and the more philosophical ideas of Universism.

On 5 December 1940 Quisling flew to Berlin for negotiations with Dr Lammers at the Chancellery about the future of Norway. During the days that followed he had talks with several of the legal experts in the Chancellery and with the new SS Service responsible for recruiting foreign volunteers, led by Gottlob Berger. Here the question of common armed forces with Germany came up in an unexpected manner – through the prospect of Norwegian military support for the joint cause directly by the voluntary participation of individual Norwegians, which would not involve the difficult questions of diplomatic or constitutional issues. Quisling's willingness to co-operate at this point resulted in a breakthrough with all the authorities, and Berger quickly summoned Paul Dahm, the SS recruitment specialist in Holland, to go to Norway and within four weeks provide at least 200 volunteers. They had of course to fulfil the usual SS requirements: height 170 cm, physical fitness and spotless racial pedigree, so as to be able to serve in the recently established Nordland Regiment of the Waffen-SS. The SS expert accompanied Quisling and Terboven back to Norway on 13 December.[22]

Quisling set out to prepare the Norwegian public for this change of policy from the NS. 'I am talking', he said in his new year broadcast to the Norwegian people, 'not to the many who have been unbalanced by the overwhelming events of the past year. These people are hanging on the "siren calls from London" and are inaccessible to reason.' Instead he addressed 'normal Norwegians ... whether NS members or not', in order to explain the great events which had taken place in the country in 1940. And

---

[22] The origins of the Norwegian participation in the SS are debatable. See Quisling to Lammers 6 September 1940, *Straffesak* pp. 99, 262; RA LD 29 Q. Various documents in BA NS 19, RFSS Persönlicher Stab. suggest that Lammers took the matter to Himmler, not the other way round. Svein Blindheim, *Nordmenn under Hitlers fane* (1977), argues that Quisling had approached Himmler as early as the summer of 1940 with the idea of NS volunteers in the SS, but there is no evidence to support this. Quisling visited the Reichsführer somewhere around 8–12 August 1940, but the only remaining record of the meeting (Scheidt's memo for Reichsleiter Rosenberg 30 May 1941, BA NS 43/27) does not mention the question.

the explanation he offered was that the revolution which Europe was now experiencing under German leadership had much in common with the American War of Independence 170 years before. Germany was now calling on the Norwegians, Quisling asserted, 'as an equal, kindred Germanic people to join her in building a new Europe'.

What this 'calling on Norway' meant became clear when on 28 January the Reichsführer-SS Heinrich Himmler arrived in Oslo. Shortly before that Goebbels had been in Norway as the first official envoy from the German government. The visit in late November was uneventful and had no political outcome.[23] Now Himmler had come to swear in the first volunteers. The SS expert had met the quota: approximately 300 had presented themselves in the two weeks following Quisling's call-up, and of those a good 200 were selected. The public accounts of the celebration in the Hippodrome at Vinderen near Oslo on 30 January studiously neglected to mention anything about the number of young men, some in civilian dress, others in Hird uniform, who had been deployed there to listen to the speeches delivered by Quisling, Terboven and Himmler. The SS recruitment office, however, was pleased with the result.[24]

Even if the first crowd was not large, the words in the Hippodrome that day in January resounded with all the gravity that the situation demanded. This was indeed a turning-point in the relationship between the two nations, brought about by a change in Quisling's strategy, which in its turn was calculated to secure maximum Norwegian sovereignty during the war. If Norway made common cause with Germany on the battlefield, surely there would be all the more reason for Hitler to stabilise the relationship between the two countries by guaranteeing Norway's independence, since that would be the best way to promote volunteers from that country. The events in the Hippodrome consequently sealed the two countries' common destiny. At the youth rally at the Coliseum the same night, Lunde remarked that this was nothing less than a 'milestone in the history of the Germans'.[25]

---

[23] Goebbels's visit to Oslo: Goebbels, *Die Tagebücher*, pp. 413f; see also Skodvin, 'Det store fremstøt', pp. 623f; Dahl, *Dette er London*, pp. 219f; T. Hamsun, *Efter år og dag* (1990) pp. 210ff.

[24] Terboven later gave the figure of 350 volunteers, of whom 230 were recruited: see Boehm's report to Raeder 5 February 1941, Paulsen, 'Terboven i konflikt', pp. 80f. Paul Dahm was pleased with the result: 'Betreff: Werbung germanischer Freiwilligen' (undated), INO. Quisling's new year speech: printed in *For Norges frihet og selvstendighet* (1942) pp. 47–58. For the Hippodrome speeches, see *FF* 30 January 1941; NRK ho 3136/3.

[25] Lunde in *FF* 5 February 1941.

ATTITUDES TO BRITAIN AND TO THE JEWS

Six weeks later Quisling himself undertook the reinterpretation of this same part of Germanic history in the light of recent developments. His speech to the party leadership and officials at the Coliseum on 12 March 1941 was delivered forcefully, showing him to be both a realist and a visionary, uncompromising and magnanimous at the same time. He greeted the crowd with the words of Ibsen: 'What Norway once was, she will become once more.' In a sweeping overview he then went on to remind his listeners of the old Norse colonisations from AD 800 onwards, pointing out the formidable strength shown by the Norwegian people through the ages, embedded in the 'old Norse sailor and farmer principle' – against which, alas, stood England: ever since 1066, when Norway's colonisation in the west was brought to a stop by William the Conqueror, England had been an obstacle to this fundamental Norwegian principle. With William came French influence, and shortly after that Jewish influence on the English, who gradually, through history, became Norway's enemy instead of blood brother. 'It is for this reason that England, the British dominions and America today speak half Latin and half German instead of Norwegian,' he explained to his supporters.[26]

A few days earlier, on 4 March 1941, the British themselves had demonstrated their real interests. In a surprise commando raid they had landed in Svolvær and set fire to stores and herring oil factories, capturing German soldiers and Norwegian NS members and taking them back to England together with those of the local island population who were willing to go with them.[27] This, said Quisling, was simply the last in a long series of English acts of aggression. For centuries the English had been using Norway as 'a sort of English province', now headed 'by a Danish prince as an English vassal king in Norway'. Haakon VII, through his defence of the Svolvær raid, had 'severed his last remaining ties with Norway and the Norwegian people, and has gone from being the father of the nation to the enemy of the nation'.

The Coliseum speech was seen as a turning-point in party propaganda. From that point on, NS agitators were to direct their attacks equally against England and the King in exile. All party speakers received instructions to use Quisling's speech as a model, 'without actually copying it', and were given

[26] *FF* 13 March 1941. There is no recording of the speech, and the version in *For Norges frihet og selvstendighet* (1942) is incomplete.
[27] Sverre Kjeldstadli, *Hjemmestyrkene* (1959) pp. 60ff; Olav Riste, *London-Regjeringa* I (1973) pp. 117f; Paulsen, 'Terboven i konflikt', pp. 84ff.

central instructions on how to interpret Norwegian history, for example, that the year 1066 when '300 ships set sail for England with approximately 30,000 men' could be seen as a high point in the country's social and constitutional history, which was followed by a period of decline that was just coming to an end. At the same time the educational authorities announced that from that time on German would be taught in Norwegian schools instead of English.[28]

For Quisling the speech meant a complete ideological break from his earlier conception of England as a Nordic nation. The Greater Nordic Union he had advocated in *Russia and Ourselves* in 1930 and delineated in greater detail at the party congress in 1936 ranked England among the Nordic powers, and had in fact placed the country ahead of Germany as Norway's natural Nordic ally. Even the peace plan outlined to Chamberlain in 1939, which he had also shown to Hitler, listed the same Germanic nations: England, Germany and Scandinavia. This was a time for reappraisal.

Two weeks later he made common cause with Nazi Germany on another important issue: the Jews. Invited to speak at the opening of Rosenberg's Institute of Research into the Jewish Question in Frankfurt on 26 March 1941, he ventured to persuade his audience – racial experts from all over German-occupied Europe – that if they thought that Norway was relatively free of Jewish influence and subversion compared to other countries, they should think again. The opposite was true: Norway was in fact being increasingly undermined and perverted by international Jewry, economically, culturally and in the area of foreign policy; indeed, the subversion was so much more effective there as it had been going on for centuries in the form of a gradual 'process of conquest', which most people had only recently noticed. By this time it was almost too late. A total of 10,000 Jews and half-Jews (the most recent census reported only 1,350) were in fact 'corrupting' Norwegian blood like 'destructive bacilli', with individuals like the Storting's president C. J. Hambro and the sexual prophet Wilhelm Reich, who wanted to introduce sex education in schools, as particularly ominous examples. He concluded his lecture in the Frankfurt Römer Hall by recommending nothing less than common European legislation against the Jews, partly to put a stop to intermarriage and to deny the Jews their civil rights, and partly to secure a more radical solution. What this solution implied was not quite clear. Neither extermination nor compulsory sterilisation were viable methods, he said; someone had to find a homeland for the Jews and 'send

[28] *NSPM* 1941/3 p. 41; 1941/4 pp. 67f.

the whole lot of them there'. As the land could not be Palestine, 'which for centuries has belonged to the Arabs', some other place would have to be found to create a 'geographically and politically separate state' for the Jews. At least, this was what he was intending to suggest to the conference. One of his acquaintances who was present, the leading German racist theorist Hans Friedrich Günther, managed to warn him in advance that such an idea was out of the question in German National Socialist priorities. Quisling duly deleted the sentence about a separate state for the Jews from his script before delivering his talk to this influential congregation of experts.[29]

It was, however, a mistake on Quisling's part to believe that the solution to the Jewish question lay in the hands of Rosenberg and his staff, just as it was naive of him to hope that he would be able to bolster Norwegian independence by showing support for Rosenberg's racist ideas. Rosenberg was without influence in this, as in other areas. Rather, it was Himmler's SS which was now increasingly carrying responsibility for European racial policy. In the spring of 1941 the essential features of the Third Reich's particular 'solution' were already beginning to be apparent. The Jewish question had gone from being a subject of academic research and an ideological issue, in which Quisling's German contacts played an active role, to a political issue firmly under the jurisdiction of the SS and integrated into Himmler's collection of obscure and covert activities.

At about the same time as Quisling made his Frankfurt speech, the German presence in Norway was becoming an increasing threat to the local Jews. Their radio sets had already been confiscated, presumably to provide receivers for Germans. By April 1941 the Jewish community in Trondheim was deprived of its synagogue and some Jewish citizens of their homes to meet Wehrmacht requisitions. Many Jewish men in Tromsø and Narvik were arrested in June as part of a larger wave of arrests, which soon afterwards could only be interpreted as part of the temporary activities which preceded the German campaign against the Soviet Union.[30]

---

[29] Quisling's original manuscript, private archives,* printed (with some additions) as *Kampen mellem arier og jødemakt. Vidkun Quislings tale i Frankfurt 28. mars 1941 om jødeproblemet* (Oslo 1941); sound recording NRK ho 5419/2. Information on the congress in *Welt-Dienst. Internationale Korrespondenz zur Aufklärung über die Judenfrage* no. VIII/8, 15 April 1941, pp. 1–9, and Draeger to Steengracht 18 February 1941, PAAA 11/63, Handakten Luther, Schriftenverkehr. Hans F. Günther, *Mein Eindruck von Adolf Hitler* (1969) pp. 134ff; various correspondence in the Günther archive, Freiburg.*

[30] P. O. Johansen, *Oss selv nærmest* (1984) pp. 136ff; Nils Johan Ringdal, *Mellom barken og veden* (1987) pp. 230f; O. Mendelsohn, *Jødenes historie i Norge* II (1986) pp. 17f.

However, there were also clearly anti-Semitic initiatives on the Norwegian side. In the spring of 1941, Justice Minister Sverre Riisnæs was working to alter the legal position of Jewish citizens. An amendment to the marriage laws designed to prohibit 'mixed marriages' was given a hearing in the Church, in the first instance by the Bishop of Oslo. In the autumn Riisnæs went on to prepare a change to the concessions laws which would take away the right of Jews to own Norwegian land, together with an amendment to the Constitution, reinstating the paragraph prohibiting Jews from entering the country.[31] Both measures were certainly prepared after consultations with Quisling, and were designed for a situation in which the NS itself would take over the legislature.

SS NORWAY

Immediately upon his return from Frankfurt in early April 1941, Quisling became aware of a deadly threat to the very existence of the NS. The SS Hauptamt in Berlin announced its interest in setting up a Norwegian formation of the Allgemeine-SS, a Norwegian SS directly responsible to Head Office and bound by life-long loyalty to Hitler. The Germans' first choice for head of this SS Norway was the former renegade Jonas Lie. Himmler himself was to come to Norway in order to swear in the first contingent.

How was Quisling supposed to justify his long-term goal of Norwegian freedom and independence with this Hitler–Himmler alliance within his own movement? And what was to become of the NS and the Hird if a new élite corps in SS black shirts started to have influence among the ranks? 'Disaster,' declared Scheidt from Berlin when he received news of the enterprise, 'the best way to destroy the party.' Scheidt naturally interpreted the initiative as part of Himmler's way of manoeuvring himself into the position of Administrator of the Germanic Countries, an appointment which would not only have consequences for the NS but would also threaten the entire Nordic policy of Rosenberg's office. If Scheidt was right, not only Quisling's organisation in Norway but also his loyal supporters in Berlin would be outmanoeuvred, which would mean the end of the NS.[32]

In the middle of this crisis, Anna Quisling died peacefully at her home in Oslo and was buried at Gjerpen on 20 May. Quisling, deeply affected,

---

[31] Mendelsohn, *Jødenes historie*, pp. 15ff.
[32] Scheidt, Memo for Reichsleiter Rosenberg 30 May 1941, BA NS 43/27.

followed the coffin with Jørgen and Maria. He had been closer to his mother than anybody and had helped her in her old age as much as he could, displaying a filial affection and a tenderness which his relatives found very moving. Now, on his last walk with his mother, he was reminded of his position in politics as a great number of German and NS leaders joined in to pay tribute to the mother of the Fører. 'Mama would have been surprised to see so many uniformed representatives of the Reichskommissariat and the NS gathered around her tomb,' Jørgen wrote wryly to Arne in New York – in one of the very few family letters that was permitted to pass through the German postal censorship and which reached the Quislings in America.[33]

The SS was not the only political problem to emerge in the early summer of 1941. At the same time as Himmler was reaching out to annex Norway, new conflicts were building up with the Reichskommissariat. The cost of the occupation was rising at a disturbing rate. In a meeting with Quisling, Hagelin and Hustad on 16 June, Terboven confirmed that, of all the occupied countries, Norway was making relatively the highest payments to Germany. A stern communication addressed to the ministers from Terboven's finance division at the end of May, with instructions that all ordinances were to go through the Reichskommissariat, was interpreted as a restriction on freedom of political action and provoked strong resentment among the NS ministers.[34] Quisling went to Terboven and asked him outright whether it was his intention that the ministers should be obliged to take orders from the Kommissariat finance department, because, if so, he was ready to resign, as this meant that the ministers who were supposed to be preparing for the NS's eventual takeover of power were simply executors without any real political power. This was the first time that Quisling directly threatened Terboven with resignation. Terboven had to stress the importance of co-operation and of resolving their differences round the table, adding that he was willing to help settle these conflicts personally.

The tug-of-war with Himmler and the SS entailed further compromises. The new SS organisation in Norway was eventually set up as a section of the Allgemeine-SS, with Lie at its helm and Riisnæs his deputy. But at the same time it was established as a special branch of the NS, within Quisling's

---

[33] Jørgen to Arne Quisling 24 May 1941, Collection Arne Quisling.*

[34] Memo of Hans Korff, leader of the Finance Division. RK in Hauptabteilung Volks-wirtschaft, with ref. to the Wegener–Otte–Berghold–Korff meeting on 22 June 1941, and various papers and meetings relevant to the case, dated 25 July 1941, BA R 2/351. Quisling to Hitler 19 June 1941 (marked 'not sent'), RA UKA (in Quisling to Hitler 2 August 1941, wrongly dated 17 June 1941).

jurisdiction, and as an organisational offshoot of the Hird whereby the Hird would furnish the first section with members and also work later with the new organisation. The paper, Hirdmannen, became a joint publication. 'I have decided on the name SS Norway,' declared Quisling in his proclamation of the initiative on 16 May 1941, thus giving the impression that the whole thing had been his idea. Altogether 150 Hird members were quickly rounded up and informed of the honour that was being bestowed on them. When Himmler arrived in Oslo five days later and swore them in as the first Norwegian SS men in a simple ceremony, he made it clear to them that their task would not simply involve marching around as political soldiers. From then on their job was to 'protect the fellowship of Germanic blood'. Jonas Lie balanced these bizarre utterances with a simple reassurance to Quisling that 'we will not permit anything to compromise our loyalty to you', stressing that the Norwegian SS was a part of the NS. The 150 oaths to the Führer had to be seen within the context of a prior loyalty to the Fører.[35]

When Himmler left Norway after this ceremonial visit, he was accompanied by Quisling and Lie. The three of them went to Heuberg to visit the Norwegian volunteers from the Nordland regiment. Quisling talked while the Reichsführer-SS drank beer with the Norwegians in a spirit of camaraderie. The visit to the camp could almost be seen as an assertion of a new and co-operative spirit despite all the difficulties between the SS and the NS.[36]

It soon became apparent that Quisling had very little to fear from the SS Norway. Himmler's corps in Norway was never any real threat, either to the party or to the Hird. Recruitment was slow, and never amounted to more than about 1,200 members. It was quite unusual that the SS willingly allowed itself to be dictated to by a national party outside Germany; in fact, Quisling had good grounds for thinking himself the victor.

On 22 June 1941, only a month after Himmler had sworn in the new recruits, and while the first SS contingent was still being trained at Elverum, Germany invaded the Soviet Union. The war with Russia developed into a lightning campaign. In Berlin, the focus of attention was on the Russian theatre of war and all available forces had to be diverted to it. The new SS men from Norway therefore never got the opportunity to compete with the NS as representatives of the Greater Germanic cause. They were immediately sent to the front, where their precious Germanic blood was soon shed in a war which had already run into serious difficulties by Christmas; this, in

35 Hirdmannen 1941/25.   36 FF, various reports at the end of May 1941.

turn, had consequences for both the civil and the military situations in all the German dependent and occupied territories, not least in Norway.

The war with Russia came as an enormous relief to Quisling. At last there was an eastern front, which he had always insisted was necessary. Ever since his youth he had considered the most important task of the West to be the 'recapturing of Russia for European civilisation'.[37] He had of course accepted certain commitments as a result of the Hitler–Stalin pact, and had shown a certain diplomatic caution in speeches and articles between 1940 and 1941, but personally he was clear on his position on Bolshevism and did not doubt for one moment that a war in the East was inevitable.

When, on the day after the outbreak of war the NS celebrated midsummer on Bygdøy, *Fritt Folk* commented on how 'serenely happy' Quisling looked. The following day the Fører started discussions with Terboven on how Norway should contribute to the war. The discussions were followed by a larger conference at Skaugum between the NS ministers and German civil and military leaders. It was decided that a voluntary Norwegian division, to be called the Norwegian Legion, would be formed and put at the Wehrmacht's disposal. It would be something very different from the contribution to the Nordland regiment of the Waffen-SS.[38]

Terboven made grand promises when he announced the formation of the legion on the radio on 29 June. He said that he had been urged from several quarters to allow Norway to participate in this historic war, and that the Führer 'has fulfilled the wishes of the Norwegian people' in that the Legion was to be formed 'under exclusively Norwegian command and according to Norwegian guidelines'. A week later Quisling responded by arranging for the Oslo party to gather in University Place with everything that it could muster in the way of flags and banners, and in a long speech he unfolded the entire 100-year-long history of communism: 'A spectre has been appearing in Europe ever since that Jewish-German emigrant Karl Marx wrote his Communist Manifesto in 1847–1848 ... it will now be eternally laid to rest!' The forming of the Norwegian Legion, he explained, was 'a great thing for us ... a step down the road towards our complete freedom and indepen-

---

[37] Quisling's speech in Universitetsplassen 4 July 1941, *FF* 5 July 1941.
[38] For the call-up for the Norwegian Legion, see Blindheim, *Nordmenn under Hitlers fane*, pp. 35ff, and *FF* 17 July 1941.

dence'. But he explained that the Legion was above all fighting on behalf of Finland. The Finns had declared war and joined forces with Germany against the Soviet Union in order to recapture lost territory. If Quisling had once had reservations about the Norwegian volunteers in Finland, he was now making up for it with an impressive solidarity campaign. The Legion was presented as a contribution to 'the struggle for Finland's freedom'.[39]

During the course of the summer some 1,700 Norwegians volunteered for the Legion, and through the autumn the number increased to 1,900. However, these young volunteers were quick to notice that German influence was greater than had been represented to them. Nothing came of Terboven's promises: the Legion was no Norwegian force but subordinate to the Waffen-SS; its uniform was German rather than Norwegian and its staff in Oslo were under German supervision. The Legion, which had started out full of promise as an independent institution, thus became a means of winning sovereignty through sacrifice, rather than a force to help build up an independent government directly.

The political demands which followed from the war with Russia were no less exacting than the military ones. Everywhere in German-dominated territories the battle against the Soviet sympathisers in local Communist Parties was stepped up. There was a formidable wave of arrests of Norwegian Communist Party members in the summer of 1941. At the same time the state police, which had been abolished by the Nygaardsvold government in 1937, was resuscitated on 1 July to co-operate with the Gestapo.[40] Towards the end of the month Terboven announced that he was giving himself the power to introduce a state of emergency, which he, not the Wehrmacht, would personally administer, 'in order to deal with events of an unusual nature in Norwegian public life'. In such cases, courts martial would be set up, with the possibility of the death sentence. From the tone of this announcement it was clear that Terboven's first priority was putting a stop to trade union opposition.[41]

Quisling did not voice any opposition to the harsher German line. In fact he agreed with it. The most prominent figure in the Trade Union Association was the lawyer Viggo Hansteen, in Quisling's view an ardent Moscow Communist and a Red Army colonel to boot. Hansteen should be perma-

[39] For Quisling's speech see *FF* 5 July 1941; for Terboven's see *Straffesak* p. 353.
[40] Ringdal, *Mellom barken og veden*, p. 195; G. Reitinger, *The SS: Alibi of a Nation* (1981) pp. 206ff.
[41] *RKVB* 1941/7; see also Skodvin, *Norsk historie*, pp. 140f; B. Nøkleby, *Nyordning* (1985) pp. 182f.

nently removed, Quisling thought. In July he signalled a change in the party's position on all those who now opposed the new order. 'These treacherous cliques must be broken up. And they will be.' Now that there were 'clear lines and fronts' in the great struggle, there was no longer any excuse. He would have to employ the most extreme measures in order to make these traitors see reason; failing that, he would have to 'render them harmless'.[42] Jonas Lie's department was meanwhile preparing an ordinance which would empower the police to hold indefinitely anybody who gave 'reasonable grounds for suspicion' of conducting organised resistance or producing propaganda in favour of the royal family. Quisling himself worked out a detailed list of every single official known to be representative of the forty Communist undercover organisations and other left-wing groups.[43]

The most damaging effect of the growing resistance to the new order was that it scared people off from the NS. An informal 'ice front' threatened to isolate Quisling's followers from the rest of society. Derision and contempt, being given the cold shoulder, family conflicts, friends who stopped talking to them – this was what NS people experienced in their everyday lives. No wonder people hesitated to join the ranks. Recently, Quisling had himself been receiving personal threats from London, as one of his old acquaintances, a captain in the navy, Riiser-Larsen, made a speech on the BBC which directly threatened both him and his party leadership with nothing less than the death penalty once Britain had won the war. 'And I would like to remind Mr Quisling that people do not traditionally waste bullets when it comes to traitors. He will be hanged.' A little later Riiser-Larsen elaborated on how Quisling should fear the gallows: 'Remember, Quisling, each time the pendulum of the clock in your sitting room swings, your doom draws closer ... As you lie awake at night your hands are gradually reaching up for your neck.'[44]

However, the propaganda from London soon dried up. In August 1941 the head of the SS and German police, Heinrich Rediess, confiscated all radio sets in Norway, starting with the coastal areas, then the regions bordering Sweden and during September completing the process with the

---

[42] *FF* 19 July 1941 'Føreord på 54–årsdagen'.

[43] List of organisations given to Quisling by H. N. Østbye, 3 July 1941, RA LD 5/49–50 H. N. Østbye, document no. 77.

[44] Speeches on the BBC Norwegian Service 18 July and 8 August 1941, cited in Dahl, *Dette er London*, p. 240. Amendments to military penal law to extend the use of the death penalty were made by the government in exile in London on 3 October 1941.

Oslo area and North Norway. Half a million receivers were handed in to the police stations in what was the most comprehensive round-up ever to have taken place in Norway. The order in itself was relatively mild: the sets were to be marked with the owner's name and address and remained the property of the owner in question; failure to comply would result only in confiscation and a fine. Even so, people lined up to hand in their radios, displaying a respect for the law which astonished even the German security police.[45]

German opinion on the initiative was divided. Listener support for the BBC was naturally curbed by it, but the relatively small section of Norwegian listeners who regularly followed the news bulletins on the BBC had plenty of opportunity for clandestine listening as there had been no cross-checking with the NRK's licence records of the radios which were handed in. It was therefore quite easy to hide away a receiver and thereby spread the contents of a news broadcast by writing them down and circulating them in the form of a chain letter.

From the party's point of view the round-up must have seemed even more dubious, as it was not only the BBC that was thus cut off but also the state radio, on which the party relied heavily for disseminating its propaganda. Quisling nevertheless approved of the German action. He had already prepared the way by his own diatribes against the London broadcasts in his public speeches ever since the summer of 1940. But whether the confiscations were carried out at his direct insistence remains unclear. At least two other factors were pertinent. Jamming the BBC had proved impractical as the signals interfered with the Wehrmacht internal radio communications. Because of that, confiscation had immediately been suggested as the only way to curb the BBC's influence. Another factor was a fresh report of public opinion made by the Sicherheitsdienst (the SD, German Surveillance), showing that public opinion in Norway immediately after Germany had marched into Russia had been uncertain and even ambiguous, leaving some room for German and NS propaganda. After the broadcasts from London had transmitted the point of view of the government in exile, public opinion turned towards support of the Allies in the course of just a few days. Terboven thus had several motives for confiscating the radios.[46]

While people handed in their sets, Quisling made another long speech at the Coliseum, this time speaking out against NS enemies, within and without. His attacks came as a surprise to the party. 'Nobody could have

---

[45] Dahl, *Dette er London*, pp. 308–12.

[46] Ibid. Only NS members were allowed to possess radio sets after September 1941.

guessed beforehand,' wrote *Fritt Folk*, that the meeting would contain 'the introduction to the most merciless showdown with the enemies of National Union inside Norway and abroad'.[47] After having compared Napoleon's and Hitler's Russian campaigns, the Fører made a bitter and detailed attack on the BBC's Norwegian broadcasts, on the Swedish press's libellous stories about the NS, and on the resistance groups who 'insinuate themselves between the party and the people'. He declared the Norwegians in London to be 'traitors' and added that there was no point in discussing reprisals as they would never be able to return to the country anyway. Were Germany to lose the war, it would be the Bolsheviks who would come – the Nygaardsvold government and King Haakon now being branded as traitors in an alliance with criminals.

As to the resistance's influence on public opinion, the Fører insisted that its cells had to be smashed, and that 'terror will be met with terror' in order that the tens of thousands of NS supporters who did not dare reveal their allegiance would be able to defy the resistance movement, in particular the plutocratic intellectual and Marxist cliques – a list which reflected the growing opposition to the new order from industry, the bishops and the trade unions.[48]

Five days after Quisling's speech Terboven did introduce a state of emergency following a wave of protest strikes in Oslo against the fact that milk was no longer supplied to work-places at breaks. Norwegian housewives had long been used to rationing and food shortages, but in the factories denying this harmless practice almost caused riots, with workers walking out in rage. Whether the Germans feared further trouble, or whether they were simply exploiting the situation of the milk strike, is not clear. Even at the time there was some speculation that Himmler's deputy, the notorious Reinhard Heydrich, had visited Terboven at Skaugum only a few days before the strike and that they had made plans for the introduction of a state of emergency. But the meeting was a private one, arising from Heydrich's need to confer with a colleague as he had just been appointed Vice Protector of the Reich in Bohemia and Moravia. Quisling did not meet Heydrich, and no connection between his visit and events in Norway has ever been established.[49]

Rediess announced a series of restrictions on normal civilian life in Oslo

---

[47] Quoted *NSPM* 1941 p. 139, 1942 pp. 50, 122.

[48] Reprinted in *Mot nytt land* pp. 23–50. The speech received considerable attention from both the Swedish and Danish press. Cuttings in BA 58-Zsg 117/1172.

[49] See also Berit Nøkleby, *Josef Terboven. Hitlers mann i Norge* (1992). Harald Berntsen, *To liv – en skjebne* (1995), argues that a report which Heydrich later wrote to Ribbentrop about

and its environs, with severe punishments for failure to comply: 250 people, most of them from the Labour movement, were arrested by the Gestapo and taken into police custody without trial. At the same time the court martial began its work. Twenty-eight trade union leaders, most of them former Communists, and two bourgeois intellectuals were given harsh punishments: five were sentenced to death, two of whom were executed on 10 September 1941. Terboven had refused to pardon Viggo Hansteen, who was held responsible for the troubles, and the shop steward at Skabo, where the milk strike had been complete.

Terboven and Rediess's hard line was widely discussed among the Germans in Norway, who felt Terboven to be tough, perhaps too tough, while among the NS his approach was causing extreme alarm.[50]

However, there is nothing to suggest that Quisling regretted the incident; on the contrary, he had always maintained before Terboven that the growing resistance in Norway could only be met with 'a certain toughness', 'as in a war'. For Quisling, Hansteen was a dangerous Communist who should be disposed of in one way or another, whereas to most influential Norwegians he was a member of one of the country's most respected academic families, a gifted lawyer with friends in high places. His execution was deeply shocking to them, and later came to be seen as a watershed in the history of the occupation, dividing it into an earlier period of innocence and a later deadly serious phase in which Quisling's regime came to be regarded as an increasingly brutal oppressive power.[51]

PREPARING THE ACT OF STATE

The government Quisling was preparing to form could not be expected to differ from Terboven's in its approach to the resistance. On the contrary, when he was dealing with the need to fight his fellow countrymen, Quisling asserted that he did not intend to give up that fight at all. He told Hitler that a national government would be able to quell the resistance much more easily than a government installed by the Germans. During the autumn of 1941 he sent several communications to Hitler explaining why most people in Norway resisted the new order: it was because it was seen as imposed by a

the events in Oslo gives proof of his involvement. There is, however, nothing in the report which supports that view.

[50] Boehm, *Norwegen*, pp. 137ff.

[51] Quisling (according to Wegener) to Terboven 16 September 1941, RA LD 29 Q 1, printed in *Straffesak* pp. 122f.

foreign power. The same measures would be accepted more easily if they were introduced by a Norwegian government. An NS government would therefore be in Germany's interest, he argued.[52]

It was hardly surprising that neither Hitler nor Terboven accepted this logic; not even Quisling's staunch supporter Boehm did.[53] The Reichs-kommissar had, on the contrary, repeatedly warned Quisling of the burden of taking responsibility for the unpopular decisions of the occupation. His reasoning was sound. The experience so far of a combined NS and commissarial government had shown that even the slight portion of blame that had fallen on the NS had been enough to turn most people against the party. What then if the NS were to take full responsibility, including that for the harsher demands of the war with Russia? Quisling countered this objection by arguing that the unrest in the factories had nothing to do with the NS but was a question of rationing, which was under the jurisdiction of one of the non-NS ministers, a man who was openly opposed to the party. The movement could not therefore be blamed for what had happened.[54]

Besides he had other arguments for a straight NS government: first of all the promise from Hitler which he always cited; secondly the consideration that it was humiliating for Norway to continue to be governed as an occupied territory, without Germany bothering to formalise in law the *de facto* relationship of peace between the two countries. Finally, his own reputation was at stake. He pointed out to Hitler the necessity of being able 'to look my fellow countrymen in the eye as a patriot' once again.[55]

The absence of formal agreement with Germany, he maintained, led to enormous practical difficulties. Among other things, Norwegian ships were regarded as prizes and confiscated by the German shipping authorities on the grounds that Germany and Norway were at war. In the spring of 1941 the entire home fleet, with an insured value of around 400 million kroner (a significant proportion of the nation's assets) was in real danger of being seized by the German courts. This was certainly a gift for the government in

---

[52] Quisling to Hitler 19 June 1941, RA UKA (the letter never got as far as Hitler, see Scheidt to Hagelin 24 June and 26 June, Hagelin to Scheidt 4 July 1942, RA LD 115 Q 1); also Quisling to Lammers 2 August 1941, RA LD 29 Q1, and Lammers to Quisling 17 August 1941, copy in BA NS 43/27; also Wegener to Quisling 16 September 1941, Wegener to Terboven 1 September 1941, BA NS 43/27; *Straffesak* pp. 523 and 121ff.

[53] Boehm, *Norwegen*, p. 136.

[54] Quisling, memorandum to Terboven 17 September 1941, RA LD 29 Q, *Straffesak* pp. 122f; Hagelin to Quisling 18 October 1941, complaining about the three non-NS ministers. German translation in RA LD 29 Q.

[55] Quisling to Hitler 19 June 1941, RA UKA.

exile in England, and moreover put the NS in the impossible situation when
certain German authorities considered Norway to be at war with Germany,
while others did not, because no official peace existed between the two
countries. True, the Kriegsmarine did withdraw its threats of confiscation,
but the conflict had not been resolved but simply deferred to later negotiations at the prize court, where further offensives could be expected if the
legal position between the two countries were not clarified once and for
all.[56]

In the autumn of 1941 even the *Deutsche Zeitung in Norwegen* reported
that Norway and Germany were still at war. This was in the context of a
court ruling in the prize court in Hamburg of 23 October which concerned
ships in Allied service. Quisling immediately summoned Admiral Boehm's
adjutant and pointed out to him that this ruling implied not only that the
Norwegian ministers were working for the enemy but also that the
Norwegian SS volunteers were fighting for the enemy, and, moreover, that
the British were right to have dragged off party members with them during
their coastal raids. This was an intolerable situation since peace did exist *de
facto* between Norway and Germany.[57] He explained to Dr Lammers that a
peace treaty should therefore be negotiated without delay between Oslo and
Berlin, ready to be signed by the two countries as the first action of the new
National Government. The treaty would put an end to the 'confusion' which
so many Norwegians felt as to which country they were actually at war
with.[58]

And indeed there was a certain movement from the German side. By late
April 1941 Terboven himself started to work on the government question by
sending his legal adviser to Berlin in order to sound out Scheidt on the
subject. This might seem an extraordinary move, if it is not interpreted as an
attempt to find out how things stood with Quisling's supporters in Berlin –
with Rosenberg and Raeder – on the government issue.[59]

On 20 May Wegener remarked that in his opinion membership of the NS
was now high enough for the NS to form a government.[60] But Hitler was

---

[56] Atle Thowsen, *Den norske krigsforsikring for Skip-Gjensidig Forening – 1935–1985 I* (1988)
pp. 329ff, ch. 'Den store prisesaken'.

[57] Settlement of the Prize Court re 'Solglimt', announced on 23 October 1941, BA-MA RM
45/1960; Memo, following conversations between Quisling, Schreiber and Hagelin, 17
January 1942, sent to the Skl. the following day, BA-MA RM 7/537.

[58] Letter in RA LD 29 Q, extracts in *Straffesak* pp. 538f.

[59] Conversation Schiedemair–Scheidt related by both in Hartmann, *Nytt lys*, pp. 124ff.

[60] *Straffesak* p. 538, Quisling to Lammers 2 August 1941.

clearly not of the same opinion. In early June 1941, Lammers told a visitor from Norway that he was no longer sure what Hitler's views on the government question were. 'The Führer had on the one hand stressed his gratitude and his indebtedness to Quisling, whom he did not want to abandon', but on the other hand he was obviously concerned that there would not be any 'progress in Norwegian matters'.[61] Thus Quisling worked in vain all summer in preparation for 25 September, the anniversary of the commissarial government as the date for the hand-over. By this time it was becoming increasingly difficult to communicate with Hitler as he had moved from Berlin to the new headquarters of the Führer, Rastenburg in East Prussia. Hitler was now focusing more and more on the progress of the war in general, not to mention the situation in Germany itself, and less on political developments in particular occupied territories. The meticulous attention to the details of the Norwegian plans which he had shown in the spring and summer of 1940 was definitely absent.

In September Quisling sent a memorandum to Hitler containing an urgent plea for independent government in Norway, warning that many people in the movement were on the way to becoming 'disaffected idealists'.[62] On 25 September Terboven announced a slight change to the government, promoting the heads of ministries to ministers, and making the Fuglesang party secretariat an independent ministry as it was in Germany. Both changes implied upgrading, possibly the furthest Terboven could go on his own initiative.

On 4 October 1941 at a grand harvest festival at University Place in Oslo, Terboven spoke of imminent changes to the government, saying that the country would be able to win back full sovereignty within a Greater Germanic Union, if only the people would join the NS. No dates were mentioned, but the Germans present remarked on how the words of the Reichskommissar had gone down better than ever before.[63]

In November Germany threw fifty-one divisions into its final assault on Moscow, and in December Japan joined the war on Germany's side, leading a devastating campaign against British and American naval powers in the East. Hitler declared war on the United States.

Quisling had been invited to the Reichstag on 11 December to listen to the Führer's important speech in which both the declaration of war on

---

[61] Boehm to Raeder 12 June 1941, in Boehm, *Norwegen*, p. 133.

[62] Quisling's memorandum 17 September 1941, RA LD 27 Q 1, *Straffesak* pp. 122ff.

[63] *FF* 6 October 1941; *Deutsche Zeitung in Norwegen* 7 October 1941; Boehm, *Norwegen*, pp. 141f.

America and the pact with Japan were publicly announced. On the same occasion Hitler gave an overview of the campaign in the East, and praised those countries which were united with Germany in the attempt to protect Europe from the Hunnish hordes of uncultured Soviet barbarians: Finland, Slovakia, Hungary and Romania. The Führer also commended those who had sent in their own divisions: Italy, Spain and Croatia, as well as the volunteers from northern and western Europe – 'Norwegians, Danes, Dutchmen, Flemings, Belgians, and even Frenchmen' – who contributed to turning the war with Russia into a 'European crusade in the true sense of the word'. Quisling must have purred to hear Norway heading the list, even though he was still waiting to realise his goal of promoting Norway into the line of sovereign Axis states.[64]

At the beginning of 1942, then, things suddenly started moving in earnest. Terboven actually spurred on the process by contacting the naval leadership in Berlin repeatedly in order to have the prize judgement from October annulled, referring to Quisling's position in Norway in his justification.[65] On 9 January he assembled all his leading officials from the commissarial departments and regional representatives from Bergen, Trondheim, Stavanger, Kristiansand, Tromsø and Narvik, together with SD leaders from all over the country in order to present the aims for the coming year's policy. Terboven asserted that the German administration was thenceforth to be wound down. His people were instructed to give the 'NS greater scope', and no longer to concern themselves with 'all sorts of things', but to intervene only in cases that had a bearing on the war.[66]

In the middle of January Terboven returned from Rastenburg, where he had been discussing the Norwegian situation with Hitler, bearing news which determined more than the prize issue. He summoned Quisling on the 17th and announced that the handing over of power had now been approved by Hitler and was to take place on 30 January in Oslo, after which Hitler would expect him in Berlin on a state visit.[67]

Quisling was obviously delighted with the news, but almost immediately

---

[64] Domarus, *Hitler*, pp. 1794–1811; on volunteers p. 1789. Quisling's visit to Berlin was reported in *FF* 15 December 1941. He visited Rosenberg with Hagelin: see Rosenberg to Quisling 7 January 1942, IfZ MA 110.

[65] SKL KTB 6 January 1942, BA-MA RM 7/32, and Skl. 1 Abt. Icb Wochenbericht 5–11 January 1942, BA-MA RM 7/113, KTB Völkerrecht, Politik u. Propaganda.

[66] Notes by Dr Alfred Huhnhäuser printed in H. Lødrup, *Læreraksjonens sanne bakgrunn* (1948) pp. 48ff.

[67] Hagelin to Schickedanz 29 January 1942, IfZ MA 11.

beset with doubts. He tried to analyse Terboven's exact words. The Führer wanted him to 'take over' in Norway. What would this mean for the peace treaty and the declaration of independence? Terboven explained that after the hand-over the Reichskommissariat would eventually be closed, as soon as peace negotiations between the two countries began. But the peace treaty itself had to be postponed until the conclusion of the war on the eastern front. Following the Russian counter-offensive, it was clear that this would not happen before the spring.

Quisling, Terboven and Paul Wegener had several discussions about the contents of the forthcoming ceremony. Between 20 and 24 January Wegener was in Rastenburg to present the results of these talks to Hitler, and to bring back final approval. No progress was made on the matter of a declaration of peace or even of independence.[68]

They also discussed how the new Quisling government was to be appointed. The Reichskommissar agreed that he would not appoint the Norwegian Prime Minister himself, and that Quisling was to make whatever arrangements he wished, using the NS power base. Neither was there any question of an announcement from the German authorities, nor any further discussions of the constitutional aspects of the situation; this was to be entirely a Norwegian concern.[69]

However, there was disagreement over the fate of the Reichskommissariat. Quisling wanted to see it closed as soon as possible, while Terboven was bound by Hitler's instructions that it was to remain at least until the conclusion of peace. On the question of peace, Terboven suggested that it might be possible to make an interim treaty in the context of the hand-over, whereupon the remaining negotiations could be concluded before 1 May when the war with Russia would certainly be over. Quisling did not agree to this as he had personally heard Hitler say that he considered the war already won, even though the army had had to set up camp for the winter outside Moscow. Quisling's advisers were in any case sceptical. Hagelin considered the entire discussion to be a sly manoeuvre on Terboven's part, designed to frustrate Quisling's chances of securing sovereignty. 'The man is a liar!' Boehm's aide-de-camp exclaimed in despair. Wegener's last discussions in Berlin had achieved only slight alterations to the plans as set out by Terboven: the ceremony was to be postponed for two days until 1 February.

---

[68] Boehm, *Norwegen*, pp. 150f and 143ff. The Wegener–Hitler meetings, dated by Wegener to December 1941, must have taken place in late January 1942.

[69] Hagelin to Schickedanz 29 January 1942, IfZ MA 110; in German in BA-MA RM 12 II/172 (Schreiber).

The remaining days were taken up by furious preparation for the ceremony. Riisnæs called together two of the new Supreme Court judges he had appointed to take over from Paal Berg and his colleagues who had left office in protest against the Reichskommissariat, and asked for their assistance with the orders he had received from Quisling. The new government was to be formed on the initiative of the existing ministers, who, on the advice of the Supreme Court and with the authority of the constitutional *jus necessitatis*, were calling on 'the Fører of National Union, Vidkun Quisling, to form a national, Norwegian cabinet to take over the reins of government'. The two judges chose their words very carefully and finally concluded that the Supreme Court could not see any 'conclusive constitutional obstacles' to the suggested procedure.[70]

Not until Friday 30 January was it made public that something big was about to happen in Oslo. The area around Akershus had been lavishly decorated, and Hird members from all over the country were summoned to the capital for the weekend, soon filling garrisons and camps around Oslo. The NRK was getting ready to record the ceremony, as was Norsk Film, which that autumn had started a regular weekly newsreel. On Saturday evening and night posters and placards with Quisling's portrait were posted on to billboards around the city, bearing the simple legend 'NORWAY' in capital letters. All this gave rise to much speculation and consternation in the city. A great change was expected, but no one could tell what exactly the Germans and the NS were moving towards. Norway was holding its breath.[71]

CLOSE TO HIS GOAL

At the age of fifty-four Quisling was close to his goal: that the Norwegian people be led by the one, Universistic party, with himself at the helm. The circumstances of his rise to power were not those he had envisaged in his Universist dreams, however. The country was heavily occupied, with German garrisons everywhere. Concrete bunkers with barbed wire barricades

---

[70] The ministers' decision and the pronouncements of the Supreme Court are printed in *Lovtidende 1942*; also Debes, *Sentraladministrasjonens historie*, pp. 75ff, and Skodvin, 'Det store fremstøt', pp. 725ff. Both Hartmann, *Nytt lys*, and Skodvin, 'Det store fremstøt' and *Norsk historie*, assume that Quisling wanted 30 January to be the day of the takeover of power in order to imitate Hitler in 1933, but that Hitler's jealousy prevented the use of 'his' day. There is no evidence for this other than the change of date.

[71] Skodvin, 'Det store fremstøt', p. 727.

and ominous bullet holes in the buildings were becoming a familiar sight, as were German anti-aircraft batteries appearing on the hillsides around every city. The coastline defences from Oslo to Kirkenes were constantly being reinforced as the country was fortified as it had never been before – by the occupying forces. This second winter of war had also brought in stricter food rationing, partly because of the war in the East. Policing was stepped up, with blockades and identity checks, warnings and prohibitions everywhere. Many aspects of civil life in Norway had changed beyond recognition since April 1940.

To Quisling, this burdensome occupation of his country was just the local manifestation of a world-embracing, universal process of global unification, with Germany on course to unify Europe, and Europe uniting the world. From this Olympian perspective the occupation, even with its pressures and problems for a country so out of tune with the grim realities of history as Norway, was simply necessary in order that the grand idea of Norsk Aktion, a Nansen party, or a Norwegian folk rising might materialise in the midst of the general international upheaval.

At last the trial period had come to an end. Since 25 September 1940 there had been gains and losses in regard to both Quisling's and the party's future. The fact that the projected 100,000 members failed to materialise was his single most damaging defeat. However, 35,000 in the context of Norwegian politics was a respectable membership figure, comparable with that of other ruling parties in the past. If still somewhat small, the party was extremely well organised. What Quisling could perhaps have been most pleased with was his own role as the movement's Fører in relation both to the party itself and to the Germans. Nobody threatened his position, and there was no other power nucleus within the party to challenge it. There were naturally differences of opinion, even distinct factions, over how repressive or justifiable German authority was. For some in the party, concern for Norway and Norwegian interests overshadowed everything else, while for others the great 'Germanic idea' was of paramount importance. Quisling was the moderator, the diffusing force for all the tensions in the party.

Personal disagreements, especially those concerning Hagelin's position in the party, were a problem. Hagelin was distrusted by the old guard of the party who suspected that he was using his new powerful position to enrich himself for personal gain. Although rumours flourished, there was no systematic opposition to speak of. The movement was on the whole more united than could normally have been expected of such a large organisation. In addition, Quisling had the satisfaction of seeing former renegades returning to the ranks, notably Hans S. Jacobsen and Walter Fürst. *Ragnarok*, which had caused him so much embarrassment during the Ethiopia crisis of 1935, was now on the whole a loyal party magazine, encouraging its readers to join the NS. Jacobsen had also become particularly active in the party, and was soon made district governor in his native Østfold. J. B. Hjort and his closest associates, on the other hand, had joined forces with the resistance. Hjort had in fact been arrested and interned by the SS for having openly opposed the Reichskommissariat's interpretation of international law in defining the legal rights of an occupying force. However, he was not held for long in the German concentration camp at Grini, west of Oslo, where approximately 1,000 intransigent Norwegians had been locked up until then. Hjort was given special treatment because of his family connections with the NSDAP. From October 1942 he was interned with his wife and children in a palace in northern Germany.[72]

In short, the *fører* principle had prevailed: Quisling had shown himself to be an effective leader, respected by the membership nationwide. The propaganda office used him effectively as a symbol of unity by distributing his portrait everywhere. All schools were ordered to hang his picture in staff-rooms and offices, though not in classrooms for the time being. Postage stamps bearing his portrait were prepared in time for the takeover. The country's leading sculptor had produced a bust of him, and several casts were made for exhibition in public buildings and institutions. A long series of publications bore his name: *A Book about Quisling*, *Quisling Has Said* (several volumes), *Russia and Ourselves* (new edition) and *The Quisling Case*, including documents from 1932. Many of these titles also appeared in German.

Naturally he took this for what it was: vain and shallow praise, but it was he, nevertheless, who stood at the centre of the party. He had done his best – writing and speaking incessantly, travelling as much as he could, never taking a holiday; his dedication was absolute. The admiration he felt from everywhere in the movement, the eulogies, the triple *Heil og Sæl!* salute which marked the conclusion of all NS meetings whether he was present or not – all this had not appeared out of a vacuum. *He* had created the movement, and nobody else had his 'genial gift of stabilising the fickle', as one commentator wrote after his long speech at University Place on 4 July 1941.[73] 'We Quislings shall never fail. I am proud to be a Quisling!' one of

---

[72] See the account of Hjort's daughter, Wanda Heger, in *Hver fredag foran porten* (1984).
[73] Signed 'Lukas' (= Albin Einnæs) in *FF* 6 September 1941.

his ministers called out, to the sound of rapturous applause at the Coliseum two months later.[74] All this testified to the fact that he had strengthened and not weakened the movement after 25 September 1940.

Perhaps the increasing German respect for him was the surest sign of this. Despite all the difficulties with the growing opposition in the form of widespread resistance against the new order, the Germans always treated him courteously. Terboven was always most correct in his behaviour, and there were never any overtly unpleasant episodes such as had taken place in the summer of 1940, even though there were frequent clashes arising from conflicting interests. He did not share Hagelin's deep mistrust of the Reichskommissar. Indeed, Terboven had often supported him, for example when defending his honour to the other German authorities when the Swedish press launched its enormous offensive against him. Terboven might have been difficult to deal with, but he was objective.[75]

Quisling's broadcasts, like everybody else's, were subject to the censorship of the Reichskommissariat but he was satisfied that there were certain objective reasons for this. In fact, King Haakon and the Nygaardsvold government in London were no more privileged than he: they were not at liberty to say anything on the BBC without its being cleared by British censors.[76] He could also comfort himself with two victories over Terboven during 1941. First of all Terboven had been forced to back down uncondi-tionally over his attempt to do away with the Norwegian title *fører* because of its uncomfortable closeness to the German cognate. Secondly his attempt to monopolise the communication line to Hitler through Dr Lammers had been rebutted from Berlin: Quisling was welcome to write to the Führer any time through this channel.[77]

He had made five visits to Germany after 25 September 1940 – and received several more invitations which he was unable to follow up. He was always treated with great respect, despite the fact that he did not as yet occupy any official position. He could certainly not complain about the amount of attention he was receiving from the Germans; if he were to cast an eye around the National Socialist world, he would see that no other party leader was treated with such deference as he was. True, his Dutch counter-

---

[74] Hagelin in the Coliseum cinema 5 September 1941, NRK ho 627–8.
[75] Terboven to Ribbentrop 22 October 1941, PAAA 34/99 Ha-Pol Wiehl. Schweden 1941–3.
[76] Dahl, *Dette er London*, pp. 160ff; Høidal, *Quisling*, p. 411.
[77] Quisling to Wegener 14 February 1941, parts of which are in *Straffesak* p. 529; Quisling to Lammers 10 March 1941 in *ADAP* D XII no. 147 pp. 214ff. Lammers to Terboven 5 October 1941, copy in BA NS 43/27.

part Mussert had been invited to meet Hitler the previous December when they were both attending the Reichstag, but his invitation arose from the fact that he was accompanying the Reichskommissar Seys-Inquardt. The Swedish press took this to imply that Quisling's position had been 'weakened' and had become 'awkward'. But this was pure speculation, which nevertheless circulated in the international press via the United Press correspondent in Stockholm. What this journalist was in no position to know was that on that occasion Mussert had been forced to take a humiliating oath to Hitler, a position which Quisling was never put in. For Quisling the conditions of the union with Germany, both the current union of arms and the equal standing of Norway in a future Germanic federation, were ones he had set out himself, a fact which was acknowledged in his interviews with the German press.[78]

And now he was ready, indeed well prepared, to take over the reins of state, a controversial figure in his own country, but with a position within his own party which was unassailable. He enjoyed full support from the occupying power, and had secured assurances of full independence once the battle against Bolshevism had been fought and won. He was confident that in time public opinion would turn in his favour once the country appreciated what was in its best interest. He had no delusions about his current reputation, being kept up to date with both the broadcasts on the London radio and the underground literature which had been circulating widely since the confiscation of radio sets the previous September. He was actually well aware of the animosity felt towards him outside his own movement, which he attributed mainly to propaganda and ill-informed misunderstanding.

He and Maria had moved house at the end of October 1941. The apartment in Erling Skjalgssonsgate was not suitable for official occasions, besides being completely inadequate for security reasons. The police had information that so-called 'illegal groups' were plotting against his life. Hagelin directed his attention to Villa Grande at Bygdøy outside Oslo. Villa Grande was a grandiose but unfinished showpiece started by the industrialist Sam Eyde during the First World War, by this time state property and thus ready to be put at his disposal.

The villa, now renamed Gimle after the old Norse dwelling of the gods,

---

[78] Hirschfield, *Nazi Rule*, pp. 298f; Domarus, *Hitler*, p. 1812; UP telegram in *Neue Züricher Zeitung* 16 December 1941. 'Norwegens Zukunft an der Seite Deutschlands', interview given by Quisling to SS-Kriegsberichter Robert Krötz, *Völkischer Beobachter* 3 February 1941, also printed in other German newspapers, cutting in BA 58-Zsg 117/1172.

was very spacious indeed: on the ground floor there was a large hall with a fireplace, a library, a garden room looking out on to the park, a music room and an impressive dining room. All the paintings from Russia were brought out of the bank vaults and the furniture moved over from the old apartment. The antiques, arranged on the ground floor, certainly looked impressive. A wide main staircase led up to the more private second floor where Vidkun and Maria had separate bedrooms with elegant *en suite* bathrooms and dressing rooms next to the private day room with its own dining room. On the same floor were the kitchen and servants' quarters (gradually the number of servants increased to twelve). On the third floor were the guest rooms and in the turret there were two further rooms, affording a view of the fjord, the city and the surrounding hills. The Søyle (Column) Room and the Hird rooms in the basement were perfect for less grand occasions, with their medieval and Nordic decorations. The following year a full-size cinema was installed in the Hird room with two 35 mm screens, much to the delight of the domestic staff, the guard from the Hird and Quisling's own guard, which had been transferred to buildings round the edge of the grounds.[79]

Villa Gimle – home to the gods – situated on the fjord approach to the Norwegian capital, founded by one of the country's great industrialists and completed by the Fører of National Socialism and his Minister of the Interior; filled with the treasures – more or less authentic – of the tsars; decorated in a multitude of styles and guarded by a modern Hird bearing the emblem of the flaming sword on its banner of the sun cross: this was the residence of the Norwegian head of state now taking up the position of Minister President of his country.

[79] Documents related to Gimle in RA LD 29 Q Div. 7.

7

Revolution from above

The Norwegian people need a strict schoolmaster, one of their own, one who knows them intimately, and who can instil national discipline in them. *Quisling in Akershus, 1 February 1942*[1]

'In hardly any other country is it as easy ... to bring about a national revolution from above as it is in Norway,' Quisling explained to Terboven in the autumn of 1941. This was due to the country's history, and to the Norwegians as a law-abiding and sober people, who, if 'given a well-reasoned argument for change ... will soon accept it'. A determined and disciplined party that constituted 1–2 per cent of the electorate, far bigger than, say, the Bolsheviks in Russia in 1917, would certainly succeed in its revolutionary project, because rule from above in accordance with the *fører* principle fitted in well with the traditional Norwegian 'mode of government'. This mode was based on the authority of such institutions as the old Norse rule by chieftains, or the regional power of the law speakers (*lagmann*), hereditary leaders who exercised their leadership in a natural way. However, since the French Revolution, Norway had been subjected to a series of false leaders who had made themselves apparently indispensable through mechanisms that were inherent in parliamentarism and the party system. It was the remains of this rule by party which was now putting up resistance to the new order, he said. The purpose of the national revolution was therefore to free the people from these false nineteenth-century-style politicians and to replace them with a leadership in tune with the nation's history and true traditions. A revolution from above would take place as soon as 'the old bankrupt and decadent so-called élite' had been replaced by force.[2]

In this, however, he was proved wrong, and his miscalculation became particularly obvious at the time when he took power on 1 February 1942. The Norwegian civilian resistance – the self-styled Home Front (Hjemmefronten) – was more than the protests of the old élite. As old leaders were

---

[1] *FF* 1 February 1942.
[2] Quisling to Terboven 17 September 1941, *Straffesak* p. 122; speech in Klingenberg cinema, Oslo 1 February 1943, *FF* 2 February 1943.

removed by the government, new ones were taking their place. Scarcely was an old group taken over by the NS or suppressed from above, than a new one was formed, this time secret and conspiratorial, and led by people who were out for confrontation with the NS and prepared for active opposition.

Oslo University was a symbol of this ungovernable Norway. In the early days of the occupation it had been fairly co-operative, hoping that things would improve and that its own authorities would get a chance to influence the situation. Even with the appointment of three NS professors in the autumn of 1940 the institution lay low. Gradually, however, it appeared that the university, staff and students alike, was passionately anti-NS. Demonstrations and dangerous resistance work were time and again traced back to the university. When the Rector, Professor Didrik Arup Seip, was arrested by the German security police during the state of emergency in 1941 for being 'responsible for the university's and the students' hostile attitude towards National Union and Germany' and sent to Grini concentration camp (which had been opened for precisely this reason in June 1941), the university became more, not less determined to mount resistance. An NS professor was appointed Rector and granted full authority by the Ministry; the academic collegiate was disbanded in keeping with the principles of the *fører* government. However, the new government was unable to prevent the resistance from spreading, even though Quisling himself on several occasions had to intervene to sort out the problems for the NS Rector.[3] The Reichskommissar was furious, and denounced the students for their lack of judgement and their negative, arrogant stance towards National Socialism and its 'sincere revolution'. Quisling, for his part, felt that the old academic families were using their young members to whip up opposition to the new order.[4]

A similar situation was developing among the clergy and the church-going population in general. Once the opposition had taken hold in these circles nothing could reduce it, and Quisling had more than a shrewd idea whom he had to thank for this: Bishop Eivind Berggrav, a prelate with a particular talent for spreading the word of resistance, a man of the cloth who had devoted his life to the service of God, but in reality a bitter political opponent. Berggrav had been one of the first who tried to overthrow the 9 April government, arguing that it was not in Germany's interest to co-operate with Quisling.[5] During the negotiations that summer, he had, as far

[3] A. Hoel, *Universitet under okkupasjonen* (1978), particularly ch. 'Protektoratet'. D. A. Seip, *Hjemme i fiendeland* (1946) pp. 195ff.
[4] Terboven, speech at Akershus 1 February 1942, '1. Februar 1942' (1942) pp. 83f.
[5] Fjørtoft, *Ulvetiden*, pp. 176ff, 253ff.

as Quisling understood, been making an effort to influence the political
process – more precisely to prevent him and the National Union from
exercising any influence. He had then organised his fellow bishops into a
united front in a Church and Lay movement whose aim was to defend the
Christian faith against National Socialism (even though Quisling considered
the NS to be a particularly pro-church, Christian party). The bishop had
obviously got the idea that, in return for the support from Rosenberg during
the power struggle, Quisling was obliged to impose a 'Rosenbergian'
ideology on the Norwegian people and to preach the heathen gospel of
Alfred Rosenberg's *Mythos des 20. Jahrhunderts* in place of traditional
Lutheranism.[6] Berggrav's alarm was groundless on that score, but he nevertheless stirred up the country's clergy through his systematic dissemination
of the view that NS was an enemy of Christianity, and in a pastoral letter of
January 1941 even got the bishops to agree to warn their people against the
new order. On the whole, Berggrav kept a high profile politically by
condemning the Hird's action against those who had been badgering NS
schoolchildren, and openly supporting the Supreme Court judges when in
December 1940 they resigned their offices in protest against the Reichskommissar. The issue here was clearly a political one, as the judges chose to
overlook the fact that according to international law, they had no authority
to test the decrees of the occupying power against the Constitution – a fact
that was accepted both in Denmark and in Holland.[7] Berggrav was also
advising a group of actors who did not want to perform in front of Germans
in July 1941, and assisting in a protest action led by some teachers against
the Ministry. Berggrav's influence and involvement could in fact be traced in
several instances of protest and manifestations of hostility to the new order.
When asked by the Minister of Church and Education why he involved
himself in all these worldly issues, he answered by saying that it was the 'holy
right' of each man to obey the dictates of his conscience, even if it came to
protesting against the government, and as a clergyman he felt that special
responsibility to offer 'spiritual advice' in such matters as conscience was a
God-given matter. According to that principle, Quisling concluded, there

---

[6] E. Berggrav, *Da kampen kom* (1945) pp. 104, 109, in which it appears that NS priests
informed Quisling of Berggrav's arguments. Also Berggrav, *Front Fangenskap Flukt* (1966)
p. 17.

[7] Erling Sandene in *Rettstidende* (1990) pp. 1305–15; see also Ferdinand Schjelderup, *Fra
Norges kamp for retten* (1945) ch. 15; for a theoretical approach, see Ole Torleif Røed, *Fra
krigens folkerett* (1945) p. 54. Hirschfield, *Nazi Rule*, pp. 154ff, ch. 'The Supreme Court'.

would scarcely be an end to the extent to which the Church could get mixed up in secular affairs.[8]

In Quisling's opinion Berggrav simply wanted to play a political role on behalf of the old system. That was why the bishop made common cause with his fellow civil servants in the Supreme Court, with Paal Berg (whom he knew well and had worked with closely in April 1940), with the Rector of Oslo University, his brother-in-law, with the actors, teachers and all the rest. That his political opposition was dressed up in theological garb did not make it any easier to take, but it did make it harder to curb. People trusted him, the clergy listened to him, and the congregations were larger than ever.

THE ACT OF STATE

Early on the morning of Monday 1 February 1942 everything was set for a great national celebration. The Fører's portrait had been posted up everywhere and the Norwegian flag was flying from the top of public buildings. In Oslo the trams and suburban trains were festooned with flags and the city centre was decked out in columns decorated with spruce and with sun cross banners. An avenue of flag-waving party faithful lined the way down from Karl Johan Street to Akershus Castle.

At a quarter past twelve the Reichskommissar summoned the thirteen ministers to his office. Hagelin tendered their resignations, which were accepted, and he agreed that they would appoint a prime minister. The NS Fører was duly appointed and given the title of Minister President.

This was followed by a ceremony in the Knights' Hall in Akershus. Tapestries bearing the sun cross motif hung from the walls, and Norwegian and German flags and banners from the ceiling. The orchestra played music from both countries: Strauss's Feast March and the Homage March from Grieg's *Sigurd Jorsalfar,* while the Minister President and the Reichskommissar took turns to make speeches. The eagle of the sun cross shone from the backdrop and the German national coat of arms stood out magnificently. This was followed by Hird and Legion parades around the fortress, a special performance in the National Theatre with an address by Guldbrand Lunde, and in the evening a torch-lit procession to the balcony of the Grand Hotel where Quisling was greeted by the adulation of his supporters and the *Heil og Sæl* salute. Later in the evening party representatives gathered at the Saga and Klingenberg cinemas to offer their thanks to the Fører through the

---

[8] Berggrav, *Da kampen kom*, pp. 141f.

words of Ministers Fuglesang and Stang. The day was rounded off with a banquet for prominent Norwegians and Germans at Gimle, the Quislings' new home.

Enormous care had been taken in the short time available to mark this day with pomp and splendour. Quisling had given instructions that the event was to be singled out as more magnificent than either the birth of the Constitution of 17 May 1814 or the secession from Sweden on 7 June 1905. 'Our Fører becomes Norway's Fører' ran the *Fritt Folk* headline of the day.

However, the German institution of the Reichskommissariat remained *in situ*, and still showed no sign of reducing its staff. Terboven also ignored Quisling's request to declare the great day 'the last step towards full independence' in his speech at Akershus and made no reference to Hitler's decision to nullify the judgements of the German prize courts. Instead, the Reichskommissar took the opportunity to present a great deal of revealing information he had gathered concerning Bishop Berggrav's role as private peace broker in Berlin and London in 1939–40, in order to clarify the run-up to 9 April, as he put it. It must have been a relief to Quisling to hear the Reichskommissar preparing the noose for the leading figure of the civilian resistance to the NS. He knew that Berggrav had had several meetings with the Reichskommissar, including a long discussion at Skaugum in the presence of Reichsführer Himmler in December 1940. Now he was written off by the Germans for all the world to hear.[9]

In his own long speech, which was clear, well-structured and confidently delivered, Quisling made the most of the occasion. He declared that not even now had everything been achieved: there had been great difficulties over the past sixteen months, and what was to come was only an 'interim arrangement', but through it Norway would be getting a national government once more: 'We are only one step away from full national freedom and independence ... The most important foundation for a new, a free and a great nationally conscious Norway has been won.'

The National Government would now try to change the direction of Norwegian foreign policy, away from Nordic co-operation, and establish closer ties with Germany. His government would thus conduct 'an honest and sensible Realpolitik' with the great power, which was also interested in a 'strong and independent Norway'. His speech went on to take in grand

---

[9] Act of State – sources: the Norwegian press 2 February 1942 and special edition of *FF* 1 February 1942; NRK ho 3138–9; Norsk Film Ukerevy no. 18 (1942), NRK fa; see also Ukerevy nos. 20, 21; for the German view of the Act of State see Kjeldstadli, *Hjemmestyrkene*, pp. 137ff, ch. 'Nasjonal Samlings store fremstøt'.

geopolitical vistas, for the world was slowly becoming one, and it was only the really great states and federations that would be able to make progress in the future. In the West the United States had built itself up into a great power, and in the East Russia would continue to grow. Locked in between and threatened by 'these two colossi', Europe had to define her new role.

The Fører was greatly concerned to justify his government's rise to power. Because the party was the manifestation of the people's will, and had been proved right in its views about the best interests of the country, the NS now represented the will of the nation. 'Whether the minority or the majority', the party had the right to power because it had won its case. And with this revolutionary legitimation, Quisling inaugurated his government.

There were no formal changes of any enduring kind to the 1814 Constitution under the new rule, except for the reinstatement of the clause denying Jews entry to the country. However, as long as the Storting did not function and the present king had lost his right to the throne, the country enjoyed a new form of government which the party's lawyers termed 'the authoritarian state'.[10] In such a state the distinction between the executive authority and the legislature was terminated. They were combined into a new supreme body – the person of the Minister President who was to make laws in the place of the Storting and was to head the government, replacing the King in Council. The former division of power no longer held, as the *fører* principle acknowledged no essential difference between the passing of laws and administrative decisions and the Minister President exercised his double office as legislator and executive head of state.

The National Government's relationship with the occupying forces resembled that of the former Administrative Council's, as the Administrative Council had also been officially appointed by a body of Norwegians although in practice completely dependent on German recognition – indeed, Bräuer had interfered in every little detail, including individual appointments, which Terboven did not bother to do now. Both were, however, dependent on German approval. Constitutionally speaking, the new government was still an occupation government, albeit with much wider credentials than before, even though Quisling never put it in these terms. The important

---

[10] The expression 'the authoritarian state' was used for example by Georg Hasle of the Ministry of the Interior (from 1943 head of the legal department in the Ministry of Justice) in the draft Constitution, 20 August 1942: §1. Norway is an authoritarian *fører* state, quoted in Wyller, *Nyordning og motstand*, p. 349 n. 65, and in S. Østrem, 'Forerlesninger i statsrett høsten 1942', MS in the library of the Faculty of Law, UiO; see also the chapter 'Den autoritære stat' in S. Feyling, *Stat og Kirke. Kirken og Den Nye tid* (1941) pp. 25ff; RA FMK 5.

thing for him was that the NS had taken a step forward in the direction of independence by forming a National Government.

The new head of state moved his offices to the Royal Palace, renamed Oslo Palace. The state seal was put to use once more, and the mechanism for conferring honours could be put to work again. Even state visits could be arranged. Certain changes, however, had to be made. The inscription on the seal was changed from 'Haakon VII King of Norway' to 'The Seal of the Norwegian State'. The Order of St Olav was remodelled to look more up to date.

Symbolic manifestations apart, the Act of State had serious implications for the political relationship between the head of government and the Reichskommissar. Quisling had gone from being party leader without any official position to Minister President with all the honour and esteem which the title carried. Goebbels noted in his diary how Quisling's rise to Minister President had provoked an international sensation. He held out little hope that someone as universally despised would be able to improve his standing in international opinion simply through an Act of State, and become anything other than a 'quisling': 'The man has managed to become a symbol, without really having earned it.' Goebbels also found Quisling's claim to have merged royal, governmental and parliamentary authority 'grotesque' in its shamelessness, pointing out 'there is still a Reichskommissar'.[11]

STATE VISIT

Quisling's first official visit to Berlin in February 1942 was extremely successful. He and the Reichskommissar led their respective delegations – Terboven with Paul Wegener and his legal adviser and Quisling with Hagelin, Fuglesang and the staff leader of the Hird, who had just returned from the eastern front with the Iron Cross. The leader of the NS Youth, Axel Stang, also joined the delegation. They travelled by air to Stettin on Wednesday 11 February, allowing for a short inspection of the Norwegian Legion at Fallingbostel before the train journey to Berlin; for reasons of security it was decided against transporting the company by plane directly to Tempelhof. Lammers, leading an official retinue, together with von Weizsäcker of the Foreign Ministry, received the party at Stettiner station. Norwegian flags fluttered on the platform and a special company paraded

---

[11] The Goebbels Diary, entry for 2 February 1942.

outside the station; it was inspected in a solemn manner before the guests got into the cars which took them to Hotel Adlon.[12]

The accidental death of Fritz Todt meant that the Norwegian guests had to wait until the following day for their audience with Hitler. On Friday 13 February the group from Norway was received on the steps of the Chancellery at 1 o'clock by Lammers, after which Hitler spoke to Quisling and Terboven in the presence of Hagelin, Lammers and Martin Bormann – the head of the newly established Party Chancellery who, following Rudolf Hess's escape to Great Britain, had become Hitler's grey eminence. The conversation lasted no more than three-quarters of an hour, and thus could have been no more than a quick presentation of the options of the new government by Quisling: first of all a peace settlement with Germany, and the entry into a Greater Germanic Union, followed by Norwegian diplomatic representation abroad; Wehrmacht bases in Norway; a full arms union with Germany as part of a common Germanic navy and airforce, but with room for a national Norwegian army and coast guard, and so on. Quisling had developed all these points in a substantial memorandum on the new order in Norway, including a draft peace settlement between Norway and Germany, which he handed over to Dr Lammers.[13]

After their brief discussion the Führer and his guests adjourned to the Chancellery dining hall, where a large gathering of prominent figures was waiting for them: Field Marshal Keitel, Grand Admiral Raeder, Reichsführer SS Himmler, Ministers Goebbels and Frick, the leader of the Labour front, Ley, and Rosenberg. Altogether there were thirty to forty people seated at around six or seven tables. Hitler, who sat between Quisling and Hagelin, as was his wont on these joyless occasions, spoke at length, this time treating his guests to an enthusiastic account of the fortunate breakthrough which the battleships *Scharnhorst* and *Gneisenau* and the cruiser *Prince Eugen* had just made by sailing from Brest through the Channel to north Germany right under the nose of Churchill's navy. There was little opportunity for the Norwegians to talk to the interesting Germans present. The meal observed strict rituals whereby everything was centred around the Führer. The food was simple, the drink was limited, smoking was forbidden as it always was in Hitler's presence, and Quisling and his compatriots must have felt somewhat ill at ease, as did most guests at Chancellery luncheons. Goebbels found

---

[12] Account based on the official 'Besuch des norwegischen Ministerpresident Quislings in Berlin 12–15 Februar 1942', IfZ MA 110, and *FF* 21 February 1942.

[13] *ADAP* E I no. 248 pp. 466ff, 'Memorandum om nyordningen i Norge 10 February 1942'; see *Straffesak* p. 113.

Quisling rather unprepossessing. His diary entry for that evening read: 'I do not feel any particular liking for him. He is dogmatic and theoretical, and it is unlikely that he will ever make a great statesman.'[14]

In the evening Terboven entertained the Norwegians at the hotel. He spoke in pleasant and polite tones about Quisling and congratulated him on his new government, which was 'national, in the eyes of the country, and National Socialist in the eyes of the world'. The Minister President was equally cordial in return. On the following day he met the international press at his hotel. Journalists from agencies and papers in pro-German European countries had come to hear the famous Quisling discuss his new government. There cannot have been many of them, judging by reports, and the conference was concluded after only half an hour, as Quisling had an engagement to make a short proclamation to the listeners to the Reichs-rundfunk. At least he managed to answer questions concerning the composition and the plans of his new government, and was asked about Nordic co-operation: 'We have abandoned the old co-operation; it was a sham,' he declared, and explained that the other Nordic countries had simply sat back while Finland struggled against Bolshevism. The subject of Bishop Berggrav's intrigues also came up, and Quisling commented that '[i]f he thinks he is going to achieve a political martyrdom, he is mistaken: Bishop Berggrav will never be made a martyr'.

An Italian journalist wanted to hear Norway's views on the Berlin–Rome axis. Quisling answered that as soon as Norway regained her full freedom and independence, the axis could be extended as far as Oslo and much further north, and that Norway was also prepared to join the pact with Germany, Italy and Japan.

There followed a visit to Göring, where he and Terboven had a short discussion, doubtless about the development of Norway's hydro-electric plants, and where the Reichsmarschall showed that he was in favour of the idea of a Norwegian airforce in the future.[15] After this there was a reception at the Nordische Verbindungsstelle, where Quisling met a new contingent of prominent Germans from the government, the SS and the party, among them once more his old acquaintance from the days of the Agrarian cabinet, the former envoy to Oslo, von Weizsäcker, and the Secretary of State Dr Stuckart from the Ministry of the Interior whom he had met the previous year.

---

[14] Goebbels Diary, entry for 13 February 1942.
[15] Schreiber, Report, 9 May 1942, BA-MA RM 12 II/172.

On Sunday 15 February the official part of the visit was over and Terboven left with his retinue. Quisling stayed on for a few days in order to contact his special friends, Raeder and Rosenberg.[16]

The meeting with Rosenberg was particularly interesting. Since the Frankfurt congress he had been promoted to the position of Minister for the Occupied Territories, and was now administering a large Eastern Ministry which was in charge of the two Reichskommissariats in the East and the Ukraine, which were continually expanding as the areas behind the front were being declared pacified and the occupation government changed over from military to civilian rule. Parts of these areas were where Quisling had worked in his days of famine relief – Kiev, Tserkassij, Nikalajev and Kherson – and he was keen to offer his views on how the German campaign could set off a war of liberation in the East.[17]

On Wednesday 18 February he was back in Oslo. The German visit had strengthened his position. The next day, after his press conference at the Grand Hotel, *Fritt Folk* helped him by analysing the situation in its reportage:

We who two years ago were present at Prime Minister Quisling's press conference in the Storting, when the country was at its lowest level, could not avoid recalling that time. Then the Fører was truly alone ... and the rats were gnawing away in silence, ready to devour him. Yesterday the press stood before Quisling as Norway's Minister President, who had come home from Berlin where he had negotiated on equal terms with Hitler and a number of the other most powerful people in the world.[18]

Or, as Quisling himself explained to the press: 'Norway has once more become outward looking. And we know that it is undoubtedly only a question of time before the next step is taken towards the full restoration of our national life.'

But before that happened, the internal politics of the new regime were setting in motion great changes in Norway.

STRICT SCHOOLMASTER

As a result of the Act of State, the NS changed its role from being a recruiting body that needed to attract a large membership in order to shore up the party's position in the eyes of the Germans, to being the leading body

---

[16] *FF* 18 February 1942, discussion of meeting 16 February 1942.
[17] Rosenberg to Quisling 8 January 1942, IfZ MA 110. A. Dallin, *German Rule*, pp. 84ff, 588.
[18] *FF* 20 February 1942.

of the national revolution regardless of its attraction to new members. What Quisling had always maintained was suddenly true: the size of the party was in itself insignificant; what mattered was the quality of its members. The Germans stopped assessing him on the basis of the statistics issued by the Einsatzstab.

Moreover, Terboven was at last conducting a radical downsizing of the Reichskommissariat. At a conference at Skaugum on 6 February he warned all his heads of department that there would be a drastic reduction in personnel, and that the administrative machinery would be subject to 'a decisive reduction as far as co-operation with the Norwegians is concerned', the aim being 'an independent Norwegian regime'. Departmental heads were therefore no longer to give instructions to the ministers but instead were to be 'calm and wait' and allow them to take over the political leadership of the administration too.[19]

This change was enormous and affected the entire public climate in Norway throughout 1942. Suddenly the NS was in control of the state, which implied that the revolution could be carried through regardless of its popular support. On the other hand, the movement had to think in the long term, and make plans for how a party with such a limited membership could manage to hold on to all the positions of power in Norwegian society.

Quisling announced this new stage of policy at a press conference on 19 February, making the astonishing declaration that although membership was accelerating, it had to be limited. The party needed to be cleaned up and strengthened, and a raising of standards would be effected through increased investigation into applicants' record sheets and via a party decree that whoever was 'visibly intoxicated in a public place, indoors or outside,' would be excluded from the party. Approximately forty members were excluded in 1942 on the grounds of unacceptable behaviour. This was only the beginning. The number of people drummed out of the movement rose dramatically in 1943 and 1944.[20]

A significant number of the laws introduced by the Minister President were designed to protect the party's work on the new order. Regulations were introduced to combat a new crime which the old criminal law did not recognise: 'activities against the people and state'. As early as November 1940 the Ministry of Justice had established a new court to which such cases were transferred, called the People's Court even though it usually consisted

[19] Lødrup, *Læreaksjonens*, pp. 51f.
[20] Party decree of 31 March 1942, *NSM* 1942/3; list of exclusions, *NSM* 1942/3, 8, 11.

of only professional judges – three in all. Now it was to judge in 'all criminal cases which can be tried under criminal law', provided that the state attorneys found the violation in question to be 'an act of enmity against the people and the state'. This was obviously a measure designed by Riisnæs to deal with the growing resistance to the regime. Then on 12 March 1942 Norway officially became a one-party state with the passing of a law of two short paragraphs only: '§1. NS is the ruling party in Norway and closely tied to the state. §2. The party's organisation and activities and the duties of its membership are decided by the NS Fører.' The law did not guarantee any monopoly for the NS, unlike the German model, although it was clear that the party would occupy the dominant position in the future. Any crime 'against the people and the state' would thereafter apply even to the party.

In the same meeting when the law on the party and the state was passed, Riisnæs proposed a law on 'protection against certain attacks on the state and the party', which provided for up to two years' imprisonment for promoting or furthering 'mendacious or grossly distorted statements' which could harm the progress of state, the government or the party, and three years for promoting 'inflammatory or malicious utterances' about prominent individuals in the state or the party, designed to undermine the people's confidence in the government. Even harsher initiatives followed. The following week the Minister President was given the authority to confiscate the property of all those guilty of acts against the people or state, or of those who hindered the work of the party or harmed its reputation. A few months later again a punishment of up to six years' imprisonment and seizure of all property was introduced for those who simply gave financial support to activities considered to be against the people or state.

The Minister President thus provided the party with more than adequate defence against attacks from real or potential enemies. 'For one who feels for his people as much as I do, it is not pleasant to have to use force.' Thus Quisling at a press conference on 19 February. Like a strict schoolmaster he would stop at nothing to maintain discipline. 'We shall destroy them completely, if they continue to fight against the interests of Norway.' Rather like a missionary, he genuinely hoped that 'every Norwegian' would recognise of his own free will that the NS was right.[21]

The question of future recruitment to the NS was vital to the new one-party state. How to bring the Norwegian youth into the party had been settled a fortnight earlier in an interview with the leader of the NS Youth

[21] *FF* 20 February 1942.

Organisation, Axel Stang, when he presented the law on national youth service which he had drafted in the very first meeting of the National Government on 5 February: 'All Norwegian boys and girls, for the sake of the cultivation of the nation, and to serve their people and fatherland, will be required to do service in the NS Youth Organisation,' read the opening paragraph. The law was obviously modelled on the German law concerning the Hitler Youth Service. But although membership was compulsory in Germany as the Hitler Youth was a state institution, this was not the case in Norway. In Norway the NS was still a political party, and that children as young as ten years old should be made to do service for a political party was obviously alien to every liberal way of thinking; indeed, it put the NS in the same class as its contemporary Communist one-party dictatorships. Whatever was thought of Quisling and his party as a collaboration government which made common cause with the occupying forces, this was seen as a direct assault on individual rights and all the more unpalatable as it involved children.

Both Quisling and the party leadership completely underestimated the reaction that this initiative would provoke. The youth service law fanned a fire which proved catastrophic to the revolution from above. When the fire was over in the summer of 1942, Quisling's reputation had suffered so much that there was no longer any possibility that he might ever again influence public opinion. From then on he stopped referring to himself as a schoolmaster, and was no longer inclined to try to win over the people. Rather, he saw himself from then on as a military leader leading a retreating army, engaged in bringing the reluctant Norwegians through the hell of war. It was another terrible blow to his reputation. For all those who had doubted that someone with his reputation after 9 April would ever be able to succeed as a political leader, this defeat in the spring of 1942 provided ample confirmation.

The teachers' opposition was perhaps the most serious challenge. For a long time there had been friction between the Ministry and the teachers because of some local NS leaders' insistence that the teachers should join the party, something the Ministry was actually opposed to. However, when committed party teachers demanded this, Skancke found it hard to oppose them too openly. What the Ministry wanted was to get the teachers to enrol in a new organisation, the Norwegian Teachers' Corporation (Norsk Lærersamband). The law concerning the Teachers' Corporation was one in a series of initiatives to remould the country's professional organisations according to corporate structures. In addition to the organisation of teaching staff at all levels, similar laws were passed covering publishers, lawyers, the press and advertising agencies, in addition to the earlier departmental decrees concerning those employed in the health sector, the film industry and the police service. Preparations were also made to organise veterinary surgeons, chemists, doctors, dentists and engineers along the same lines. The idea was to recast the organisations 'vertically' and place superiors and subordinates in the same corporation so that they could in theory be organised into a Riksting (national assembly), and in practice could be turned into self-governing professional monopolies or guilds, as outlined in the NS manifesto. The new corporations were designed to be politically neutral and independent of party membership. However, one over-zealous local leader declared that the Teachers' Corporation was required to instil in its members 'a positive attitude towards the youth service so that the state could reach its goal with the young not only out of school but in school too'.[22]

This was a blunder on a grand scale. The association with the youth service proved disastrous for the Teachers' Corporation, as it provided the old leaders of the teachers' organisations with justification for taking action against the Teachers' Corporation, which in any case was having problems in becoming established. Now the protests were backed by the nation-wide anger against the youth service. Teachers who protested against the youth service did so on grounds of conscience and resigned from the Corporation in one and the same letter.[23] The threat of indoctrination of the children rallied much greater support around the protest against the Teachers' Corporation than might otherwise have been the case. Moreover, by some coincidence, on the same day as the teachers' protest began, 14 February 1942, the bishops issued their protest against the youth service. In the outraged tones of Bishop Berggrav's inimitable style, the letter declared that forcing children to join the party was tantamount to 'disturbing the nation to the very core of its being'.[24] Copies of the letter were circulated immediately, including to the BBC. It gave an invaluable fillip to the teachers' protest by lending moral weight to the less rousing organisational points. The letter itself was followed up by an action within the Church

[22] Orvar Sæther, quoted in Olav Hoprekstad, *Frå lærarstriden* (1946) p. 28.
[23] Magnus Jensen, 'Kampen om skolen', *Norges krig* III, pp. 82ff; Hoprekstad, *Frå lærarstriden*, ch. 'Under framanvelde', and p. 36.
[24] I. B. Carlsen, *Kirkefronten i Norge* (1945) ch. 9, 'Kampen om barna'; H. C. Christie, *Den norske kirke i kamp* (1945); L. Schübeler, *Kirkekampen slik jeg så den* (1945); B. Nøkleby, *Holdningskamp. Norge i krig* IV (1986).

which eventually led to the bishops echoing the Supreme Court by resigning their offices on the grounds that the state had committed a crime against the Church. This decisive action on the part of the bishops had such a deep effect on the country that most priests made common cause with them and resigned their office during the Easter Sunday service.

The united front of the teachers and the clergy made a huge impression. Among parents resistance spread throughout the country like an awakening via secret meetings and victorious ballot results which were printed in the underground press and broadcast on the BBC. During the winter a parents' petition was circulated and signed by a hundred thousand at least. One of the biggest waves of civil unrest in the entire war was sweeping across Norway, and news of the recalcitrant bishops, priests and teachers defying the detested Quisling government filled the columns of the Allied and neutral press. The Germans were also reaching conclusions. On 1 May 1942 the German High Command stated in its war diary that 'in Norway organised resistance to Quisling has started'.[25]

Quisling's reaction to all this was bitter, furious, even uncontrolled. It was as if he realised, as the revolt gained momentum, that his revolution from above was threatening to become a fiasco. He responded to the bishops' mass resignation with a circular addressed to all priests in the State Church: theirs was an unprecedented action, but not entirely unexpected as Berggrav had obviously been waiting for an opportunity to strike. 'It is the fate of the nations that small men in high places, with limited perspectives and no historical vision whatsoever, for the sake of imagined gains are destroying everything that has been built over generations by wise and patriotic men.' Quisling was given further opportunity to express his feelings when he summoned Berggrav to the palace three days later to interrogate him about the last days of the April 1940 government. He was determined to get to the bottom of that conspiracy, which he still regarded as the worst crime yet from Berggrav's side. The meeting in the royal dining hall on 3 April was hostile, with Berggrav alone on the one side of the table, the Minister President, Hagelin, Lie, Riisnæs and Fuglesang, as well as two adjutants on the other. Quisling fired off his charges with intense bitterness. He maintained that Berggrav, who together with Bräuer and Paal Berg had overthrown his April government, was ultimately responsible for Norway's state of war with Germany, for the bombings and fires that ensued, and thus

---

[25] P. E. Schramm, *Kriegstagebuch des Oberkommandos der Wehrmacht 1940–1945* II (1965) p. 331.

for the occupation and all its implications, not to mention the enormous costs which were now burdening the state – 5 milliard kroner, 'which is what the entire Franco-German war cost France'. Those responsible for this deserved to be executed a hundred times over, at the very least.

But Berggrav was most uncooperative and refused to give any account of the conversations he had had with Bräuer. He provoked Lie by reminding him, apparently innocently, of a letter Lie had written to him after 15 April to thank him for his action in getting an Administrative Council established. According to Berggrav, the meeting deteriorated into a bickering session. When he looked back on it he was not in the least impressed by the new leaders of government: 'Quisling [was] the only interesting person there,' he noted. 'There was something helpless about him which one could not but feel drawn to. With no sense of humour whatsoever and moreover completely intransigent, it seemed as though he was driving blindly down a road he could not avoid. Sometimes he seemed absent-minded. But even so there was something notable, or at least unusual, about Quisling.'[26]

Berggrav was quite right in his assessment that Quisling was not able to change direction in the way he was dealing with the Church. Feelings ran even higher when the Fører visited Skien the following week. The district governor welcomed him to the Telemark, 'the district which has the honour of having nurtured you, and of being the home of your family for half a millennium'. In front of a large gathering in the Parkbiografen cinema on Saturday 7 March, he made his first public speech after the dramatic events of the spring. He reminded the assembly that in Norway new realities always had to be 'introduced by force if they are to succeed'. Neither of the two medieval kings, Harald Finehair or Olav Haraldsen, had negotiated with the people, but had had to use force, and now the same course was necessary again. He made it clear that the bishops' attempt to set up a new church outside the state by keeping the church buildings, their residences and their stipends would not be tolerated. This was nothing but a veiled political attack on the new order. 'We in the NS are taking up the struggle and shall lead it.' He insisted that it was not pleasant to have to fight one's own, but nevertheless he did so with a clear conscience, concluding with the warning that '[w]hat goes for the bishops goes for all those opposed to progress'.

Here as elsewhere he referred to Berggrav as the *bagler* bishop, a term from the Sagas immortalised in Ibsen's *The Pretenders*. For Norwegians of his generation this allusion was a clear signal of what a cunning schemer he

---

[26] Berggrav, *Font Fangenskap Flukt*, pp. 30–6; S. Rødder, '*Min ære*', p. 126.

considered Berggrav to be. At the same time he made it plain which character he wished to be identified with: Håkon Håkonsson, who proved his right to the throne by 'striding forward unflinchingly on the straight way', true to his calling and assured of his victory, and imbued with natural authority.[27]

The recalcitrant Berggrav soon found himself a prisoner at Bredtvedt, where he was sent on the charge of giving a false statement to the police and subjected to interrogations both by the police and by Riisnæs and Lie, as well as the State Attorney himself. Meanwhile the prosecution was gathering evidence in order to charge him with treason and acts of enmity towards the state for having wilfully attempted to destroy the constitutional order of state and church in Norway, in a case which was to go before the People's Court. However, these were all empty threats. When it came down to it, the prosecution managed to produce no solid evidence, and worse – the German authorities started intervening in his case. Prominent German friends of the bishop's who worked in the resistance in Berlin, such as Helmuth James von Moltke and pastor Dietrich Bonhoeffer, flew to Oslo to try to use their influence on von Falkenhorst and thereby on the Reichs-kommissar himself. There were rumours that even Himmler sent a telegram asking to know why Berggrav had to be imprisoned.[28] In a dramatic government meeting Quisling was forced to repeal the indictment and had to content himself with having Berggrav interned. The possibility of banishing the bishops from their own bishoprics was also discussed, but Terboven advised against it, and for the time being only the Dean of Trondheim was removed.[29]

Thus most of the clergy were left unmolested both by the Norwegian police and the German security police. The strength of the Church's resistance was demonstrated by the fact that its leaders could not be touched. Its bloodless, but for Quisling, nevertheless fatally damaging, demonstration resulted in Berggrav being held under house arrest in his chalet in Asker outside Oslo for the remainder of the war, guarded in such a humane way that his resistance work was only briefly interrupted.

However, things did not go so smoothly for the teachers. After the underground leadership had mobilised a majority of the teachers into leaving the Teachers' Corporation by signing a petition – the Reichskom-

[27] *FF* 9 March 1942.
[28] Berggrav, *Font Fangenskap Flukt*, pp. 70ff; Arvid Brodersen, *Mellom frontene* (1979) pp. 88f.
[29] Skodvin, *Norsk historie*, pp. 194, 395. Account by Sverre Riisnæs, 1989.*

missariat registered between 6,000 and 7,000 resignations of the country's 12,000 teachers – severe punishments were discussed in the government. Word went that the Minister of Police wanted to shoot a hundred key teachers in the resistance. Instead a large-scale operation of arrests was mounted.[30] On 20 March 1942 a full thousand of the most vocal teachers in the country were rounded up. Extraordinary scenes were played out when the police drove around to local communities arresting teachers and escorting them away, sometimes followed by the whole community. After they had been taken into German police custody at Grini near Oslo, Falstad in Trøndelag and Sydspissen in Tromsø, the teachers· found themselves under the jurisdiction of the Reichskommissar. Terboven defined the teachers' protest as 'an attempted strike', thereby threatening a new state of emergency, with both military courts and executions. Enormous pressure, coupled with threats, was put on them to withdraw their resignations. By April half of those arrested had given in and been released; the rest stood firm. Late in April the hard core of the teachers' resistance was transported north on the steamer *Skjerstad* for four months' enforced labour service for the Wehrmacht. Under this treatment they began to withdraw their resignations and the Teachers' Corporation resumed its activities. But as this happened under open duress, and often under draconian threats too, the steadfast attitude of a great many teachers became a moral victory in the eyes of the world, with several columns devoted to it in the Swedish, British and American press.[31]

The Minister President interpreted this in his own way. In his view, the teachers had been successfully forced to co-operate with the new order, just as he had said unwilling Norwegians would be. Even in the case of the Church he was confident that 'resistance has been broken', although the debacle with Berggrav had meant a serious loss of prestige for him among his champions in Germany. By chance, the controversy with the Church in Norway coincided with similar events in Berlin, something which sharpened the focus on Norway even more. Goebbels chose to handle his own Church problem more delicately. Even though the Catholic bishop Preysing circulated pastoral letters agitating against the German conduct of the war, the Minister of Propaganda, with Hitler's blessing, preferred not to react until the war was over, calculating that a clash with the Church could only have

[30] F. Schjelderup, *På bred front* (1947); Nøkleby, *Holdningskamp*; Huhnhäuser in Lødrup, *Læreaksjonens*, pp. 55ff.
[31] For a summary, see Schjelderup, *På bred front*, ch. 24.

undesirable results.[32] It was therefore quite extraordinary that the situation in Norway erupted at the same time. During Easter Goebbels wrote that 'Terboven has now got a problem on his hands which will certainly not be easy to deal with'. A little later he added that 'our people and the NS have got themselves into a mess which they will have a hard time extracting themselves from'.[33]

Hitler himself never made any statement regarding the situation with the Church in Norway. He was more concerned about the teachers. On 5 May he received Terboven at Rastenburg in order to be apprised of the situation. Hitler agreed that the teachers' opposition was a cause for serious concern, as it indicated that Norway was on its way to becoming a problem area, 'one of our most difficult Kommissariate'. He also agreed with Terboven's strong line on deportation and enforced labour, arguing that it was necessary to stem the tide of resistance before it was too late. At the same time he scorned the navy, which had been so soft towards the deported teachers that it had expressed concern that there were not enough life jackets on *Skjerstad* to go round; it would be a pleasure for those Norwegians to swim around in the sea after having been torpedoed by their British friends.[34]

On Midsummer's Eve Quisling explained to his followers that the NS had now conquered Norway, and that all that remained to be done was to 'clear the battlefield'; the Norwegian people would get the new order 'whether they like it or not'. At the Fører Council he assured his local representatives that the resistance against the NS had now been broken 'at crucial points', and it was thus up to them to rid the party of all internal division as Norway was now facing a real opportunity to assert itself in a new, German-led Europe.[35]

ULTIMATUM TO HITLER

With civil resistance spreading at home, Quisling continued to push for full national sovereignty and peace talks with Germany. And indeed, spring 1942 showed some signs of progress in this crucial matter. As soon as Lammers had delivered Quisling's memorandum to Hitler on 13 February, Lammers himself began to consider its contents. The Norwegian Minister President was ambitious to the degree that Lammers considered his demands 'beyond

[32] Magne Skodvin, foreword to Goebbels, *Dagbok 1945* (1978) pp. xvf.
[33] Goebbels Diary, entries for 9, 16, 24 and 26 April 1942.
[34] Picker, *Hitlers Tischgespräche*, p. 266.
[35] Speech at Hamar, *FF* 24 June 1942. The Fører Council 15 June 1942, NS Riks-og rådsmøteprotokoll 1934–45 (private archives*).

the realms of the possible'. Goebbels deemed them simply naive. However, on certain points a compromise could be reached. After some days Lammers suggested that a change in Norway's status might be discussed during the course of the spring. He had not put the matter to Hitler as yet, as it would be pointless to do so as long as the Führer was so deeply caught up in planning the summer campaign in Russia. In any case it would not be possible to let peace negotiations take place in Norway, but the Norwegian government could certainly draft some of the conditions. Next, it would be necessary to consider Norway's status, and whether a position similar to that of Croatia or Slovakia was desirable. Both were states with a considerable degree of autonomy. If so, the Reichskommissariat would have to be disbanded and replaced with diplomatic representation.[36]

It was therefore with positive intentions that Terboven was able to invite Quisling to prepare for the talks that spring. Talks could perhaps be scheduled for May and could even be concluded as early as July or August, if the summer campaign in Russia had brought about the desired solution. However, the problem with the Church and the teachers interrupted the progress of the talks. Terboven maintained that it might be necessary to take more extreme measures, such as reintroducing the state of emergency of 1941 or executing the teachers in large numbers; in either case it would be inadvisable for Quisling to stand alone unsupported by German authority. Quisling was forced to agree that a temporary arrangement was the best until the situation had calmed down. He was confident, though, that things would soon settle down and that the resistance would slacken, arguing that it was the official state of war between the two countries that was providing Norwegians with the excuse for carrying out extensive acts of sabotage and spying for Britain. Terboven was not moved by this somewhat simplistic argument. As he saw it, a free Norway would continue to be closely allied to Germany: the Wehrmacht would remain in Norway, and both the police and politics in Norway would continue to be characterised by the alliance. Even in Denmark and Croatia this was the case, and it was thus naive to believe it possible that a mere constitutional formality would be enough to make the ever-intensifying Anglophilia of the Norwegians evaporate overnight.[37]

The stalling of the peace settlement was causing dissension in the

---

[36] Aufzeichnung des Unterstaatssekretärs Woermann 17 February 1942, *ADAP* E I no. 248 p. 465. Goebbels Diary, entry for 12 February 1942.

[37] This account follows the chronology of Quisling's memorandum to Hitler 9 June 1942, printed in Boehm, *Norwegen*, pp. 153ff.

government, where an atmosphere of increasing mistrust of the growing German presence in Oslo and its attendant problems prevailed. Hagelin was particularly disturbed by German arrogance and the fact that officers of the Wehrmacht and those in the Reichskommissariat were behaving like aristocrats, taking over all the most desirable residences and the best sailing boats, keeping mistresses and running an enormous and unnecessarily extravagant administration. The Minister of Finance, Prytz, had other, perhaps more urgent reservations. The cost of the occupation in the course of two years had reached astronomical figures, covered by an account in the Bank of Norway, but in practice settled more quickly by printing bank notes. The effect of this on inflation and the results of other financial problems were, by the spring of 1942, eating into the budget of the following year. During the spring the cost had risen to 250,000,000 kroner a month. In comparison to the other occupied countries Norway was shouldering a completely unreasonable burden, paying 1,737 kroner per capita of the population to subsidise the occupation, against 258 in Denmark and 310 in France. Norway was being choked. Quisling asked each minister to gather information and set out arguments to support his demand for governmental independence. Moreover, moves on the part of Germany to secure rights of ownership over rivers and waterfalls, the potential sources of hydroelectricity, served to intensify resentment.[38]

All these frustrations were given full expression in a memorandum Quisling sent to Hitler on 9 June 1942. In a political career not short of lengthy memoranda and highly strung arguments, this communication holds a unique position. In it, Quisling set down all his arguments and feelings, ranging from enormous pride to obsequious pleading for a peace settlement. In content although not in form it was essentially not a request but an ultimatum to Hitler.

'I consider it my duty to describe', he began, 'the material as well as the spiritual burdens which have been placed on the small Norwegian nation.' Norway, the smallest and poorest of the occupied countries, was being required to carry most of the costs of the war, a condition crippling the country's commercial policy and forcing it to tolerate a 'humbling position' in foreign policy. After a long disquisition on the strength and ability of the current NS movement, he went on to single out the peace settlement and the

---

[38] See Hagelin's memorandum to Lammers 29 May 1941 and to Hitler August 1942, and Blehr/Hagelin's draft peace agreement 9 April 1942, all analysed in Sørensen, *Hitler eller Quisling*, pp. 126–43. Also Terboven to Prytz 24 June 1942, and various communications sent to Quisling from the Ministry of Finance 27 August 1942, RA FMK 14.

restoration of sovereignty as the only way to improve the situation, suggesting the following course: a preliminary peace to be concluded and made official on 18 July, the anniversary of the battle of Hafrsfjord when Norway had been united 1,070 years earlier; followed by the declaration of Norwegian independence whereby the country would join the Anti-Comintern Pact, the ideological axis consisting of Germany, Italy and Japan, and recently joined by Denmark, Finland, Slovakia, Romania and Bulgaria. A definite peace between Germany and Norway could then be concluded 'with regard to developments of the wider situation', that is whenever the Russian war gave Hitler the opportunity to do so.

Timing, he urged, was essential. The National Government had to give the people visible results in the area of foreign policy. The organised opposition of the Church and the teachers had been broken, and there was no longer any united resistance. Although most people were not participating in the new order, and although the work of the NS – to turn the Norwegians into Germanophiles – felt particularly 'heavy' and 'onerous' under existing conditions, active resistance was now restricted to discrete groups of intellectuals and what remained of plutocratic and Communist circles. These groups were instructed by British commando soldiers and trained by secret agents who had infiltrated the whole of the country. The majority of the population, however – workers, farmers, fishermen – had nothing to do with them and did their duty as before.

This was the sharpest letter Quisling ever sent to Berlin. It was intended to bolster his pleas for Norwegian independence, but at the same time aired an indirect criticism of the Reichskommissar for not having kept Hitler fully apprised of the realities of the Norwegian situation.

Lammers acknowledged its receipt from the Chancellery, emphasising that 'The Führer did not consider the current situation suitable' for making a conclusive agreement between the two countries.[39] As Quisling himself had expressly stated the same view in his letter by suggesting that a final settlement should wait until the situation on the eastern front had been resolved, the reply was somewhat startling. Would Lammers postpone even the more pressing questions of a preliminary settlement and independence? The Fører was 'visibly shaken' by the prospect. This was an ill omen, even though it did not in any way constitute a final response from Hitler. Two

---

[39] Boehm, *Norwegen*, pp. 157f, copy of the original in IfZ MA 110; see also Wyller, *Nyordning og motstand*, p. 162.

days later he read out the letter in a meeting with his ministers, who were struck by his gravity.[40]

The NS Fører had committed himself to Germany. He intended to honour his commitment. But now at last he was expecting something in return for his pledge of loyalty.

THE FØRER AT FIFTY-FIVE

The anniversary of Hafrsfjord was not the only event marked on 18 July: it was also Quisling's birthday. His fifty-fifth birthday in 1942 was a day filled with ceremonies, parades and celebrations in his honour so conspicuously un-Norwegian that the BBC commentator maliciously suggested that all this pomp was an acknowledgement of the fact that he would never reach sixty.

'We acknowledge you our Fører and rely on you / As our ancestors relied on theirs,' wrote the NS poet Kåre Bjørgen in *Fritt Folk* to mark the occasion: 'We follow you forward where you show the way / And illuminate it with your thoughts.' These words gave a telling picture of how dependent the movement was on its Fører. He was indeed their spiritual leader, who knew and understood how his people struggled. The poet's lines did not sound like empty clichés, but had deep significance for the party.[41]

He was certainly fêted proudly that day. The telegram from Hitler and the greetings from the Reichskommissariat were obvious formalities, but the ministers' tribute at the palace and the reception which followed at Gimle, with all the uniforms and insignia on show, made the occasion one to remember. General von Falkenhorst and his staff officers, the leadership of the Einsatzstab and scores of other high-ranking officials showed up, as did representatives from the party's local organisations and special divisions. Greetings and gifts came pouring in from all the party's organisations. Telemark sent a silver axe, Aust-Viken a horse (which a boy from the Youth Organisation had ridden in from Båstad to Gimle overnight), Vestland a chalice, Oppland a Hadeland crystal vase, while the Women's Movement brought beautiful silverware to complement the government's gift of a silver bowl decorated with Viking patterns. Representatives of farmers, workers, fishermen and artisans also brought gifts, including a pictorial rug with saga

---

[40] Report dated 14 September 1942 from Dr W. Stuckart sent to Himmler, Bormann et al., BA NS 19/1982.

[41] Bjørgen in *FF* 18 July 1942, which also records the guests and their gifts. The BBC commentator quoted in Dahl, *Dette er London*, p. 230.

motifs. Prytz presented a cheque on behalf of a group of well-to-do party members for no less than 300,000 kroner.[42]

Gimle rose to the occasion. That spring Maria had enthusiastically taken on the role of lady of the house. Furniture, paintings and silverware had been brought in, much of it antique, including the furniture in the dining hall seating over a hundred, which had been bought from Oslo's largest store, Steen and Strøm. Special silverware had been commissioned from the leading silversmith Tostrup, with a special canteen engraved with the initials 'NS'. Some of the equipment was brought for safety to Gimle from the palace, to prevent further German thefts from the royal collections. His own paintings and antiques from Russia were augmented by gifts of more paintings from the municipality of Oslo and the Hird among others.[43]

Quisling himself cheerfully circulated among the guests in his Hird uniform and riding boots. His fair hair still preserved a boyish sheen, although his once impressive figure had been overtaken by middle-aged stoutness. From the park, the sound of the staff musicians could be heard, and sections of the Youth Hird, the Little Hird and the Girls' Hird paraded before the guests in the garden.

Politics were also discussed at the party. The Fører told his chief propaganda executive that a Riksting was to be held on 25 September. He had plans ready, and thus preparations for the great event could be started in the relevant ministries immediately.

Still there was no reaction from Hitler, either to the concrete proposals for a preliminary peace or for Norway's membership of the Axis. Not even a declaration of intent could be extracted from Berlin, it seemed. Thus Quisling's attempts to get things settled within a definite time frame were frustrated once more. Meanwhile, Hitler's summer offensive was well under way. After Kharkov had been taken at the end of May, the offensive on the Caucasus was launched on 28 June, and in July the Crimea and the towns of the Don and Donet basin fell one by one: Sebastopol, Voronesj, Rostov, while the panzer divisions were moving south towards the Caucasus. At the same time, Germany was celebrating its U-boat triumphs in the Atlantic; in June alone 144 Allied ships with a total tonnage of 700,000 went down, more than in any single month of the war so far. Hitler was full of praise for

---

[42] *Straffesak* p. 142.
[43] Account of palace administration of objects surrendered to the German authorities 21 November 1940 to 15 September 1942, RA FMK 5. Also Juritzsen, *Privatmennesket Quisling*, ch. 11 'Livet på Gimle'.

the Norwegian naval bases, which had been particularly useful.[44] The press also carried reports of Axis progress in North Africa and the Far East. Quisling therefore had good reason to be optimistic that Hitler would soon have time to study his memorandum more closely, and that a military victory in the East would make way for the eventual peace settlement with Norway – with luck before the scheduled Riksting meeting in September. But when he left for Fyresdal for his holiday with Maria at the beginning of August he had still not heard anything from Germany. In a tense situation such as this, there was nothing that could compare with a peaceful vacation in his home village. Quisling loved West Telemark and Fyresdal deeply; through the years it had strengthened his resolve. However, on this occasion, it was not a holiday from politics. The question of the parish priest was causing him concern. The pastor in question belonged to the Berggrav camp and had resigned his state office. Quisling had been gathering information about his resistance activities and was now ready to take action.[45]

A confirmation class was in progress at Moland church in Fyresdal on Wednesday 12 August when the priest and his pupils noticed the shadow of a large man walking up and down in the churchyard. The man came to the door and introduced himself as Quisling. What followed was an interrogation in the priest's office as the Minister President presented a list of charges against him, accusing him of inciting the congregation, holding political meetings and using the Church to undermine the state. Quisling spoke out violently against Berggrav and the bishops, insisting that they deserved at the very least to be decapitated. He informed the pastor that his own and his wife's property were to be requisitioned and that they were to leave the rectory immediately.

The locals in Fyresdal were warned to mark well what had happened to their pastor. Quisling used his vacation to visit the office of the local police chief and find out what the people's attitude to the new order was. With this information he became personally involved in local appointments, sacking the inspector of forests, suspending the head of the medical board and installing a new police chief.[46] Later on he continued to visit the community

---

[44] Speech at Wolfsschanze 24 April 1942, quoted in Picker, *Hitlers Tischgespräche*, pp. 238f.

[45] Otto Irgens, 'En episode fra kirkekampen', *Kirke og Kultur* (1946) p. 554, and Quisling's speech at Gjøvik on 22 August, in *FF* 24 August 1942.

[46] Letters concerning these appointments from mayor Eivind J. Spockelie on 26 June and 7 October 1942, and to Spockelie on 26 November 1942, Municipal archives, Fyresdal. Accounts given by Theodor Hanssen and Ragnar Austad 1986.*

as often as he could to oversee the large fencing project which was started the following year, when Lunden, Jonsborg and eventually Moland too were fenced in by a 2-metre-high mesh fence with barbed wire to discourage intruders from Quisling's home. Quite probably it was the state police, responsible for Quisling's safety, who had insisted on this measure. For the locals the grim fence stood as a more than adequate expression of the situation which their infamous son had brought on himself.

JUDGEMENT

Hitler's decision was made in the middle of Quisling's holiday on 11 August 1942. In late July the Führer had moved into his new headquarters, 'Wehrwolf' at Vinnitsa in the Ukraine, to follow more closely the operations in the Caucasus and issue instructions for the summer offensive on the entire Russian front. After two weeks in Vinnitsa he was able to receive Terboven and to hear his assessment of the Norwegian situation. Ribbentrop, Lammers and Bormann were also present.

After listening to his Reichskommissar, Hitler concluded that there was no question of Norwegian diplomatic representation, not even in the form of commercial legations, abroad. Nor was there any possibility of making peace with Norway so long as the war lasted, not even a preliminary settlement. As soon as the war was over, the German government would unilaterally apprise Norway of its future relationship with the Reich, but until such time, all initiatives concerning a peace settlement or any other issues with bearings on Norway's relations with the Reich after the end of the war were to cease. The Führer instructed Terboven to inform the Minister President of these decisions 'as clearly and firmly as possible'. In addition, Lammers was instructed to send him a letter containing the same information in order to prevent Quisling from complaining to the Chancellery about Terboven's announcement.[47]

Terboven also used the opportunity to put the question of rights over the waterfalls to Hitler. The German programme of aluminium extraction in Norway was encountering enormous difficulties from the Quisling government, which wanted to keep the hydro-electric energy sources under national jurisdiction, whereas Terboven wanted unlimited access. Quisling

---

[47] Record by Lammers, dated F[ührehaupt] Q[uartier] 12 August 1942, BA R 43 II/623a. Account of the meeting in Kjeldstadli, *Hjemmestyrkene*, p. 144.

was only prepared to commit certain waterfalls to Germany for a period of sixty years. The Führer's opinion followed promptly. He had always considered it Norway's particular mission to become 'the electricity centre' of northern Europe. The question of exploiting Norwegian energy sources should therefore naturally be a matter for Germany to decide. Terboven was thus authorised to take any steps he considered necessary.[48]

Two weeks later Quisling had Hitler's decision read out to him when Terboven summoned him to Skaugum for the occasion. He was strongly reprimanded, and had to listen to Terboven describing the incompetence of his government, admonishing him for his intrigues with Rosenberg and censuring his dishonourable ministers for over an hour. It was a terrible blow, which put paid to all his plans for Norway's independence for the duration of the war. What this meant was that the National Government was to remain an occupation government, and that the Wehrmacht troops were to remain as an occupying force. Nothing had changed, not even the intolerable situation of being Minister President at the mercy of the Reichskommissar.[49]

The message from Hitler was not of course the first time he had suffered setbacks and disappointment in his life, but this time it was so absolute, not simply in terms of a postponement, but with its demand of complete suspension of his entire project of getting Germany to end the occupation while the war was still in progress. The glamour of the birthday celebrations immediately lost its sheen. The new tone was set at the big meeting of party representatives at Gjøvik at the end of August. 'What sort of times are we living in?' he asked an assembly long accustomed to a Fører who told them of the golden age which lay before Norway in the new Europe. 'Hard times, some of the hardest which mankind in its entirety has ever faced,' he now insisted; '[f]irst and foremost, we must win this war.'[50]

In late September he received the official letter from Lammers, putting in writing everything that Terboven had told him and, moreover, was informed that Hitler no longer wished to receive letters from him. All correspondence should henceforth go through the Reichskommissar. With that Quisling was deprived of direct contact with Hitler. Terboven had probably told him this

---

[48] Hitler on 'the electricity centre', speech at Wolfsschanze 2 August 1941, in Picker, *Hitlers Tischgespräche*, p. 66.

[49] The episode is related by Huhnhäuser 21 November 1942, IfZ ED 69/14 Alfred Huhnhäuser, from the official protocol from the Terboven–Quisling meeting (lost).

[50] *FF* 24 August 1942.

during their meeting, but he may have interpreted it as an attempt on the part of the Reichskommissar to monopolise contact with the Reich.[51]

This was such an ignominious humiliation that Quisling found it hard to believe that Hitler himself was behind it. He had issued an ultimatum, which had been rejected in every particular. Moreover, he had been deprived of his most important channel for promoting Norway's cause. Whoever was denied access to Hitler was similarly denied access to any meaningful influence at all.

---

[51] Lammers to Quisling 17 September 1942, printed in Boehm, *Norwegen*, pp. 157f and *Straffesak* p. 547. The order that Quisling's letters to Hitler thenceforth had to go via Terboven does not appear in the *Führer-Weisung* of 11 August 1942, and must have evolved when Terboven and Lammers, on Hitler's orders, co-ordinated their communications to Quisling.

8

Betrayed by Hitler

> Politically I was dependent on Adolf Hitler and Germany, but on the level of political vision, Hitler was my inferior. *Quisling, 15 October 1945*[1]

Hitler's refusal was so blunt and categorical that Quisling immediately considered resigning his position. Moreover, it implied a complete realignment of the conditions on which he had hitherto offered his co-operation with Germany. He had thought a union 'in free, federal forms' would be advantageous to Germany and favourable to her fighting machine, as more resources could be put at her disposal through voluntary contribution than by forceful subjugation. What he had been proposing for Norway, peace negotiations accompanied by a declaration of sovereignty followed by entry into a German-led federation, was only what he envisaged for any country under German dominance. When Hitler rejected this plan on the grounds that the war in the East was not over and thus refused to acknowledge even friendly regimes in countries which had been drawn into the new order, it was a setback not only for him and for Norway; it augured ill for the course of the war as a whole.[2]

Hitler was refusing to discuss the matter not only because he was too caught up in the war with Russia. If Quisling had read *Mein Kampf* and particularly the passage concerning Germany's future role, not only for what it said but also for what it left unsaid, he would perhaps have understood that Hitler was quite uninterested in forming a European federation. In fact, he was not thinking along these lines at all. On the contrary, he rejected any plans of that kind, whatever their provenance, because they did not coincide with his own thinking. Nor was he concerned about making Germany's relationships with individual countries or occupied territories uniform, preferring instead to let everything take its own course. In fact, Hitler's campaign for world domination was improvisatory to a greater extent than Quisling or anyone else could possibly have imagined. Thus the relative

---

[1] Quisling in October 1945, quoted in H. F. Dahl et al., *Den norske nasjonalsosialismen* (1982) p. 11.
[2] Hans Werner Neulen, *Europa und das 3. Reich* (1987) pp. 21ff.

independence Quisling had acquired via the Act of State at Akershus was no design for future relations, let alone a blueprint for a German-led European union of nationalist states. The Norwegian Act of State actually caused Hitler immediate trouble in that Mussert and Clausen subsequently demanded increased powers in their respective countries.[3] And certainly he felt no obligation to 'fulfil' the promise of full formal independence for Norway, such as Quisling's rhetorics of the 'last step before full freedom' implied.

But Quisling was not in a position to act on instinct. Resignation and withdrawal from power was out of the question for a leader saddled with the responsibility of a movement of tens of thousands of people who were expecting him to lead them to greater things. Regardless of how Quisling saw his defeat at a personal level, the feeling that he could not let down the party prevailed, especially as the organisation was at this point ready for a major performance – the largest meeting in the ten-year history of the NS – the party convention in Oslo in September 1942.

NATIONAL ASSEMBLY OR FØRER COUNCIL?

The first draft of the programme was sent out from the party secretariat at around midsummer, with the intention of producing a constitution for a Riksting during the conference. The Riksting would naturally be a state authority but with such a close connection as prevailed between party and state it was only natural to allow the party convention to determine the constitution of the new National Assembly. The voluntary Riksting which the NS had set up in 1934 as a preliminary to a full-scale state organ had also been launched during a national convention; 25 September 1942, then, was to signal the complete merging of party and state in the new Norway.

Security was a major problem. The sheer scale of the convention – with transport arrangements, accommodation, communications, security and supplies for a projected 20,000 delegates – meant that a great deal of information which under the normal circumstances of war would be kept confidential, such as the details of the travel schedules of high-profile German and Norwegian delegates, could easily leak out during the preparations.[4]

With the publicity surrounding an event such as this, the possibility of an Allied bomb attack could not be excluded. British and American bombers

---

[3] Rente-Fink to AA 6 February 1942, and Bene to AA 13 February 1942 in *ADAP* E I nos. 212, 237, pp. 383f and 421f; Poulsen, *Besættelsesmagten* (1970) pp. 345ff; see also Clausen to Quisling 27 April 1942, RAK BA 1a, Partiføreren, Diverse.

[4] Fuglesang, various conversations 1985–7.*

were flying over Germany almost nightly in response to the Luftwaffe's intensive and extended sorties over the Channel. In Norway Allied bombs were falling over wide areas. Under these circumstances, arranging a large-scale convention was an enormous undertaking for General Secretary Fuglesang and his staff, as well as for the German police and military security departments. The Luftwaffe positioned three Focke-Wulf fighter planes in readiness at Fornebu as extra air support for the convention.[5]

Meanwhile, in the government, the task of preparations for the Riksting were under way. The concept, as it was set down in the NS manifesto, was of a highly corporate nature, as the industrial and cultural life of the entire country was to be organised along Italian lines into 'autonomous, legalised guilds'. No private or voluntary unions were to be admitted into the Riksting so as to prevent political parties in disguise from participating. Only guilds organised by the state, with authority accorded to them by law – such as the Teachers' Corporation – were to be given representation. After the priests' and the teachers' protests in the spring, planning for the future corporate structure was delayed. The guilds already in existence were the corporations for teachers, publishers, lawyers, journalists, advertisers and shipowners, which were all set up in the spring of 1942.

On 20 August, the Ministry of the Interior had succeeded in producing a general Law Concerning Organisations and Associations ready to be signed and sealed by the Minister President. All the country's organisations and associations were thenceforth to be 'led in accordance with the demands which the tasks of the people and the state produce' and the Ministry was given the authority to dissolve associations which were reluctant to comply. A central public register was set up and the country's organisations were instructed to make their statutes consistent with the new rules.

But rather than strengthening the corporate structure, the new associations law sparked off a veritable exodus from the official organisations. Fearful of the plans, which from the end of August were starting to leak from the ministries, and ignited by an illegal resistance leadership, representatives of several industrial associations were leaving the federations. However, this action was stopped after pressure from the German police, and after 9 September, following the publication of the law with its stern warnings of punishments, members and representatives returned to their posts.[6]

[5] Sem and Sten Stenersen, *Flyalarm* (1991) p. 155.
[6] Nøkleby, *Holdningskamp*, ch. 'Først riksting så fred', pp. 140–86.

In the meantime, however, Quisling had changed his mind. The whole Riksting was abandoned. There was to be no strictly corporate alternative to the Storting in the future Norwegian Constitution, the Minister President decided. By early September the party was fully informed that the Riksting had been abandoned. Something had occurred which had interfered with the Minister President's original plans. The cause of the abandonment has often been misunderstood. The civilian resistance movement took it as proof of their success, seeing that the action of leaving the associations had caused panic in the Reichskommissariat, which in turn was forcing the NS to back down and order the suspension of the Riksting.[7] However, the reality was otherwise: the Riksting was neither blocked by the resistance movement nor stalled by the Germans. Quisling himself made the decision. His original idea had been that the Riksting should consist of the country's economic and cultural bodies, arranged in two chambers, similar to the bicameral parliamentary system. By early June 1942, however, he had come to the conclusion that economic and professional organisations, even when authorised by the state, could scarcely be trusted as proper state organs. We do not know the exact reason for this change of mind, but apparently the stubborn resistance of the clergy and the teachers played a role. He may well have concluded that organisations more often than not were channels for distrust and professional selfishness instead of positive influence and authority. In any case he envisaged a new legislature in Norway of a political, not a corporate nature, based on the party rather than on the corporations.

But even to launch a politically composed Riksting would have been premature in September 1942, as Hitler's refusal in August countermanded any thought of a National Assembly ratifying an agreement with Germany. Without even a tentative peace agreement on the horizon, a Riksting would be superfluous as there were no other matters for a National Assembly to settle. Instead, the intended Riksting was summoned as a Fører Council (Førerting). Independently of this, Quisling still intended to get the Economic Chamber (Næringsting) and Cultural Chamber (Kulturting) started with new functions within the short space of time available. The two were to be purely advisory bodies, consultants to the Ministries of Industry and Culture respectively. Of the two, the Cultural Chamber came into being

---

[7] Wyller, *Nyordning og motstand*, pp. 160f; Kjeldstadli, *Hjemmestyrkene*, pp. 146–51. Tore Gjelsvik, *Hjemmefronten* (1977) pp. 76f.

as planned, but the Economic Chamber had to be put off because of the unrest in the organisations.

The Fører Council was opened in the old hall of the university on 25 September. There were 150 representatives there, three times as many as at the previous one, attendance having been bolstered by the summoning of all district governors and the leaders of the party's central organisation, together with representatives down to the level of the district party leaders in addition to the twelve members of the government. Three German observers were also present.[8]

Quisling arrived promptly at 4 o'clock, after everybody had taken their seats in the hall. Fuglesang invited him to open the meeting, and then, beginning with Hagelin, the ministers read out in turn short reports on the activities of their respective departments. While Prytz was reading out the report from the Ministry of Finance, an alarm suddenly went off, machine-gun fire and several deafening noises were heard from outside. Glass smashed, and the old university buildings shook. It was obviously an air raid, even though the sirens had not sounded. Judging by the strength of the explosions, it was possible that the attack was centred on the university itself. Prytz involuntarily took cover, and several people rose to leave the hall. But Quisling remained calmly in his seat in front of the speaker. In the silence following the alarm, he gestured to the ceiling and said, 'Greetings from the exiled King'. After that he instructed Prytz to continue. Those who had stood up returned to their places. The meeting then continued as though nothing had happened.

After the last ministerial report Quisling mounted the speaker's platform. The most pressing and basic task for the new Norway was to create 'a proper form of government and an ordered administration. It is this question which I want to address today,' he explained in a voice full of authority which managed to calm his audience. Then followed a Quisling lecture such as his followers loved to hear. In fact, never before had he spoken so simply and comprehensively about the new state's constitutional position, nor asserted with such stern authority the legitimacy of the new administration.

When the sirens sounded Quisling went on with his lecture undeterred, and soon reached his conclusion, which was that the Constitution would have to adjust to the new order inasmuch as the forthcoming representation of the people would be a one-party state, that is, a political representation

---

[8] NS Riks- og rådsmøteprotokoll 1934–45 pp. 101–4;* see also *NS årbok 1942* ed. W. Klevenberg (1943).

with a 'more personal and a wider character' than one comprising trade and industry organisations with their representation of interests could ever have. Thus it was to be primarily a representation of the party, but at the same time 'a state authority accessible also to those who do not belong to the NS'. Corporate considerations should focus on the culture and industry chambers whose tasks were to be 'exclusively of a professional and not political nature'. The time was now ripe, he said, 'in principle to assert' that such a Riksting should be organised so that it could be summoned and constituted when the circumstances made it desirable to do so. His proposal that 'the Førerting give its endorsement to this, my principal resolution', was greeted with a round of applause.

When the delegates left the building towards 6 o'clock, the streets were in chaos with ambulances and fire engines, and the areas around the university were cordoned off with German and Norwegian police working frantically in the smoke. The explosions which had been heard were the result of bombing by four British Mosquitoes which had flown in low over the city from the south, releasing their bombs on to Victoria Terrasse, the German security police and Gestapo headquarters. The building itself had escaped, but several residences in the surrounding streets had not been so fortunate. Eighty civilians were killed or injured in the worst air raid on Norwegian soil to date – several steamships trading along the coast had already been sunk. During the air battles over Oslo and Bærum which followed, in which German fighters were put into action, several British aircraft were shot down, the official communiqué stated. In fact, the British lost one Mosquito. Nor was Quisling right in his assertion that the air raid was a greeting from King Haakon in London. The Norwegian government in exile knew nothing of the raid and expressed serious concern to the British government afterwards.[9]

Quisling rushed to the scene while the fires raged and the maimed and wounded were dug out from under the ruins.

EIGHTH AND LAST NATIONAL CONVENTION

The thousands of members who streamed into Oslo in order to attend the convention on the last Saturday and Sunday in September 1942 met at a

---

[9] This account of the attack is based on Stenersen and Stenersen, *Flyalarm*, pp. 155ff. The government's concern: Riste, *'London-Regjeringa'* I, p. 50.

time when the conflict between the NS's demand for autonomy on the one
hand and the interests of the occupying forces on the other was tangible.

The occupying forces, with 300,000 soldiers, more than had ever been
seen before in Norway, wanted peace and order so as to reap the spoils of
war undisturbed. The NS for its part was ambivalent about the occupation.
On the one hand it needed it in order to force a national revolution on an
unwilling population, but on the other hand it wanted to limit the greed of
the German forces. The resistance movement deliberately reduced the
nuances of the party's ambiguous position into the blanket term 'Nazi',
which covered both Norwegians and Germans, both the nationalist and
collaborating factions. None of those concerned, Norwegian or German,
liked the term. The concept of Nazism concealed the diverse interests at
stake; as for the Germans in Norway, there was a definite divide between the
National Socialists of the NSDAP and the government officials. Both
represented the occupation, but the party people were busy engaging the NS
in a 'Germanic' co-operation, while the bureaucrats were concerned with
practical collaboration, preferably through channels other than the NS.

Among the Norwegians, the black-clad formations in the SS Norway
represented an extreme pro-German stance, while the dark blue of the – in
all senses – more solid Hird represented the national line in the NS. The
fronts between the two organisations were clearly drawn in their respective
newspapers, *Germaneren* and *Hirdmannen*, in which the conflict between the
two was being played out. Among the government ministers, Sverre Riisnæs
and Jonas Lie were keen SS supporters; most of the others were not. Hagelin
in particular was well known for his lightning attacks and forthright speeches
against the Germans. Axel Stang and the Youth Organisation, not to
mention the Labour Service, were all clearly on the Norwegian side.[10]

That Quisling himself had been banking on a peace settlement and on
Norwegian autonomy was abundantly clear from his many speeches in the
spring and summer of 1942. But he also set great store by Germanic co-
operation, always operating with a long-term strategy with far wider
perspectives than normally applied within the corridors of the ministries
and the party headquarters. After Hitler's response in August–September
1942 he was forced closer to the German line, and compelled to promote it
among his own people too. The convention showed that he was in control of
the movement and able to push the common Germanic line along with its
necessary commitment to the task of winning the war before any peace talks

---

[10] The ideological diversity of the NS is analysed in Sørensen, *Hitler eller Quisling*.

could be opened. German observers expressed surprise at how far the party, under the guidance of its Fører, was tending towards a common Germanic course.[11]

Quisling set the tone in his opening speech, declaring it the party's first duty to ensure that the war was won and consequently to 'direct our economic strength and resources towards the conduct of the war'. Germany must at all costs be supported to maintain her position in Norway as well as in Europe. The Germanic countries – including Norway – so necessary for Germany's victory were also the only European people to enjoy 'both a common blood and a common culture'. The poet-prophets Ibsen and Bjørnson had both in their time spoken warmly of a Germanic union; he quoted Bjørnson: 'The union with Germany is a matter of earnest relations ... spiritually and physically we give each other the greatest help of all people on earth.' The NS would certainly follow through this good work, reassured by the fact that 'our three great spiritual heroes, Bjørnson, Ibsen and, in our own time, Knut Hamsun, all with their unmistakable universal and national instincts' had been absorbed in the same task. He stressed the importance of being 'good Norwegians, good Germans, and good Europeans'.

Quisling's speech was immediately, from the moment it was made, interpreted in various ways. German observers, including Paul Wegener, who had recently been replaced as leader of the Einsatzstab by the 32-year-old SS Obersturmbannführer Hans-Hendrik Neumann, said that Quisling was clearly taking 'a greater Germanic union' line. The SD reports drew the same conclusion, as the SD people really believed that the salutes of his audience indicated that Quisling's Germanic sentiments were shared by his audience, and greeted them as signs of a swing of opinion within the party. However, the pro-Germanic messages were received with little enthusiasm in the organisation, particularly in the Hird. Many Hird members did not like this Germanic tendency at all. Soon after the convention an SD report stated that party opinion had reverted to a more nationalistic mood.[12]

BLACK AUTUMN

The months following the NS convention were a black period for both the Fører and the party, heralding a decline which was to last for the remainder of

---

[11] Appendix to the 'Meldungen aus Norwegen' no. 46: Das Reichstreffen der NS in Oslo, BA NS 43/61.

[12] Ibid.

the war years. Unrest in the party, painful personal losses, heavy measures on
the part of the Reichskommissar – and finally the disastrous action against the
Jews – resulted in neutralising everything the convention had managed to
achieve in terms of approval and morale within the party ranks. At the close of
the year Quisling was left with a movement held together by the threats of
gloomy events, further from his goal than ever.

Early in October Terboven introduced a new state of emergency, this time
in the Trøndelag region. Ten random arrests were made, most of them of
well-known citizens from the city and the surrounding districts, who were
shot as 'a warning against further attempts at sabotage', a devastating act of
terrorism executed without any pretence of justice. Immediately afterwards,
more executions were carried out, and another twenty-four men, prisoners
in the German concentration camp south of Levanger who had been
rounded up after the fighting earlier that autumn between the Wehrmacht
and the Norwegian resistance at Majavatn in Nordland, were shot. These
men were local civilians, and their executions thus entailed more than
reprisals.[13]

Quisling had always stressed that the resistance groups were morally
accountable for the necessarily repressive initiatives in Norway. He had long
been impressing on Terboven his view that Germany would have to take
increasingly tougher measures against the resistance, and that only independence and freedom for Norway would calm the errant Norwegian freedom
fighters.

On Monday 12 October the state of emergency in Trøndelag was lifted,
but this time the NS was not in a position to claim that the initiative had
been unilaterally German. Terboven had given the NS district leaders, as well
as local party leaders, extensive extraordinary administrative powers during
this period. District leader Henrik Rogstad exploited this to effect a large-
scale purge of municipal and district personnel and to some extent of
private institutions too, providing local businesses with pro-NS heads.[14]

The Fører had only a few days to think this over before trouble erupted
again, on a much smaller scale, but serious nevertheless. For the first time
since 1937 there was dissension within the party organisation. The forming
of factions had been expressly forbidden but dissatisfaction was now crystal-
lising in a conspicuous opposition to the main circles in the party. Young
men from the Hird's air corps started walking around in party and

[13] Nøkleby, Holdningskamp, pp. 206ff.
[14] John Lyng, Brytningsår. Erindringer 1923–53 (1972) pp. 65f.

government offices slapping senior officers in the face, staging an ostentatious demonstration against Freemasons in the top party ranks: all their victims were former members of the long since abandoned Lodge of Freemasons which had been closed down on a German initiative in 1940. The demonstration was supported by the SS paper *Germaneren*, whose policy was hostile to the bourgeois upper echelons of the NS.

To the Fører this was not only unwelcome and embarrassing but also deeply unsettling. Young idealists, valuable assets to the organisation, were proving so blinkered they were taking an otherwise noble cause, the struggle against international Freemasonry, to extremes, thereby opening new wounds in the party organisation. He gave full vent to his feelings in the main issue of *Fritt Folk* on 7 November, in which he attempted to lay the matter of the Freemasons to rest. 'Freemasonry in Norway is long dead and no longer of any real political importance,' he wrote. The childish actions were simply an outburst of 'foolish fantasies which not only betray a lack of judgement but are also directly detrimental to the cause'.[15]

At the height of these problems with the activists came news of Guldbrand Lunde's sudden death. It was almost like a sign: Lunde, the most nationalist of all, had died in a road accident during a lecture tour in Vestland while the young and thoughtless in the party were carrying out their acts of provocation in the capital. Lunde's death was painful in many ways. Quisling lost a trusted and much valued adviser, and the movement was bereft of not only a remarkable administrator but also one of its founding ideologues, whose compelling speeches throughout the country nurtured the growth of National Socialism on Norwegian soil and animated it through the sagas, history and national poetry. No one was able to anchor the position of the movement in the common cultural history as Lunde was, or to condemn the 'un-Norwegian' resistance – as, for instance, when he had recently put the Swedish press in its place for its 'shamelessly biased reporting' of the new order in Norway.[16]

Lunde and his wife died on 26 October 1942 in the car they were driving from Ålesund to Åndalsnes in a ferry accident at the Våge ferry port in the

---

[15] The episodes are referred to in the party judgement (5 June 1943) against Reidar Aagaard, RA NS Partirett 1, and the background is sketched in Sørensen, *Hitler eller Quisling*, pp. 195ff. Quisling's reaction is printed in a collection of his speeches, *Mot nytt land* (1944) pp. 166ff.

[16] See Guldbrand Lunde, *Kampen for Norge* I–III, lectures and articles (Oslo 1941–3); Marie and Guldbrand Lunde, *Liv i kamp for Norge* (1943). A detailed analysis of Lunde's ideological position is given by Sørensen, *Hitler eller Quisling*, pp. 29–46 and 144ff.

Romsdalsfjord. There was an inquiry into the incident later by both the Norwegian and the German police. Rumours were rife within both the government and the party that the accident had been arranged by the Gestapo in order to weaken the nationalist front in the party. These rumours were never substantiated, but neither were they conclusively disproved.[17]

The state funeral at Trinity Church in Oslo was a grand ceremony including the Hird, Labour Service, German SS, Legion and party parades. Hitler sent a telegram conveying his condolences and there was a large representation of German dignitaries. This was the first time that a member of the government had died in office under the current regime and it was marked with all due ceremony. After the cremation the urns were taken on a garlanded boat to the Lunde family home at Vik in Sogn, to be placed outside the Hoprekstad stave-church. The Minister of Justice, Riisnæs, also a native of Sogn, accompanied the urns. 'Like so many pioneers, Lunde has not been appreciated,' he declared at the graveside. 'Indeed, not even the people here in his own village understand the contribution Lunde has made for the people and the country.' Riisnæs's words were certainly pointed: in Vik there were hardly any NS members at all, and only a handful in the whole of the county of Sogn and Fjordane.[18]

QUISLING AND THE JEWS

From the beginning, Quisling and his government suspected the Jews, more than any other group, of what the new criminal code defined as acts of enmity towards the state and the people. Their suspicion, although based on racist theories and thus falling on all Jews without exception, was also born of the belief that individual Jews comprised a clandestine network with links in all the Allied countries, which in turn were under the leadership of people with the power to co-ordinate the activities of their fellow Jews world-wide. In this sense the Jews constituted a potential conspiracy against Germany and her allies. 'It is hardly a coincidence', a friend of the Oslo government noted in his diary, 'that nearly all [Norwegian] Jews are anti-Nazis.'[19]

---

[17] Fyrst, *Min sti*, p. 252, and Ringnes, *Bak okkupasjonens kulisser*, p. 265. C. Astrup, who followed the car, denied both at the time and later that the accident could have been an act of sabotage: see C. Astrup to *Morgenbladet* 11 August 1981, and an unsent letter of 12 August 1981 (private archives*).

[18] *FF* 2 November 1942. Marie and Guldbrand Lunde, *Liv i kamp*, p. 93.

[19] Gustav Smedal, *Patriotisme og landssvik* (1949) p. 62. See also Quisling in *Germaneren* 1942/1, quoted in *FF* 25 July 1942.

The German police thought the same. Jews were frequently arrested for illegally listening to the BBC and for disseminating the information gleaned from it in a conspiratorial manner. In March 1942 five Jews from Trondheim were shot by the SS for illegally spreading news. The punishment was harsh, but the situation was considered extremely serious. However, Quisling would not hear of persecution, and when some young Hird members daubed anti-Semitic slogans on Jewish-owned shops in Oslo on 30 March 1941, he had them brought in. The furthest the government went in discriminating against Jews was revoking the licences given to Jewish doctors and lawyers, and the restoration on 12 March 1942 of the constitutional prohibition on any further immigration.[20]

However, the Jewish policy in Norway was not in the hands of the NS. On 22 January 1942, following an order from the occupying forces, the police announced that all identity cards belonging to Jews were to be stamped with a 'J' in order to be valid. The criterion given was that the individuals concerned should have at least three 'completely Jewish' grandparents, that is, adherents of the Jewish religion, or two in cases where the person in question was married to a Jew.[21]

Jews were also to be registered with the police, something which the German police had tried to start very early on in the occupation. The party itself organised the registration, with the head of the NS Statistics Bureau in charge, thus providing a basis for further initiatives which in time would be introduced and effectively enforced, above all further laws discriminating against the Jews in the labour market and a marriage law planned to set up a future apartheid system for the Norwegian Jews.[22]

The Jews were not the only group to be registered in 1942. At the same time a corresponding list of actively anti-government Norwegians was being compiled, in this case prompted by the British commando raids of the previous December, during which NS members at landing points had been arrested by the British and taken back to Britain as prisoners. The same thing had happened during the Solvær raid in March 1941. These incidences of the abduction of civilians had, almost without exception, the most demoralising effect on the party during the war and provided the warrant for the listing of anti-NS citizens. Even so, it proved more difficult to

[20] Mendelsohn, *Jødenes historie*, pp. 63f, 68ff.

[21] Johansen, *Oss selv*, ch. 'Spørreskjemaet "Jøder i Norge"', pp. 144–7.

[22] Østbye to Quisling 7 October 1942, RA LD 5/49–50. Leif Salicath to H. N. Østbye 16 January 1942, RA PA H. N. Østbye. Per Ole Johansen, *Oss selv*, ch. 'Spørreskjemaet "Jøder i Norge"', pp. 144–7. For the police action see Ringdal, *Mellom barken og veden*.

compile these lists than to compile answers to the police questionnaires about the Jews, and not simply because the police were much more competent than the party apparatus to carry out such tasks. Many local party officials found having to report on political opponents in this manner distasteful. Several district and group leaders shrank from informing on their neighbours and as a result few names were given.

The registration of Jews turned out to be of great use – to the Germans. The German police gave the order that all Jews in Norway should be arrested in two round-ups, Jewish males on 26 October 1942 and Jewish females on 26 November. The criterion for arrest was the possession of an identity card marked 'J', but during the search and the subsequent arrests the police and the additional manpower from the Hird and the SS Norway also made use of the lists from the party and the police's joint registers to track down Jews.

Quisling made his contribution to the German Jewish action in two pieces of hastily drafted legislation: the first an extension of the criminal code's provision for detention (which in fact provided the authority for the arrests; such provision was necessary because it was the Norwegian police who were to carry out the arrests), and second, a special law on the expropriation of Jewish property. These two laws, of 24 and 26 October 1942 respectively, were passed during a period of frantic preparations inside the police department, but despite the fact that they followed each other closely, they must be seen as discrete cases.

On 22 October a Norwegian border policeman conducting a passenger check on the train to Halden, a town on the border with Sweden, was shot by a young fireman who was in the process of taking a group of Jews through to Sweden. The 'Jewish' murder of the policeman was front page news in the NS press, and both Quisling and Terboven attended the funeral. On the same day as the episode was receiving extensive coverage in the morning papers, Saturday 24 October, the chief of police, General Karl Marthinsen, received notification from the Gestapo that all Jewish males were to be arrested the following Monday. Simultaneously, the Minister of Justice, Riisnæs (who was also running the Police Department during Jonas Lie's absence at the front), received instructions to make legal provisions for the authorisation of arrests. He prepared a proposal for Quisling that evening, that anyone 'who with good reason is suspected' of acts of enmity towards the state or the people could be detained without the case going to court. The arrests, which, on this authority, were started early on the Monday morning, led to around 300 Jewish males being rounded up in the

Berg concentration camp that week, while the women had to report daily to the police.

What did Quisling think of this? There is no trace of evidence to suggest that he reacted negatively to the Gestapo's action, let alone that he stood up to defend the Norwegian citizens in question. Quite probably he regarded the fate of his country's Jews as a legitimate domain for the occupying power. And indeed, the arrests were the result of long-standing German preparations for Jewish arrests in Norway, as in all occupied territories. In France, Holland and Belgium the arrests had started as early as the spring of 1942, and in July and August they were in full swing. In September the first preparations for Denmark were planned, and by October Norway's turn had come.[23]

There is no reliable documentation to show what the leading NS people imagined would happen to the Jews. Both in 1938 and again in 1941 Quisling had maintained that only a common European or international solution to the Jewish problem could be effective. On the other hand, it is probable that neither he nor other NS leaders imagined that the final international solution would come at that time, and so quickly. Quite possibly they envisaged concentration camps or work colonies in Norway as the most feasible solution.

The German deportations provide the background for the second law that Quisling signed that October, concerning the confiscation of Jewish property. In this case, his concern was contrary to that of assisting the Germans.

As the German police had instructed those arrested to bring with them only the basic necessities, leaving all their possessions at home, all Jewish property was in danger. Perhaps it was the vigilant Hagelin who first decided that the property of the detainees should be secured in Norwegian hands. On Monday 26 October, on the same day as the police started the arrests, he and Riisnæs met with Quisling in order to sort out the law on this point. Riisnæs had a draft ready, which Quisling, after his usual detailed study of the text, amended on several points before he signed: the property of all Jewish persons was seized and confiscated by the state. Every Jewish estate was accounted for, with the administration of the liquidation left to a board

---

[23] Martin Gilbert, *The Holocaust* (1989) chs. 23, 24; H. R. Kedward, *Occupied France: Collaboration and Resistance 1940–44* (1985) pp. 62f; J. C. H. Blom, 'The Persecution of the Jews in the Netherlands: A Comparative Western European Perspective', *European History Quarterly*, 19 (1989) pp. 333–51. Denmark: Luther to von Weizsäcker 24 September 1942, PAAA 11/64 Handakten Luther, Schriftverkehr.

of auditors. Through an ingenious process of resolutions covering all possible eventualities, the liquidations dragged on and the property was thereby held in the form of unmaintained estates for the duration of the occupation. Even though a number of greedy hands were after the Jewish fortunes, at least German demands were circumvented and the Jewish estates remained in Norway. All the German police got were the watches and the jewellery of those arrested, much less than they were to collect from Jews in other countries.[24]

Further action on the part of the Germans was only to be expected after the arrests of 26 October. Male detainees remained in the Norwegian state police concentration camps, most of them at Berg. The Norwegian government therefore had something to say: and it did. On 7 November all those over the age of sixty-five were released. Jewish women remained at home with their children. However, on 26 November 1942 all those who had been arrested in October, together with their families who were now rounded up as well, were deported overnight. The order went first from Reichssicherheitshauptamt to the Gestapo in Oslo and from there directly to Police Chief Marthinsen. Jonas Lie, now back in Oslo, only heard about the action after the event. The Norwegian police, with reinforcements from the Hird and the Norwegian SS, were once more mobilised throughout the country, this time to round up the women, children and the elderly. The steamship *Donau* was to take the families to an unknown destination.[25]

Both the nocturnal arrests and the assembling of the Jews at the pier on 26 November took place without the knowledge of the Minister President. The palace was in complete ignorance, until Helene Stang, Axel Stang's wife,

---

[24] Regulations concerning the requisitioning of Jewish property 20 November 1942; circular and instructions from the Ministry of Finance and the liquidation committee cited in Mendelsohn *Jødenes historie*, pp. 91–5. The range and scope of the Quisling government's seizure of Jewish property during the war has been a subject of much recent discussion, as the members of the royal commission which was set up in 1995 to investigate the Jewish losses disagreed profoundly both on the question of how much was seized and on what was actually referred after 1945. According to the majority of the commission, the total value of the Jewish fortunes confiscated was about NOK 18 million, of which NOK 10 million were paid out in compensation to the survivors after 1945. The minority hold the loss to be NOK 23 million, of which only some 8 million were paid back after 1945 (all estimates in 1945 currency rates) (NOU 1997: 22: 'Inndragning av jødisk eiendom i Norge under den 2. verdenskrig'), as summarised by H. F. Dahl, in *Dagbladet* 7 August 1997.

[25] Documented in the Wagner case: see 'Riksadvokatens meddelelsblad' no. 36, August 1947, pp. 19–34.

telephoned in a state of panic to find out whether the rumours that the Jews were to be sent away were true. She was told that they were not.[26]

Although the deportation was never officially announced, word of what had happened leaked out illegally and was passed on by the Swedish press to the BBC. It appeared that the *Donau* had not followed the Norwegian coastline northwards towards North Norway as so many had thought. It was heading south, through Øresund, towards the German Baltic, and docked at Stettin, from where the Jews were sent by train to Poland. In Sweden the news was given extensive publicity and thus reached Denmark, where it also made a deep impression. The fact that Norway's Jewish population could be rounded up by an occupying force and deported to an uncertain fate in order to satisfy certain central European racist ideologies shocked Scandinavia. The fact that two-thirds of the Jews from Norway were already safe in Sweden was unknown at the time.[27]

What outraged public opinion in Norway more than anything was the seizure of Jewish property: it smacked of cynical exploitation and was moreover made public though detailed records of all estates in the press. Even when the underground leadership of the Church registered its protest against the treatment of the Jews (the only Norwegian institution to do so), the confiscations headed the list of complaints as the single most appalling assault.[28] Quisling answered his critics in two speeches. On both occasions he talked of 'tragedy', but in the context of international Jewry being one of the main impulses behind the war. Stating that his government had 'protected itself against the Jews', the fact that the driving force behind both the arrests and the deportations had been the German police was something he neglected to mention. Instead he gave the public to understand that the whole operation had been a joint decision of the German and Norwegian authorities, perhaps even initiated by his government. It was thus clear that he, at least officially, sanctioned the deportations, and the tragedies he was referring to were mainly those concerning the marriages of Norwegians to Jews, and not the deportations as such.[29]

---

[26] Maria Quisling to Henrik Bergh summer 1945 (no date), UBO MS fol. 3920 IX, 3.

[27] The royal commission (NOU 1977: 22) estimates the number of Jews in Norway by 1940 to have been 2,173, of whom around 770 were deported and 747 died in Auschwitz. Also Kr. Ottosen, *I slik en natt* (1994).

[28] Christie, *Den norske kirke*, pp. 267ff.

[29] *FF* 7 December 1942, which contains reports of Quisling's two speeches in Trondheim. Extracts of the speech at the Filmteatret in a revised form in *Mot nytt land*, pp. 170–6, but *FF* is here taken as the more authentic source.

A similar shipment to the one in November left Oslo harbour in February 1943, bringing the total of Jewish deportations to 759, including 250 non-Norwegians, destined – so Quisling thought – for Poland or the Ukraine. On his visit to the eastern front in May 1942 he had had a unique opportunity to apprise himself of the situation there, paying particular attention to the conditions in the Ukraine, his old district, with its traditionally large Jewish population. 'The Jews here are not being treated brutally,' he had related at a press conference on his return to Norway. 'They are marked with white armbands and a yellow patch on their backs, and forced to work' but were not otherwise maltreated.[30] From his statements to the press at the time, it seems that he thought that Norwegian Jews would be treated reasonably well. Likewise, those who asked the Germans whether the deported Jews would suffer or even perish were reassured: 'Aber gnädige Frau, das ist Wahnsinn!' (But Madam, that's absurd!) At least that was the reply Helene Stang received when she expressed her concern. She was told that the Jews from Norway would be settled in a new home, employed in handicrafts and on the land. This was the official version, and there is no evidence to suggest that Quisling seriously doubted it at the time. However, the Jews who set sail on the *Donau* from Oslo, contrary to what they had been told, were destined for neither ghettos nor labour camps, but for extermination at Auschwitz.[31]

There is only scant documentation to shed light on the NS attitude to the deportations. The matter was simply not discussed within the party leadership. But the government must have known, or at least suspected, what was really going on. In the spring of 1943, during a visit to Berlin, Frederik Prytz took the opportunity to visit his eldest daughter, who was living in Breslau, where her husband was Oberbefehlshaber for the SS-SD. They discussed the fate of the Jews. Earlier in the year, Prytz's daughter had seen the local Jewish population being carried off like cattle in trucks. It was said that they were to be retrained as craftsmen. But her father countered, 'Do you know what happens to the Jews in those camps? They are exterminated.' Prytz used to listen to the BBC, and advised his daughter to do the same, illegally. Rumours of the extermination of Jews were in fact circulating within the party, and it seems highly implausible that they never reached Quisling. Unlike Prytz, however, he disregarded the rumours altogether. Prytz was an

---

[30] Quisling at a press conference 18 May 1942 in *FF* 19 May 1942. More details in the radio recording NRK ho (transcript with the author). Riisnæs, who accompanied Quisling to the front, gained much the same impression: see N. J. Ringdal, *Gal mann til rett tid* (1989) p. 107.

[31] Helene Stang, 1986.*

ardent Anglophile. He viewed the Germans with scepticism and was certainly not anti-Semitic. Since the years around 1920, when they shared so many ideas, Quisling had taken a different ideological turn and during the war he went a long way towards accepting German National Socialism.[32]

At about the same time as Prytz was revealing the terrible truth to his daughter, Quisling gave a lecture which in highly scathing and sarcastic tones painted a picture of what could be expected if the exiled Nygaardsvold government ever returned to Norway: What did they plan to do once they had killed off the Nazis and done away with the new order? Immediate introduction of Russian conditions? Or just the same old party politics, the class struggle with its lockouts, strikes, unemployment and *Dagbladet* – 'and of course, Aronstam, Cohn, Fein, Glick, Goldberg, Goldenheim, Goldfart, Goldwasser, Levenstein, Levinson, Nachtstern, Nathan, Rabinowitz, Rosenblum, Rubinstein, Salomon, Steinsaphur, Weinstock and Moses Apelsin, with Hambro at their helm'? The satire on Norwegian Jewish surnames was certainly designed to impress his audience, and to make it clear that the new Norway could manage without these people – and should be thankful that a man like Hambro was in exile and that *Dagbladet* and *Morgenbladet* had finally been shut down. These words indicate that Quisling actually believed what he heard officially in 1943–4: that Norwegian Jews were living in reservations and concentration camps in Poland, awaiting eventual repatriation to Madagascar or some other place after the end of the war.[33]

'ONE DAY THE LIGHT WILL COME'

During Quisling's winter of discontent, the wider parameters of the war were changing, with December 1942 the bleakest month of the war so far. What in November could still be regarded as isolated episodes – the Germans being surrounded at Stalingrad, and their desert tanks under pressure in North Africa – now emerged as distinctly disturbing tendencies in the overall picture of the war. Both on the Volga front and in the southern Mediterranean the Germans were sustaining defeats of obvious strategic significance.

[32] Anne Margrethe Prytz, 1986.* This visit in April 1943 was the last time she was to see her father; see Prytz's report of his meeting in the Reichsfinanzministerium, printed in *Norges Bank under okkupasjonen* (1945) pp. 103f.

[33] Quisling's speech, Klingenberg cinema 17 May 1943, in *FF* 18 May 1943. For the opposite view, that Quisling was very well aware of German genocide and the 'final solution' when the Jews were deported from Norway, see Høidal, *Quisling*, pp. 469, 677n. There are no sources to support this view, however.

At the end of the year it was clear that the tank battle at El Alamein in Egypt heralded an Allied victory in North Africa, while all Germany's gains in the East in 1942 were about to be lost in the Russian campaign that winter. Particularly crucial was the situation of the Sixth Army at Stalingrad. The rhetoric of war thus changed. The words 'enemy offensive' were increasingly heard in the long series of daily war announcements.

Quisling too changed the tone of his generally optimistic analysis. In Trondheim on 6 December 1942 he summarised the position of the fortieth month of the war by comparing the situation to that of the same month of the previous world war – January 1918. From that perspective the situation did not seem too bad, or at least quite different from January 1918. If Germany and her allies were counted up, a total population of 300 million was reached in Europe alone. Added to this was the fact that Japan had now emerged as a formidable world power in the Far East, bringing the Axis population to somewhere between 500 and 550 million people. On this calculation, the Axis could still be seen as a superpower, at least in comparison with the previous war. Some weeks later, however, his words had a very different tenor: 'Today as we celebrate the winter solstice, we should remember that even when there are difficulties, the light will come one day,' he told the Hird in Oslo.[34]

Naturally, such pessimism was entirely absent from the official greetings telegrams he exchanged with Hitler, Terboven, von Falkenhorst and Rediess in the new year, which still smacked of the customary triumphalism. In his telegram to Terboven, Quisling thanked him warmly for his co-operation in 1942, and the Reichskommissar saluted him cordially and at length. Indeed, the relationship seemed to have improved. To a delegation of leading Norwegian industrialists and top civil servants, many of whom were opponents of the NS, whom he invited to Skaugum in December 1942, Terboven praised Quisling in a eulogistic speech. A more neutral observer, however, the newly appointed Reich plenipotentiary in Denmark, Dr Werner Best, who came to Norway to familiarise himself with the neighbouring situation, noted that there had scarcely been any improvement in Quisling's relationship with Terboven.[35]

The gravity of the changing situation was discernible between the lines in

---

[34] *FF* 7, 22 December 1942.

[35] Best, in his portrait of Quisling dated December 1948, in Siegfried Matlock, *Danmark i Hitlers hånd* (1989) pp. 294f. His report after the visit to Oslo: Report to AA 14 December 1942, *ADAP* E IV no. 287 pp. 523f. The new year telegrams were recorded in *FF* on 2 and 4 January 1943.

the telegrams Quisling exchanged with Hitler. Quisling's message expressed the wish that the 'new year bring the triumphant German armies a decisive result'. Hitler replied that, 'whatever may occur in the new year it will definitely bring us closer to a decisive result, which we are determined to fight for with all our fanaticism'. There was no mention of Norway's situation or of what the country's role in the Europe of the future would be. In fact, Hitler was already resenting the relatively independent position he had granted to his Norwegian protégé. On 14 December the Führer faced a similar demand from the leader of the Dutch National Socialists, Anton Adriaan Mussert, who requested appointment as Prime Minister in the manner of Quisling in Norway. Hitler refused on the grounds of the negative experiences of the Norwegian situation, stating that it might have been better had Quisling not been made Minister President at all; better for Germany in any event, but also better for Quisling himself. The assessment not only scotched Mussert's ambitions but also augured ill for Quisling. Ignorant of what was said in the Reich Chancellery, the Norwegian Minister President was at this time complaining to a high-ranking German official in Oslo that Hitler now treated Norway even worse than the Russian Tsar in former years had treated the Finns. Anti-German sentiments were indeed bound to spread within the NS movement, he predicted.[36]

The Norwegian Fører therefore saw the new year in with great apprehension, no longer the optimistic collaborator of earlier times, but worrying about allying himself to German policy in Norway, and bitter about having been abandoned that autumn. Everything contributed to his decision not to broadcast his customary new year address on radio that year, but to delegate the task to Fuglesang – Lunde's successor as Minister of Culture and Public Information. In addition to this new appointment, Fuglesang continued as Secretary General and Party Minister, thereby strengthening his position in the party to the extent that, at thirty-three, he was generally regarded as Quisling's tacit choice of successor.

However, on 1 February 1943 Quisling was forced into the fray himself. No matter how depressing the situation of the war in general and the NS's position in particular seemed, the anniversary of the Act of State at Akershus had to be marked with a speech from the Fører. And so it was: the speech actually signalled a turning-point in the conception of the war, and a new

---

[36] Admiral Fein to Boehm 26 December 1942, BA-MA RM 7/127. Hitler and Mussert: *ADAP* E IV no. 284 pp. 506ff. For the background to Mussert's visit see Hirschfield, *Nazi Rule*, pp. 303ff.

direction for the party propaganda. The old themes of freedom and independence were now abandoned. The Sixth Army was about to be annihilated at Stalingrad. Thus the burning issue was the danger which more than ever threatened the lives and integrity of the Norwegian people: the danger of a possible Russian victory in the East: 'If Germany's hold on Norway should slip, or if Germany herself goes under', nothing could save Norway from Bolshevism – in comparison to which the German occupation that his countrymen complained about would seem more of a protection than an occupation. 'If Germany loses the war, there is no hope for Scandinavia': deportations, killings, persecutions would be inevitable. He reminded his listeners that, only ten years before, Stalin had starved 6 million farmers to death in order to accelerate the process of collectivisation. His speech indulged in apocalyptic visions: 'The whole world is struggling and quaking in the midst of a crisis of such proportions ... such that never in the history of mankind has its like been witnessed.' His fellow Norwegians had 'grossly offended' against holy promises and thus had to 'acknowledge their own guilt and sin' by accepting the punishment now upon them by doing as the Germans and the Finns had done: sacrificing themselves heroically in the struggle to defend themselves.[37]

And the people did indeed make this choice – in their own way. After Stalingrad the shift in public opinion became obvious to everyone. Even before the catastrophe, the general view of the NS had been hostile to the point of maintaining an 'ice front' between them and the rest of the population. 'People stare openly at NS members in the street and in passing purse their lips,' an NS sympathiser noted in his diary in November 1942. After Stalingrad the climate sharpened, according to the same source: 'The hatred between Norwegians is intensifying. Here in Oslo there is a mentality of civil war. Recently I heard of two NS men who had been murdered ... set upon in their own homes and stabbed to death. If the Allies win, all NS people in Oslo will be in the greatest danger.'[38]

COLONISATION IN THE EAST

On 2 February 1943, the day after the celebrations and the same day as General Paulus signed the official capitulation at Stalingrad, Quisling put his

---

[37] Speech printed in *FF* 2 February 1943 and reprinted verbatim in *Mot nytt land*, pp. 181–203; sound recording in NRK ho 3146.

[38] Smedal, *Patriotisme*, p. 58 (entry 14 November 1942) and p. 68 (9 April 1943).

signature to a document of some forty pages intended for Hitler and other high-ranking Germans, entitled '*Aide-mémoire* on the Russian Question' (*Denkschrift über die russische Frage*).[39]   When Quisling finished it on 2 February, the military aspect of the Russian question was completely different from what it had been when he started on the first draft in the autumn of 1941 with the purpose of presenting to Hitler a strategy for avoiding Napoleon's mistakes and conducting a victorious campaign. But twenty months later neither Leningrad nor Moscow had been taken, and the way to Vladivostok looked more difficult than ever.

Nevertheless, 'Denkschrift über die russische Frage' was given to Terboven to forward to the Führer. Terboven read the document closely, and concluded that Quisling was clearly an expert on the situation; it occurred to him that Hitler might appoint him Reichskommissar somewhere in Russia. If so, it might open a welcome door for a change in the deadlocked situation in Norway. With this in mind Terboven sent the document round to other offices, including a copy to Gottlob Berger at SS headquarters in Berlin, who in turn provided Himmler with a copy at his headquarters in East Prussia. The Oberkommando der Wehrmacht received a copy from von Falkenhorst's staff. Goebbels also received a copy, and commented in his diary that 'Quisling here displays clear and objective judgement'. Rosenberg and his colleagues naturally received copies too. Quisling himself intended to take one with him to his next meeting with Hitler which was scheduled for February 1943.[40]

'In Russia the fate of the world is being decided. The Russian question is the main problem in world politics today,' read the introduction. This was followed by a formula for how Germany could most effectively quell resistance and take the occupied areas of Russia for good. 'Russia is a country which cannot be conquered and occupied without the support of the population,' Quisling stated. Napoleon had made a mistake in stopping the peasants from rising up against the Tsar. Von Clausewitz had shown through his detailed analyses why he should have permitted such an uprising and exploited domestic conflicts, which would have been all that was necessary to win Russia. Quisling emphasised that it would not be enough to rely on minorities in this struggle, although the Baltic nations, the Byelo-

---

[39] The only known version of this document is a copy Berger sent to Himmler on 1 March 1943, BA NS 19. Quisling's handwritten notes, mainly statistics and calculations, are in RA FMK 17.

[40] Note by Rudolf Schiedemair 28 April 1948, IfZ MA 110. OKW KTB March 1943. The Goebbels Diary, entry for 14 April 1943.

russians, Caucasians, Finns and the Turkish Tartars should all be mobilised. The main weight must be laid on Russia itself, the Communist heartland, if the Bolsheviks were to be prevented from exploiting greater Russian nationalism for their own benefit.

The 'Denkschrift' drafted a number of proposals for a geopolitical solution of the Russian question, suggesting the Dnieper line as a clear border between western Europe ('Germania') and Russia. This necessarily involved the division of the Ukraine, but even so could be defended from geographical and historical perspectives. When it came to Russia's borders in the south-east, he proposed that Georgia, Armenia and Azerbaijan should all become independent states, while the Central Asian regions remained Russian. Karelia should remain Finnish, Crimea should be established as 'a German colony state under German military administration', and the Kola peninsula he suggested should either remain Russian or be transferred to Norway.

These plans, which in fact went far beyond Hitler's petty bourgeois, anti-Slav prejudices, assumed that Germany would apply certain principles, which Quisling was at pains to define: 'It is not possible at the same time to unify and occupy Europe's nations,' he insisted. Napoleon had tried and failed. 'Europe must be united and pacified through adequate timely (*"rechtzeitige"*) concessions to the individual states and national freedom and independence of the people of those states.' If Germany were to try another approach, its leaders would find that the situation in the long run would be 'extremely difficult ... The basis for the peaceful conquest of the world must be the use of only a limited number of exceptional men who know and understand the country and the people; energetic but also just and respectable men.'

The 'Denkschrift' is only one document among several containing Quisling's visions of German conquest. Enormous areas were in the process of being taken, and the question of how they would be divided, administered, populated and developed in the future was one of the most hotly debated issues in the comprehensive German Ostpolitik and Ostforschung,[41] as well as an object of notorious rivalry among the various authorities in the Third Reich: Hitler himself, his party leader Bormann, Rosenberg's Eastern Office, Ribbentrop and the Foreign Ministry, Göring's four-year plan, Himmler's SS empire, Goebbels and the Propaganda Ministry, as well as the

[41] Catherine Andreyev, *Vlasov and the Russian Liberation Movement* (1987) pp. 29ff; Michael Burleigh, *Germany Turns Eastwards: A Study of* Ostforschung *in the Third Reich* (1988).

Wehrmacht in all its various combinations.[42] In any case Quisling's proposals were quite remote from the ideas of Hitler, who considered the Slavs to be subhuman, and not at all the God-fearing and tolerant peasants Quisling was depicting. Hitler had therefore long dismissed any thought of Germany taking on a civilising mission, and instead regarded the East as a single area suitable for colonisation. It was also out of the question for Hitler to enter into discussions on the constitutional position of the various Baltic countries at this point, in the middle of the Leningrad episode of the war. In all, Quisling's view that Germany could put the civilian population to military use was so far from Berlin policy that he could hardly have expected it to have any purchase there. Himmler's Einsatzkommando was hostile to the civilian population in such a way that it has since established itself as a paradigm of the horrors of warfare. At the time when Quisling wrote his 'Denkschrift' this stance was less apparent. When he visited the front in the spring of 1942 he had remarked that in the Ukraine 'the relationship with the civilian population is very good'. 'A sigh of relief on the faces of the people after Bolshevism,' he said to Oslo journalists on his return. But by the time the 'Denkschrift' was finished, things were much clearer. Hitler was no civiliser, rather a new and harsher Napoleon.

With hindsight it seems strange that Quisling did so little to further Norwegian interests in his 'Denkschrift'. In view of his strong feelings about Norwegian racial superiority and Norway's historic claims in the northern hemisphere, one could have expected more references to Russian–Norwegian issues. The only such reference was in fact the suggestion concerning the Kola peninsula.[43] His modesty on this occasion did not mean, however, that the NS regime had no plans for penetration into the Russian sphere.

As soon as the German campaign started in the summer of 1941, an old colleague of Quisling's, Colonel Konrad Sundlo, offered to make a contribution for 'a greater Norway' in the East. Sundlo, the former commander of the Norwegian forces in Narvik, had taken up party work after the campaign

---

[42] Dallin, *German Rule*, ch. 2.

[43] A few weeks after the launch of Operation Barbarossa, Göring suggested to Hitler that they 'give Kola to Terboven to exploit', to which Hitler agreed, according to Bormann's report of the conversation with Hitler 16 July 1941, *ADAP* D XIII 1 no. 114 p. 128. The idea came to nothing. But rumours that Norway was after Kola had got as far as Helsinki at least, and led to a worried communication from the former President, Svinhufvud, to Ribbentrop. Von Blücher in Helsinki to Ribbentrop, 21 March 1942. Reply from Ribbentrop 4 April 1942, *ADAP* E II no. 111 p. 191.

in 1940 and declared himself 'very anxious to be involved if the question of pursuing Norwegian interests in Russia arises'. Sundlo had been a businessman in Russia for many years, including a spell in the Caucasus in 1919–20, and was full of ideas as to how the task should be continued.[44]

At the same time, Frederik Prytz had a full memorandum translated and distributed in German. The memorandum was based on the document he had prepared as trade attaché in Petrograd for the Foreign Ministry in November 1918, and argued for diverting the flood of Norwegian émigrés away from America and encouraging them to settle in northern Russia and Siberia instead. Under the heading 'Bjarmeland – Europe's Canada', the memorandum was distributed to Himmler, among others, who saw reason to make a detailed and mainly positive comment on it. Hitler also entered the discussion, and in one of his table talks in September 1941 he said that Northerners should no longer be given permission to go to America. 'Instead we must lead Norwegians, Swedes, Danes and Dutchmen into the eastern regions.'[45]

Quisling was clearly thinking along these lines too. In his inaugural address at Akershus on 1 February 1942 he made a pledge to ensure that Norway made a contribution to the forthcoming 'clearing up and reorganisation of Russia'. A few months later he explained to Oslo journalists the potential of, for example, the Ukraine: 'When we survey that extraordinarily rich country, the black soil, just waiting to be ploughed, and the vast uninhabited and undeveloped areas, then we realise that this is the country of the future, far richer and greater than America.'[46] He had already gone into the matter in greater detail both with Himmler when he visited Oslo in 1941 and with Rosenberg in Berlin, who was very enthusiastic, asking Quisling to return for further consultations at the earliest date possible.[47]

Quisling's government had set about opening a Russian Office as early as 1942; from December that year it was put directly under Quisling's Chancellery at the palace. Preparations for 'the new colony in the East' were made here in a number of ways, modelled on the Dutch initiative for an

---

[44] Sundlo to Hagelin 18 November 1941, RA FMK 16.

[45] Speech 9 September 1941, cited in Picker, *Hitlers Tischgespräche*, p. 70; see also speech 27 July 1942, ibid., p. 471. Prytz's memo is in RA PA Prytz 8; see also Ole Kolsrud, 'Kollaborasjon og imperialisme. Quisling-regjeringens "Austrveg"-drøm 1941–44', *HT* 1988/3 pp. 241–70. Himmler's comment: Himmler to Heydrich and Rediess 16 February 1942, BA NS 19/2375.

[46] Quisling at press conference on 18 May 1942, in *FF* 19 May 1942.

[47] Rosenberg to Quisling 7 January 1942, IfZ MA 110. Kolsrud, 'Kollaborasjon', p. 243.

Eastern Company, along with courses in Russian and the compilation of a
Russian dictionary. The office had a good relationship with Rosenberg's
ministry and went on planning for Norwegian expansion in Byelorussia and
the Ukraine after the stalemate of Hitler's campaign had made Siberia less
probable. By 1943, however, Terboven declared the whole project to be
under the aegis of the Reichskommissariat, and soon the development of the
war made clear that there would be no expansion at all.[48]

Thus the Norwegian industrial offensive came to a halt, overtaken by the
events of the war. But even as Quisling was penning his 'Denkschrift', there
was still some hope. The consideration he was giving to a possible
Norwegian colony was made only indirectly. After having made his main
point that no colonisation of Russia should be carried out without genuine
consideration of the population's feelings of pride and honour, he concluded
his text with a somewhat unexpected turn: perhaps it could come about
even so with a 'greater Germanic colonisation' which under certain circumstances would be 'not simply conceivable but even necessary'. It may be that
one of his associates had pointed out to him that a document which rejected
out of hand any question of foreign colonisation east of the Baltic, would ill
serve as the basis for a potential Norwegian initiative whenever the
opportunity presented itself.

But such an opportunity never did present itself. On 13 January 1943, at
the same time as Quisling was adding the finishing touches to his text, Hitler
gave the order to cease all long-term plans for the East until after the war.
With mounting pressure from the Volga front, and the Russians breaking
through the iron ring around Leningrad, there was no longer time for
speculation about how to clean up and reorganise Russia in the future. What
was necessary was to concentrate efforts on the war in the here and now.
The catastrophe at Stalingrad followed two weeks later.[49]

For Quisling this meant that the very moment that he put his signature to
it, the 'Denkschrift' became totally and absolutely irrelevant.

TOTAL WAR

The defeat at Stalingrad signalled a turning point in mobilisation over the
whole of German-controlled Europe. All efforts had to be made to avert

---

[48] For the Dutch company, see Dallin, *German Rule*, pp. 285f; Hirschfield, *Nazi Rule*, p. 308;
Terboven's declaration: Kolsrud, 'Kollaborasjon', pp. 254ff.
[49] Dallin, *German Rule*, p. 288.

catastrophe. The National Work Effort (Arbeitseinsatz), with universal registration, was introduced into Germany at the end of January 1943. Besides, there was a large-scale importation of workers from the occupied territories, which by the end of the year reached approximately 5 million, the majority of whom came from Poland, the Soviet Union, France, Czechoslovakia and Holland.

Norway and Denmark had so far escaped sending workers to Germany, but the gravity of the situation meant that the work effort had to be extended to the Reichskommissariat Norwegen too. On 7 February 1943 Terboven and other national and *gau* leaders listened to the Führer's analysis of the situation at the headquarters at Rastenburg. Hitler stressed how every effort must be made to mobilise whatever resources were available. This was followed on 18 February by Goebbels's famous speech 'Do you want total war?' in Berlin's Sports Palace. With rehearsed triumphant cries coming from loudspeakers scattered among the audience to rouse the already excited crowds, and stirring rhetoric accompanied by sophisticated lighting, the evening in the Sports Palace reached its hysterical climax in support of total war. Terboven telephoned his congratulations to Goebbels afterwards.[50]

Towards the end of February preparations in Norway had reached the point of implementing the necessary decrees. At very short notice a joint Norwegian and German meeting was called at Klingenberg cinema on Monday 22 February, where the occupation forces and the National Government were to announce the new policy. It was the first joint meeting since the Act of State at Akershus, with Fuglesang as Norwegian and Neumann as German organisers. Both national anthems were sung and there was meticulously equal coverage of Quisling's and Terboven's speeches in the party press, besides a joint telegram to Hitler.[51]

At the time the work effort was seen as a German imposition and as part of its exploitation of Norway. Quite naturally it was experienced as a new pressure in the Germans' increasingly aggressive domination of the Norwegian economy. Cabinet ministers now spoke openly of 'German imperialism'

---

[50] The Goebbels Diary, entry for 17 March 1943; Ralf Georg Reuth, *Goebbels* (1990) pp. 516ff; David Irving, *Goebbels. Mastermind of the Third Reich* (1996) pp. 421ff; D. Welch, *Propaganda and the German Cinema* (1983)' pp. 22f, and Welch, 'Goebbels, Götterdämmerung and the deutsche Wochenschauen', in K. R. M. Short and Stephan Dolezel (eds.), *Hitler's Fall and the Newsreel Witness* (1988).

[51] Quisling and Terboven's speeches in *FF* 23 February 1943.

as a growing, destructive and oppressive force directed against their own efforts to shield the nation's resources from the conqueror.[52] That the initiative was clearly a German one did not, however, prevent the Norwegian government from benefiting from it in certain ways. Compulsory registration of the work-force at municipal work offices had been going on since 1941 as a provision of ordinances made at the time. The state had acquired the right to demand a national work effort for the common good in times of need, such as harvesting and forest work. With greater weight behind the authority of the Ministry of Social Affairs, registration of the labour force, which was already compulsory, now became much more effective.[53]

Quisling chose to word his own speech at the Klingenberg cinema on 22 February in a strikingly anti-Semitic form. In fact, his anti-Jewish rhetoric on this occasion resembled his Frankfurt speech in March 1941. It was as though he were deliberately playing to the German civilian and military authorities, who sat there in the hall in their glittering regalia, concentrating on the danger facing them all if the fortunes of war did not turn, and presenting a nightmare vision of Judaism, that 'international conspiracy', the 'universal plague which strikes whole peoples, splits and destroys their national bodies, and will result in a brutal conquest of the world'. His words produced a terrifying portrait of the enemy in the shape of a secret Jewish conspiracy which extended from Wall Street to the Kremlin, so far divorced from any reasonable assessment of the world that it did not resemble his customary style in any particular. To picture Germany's invasion of Russia as a response to a 'consciously and carefully planned and prepared' offensive on the part of world Judaism was not even consistent with his own analysis. The speech had to be understood as Quisling's moving towards Germany. Anti-Semitic rhetoric constituted an affective common language in German Europe, a frame of reference within which a minor national politician could demonstrate verbally that he was on the right side. And indeed, at the time, Quisling did need to build up his standing with the German authorities after the disastrous blows of the previous autumn. January and February 1943, moreover, saw another setback, in that his constant support in the German leadership, Admiral Raeder, was poised to fall. Hitler, who was displeased with the navy's surface offensive in the battle over the Atlantic, resolved to give priority to the building of U-boats over Raeder's own programme. The

---

[52] Notes by Regierungsrat Hagemann 16 April 1943, *ADAP* E V no. 310 pp. 609ff.

[53] Ø. Sørensen, *Solkors og solidaritet* (1991) ch. 'Nasjonal Samlings store triumf', pp. 102ff.

Grand Admiral saw this as a vote of no confidence and resigned. On 2 February, he was replaced by the head of the submarine fleet, Admiral Dönitz. This had wide repercussions in the navy, in that Admiral Boehm and his adjutant were recalled from Norway. Admiral Ciliax, a man unknown to Quisling, took over as the navy's commanding officer.[54]

This was a heavy blow. Boehm's recalling meant that the only high-ranking Wehrmacht representative who had any genuine interest in Norway had gone. Boehm and Quisling had worked very well together for almost three years. Invitations and small gifts, birthday greetings and good wishes were frequently exchanged. In addition, the Admiral was an extremely friendly, well-educated and cultivated man. 'I deeply regret your departure from Norway,' wrote Quisling in his farewell letter to Boehm on 25 February. Terboven was of course delighted at Boehm's departure, as the well-known tensions between them had escalated irreparably in the previous year.[55]

One month later the results of the Folketing elections in Denmark on 23 March sent a shock through the NS. Frits Clausen and his National Socialists suffered a crushing defeat, with only 2 per cent of the vote, only a slight increase on the previous election in 1939, despite considerable German subsidies and a German occupation policy which should have ensured that Danish hostility towards their NS movement would be far less than Norwegians' loathing of the NS. The defeat resulted in Clausen's declining further subsidies and retiring from Danish politics for good.[56]

Norway was obviously not Denmark, and Quisling considered himself a Fører of a different class from Clausen. Still, the fate of the Danish movement was a sign that German imperialist attitudes threatened the whole project of securing National Socialism through collaboration in Norway.

BACK TO HITLER

Stalingrad also had consequences for Hitler's health. In March his doctor told him to leave Wolfsschanze, the cramped and unhealthy headquarters at Rastenburg in East Prussia, and go home to the fresh air of the Salzburg Alps. Hitler duly relocated to his light and airy home, Berghof in Obersalz-

[54] M. Skodvin, *Krig og okkupasjon* (1991) pp. 204ff; J. Noakes and G. Pridham, *Nazism* II (1983–6) ch. 32, 'The Battle of the Atlantic'.

[55] Quisling to Boehm 25 February 1943, RA FMK 14; Paulsen, 'Terboven i konflikt'.

[56] Poulsen, *Besættelsesmagten*, pp. 380ff; Clausen to Best, 23 March 1943, RAK BA 44d/1; Werner Best, report concerning Dr Frits Clausen and the DNSAP 28 January 1946, RAK Rigsadvokaten, Clausen-Sagen.

berg. During the spring he received streams of foreign visitors and associates, some at Berghof and some at nearby Schloss Klessheim, which was used for official entertainment. King Boris of Bulgaria, and a delegation from Italy led by Mussolini, Marshal Antonescu of Romania, Admiral Horthy of Hungary, President Tiso of Slovakia, Prime Minister Pavalic of Croatia, Prime Minister Laval of France and Norway's Minister President Quisling were numbered among his guests.[57]

Quisling travelled alone on this occasion, which was exceptional, as on all previous visits to Hitler he had been accompanied by Hagelin. Although Hagelin was not to be present on this particular state visit, he did play a part in the preparations leading up to it. On 12 April he invited Quisling to his home on the Bygdøy peninsula, to a small gathering attended only by himself, Neumann from the Einsatzstab and Ernst Hagemann from the Reichskommissariat – two reliable and honourable Germans who really appreciated the difficult position of the NS. The Germans had asked for the meeting and Hagelin now steered the conversation in such a way that Quisling was given the opportunity, for once, to air his opinion of German policy in Norway. He took advantage of the situation, and spoke for several hours on the subject. Hagelin, who had so often in the past been obliged to encourage the hesitant Quisling to speak out and to fashion what he said into a suitable form, was able to remain in the background that evening. Hagemann kept notes, and Neumann made the occasional comment, but otherwise this was Quisling's evening, with all his bitterness and pent-up frustrations pouring out into the open.

German policy in Norway, he said, was now assuming the character of organised treachery against his people. For, as Germany was constantly refusing to make known the principles on which post-war Europe would be organised, and at the same time continued to demand increasingly greater sacrifices in terms of the war effort, people could only see this as an attempt to cheat the smaller nations out of their independence and freedom. Not even in the communiqué which followed Mussolini's recent visit to the Führer was anything approximating concrete aims of the war mentioned. The wording was kept deliberately vague, not because the aims of the war would have to be abandoned in the future, but because it was so obviously German and Italian policy to make a fool of the smaller nations: 'German

[57] Andreas Hillgruber, *Staatsmänner und Diplomaten bei Hitler* II (1970); Domarus, *Hitler*; M. Hauner, *Hitler: A Chronology* (1983).

policy is intrinsically dishonest, and thus she cannot be honest with her partners,' concluded Quisling.[58]

No European union could be organised from either Germany or Italy. German policy, based on violence, on cunning and betrayal, could only unleash the forces of opposition, and lead the European people into a union against Germany. In response to Neumann's comment that it would therefore be worth while to stimulate a common belief in National Socialism and bolster faith in Hitler's capability as a genial leader, Quisling replied that in this context he would only be able to see National Socialism as 'little more than a form of spiritual imperialism'.

The two Germans were astounded by what they heard. Quisling's words were noteworthy enough in themselves, without the unprecedented emotional charge. 'He is embittered to an extent which we have never witnessed before,' reported Hagemann. 'It was as if a profound human disappointment had unleashed emotions in him which completely displaced his reason and made any kind of discussion difficult.' The four men discussed what Quisling should do. Neumann and Hagemann recommended that he present at least some of his points to Hitler at their forthcoming meeting 'to hear what the Führer himself had to say'.

The visit to Schloss Klessheim was to take place the following week on Monday 19 April. The circumstances were normally treated as state secrets. But among the Norwegian journalists in Berlin the news of Quisling's visit was known a few days in advance, even though they were not at liberty to report it. *Aftenposten*'s correspondent noted that on this occasion Quisling was being put up at Bellevue Palace on his way through the capital, a big step up from Adlon or Kaiserhof, as 'only heads of state or prominent statesmen in the Axis agreement stay at Bellevue'. Terboven and Neumann, who accompanied him, were given hospitality elsewhere.

In between meetings with Rosenberg and Himmler, the Minister President and Terboven also had tea with the official Norwegian News Bureau (NTB) correspondent just before they left for Munich and Obersalzberg: 'Quisling looms large, says nothing, and looks as though he is imagining Terboven dead.'[59]

---

[58] Hagemann's report is dated 16 April 1943, printed in *ADAP* E V no. 310 pp. 609–15. It is not known who received the report or who read it, but it must have been circulated fairly widely for it to have reached a subordinate such as Ernst Züchner in the German Propaganda Ministry – see his statement of June 1945 in *Straffesak* pp. 602ff, in which the conference is wrongly dated to February 1943.

[59] Theo Findahl, *Lange skygger* (1964) pp. 115f. Detailed schedule of the visit in BA R 43 II/

On the day of the audience, Hitler, Bormann and Lammers first received Terboven alone. Then Quisling was invited to an official reception. After twenty minutes of polite formalities a midday meal followed at 2 o'clock and was attended by several prominent officials, including Reichsführer-SS Himmler. Hitler used the meal to express his anger at King Christian X of Denmark, who had insulted him by acknowledging his friendly birthday telegram with a terse greeting. The Danish King's telegram read 'Thank you very much'. 'So eine Unverschämtheit!' declared Hitler, still greatly vexed, despite the fact that the incident had taken place more than half a year before. Quisling tried to calm him, explaining that the King's clumsiness could have been caused by linguistic difficulties.[60] After the meal there was a long conversation between Hitler, Quisling and Terboven, with Lammers and Bormann present, before Hitler returned to Berghof to meet Göring in the evening.

Fourteen months had passed since their last meeting, and the events of those months had taken their toll on both men. Quisling had become more corpulent while Hitler was much thinner, a result of his steadily declining health. Their meeting, which lasted almost three hours, was monopolised by Hitler, whose monologue sounded fluent and unrestrained as always, but with more repetitions and circular arguments than usual. It proved impossible for Quisling to find an opening.[61]

The main point was painfully clear. Hitler was not prepared to make any promises whatsoever over Norway. Whether or not he had been briefed about Quisling's latest outburst is not known, but he completely dismissed the points Quisling was most concerned with. He repeatedly stressed that his integrity prevented him from making promises which he was unable to honour, as he wanted to go down in history as 'a man of absolute integrity', and was at pains to point out that he was a historical and not a political figure, thus honesty and keeping his promises were of paramount importance to him. Moreover, he could not end the state of war with Norway, because if he did, Laval in France, among others, would 'immediately make

1172. Hitler's agenda 1943, IfZ München F 19/4; official announcement in *FF* 21 April 1943; German version in Domarus, *Hitler* II, pp. 2006f. P. A. Jahr's account of the visit (wrongly dated as late summer 1942) in J. O. Jensen, *De nære årene* (1986) pp. 137ff.

[60] Jahr's account in Jensen, *De nære årene*, pp. 138f; see also Quisling's statement to the Danish police on 10 September 1945, quoted in Sehested, 'Sandheden om 9. April', stencil (no year) pp. 171f, 197f; on the 'telegram crisis' see further Jørgen Hæstrup et al. (eds.), *Besættelsens Hvem Hvad Hvor* (1985) pp. 235ff.

[61] Report dated Oslo 3 May 1943, probably by Neumann, in RA LD 29 Q.

the same demand'. Peace and the reorganisation of Europe would thus have to be settled at one and the same time, when the time was right. And from Quisling's point of view, the Führer was working within a depressingly long time-scale: the war in Russia would come to a conclusion in either 1943 or 1944 – perhaps later, after which new tasks awaited them as the situation in Britain and their stance on Mosley's movement were included as part of the final settlement. He would not shy away from introducing a military dictatorship in Europe if it was needed to break Britain, Hitler said. And whatever arrangement he decided on for Europe could at this point only be considered in the most general of terms.

All in all, Hitler was vague on the question of a time-scale, categorical in his rejection of the peace settlement, and dismissive of any move which might be interpreted as a federal initiative, while naturally uncompromising in his resolve to fight the battle to the end, a battle which, he explained, could in several respects be a long and demanding one. Hitler's insistence that Britain had to be conquered and his colleague Mosley perhaps taken out of prison and set up as Germany's man in London before any arrangements for Europe could even be discussed, meant that Quisling might have to wait several years for a settlement. The only firm promise for the situation ahead was that he and Hitler would 'meet at least once every two or three months', for what it was worth.

The meeting was a disaster, worse than if he had not seen Hitler at all. Quisling failed to hide his disappointment to *Fritt Folk*'s correspondent afterwards. The paper had made preparations for a special issue back in Norway, but Quisling told them that there was to be no special issue. Demands and empty promises were the only outcome, nothing positive on the question of peace. The NTB correspondent was also deeply disappointed: 'Hitler, the world's greatest crook and traitor, and Quisling actually believes in him!' The Norwegian Fører came back empty-handed, disappointed and humiliated. All the principles he had worked out for his co-operation with Hitler – the reorganisation of Europe along federal lines, the Europeanisation of Russia, together with Norway's supremacy in Scandinavia – had been brutally dismissed.

Two weeks after his return to Norway Quisling attended the Norwegian–German Society meeting at the University Aula to listen to Goebbels's Secretary of State, Leopold Gutterer, speak on the war effort and the European new order. Gutterer, who appeared in his SS general's uniform, talked with great authority. The new order which the Axis powers were bringing forward, he said, aimed to secure the very goals which the Bolshevik and economic-imperialist world are threatening, that is, 'national qualities, the right to life and the possibility for development for the individual peoples in our European continent'.

For Quisling, who was fully aware of Hitler's standpoint, all this rang utterly false, with its empty phrases, non-committal talk, perhaps designed to make fools of Europe's small nations. The experience he had had at Schloss Klessheim had been an eye-opener; he could plan as much as he liked – for after the war. In reality, Norway's freedom had been postponed to an indefinite and increasingly distant time. Three years after he had put himself at the disposal of German policy in Norway he had been betrayed by Hitler.

9

On the edge of the volcano

The war now in progress is a total war ... King Haakon and his allies
are bombing ships on peaceful missions along our coast and murdering
innocent women and children in the most gruesome way. Indeed, they
are systematically advancing the lines into civilian life itself, organising
illegal resistance and terrorist groups, opting for boycotts and sabotage;
working with explosives, lies and poison. *Quisling at the* Hird *inspection, Oslo, 17 October 1943*[1]

Every morning during the last years of the war residents of the west end of
Oslo witnessed a low armoured Mercedes 700, followed by a police escort,
driving through the streets from Bygdøy to the palace: Quisling on his way
to begin his day's work. 'Nobody can deny his courage,' a local resident
noted in his diary one morning as the Minister President's car drove past.
Others were of the same opinion. The armoured car notwithstanding,
Quisling showed no signs of fear or despondency but rather a steady
resoluteness, even though the fortunes of the war had turned and everything
was pointing to Allied victory with his own downfall as an inevitable
consequence.[2]

Actually he was leading his movement towards disaster. From the autumn
of 1943 it was clear that only a miracle, perhaps internal collapse in the
Allied ranks or a breakthrough in weapon technology, could save them. He
no longer indulged in optimistic rhetoric. During this period none of his
public statements displayed such *naïveté* as Hitler or Goebbels showed, even
though he was obliged to keep up the appearance of believing in a German
victory.

The chances of such a victory were in fact diminishing daily. In July 1943
Mussolini fell, forced out of office after the Allied landing on Sicily brought
the war into Italy. In August the conditions prevailing in Denmark came to
an end after the government was replaced and Dr Werner Best introduced a
state of emergency to deal with the growing problem of sabotage. In October
Italy capitulated to the Allies, although Germany still held the northern part

---

[1] Quoted in *Mot nytt land*, p. 291.
[2] Smedal, *Patriotisme*, p. 96, entry for 10 April 1945.

of the country, and Mussolini was reinstated as leader of the symbolic republic of Salò on Lake Garda. During 1944 Hitler's federal republics fell one after the other: Hungary in March, Romania in August, Finland and Bulgaria in September, while France, after the Allied landings in June 1944, was slowly being occupied from the west. The Red Army was constantly stepping up pressure, driving the Axis out of the Caucasus and the Ukraine in 1943 and of Crimea and Byelorussia the following spring. In the summer of 1944 Hitler himself narrowly escaped the Wehrmacht generals' attempt on his life in a bomb attack at Rastenburg. Not even individual German triumphs such as the new rocket weapon against Britain in the summer and autumn of 1944 or the December offensive to recapture Belgium the same year could break the heavy pattern of the disastrous setbacks Germany was constantly suffering.

All of this exhausted Quisling, and Maria became deeply concerned about his health: 'He was plagued by worries about the future of the Norwegian people,' she stated. 'What kept me going was the fact that I believed that my turn had come to support *his* people, just as he for so many years had helped *my* people through times of famine.'[3] The truth was that his position allowed him to do little other than express his continuing faith in Germany in his public statements and speeches to the bitter end, although he held no illusions about Germany's prospects. Among his ministers the opinion prevailed that America's entry into the war in 1941 had in fact signalled the end for Hitler, while he himself commented to an associate that in view of America's air capacity, it was only a question of time before Germany would be defeated.[4] He was nevertheless committed to an obligatory optimism, which he exhibited until January 1945.

Apart from the moral obligations, he also considered it vital that the NS should be on the alert because the German presence was now more dominant than ever in Norway. The fear of a joint British and Russian invasion, backed by the exiled Norwegian forces, and supported by the underground military organisation which was obviously being built up, prompted Hitler to strengthen rather than weaken his colossal, expensive guard along the Norwegian coast. Expansion was in full swing in both 1943 and 1944. Islets and skerries were filled with cannons and aircraft, and naval reconnaissance was continual, as was the extensive laying of mines in all the

[3] Maria Quisling to Henrik Bergh 8 September 1945, UBO MS fol. 3920 IX, 3; also to Henrik Bergh 16 August 1945 in *Straffesak* p. 316.
[4] Finn Thrana's account, 1987;* Knudsen, *Jeg var Quislings sekretær*, p. 195.

main waters. In the autumn of 1944 no fewer than 400,000 Wehrmacht soldiers were garrisoned inland. Terboven, moreover, was constantly assuming more and more military authority, and emerged as the central authority in Norway from 1944 onwards.

Thus the final settlement would in any case involve a mobilisation of frightening proportions, which meant that Quisling's government could at least have a mitigating effect. The days of the government were numbered, however, as it had little direct bearing on the settlement, and none at all on any plans for after the war, for it was painfully obvious that there would be a completely new government after the armistice. The pace of his own initiatives was also weakening noticeably: in 1942 the Minister President passed 231 laws, in 1943 166, the following year only 139 – the opposite of what one would expect of a new revolutionary regime. He had no choice but to try to maintain order in the party, and otherwise make *ad hoc* moves whenever the situation afforded him any room for manoeuvre. Order in the ranks was after all no insignificant contribution to a peaceful settlement after the war, and in this he was successful. In a world of cowardly betrayals and renegade leaders, Quisling stood firm in the NS, and the NS's position as Norway's only legal party was unassailable. The intermittent flurries of unrest in the movement did not threaten his position. Moreover the party was steadily attracting new members, albeit in somewhat smaller numbers than before. Nothing on the scale of the Freemason episode of 1942 ever took place again.[5]

To the world Quisling was not only Hitler's most notorious collaborator but also his most faithful. By the autumn of 1944 nearly all the others had fallen away: Clausen, Mussolini, Antonescu, Horthy, Ryti. Only Quisling in Norway and Mussert in Holland were still firmly in place, Mussert basically as a nonentity whose function was simply to give advice to the Reichskommissariat through his political secretariat. Quisling's situation was different. He was leading a government from his offices in the palace, and even if his powers were limited and his position in relation to the German occupation ambiguous, he was still the one who 'temporarily exercises the King's authority as fixed in the Norwegian Constitution'.

---

[5] Statistics of party growth in RA FMK 58.

VOTE OF CONFIDENCE

In the course of 1943 a worrying climate of defeatism was spreading through the NS Party, brought on by the rumours surrounding the last unfortunate visit to Hitler, within the rank and file, in addition to the general feelings of hatred and contempt now being directed against party members. The new harsh rationing measures and all the other burdens the Germans were laying on the civilians hit party members particularly. Party members, and officials in particular, for moral reasons could not take advantage of the flourishing black market to supplement their basic needs, while in the population as a whole the opposite held true: here, participating in black market activities was seen as an expression of the spirit of resistance. Thus belonging to the state party was turning into a liability.[6]

German recognition of Norwegian independence was the only move that could rectify the situation, the district governor of Hamar, Ole Vries Hassel, reported to Quisling: 'We should point out to the Germans that now even Burma is independent.' Party members demanded that the government should not compromise, and if necessary resign from office. Were the attempt to secure a peace treaty to fail, wrote the district governor, it would be natural not only for the government but also for all the NS district governors 'and other party members in prominent positions' to consider their task finished and to resign their offices.[7] Quisling regarded this as tantamount to treason and to be dealt with harshly. He actually considered the death penalty, but later compromised with the house arrest and dismissal of Hassel. The episode was widely discussed inside the party, and Quisling's appeals for unity thereafter carried the threat of severe reprisals.[8]

On Sunday 25 July 1943, while the Minister President was heading a delegation of senior civil servants to North Norway, and was on the way from Hammerfest to Tana, he received the devastating news from Italy that the Fascist Party had decided to strip Mussolini of his command of the armed forces. The Duce had been arrested, and Marshal Badoglio had taken over as head of government. Immediately, a group of ministers went to see Maria Quisling, ostensibly to support her in the face of this depressing news, but also to find out whether she was in touch with her husband. During

---

[6] Guri Hjeltnes, *Hverdagsliv. Norge i krig* V (1968) pp. 147f, 257.
[7] Ole Vries Hassel to Hagelin and Quisling 16 August 1943, private archives.*
[8] Th. Dahl, Report 15 January 1946, RA LD 4088.

their deliberations on what should be done, Maria noted that Prytz was clearly in favour of Quisling breaking off his trip and returning to the capital to head his cabinet in this time of crisis.[9] On his return, Quisling discovered that Hagelin had actually been taking certain initiatives during his absence. He had summoned seven members of the government to a conference at his home, where he managed to get approval for a document on the subject of the ministers being forced to 'step down'. The long-standing dissatisfaction with the occupation forces and resentment over Norway's position was well known. What was new was that even the ministers themselves were now considering resignation.[10]

There was, however, something very amateurish about Hagelin's agitation, which the protagonists themselves soon reported to Quisling. Hagelin was a relative newcomer to politics and readily interpreted all conflicts as expressions of personal ill-will, if not malice. Thus his complaints about Terboven and his associates were all based on the alleged unreasonable and difficult personalities of the individuals concerned, not taking into account the reality of the situation in which these Germans found themselves.

To Quisling it was the objective realities which mattered – geography, geopolitics, power conditions. Geographically, Norway was caught between the great powers, and there was a danger of both an Allied invasion from the west and a Russian invasion from the north, either of which could have catastrophic consequences. In June 1943 there was another Soviet air attack on Vardø and North Varanger, followed by an attempted invasion on the Varanger peninsula, and renewed air attacks later in the autumn. Trondheim was attacked from the air in July, and on 24 July the British and American strike forces bombed the Herøya factories near Porsgrunn, leaving forty-seven dead and sixty-nine injured.[11] The situation became so grave that for Quisling the question of Norway's legal position *vis-à-vis* Germany and the question of the state of war or peace paled into insignificance in the face of the reality that the country was *de facto* at war – at war with the Allies. In such a situation it was necessary to stand closely by Germany and at the same time try to improve Norway's position as far as possible. In this case, to get caught up in trivialities such as personal attacks on the Reichs-

[9] Maria Quisling to Henrik Bergh, summer 1945 (undated), UBO MS fol. 3920 IX, 4.

[10] Memorandum of 2 August 1943 in RA LD 846 Hagelin; see also Sørensen, *Hitler eller Quisling*, pp. 209ff.

[11] Report to the government based on reports from the country's district governors for the year 1943, dated 31 January 1944, RA FMK 17.

kommissar's subordinates was to travel down a hopeless dead end at a time when the country was facing a truly threatening situation.[12]

Furthermore, there was nothing to be gained from an opposition led by Hagelin. Hagelin was *persona non grata* at the Reichskommissariat, and with good reason. His latest memorandum had contained inexact, not to say misleading, information. Moreover, allegations of corruption which had been dogging Hagelin from the very beginning, by the spring of 1943 had intensified to such a degree that both he and his closest associates were removed from key party positions. A special commission headed by the Minister of Justice worked from October 1943 to March 1944 to investigate the various allegations. The result – Hagelin's unexpected acquittal – did not lay the case to rest; on the contrary, the rumours continued to circulate, and they were particularly damaging because they concerned the man in the government who was the most uncompromising in his opposition to the Germans. This was to become obvious during the next government crisis, the Eilifsen case and the turmoil within the police force.[13]

THE AUGUST CRISIS

The Norwegian police force was rapidly expanding under the new order, and by the summer of 1943 had almost trebled in size since April 1940. Although several of the country's policemen had joined the party in the autumn of 1940, an almost equal number chose to leave it in 1942; however, as new policemen were recruited, mainly from party ranks, the number of those loyal to the party remained more or less constant. Nevertheless, the desertion of the party members was sorely felt. In addition, an increasing incidence of direct professional disloyalty was noticeable within the force. Wilhelm Rediess and the German security police were particularly disturbed by this tendency and its perceived repercussions for the effective running of the force as a whole.

In August 1943 the German police were informed of a particularly ugly case of disobedience within the force. The assistant Police Chief in Oslo,

---

[12] Department head Georg Hasle, 'Statsrettslige og andre konsekvenser av loven av 14 August 1943', undated memorandum in RA NSRG Sentralavd. 1. For the official NS position on the question of war, see Judge Andreas Mohr in *Aftenposten* 20 and 21 November 1943.

[13] Sources for the Hagelin affair are: *NSM* 1943/4 and 5; see also press announcement in *FF*; Quisling to Norvik 17 August 1943, RA FMK 19; various documents in RA FMK 50; and Quisling to Dysthe 18 August 1943 (private archives*); see also Sørensen, *Hitler eller Quisling*, pp. 215ff and H. F. Dahl, 'Ledelse i en førerstat', *NNT* 1992/2.

Gunnar Eilifsen, a former NS member, refused to arrest two young girls who had been called up for compulsory Labour Service (AT) for some weeks that summer. Eilifsen's insubordination was considered flagrant, and things were not helped by the fact that his action seemed to have been motivated by an order from the clandestine resistance movement.[14]

On Friday 13 August Terboven summoned Quisling, Riisnæs and Lie to his office. The German Chief of Police, Rediess, was also present. Terboven issued strict instructions that Eilifsen was to be executed immediately, arguing that in the present situation with the threatening British and Soviet invasion attempts, this kind of action from the police could not be tolerated. Quisling and his ministers were given the choice of whether the death sentence should be passed and carried out under German or Norwegian law. Jonas Lie suggested the latter. Quisling agreed.

The decision caused a bitter controversy in the party. Most of the party lawyers and several of the moderates considered the case tragically mishandled: Quisling should let the Germans implement their own draconian measures. But he calculated that if Norway and Germany were to maintain a union of forces, unnecessary displays of German superiority had to be avoided, and to punish a Norwegian police officer was clearly a government task. However, there was no authority for such a death sentence. Only in cases of life imprisonment could punishment be escalated to execution, according to the latest revision of the penal code. The provision had never been implemented, and in any case did not apply here. When Riisnæs mentioned this to Terboven, he replied: 'So make a provision for it!' Quisling nodded and Riisnæs promised he would do so.

But the Justice Minister encountered problems in his own department. Several secretaries refused to participate in the drafting of the law, as did one Supreme Court judge who was called in. Eventually Riisnæs was assisted by a department head who was also a party member. Together they drafted the law of 14 August 1943 'Concerning Actions to Maintain Calm and Order in Time of War'.[15]

This *lex Eilifsen* (which, along with the law on youth service of 1942, soon earned notoriety as Quisling's most controversial act) was conceived as an emergency measure, to be passed in order to accommodate the categorical demands of the Reichskommissar. However, Riisnæs found that a death

---

[14] This account is based on Ringdal, *Mellom barken og veden*, pp. 289ff; Ringdal, *Gal mann*, pp. 110ff; Rødder, '*Min ære*', pp. 157ff; see also J. B. Hjort, *Justismord* (1952) pp. 227–35.

[15] Georg Hasle, 'Statsrettslige og andre konsekvenser av loven av 14 August 1943', undated memorandum in RA NSRG Sentralavd. 1.

sentence could only be passed if Eilifsen's insubordination were considered an act of agitation under military law. Consequently the police would have to be defined as part of the country's armed forces. However, following capitulation to Germany in 1940, Norway did not technically have its own armed forces as the volunteers who subsequently joined up belonged to the Waffen-SS. Riisnæs's solution depended on whether he could define the police, the Hird, the SS Norway and the Fører Guard as formations belonging to the country's armed forces under military law. If he could, insubordinate policemen could be dealt with effectively, but just how effectively was not evident, for the death penalty was only applicable during 'times of war'. But was Norway at war, and if so, with whom?

Riisnæs and his aide pored over this legal problem on 14 August while Jonas Lie paced up and down the corridors of the Ministry impatiently and Quisling waited at the palace, trying to resolve the 'wartime' question. The most pressing and delicate juridical problem of occupied Norway was the country's status under international law after the capitulation of 1940: fighting had ceased but just as no official peace between Norway and Germany existed, there was no official war either. The two lawmakers found that circumstances had come to the aid of the government. The undeniable acts of warfare committed by Russian, British and American forces against Norway that summer doubtless constituted a 'time of war' for the country, even if the term 'time of war' was not defined in international law. Irrespective of the legal complications in the situation regarding Germany, a *de facto* state of war with the Allies could be said to have been established between 21 and 24 July with the attacks on Varanger and Herøya: thus the emergency provision in its preamble stated that a 'state of war exists in Norway because of the Soviet and American acts of aggression ... In this state of war the police have been constituted as part of the armed forces.'

Even this did not eliminate all the difficulties, however. After Quisling had signed the law, it proved very difficult to find a judge willing pass the death sentence on Eilifsen. Pressure was exerted, threats were made to the special court that was set up, until two judges from the senior police corps gave in and outvoted the presiding judge, thus passing the death sentence. The whole case was a parody of justice, giving Eilifsen's defence an easy time of ripping the prosecution's case to pieces, as a retroactive law like this one was in flagrant contravention of the Constitution and indeed an outrage to any rudimentary sense of justice.

To complete the mockery, the court had been led to believe that Quisling would pardon Eilifsen. But this he could not do. When Riisnæs and Lie arrived at Gimle with the judgement on 15 August, all that remained was for Quisling to refuse clemency. Early the following morning Eilifsen was executed by a state police firing squad.

The execution prompted a large-scale clean-up operation by the Germans, who launched the Aktion Polarkreis to rid the police force of insubordinate elements. The same morning as the macabre execution took place in Oslo, the German police arrested nearly 500 policemen nation-wide, following a list drawn up by the Norwegian chief of the state police, General Karl Marthinsen.[16] Those arrested were transported to Grini. Nearly half of them were released during the autumn, while the remaining 271 were sent to camps in Germany at the end of the year – some even to secret *Nacht und Nebel* camps. At the same time as the police arrests were taking place, approximately 1,100 army officers were placed in Wehrmacht custody, on the grounds that several Norwegian officers who, following the campaign of 1940 had been pardoned by Hitler after having taken a solemn oath of loyalty, in the meantime had broken their pledge not to take up arms against Germany by participating in underground military activities.[17]

The Eilifsen case and the arrests of 16 August marked a new watershed in the history of the occupation. It was the first death sentence carried out under the Quisling regime, and the most flagrant violation of the Constitution since the April coup. The events took on the same dimensions in public opinion as the execution of Hansteen in September 1941. German reports lamented the enormous unrest spreading through the country, signalling the end of the period of calm and order in industry and production plants which the occupation forces had maintained so effectively throughout the spring and summer of 1943.[18]

For the police, this clean-up operation within the force put an end to recruitment, as nobody other than loyal party members would even contemplate joining it. More policemen from this time on were involved in underground activities. Moreover, it soon turned out that the sacrifice Quisling, Lie and Riisnæs had made by choosing to condemn Eilifsen under

---

[16] Rødder, '*Min ære*', p. 165; see also Ringdal, *Mellom barken og veden*, who assumes that Sipo worked from a list of 120 'politically unreliable' which was drawn up in the Police Department in spring 1943.

[17] Von Falkenhorst's announcement in the press 17 August 1943; also I. Kraglund and A. Moland, *Motstandskamp* (1987) pp. 149ff.

[18] Oberregierungsrat Korff to Ministerialrat Dr Breyhan at the Reichsfinanzministerium 28 August 1943, BA R 2. A watershed: see Ferdinand Schjelderup, *Over bakkekammen 1943–1944* (1949) ch. 13 'August 1943'.

Norwegian law or, rather, pseudo-law, had been for nothing. What was the point in exercising one's own disciplinary authority in one individual case if the Germans subsequently went ahead and rounded up one-tenth of the entire police force? The argument that they were protecting the sovereignty of Norwegian authorities certainly did not convince anyone.

The controversy over the Eilifsen law split the government into a civilian and a military wing.[19] The 'civilians', headed by Hagelin, were fiercely opposed to Riisnæs and Lie on the other side, but their influence was modified as there was not much point in insisting on constitutional law when Germany was said to be an 'allied state' and when the consideration that the allied states should win the war was paramount. During 1944, one after another of the dissenting 'civilian' ministers resigned from the government: one in February, two in June and eventually Hagelin himself in November 1944.

Doubtless all of them could have been dismissed after the events of August 1943, but Quisling, who dreaded confrontation, was slow to act in such delicate personal situations. Moreover, there was good reason for keeping an appearance of unity within his government at this time. Mussolini's downfall in Italy was keenly felt in the Norwegian movement, as it was in all National Socialist organisations. 'It surely came as a shock,' Quisling confessed to his followers, 'the oldest representative of the European new order has collapsed like a house of cards ... it might seem as though the whole order has run aground.'[20]

Curiously, Prytz's position in the government strengthened with the waning of Hagelin's. Politically Prytz was moving closer and closer to Quisling, conducting weekly private conferences on the economy with him at the palace, where he pursued his efforts to counter the damages caused by the growing German economic demands.[21] Unlike any minister apart from Fuglesang, Prytz enjoyed unrestricted access to Quisling. His star was also in the ascendant in the party in general, for a somewhat peculiar reason: his growing circle of prominent sons-in-law. One of his daughters married the head of Quisling's Chancellery who was also deputy General Secretary during the war. Another married one of the party's most promising young

[19] Sørensen, *Hitler eller Quisling*, pp. 225ff. See also B. B. Borge, 'NS og makten', pp. 99ff.

[20] Quisling in the Klingenberg cinema 25 September 1943, *FF* 27 September 1943.

[21] *Norges Bank*, pp. 42ff, 59ff, 77, 82ff, 103f; S. Hartmann and J. Vogt, *Aktstykker om de tyske finanspolitikk* (1958) pp. 126ff. A frank report from Hans C. Korff of the Reichskommissariat to the Reichsfinanzministerium on 5 May 1943 concludes that Quisling was behind Prytz's unbending rejection of German demands, BA R2/352.

academics, who then became district *fører* in Bergen and Hordaland, and a third a high-ranking SS officer in Germany. 'Prytz and his sons-in-law' were considered, at least by his enemies, to be a political circle of growing influence.[22]

The August revolt of the 'civilian' ministers of 1943 was followed by an unexpected concession from Hitler. At the party gathering celebrating the first three years of power on 25 September, both Quisling and Terboven rose to speak – Quisling mainly on the progress of the war, and on the subject of how the strain from Mussolini's fall and his opponents' war of nerves were taking their toll on the party, declaring that the 'tragic fate of Italy is a warning to us all'. The Reichskommissar had a more positive message to impart, for once. He began with a vicious attack on the party moderates, but kept a personal message from Hitler to the end. This message was so appeasing and accommodating that it overshadowed the hatred felt towards its bearer. What he announced was Germany's commitment to the very same European policy as Quisling had been championing for years, and which Hitler had only discussed in the most conditional and theoretical of terms at Klessheim: 'It is the Führer's firm intention to allow a free and independent, national and socialist Norway to come into being once the war has been brought to a victorious conclusion' the message read. After the war, 'Norway will be free to delegate only those functions to the general European community that will be deemed absolutely necessary to secure the safety of Europe, as only such a community can take on the guarding of European security at large'.[23]

Perhaps Hitler was less of a Napoleonic conqueror and more of a European architect after all? The announcement was in fact unexpectedly generous, bearing no traces of the Reichskommissar's customary ambiguous 'Germanic' expressions.

No satisfactory explanation has ever been given for this extraordinary move of Hitler's. But the negative reaction within the NS following the Klessheim visit was certainly one factor behind it, as was the opposition led by Hagelin within the government. At any rate, Quisling was able to relish this promise of future freedom which was more far-reaching than any assurances ever given to his counterparts. A Norwegian in Berlin even heard

---

[22] Hagelin's account 15 October 1945, RA LD 846 Hagelin. On the Hagelin–Prytz conflict, see also Prytz to the members of the government 8 April 1943, IfZ MA 110.

[23] Reprinted in *Straffesak* pp. 552ff. The speech was not reported in the press. Quisling's speech was quoted in *FF* 27 September 1943.

a high-ranking official stating that Norway would soon come under the Foreign Ministry, which, if true, was a promising sign.[24]

Hitler's pledge was given prominence in NS propaganda for the duration of the war. It provided the movement with a post-war programme, even though this programme soon disappeared from sight. Pressure resulting from the Allied landing in Italy and the Red Army victories on the southeast front, coupled with the prospect of an invasion from the west (possibly on the Norwegian coast), intensified, thus reducing the practical worth of the proclamation week by week. At the same time Terboven was demonstrating ever more energetically that he was responsible for public order in Norway. In October 1943 he put five prison hostages to death for an act of sabotage in Mjøndal, and in November he ordered the arrests of students and lecturers at the university.

The latter action was particularly dramatic, bringing German activity in Norway to international attention once more. The Swedish reaction in particular was very strong. Terboven had anticipated this, but had explained to his advisers that he had been waiting for an opportunity to eliminate this hive of opposition. An Allied invasion was expected in the spring, and it was thus better to deal with this problem in good time rather than risk allowing the university to develop into an effective support for the Allies. During the night of 28 November the opportunity presented itself. A sabotage group of Communists set fire to the University Aula. The fire was contained and damage was limited, but it was still an invitation for the German police to strike.

The Reichskommissar's move against the university came as no surprise to Quisling. Ever since 1942 his Education Minister, Skancke, had been clashing with the deans on the subject of admitting a quota of NS students to the Faculty of Medicine without the requisite matriculation grades. The conflict was never properly resolved, much to Quisling's irritation. On several occasions he had intervened, with Terboven firmly behind him. However, threats of arrest and the prospect of a summary settlement did not avail, and the deans continually went through all manner of formalities in order to buy time. Eventually, in mid-October 1943 the Reichskommissar visited Quisling at the palace and told him that this situation was intolerable.

---

[24] 'Willensäusserung des Führers über Norwegens Stellung in Europa', printed in *ADAP* E VI no. 353 p. 595. For the effect it had within the NS, see Report of the RSHA Amt III (undated) Germanische Leitstelle Norwegen, Berger to Himmler 5 November 1943, BA NS 19/3889. A Norwegian in Berlin: Støren to Sundberg in Berlin (?) October 1943, IfZ MA 110.

Quisling agreed. He summoned the NS student leaders and Police Chief Marthinsen to announce that 'in order to gain respect' they would have to go ahead with some arrests. The 'respect' Quisling spoke of referred mainly to the Germans, for if the Norwegian authorities did not act immediately, the Reichskommissar surely would. Marthinsen made the necessary preparations and between 15 and 17 November ten university dons and sixty-four students were arrested by the state police and taken to Bredtvedt.

The arrests provoked fierce protests in the academic community, forcing the government into countless conferences on the subject. The NS Rector campaigned tirelessly for the release of the prisoners, as did several of the ministers. A release date was negotiated and renegotiated, and on 18 November Quisling gave the Rector the impression that he was prepared to release the prisoners and grant them an amnesty, on the understanding that, were they to cause any further trouble, they would risk the German authorities 'closing the university and carrying out widespread arrests'.

The Aula fire ten days later was a golden opportunity for the Germans to move in and make arrests. After consultation with Terboven on 29 November, the university was closed the following morning and all male students and lecturers were rounded up in the Aula. German police cars and motorbikes circulated through the streets of Oslo the whole day and well into the night hunting down any university people who had escaped them.

That afternoon Terboven and Rediess entered the Aula, where the students had been assembled. Terboven sat down while Rediess mounted the rostrum and delivered a ferocious speech enumerating the complaints against the students: ever since 1940 they had opposed the Germans and the NS. Illegal organisations flourished and their numerous acts of sabotage had culminated in the Aula fire. The Reichskommissar had therefore decided to transport all male students present to a camp in Germany – not a concentration camp, but a special camp, after an appeal from the Minister President. Female students would be permitted to go home. Loyal students would be allowed to continue their studies in Trondheim and Bergen. The students were immediately herded on to buses waiting outside the building. There was a total of 1,100 arrests, which constituted approximately one-quarter of all registered students; 650 of these were sent to Germany in two groups.[25]

---

[25] *FF* 1 December 1943; see also M. Sars and K. E. Tranøy, *Tysklandsstudentene* (1946). A high-ranking officer of the German military High Command, Theodor Steltzer, tried to warn the resistance of the impending arrests, but the warning did not reach the students in time: see T. Steltzer, *Sechzig Jahre Zeitgenosse* (1966) p. 145. See also Hartmann, *Nytt lys*.

The new deportations threatened to become another disaster for Quisling's regime. Not only Quisling but every member of the government who had contact with the German authorities did their utmost to intervene. NS students lined up beside their colleagues. Fuglesang, who fortunately was in Berlin at the time, took the matter up with the Reichssicherheitshauptamt, with Himmler and Berger. His efforts were not entirely wasted: the majority of the students were freed, and the German police made no further attempts to arrest the remaining ones. Hitler, according to Goebbels's diary, was furious. The comprehensive arrests were a serious error: rounding up the few students directly responsible for the fire would have sufficed. Himmler too was incensed, and considered Terboven's action to have thwarted his own chances of recruiting the 40,000–60,000 men who would otherwise have volunteered for the Waffen-SS. The worst thing was that Berlin could do nothing to repair the damage: because of the unusually strong letters of protest from Sweden it was politically impossible to risk losing face by recalling the arrest orders and reversing the action.[26]

For Quisling, the turbulence behind the scenes could not soften this overt humiliation. First the Jews, then the officers, and now the students. His government had genuine cause for concern: the absence of academics with the right qualifications represented a chronic problem for a regime which was already weakened by the fact that its own youth were away, fighting on the eastern front – where they were facing death in their hundreds.

In December 1943 the atmosphere was very grim indeed, with the Fører under enormous pressure. The unfortunate explosion in Fillipstad in Oslo on 19 December, in which fifty civilians and an unknown number of Germans lost their lives, sent a new shock through the government. It was not only a disaster in human terms: the uncertainty over who was responsible added the episode to the growing list of setbacks for the regime. Once again, he refrained from making his new year radio address.

LIFE AT THE PALACE

The winter of 1944 was particularly harsh in northern and central Europe, affecting both living conditions and social life, and even war itself, through frozen machinery and idle engines. The daily hunt for fuel, coupled with

---

[26] Fuglesang in Berlin: related to Anders Buraas 1972, NRK fa. Terboven's action caused great concern in the SS in Berlin; see Interrogation Report of the Obersturmbannführer Professor Dr Richard Frankenberger 1 June 1946, BA Z 42 VII/1836. Hitler was furious: Goebbels Diary, entries for 5 and 6 December 1943.

desperate food shortages were the dominant concerns of the civilian population. Oslo suffered the harshest winter in generations.

The palace did not escape the cold weather, although the heating system had been modernised. The Minister President had had a modern fireplace installed in his study (formerly the Queen's private salon), which, in addition to the radiators, made the cold tolerable. The refurbishment of this room was the only real change Quisling made to the royal decor. Bookshelves, lighting and comfortable leather furniture were brought in, making the room resemble the offices of a shipping company more than a room in a neo-classical stucco palace.[27]

The palace had not been Quisling's first choice of headquarters in 1942. King Haakon's growing popularity made it a less than ideal option, but there was a desperate lack of suitable premises. The Storting had been taken over by the Reichskommissar. Neither the parliament nor the government offices had sufficient space; even the Ministry of the Interior was struggling to find office space. As the palace was available, and had been stripped of hundreds of antiques, paintings and carpets by the Germans, Quisling considered it sensible to install himself there to prevent a total German take-over.[28]

This meant that there was a continuity in the state budget's grant for the maintenance and running of the palace. Quisling, like his predecessor, was given 20,000 kroner a month to live on, tax free, with all expenses covered, rising to 50,000 kroner in 1943–4.[29]

When he was assuming the power of Minister President, Quisling set up a new state office, the Chancellery, his permanent staff at the palace. The Chancellery took over some of the functions of the Fører's secretariat but also assumed many new governmental duties. It was staffed by a Chancellery head with the rank of permanent secretary, with four officers under him, each with his own department head. These department heads were, just like the additional thirty secretaries and assistants, party members of proven calibre, several of whom had been recruited from NS student groups in the 1930s, and the majority recommended on objective criteria of competence rather than excessive political bias. The same went for the government

---

[27] Hannes Rein (= Hans-Reinhard) Koch in *Der Weg*, Buenos Aires 1950/7. Also documents in RA FMK 47; see also *Straffesak* p. 176.

[28] Account given by the estate manager of the objects surrendered to the German authorities from the palace, Oslo 21 November 1940–15 September 1942, RA FMK 5.

[29] Prytz to FMK, RA FMK 20; Finance Ministry to Fuglesang 13 March 1942, RA Statsrådssekretariat NS-Adm. 1.

secretariat, which under the leadership of the secretary took care of all the Minister President's government business, together with a special Foreign Directorate which was also run from the palace. All in all, the members of these different entities numbered forty, plus the chauffeurs, assistants and guards, which made a total staff of sixty.

'Quisling is no martial dictator,' remarked a high-level civil servant at the Reichskommissariat, for the Minister President normally listened to his staff and made his decisions according to proper procedures.[30] In this sense, the Fører ruled in a way completely unlike the explosively intuitive Adolf Hitler, and his government was a dignified and civilised assembly in comparison with the boorish revolutionaries surrounding the Führer.

Quisling would get up at 6.30 every morning and put in a good few hours' work at home at Gimle before arriving at the palace between 9.30 and 10 o'clock, where he started the day by dealing with his correspondence. He always opened his own letters. All mail addressed to the Chancellery went to him directly. Quisling read each letter carefully and often wrote detailed instructions for action to be taken. No detail was too insignificant for him not to make a decision on, which his subordinates would carry out. In fact he was meticulous to a fault, involving himself directly in every matter, making statements and arranging appointments. His Chancellery functioned as an independent administration under active political leadership, being kept up to date with the situation in the party via weekly reports from district leaders, and from the more comprehensive monthly reports from the district governors, which were edited and collated by the Ministry of the Interior. The party's own information service furnished the Fører with several hundred reports. More important than these documents were, however, Quisling's daily meetings with Fuglesang. The Party Minister was well briefed on the atmosphere in the organisation. As a conscientious politician, he laid great emphasis on keeping an overview of the activities of the various groups via the extensive contact and information networks, which he had built up. In addition, the General Secretary held secret meetings with all the state and national leaders, and duly briefed Quisling on their contents.[31]

As Minister President Quisling received communications from a large number of individuals. People wrote to him from all over the country,

[30] Koch, *Der Weg* 1950/7.
[31] Scattered reports survive in RA FMK 15 et al. On the NS Information Service, see Sørensen, *Hitler eller Quisling*, pp. 282f, 413.

trying to secure his help and personal favours. Quisling was generally accommodating in such cases, noting down 'if we can do anything to help', or 'the Ministry of Finance will be asked to help' on an astonishing number of the appeals he received. On the other hand, appeals from party members asking for special consideration on the grounds of membership were usually rejected.

The surviving records suggest that at least 10 per cent of requests concerned appeals for release from German prisons and camps. Hundreds of people wrote each year to the Minister President, including his political opponents, asking him to intervene and secure the release of their relatives. The majority of such requests concerned German police custody, as the few detainees the Norwegian police authorities had found it necessary to send to Bredtvedt or Berg were generally released after a short sentence. Appeals for release from German prisons and camps were strictly speaking none of the Chancellery's business. Quisling and his office colleagues nevertheless took it upon themselves to try to secure the release of Norwegian citizens from Terboven's and Rediess's hands as if the victims were after all Quisling's responsibility. At the end of the occupation a special office within the Chancellery was set up for this purpose, but it enjoyed limited success. In the majority of cases the Germans refused to release the prisoners.[32]

In addition to this, Quisling devoted himself to large-scale policies. He wrote speeches, memoranda, plans for European and world peace based on press cuttings, telegrams and other information in an attempt to keep up to date with world events. He relied heavily on the Swedish press: *Dagens Nyheter, Svenska Dagbladet, Social Demokraten* and *Stockholms Tidningen*, as censorship and postal restrictions prevented him from consulting the international papers he used to buy before the war: *The Times, Istvestija, Die Presse* and *Le Parisien*. He also kept up with more tendentious publications such as the outwardly anti-Nazi papers *Trots Alt* and *Göteborgs Handels och Sjöfartstidning*. The Chancellery had obtained permission from the Reichskommissariat press office to subscribe to some eight or nine Swedish papers.

London was also a source of information. Transcripts of all BBC Norwegian broadcasts were placed on Quisling's desk every morning, keeping him up to date with the activities of the Nygaardsvold government. The government in exile seemed particularly anxious to stress the increas-

---

[32] Documents in RA FMK 7, 8, 9, 14, 16, 19, from which it appears that these questions, at least in 1945, were dealt with by a separate office. Testimony of Herberth Noot 23 June 1948, RA LD 933 Vest-Oppland police station, case of F. Thrana.

ingly tough measures against the NS it was considering introducing in the event of liberation. He noted this, but did not accord much importance to it: he took it as the sign of a guilty conscience that London was constantly threatening 'the sadistic revenge which they will take on us in the NS when the Allied troops, according to their own pronouncements, in the very near future, will have brought them back to the country which they so shamelessly betrayed, left and betrayed anew'. Later in the war he was forced to follow Nygaardsvold's foreign policy more closely. Spring and summer 1944 was an active period of international conferences, declarations and proclamations concerning the peace settlement the Allies wanted to implement once they had forced Germany into unconditional surrender. Quisling followed both the Dumbarton Oaks and the Bretton Woods conferences closely.[33]

The policy of the government in exile both surprised and shocked him. On 25 April 1944 it officially invited the Soviet Union to conduct military talks, so that the Red Army could participate in the capture of German forces on Norwegian soil. On 9 May Reuters announced that the Soviet Union had decided to contribute to the liberation of Norway. On 16 May the Soviet–Norwegian 'liberation agreement' was signed at the same time as the Nygaardsvold government went into identical discussions with the US and Britain. In Quisling's view the government in exile in London was playing a dangerous game with Norwegian interests, but his interpretation fell wide of the mark. Despite the government's revolutionary past, Nygaardsvold's ministers did not made their overture to Russia out of any secret wish to promote class struggle, as Quisling thought. Their concern was rather to commit even the western Allies to participating in the forthcoming liberation of Norway, something which they actually succeeded in doing. Quisling was in every sense out of touch. In a speech of 15 May he declared that this 'alert from London is the most serious alarm signal that the Norwegian people have heard so far'. He also proclaimed that anyone who worked against the NS national struggle 'or otherwise acted disloyally' would be held responsible for acts of enmity against the people and the state.[34]

---

[33] Quisling on Bretton Woods, speech at Stiklestad 29 July 1944 in *FF* 31 July 1944. 'Sadistic Revenge': *FF* 16 May 1944. See also Dahl, *Dette er London*, p. 241.

[34] Distributed by leaflets and the larger newspapers 16 May 1944, UBO Krigstrykksamlingen. *FF* 16 May 1944. For the negotiations of the Norwegian government in London, see Riste, *London-Regjeringa* II, pp. 166ff; see also Riste, *Utefront*. Complete press coverage, with commentaries from Swedish, German, Finnish and Danish newspapers in *NSPM* 1944/6.

The BBC's Norwegian service no longer restricted itself to propaganda and warnings of the reprisals which would follow the Allied liberation. From mid-March 1944 directives were broadcast directly to the people over the air waves, the so-called 'paroles' addressed to all Norwegians. What was new about these orders was that they were issued in the name of a body which called itself the leadership of the Home Front. Quisling warned against this tendency to obstruct the work of the country's authority once more in his proclamation of 15 May: 'The emigrant government in London does not represent the Norwegian people and has no legal or moral rights,' he reiterated.[35]

The body which did carry these responsibilities, at least according to its own understanding – Quisling's own government – underwent a curious change in its *modus operandi* during its last year in office. From late 1943 nobody any longer referred to the meetings which took place every Thursday at the palace as 'government meetings'. It was no longer a requirement that all members of the government be present when matters of the state were dealt with. Instead, every Thursday morning the ministers were to make themselves available, each in his own department, for a possible summons. Only ministers who had matters to put before the Minister President would be called to the palace. The ministers, or at any rate the dissenters among them, were sceptical about this, as it meant that Quisling could not be forced to listen to any counter-arguments he knew they would present. The government thus ceased to function as a collective body in any real sense, and Quisling no longer had anything resembling a cabinet to advise him. From this point on it was the opinion of individual ministers which counted, for what that was worth. That such a change could take place without any formalities was due to the nature of the authoritarian regime's Constitution, which did not define the government as a collegiate body but simply as an assembly of department heads, who could just as well be summoned one by one. In the early days of the regime, much emphasis had been put on the importance of continuity with previous forms of govern-ment. Government decisions were published in the press every Saturday under the heading 'Officially from the Cabinet'. Now it read 'Officially from the Ministerial Meeting', with matters often concerning only one depart-ment. These meetings – mere formalities – had replaced the government's most important political task.[36]

---

[35] NRK ho 3793/3.
[36] Irgens's statement of 11 October 1945 in Irgens-saken (1948) pp. 90f; account of T. Dahl 15 January 1946, RA LD 4088 Dahl. Also RA Statsrådssekretariat, NS-administrasjonen 1.

Quisling was thus an elevated legislator working alone in his palace during the last year of the occupation. When he passed a law in the presence of one of his ministers, the seal of the kingdom would be added. The seal itself also underwent a change in the last year of the regime. The movement's expert on heraldry, by that time a justice of the peace in Oslo W. F. K. Christie, had discovered that the Norwegian lion had been corrupted over the centuries and that the mould made in 1905 was inaccurate in heraldic terms; this was now rectified. The lion's front paw and the axe were raised, while the tail was made to point down instead of up. But this new seal was little used, as there were increasingly longer intervals between law reforms. This legislative restraint was particularly noticeable in cultural matters. In comparison with all the reforms and initiatives which Lunde had been responsible for, his successor Fuglesang maintained a very low profile. Propaganda matters alone seemed to encourage some legal reforms. It was as though the events of autumn 1942 had sapped the reforming zeal of all momentum. There was an attempt to resuscitate the Cultural Chamber (Kulturting), but the only two meetings held, in Oslo 1943 and in Trondheim 1944, produced little of lasting value.[37] And the law to privatise state broadcasting was never put into force. There was a little more progress in the area of industry. The Post Office Savings Bank was set up in December 1944, on the initiative of the new Traffic Department. Then a prolix law on the Association of Norwegian Industries was passed.

In one area, however, Quisling's later regime did prove remarkably active. From the spring of 1944 to spring 1945, there was a wave of social reforms: health insurance, which had been introduced in 1930, was substantially extended, as were old age pensions from 1936. From January 1945 child allowance was introduced. Labour legislation abounded. It was as if the strains of war triggered off a thrust for radical reforms, sometimes quite akin to those contemplated by Beveridge in Britain.[38]

One aspect of the regime's later social policy concerned initiatives against vagrancy. Like many rural children, Quisling had grown used to gypsies and vagabonds on the country roads in his childhood, seeing them as an alien or even disruptive element in society. The case was discussed in the government in the summer of 1943, and it was unanimously decided to 'take up the question of the gypsies on all levels ... including the aspect of racial purity',

[37] Reports in *FF* 23–25 September 1943, 25–30 July 1944.
[38] Sørensen, *Solkors.*

as the Minister President himself had instructed.[39] Various measures were
prepared by the Police Department, whereupon it was decided on the
establishment of special labour camps for all 'vagabonds with gypsy blood'
who could be defined as habitual criminals, in addition to racial investigations and compulsory sterilisation of 'gypsies with criminal genetic disposi-
tions'. Sterilisations were to be conducted in accordance with the law on
compulsory sterilisation of 1934 which had been sharpened in 1942 and to
which an amendment was now prepared to widen the scope of the cases
under consideration. 'The interests of society must override those of
individuals and there is no reason in these cases to uphold a false
humanism,' wrote the Director of Public Health. The initiative came to
nothing as the amendment had not been carried through by 1945. Sterilisations were thus kept on a modest scale.[40]

Unemployment was a another special concern of the regime. The Social
Ministry, led by Johan Lippestad, had been prepared for the eventuality of
mass unemployment ever since 1940. But threats of unemployment passed,
mainly because of the Wehrmacht's comprehensive building works. In the
following years German military installations took on considerable numbers
of forest and agricultural workers. During the winter of 1944 the demand for
workers was greater than ever. German coastal fortifications were to be
extended on direct orders from Hitler, who was anticipating an invasion
from the west. But the Reichskommissariat could not foresee any possibility
of meeting the labour demands and the Ministry was unable to help. The
national work effort, which was supposed to register all available workers for
this purpose, had barely got off the ground. In the discussions which took
place between Quisling and Terboven concerning this problem an unexpected solution was found: that of conscription, based on the registers of
current age groups which had been built up since the autumn of 1940 in
Axel Stang's department for the use of the Labour Service (AT). According
to a statement from a Reichskommissariat representative, Quisling himself
came up with the proposal. This was a misunderstanding. What the Minister
President had in mind was simply to use the AT registers as lists of possible

---

[39] Ted Hanisch, *Om sigøynerspørsmålet* (1976); also Anders Gogstad, *Helse og hakekors* (1991)
ch. 10; Lie to Quisling 23 December 1944 RA FMK 24.
[40] Ministry of the Interior circular no. 70–1943; Getz, *aide-mémoire* of 12 January 1945, RA
FMK 21. A total of 580 persons were sterilised in the years 1943–5. How many of these
were of gypsy (or rather Norwegian *tater*) origin is not known. Information provided by
Per Haave, Historical Institute, University of Oslo, 1998.

employees. In fact he had resisted any idea of compulsory conscription, both in 1942 and again in 1943. It was the Germans who took the ill-fated step into forced labour. Terboven was initially sceptical because Germany had had bad experiences of forced labour in other countries, particularly in France. But the Wehrmacht was adamant and he yielded to their wishes.[41]

Meanwhile, the resistance movement was issuing orders which extended its struggle against the AT into a wider opposition to the work effort in general, and to the threat of forced labour. Not only did resistance leaders require all young Norwegians to refrain from registering, but all undertakings in accordance with the law on the national work effort were discredited on the grounds that forced labour might be extended to full war service for Germany. Rumours spread through both the London radio and the illegal press that the work effort was a covert mobilisation. When all men between the ages of twenty-one and twenty-three were required to register, in accordance with the Terboven–Quisling labour agreement, many young men promptly disappeared into the forests. This act of civil disobedience spread into a general boycott of all forms of registration for labour. In fact the collapse of the nascent national work effort was on its way to becoming a new and dangerous problem for the new state. 'The action against the work effort must be considered 100 per cent successful on the part of the resistance,' reported a district party leader at the end of May 1944.[42]

The disturbances in the labour force, endemic during spring and summer 1944, soon calmed down, however. By autumn most people were back at work. Altogether some 200,000 Norwegians took up work for the Germans, voluntarily this time, as the 'labour refugees' of the summer were widely pardoned and no strong measures applied. It might be thought that a soft line was out of tune with the Minister President's will, in the light of his frequent public threats and draconian utterances. In fact the sequence of events was quite typical. After rumbling and thundering in public, he quite often committed himself to reasonable solutions in private.

PERSONALITY

All the crises in the party and the government after the summer of 1943 naturally took their toll on the Minister President. Judging by the photo-

---

[41] Fritz Johlitz, Report 25 November 1945, RA LD 29 Q. For Quisling's view, see entries 'Tvangsarbeid' and 'Arbeidsmobilisering' in *Norsk krigsleksikon* (1995).

[42] Related at a Fører meeting 24 May 1944, RA FMK 15.

graphs from this period, he seemed to be holding up well, nevertheless. His tendency to gain weight, so obvious in 1942 and 1943, was being kept in check. In the summer of 1944 he was in better shape than he had been for years: his complexion was smooth and he often looked happy. At least, the official pictures released that autumn did not give the impression of a harassed leader, but of a decisive and serious man.

Even in the face of all his setbacks, Quisling always had to look certain of victory in front of his supporters; he was fond of remarking that 'History, which has a great deal to teach us in this case, shows how victory can be achieved in spite of all defeats' – then citing examples of the early history of Rome, Prussia under Frederick the Great or the Bolsheviks' seemingly hopeless struggle during the civil war, to show how radically situations can change. Nevertheless, the existing state of affairs was indeed a grave one: his old talent for apocalyptic rhetoric resurfaced in the final phase of the war, in view of Germany's impending collapse.

To his followers and his opponents he remained two entirely different persons. His political followers regarded him without exception as conscientious, knowledgeable, well informed; administratively first class, with a great eye for detail, but also with a certain preponderance for drawing up abstract plans instead of making concrete decisions. His weaknesses notwithstanding, Quisling was regarded as a balanced and gentle person, perhaps too gentle in many ways, and therefore not resolute enough when dealing with people, but with his humanity shining through his high moral seriousness.

His political opponents experienced an entirely different Quisling. There is hardly a quotation from any conversation with Quisling between 1940 and 1945 which does not give the impression of an unstable and undisciplined personality. To his adversaries, Quisling was the man with the shifty eyes and the abrupt, threatening manner.[43]

This discrepancy is so striking that it requires some explanation. It is evident that people reacted to Quisling emotionally: by Norwegians outside his own movement he was regarded as the devil incarnate. Quite naturally, in the illegal slogans plastered across walls and fences, in the broadcasts sent from London and Boston, as well as in propaganda the world over, the name of Quisling had, ever since April 1940, acquired both moral and emotional connotations which inevitably prejudiced those who had to deal with him in person. That his opponents thus fastened on to the picture of the irresolute and unattractive personality, and his followers on to the humane picture,

---

[43] E.g. Nansen, *Langs veien*, pp. 147–57; Berggrav, *Front Fangenskap*, pp. 30–6.

provides a natural point of departure for evaluating the two contradictory opinions.

However, the two interpretations could both be objectively true, in that they point to different sides of his character. It is reasonable to assume that Quisling was more hesitant, exercised less self-control, and could be gruff and even threatening when confronted with opponents than he was with his own people. His abrupt manner came to the fore when his routine was disturbed and he had to deal with urgent business on the spot, often letting slip shocking or dramatic statements such as 'he deserved beheading one hundred times', 'total annihilation, total'. It could be argued that it was scarcely intelligent behaviour for a politician to be more aggressive in word than in deed. His abruptness has been variously interpreted by experts. Odd Nansen, the son of Fridtjof Nansen, found him morally crippled and deeply insecure. Professor Monrad-Krohn, the neurologist who met him at a stormy conference at the palace in 1942 in his capacity as Dean of the Faculty of Medicine, interpreted his behaviour as calculated to frighten the university leaders into submission. Once he realised that threats were not going to work, he resumed his normal manner, and the discussion continued more calmly.[44]

Several people who knew Quisling well described him as politically open and tolerant of criticism on a one-to-one level. Indignant colleagues with complaints were met by calm understanding, and even strangers who came to protest against the deportation of the Jews or the student arrests were told patiently to leave. However, when he was facing a united group, he always smelled conspiracy, and was not to be trifled with. People soon learned that it was inadvisable to approach him in groups.[45]

His famous talent for avoiding social contact and sitting through entire banquets without saying a word, irrespective of whom he was sitting next to, was not so much a sign of self-control as shyness disguised as philosophical seriousness. Were he to take the initiative in such a situation, his words would usually come cascading out in a cataract of dramatic rhetoric, after which he would become taciturn once more. After a short pause, his inscrutable smile would be a signal for the conversation to resume. He certainly felt he was above the everyday trivial chatter of his colleagues as well as Terboven's lively Rhineland conversation.

[44] Monrad-Krohn, memo on his meeting with Quisling on 16 September 1942 of 30 June 1945, RA LD 29 Q, Div. 7.
[45] Hustad, according to Hagelin's account 15 October 1945, RA LD 846 Hagelin; and Smedal, *Patriotisme*, p. 60.

The people closest to him accepted these character traits. The exaggerated sense of his own importance as a politician, the fact that he repeatedly reached conclusions of a far-reaching nature independently of his advisers, were not only a result of his inability to communicate but suggestive also of the sort of politician he wanted to be. His plotting in Berlin in 1939; the *coup d'état* in 1940; the sudden restructuring of the Riksting in 1942, and the changes to the government in 1943–4, are all examples of unilateral decisions taken without reference to anyone, not even his most intimate circle. The truth was that there was nobody he trusted unconditionally. As Fører he took sole responsibility and stood alone. In this way the principles of the *fører* system merged with the image which he had cultivated as a statesman and wartime politician in the style of a Frederick the Great, or a Napoleon or a Mannerheim, complemented by a withdrawn personality.

Curiously enough he did not consider it his moral duty to share the hardships of his subjects. The country was enduring strict rationing of food, except of course at Gimle. Gifts were showered upon him. The Ørneredet (Eagle's Nest) estate at Leangkollen in Asker was given to him personally, and expensively decorated at public cost. Moland parsonage in Fyresdal was offered to him free of charge, restored at the expense of the Ministry of Churches' budget. This might perhaps be justified in the case of a royal head of state, but Quisling, who was only temporarily exercising supreme authority, could not in any way be considered an institution that required gifts on a scale out of proportion to a Norwegian prime minister.[46]

However, he did not live extravagantly. The few parties he and Maria gave for the relatives they kept in touch with – Jørgen (although he kept himself very much to himself), Aunt Hildur, Uncle Rasmus's widow, Cousin Konken Langaard and her children (two of them were front-line soldiers, one of whom died), and Cousin Eli and her daughter – were relatively modest occasions. The gifts he received were not put to personal use. In his account 874 at the Oslo Savings Bank there were monthly deposits of 50,000 kroner in appanage, as well as private donations, including one of 400,000 kroner from Consul Hildisch in September 1944, of which 300,000 were refunded as part of a tax agreement, and a further 150,000 from the Public Assistance Fund collected through a tax of one øre on the price of each matchbox since 1942. There were 1.2 million kroner in Quisling's account in May 1945, but from the same account he dispensed charity in grand style – via the party organisation.[47]

---

[46] RA FMK 27, various documents.   [47] Document in UBO MS fol. 4096 IV.

Most striking of all was his concern for his native Fyresdal. The special treatment the village received, in his attempt to control the local administration from Oslo, exceeded the powers of a Norwegian head of state, but nobody in the Chancellery or the party leadership seemed to object to 'the Fører's native village' playing a special role in the new Norway. The same went for Gjerpen, because his family had lived there.

The full restoration of Lunden in Fyresdal, as well as the completion of the grotesque surrounding fence, went on into 1944. But the purchase of the parsonage did not go down well in the village. Even among party members there was stinging criticism of the Fører. It was said that Quisling wanted a large estate, and that the agricultural produce from the extensive farm was already being sent to Gimle.[48] The truth was somewhat different. Quisling had definite plans: he wanted to retire as parson in the parish once he had completed his great task as Minister President. Lunden was to become his residence, Jonsborg his retirement home; in this way Moland's large, old-fashioned main building could be used for charity events, which he would personally take pleasure in organising.

Indeed, he had a vested interest in fostering his native village: he imagined himself following in the footsteps of his forefathers, of whom no fewer than eight had been parsons at Fyresdal and at Lunden, which his grandfather had turned into a model farm, and finally retiring to Jonsborg just as his parents had done. It was a pleasant dream, which seemed all the more attractive to a head of government who at the time of the troubles with the Church had been forced to introduce a general entry for particularly well-qualified lay people to be appointed to vacant positions in the state church. Quisling, with his vast knowledge of philosophy and theology, considered himself an obvious candidate for such a post.

He was a dreamer, and his fantasy about the life of a quiet country pastor took shape amidst a private project he was working on towards the end of the war. When he was looking for escape during difficult times he entertained himself by tracing his family tree back as far as he could. This took him far back into the past – beyond Fyresdal, beyond history in fact: through the Hvide family, from which his mother had come, he managed to trace a line back to Harald Hårfagre, Ragnar Lodbrok and Sigurd Ring, and from there back through to the Voldsungs, 'a northern Germanic line of

---

[48] Report to the Fører concerning his visit to Fyresdal 20 November to 5 December 1944 from Willy Andersen, Kåre Vik and Rolf Hessvedt, p. 3, Municipal archives Fyresdal, also published in *Vest-Telemark Blad* 27 and 29 September and 13 October 1984.

chieftains', who were said to be descendants of Odin himself. Perhaps the findings gave him an added sense of authority when he was facing German assertions of racial superiority. Norway, he asserted, was 'the oldest nation in our cultural sphere', 'the people who made the British Empire'.[49]

SECURITY

Quisling, one of the most potent symbols of the Second World War, was – like no other man in the country – a target for planned assassinations. Scarcely a resistance group activist, at least in the Oslo area, had not considered attempts on his life. In Fyresdal, there had been long-standing plans for his murder. The leader of the armed resistance group in the village also discussed the possibility of kidnapping him on one of his visits to his hut in Homvatn. If a British plane had been ready then, it would have been relatively easy to attack his companion, drown him and let it look as if Quisling had gone under too, and then administer chloroform and transport him to London.[50]

For the regime the question of the Fører's security presented a real headache. A system of three partly interdependent security systems was therefore set up: adjutants, police and Quisling's own guard.[51] The adjutants were the ones closest to him. In line with prevailing military norms, Quisling had neither a secretary nor a secretariat, but adjutants. The police were responsible for the next level of security. Uniformed officers patrolled the palace and the area around Gimle. A guard from the detective force, backed up by manpower from the state police, played a more important role as undercover protection for the Fører wherever he went. This complex security arrangement was without precedent in Norway. Whenever Quisling wanted to attend a meeting in the city, the locale had to be checked out in advance, his route investigated and a detailed minute-by-minute plan of his movements had to be drawn up.

On 21 September 1943 he was expected at the opening of the Norwegian

---

[49] Speech at Steinkjer 6 June 1943, *FF* 7 June 1943; speech in Hamar 20 June 1943, *FF* 21 June 1943.

[50] Related by Ragnar Austad, Fyresdal 1986; see also Jon H. Ofte, *Me ville vera med* (1984) pp. 22f, and Harald Sandvik, *Krigsår* (1979) pp. 146f; Olav Straume in *Telemark Arbeiderblad* 7 May 1985; Olav Skogen, *Ensom krig mot Gestapo* (1992).

[51] Memo concerning the Minister President's security service 7 August 1942, and an undated directive for the Minister President's civilian bodyguard, both in RA FMK 16, as well as orders concerning the Fører and Minister President's guard 18 January 1944, RA FMK 21.

Cultural Chamber in the university's Old Hall. The agenda included subjects such as the establishment of a new national organisation for conservation (a subject very dear to the party, and which subsequently led to the opening of the country's first national parks), a music academy and a language academy. Security arrangements behind the scenes were very complex. The hall and the gallery of the old Aula were searched and the corridors closed off. The police had to close Karl Johan Street in good time and position guards on the stairs, and in the passages and cloakroom for the duration of the meeting. The three hundred metres between the palace and the university were put under full surveillance.[52]

His travels presented a challenge to the police guard, even though local forces of both Hird and police followed him closely wherever he went. The most difficult arrangements were those for Quisling's long journey to the north, which he made with a select group of ministers in the summer of 1943, the only visit he made to that part of the country during the war. After the disastrous explosion in Bergen on 22 April 1944, the worst explosion of the war, which claimed around 200 dead and 2,000 injured according to contemporary accounts, Quisling visited the devastated city to inspect the damage, his visit publicly announced in advance. On this occasion the train schedule was altered so as to avoid railway sabotage of the Fører train to and from Bergen.[53]

Several prominent NS people were killed, either with or without advance threats. The autumn of 1944 saw the death of no fewer than fourteen state policemen, including two inspectors and an adjutant – victims of the resistance movement's liquidations. In February 1945 the security police chief, Marthinsen himself, was ambushed in his car on his way to the office. In each case the victim was given a state funeral surrounded by a great deal of publicity, and in Marthinsen's case both the Minister President and the Reichskommissar were present, which demanded careful security arrangements in itself.

The party was nervous. The weapon question, the demand for the distribution of pistols to 'particularly vulnerable political leaders', often came up within the party leadership. The government and heads of departments were all armed during the course of spring 1945. At least from the standpoint of the NS and the security forces, in the last year of the war

---

[52] Plan for the opening of Norway's Cultural Chamber 20 September 1943, RA FMK 17.
[53] Police order of 3 June 1944, RA FMK 19.

the political struggle in Norway was turning into a violent uprising bearing all the marks of civil war.[54]

The third level of Quisling's security was the most prestigious. He had his own guards division, normally of three companies, who adopted a Royal Guards uniform bearing Quisling's initials on its central emblem. The Fører Guard originated from the Hird, which had taken on the task of guarding the palace, armed with police truncheons, in February 1942. It developed into a separate entity in April 1942, armed with rifles from the same autumn, and was financed directly out of the state budget from 1943 as the Fører Guard. It was a crack division, and 200 or so Hird youths were recruited and trained for the two original companies which were stationed at Bygdøy and Ullevål schools.[55]

This uniformed guard was later expanded with forces from the SS Nordland Regiment and the Norwegian Legion discharged from service on the front. A fourth company consisting of veterans from the eastern front was formed in the autumn of 1944.

NORWAY ARMED

Quisling's political thinking was of a highly military character; he always assessed situations from a strategic point of view. While others were focusing on the growing political opposition in Norway, the possibility of civil war and the collapse of the new regime, he had his eye on the world war and how the fate of Norway was being determined by events abroad. In a sense the war situation provided a clearer perspective for what he had always maintained: that foreign policy in the final analysis always determines internal affairs. What was decisive for Norway after 9 April was not so much how the government succeeded internally, but the position it managed to create for its country in the relations between nations, the balance of which was defined by arms. All political planning had therefore to work on the assumption that the war would be over after a relatively short time and that Norway would have to try to secure for itself the most advantageous position possible in the subsequent regroupings of nations. This position would not come of its own accord, and certainly not in such a way that it would be possible to concentrate exclusively on internal affairs. It could only come

---

[54] Discussions at Fører meetings 31 May to 2 June 1944 and 23–25 September 1944, NS Riks- og rådsmøteprotokoll (private archives*).

[55] Various documents in RA FMK 5 and 16.

about as the result of energetic efforts to make the country assertive in foreign policy in the present circumstances, that is by force of arms.

Norway, *his* Norway, had to take sides, then, and through the events of 1940 it had made its choice. It was important not to waver in this choice but to stand firm, with a resolute government working on the premiss that Germany would win. Were Germany to be defeated, Norway's position would be significantly weakened. A German victory, on the other hand, coupled with intelligent policy, would secure Norway's place in the new Europe, provided that it made a military contribution to the common cause.[56]

However, little progress was being made on this front. The seven battalions which Quisling had dreamt of when the Norwegian Legion was formed in 1941 as a Waffen-SS unit totalled only 900 volunteers in its first year. A party decree issued the following year to district leaders, that they were required to find 2,700 new recruits for the Legion so that it could be built up into a regiment, was not met. The potential for voluntary service was thus far smaller than Quisling had supposed.[57]

The same thing happened every time there was an initiative to form new divisions. The Panzer Grenadier Regiment Norway, which succeeded the SS Nordland Regiment in 1943, was supposed to have been between 3,000 and 3,500 strong but reached only 700. The Ski Battalion, which absorbed part of the Legion for a mission in Finland, was an élite force, including Minister Stang himself; despite an energetic recruitment drive it lacked a significant base. At the end of 1943 Norwegian volunteers totalled 3,878 soldiers, the following year barely 500 more than that, but by then 750 were lying dead on the battlefield.[58]

In December 1943, Quisling declared that five or ten times as many should have gone to the front: 'Then Norway would have been stronger today.' The NS Party apparently backed its Fører in his demand for more and more volunteers. In reality, however, the question of war volunteers provoked a great deal of controversy within the movement. The question of front-line service got mixed up with the general polarisation between the moderates and the activists in the movement. The activists' charges against

[56] Quisling, Fører resolution 1 April 1942, RA NSRG Sentralavd 1.

[57] Blindheim, *Nordmenn under Hitlers fane*, pp. 35ff; decree of 6 August 1942 on recruitment to the Norwegian Legion, RA LD 1099 Fuglesang.

[58] Rediess, Report 4 October 1944, BA NS 19/2135; Karl Leib, 'Die germanische Leitstelle Norwegen', 9 November 1945, RA LD 1099 Fuglesang; H. W. Neulen, *An deutscher Seite* (1985) p. 159.

the 'indolent' free riders, and their attacks on 'the rats gnawing away in the party basement', were so insistent and aggressive that the party leadership in January 1945 had to censure Leif Schjøren, the SS Norway leader, and the editor Egil Holst Torkildsen to try to muzzle the worst extremists.[59]

The question of front-line service also had its practical side. Party Minister Fuglesang, who in addition to his many other tasks was also responsible for the movement's personnel, clearly sensed the drain of talent which the volunteers represented. Not only would valuable young men by the thousand disappear east instead of working for the party or in the police, but the duty to serve on the front would necessarily appeal more strongly to the most valuable party functionaries, including district leaders and ministers. There would also be a flood of applications from people who for various reasons would welcome the chance to be released from their duties at home. This was something the NS could little afford as it was way below its membership targets and even lacked people in the key leadership positions needed for both the public and party administration. Quisling had been over-optimistic when he declared that a membership of 1 per cent of the population would be enough to sustain the new state. He reckoned that under normal circumstances an élite of between 40,000 and 50,000 dedicated individuals would suffice. But circumstances were far from normal and army volunteering made the situation even worse. There was strong opposition to the party in both industry and the civil service, with officials everywhere refusing to take orders from the NS leadership, Fuglesang reported.[60] Moreover, from the spring of 1944 onwards there was a mass exodus from the country, and several people, including many in prominent positions, simply disappeared over the border into Sweden, often taking their families with them. It seemed impossible to stem the tide of escapees. Some 607 people were reported missing by the security police in July 1944 and a further 745 in August, and in October the number reached 916, that is approximately thirty people a day, and the number was growing.[61] The borders were not too heavily policed, and the few guards from the border police who were there were unable to prevent the crossings. Moreover, the party was divided on the subject of the lengths it should go to to reverse the trend. Quisling was of the view that they were well rid of these dissenters,

---

[59] Sørensen, *Hitler eller Quisling*, p. 268; see also documents in RA FMK 16.

[60] Fuglesang at the Fører meeting 31 May to 2 June 1944, NS Riks- og rådsmøteprotokoll 1934–45.*

[61] Security police, monthly report on missing persons, August–October 1944, RA FMK 12. Ringdal, *Mellom barken og veden*, ch. 'Flukt og flyktninger'.

while the Reichskommissar took the matter more seriously and wanted to take hostages on a large scale, but Terboven's hostage-taking simply resulted in entire families, instead of just individuals, escaping. Policemen also left in droves, some of them precisely because the German security police had ordered them to take hostages.[62]

Quite how such a small party was to maintain control, let alone function successfully as a government when faced with an overburdened public sector, was a problem which above all preoccupied Fuglesang among the leadership. He got the reputation of being neutral, if not anti-SS on the subject of recruitment: reports from Himmler's people in Norway increasingly complained about his ideological bent – he who had once been so pro-SS was now very obviously resisting further recruitment for the front, a position which provoked fierce conflicts both with the SS leadership and within the party.[63] However, it was clear that Fuglesang's position was valid; not only would the NS have to deal with the absence of valuable colleagues but they also had to face the eventuality that several of them would not come back alive. It seemed meaningless that the party's most able Supreme Court judge, for example, should risk his life and die at the front, as there was no chance of appointing new judges. Neither was it encouraging that a large number of the young aspiring leaders which the party had been training at the Fører school at Jessheim at vast expense were so anxious to join up to lose their lives in their scores. During the devastating battle of 'the last hill' in June 1944, of the 300 men in the Ski Battalion in Finland, 141 never returned to their own lines after two days of siege. With the cry of 'Long live Quisling!' these young Norwegians put themselves in the path of advancing Russians.[64]

Such compelling arguments notwithstanding, recruitment did go ahead throughout 1943 and 1944, and a welfare apparatus was developed. The office responsible for the front-line units collected vast sums of money through appeals and more or less voluntary contributions from the country's municipalities and businesses. From the palace Quisling was anxious that

---

[62] Herbert Noot's testimony 23 June 1948, RA LD 933 Vest-Oppland, and Thrana to Noot 10 June 1943, ibid.; Fuglesang to Lie 21 April 1945, RA FMK 12. Also Thrana to Ministry of the Interior 29 December 1944, RA FMK 18.

[63] Rediess to Himmler 20 April 1943, 2 December 1944, BA NS 19/3451; telex 18 December and 30 December 1944, BA NS 19/2135.

[64] Eye-witness account in a letter from Arild Jadar, printed in NS Månedshefte 1945/1. See also Blindheim, Nordmenn under Hitlers fane, pp. 85f.

confiscated and requisitioned farmland should be turned over to discharged volunteers, as tenants or for possible sale.[65]

The pitiful recruitment in Norway stood in sharp contrast to the situation in Finland, so much so that Finland was constantly held up as an example by the Germans. But Finland's business was also Quisling's business. After his two and a half years in Helsinki as military attaché between 1919 and 1921, he was well informed on the situation, and had kept up with developments by reading the *Hufudstadsbladet* regularly. After Finland declared war on Russia in 1941, he felt an even stronger identification. The attractive thing about the Finnish initiative was that the struggle against the Bolsheviks was being fought as a national cause, despite the bitter class conflicts which had erupted during the civil war of 1918–19, just before Quisling's arrival in the country. Even Finnish labourers and smallholders were loyal members of Mannerheim's army of uniquely brave conscripts, dedicated to a true war of attrition to win back territories lost to Russia in 1940. He wondered whether such a show of unity were feasible in Norway, and whether Norwegian workers and peasants might mobilise to the extent that the problem of voluntary recruitment could be abandoned in favour of mass conscription, thus contributing to what had become a many-sided issue: the question of future Norwegian independence in the Germanic struggle for a new European order.

In the winter of 1943, General von Falkenhorst received several reports indicating that the Norwegian Minister President had taken an interest in the developments in Scandinavia, especially in Sweden and Finland. 'Quisling is of the opinion that we Germans are underestimating the danger of the developments in Sweden and perhaps in Finland too,' wrote von Falkenhorst in his report to OKW. 'He no longer regards the idea of a war on two fronts in Norway as fanciful, but as a real possibility.' Von Falkenhorst, however, was careful to distance himself. He considered Quisling sincere enough, but the problem was that he had only Norwegian interests in mind, thinking of the political advantages to be had if the Wehrmacht withdrew one or two divisions from the Mediterranean and sent them to Norway.[66]

Two days after von Falkenhorst had sent in his report, Quisling was sounding out the leading Germans in Norway on whether the recruitment of

[65] Documents in RA FMK 7; on the Fører school, *NS Månedshefte* 1944/5, 1945/1 and *FF* 21 September 1944.
[66] Von Falkenhorst to Keitel 8 March 1943, PAAA Ges. Helsinki 24/2, Schriftwechsel Geheim; Woermann to Blücher 24 March 1943, ibid.

Norwegians for the eastern front should be replaced by conscription. Compulsory military service could be reintroduced, he suggested, making it possible to enlist 60,000 men from the male population aged between twenty-one and thirty-two, and thus ensuring that key men in industry and the economy were retained.[67]

This was an astonishing proposal, which Rediess considered necessary to report to Himmler immediately. He objected, though, that conscription for fighting on behalf of Germany would only provoke further flight into Sweden. Quisling disagreed. In any event the number of those escaping over the border would be compensated for by those who did join up. He stressed the law-abiding nature of his fellow countrymen, although they did demand fair treatment in return, and therein lay the rub: the Germans were keen to accept the volunteers he could raise for them, but refused to give his government the authority and independence it needed. Rediess nevertheless seems to have been captivated by the idea that the Norwegians could be required by their own Constitution to enlist for front-line service, and made a cautious recommendation to Himmler. Von Falkenhorst declared himself interested. The three men were, however, aware of Terboven's unqualified opposition to the plan, and the whole matter foundered temporarily on the Reichskommissariat's negative stance.

However, neither Quisling nor the SS had abandoned the idea of conscription. The head of the Waffen-SS recruitment office in Norway, who was a son-in-law of one of the men most close to Himmler, Gottlob Berger in Berlin, kept a particularly keen eye on the Labour Service (AT). Each year the new age group of 18-year-olds was required to register for socially useful work such as digging ditches, building roads and dams. Even if the Labour Service itself was not sufficiently developed to take on more than a part of each age group, its registration system was fully developed, as it was to all intents and purposes an extension of the army's conscription body.

SS interest in the Norwegian Labour Service was actively rebuffed by the AT leadership itself, which considered it essential to distance the Service from any allegation that its camps were used for recruitment. However, pressure mounted during the autumn of 1943, and Axel Stang's department was instructed to prepare itself for the conscription of all registered AT manpower for front-line service. The Ministry itself was vehemently opposed to this, stressing all the negative consequences such a mobilisation would have. It 'would inevitably assume the character of a mass deporta-

[67] Rediess to Himmler 13 March 1943, BA NS 19/3451.

tion', which would certainly bring things 'to boiling point'. Opposition to Germany and the NS would increase 'to an overwhelming extent', and result in disturbances everywhere, not to mention the outrage it would provoke in Sweden.[68]

In spite of this Quisling was determined to go ahead. With conscription he would kill two birds with one stone: put men in the service of the joint struggle and thus secure a favourable position for Norway in the new Europe, and at the same time strengthen the authority of his government as the supreme power in the country implementing the Norwegian law and Constitution, depending, of course, on a certain measure of formal independence from Germany, perhaps even on a peace treaty.

During a visit to Germany at the end of November 1943 Fuglesang and Stang conveyed the following information to Berger in Berlin, which he duly passed on to Himmler: 'Quisling informs us that he now, as before, intends to mobilise four age groups of around 40,000 men registered at the Labour Service. It is suggested that AT installations are used.' Quisling repeated his intention to Neumann a fortnight later, but gave a figure of 50,000. This discrepancy suggests that the estimates were verbal and approximate. Neumann for his part reported what Terboven had so often said, that a conscription of Norwegians initiated by Quisling was out of the question. In his written justification, Neumann presented the objection typically raised by Stang's colleagues at the AT, namely that it would be impossible to keep a planned mobilisation secret, that it would cause great unrest and precipitate a mass exodus to Sweden, and that there were insufficient reliable policemen for them to be confident of successful arrests. The mobilisation Quisling proposed 'will have only two results: either it will serve as a trigger for an enemy invasion, or, if this fails to materialise, will undermine government authority'.[69]

In January 1944 the opportunity to take up the whole issue with Hitler personally presented itself. Quisling's long-awaited state visit to Germany was about to take place. During their previous discussion at Schloss Klessheim in April 1943 Hitler had solemnly promised to consult Quisling more frequently, and had suggested a meeting every three months. Not surprisingly, nothing ever came of this. An audience was scheduled for 21 January 1944 at field headquarters, Wolfsschanze at Rastenburg in East

---

[68] Undated memorandum on the mobilisation of 25,000 men, RA LD 29 Q, unsubmitted document.

[69] Neumann to Quisling 18 December 1943 in *Straffesak* p. 113; Berger to Himmler 26 November 1943, BA NS 19/3451.

Prussia. From the German side Himmler, Lammers and Martin Bormann were to attend. This time Quisling was permitted to bring a small delegation: he chose Fuglesang, Lie and his new cabinet minister Alf Whist. Terboven, who was also to be present, brought Neumann with him. The Norwegian delegates were put up at the Park Hotel in Köningsberg, two hours' drive from Rastenburg.[70]

According to Quisling's young adjutant Per Jahr, Terboven arrived ahead of the Norwegians. All the same Quisling managed to speak to Hitler alone first, possibly in order to give his opinion on Terboven. Then he presented his plans for conscription to Hitler, who rejected them. He nevertheless had a 'definite feeling that he had the Führer's confidence', as Hitler explained the situation to him clearly and openly; despite all the military and political difficulties, he was encouraged because he had been shown such trust.[71]

The following day, the Norwegian delegation was received by Reichsführer SS Himmler at his field headquarters near Rastenburg. In the evening the question of mobilisation was discussed in detail. Quisling argued strongly for the establishment of a Norwegian conscript army which would be instructed by a command trained at the Norwegian Military Academy. It took Himmler a long time to convince Quisling that he was wrong, and that the Waffen-SS should still be the joint European force, based on voluntary participation. According to his own minutes he finally succeeded in persuading Quisling to see that the best way to further the Norwegian cause would be to allow Norwegian volunteers to join the SS, but to allow them to fight under Norwegian command and to be given ranks and insignia which would indicate their nationality more clearly than hitherto. But Himmler also argued for stepping up recruitment among the AT youths.[72]

Thus Quisling's proposal was not accepted. But he had by no means abandoned the idea: his offer to Germany stood, as long as it came with a watertight guarantee of Norway's future independence.[73]

---

[70] FF 25 January 1944; Domarus, Hitler II, p. 2080. Bills from Park Hotel Köningsberg in BA R 43 II/673. Information from Per Jahr related to Johan O. Jensen, De nære årene, pp. 139f.

[71] No contemporary record exists, only a report given some weeks later by Neumann, Neumann to Himmler 9 March 1944, BA NS 19/2135.

[72] Aktenvermerk by Himmler on the discussion 22 January 1944, BA NS 19/1576.

[73] This is evident from Neumann's lecture at Ic-Tagung in Oslo 28–30 March 1944, reference in Bericht Oberstleutnant Ogilvie Reise Norwegen–Schweden 25 March to 5 April 1944, PAAA 11/46, Handakten Etzdorf.

PERFIDIOUS NEWSPAPERS, COWARDLY DESERTERS

When the Norwegian delegation returned to Oslo on 24 January 1944, it appeared that their colleague Riisnæs had been active in their absence. The Minister of Justice had produced a detailed memorandum, which he considered sending to Berger, on the mobilisation of no fewer than five age groups, that is, 75,000 men, who would be sent on to Germany for training. The document was immediately copied by his secretary and forwarded to the resistance, which, panic-stricken, published it in full in its main underground paper *Bulletinen* ('The Bulletin') at the end of January. This document caused a major sensation all over the world, and was taken as final proof of how desperate the Germans and the NS government had become. It was given extensive coverage in both the BBC's and Moscow's Norwegian broadcasts, not to mention the Swedish and the Allied press.[74]

This publication was particularly unwelcome to the Germans. The Reichskommissariat felt it necessary to issue a special disclaimer which was published all over the country on 1 February 1944, categorically denying that any German or Norwegian authorities had ever considered introducing such a measure. The whole story was set up by the Swedish press in order to 'cause the hasty escape of young Norwegians so that the government in exile could hand them over as cannon fodder for the Bolshevik-plutocratic powers'. It is doubtful whether anyone believed it. To the resistance movement, which throughout the autumn of 1943 had been suffering from a disabling rift between the Communist and official, London-supported factions, the episode was a signal for unity and revitalisation, something which the NS government soon came to recognise during its attempts to introduce the national work effort that spring.[75]

During the Fører meeting at the palace at the end of January 1944 the crisis over the Riisnæs letter was discussed in detail. But Quisling brushed aside their anxiety: the leakage, he said, was of no consequence. 'The matter would have come out anyway.'[76] In a sense, he was standing by what he had said. He wanted to go ahead with the mobilisation project, and would therefore sooner or later have to face public reaction. However, the problems proved greater than he had anticipated. Both the AT registration and the

---

[74] Schjelderup, *Over bakkekammen*, ch. 23; Ringdal, *Mellom barken og veden*, pp. 120ff. There is no evidence, at least in the Reichsführer-SS or the SS-Hauptamt archives, of this letter ever having been sent to Berger.

[75] *FF* 25 January 1944.

[76] Related by Sverre Riisnæs to Per Bøhn, NRK ho.

order for the national work effort in May suffered heavily from the suspicion surrounding the government's motives. The problem was exacerbated by the Reichskommissar press office, which altered the text of the government announcement so that the call for registration was referred to as 'mobilisation', thereby fuelling rumours that the entire initiative was an implementation of the Justice Minister's plans. Several newspapers referred to the work effort as 'mobilisation'. Consequently both the work effort and the AT were sabotaged by the age groups concerned in a large-scale action of civil disobedience which became a triumph for the resistance movement.[77]

Once again the Swedish press rehearsed Quisling's government's fiascos with glee. The Jews, the officers, the policemen, the students, and now this. It seemed that Swedish journalists stopped at nothing to disgrace him in the eyes of the world. But now he struck back: early in March 1944 he had a lengthy discussion with von Falkenhorst's Chief of Staff, Lieutenant General Rudolf Bamler, whom Neumann had suggested he invited to Gimle. Quisling warned that if Germany did not abandon its passive stance and adopt a definite policy based on a strategic conception of Scandinavia as a single area, with Sweden playing a temporary key role, the whole area would soon be lost. Finland was already about to make a separate peace with Moscow, in which case North Norway would have to be given up. The danger of Sweden joining the Allies and entering the war on their side was imminent and had to be dealt with at once. Germany should invade the north of Sweden and secure the area between Finland and Norway in Torneå. At the same time an independent eastern Karelian state would have to be established as a base for the continuing Finnish resistance to Russia. After that, south-west Sweden should be taken in order to establish an unbroken transport route. While German troops would be moving forward through the Baltic islands towards the Stockholm area, the Swedish defence would be tied up and the operation could be concluded in a short time. After these losses, Sweden would be forced to capitulate. General Bamler took notes of Quisling's proposal and sent them on to General Jodl at the Wehrmacht headquarters while Neumann sent a report to Himmler.[78]

The feeling that he had got the attention of these prominent Germans pleased him. He continued to work on the Swedish question, with the co-operation of his unofficial foreign minister, Consul Støren. Three weeks later

---

[77] Lippestad to Quisling 22 May 1944, RA FMK 17.
[78] Bamler to Jodl 9 March 1944, BA-MA RW 39/57; Neumann to Himmler 9 March 1944, BA NS 19/2135.

he had prepared a comprehensive memorandum entitled 'Die schwedische und nordische Frage' (The Swedish and Nordic Question), offering political and historical arguments as the basis for the plan he had presented to Bamler. In this document, the history of Sweden's ambitions as a great power was traced back to the time of Gustavus Adolphus, and provided the reader with a detailed lesson in Swedish ambitions in the rest of Scandinavia, in Norway in particular. Himmler noted on his copy that 'the historical parts are interesting', but as for the political analysis he had several reservations, primarily because Quisling was so obviously motivated by self-interest. In his attempt to justify the need for a German campaign in Sweden he argued that it was vital to stop 'the only remaining Jewish free state in Europe' and the political opposition it was putting up to the new order in its neighbouring country. In particular he pointed to the 'perfidious and scandalous manner in which the Swedish press treats the Norwegian situation, and the distribution of its propaganda by illegal pamphlets which do not stop short of dishonesty and malice'. The way to stop all this would be, it seemed, to grant the National Government full sovereignty once more – so as to be able to undercut the arguments of the 'perfidious editors'.[79]

While Quisling was elucidating the need for German action against Sweden, the question of an independent Norwegian armed force was approaching a solution. It seemed that the Labour Service was not the way to go about it after all. Instead, the Hird, the paramilitary party division, was emerging as the institution which was gradually being developed into an armed force, with a view to establishing the core of the post-independence Norwegian army. After the Eilifsen episode the need for separate Norwegian forces increased as the country was obviously facing possible attacks from both Allied troops and troops in exile, who in turn would join forces with the underground army. Specially trained Hird men, following meetings with Rediess in April 1944, were allowed to form into a special division – the Alarm Unit – soon to be combined with another division. Provisions and pay were met by the state budget, even though the Hird was clearly a division of the NS. The German Police Commander General Rediess was in charge of operations, but the two divisions could not be called in without first obtaining Quisling's approval. Thus, in a sense, the new force had two high commanders.[80]

---

[79] Memorandum signed and dated Oslo 30 March 1944, enclosed in Berger to Himmler 26 April 1944, BA NS 19/2135. Only this copy appears to have survived. A preliminary version, 'Sveriges hegemoni i Norden', in UBO MS fol. 3920 VII, 10.

[80] *FF* 17 April 1944; Kraglund and Moland, *Motstandskamp*, pp. 57f.

On Saturday 15 April 1944 the first division paraded through the streets of the capital in steel helmets and full combat uniform. By the end of September 1944 the armed Hird forces consisted of 2,000 men. At that same time there were 1,400 Norwegians fighting on the eastern front.[81]

But if he had really hoped to raise a Norwegian conscript army from this initiative, Quisling must have been greatly worried by the opposition to it. It soon became clear that the establishment of the two divisions was unpopular, even among his own people. At the Fører meeting of 2 June 1944 a party official confessed that the introduction of armed service to the Hird had led to people leaving both the Hird and the party. In fact, growing numbers of young men who did not wish to fight were resigning from the party.[82] At a similar meeting later in the month, the number of reported resignations was so high that drastic measures had to be taken. Quisling accepted, on the advice of the party leadership, that resignations due to the call-up 'should be ignored'.[83] A form of compulsory service had thus been introduced for registered NS members after all. The desertions in advance of the implementation of compulsory service, however, did not bode well for the formation of the country's future army.

LAST VISIT TO HITLER

On 20 January 1945 Quisling went to see Hitler for the last time. As usual, he travelled in the Reichskommissar's official aircraft, a Junker 111, this time over a Germany which, since his last trip, had been dramatically reduced by advancing armies from both the east and the west. As he and his sole escort, Consul Støren, could see from the plane's windows, the Second World War was clearly coming to an end. Besides, developments back in Norway had taken a dramatic turn since his last visit with the Soviet incursion into Finnmark in October 1944 as the first stage of the planned Allied liberation of the country. Norway had become a theatre of war once more, just as it had been in 1940, but this time the Allies were not on the defensive.[84]

In November Hitler had been forced to give up Wolfsschanze and was now back at the Chancellery in Berlin, where he received Quisling on no fewer than three occasions: for unofficial discussions on 21 and 22 January and finally for an official visit on 28 January, which was to be Hitler's last

---

[81] Report from Fehlis 4 October 1944, BA NS 19/2135.
[82] NS Riks- og rådsmøteprotokoll 1934–45 (private archives*).   [83] Ibid.
[84] The Ju 111 is described in Rødder, 'Min ære', p. 169.

diplomatic appointment.[85] In between his discussions with Hitler, Quisling had meetings with Lammers, Goebbels, Ribbentrop, Rosenberg and Berger. In this way, this visit recalled his visits of 1939 when all doors were open to him and weighty matters were discussed, the only difference being that on this occasion the discussions were characterised by complete confusion. Hitler frequently broke off to consult with Göring, Jodl or Guderian, the new army Chief of Staff. Lammers was unable to do anything for the Norwegian Fører; Rosenberg explained that he was powerless. Berlin was dominated by an indescribable atmosphere of resignation, relieved by only intermittent bursts of optimism. Air raid warnings sounded nightly as bombings were being increased.[86]

Quisling was well prepared for this meeting, having produced no fewer than four documents, including a draft peace settlement and a draft for both a Germanic and a European pact.[87] If Hitler were to rely on Norwegian support in this final stage of the war, he would have to agree to a settlement that would secure the country's sovereignty, put an end to the occupation, remove the Reichskommissariat and the German police, and stop interfering in the Norwegian administration. Quisling wanted the draft peace settlement which he brought with him signed immediately, together with the draft for a European pact, which all Germany's allies could join in time. He insisted that on this occasion there would be no talk of any automatic German domination in the projected Germanic and European federations. In the cases of both the European pact and the Germanic federation which he had outlined, Germany's vote would carry only as much weight as that of the other members. In short, it was time to realise the principle of free, federal forms once and for all. According to Article 9 in the European pact, each

---

[85] Domarus, *Hitler*, p. 2192. The sources for the Quisling–Hitler encounters are: written statement of Ole Brunæs 1 November 1951, INO; Johan Scharffenberg in *Morgenbladet* 8 May 1954 with references to a report from Støren; information given by Jan Sundberg 1991.

[86] Theo Findahl, *Undergang* (1945).

[87] (1) Entwurf [Draft]: Vorläufiger Traktat zwischen dem Grossdeutschen Reich und Norwegen, RA FMK 40; (2) Entwurf: Vorläufiger germanischer Gemeinschaftsvertrag zwischen dem Grossdeutschen Reich, Dänemark, Niederland und Norwegen, and (3) Grossgermanischer Vertrag, both RA FMK 40; (4) Entwurf Europa-pakt. Printed in fifty numbered copies; one copy INO; printed in translation in *Folk og Land* 1980/4. See also 'Exposé der Beweggründe für das Memorandum vom 2 November 1944 über die Regelung des Verhältnisses zwischen Deutschland und Norwegen' of 2 November 1944 (the memorandum itself is unknown), in RA LD 29 Q.

country should explicitly enjoy full domestic sovereignty in the future union.

The utopian element of his vision was matched by the desperation felt by all Hitler's allies at this point. The war could only go one way: the unconditional defeat of Germany and of National Socialism. However, there was some rationale behind the logic contained in Quisling's documents. The impetus for his renewed attempt to wind up the Reichskommissariat and to put an end to the occupation was the unrest which had become so prevalent within his own government in the previous four to five months, fuelled by concern that the final phase of the war could put the government and the Minister President in an even more difficult situation than before. As soon as it became clear that Finland was about to seek a separate peace with Moscow, the German forces would be compelled to cut short the front in the north and move down south through Norway. Parts of North Norway would then be occupied by Russian and other Allied troops, the government realised, and if the government in exile returned from London and established itself in North Norway, the country would have two governments.

Finance Minister Prytz was particularly worried about this possibility. It was obvious that the government in exile had already gathered considerable support for itself from London, maintaining that Norway was occupied, which meant that a state of war existed with Germany. If the government in exile were to set itself up in North Norway, its influence would increase considerably, and there was good reason to believe that the people would take their cue from it and not from the National Government, which could then be said with 'some justification' to be an occupation government 'under German leadership', and not an independent government. Moreover, if they had to face a rival government on Norwegian soil, one guaranteed by royal authority, the situation would become utterly intolerable.[88]

Prytz had the rest of the cabinet behind him in this evaluation, and they all agreed that Quisling had to resume negotiations with Hitler to end the occupation and recall the Reichskommissar before the government in exile had time to establish its counter government. Even Lie and Riisnæs were with Prytz in this matter. Quisling set to work in October with his adviser on foreign affairs, drawing up various plans for speeches and tracts, but even as they wrote, Prytz's prophecies proved self-fulfilling. Germany retreated

---

[88] Memo from Prytz presented to the Cabinet meeting on 28 September 1944, *Straffesak* pp. 563ff.

from the Finnish front and brought its troops south through North Norway. However, they did not leave the area clear for a Russian incursion. To Quisling's and his government's bewilderment, the troops had received orders to devastate the country, and to evacuate the entire population south as soon as possible to escape the front line between the retreating Germans and the advancing Russians. Their protests were ignored. Terboven ordered immediate evacuation of all civilians from the north of Norway, and the government was forced to co-operate.[89]

To Quisling this seemed 'the greatest tragedy in recent Norwegian history'. On 8 October he appointed Jonas Lie and Social Minister Lippestad regents in Finnmark and North Troms. They left immediately. However, the local population did not want to be moved out, and evacuations were therefore sluggish.[90] Moreover, both the NS and the state officials were caught in the cross-fire between the conflicting interests of the Reichskommissariat and the Wehrmacht. The entire episode blew up into one chaotic and mismanaged scandal. On 28 October Terboven got Hitler to order the removal of the population by force. All homes were to be burnt. General Rendulic, the commander of the retreating Twentieth Mountain Army, was made responsible for implementing the order.

The compulsory evacuation of Finnmark and North Troms in October and November 1944 cast a shadow over Quisling's plans to persuade Hitler to agree to changes in Norway. He was receiving grim reports of how much the people in the north were suffering, and Lie himself added to their misery by having civilians shot for trying to prevent the evacuations. On 23 October the first Soviet forces crossed the Grense Jacobs River and Pasvik River. The plundering of Norway by the Bolsheviks had begun. Surprisingly, they soon stopped, and the danger Quisling had so often talked of failed to materialise. Early in November, it became known that the government in exile's Foreign Minister Trygve Lie was in Moscow, presumably to negotiate for a Norwegian government in Finnmark.[91] But this was not the case. The Quisling government wildly overestimated the government in exile's freedom of manoeuvre; in reality it was almost as restricted by the Allies as they themselves were by Germany, and there was no discussion by the Allies on re-establishing the Norwegian government in the north of the country.

The 'revolt' in the government of autumn 1944 caused concern at the

---

[89] K. E. Eriksen and T. Halvorsen, *Frigjøring* (1987) pp. 20ff.

[90] Rødder, '*Min ære*', pp. 172–88; see also Lie and Lippestad's report of 28 February 1945, RA LD 3802 Lippestad.

[91] Jonas Lie's diary entry for 7 November 1944 in Rødder, '*Min ære*', p. 185.

Reichskommissariat. It soon became known that Quisling wanted an audience with Hitler, and that he was planning to make far-reaching demands. Terboven, for his part, proved more co-operative in the months that followed than ever.[92] The thaw was a refreshing change for Quisling. Nevertheless, while he was waiting for the message from Lammers to leave for Berlin, the seriousness of the situation weighed ever more heavily on his shoulders. Allied bombings of Bergen in October and Oslo in December 1944 claimed hundreds of civilian lives, including those of schoolchildren. Coastal traffic of all kinds was constantly disrupted by Allied air raids. In November a Bergen ship, the *Rigel*, went down with 2,570 Russian prisoners of war – the single greatest loss of life in wartime Norway. Acts of sabotage multiplied, becoming increasingly destructive. There were almost daily reports from the state police of explosions in factories, on rail tracks and on docks all over the country. At the end of November six ships in dry dock at Aker and Nyland in Oslo were blown up in the course of a single night.

Disturbances and unrest also characterised the occupation force. In December 1944 von Falkenhorst was dismissed, and after only one month his successor Lothar Rendulic was replaced by Franz Böhme. The Wehrmacht moved its headquarters to Lillehammer. On the civilian side, there were several replacements at the Reichskommissariat. The departure of the co-operative Neumann was a blow to Quisling.

Eventually, on 19 January 1945, he received the go-ahead to leave for Berlin early the next morning. He boarded Terboven's plane, which had just returned to Fornebu after having taken Terboven and his escort to Berlin. On his arrival Quisling was put up at the Gasthaus des Reichs, a complex of lodgings in Tiergarten next to the Chancellery.

The first meeting with Hitler on 21 January was encouraging, as the Führer seemed anxious to reach a settlement. The discussion, which took place in the presence of Terboven and Bormann, showed, however, that he was above all determined to put a stop to acts of sabotage in Norway, and he admonished Terboven for failing to stamp them out. The Führer was so incensed over this matter that Quisling felt obliged to try to calm him down. He pointed out that the majority of Norwegians were not saboteurs; on the contrary, half a million were working loyally for the Germans, both directly and indirectly. But Hitler was obsessed with the subject. He had just read the Wehrmacht reports on the full extent of the railway line sabotage at Jørstad bridge in North Trøndelag on 13 January and was furious. He had,

---

[92] Korff to Dr Breyhan 24 December 1944, BA R 2/532.

moreover, aged considerably since their last meeting: he had clearly been disturbed by the assassination attempt in July, and the course of the war had affected his nerves. He shook and trembled, and spoke in a grotesque, hoarse voice. But the direction of the conversation remained unchanged. The Führer's monologue gave Quisling to understand that the Allies had won a Pyrrhic victory in the Ardennes, and that his new secret weapon would soon prove its capability, ensuring the imminent collapse of the alliance of his enemies. He was willing to receive Quisling the following day, and Lammers would be instructed to make the arrangements for the official visit.[93]

By the following day, however, Hitler had almost erased what had been said the previous day from his memory, and refused to contemplate any kind of new settlement for Norway. Quisling, who wondered whether Terboven had influenced him in the meantime, was much disheartened. Over the next few days the Norwegian delegation took care to meet as many influential individuals as possible in the hope of gaining indirect support for their cause. Himmler was not present, and Quisling had to make do with Berger, who seemed sympathetic to the NS, although he was not at liberty to say as much. He called on Goebbels, who listened to the Norwegian demands, read through some of Quisling's proposals and even reacted positively to the draft European pact, which contained 'a good many attractive points', according to his diary. A few days later, after having seen Hitler on 24 January, his comments changed, and he reacted strongly against the proposal for giving each country in the federation one vote each, declaring it to be a 'nonsense'. The Führer strongly opposed the suggestion, telling his colleagues that Quisling must 'be utterly crazy, out of his mind, have taken leave of his senses'. Himmler's reaction was similar.[94]

During the talks, then, Quisling provoked suspicion and opposition. The adjutants gained the impression that the German officials considered him to be out to try a 'Horthy manoeuvre', a 'Badoglio affair', and to be threatening to abandon the fold and to turn to the Allies. Quisling, however, had no such intentions. Instead he took the opportunity of talking at length to Rosenberg at the Ministry for the East. One of the young adjutants was struck by the bitterness that marked both these men who had seen their

---

[93] Quisling, speech at the Fører meeting at the palace, 6 May 1945, INO; J. C. Fest, *Hitler* (1973) ch. 'Ragnarok'.

[94] The Goebbels Diary, entry for 25 January 1945; Berger to Himmler 6 February 1945, BA NS 19/3822, and Brunæs 1 November 1951, INO.

plans crumble. Quisling complained that he had been made a traitor, while Rosenberg lamented his impotence in the situation.[95]

Within the small Norwegian delegation there was much discussion about what should be done. The fact that Terboven was in Berlin to raise warning signals about their intentions was certainly an obstacle, but it was also clear that he did not have his former influence with Hitler. The Führer was furious at his Reichskommissar's inability to stamp out sabotage in Norway. As the proposals for peace talks and for an equal standing in a Germanic federation had been rejected out of hand, it was thought wise to promote certain subsidiary demands, a list of which was subsequently drawn up. It included putting an end to German military courts and an end to the execution of hostages, the return of Norwegian students and those incarcerated in concentration camps, as well as opening trade agreements with Germany to protect Norwegian supplies. These subsidiary demands had already been put to Hitler and Bormann in the meeting on 22 January. However, Quisling was told that there was no prospect of trade agreements, and as far as the return of prisoners was concerned, Hitler merely promised to think it over. As to the question of growing sabotage, Hitler had originally been disposed to stop the shooting of hostages. After having read the latest Wehrmacht reports he viewed the matter differently and demanded that Terboven put an end to it altogether. The tensions over this question cast a shadow on the official visit. At the banquet given by Lammers for the visiting Norwegians and Germans Terboven demanded that thousands of hostages be shot immediately. Quisling was requested to sign a document giving his approval. He declined, whereupon Terboven exploded and stormed out of the room.[96]

---

[95] Related by Jan Sundberg, 1991; see also Scharffenberg in *Morgenbladet* 8 May 1954, and Brunæs 1 November 1951, INO.

[96] Quoted by Scharffenberg in *Morgenbladet*, and used as the basis for several later accounts. According to Lammers's statement at the war crimes tribunal in Nuremberg it was Hitler himself who blocked Terboven on the shooting of hostages, see *Der Prozess gegen die Hauptkriegsverbrecher vor dem Internationalen Militärgerichtshof Nürnberg 1947–48* XI, p. 138, 9 April 1946; see also documents from the Reich Chancellery of 2 February 1945, which repeat Terboven's proposal and Hitler's decision that hostages not be shot, but rather that influential citizens be threatened, as stated in Jodl's trial, ibid. XV, pp. 547f. Six months later Quisling claimed it was Hitler who had ordered Terboven to introduce the strictest measures: see Quisling's 'Bemerkninger til nytt i tiltalebeslutningen 7 August 1945', *Straffesak* p. 621; see also oral statement p. 134. It is unclear whether the sources refer to the taking of or the shooting of hostages. Terboven was empowered to take hostages, but not to execute them without clearing it with RSHA in Berlin, according to the testimony of Fridtjof Hammersen in *Straffesak* p. 217. The banquet probably took place on 23 January.

Energetic attempts were then made on the part of the Norwegians to persuade both Goebbels and Himmler to dissociate themselves from Terboven's line against hostages, and Terboven left Berlin ahead of them without having obtained any special authority from Hitler. Although Hitler was determined to put a stop to the sabotage (the Führer had actually castigated his Reichskommissar in full view of the Minister President), he would not countenance the shooting of hostages and, according to Lammers, instructed Terboven to find some other means of dealing with the problem. But this did not mean that Quisling had got his way. During the official and final visit to the Chancellery on 28 January, Hitler expressed interest in his proposed treaty, and said that it would be signed as soon as the war was over. Foreign Minister Ribbentrop was present on this occasion in order to highlight German diplomatic interest in the matter. Hitler replied to Quisling's question about the end of the war that Germany would win, thanks to her new, secret weapons, and said that he only wanted to beg God for forgiveness 'for these weapons which I shall introduce in the last four days of the war': that was all it would take for the new rockets to devastate Britain.[97]

Quisling brought up the Norwegian weapon question, and suggested placing arms at the disposal of NS officers. The Wehrmacht and the German police had hitherto been against arming the party in any way, and even the members of the Fører Guard itself had only been given a handful of cartridges each. This had consequences for security; his own chauffeur had only three cartridges, and his reserve driver went about with an empty pistol. There was considerable discontent among the party officials. Hitler listened to all this and promised to dispatch 10,000 pistols.[98]

The two leaders parted after the usual warm handshakes and mutual assurances of undivided loyalty – a ritual which Hitler himself liked to describe as 'hypnosis'. But the grand words could not disguise the fact that Quisling was, once again, going home rather empty-handed. Sure enough, the communiqué from the meeting was worded in a satisfactory manner to the effect that Norway had been promised full independence and freedom, even more unconditionally than in Hitler's declaration of September 1943, but not 'until the struggle for the fate of Europe ends in victory'.

On the way home, Quisling stopped over in Copenhagen and expressed

---

[97] Domarus, *Hitler*, p. 2193; Smedal, *Patriotisme*, pp. 94f. Quisling's statement to the High Court, *Straffesak* p. 219.

[98] *Straffesak* p. 219.

all his bitter disappointment to Dr Werner Best. With tears in his eyes he explained that 'a peace settlement would have legitimised me. But now it won't be long before Norwegian troops are once more fighting Germans on Norwegian soil, and I am branded a traitor.'[99]

[99] Best in Matlock (ed.), *Danmark*, pp. 297f; Hartmann, *Nytt lys*, p. 174.

10

An enemy of the people

People talk of the 'Quisling enigma', but I think it is more a case of the 'enigma of the Norwegian people' ... Why I am sitting here like a traitor I do not know. How can the Norwegian people be like this?
Quisling at the High Court, 6 September 1945 [1]

Many of Henrik Ibsen's dramatic creations were living realities for Quisling. This was particularly true of Brand, with whom he had identified ever since his youth. He recognised several parallels between the subject of *The Pretenders,* of Haakon Haakonsen's medieval struggle against Duke Skule and Bishop Nicholas, and the power struggle in Norway during the war. On the whole, Quisling regarded Ibsen as much more than a playwright: he also was the poet-prophet and truth-teller, a spiritual hero whose work showed the way forward for the nation in much the same way as the Old Norse myths and the medieval sagas had done in earlier times.

However, he scarcely saw the most striking parallel of all, that between himself and the character of Dr Stockmann in *An Enemy of the People,* an account of how social and psychological mechanisms can gradually force someone who starts off as an altruist into the role of a rejected sectarian, and finally combine to make him the reviled enemy of the overall majority.

The similarities are indeed obvious. The idyllic little spa town of the play, with its petty bigotry, was symbolic of the Norway Quisling returned to from Russia in 1929, only this time the poison in the waters was Marxism, which had taken hold of the Labour movement. Quisling had then become the hero of the day, congratulated by the Storting Special Committee and applauded by the people, who flocked to hear him speak during the summer of 1932. But as soon as the consequences of the revelations became clear, the supporters disappeared. This self-interest first of all manifested itself behind closed doors (as in the 1933 elections) and later in open hostility. His words, which people had been so eager to hear, fell on increasingly deaf ears. Fired by the passion of his own voice, he then stepped up his warnings, suggesting ever more drastic solutions as the majority showed only indifference in the face of the impending crisis. Reaching an understanding with Hitler was

---

[1] *Straffesak* p. 327.

imperative. But even that was misunderstood. By some unfortunate process his name was blackened, his endeavours misinterpreted and derided. Had the Fører Guard not been stationed outside the Oslo palace, the people would surely be hurling stones at his window, just as they did to Stockmann in the fifth act. He had been branded a traitor, an 'enemy of the people', in his own mind simply because he had had the courage of his convictions, and had fought for the truth.

It is not entirely clear at precisely what point Quisling started to prepare himself mentally for the eventuality that he would be brought to trial. His ministers occasionally discussed the possibility of facing investigation by some sort of an official commission. In view of the speed and conciseness with which he wrote his own defence speech after his arrest, it is highly likely that he had been working on this project a long time before the final collapse of the regime. Indeed, self-justification had been a constant feature of everything he said and wrote during the occupation – about 9 April 1940, about his collaboration with Hitler, about the National Government and its 'heavy burdens'. In a way he was well prepared for a coherent speech in his defence, using legal arguments and delivered as a soliloquy before a sceptical but just college of judges. He had to prove that the policy of collaboration which he had embarked upon in the establishment of his government of 9 April had been in the best interests of the country, and persuade his judges that he himself had been motivated by the same patriotic and selfless sentiments that had characterised his previous activities: in Russia, in the Agrarian government and in the pre-war NS leadership.

His defence must have been rehearsed silently on several occasions well in advance of his defeat, in preparation for the final act of the drama which was played out in the spring of 1945.

DISSOLUTION

Three weeks after his return from Berlin came the news of Frederik Prytz's death. Quisling's oldest and closest friend died at his Oslo home on 19 February 1945. From the autumn it had been clear that his illness had become terminal. After his last contribution in the government, when he succeeded in rallying the ministers behind Quisling's demand that Hitler end the occupation, he asked to be relieved, and handed his ministry over to his financial adviser. Quisling decided to award him the St Olav Cross before it was too late; this was the first and only time that he used this prerogative and he went in person to Prytz's sickroom to award him the medal. The two of them finally discussed the subject which had cast a shadow over their friendship for five years: Prytz's desertion in April 1940, a matter which bothered Prytz more than it did Quisling. When Quisling left, it was with the realisation that they would never meet again.[2]

With Prytz gone, there was only one remaining member of the original circle of five, described in the NS party records as 'the founders of the movement', and that was Quisling himself. Of the others, Hjort was interned by the Gestapo in Germany, Adolf Munthe was being held in a prisoner-of-war camp in Germany and Ragnar Hvoslef had died in the autumn of 1944. Of former prominent members of the inner circle, Dr Mehle and Dr Aall had both left the party at the end of 1944. Aall's resignation meant that the so-called Aall Commission, an investigatory body instituted in 1943 to collect information on the background to April 1940, and in particular on Great Britain's supposed role in it, had to proceed without its expert in international law.[3]

But a more serious threat than the falling away of the old guard was that of liquidation and assassination which had intensified during the final phase of the war. Information suggested that the government in exile had drawn up a hit-list consisting of members of the party leadership. This, coupled with acts of sabotage, intimidated the movement's inner circle.[4]

Quisling tried to stop the sabotage by convening a group of prominent men from industry and insurance at the palace on 3 February, where he reprimanded them and gave strict instructions that these activities had to stop, or else the Germans would take extreme measures, and 'those present and other good citizens would be shot'. His threats, however, sounded more like a plea.[5]

Liquidations were even harder to pre-empt. Those which were carried out by the German police, called *Blumenpflücken* ('flower picking') were not, of course, reported in the press, while the killings of the other side were. A considerable number of the 100–200 liquidations carried out by the resistance movement and in the first instance directed against personnel employed by the German and Norwegian police took place that winter and spring. When even the head of the Hird and chief of the state and security police, Karl Marthinsen, was shot on his way to work, no one could feel safe. There was a strong reaction to Marthinsen's assassination. Thirty-four

[2] *FF* 3 November 1944; reporting of Prytz's funeral 24 February 1945 in *FF* 26 February 1945.
[3] The remaining minutes of the Aall Commission in RA UKA archives.
[4] Quisling's statement to the High Court, *Straffesak* p. 134.
[5] Ole Kristian Grimnes, *Hjemmefrontens ledelse* (1977) pp. 446ff; also *Straffesak* p. 134.

imprisoned resistance members were sentenced to death, thirteen of them by a Norwegian special court and the remainder by the German military court. Quisling refused to pardon the thirteen, none of whom were hostages in the ordinary sense but charged or sentenced for various resistance activities. It thus seemed that Terboven really had been forbidden by Hitler to carry out any large-scale execution of hostages in Norway. Reprisals consisting of the execution of innocent civilians such as had taken place in Trøndelag in 1942 or Mjøndal in 1943 were not used any more towards the end of the war.

Security at Gimle was tightened. As early as the autumn of 1944 an extra guards division was formed, and a cell group of absolutely reliable party members (the majority erstwhile front-line fighters) was entrusted with the personal safety of the Fører. A speed-boat was procured and placed in readiness at the bridge at the bottom of the park so that the Minister President could escape across water if necessary. He himself preferred to continue to work on the routine matters of the administration and to develop the party's long-term plans. As late as 18 April 1945 he set up a commission to handle new tax reforms.[6]

However, it was clear that the resistance movement (now universally called the Home Front) was working up to a showdown. Radio messages from London were more and more detailed and sabotage was increasing. On 17 April Bishop Berggrav escaped from house arrest in Asker. However, Norway's position as Germany's strongest fortress in Europe remained uncontested, and nothing suggested that Hitler was about to concede this advantage without a fight. Quisling found himself busy with the planning of how to avoid a bloody battle between the 365,000 German troops and the Allied liberation forces which were expected to arrive in Norway at any moment. The armed groups of the NS could not be wound up in the face of the expected Allied offensive. If foreign forces were to fight on Norwegian soil, there would actually be an urgent need for a Norwegian force, at least for police purposes. In short, it was necessary to mobilise all available resources and at the same time to manoeuvre in such a way that in the end Quisling, not the Germans, would be in control of them, so as to avoid bloodshed. Until then the NS forces would also bolster his own position against the Home Front.

By 20 February the mobilisation plans for the Hird were ready. The Hird, which was now referred to as the 'nation's armed force', was to be mobilised through a strict process of conscription of all male party members aged

---

[6] Draft press announcement from Ministry of Finance 5 May 1945, RA FMK 41.

between eighteen and fifty-five. Draft refusals and desertions diminished the number to some 2,000 men. The Norwegian SS soldiers constituted a force of 1,800 men at the front and an equal number of discharged soldiers back in Norway – élite groups of exceptionally experienced soldiers according to Norwegian standards. However, Himmler and his staff were most reluctant to let go of their volunteers. Quisling's request for their return to Norway, although supported by both Terboven and Rediess, was turned down.[7] Relations with the SS thus became very strained, and things did not improve when rumours started to circulate that Himmler's organisation was out to liquidate Fuglesang because of the 'unfortunate' influence he had on the Fører. Quisling and his General Secretary had for some time been moving away from the 'Germanic' line. Himmler and Berger were also dissatisfied with Jonas Lie, and were trying to get him replaced as leader of the Norway SS. For one reason or another they seemed to think Riisnæs more suitable for the job, despite the fact that the Justice Minister at that point was showing signs of depression and mental instability, a condition which, astonishingly, they failed to register.[8]

Only at the end of April, after Himmler's organisation had been discredited by the Reichsführer's betrayal of Hitler through his unilateral negotiations with the Red Cross and Folke Bernadotte on the repatriation of concentration camp prisoners from Germany, was Quisling able to ignore the opposition from the SS. What Berger and Himmler said was no longer of any importance. On 30 April the Minister President sent out the order for mobilisation, 'in accordance with paragraph 109 of the Constitution', to all discharged front-line soldiers for military service 'in order to aid the Norwegian state authorities by upholding law and order in the country'. The men were organised into a separate battalion.[9]

By that time his relationship with the Reichskommissar had deteriorated into open hostility. Terboven wanted to fight in Norway down to the last cartridge, while Quisling wanted to avoid combat as long as possible and use the forces politically. On 20 April, when Quisling sent greetings to Terboven on the occasion of the fifth anniversary of the Reichskommissariat, the time had come to show magnanimity. The Norwegian Fører thanked him for the

[7] Report on interrogation of Bereichsleiter Heinrich Schnurbusch, IfZ Prisoner-of-war interrogations (Norway)/65.
[8] Ringdal, *Gal mann*, ch. 'Bøddelen'. Rediess to Himmler 18 and 30 December 1944, Himmler to Rediess 1 January 1945, BA NS 19/2135. Liquidation of Fuglesang: related by Fuglesang, 1987.
[9] Order of 30 April 1945, sent to district *førers* 1 May 1945, RA FMK 12.

friendship and understanding he had shown during their collaboration, which had also developed 'on a personal level', and expressed his hope that they would be able to overcome the difficulties which lay before them. On the same evening, however, he expressed his real feeling to Dr Werner Best, recently arrived in Norway to consult with him and Terboven on the question of the impending crisis: it was no longer viable for him and the Reichskommissar to work on a joint policy, he stated. Best, Quisling and Dr Koch from the Reichskommissariat sat at Gimle and discussed the situation. It was Hitler's birthday, usually the high point of the National Socialist calendar, a day celebrated with a German gathering at the Coliseum cinema at which the Reichskommissar officially promised the Führer that Fortress Norway would be held to the very end, something Quisling was not prepared to commit himself to.[10]

In the week which followed Best's return to Denmark, there was feverish activity at the palace to secure the return of Norwegian prisoners from Germany. The party's liaison officers in Berlin and Hamburg had been trying for years to monitor which Norwegians had been placed in what camps and prisons, information which the German security police was loath to disclose. It was Fuglesang who led the initiative, which also included the sending of food parcels and vitamins to the camps.[11] Quisling had raised the issue with Hitler in January and was assured that the matter would be looked into. After that he heard nothing. During the spring it became known that Count Folke Bernadotte had been negotiating directly with Himmler on the joint release of all Scandinavians. On 19 April the Count was given permission to take across the Danish border all Scandinavian prisoners who were gathered in Neuengamme. Now that the Germans were no longer able to put up further resistance, it was time for the government to follow up the matter. A delegation with the authority to protect Norwegian citizens under evacuation travelled to Germany. Three days later, the delegation was authorised to negotiate a loan with the National Bank of Denmark for 10 million kroner to pay for the transport. The prospects for this semi-diplomatic mission were, however, short-lived. The delegation had not managed to raise any of the money from the Danish bank before they were arrested by the Danish police in their hotel room.[12]

---

[10] *Straffesak* p. 231. Telegram to Terboven: Quisling to Terboven 21 April 1945, RA FMK 12. Best, in Matlock, *Danmark*, pp. 298f.

[11] Related by Fuglesang in an interview with Anders Buraas 1972, NRK fa.

[12] *Politiken* 22 May 1945: 'Quisling-Minister arrestert paa Angleterre'. RA Statsrådssekretariat, NS-administrasjonen 2.

With Hitler's suicide on the night of 1 May 1945, both German and Norwegian NS morale finally collapsed. Unconditional loyalty to the Führer, informed by a wholly irrational belief in his capabilities, was what had kept National Socialism together even as an international movement. Now defeat seemed inevitable.

For Quisling it came as something of a relief. At least he was now at liberty to speak his mind. Even as late as 22 April he was still constrained to take the official, optimistic line and talk of 'victory in the long run', out of consideration for morale in his own ranks.[13] Now he could work through this final phase from a realistic basis, both publicly and privately. Privately, he had long accepted the inevitability of defeat. On Sunday 29 April, he had convened a meeting of his ministers at the palace to discuss the new situation emerging from the irreparable schism between Hitler and Himmler, following Himmler's behind-the-back offer of capitulation to the Allies. Now anything could happen. The meeting produced a document declaring Norway's neutrality and forbidding the use of Norway as a theatre of war. The ministers made their positions available so that Quisling could 'call in people from other camps' to facilitate the necessary transition of power, and at the same time gave him a vote of confidence to remain in office. Through this action Quisling wanted to stress that the country had entered an interregnum. His own government was on the way out and was opening the door to a new administration which would be formed through the offer of a partial substitution, although it was not yet clear who was going to participate in this new government.[14]

This of course was sheer *naïveté*. To believe that either the Nygaardsvold government or the resistance leadership would come anywhere near the palace to negotiate a transfer of power with him was completely unrealistic; on the contrary, the government in exile had long since declared that it considered the Quisling government liable for arrest and sentencing. However, the war was not officially over, and the German build-up of strength, together with his own control of the state machinery, might possibly be put to use by forcing his enemies to compromise. As he still nursed some slight hope that the war would be concluded through a

---

[13] Speech at Jessheim, *FF* 23 April 1945.
[14] Government announcement 29 April 1945 (document in private archives*), and Quisling's statement in *Straffesak* pp. 231f.

settlement negotiated by the German and Allied High Commands, instead of the terrible unconditional surrender, he chose to gamble on a transfer settlement in one form or the other.

But his proposal for a peaceful transition had a difficult birth. He would have liked to announce it on the NRK that very evening, but was advised to consult Terboven first in order to avoid misunderstandings. Terboven was firmly against the idea, and went out to Gimle to try to dissuade Quisling from making any public announcements. In the course of a long conversation, Terboven made it clear to Quisling that his proposal gave the impression that he was turning away from the common cause or, worse, of thrusting a dagger in the Führer's side. This line of argument had the desired effect, and Quisling reluctantly agreed that instead of making the announcement as originally planned, he would broadcast a speech outlining the government's position in more general terms.

But the speech (his last) was postponed for six agonising and frustrating days, as the preparations were broken off by news of Hitler's death, announced on the evening of 1 May. Terboven and Franz Böhme, the new Commander-in-Chief in Norway, were immediately summoned to Flensburg, the new headquarters, to meet with the new Chancellor and Commander-in-Chief, Admiral Dönitz. The occasion was postponed from 2 to 3 May, and the Reichskommissar and the Admiral returned to Norway late on 4 May. Quisling contacted Terboven on 5 May.[15] The Reichskommissar was reluctant to reveal the dour realities of the situation, that he had in fact secured no approval for his plans to hold on to Festung Norwegen, and that things were moving towards a hand-over of power in Norway too. Quisling nevertheless must have had some inkling of the situation, if from nothing else than the fact that Germany had capitulated quietly in both Denmark and Holland the previous day. Moreover, the diplomatic courier he had sent to Himmler on 18 April, the young Jan Sundberg, had returned the same day, 4 May, with a lively account of the collapse of Germany and Denmark after a hazardous journey from Berlin to Oslo.[16]

At last, on the evening of Saturday 5 May, Quisling was able to make his radio speech. That weekend the district leaders and the party leadership assembled at the palace. Fuglesang stressed the necessity of maintaining law

---

[15] Quisling's version in *Straffesak* p. 232.

[16] Sundberg's mission and eventful journey from Oslo to Berlin and back again is recounted in C. Christensen, *Den andre siden* (1988) pp. 15ff.

and order to avert civil war, anarchy and chaos, and the need for the party to 'stand firmly and resolutely behind Vidkun Quisling'. The atmosphere was calm in the expectation of a quiet capitulation, which was the favoured solution although people like Jonas Lie and Sverre Riisnæs seemed to prefer armed defence, even if Germany did capitulate. 'We do not want civil war,' Lie said at the official opening of an SS exhibition on that very Saturday afternoon. 'But if others are set on it, if others start one and want one, they will find us prepared.' A time was set for the Fører himself to come to the microphone to clarify the situation.[17]

His sombre broadcast was put out over the network of loudspeakers which the party propaganda department had rigged up all over Oslo and half a dozen other cities in Norway. There was a lot of traffic that Saturday afternoon and an atmosphere bursting with anticipation. 'The streets were suddenly full of people who were listening, standing there and listening to a voice which nobody could mistake for anyone but a very moved Minister President urging solidarity, national solidarity at this critical time,' recalled a passer-by. 'It was one of those remarkable experiences of the importance of the moment, following the final, dramatic winter of the war in the area, of shootings in the streets, sabotage and raids.'[18]

Quisling opened with a tribute to Hitler, who according to the official German version had died 'a hero's death' in his commando position in Berlin. But his tribute sounded somewhat ambiguous. On the one hand Hitler had 'through his life's great achievement' rescued Europe from Bolshevism, but on the other hand his failure to secure the co-operation of Britain, which alone could guarantee world peace and counteract Bolshevism, had to be considered 'the great tragedy of his life'. As a result, almost three-fifths of Europe was under Moscow's domination, he reminded his listeners.

He himself had experienced Bolshevism in Russia, and ever since his return to Norway fifteen years earlier he had dedicated himself to saving the country from war and from communism. At the end of the 1930s he had tried to prevent war by seeking a reconciliation between Britain and Germany. When that failed, there was no option but to lead the country into closer alliance with Germany, as it would have been impossible for Norway to defend herself in such a war. He had formed his government on 9 April in

[17] P. Hansson and J. O. Jensen, *Den farlige våren* (1983) p. 139; *FF* 5 May 1945.

[18] B. H. Johnsrud in a letter to the author 19 April 1985. See also Dahl, *Dette er London*, p. 340.

order that Norway avoid the fate of Poland and be divided in a struggle between Germany and Russia; for this reason a peaceful German occupation had had to be accepted.

And now to the forthcoming change-over of power: as his own government was a legitimate one, it could not be removed by illegal means without plunging the country into chaos. What he considered to be 'legal' in this context was suggested by his declaration that he was not prepared to 'deliver the country up to lawlessness and Bolshevism', thereby ruling out the Communist faction of the Home Front, while he was fully prepared to negotiate with others in the movement. Abundant quotations from the speech of the father of the Constitution C. M. Falsen at Eidsvoll on 17 May 1814 reminded the listeners that the situation now was similar to that of the end of the Napoleonic wars.[19]

Now he had shown his hand. He was willing to back down, but the process had to be legal. That evening, however, he heard nothing from either the government in exile or the Home Front. Thus the Fører meeting continued on Sunday. The ministers reported their activities as usual. After the police report from Lie, there was discussion of a possible co-operation between the Home Front units and the Hird, and of what marks of rank such a force would eventually carry. It was clear that Lie was determined to fight.[20]

As the meeting was drawing to a close, a man in an SS general's uniform checked into the Hotel KNA in Oslo. It was Brigadenführer Leon Degrelle, the former leader of the Rex movement in Belgium, who had earned considerable renown for his leadership of the Walloon division of the Waffen-SS. Degrelle had just completed active service in northern Germany and, following defeat, had arrived in Oslo via Copenhagen with his adjutant to continue the struggle in Norway. He arrived in a peaceful capital bathed in spring sunshine with people strolling through the city streets. He immediately made contact with Terboven and Rediess out at Skaugum to investigate the possibility of an initiative at least in the north of Norway. The following day he was to meet his Norwegian colleague for the first and only time.[21]

During the night Jonas Lie was taken ill, suffering from a fever that he had

---

[19] Speech printed in FF 7 May 1945 (the last edition of the newspaper to appear), UBO Krigstrykksamlingen.

[20] Speech at the Fører meeting 6 April 1945 at the palace, INO.

[21] Egil Ulateig and Tom B. Jensen, interview with Degrelle in Vi Menn 1990/20, which in turn is based on Degrelle's notes.

contracted while on service in the Balkans. Quisling immediately appointed Major General Erling Søvik in his place and gave orders that he was to consult him directly on all important issues. Shortly thereafter Søvik received the order to instruct the police not to offer armed resistance except in self-defence, not even against 'troops wearing the armbands of the Home Front'. With that, the police force was, to all intents and purposes, instructed to let itself be arrested by Home Front forces.[22]

Quisling drove out to Skaugum on 7 May to confer with Terboven. With Degrelle, who returned to Skaugum the day after his first visit, he discussed the possibility of getting a seat on Terboven's plane which was ready at Fornebu after his trip to Flensburg. The Reichskommissar himself did not want to go, but was willing that others should. In the end only Degrelle and his adjutant boarded the plane and took off to Spain at around midnight.[23]

Back at the palace, Quisling was hard at work. Selmer Alm from the Social Ministry had visited him two days earlier and reported that contact had been sought with some representatives from the Stockholm legation, who could be used to liaise with the government in exile in London. Quisling doubted the value of contacting the Nygaardsvold government in this way, and considered that *they* should rather approach *him*, as he had declared himself willing to negotiate. His position was not so hopeless that he needed to throw himself headlong into any kind of project. He still had time, as Terboven had promised to brief him as soon as he had news from Flensburg.[24]

Suddenly one of the adjutants burst into the room, reporting rumours of a German surrender. Quisling and Fuglesang immediately turned on the radio to hear the declaration of surrender read out on the NRK at 3.50 p.m. Fuglesang noticed that Quisling, who had been otherwise calm that day, was 'profoundly affected' by the news. He had been assured that he would be informed beforehand of any such turn of events. Moreover, his own position was now impossible, as any prospect of a peace settlement had evaporated. After a brief consultation it was hurriedly decided that they should go ahead and send a delegation to the border nevertheless to try to make contact with the people from the legation, even though the deadline could not be met.

---

[22] RA LD 3721 Erling Søvik; Quisling to the Police Department 7 May 1945, RA FMK 32. Lie's illness: Rødder, 'Min ære', p. 204.

[23] Degrelle in *Vi Menn* 1990/20. In Christensen, *Den andre siden*, p. 21, Jan Sundberg states that the offer of escape was made to Quisling by Terboven and Degrelle together at the palace. Quisling expressly contradicts this in *Straffesak* p. 327.

[24] Alm's account in E. Werner Svendsen, *Konsentrasjonsleiren Ilebu* (1950) pp. 109ff.

Fuglesang and two other ministers invested with the necessary authority were sent off with Alm, leaving for the border at about 5 o'clock. They agonised over what they were to say if they were stopped by the Germans.[25]

Meanwhile, Quisling instructed all party members to stand guard, but at the same time to try to make contact with 'all good Norwegians' and otherwise behave in an exemplary manner. The appeal was read out on the NRK at about 6 o'clock. Four hours later followed General Böhme's order of the day and speech to the German soldiers informing them that they too were about to surrender.[26]

There are two versions of what happened in the forest near Eda on the Swedish border that evening – the only occasion ever when anything resembling a negotiation between the Quisling government in Oslo and the government in exile in London took place. When Alm announced that a delegation from Oslo was on its way, the two representatives of the legation withdrew and telephoned their office in Stockholm, which gave firm instructions that the NS delegation should be sent away, whereupon the two returned to Stockholm, according to their own account.

According to Alm, when the ministers arrived at the meeting place the deadline had passed and the representatives of the other side had gone back to Stockholm. The local police chief, with the help of his colleague on the Swedish side, managed to get hold of them and the representatives were indeed stopped and brought back to the meeting place, only to report that Germany had capitulated, thus obviating the need for further discussion. With that, the ministers turned round and returned to Oslo.

'It was a somewhat peculiar journey,' Fuglesang recalled later. 'Everywhere we could see people celebrating ... There were Norwegian flags everywhere ... and I cannot pretend that even those of us who were sitting in the car driving into Oslo, despite the gravity of the situation facing us, did not feel a certain sense of release that the whole thing was over.' At approximately the same time Quisling went for a drive around in the suburbs of Oslo to observe the festivities. 'For me this was a moment of the greatest relief and release.'

---

[25] Main sources of the mission are Alm's report in ibid. and Fuglesang in an interview with Per Bøhn 1982, NRK ho, and Arnvid Vasbotten, 'Referat av hva jeg opplevde 7.–9. mai 1945', dated 12 September 1951, INO; Per Jahr's account in Jensen, *De nære årene*, p. 143; Oddvar Aas, *Norske pennekneter i eksil* (1980) pp. 194f. There are several discrepancies between these accounts.

[26] Appeal to all members of NS 7 May 1945, RA FMK 32, report transmitted in the NRK log, NRK ho.

Finally, at 1 o'clock in the afternoon on 8 May, Dr Bjørn Foss, sent by the Home Front military wing Milorg's local district command, presented himself at Gimle to negotiate with Quisling. Quisling could of course entertain only the slightest hope from these talks. With Germany's defeat and the Wehrmacht's capitulation, and his own forces preparing to give themselves up, there was not a great deal left to bargain with. There would certainly be no discussion of any NS influence in the country's new government.

Yet the talks did have a particular significance, if not on a personal then on a symbolic level, on how he was to be arrested. He preferred internment in the grand style, a *custodia honesta* worthy of his position as the most high-ranking prisoner of war on the defeated side. Thereafter, the investigating committee could reach whatever conclusion it pleased.

He had come home late from his drive the night before. There was no word yet from the delegation he had sent to the Swedish border, only the noise of joyful celebrations in the city floating through the air all the way out to Bygdøy that night. Early the following morning he sent his adjutant out in a car to bring his ministers to Gimle. By the late morning most of them had arrived, including Fuglesang, Skancke, Lippestad and Stang, but there were some conspicuous absences. One of his ministers had left town, another had turned himself in to the police (the new police, at the headquarters at Møllergaten 19). Police Minister Lie, on sick leave, and his SS colleague Minister of Justice Sverre Riisnæs, had fled the day before to a police base in Bærum where they holed themselves up under the protection of the tiny section of the police which was determined to keep fighting.

During the early afternoon, after events on the border had been discussed among the ministers at Gimle, the Home Front representative was announced. The meeting had originally been scheduled for the morning but Quisling requested a postponement until all his ministers had arrived. At 1 o'clock Foss drove up.[27]

Bjørn Foss was unknown to the ministers, as they were to him. He was an ophthalmologist, head of hygiene for Milorg's district 13, the Oslo area, and had been selected to negotiate with Quisling because in his capacity as a health officer in the civilian airforce he had had several dealings with NS

---

[27] Bjørn Foss, 'Møte med Quisling 8 May 1945' (undated), report based on notes made 'immediately afterwards', copy in INO.

people, and had shown that he knew how to handle them. However, he had never acted as a diplomat before, and felt somewhat apprehensive about the task. And indeed, when he was shown into the meeting room on the lower floor and introduced himself to Quisling, Fuglesang and Lippestad, a heavy silence descended. Foss, who was under the impression that Quisling had sent for him, sat and waited for someone to speak. Quisling, who regarded Foss as a representative of the Home Front who had asked to see him, waited for him to begin. The atmosphere was extremely awkward: four men had met in order to negotiate, yet nobody said a word; only the sounds of celebrations in the city penetrated the silence.

Eventually Foss found the situation so painful that he took the initiative and communicated the Home Front's position on Quisling: internment in a building decided by the Home Front and guarded by men from Milorg. Quisling asked to be interned at Gimle, or eventually at the country house at Eagle's Nest in Asker. Foss refused. Quisling then asked whether the offer included his ministers. Foss said that it did not. Quisling replied that, in that case, he did not want any preferential treatment over his friends who had stood by him loyally through the most difficult years of his life. At this point he was visibly moved and declared in an emotional voice: 'I know that the Norwegian people have sentenced me to death, and that the easiest course for me would be to take my own life. But I want to let history reach its own verdict. Believe me, in ten years' time I will have become another St Olav.' He followed with a long defence, which according to Foss lasted well over an hour, outlining the dangers represented by Russia, sketching the constellations of the great powers and relating the problems he himself had encountered in his collaboration with Germany.

When he finished, Foss asked if he wanted to keep fighting. 'You have indeed seized victory prematurely,' Quisling replied. 'Capitulation in Norway has not even been signed. I have 30,000 men in Oslo at my disposal, while you have only 4,000. But I do not want to turn my Norway into a battlefield.' He wanted to surrender with good grace, and gave his assurance that he had refused to send reinforcements to Jonas Lie at Bærum. He wanted to do everything possible to ensure that there would be no armed resistance from his people.

After a short account of the atmosphere in Oslo, Foss was careful to say that the forthcoming settlement with the NS would not degenerate into any kind of mob violence. None of the ministers or any other member of the NS was to be sentenced without trial or without presenting his own defence before the court. This news came as a great relief to all of them, and with that the negotiations came to an end. Quisling repeated that while he would do all he could to prevent fighting, he was not prepared to abandon his friends. He thus rejected Milorg's offer, but said he had no objection to the Home Front guarding Gimle. However, he rejected the idea that his Fører Guard should be removed first, and made it clear that he favoured a joint force to take on the task in shifts. He added that he and his colleagues would 'report to the authorities' as soon as they had official notice that the new legal authorities had taken over the ministries. Foss informed him that this would happen in the course of the day, at which Quisling gave him a friendly smile and told him that it would thus not be long before he 'reported himself'. Quite what he meant by this is not clear. Possibly Foss misunderstood him; it is highly improbable that he would both turn down Milorg's proposal and at the same time volunteer to give himself up.

At all events, he accompanied Foss to his car. He was reassured by the promises of a fair trial, and happy that his actions would be publicly examined, even though he harboured no illusions about the outcome. History, he felt, would rule in his favour. After Foss had given him his telephone number and told him that he could ring whenever he wished to contact the Home Front leadership, he returned to police headquarters.

When they were briefed on the contents of the meeting, the other ministers were much encouraged. Dr Foss had certainly been amenable and understanding, giving the impression that their wish to be interned would be respected, and that they could now wait safely for his return, if not later the same day, at least by 11 o'clock the following morning. 'After that we felt calm and almost optimistic,' one of the ministers related. 'We talked quietly among ourselves and strolled in the garden on that beautiful spring day.' An NS man from the neighbourhood telephoned and asked whether a flag should not also be hoisted over Gimle as this was 'a happy day for us all'. Quisling was enthusiastic at first, but later decided that it would be bad taste for him to raise the flag in celebration of Germany's defeat.[28]

Strangely enough, none of them thought to turn on the radio. The NRK did not broadcast anything that day, but London and Motala were certainly on air. The most important announcement, that the German surrender in Norway would come into effect from midnight, would have the most serious consequences for all those present, as from that point forward all members of the NS would theoretically be hunted down by the new authorities.

---

[28] Speech made by Quisling at table on the evening of 8 May 1945, INO; story related by Bjørn Østring, 1989; Vasbotten, 'Referat av hva jeg opplevde'.

However, the party leader remained in ignorance of this for the time being. Instead, they concentrated on the fact that a division of the Ski Battalion, bent on resistance, had appeared at Gimle to replace the Fører Guard, who had disappeared first one by one and then in whole groups. The Battalion raised the cry that they would 'fight down to the last cartridge'. But Quisling issued the order to lay down arms and go home. He similarly declined an offer of protection from a German division in the nearby Frogner Park. Neither he nor his ministers wanted to resist what, upon capitulation, were to be the country's legal authorities, with whom they were still in negotiation.[29]

Their only remaining cause for concern was the possibility that illegal forces, namely the Communists, who were still thought to be receiving instructions from Moscow, should interfere with the transfer of power. Even if the Allies took control, some Soviet representation had to be reckoned with, perhaps even taking over a certain degree of police authority around the country. The party had already taken pre-emptive measures on that score. On Sunday 6 May, the party office and the Chancellery had received instructions to burn all sensitive documents, correspondence with party officials, party lists, membership lists as well as other parts of its archives. Late that evening smoke was seen billowing out of the main chimneys of the palace and of Rådhusgata 17.[30]

At Gimle nothing was burnt. On the contrary, Quisling used the time to pack some of his most important papers. His library was full of papers, as was his small private study on the second floor. On one shelf lay his Universism manuscript; his personal papers, including his father's and grandfather's notes, were stored in drawers and cupboards. Quisling never threw anything away, including personal letters and cards from the young Arne and Esther after he had left home in 1905. All the letters he had sent to his brothers and parents from abroad between 1918 and 1929 had been left in a chest at Jonsborg. His political papers, manuscripts, notes, literary endeavours, private correspondence from his time as cabinet minister were all kept in the library at Gimle. In a safe in the dressing room on the second floor he had filed the documents pertaining to his dealings with Germany from 1940 onwards, all marked 'Confidential'. The most important of these

---

[29] Related by Kåre Hansen, 1991. The Ski Battalion left Gimle for Skallum, but was sent back to its quarters in Bygdøy later in the day to demit.

[30] Fuglesang to Bøhn, 1982, NRK ho; statement of head of personnel in the general secretariat Erik Arveschoug 20 July 1945 in RA LD 1099 Fuglesang.

were now gathered up and packed into suitcases and bags and made ready for transport to the place of his internment.[31]

At about 8 o'clock Maria served dinner. Quisling made a short speech: 'What the last twenty-four hours have brought us is something I have been fearing for a long time,' he said. 'But I never believed that the defeat would be so absolute and complete.' The day was 'despite everything a day of liberation': the occupation was over and the country had won its independence, and all the efforts of the NS had not been in vain: supplies had been secured, German demands and requisitions had been resisted, and the administration was safely back in Norwegian hands. The hard times facing the NS would be a necessary sacrifice he had to face with equanimity, because it had all been in the country's best interests. 'Each NS man can now withdraw from this struggle with a clear conscience.' He expressed one final hope that everyone around the table might emerge from the situation in the best possible way.

Meanwhile, Dr Foss seemed to have vanished into thin air. All attempts to reach him by telephone came to nothing. The Home Front's silence was beginning to cause concern. Several of the ministers considered that the matter should be settled by the 11 o'clock deadline. Lippestad, the Social Minister, with his many contacts in industry, suggested approaching the director of the Federation of Employers whom he knew personally, and who might be able to help make an unofficial contact. The director duly set up a meeting at Møllergaten with the chief of the Home Front's newly installed head of police Lars L'Abbée-Lund and a delegation from Gimle. Lippestad was guaranteed safe conduct and escort through the city streets.

This meeting at the police headquarters signalled a change in the Gimle group's official status, as they had gone from negotiating with Milorg and the country's armed forces to submitting themselves to the civil police authorities, albeit without realising this important distinction. Soon, however, the change was to manifest itself.

---

[31] Maria Quisling, handwritten 'Erklæring 8 May 1945', INO; various statements in UBO MS fol. 3920 X, 3. The main bulks of Quisling's archives have been organised as follows: (1) UBO MS fol. 3920 – papers (mainly from Gimle) which were in Maria Quisling's keeping from the lifting of their confiscation in 1952 until her death in 1980, when they were donated to the Oslo University library; (2) UBO MS fol. 4096 – papers confiscated in 1945, some at Gimle, others at the palace, transferred to the Oslo University library in 1986; (3) RA LD 29 Quisling, various documents confiscated as evidence in the trial: (a) documents submitted during the trial (b) documents not submitted during the trial; (4) RA PAQ, documents of various provenance confiscated in 1945 which were not used during the trial; these were in UBO until 1970, when they were transferred to RA.

Lippestad drove off from Gimle at about 11 o'clock in the evening. The police escort was waiting halfway. As they were approaching the police station, a group of intoxicated German sailors opened fire in the vicinity, but Lippestad's car escaped unscathed.

Once inside the police station, Lippestad met with L'Abbée-Lund, who denied all knowledge of a Dr Foss, or of any negotiations with Quisling. But he was not completely opposed to the idea of internment. However, he was anxious that the new supreme chief of Oslo police installed by the Home Front, Heinrich Meyer, should be present. When Meyer arrived, Lippestad reiterated that in view of all the services which Quisling had rendered the country over the past five years – which he duly rehearsed – he was not prepared to climb down without an honourable departure, and in any event would refuse to be imprisoned like a common criminal.

While he was explaining all this, they were joined by the new State Attorney Sven Arntzen, who was there in his additional capacity as national chief of police. Lippestad went over his main points once again, stressing that there was no point in trying to treat Quisling like a common criminal. Arntzen broke in: 'Why not?' he asked gruffly. 'He *is* a criminal.' Lippestad gave a start: 'But you cannot say that! What crimes has he committed?' Arntzen replied, 'Murder, among other things.' Lippestad protested and demanded that Arntzen name even one murder that Quisling was responsible for. The answer came without delay – Eilifsen's.

Lippestad was then informed that there was no question of any negotiations taking place with Quisling or any of his ministers, and that they were all to report at the police station at once, and if they failed to do so they would be arrested and brought in. Bloodshed would only be avoided if they gave themselves up. Following their arrests, they would be held in custody, and be given equal treatment with other prisoners. The 'clear, cold path of justice' was to be taken. Arntzen refused even to shake hands with Lippestad as he left.[32]

Lippestad drove back to Gimle in shock. His colleagues were equally stunned. It seemed that their trust in Foss had been completely misplaced, and they wondered whether they had been duped. In the confused atmosphere it was not easy to see that they had been the victims of a power struggle between Milorg and the police, and between the military and civil authorities of the new Norway. Remarkably, it was the civil authorities

[32] Kåre Norum, RA D 29 Q, unsubmitted document 2; C. Erlandsen, reference to memorandum by H. C. Erlandsen, *Aftenposten* 7 May 1988.

which had proved the harsher opponent. Arntzen, said Lippestad, had burst in on his otherwise calm meeting with L'Abbée-Lund and Meyer 'like a madman' and had issued a stern ultimatum, accusing them of having Eilifsen's blood on their hands. Quisling objected that 'Eilifsen was found guilty in a court of law'. One of his ministers quietly remarked that since he had been sentenced retroactively, they would have to be prepared for the eventuality that the other side would perhaps consider the Eilifsen case to be murder.

While the others retired to get a little sleep, Lippestad and Quisling sat up talking, taking and making telephone calls. After a while the others were woken up. The situation was deteriorating rapidly. Quite a lot of people approached Quisling and Stang at Gimle by telephone that night, trying to persuade them to turn themselves in. The director of the Federation of Employers continued to act as unofficial middleman. The deadline for reporting at the police station was first said to be 3 o'clock, then 6 o'clock and then 6.30. This final deadline was issued by Arntzen himself. They tried to reach Chief Justice Paal Berg and the leadership of the Home Front, and once more contact Sven Arntzen to remind him of Foss's promises. They even considered telegraphing Crown Prince Olav, to say that they were putting themselves under his protection. A call was made to the police station to enquire whether the telegram could be sent from there. They were informed that it could not. The women at Gimle were active too, with Maria and Prytz's daughters constantly at the receiver. They wondered whether Prytz's cousin, Pastor Johan Prytz, might ask Bishop Berggrav to ensure Quisling's safe passage through the crowds. All this went back to the police station. Calls went back and forth through the night repeatedly, escalating into a network of appeals, threats and warnings, gradually closing in on Quisling.[33]

Eventually, at 5.45 in the morning, he placed a direct call to Arntzen. The conversation was extremely hostile as Arntzen denied having ordered any kind of communication with Gimle during the night, and categorically refused to recognise that there had been any negotiations or to listen to Quisling's protestations. Quisling for his part tried to remind Arntzen of the discussions with Foss, insisting that it was disgraceful that they were planning to arrest him; he complained about Arntzen's rude denials, but in the end had to hang up having achieved nothing.

---

[33] Norum, in RAD 29 Q, Fuglesang to Bøhn 1982, Vasbotten, 'Referat av hva jeg opplevde'; see also A. Kvaal, diary entry 11 May 1945, RA LD 29 Q, unsubmitted documents 2.

At this point Maria entered the room and overwhelmed by grief threw herself weeping into her husband's arms. Quisling gently asked her whether they should seek refuge in death together. She said nothing, and after a short while Quisling went downstairs to join his ministers.[34]

The die was cast; they had decided to turn themselves in. Provisions were packed and the ministers emptied their pockets on to a table in the hall of money, weapons and personal effects. Quisling's luggage was ready, and Maria appeared at the last moment with a scarf for her husband to keep him warm in prison.

At 6.15 the cortège set off with Quisling alone in the first car followed by the ministers and the others in a further four cars. It was a quiet grey morning. The streets were deserted after the previous day's celebrations. In the big square between the public library and police headquarters in Møllergaten the escort waited for them. With Milorg forces armed with sten guns on the running board, the motorcade drove the last few metres to the police station. At 6.22 on the morning of 9 May 1945 Quisling's car reached the main entrance.

PRISON AND INTERROGATION

The imprisonment followed normal procedure. The guards on duty took the prisoners in, gave them a routine examination, did the usual paperwork and checked their identity. Warrants for arrest were drawn up and signed by L'Abbée-Lund. Quisling was led to the medical officer and submitted to a body search, protesting vociferously. Afterwards, he registered an official complaint that as he had given himself up, he had expected better treatment. Chief of Police Arntzen watched everything covertly, concealed in the telephone booth in the interrogation room.

Quisling was then led to his cell. From this point forward he would never be alone again, guarded day and night to prevent suicide attempts. The food, a diet composed almost entirely of salted herrings and mostly rotten potatoes, had to be eaten with a spoon; he was not trusted with either a knife or a fork. The light in his cell was never turned off. He was allowed to read no newspapers.

After some ten weeks in police custody, he was transferred to Akershus Castle, where he was held in a cell at the top of the old prison tower. The round-the-clock watch continued through the open door of his cell, and the

[34] Vasbotten, Fuglesang, 'Raferat av hva jeg opplevde'.

same routine for meals and visits to the toilet was observed, and the same incessant light, which he was only allowed to dim a little at night by placing an old newspaper around the bulb.[35]

This way of life soon started to take its toll on his health: he lost weight rapidly and was struck by the deficiency disease polyneuritis, a neurological disease resulting in partial lameness in the feet. As soon as he had got used to it all, however, he started working hard and regularly on his case, looking forward to the daily walks in the yard as a welcome change. He never complained, and behaved in several respects as a model prisoner. He was very cordial with his guards, and even gave them small gifts now and then. The nurse responsible for health and hygiene in the prison found him exceptionally calm and peaceful, and thought he was a truly good person. He also made a good impression on the psychiatrist Jon Leikvam who, in his capacity as prison doctor, had several long conversations with him. In Leikvam's view he was certainly an exceptional character, with a peculiar mixture of deep inhibitions and a high opinion of himself. In contrast to his brother Jørgen (Leikvam gained the impression that there was something about him that was more than just peculiar), Leikvam was unable to detect signs of any pathological disorder in Quisling. On the contrary: 'If Quisling is to be considered insane, I don't hold out much hope for the rest of us,' he would say when asked for his diagnosis.[36]

Reluctant to take on full responsibility when the prosecution wanted to know whether they had to reckon with a judicial assessment in order to ascertain whether Quisling was criminally responsible, Leikvam brought in another experienced psychiatrist, Johan Lofthus, for a second opinion. The matter was a serious one. If a full assessment were initiated, there was a risk that conclusions would be drawn which would have far-reaching consequences for the case. However, the two doctors signed a declaration stating that assessment would not be necessary as they found no indication of mental disorder of a kind relevant to the law's concept of diminished responsibility.[37]

Immediately after Quisling's arrest, rumours spread in police circles that he was an alcoholic. These rumours had been going around during the war too, and were obviously reflected in the police record of the morning of 9

---

[35] *Straffesak* pp. 244f.

[36] Leikvam to *VG* 13 September 1945; to *Arbeiderbladet* 5 November 1969; also letter to the author, 1986; *Straffesak* pp. 441f. Interview with guard Tiedemann Olsen, *Fredrikstad Blad* 2 June 1990. Personal communications to the author.

[37] All legal documents printed in *Straffesak*.

May when it stated that 'Quisling's face is ravaged and ugly. It seemed fat and clammy, red and bloated.' Young investigators remarked that he smelled of alcohol, and that the stench from the cell was overwhelming.[38] When he met the press in connection with his main charges, *Aftenposten* reported that 'traces of drink and carousing' had been wiped away from his face by the routine of prison life. However, Leikvam and other doctors who actually examined him found no grounds for these rumours; on the contrary, it was established beyond doubt that all such rumours were false. Quisling's tendency towards regularity and moderation, as well as a very strong constitution, helped him to adjust remarkably well to this new ascetic life.[39]

Within three weeks the question of extended custody came up. He was to appear before a preliminary hearing, and the question of his defence had to be sorted out. He had never had a lawyer, having always acted for himself whenever he had been involved in any court cases, for example the one against the art dealer Warberg at the end of the 1930s. But this time he was to be assigned a publicly appointed defence lawyer of his own choosing – his choice, however, was limited by the fact that all the lawyers he knew were NS members and now under prosecution.

It was Leikvam who recommended Henrik Bergh, a barrister with an impressive track record. Bergh was eight years Quisling's senior, a liberal-minded conservative who remembered well what an odious opponent the NS had been in the 1930s – his own secretary had once belonged to the party. Even if he had had some understanding of why young people could have fallen under Quisling's spell then, things were very different now after five years of occupation and NS government. Bergh felt no sympathy whatsoever for either the man or his cause, and, moreover, trying to take on Quisling's defence in 1945 was a hopeless task. Initially he turned down the request, not wishing to pass into the records as 'the man who defended Quisling'. However the pressure put on him to take on the case mounted until Arntzen as good as ordered him to do it.[40]

The first meetings between him and his client turned out to be fairly productive. Quisling immediately trusted Bergh, who, in turn, appreciated Quisling's clarity over the details in his case, and the fact that he was

---

[38] T. Bratteli and H. B. Myhre, *Quislings siste dager* (1992) p. 65 and *passim*.

[39] *Aftenposten* 21 August 1945. Statements by Jens Evensen and Hans B. Myhre to the author 1988. Norum, RA LD 29 Q, unsubmitted document.

[40] Private correspondence made available by Olof Rydbeck.* RA PANS 23 and 27, file: Frogner 1933–5.

determined to fight. Whether or not it would be intelligent for him to throw himself behind Quisling's line of argument was something he had to consider carefully since the defendant and the court were divided by an unbridgeable gulf. Quite possibly any energetic line of defence would only serve to harm his cause. Bergh soon came to the conclusion that he had to take a more careful approach, basing the defence on Quisling's motives and idealism rather than on his version of events; not that this was any more attractive a task, as public opinion in the summer of 1945 was thirsty for blood and revenge to a degree which was felt incompatible with a mature lawyer's concept of justice. Even among prominent criminologists the NS movement was regarded as a 'vicious conspiracy of the country's most spiritually depraved' individuals, as Professor Langfeldt, who later also characterised Knut Hamsun as a man deprived of normal mental abilities, said. In the light of this hostility it would certainly be a thankless task to argue Quisling's good faith and noble intentions. Nonetheless, from the numerous interviews he had with his defendant, Bergh was convinced that the man genuinely did believe in his mission, and that he quite seriously felt himself called to deliver Norway from the terrible crisis he had seen approaching in the early 1930s.

On 26 May Quisling was brought before the pre-trial court to be remanded in custody for a further three months. Bergh was officially nominated as his defence lawyer at the same time. During the proceedings, attended by the press, Quisling heard the formal list of charges brought against him for the first time. First, the coup and the withdrawal of the mobilisation order on 9 April 1940, which were considered to be in contravention of both the military and the civilian penal codes regarding treason during wartime, and illegal attempts to bring the country under foreign domination. This was followed by charges concerning his activities as NS Fører and Minister President, which were said to involve assisting the enemy during wartime, inasmuch as he had encouraged Norwegian citizens into bearing arms for Germany and thus had put them and Norwegian material resources at the disposal of German forces. His governmental decrees, both at the time of the coup and in conjunction with the Act of State of 1942 were also said to constitute an attempt to change the Constitution by illegal means, which was in contravention of the civilian penal code which expressly forbade revolution in Norway. The final charge was that of the premeditated murder of Eilifsen, through his passing of the notorious law of 14 August 1943 and his refusal of clemency.

In his reply to the pre-trial court he was given the opportunity to present the main points of his defence. Rather than contesting the facts, he wanted to clarify that his intentions and motives had been misrepresented in the charges. He had not delivered Norway into enemy hands, as he had been as unaware of the German invasion of April 1940 as anyone else. He conceded that he had made contact with Germany prior to 9 April and even told the court that he had met with Hitler in December 1939, a fact which was now revealed to the world for the first time. He did not try to hide the truth, insisting that nothing illegal had taken place during this meeting. When forming his government on 9 April, his purpose had been to replace the one which had fled; by calling off mobilisation, he had acted in the best interests of the Norwegian people, and moreover in line with the people's wish that the country should remain neutral and not be turned into a theatre of war of the great powers. He had thus not sought to bring Norway under foreign control; on the contrary, he had tried to keep foreign powers out of the country, and once Germany had moved in, he did all that was in his power to secure Norwegian independence and freedom. Furthermore, he had never had the opportunity to raise troops for the Germans as the charges claimed. What he had done was to encourage Norwegian citizens to volunteer for German military service, and nothing else. Beyond what had been demanded by the Germans he had done nothing to hand over Norwegian resources; rather, he had worked hard to limit such demands. He also denied having taken part in any illegal revolutionary activities. His government of 9 April was an emergency measure, and he claimed to have no recollection of the press conference of 12 April cited by the prosecution when he had proclaimed a change towards a corporate constitution. He requested permission to address the subject of the Act of State at a later stage. On the matter of the Eilifsen case, he insisted that the law provided for the avoidance of court martial, in a situation in which the Germans were threatening military dictatorship and the execution of not only Eilifsen but a great many others. Finally, he wanted to point out that these few remarks he was permitted to make could not in any sense cast sufficient light on the charges levelled against him, and added that he therefore intended to present a complete account in writing of the points in the charges.[41]

Back in his cell he set to work on this account. He had only his memory to rely on as he had been denied access to his own archives, which were now in the possession of the police. His lawyer furnished him with as much

---

[41] The record of the pre-trial court proceedings in RA LD 29 Q Div. 7.

information as he could, and in the course of four weeks he had completed sixty full pages giving a point-by-point rebuttal of the charges.

While he was working on the text, he was interrogated by the investigators in the case. The assistant chief of police in Hamar, Simon Østmo, was asked by Arntzen to head the inquiry. The case against Quisling, which the prosecution was anxious to conclude as quickly as possible as the beginning of the fully-fledged legal purge of all NS members, was given high priority and conducted at breakneck pace. From the start, the intention had been to set the deadline for the preliminary hearing at three months in order to avoid another order of commitment. Østmo was appointed police inspector and was authorised to select colleagues of his choice, and set up his headquarters in an empty office next to the city hall. He received assistance in the task of interrogation and examining the considerable documentation from experienced police officers, who like himself had been summoned to Oslo after the liberation. In the first instance they went through the documents confiscated from Gimle, both before and after Maria was forced to leave the house on 14 May. In addition, a plethora of archive material, and the interrogation reports of implicated German officials such as Rosenberg, Ribbentrop, Göring, Keitel and Jodl, were examined through the comprehensive and willing co-operation of the office for the Allied trials for war criminals in Nuremberg. Two young civil servants were mainly responsible for this contact, visiting Germany twice in July to collect documents for the prosecution under the assistance of no less than Milorg supreme chief Jens Christian Hauge.[42] Quisling, when asked if there was anybody else in particular he wanted to be questioned to help his case, said there was no one.

From the points he was questioned on in the long series of interviews with Østmo and his colleagues, he gained some insight into how the prosecution was intending to build its case. Moreover, from his frequent conversations with Bergh it gradually became clear to him what the state prosecutor, Annæus Schjødt, wanted. He had met Schjødt once, in Moscow in 1926 when they were both representatives of Prytz's Russian-Norwegian timber company.

While he was adding the finishing touches to his own written account, he was one day taken by the police to Trandum, where a large inspection of the recently uncovered mass graves used for German executions had been arranged. The bodies of Norwegian patriots in varying states of decomposi-

---

[42] Jens C. Hauge in *Arbeiderbladet* 22 August 1945.

tion were on display. That the prosecution was to place some of the responsibility for this on his shoulders was something which Quisling had suspected from the interrogations, in which Østmo and his people had shown a great deal of interest in the petitions for clemency he had dealt with in the last year of the occupation.

His written statement was ready on Friday 21 June and copied out at Bergh's office. Basing his arguments on points of constitutional law, Quisling first of all tried to demonstrate that the reinstated authorities, 'the restoration' as he called them, did not have the right to stand in judgement over the NS, or to declare the organisation illegal and to bring its members to trial. The government in exile, he argued, had forfeited its rights after six months' absence from the country, and certainly after the Storting had rescinded its authority in the summer of 1940. Both the commissarial ministers and the National Government had therefore acted as the legitimate Norwegian authorities during the occupation. There was no state of war in Norway after the armistice of 10 June 1940; on the contrary, there was a *de facto* peace with Germany. The government in exile's declared war was its own concern and was not binding on the Norwegian state. Thus the NS activities 'have been legal in every respect'. Only German policy and 'the obstacles it put in our path ... prevented us from gaining the full support of the people'. He urged that the present actions against the party come to an end, and declared bombastically that he, for his part, would demand redress and compensation for the wrong and the injury he had suffered since his arrest in May.

He went into the Berlin visit in December 1939 in great detail, but without mentioning either Grand Admiral Raeder or his discussions with Rosenberg and his people. Hagelin did not feature in his account at all. Instead, he focused on his discussion with Hitler, which he argued was purely a discussion of world politics, even though the issue of the government in Norway was briefly treated. His main line of argument was now that throughout the occupation his aim had been to secure Norwegian independence from Germany. He was fully aware that many people would hold him responsible for German actions during the occupation and even seek to punish the NS for everything the Germans had done in Norway. But to do so, he argued, would be misguided, for although he had been compelled to emphasise the two countries' common interests 'for tactical reasons', the truth was that German control and surveillance of both party and state had been an 'intolerable regency'.

Arguments along these lines committed him, logically, to emphasise his achievements, such as they were. At no point would he concede that his attempt to secure independence from Germany had been futile, or even of limited value. Consequently he was constrained to play down his disagreements with Hitler, and conceal the defeat he had sustained at the hands of Germany, so bitterly and so often lamented during the war. To his judges as well as to his fellow Norwegians the self-acclaimed success story of his achievements with Germany sounded completely contrary to the real situation.

Equally misleading was the line of argument that he had never attempted to change the Constitution. He now stated that the Minister President's government was a temporary one intended only for the duration of the war, and that it should be replaced by 'the election of a new Storting' as soon as circumstances permitted. In fact he had expressly denounced the Storting as a constitutional body ever since his election defeat in 1936, and both he and his party had consistently championed the Riksting as the constitutional body of the future. By this line of argument he simply did not stand by the revolution which he had tried to lead, claiming instead that it was the others, the 'restoration' people who were the revolutionaries.

Through his statement, then, Quisling had established both the tone and the line of his defence, above all in his assertion that *others* had been responsible for bringing Norway into the war, that *others* had been trying to bring the country under foreign control and thus were guilty of treason. The struggle for independence, the real 'Home Front' had been led by *him*. The tenor of his statement was that of a wounded man, complaining bitterly at those who were now sitting in judgement over him, a man whose actions had been exclusively determined by his concern for his country.

Such underlying mental constructions would force him time and again during his trial to tread a fine line between truth and falsehood, falling short of presenting a rational account of what had really taken place. He, who for his adherents had represented objectivity, light and morality, appeared to the court as a cowardly perpetrator of half-truths, a defendant who, in presenting his pathetic self-defence, emerged an elusive and often pitiful figure.

INDICTMENT

Immediately after he had completed his written account, his case took a new turn. The investigators started taking interest in issues beyond the specific charges that had been brought up so far, by looking into his German connections prior to 9 April. In an interrogation on 2 July he was confronted with a draft letter to Hitler dated 10 June 1940, in which he insisted that he himself should assume power in Norway once more, on the basis of the December talks of the previous year. He explained to Østmo that the letter was not his own text. It had been put together by Rosenberg's Chancellery head, Schickedanz, on the basis of talks which had taken place during his visit to Norway in June 1940. The investigators continued to question the nature of the Berlin talks, including whether Quisling had received any financial support. The prosecution had now obtained access to Rosenberg's archives in Berlin, and to naval documents in which many secrets had lain buried. At about the same time the first statements from witnesses on the German side were suggesting that the December talks with Hitler had focused on much more than general conversations about world politics.

The fact that the list of charges against him was dramatically extended became painfully evident on 11 July, when Schjødt's indictment was completed. The new document, which was to be the basis of the case against him at the High Court (Eidsivating lagmannsrett) in August was indeed a terrible blow to Quisling's defence. The charges were expanded in the light of a whole list of individual cases of treason and revolution from April 1940 onwards. And he was facing the charge not only of Eilifsen's murder but also of Viggo Hansteen's in 1941, which he was accused of having encouraged the Germans to accomplish, and of fourteen others' who were executed by the same law as Eilifsen as reprisals for Marthinsen's death. There was also a long list of charges of theft, embezzlement, and even receiving stolen goods now being presented by the prosecution, which referred to detailed accounts of his use of furniture from the royal palace and other places, which the prosecution stated had been brought to Gimle or to Fyresdal illegally, and of his government's disposal of funds from a number of confiscated fortunes and requisitioned properties, as well as the appanage he received as Minister President and the gifts his own cabinet members had presented to him, including the Moland parsonage. The prosecution made no secret that it was out to defame Quisling with these accusations of economic malfeasance, and to demonstrate that he was a villain in small things as in great, and thus thwart any attempts to create a martyr of him. But damaging though these accusations were, they paled in comparison with the new charge that he had been conspiring with Hitler over the occupation of Norway prior to 9 April.

The indictment had to be answered, and Quisling was determined to produce a rebuttal of all charges, which he did in a new, bulky document with sixty fresh pages of 'remarks on the new indictment of 11 July 1945'.

The new document did not prove to be significantly more concrete than the previous one. With no access to his own files, and no documents at hand, he had to rely on memory alone and concentrate on his line of argument, rather than on specifics. Thus the same ambivalence as before came to characterise his basic reasoning, particularly regarding his claims about the National Government after the Act of State in 1942: his had been a legal and sovereign government, ruling the country with positive success; it had nevertheless had to bow to German demands on all points now listed as charges against him.

He also felt compelled to correct a number of factual errors in the grounds presented by the prosecution before the main trial. During his peace initiative with Chamberlain and Hitler in 1939 he had presented his idea of a Greater Nordic or Greater Germanic Union: an association of Germany, England, Scandinavia, Holland and other Germanic and Nordic states. The prosecution had mixed this up with the later, partly SS-inspired concept of a 'Greater Germany', which implied something quite different from a union of free states on both sides of the North Sea.

Under the charge of murder, he was accused of contributing to Viggo Hansteen's execution in the autumn of 1941. The prosecution had based the charge on a memorandum sent to Terboven a week after the execution, in which he said that he had 'often noted the dangerous activities of the now dead lawyer Hansteen'. But how this proved that he was complicit in the man's death was a mystery to him.

He was also charged with the premeditated murder of 'several hundred Jews', having supposedly urged the German security police to organise the immediate deportation of the Jews to Poland, although he knew that many of them would face certain death there. The prosecution seemed to build their version of events on the testimony of an employee in the Gestapo, Wilhelm Wagner, head of the Jewish and Ideological Office in Viktoria Terrasse, who claimed that the action had been put into motion after Quisling's initiatives with the Reichssicherheitshauptamt in Berlin. Quisling maintained that this was a completely distorted version of the facts, as he had not been aware of any impending action against the Jews in advance, and had not been notified of the deportations before the *Donau* had set sail. As for the conditions experienced by the Jews in Poland in general, he said that during his visit to the front in spring 1942 he had seen 'various Jewish colonies and work stations' which by no means invited disturbing comparisons with what he had seen in peacetime.

In addition, he rebutted the charge in the strongest possible terms that he had made use of pay, entertainment expenses, palace furniture and effects and the requisitioning of personal fortunes with a view to personal enrichment. All this had been the consequence of his position as temporary head of state, he argued.

TRIAL

On Monday 20 August 1945 the case finally came to trial.[43] As usual, Quisling rose early. From Maria, who had moved in with Prytz's widow that summer, he received his fine dark grey suit and some clean shirts and ties for the three weeks in court ahead. Noticing that his clothes hung a little loose, he nevertheless dressed carefully, and at around 9 o'clock was fetched by a group of guards who accompanied him on the short distance from the tower to the old Masonic Lodge just outside Akershus.

The great hall of the Lodge had staged many important moments in his career, particularly at party meetings in the 1930s. It was here that he had proclaimed the party manifesto on 6 February 1934, and had made the Ibsenesque pledge that 'Norway is a kingdom, it shall become a nation'. It was also here that he had made speeches on security policy and the Jewish question, and had agitated against the Storting after the presidency had refused to consider the NS's proposed amendments to the Constitution.

But the hall was barely recognisable. Instead of the usual raised speaker's dais, a platform had been erected along the back wall, where nine high-backed chairs had been set out behind the central table. On each side was an exclosure, the left for Bergh, his assistant and the defendant, with the right side reserved for the prosecution. Under the judges' platform was the table at which the clerks were seated.

Across the hall was the barrier which separated off the public and the press. Bergh had told him that there were several representatives of the largest papers and press agencies in the world present. Behind them sat members of the public. He also spotted many of the case investigators, besides friends and colleagues from the 1920s and 1930s.

Maria was not there. She had wanted to be present but the court had ruled that she should not be admitted into the courtroom. She begged Bergh to put in a word for her, and give assurances that she would simply sit there quietly at the back of the court incognito and would be brave, would not

---

[43] Description based on contemporary newspaper reports, and the verbatim report in *Straffesak*.

faint, or even react audibly. All she wanted was to follow the proceedings so that she would be in a position to point out any inaccuracies concerning her husband to the defence afterwards. She felt that if everything which the papers were writing about Vidkun's alcoholism, his malice and his debauched existence were to be taken up by the prosecution or by the witnesses, she should be given the chance to correct it through Bergh. Throughout the summer she had done her utmost to collect material for his defence by talking to the wives of his ministers and other women in the movement, most of whose husbands were in prison, by writing numerous letters to Bergh and visiting him at his office. Quisling had been denied visiting rights, so she was unable to see him, and now Bergh was telling her that she would not even be able to attend the trial.[44]

As soon as Quisling was led into court, the murmur of voices increased in pitch before the room fell into a heavy silence which did not break until he sat down, whereupon a swarm of press photographers rushed to the barrier, flashlights exploding incessantly at Quisling's serious, emaciated face. The more persistent photographers had to be driven back by security guards.

The court rose on the announcement of the arrival of the jurors, whereupon the five laymen and four professional judges paraded into the courtroom. It was customary for such a panel to consist of only seven members, but in this case it was decided that nine should serve, in case of illness.

The presiding judge, a former member of the Supreme Court, Erik Solem, took his seat in the middle of the panel and declared the court in session. With that the trial began. After the standard formalities, the indictment was read out. The nine charges with innumerable examples, the many references to laws and citations of the relevant paragraphs from the civilian criminal code's rulings on treason, murder and theft, as well as the military penal code's rulings on wartime treason, took over half an hour, after which the accused was called upon to give his full name. He rose, now standing before his main judge Solem face to face for the first time.

Bergh had strenuously protested against Solem's appointment as president of the court. Immediately after the liberation Solem had published three newspaper articles in which he discussed the new special law which was to serve as the basis for the indictments in the general purge against the NS. As

---

[44] See Maria's many letters to Henrik Bergh July–August 1945, in the Bergh archives* and UBO MS fol. 3920 IX, 3, some of which are printed in summary in Juritzen, *Privatmennesket Quisling*, ch. 'Vidkun Quislings siste dager'.

the articles contained a great deal of strong language against Quisling, Bergh found it inappropriate that the author should pass sentence on him. But the Supreme Court overruled the objection, insisting that Solem had not said anything about Quisling that 'any Norwegian' would not have said.[45]

Nevertheless, Solem's bias did manifest itself during the first day in court. On several occasions he interrupted Quisling in quite an aggressive manner, making sarcastic comments and behaving generally in such a hostile way that he overstepped the mark of what was appropriate. He did moderate his language a little after counsel from his colleagues, but the impression of the biased president held sway for many days in the court.[46]

After Quisling had pleaded not guilty to all charges, Prosecutor Schjødt began his introductory statement. He spoke for nearly three hours, presenting a catalogue of offences which in both breadth and depth sent shockwaves through those present in the courtroom. It was much worse than any of the press representatives there had imagined: Schjødt described how Quisling had conspired with Hitler and Rosenberg prior to 9 April, and explained, step by step, how a comprehensive plan for a coup in Oslo had been worked out to help German troops take over the country. He could give details of how the NS had been in receipt of substantial sums of money for putting these plans into action. Hagelin and Scheidt's role was revealed in detail. Quisling had given military information, both to staff officers in Berlin and to a German colonel in Copenhagen at the beginning of April, a fact which had been corroborated by Keitel and Jodl in Nuremberg a few days earlier. There was an overwhelming supply of evidence which had just come to light in Nuremberg and in the archives of Rosenberg's office, which proved that Quisling's role in the preparations for the assault on Norway had been more central than anyone had hitherto imagined. The prosecution laid particular emphasis on a comprehensive memorandum from Rosenberg's office entitled 'The Political Preparations for the Norwegian Action', from June 1940, which also provided a basis for the indictment, in addition to other documents which had just come to light.

A long description of other circumstances showed how he had also been guilty of treason during wartime from 9 April on, according to the military penal code, in addition to treason as defined by the civilian criminal code. That Quisling himself claimed he had acted in the best interests of the country in a desperate situation was rejected out of hand by the prosecution:

---

[45] Erik Solem, 'Rettsoppgjøret', *VG* 27, 28 and 30 June 1945.
[46] *Straffesak* pp. 8–25; Johs. Andenæs, 'Rettssaken mot Quisling', *Lov og Rett* 1988/5.

the coup and the formation of his government had not been forced by circumstances but were simply the final step in the execution of a carefully considered plan, motivated by the same personal ambitions as had always, right from the 1920s, underpinned his political activities with the 'desire for power ... characterised by a cynical opportunism and disregard for his country and the ideas, interests, feelings and suffering of others'.

Schjødt went on to give the court a lengthy account of Quisling's activities as legislator during the occupation – first as a politically responsible behind-the-scenes man for the commissarial government and then as Minister President from 1942. Oppression, censorship, dictatorship, ruthless implementing of the *fører* principle – 'pure Nazism after the German model' – was what he had aspired to throughout. As for Quisling's many attempts to obtain independence from Germany, Schjødt said that he could furnish the court with incontrovertible evidence that Germany had never considered giving Norway anything which resembled independence or freedom, even once the war was over, and that Quisling had always been well aware of this fact: 'Quisling clearly never wished for such freedom, because he knew that he would cease to have any power in this country the minute German domination came to an end.' All his efforts in this direction were in fact designed to bring Norway into a Germanic or European federation which under German leadership would have common foreign and security policies, establish a common market and a currency union, reciprocal rights of communication, residence and work, something which would in practice turn Norway into a 'German colony', as Schjødt put it, arguing that the only reason Quisling tried to make peace with Germany was to facilitate the conscription of Norwegians to fight for Germany. 'All the time he was in power ... Quisling's actions display a continuous, consistent and extensive act of treason', his sole purpose having been to 'secure the government in Norway for himself' with the help of a constitution based on the *fører* principle.

Finally, the prosecution presented the grounds for the charges of theft, embezzlement, and the use of stolen property in bad faith so that the Norwegian public could see what sort of man had been governing them for the previous five years. And if Quisling were to insist that his actions had been motivated by his concern for society, the prosecution would simply say that his attitude to other people could best be defined by the way he had treated the families of people he had prosecuted, the families of political prisoners and fugitives and Jews, 'and perhaps, even worse, the families of even more murdered Norwegians'.

With this parting shot, Schjødt finished his introductory remarks and sat down. It was 1.45 in the afternoon. In the tangible silence which followed, Quisling rose to submit himself to the questioning of the presiding judge, and to make a statement.

He began rather hesitantly, saying that it was a difficult and complex case and he would prefer to present a general view of things as background to all the particulars. However, the president interrupted him, assuring him that he would be 'given the opportunity to give an account of Norwegian history at a later stage'; but now the court wanted to hear about his connection with Rosenberg. A somewhat incoherent exchange between Quisling and Solem on the subject of his relationships with Rosenberg, Hitler and Hagelin ensued, until Solem suddenly changed the subject by asking Quisling whether he had met any Germans on his trip to Copenhagen in early April 1940. Quisling cannot have been entirely surprised by this question. Schjødt had mentioned the testimony from Keitel and Jodl. Even so, he chose to deny it. Solem persisted, and Quisling resorted to tactics of evasion, claiming not to have any recollection of the meeting, and if there had been one, the alleged German must have appeared incognito. Asked whether he would have remembered if a German major, albeit incognito, had demanded information pertaining to the state of the Norwegian forces, he replied that he would have remembered if he had been questioned in detail, but claimed not to have any general recollections of that nature.

The exchange made a very poor impression. Although he was blessed with a formidable memory, he was trying to extract himself from a difficult situation. The consequences for his defence were disastrous, as the exchange destroyed the credibility of his testimony in general. However, his prevarication and stuttering that day could be attributed also to the aggressive style of examination which was apparently designed to humiliate him.

He did not make a significantly better impression when he denied all knowledge of German financial support of the NS, explaining that he had never had anything to do with the party's finances. A leader who repeatedly answered 'I do not know' when questioned about his party's basic outgoings could scarcely inspire much confidence, irrespective of the situation.

Why did Quisling lie about the meeting in Copenhagen? If he had told the truth, that he had initially refused and only later agreed to meet Colonel Piekenbrock under pressure from Hagelin, and that he was careful not to say anything of significance, things would have gone better for him, as it turned out. But as he saw it on the first day of the trial, such an admission would have broken his chosen line of defence, namely that his contact with Berlin and Hitler exclusively concerned his peace mission, and, moreover, that Hagelin had played no part in it whatsoever.

However, he was unable to persuade the court of this. Solem then focused on the overwhelming documentary evidence, which was read out alternately by the prosecutor and the presiding judge, without the accused or his counsel having any prior knowledge of its contents. Solem started with Rosenberg's memorandum on the political preparations for the Norwegian action, and followed this up with several notes of Scheidt's from the spring of 1940, finishing with Rosenberg's diary from December 1939 to April 1940, which had recently come to light during the war crimes trials at Nuremberg. These papers bore ample witness to wide-ranging plans for a coup, a secret network, espionage, information and secret contacts between Oslo and Berlin, and described in uncomfortable detail Scheidt's conspiratorial adolescent style, Hagelin's characteristic rashness, and Schickedanz's far-reaching ideological interpretations. When the presiding judge finally announced that the court would resume the following morning, it was almost a relief. But Quisling turned to Bergh and said, 'It went rather well today.' Bergh was astounded. During the summer he had had several intimate conversations with his client, in which Quisling had shared his memories of his youth, spoken freely of his personal life, and discussed many mutual acquaintances. Bergh had thus got to know him quite well. However, that Quisling should be so completely absorbed in his own universe that he was able to assess the day's proceedings in a positive light came as a shock to him. Bergh felt compelled to tell him that he did not consider the documentary evidence from Germany to be propitious at all.[47]

INTO THE CROSSFIRE

When Bergh and Quisling arrived in court the following morning, they found that the prosecution had presented a new, thick dossier of copied documents. Much of the morning was taken up in the reading of still more evidence from Raeder, Scheidt and Rosenberg, as well as the copious records of Colonel Amen's examination of Rosenberg in Nuremberg on 14 August. Scheidt's notes proved, moreover, that the secret subsidies to the NS had run to as much as 200,000 Reichsmark.

Quisling was cross-examined on all this, and squirmed. He denied all knowledge of the money, as well as the contents of the conversation with

---

[47] Private correspondence made available by Olof Rydbeck.*

Raeder, maintaining that this was the first he knew of any minutes having been kept from the meeting. He denied having offered naval bases to Germany in 1939, or that he had ever planned a coup or any large-scale action in Norway: 'These statements which are constantly ascribed to me must have arisen from either some misunderstanding or from the wrongful use of my name.'

There was some truth in this claim. The conversations which he personally had been party to had in fact been conducted in fast-flowing German by Hagelin, and were thus difficult for him to follow. The promise of naval bases, for instance, was something which Hagelin almost certainly had said on his own account, without Quisling either having understood or seeing any reason to correct him; besides, it was not always easy to correct Hagelin when he was speaking. During the spring of 1940 Quisling's most energetic collaborators had taken on the responsibility for planning, based on the understanding that he himself should not be involved. He was therefore unable to explain where exactly his own involvement ended and where Hagelin and Scheidt's began. 'I have never been party to any plans for a surprise action in Oslo,' he asserted confidently. He told the court how, during the December talks in Berlin, he had highlighted the danger of an Allied invasion of Norway to both Raeder and Hitler, explaining that if Britain and France did move in on Norway 'it is possible that we [the NS] will not tolerate it'. Whatever he asserted now, such utterances implied an admission that he *had* conspired with Germany over a possible invasion of Norway, and over a potential coup, even if the details were left to his collaborators Hagelin and Scheidt.

When the fateful 9 April was mentioned, he agreed that he had indeed seized power, but not as the fulfilment of any kind of plan or of the December talks, but simply because 'the government was away'. 'Away?' queried Solem, adding that '[e]ven those not in the business of forming governments were fully aware of the fact the Storting was meeting at both Hamar and Elverum'. Quisling insisted that he was unaware of this, as he had not listened to the radio that day.

Thus his version of the events between December 1939 and April 1940 sounded unconvincing. With constant interruptions from both the judge and the prosecution, it was difficult to come through with a coherent account of his own motives. The same went for later events. His motives for presenting proposals to Hitler for peace with Germany and a European federation were distorted. Solem and Schjødt completely rejected the possibility that Norway would have been granted anything resembling self-determination in a Europe dominated by Germany. In the crossfire he did not succeed in presenting his most convincing argument, namely that leading Germans such as Ribbentrop and Goebbels had in fact agreed to this, and that Goebbels himself had even expressed the possibility of democratic constitutions in the Europe of the future. If indeed Quisling had been mistaken in his assessment, he was not alone. However, to the court he appeared to be nothing more than a solitary ingénu. Nor did the court believe that his administration had benefited the country in even the slightest respect during the war. All his actions, all the motives behind them, were in fact compromised from the start by his negotiations with Germany and his treason of April 1940.

He fared somewhat better on the question of police maltreatment and torture of prisoners. He was quite convincing when he stated that he had not been informed of more than two or three incidences of torture, however strange that might seem in retrospect, and that he had taken action. At least one state police constable had been sentenced for police violence at the time. However, his case was much weaker when it came to the teachers and the Church action of 1942. As for the state police action against Berggrav, he tried to play down his own involvement, and made the astonishing claim that it had been the Germans who had arrested the Bishop, when it had in fact been the state police, the Minister of Justice and above all himself. He was also unlucky in his defence against the charge brought against him concerning the Jews. In the crossfire from Schjødt and Solem he was barely able to make the point that the legislation concerning the requisition of Jewish property had been pushed through in order to pre-empt German confiscations.

Altogether he made a poor impression under cross-examination. His standard reply was 'No, not in that sense'. Solem asked him on several occasions if he might not do the court the courtesy of providing a direct answer. Quite often it was as though he was making excuses, his semi-rehearsed answers sounding like half-truths, his frequent hesitations the prelude to a lie. However, apart from his account of what had taken place in Copenhagen, it was only in his statements concerning Berggrav that he directly misled the court.

TESTIMONIES

After three and a half days it was time for the witnesses to be called. The order in which the prosecution had arranged for their witnesses was designed for dramatic effect. First of all the court heard the testimony of an employee at the Reichskommissariat who spoke of Terboven's policies in Norway. Then the Labour leaders Jacob Friis and Martin Tranmæl were called to recount how Quisling had approached them in the mid-1920s offering to spy on the General Staff and to organise Red Guards, to prove the prosecution's point that Quisling had been an unpredictable opportunist as early as the 1920s. Next several of Quisling's fellow officers gave evidence about the mobilisation of 1940 and Quisling's part in it. But the really sensational testimony came from Dr Leo Eitinger, a 33-year-old Jewish psychiatrist who had come to Norway from Czechoslovakia in 1939, and was later debarred during the occupation. Eitinger was arrested together with a number of other Jews in May 1942 and sent to Poland in February 1943 as part of the second wave of deportations. He told the court in detail how on arrival at Auschwitz the prisoners were sorted into two groups: those who were fit for work, who were sent to forced labour; the others went to the gas chambers. He also explained how the gassing of women, children and the infirm was carried out. Earlier that summer he had given the press his account of the horrors which had befallen the estimated 11–12 million murdered Jews and others, explaining that he considered Quisling responsible for the particularly harsh fate met by Norwegian Jews. In court his account made a profound impression, even on the defendant, an impression reinforced by the testimony of a young Jew, Ariel Hirsch from Trondheim. A Danish reporter noted that at last a human reaction was discernible on Quisling's face. The reporter of *Verdens Gang*, the Home Front paper, however, gave a somewhat different account: the accused 'sits the whole time looking at the witness with a look full of stupid hatred mixed with indescribable terror'.[48]

The following day, Wagner from the Gestapo entered the witness box and testified that in the summer of 1942 they had received instructions from Berlin that 'the Jewish problem in Norway should ... be solved in accordance with the wishes of the Norwegian government'. Wagner admitted that he had not actually seen the order himself, but had heard it read out.[49]

Then Hagelin was called. Solem's cross-examination turned into a bizarre performance, in which the former Minister of the Interior simulated amnesia. He claimed to have absolutely no recollection of the events of

---

[48] *Straffesak* pp. 146–59. (Alphabetical list of witnesses with page references, ibid. p. 647.) *Dagbladet* 24 May 1945, *Nordlys* 25 May 1945, *Politiken* 24 August 1945, *VG* 24 August 1945.

[49] *Straffesak* pp. 203f.

1939–40, but did not manage to sustain this performance entirely consistently. With his numerous peculiar and often barbed replies, his supposed blackout acquired a decidedly comic gloss. Solem, for his part, gave in to cheerful malice on the subject of the coup. Were any general conclusion to be drawn from the extraordinary impression Hagelin's testimony made, it would be that the preparations, just like the execution of this hazardous action, bore the marks of almost operatic irresponsibility.

Of the potential German witnesses, there were many who could have shed considerable light on events, including Raeder, who was being held prisoner of war in Moscow; Terboven and his two police chiefs had all committed suicide that May. There were other Germans who could similarly have given invaluable evidence, such as Schreiber, Boehm, Wegener and Neumann, but the prosecution had scarcely investigated the case sufficiently to have a clear picture of what part they had actually played in events. Scheidt, however, was considered a key witness, but as early as April he had gone into hiding somewhere in Germany and his Norwegian wife in Flensburg had no idea of his whereabouts. Nor were the Allies successful in their hunt for him. Thus, the combination of Scheidt's absence and Hagelin's amnesia meant that there were significant gaps in the story of how the government of 9 April with all its implications for Quisling's future, actually came into existence. The gaps were filled by a general assumption that he had carefully planned and staged the coup in accordance with Hitler's wishes. A short testimony by Fuglesang modified the prosecution's claim that the whole thing had been prepared in detail within the party organisation; in fact, after Fuglesang's testimony the prosecution was more moderate in its descriptions of events. But this was a minor victory only, and of little significance in the end.[50]

Saturday's proceedings ended with the defence's examination of its six own witnesses. Following a week of heavy court procedure, this brought Quisling a much welcomed change of scene. Bergh had wanted an additional seventh witness, namely Maria Quisling. Maria had indeed been campaigning for her husband through the summer, and was keen to testify. She certainly had a lot to tell, both about Quisling's time in Russia in the 1920s and of his deep sense of responsibility in the war years, which was so taxing that he had scarcely had a single happy day. He had taken the Eilifsen case in particular very hard. On two separate occasions he had told her that he wanted to step down in protest over the Reichskommissar, but on both occasions he had come to the conclusion that the country needed him after

---

[50] Ibid. pp. 188f; see also p. 9.

all, and he was not prepared to have a German military dictatorship on his conscience. She was anxious to relate all this to the court. Her husband, however, would not allow it. He felt that it would be too much of a strain on her to take the witness box with him right next to it, and to defend him before a hostile court. Instead Maria wrote a letter to Bergh in which she set out everything she would have said. He advised her on which parts of her account she should stress, in case he wanted to use her in his plea.[51]

The one witness who really stood up for him was no less than General Otto Ruge, the hero of the campaign of 1940. With objectivity and authority Ruge outlined his impression of Quisling from the three different periods he had been involved with him: as a cadet in the General Staff prior to the First World War, as General Staff officer in the 1920s, and finally as Minister of Defence 1931–3. In the last case, Ruge had been secretary to the parliamentary committee which dealt with the revision of the organisation of the army, the single most important case from Quisling's ministerial term.[52]

Ruge's testimony caused a sensation, perhaps not so much because of what he said as the fact that he was testifying at all. To defend Quisling in the summer of 1945 implied serious consequences for someone holding an official position. Bergh, for example, received several threatening letters and was more than once spat at in the street.[53] This was all part of the extreme anti-Nazi sentiment; the passion for revenge ran high, fanned by radical papers such as *Dagbladet* and *Friheten*. The hatred towards Quisling and the call for the death penalty was almost universal. Even the guards officially responsible for his safety during the trial decided solemnly to murder him in the event that the court did not invoke the death penalty.[54] Therefore, the fact that Ruge, despite the drawbacks and without any obligation to do so, decided to testify on behalf of his former colleague was remarkable. Second only to King Haakon, Ruge was undoubtedly the one who stood highest in Norwegian public opinion in 1945. And now he spoke positively of Quisling – at least of the young Quisling, who had made such an excellent impression in the General Staff. He was intelligent, hard-working, ambitious and ascetic. As Defence Minister, on the other hand, Ruge had been somewhat less favourably impressed by him, but overall his judgement of him even in that capacity was positive.

---

[51] Maria Quisling to Bergh 16 August 1945, ibid. pp. 314 and 316f. Also the Bergh–Maria Quisling correspondence in the Bergh archives.*

[52] Ibid. pp. 235f.

[53] Private correspondence made available by Olof Rydbeck.*

[54] Related to the author by Kjell Juell, one of the participants, in 1987.

Quisling's close friend from the General Staff, Halvor Hansson, who had just been appointed major general on his return from a prisoner-of-war camp in Germany, also spoke well of him. He had worked closely with Quisling in the 1930s, he explained, and his testimony now, like Ruge's, was exclusively positive in its evaluation of Quisling from the years before he became party leader. When Bergh asked him if he saw any relation between the Quisling he knew then and the Quisling who was standing trial, Hansson concluded that they were 'two entirely different people'.[55] This was also former ambassador Andreas Urbye's conclusion. He was asked to give an account of Quisling's diplomatic work in Helsinki and Moscow in the 1920s, and strengthened the positive impression of the young Quisling made by the previous witnesses. Urbye also explained how the two most prominent figures from the national surge of 1905, Fridtjof Nansen and General Holtfodt, had both spoken highly of Quisling.[56]

His testimony was followed by that of Quisling's closest childhood friend, Vilhelm Ullmann, whose account was so moving that the defendant had difficulty holding back his tears. Ullmann described how much Quisling's school friends had looked up to him and respected him as a genius, as a helpful friend and as a kind-hearted person, adding that he was speaking on behalf of them all. However, even Ullmann was much taken up with the question of whether Quisling was the same person he had been in his youth. In an additional testimony two days later, he gave a detailed account of an episode in January 1940 when some of the old friends had been together at an Oslo café where Quisling had explained to them that Norway was in great danger on account of the government's compliance over the Finnish war. During his speech he had become extremely agitated, attacking the government so violently that the others concluded him to be 'utterly mad'. Ullmann, who was unaware that Quisling had been suffering from a virulent infection that winter, took the episode to mean that his old friend was actually suffering from deep-seated political delusions.[57]

A DIFFERENT PERSON?

Thus nearly all witnesses for the defence – Ruge, Hansson, Urbye and Ullmann – each in his own way maintained that the man before them was a completely different person from the one they had known so well in the past, and that they had all observed a change, or rather a 'decline' in

[55] *Straffesak* pp. 236ff.   [56] Ibid. pp. 238f.   [57] Ibid. pp. 273–6.

comparison with the old Quisling. To a great extent their impression could be explained by the fact that they had all more or less lost touch with him since the 1930s, and had to compare their personal memory from the past with that of his image from the occupation years. Many of Quisling's NS and wartime colleagues and acquaintances would have used more or less the same words as his old friends – that he was loyal, helpful, even kind.

All the same, the possibility of a serious character change was put to the court. The psychiatrists Leikvam and Lofthus had excluded any kind of mental disorder. The explanation for Quisling's 'impairment' (as Ruge put it) had to be found in what the prosecution described as 'the difficult art of psychology' or else be regarded as the symptom of a physical condition. Leikvam and Lofthus had considered this possibility too. They had come to know Quisling quite well, at any rate better than was usual during psychiatric observations carried out on behalf of the court. They found him to be in astonishingly good health, with nothing to suggest any kind of malady which might have repercussions for his mental health. However, Professor Monrad-Krohn, the leading neurologist at the national medical centre Rikshospitalet, urged them to allow him to carry out more thorough tests on Quisling. To Solem he insisted that the character change between the shy and gifted Quisling of the old days and the evil dictator of the war period could well be attributed to a lesion in the brain, and more specifically to a tumour in the region of the forehead, which could have taken years to develop.[58]

Monrad-Krohn already knew Quisling. He was consulted when Quisling had experienced an attack of fever in the 1930s and possibly on the occasion of his mysterious infection in the winter of 1939 too when Quisling was a patient under Dr Scheel at Ullevål Hospital. He had also met him during the war, under circumstances which had aroused his interest in the Minister President as a personality type: during a stormy conference concerning the extraordinary admission of NS students into the Faculty of Medicine in 1942, when Quisling's behaviour had shifted between rage and compliance to such a degree that the professor's suspicions were raised. He explained to the court that a lesion in the brain could have brought about 'a falling off from, or a weakening of normal inhibitions', which could in turn explain the 'lack of inhibition' and 'delusions of grandeur' which the professor thought had been demonstrated during the trial.

Leikvam was not convinced, nor did he regard Quisling as abnormal, but

---

[58] Ibid. pp. 244ff. Related to the author by Jon Leikvam 1988.

simply peculiar. But Monrad-Krohn managed to persuade others of his theory, and thus Leikvam was forced to give in, as it would be unfortunate if the professor, a powerful figure in the medical establishment, were to go around in the future declaring that Quisling might have suffered from a brain tumour which was not investigated. Moreover, a post-mortem was out of the question, as the special rules recently provided by the government for those executed in fulfilment of the death penalty required the immediate cremation of the victim.

Immediately after the court recessed on 25 August, Quisling was taken to the Rikshospitalet Department of Neurology, while the court went to inspect Gimle and Ørneredet. Quisling gave his consent, and three professors and three doctors started their explorations. The doctors ran tests on Quisling for three days, and the results were quickly analysed. The tests did not indicate the presence of either a lesion or any other form of abnormality.

The examination did, however, have its consequences. Quisling was completely exhausted, and remained seriously weakened for the rest of the trial. His defence from now on became considerably confused and incoherent, significantly weaker in both content and presentation than hitherto. The reasons for this were strangely never publicised. Solem explained to the court that the accused's 'state of health has been somewhat impaired' mainly as a result of the exhausting days in court, in addition to his polyneuritis – the neurological tests were briefly mentioned in this connection. The official Norwegian news agency NTB announced quite misleadingly that Quisling had been taken to the Rikshospitalet because 'he felt a little unwell'. The announcement was automatically reported in most newspapers. The real circumstances surrounding Quisling's condition towards the end of the trial thus remained unknown.[59]

The doctors understood very well why this should be so. The methods and the instruments available then were such that they inevitably took their toll on a patient subjected to such intrusive tests over such a short period of time. Monrad-Krohn's request for a complete ophthalmological examination, for example, required the following procedure: with the help of a tube, compressed air was blown into the patient's spinal marrow, from where it passed directly into his brain cavity. While high pressure was applied to the brain, X-rays were taken. The whole process was carried out without anaesthetic. The so-called angiographic examination was even more painful,

---

[59] *VG* and several other newspapers 28 August 1945.

involving the injection of large quantities of iodine contrast medium into the main artery in the neck so that X-rays could be taken of the frontal lobe. The strain on Quisling was so great that Monrad-Krohn refrained from testing the left side after results from the right side indicated that there was no lesion there. In addition, tests were performed on his spinal cord, and an electro-encephalogram was performed.[60]

When Quisling was returned to Akershus on the Monday evening, he was forced to walk up all the stairs to the top cell of the tower, although medical rules prescribed the angiography patient should be carried horizontally on a stretcher. In fact he was so weak that Leikvam considered it unacceptable that he should appear in court the following day, and thus the court was recessed until the Wednesday. As the accused had not recovered by then either, it was decided that the court would meet for a short time only. After Monrad-Krohn's results were read out, Solem informed the court that the defendant, for various reasons, was suffering from health problems and thus should not be required to appear in court until Friday. But when Friday came, Quisling was still too weak even to present the points he had prepared concerning his protests at the recent reintroduction of the death penalty, which had been brought in as a provisional decree from the government in exile in London in 1941 and again in 1942 and had been made formal law by the Storting during its short session after the liberation. His protest had to be read out by Bergh's assistant – Bergh himself had also been taken ill. With the accused in a pitiful state, and his defence lawyer on sick leave, the prosecutor then rose to make his formal summation of the case.

During the four hours in which Schjødt addressed the court, the accused sat upright with his gaze fixed on the speaker. Journalists who were following the case had always been struck by how attentively Quisling followed the proceedings and the interest he showed in the statements of the witnesses and of the prosecution, leafing through the documents and always keeping notes. He clearly found his own trial fascinating. However, that day he sat motionless, with only very intermittent jottings on the notepad in front of him. And indeed Schjødt's summation – to the extent that he could follow it at all – was devastating from start to finish. The fresh evidence which had come to light over the previous few days concerning the events of 9 April established a treason 'more extensive, more terrible and more consistent

---

[60] *Straffesak* pp. 247ff.

than anyone could have imagined possible', he maintained. Quisling had simply pushed Germany into the occupation, as shown by the recently discovered Scheidt–Hagelin–Schickedanz correspondence. Schjødt went on to refer to various speeches Quisling had made during the war which demonstrated his intransigent and threatening stance towards public opposition to the NS in general and towards the resistance movement in particular.

The most discouraging thing from Quisling's point of view was that the prosecution not only cast doubt on the reliability of his own testimony but actually placed confidence in the stories of the Gestapo and other Germans, which were now presented as proof, for example, of his alleged responsibility for the arrests of the teachers, for the arrests of 250 officers, for the murder of Hansteen and for escalating the executions of hostages. No single accusation seemed more distorted to him than the one presented by the prosecution on the Jewish question. It was claimed that Quisling had actually compelled the Germans to pursue a Jewish policy which was 'strictly counter to their Jewish policy in Denmark'. What this accusation overlooked was that Norway's relationship with Germany in general was very different from that of Denmark, and that he had actually striven to obtain a 'Danish solution' for his own country.

Schjødt's powerful speech, which was delivered with ease and authority and informed by an unremitting contempt for the accused, was about to reach its conclusion when he declared: 'As prosecutor in this case I demand the death penalty.' Although it was a foregone conclusion that he would do so, his words nevertheless made a great impression on the court. All eyes were on Quisling, who sat motionless with his stiff gaze fixed on Schjødt.[61]

The military penal code provided for the death penalty in cases of treason in time of war. During the occupation this section of the law had been supplemented by a provisional decree from London to the effect that the death penalty could also be used after the end of the war. If anyone should doubt the applicability of military law in this case, the civilian criminal code contained resolutions concerning treason and murder, which had now been extended by the Storting's sanctioning of the use of the death penalty. The first death sentence had, in fact, already been passed on a Norwegian torturer employed by the Gestapo. In general, Schjødt did not allow any doubt concerning the applicability of the sentence to surface, and did not feel

[61] *VG* 1 September 1945.

constrained to argue the legal position in detail as the evidence was overwhelming.

When Bergh rose some days later to give his summation on behalf of the defence, the court was filled to capacity. According to one newspaper, 'the spectators waited in suspense to hear what the defence could come up with to benefit the world's most infamous individual'.[62] In fact, Bergh's summation was well organised, well documented, and intelligently pitched. If he had been somewhat unforthcoming, offering only limited assistance to his client during the main part of the trial, he more than compensated for that now.[63]

In his introduction Bergh asserted that it was not easy for anyone to understand Quisling because of the enormous gulf which separated almost everybody else from his understanding of reality. How was it at all possible that Quisling, who had made such an honourable contribution to Nansen's great humanitarian effort and who had been regarded by all as morally and intellectually first-rate, was now being tried for high treason? This was the 'Quisling enigma', which was to provide the key concept around which Bergh based his defence. While his loyal supporters had seen Quisling not only as an important figure and as a good and genuine man of impeccable character but as a leader and a prophet, the general public viewed him as one who 'did almost anything for power or money'. It was the duty of the court to try to understand Quisling's personality as far as possible, because it was necessary to establish his subjective guilt too if he was to be sentenced. Rebutting the prosecution's allegations of megalomania, Bergh argued instead that Quisling had fallen victim to his own dogmatism. In particular two dogmas had taken hold of him over the past years. The first, that Marxism and Bolshevism were an evil poison leading him to favour a co-operation between the Germanic, Nordic peoples which he had advocated since the 1920s, after first having been sympathetic to the Russian Revolution. Secondly, the belief that parliamentary government was a rotten system, which he developed during his term in the cabinet and which was reinforced in the course of the 1930s when he found the Storting less and less able to serve the country's most pressing need: strengthening Norway's defence. As these beliefs had taken on the dimensions of a dogmatic quasi-religion he saw himself as 'chosen' to apply them to practical politics.

Bergh insisted that it was from such a perspective that Quisling's actions

---

[62] Ibid. 6 September 1945.   [63] *Straffesak* pp. 278–319.

had to be judged. He proceeded to address the substance of the charges one by one, concluding in each case that his client considered that he was serving the best interests of his country.

The main purpose of the defence, however, was to save Quisling's life. The prosecution's call for the death penalty rested on no less than three legal bases: the treason clause of the military penal code; further, on the civilian criminal code's articles concerning the state's independence and security; and finally on the criminal code's resolutions on murder. The provision for the death penalty for murder had been brought in by a provisional decree of January 1942, and Bergh argued that it could not be applied retroactively. The death penalty for crimes against national security and independence had been introduced by another provisional decree of October 1941, and thus could not apply to the Berlin talks, to 9 April, or to the commissarial government of 1940–2. As for the events of 9 April, Bergh also insisted that they were not even covered by the military penal code, as it only applied to wartime and a state of war between Norway and Germany was not established until two days after 9 April when negotiations finally broke down. In other words, the death penalty could only be related to the events following the establishment of the National Government in February 1942, and in particular to what Quisling had said and written concerning the SS volunteers and the various laws he had passed, as well as his initiatives against the resistance and the general conditions under the occupation – that is, all the events which the trial had given the least attention to. 'Is the death penalty really applicable in this case, based on everything the court has heard during these weeks of trial, and in view of what the court knows of the defendant's personality?' Bergh did not need to answer that question. After reminding the court once more that Quisling was an 'enigma' whom nobody, not even the doctors, understood, he submitted his request to the court that it reach a verdict of not guilty, or, as a subsidiary request, that if found guilty, his client be treated as leniently as possible.

When Bergh sat down, something extraordinary took place. The president, Judge Solem, told the court that he wanted to make it clear – because of misunderstandings in the press and fierce public criticism of the possibility that Bergh might try to argue Quisling's innocence – that the counsel for the defence could logically do nothing else and that it was Bergh's duty to go for an acquittal. That the presiding judge should find it necessary to justify the plea of the defence out of concern for his reputation and perhaps his safety was indeed a rare occurrence in Norwegian legal procedure. Apparently Bergh himself had requested this intervention so as to take the edge off the unavoidable criticism his plea would raise in public opinion.[64]

In the ensuing exchange of polemics between the prosecution and the defence Schjødt pointed out, among other things, that Quisling had evaded the meeting in Copenhagen of 3 April 1940. Bergh claimed that there had not been sufficient proof that the meeting had taken place. Schjødt immediately went on the offensive against what he called Bergh's 'sentimental enigma theory', which he feared might create a Quisling myth, and countered Bergh's theory with a new reading of Quisling as a weak, irresolute character. Democracy and parliamentarism were forms of government which 'demanded a strong man, ready to fight and ready to defend, who had the will and the ability to take up the struggle', whereas Quisling was a weak man, easy to flatter, and an inveterate liar. On the question of the applicability of the death penalty Schjødt simply declared that it was necessary to accept the fact that the death penalty was now a feature of the Norwegian legal code, and if it were to be employed at all 'it must be against the man who has committed this odious and widespread treason'.

Following this exchange, the court adjourned for lunch. Quisling used the break to tidy up his notes and prepare himself for his own defence.

THE SPEECH OF DEFENCE

He was clearly weak, suffering from severe headaches and physical exhaustion. His legs could barely support him. Although he had been reassured by Bergh's efforts, he was almost unable to communicate this fact to his lawyer. The task which lay before him was formidable. He was to present his own defence, both against the specific charges brought and against the call for the death penalty.

He made an extremely good beginning, his speech fluent and animated. He allowed himself to furnish the court with some personal details, as it had taken such an interest in him as an individual. He shared a few anecdotes from his childhood in Fyresdal, a glimpse here and there into his schooldays in Drammen and Skien, and a short account of how he, as a young officer, gradually became confident of the nature of his vocation to serve the nation. Throughout, he spoke without the use of notes.

After half an hour, he turned to the subject of Russia, unfolding his experiences when he worked with Nansen, and held forth on the matter of

---

[64] Ibid. p. 319.

his leave of absence from the General Staff. He stated five times in as many minutes that he was not in the least bitter that his request for an extension had been turned down. Soon repetitions started making their way into his hitherto coherent speech, his arguments constantly losing their cogency and giving way to exaggeration as if he was in considerable pain. His work in Russia had been unbelievably varied and hard, taking in the whole of southern Russia, if not the entire country, and everywhere he had earned the trust of the leadership, and the people came flocking to him anxious to hear what he had to say to them, including Trotsky, who wanted to offer him a prominent position, any position he cared to mention, in fact. Compared to this, being Fører of only three million people was child's play . . .

He was clearly becoming muddled. His account of his life as an aid worker sounded unlike anything he had ever said or written on the subject in the previous twenty years. His diffidence deserted him, as did his sense of moderation and his unswerving loyalty towards Nansen which always permeated his descriptions of his own efforts. Exaggeration followed upon exaggeration. Then, with an enormous show of strength, he managed to pull himself together and talk about his activities in Norway. His account of his time in the Agrarian government was relatively coherent. He regretted not having exposed all the lies in parliamentary life, and that he had never gone public with everything he knew and thereby 'stamped out this filth'. Instead he had founded his own party. Just as he was about to talk about the NS, he went off at a tangent, describing his reform bills, his brother Arne in New York, his plans for dealing with his financial crisis, all his lectures and talks, and of the 100,000 followers who had flocked to him . . .

At this point Solem interrupted and advised Quisling of the unsuitability of the defendant agitating from the dock. Quisling had been speaking for over an hour, without once referring to the events which led up to 9 April, and Solem urged him to come to the point.[65] But Bergh, who had been following his address with increasing anxiety realising that he was in great distress, took advantage of the interruption to request that the court adjourn until the next day as his client was clearly in extreme physical discomfort. Quisling confirmed that standing up indeed caused him great pain, and his face showed signs of debilitation; according to one newspaper his wide staring eyes gleamed 'with fanatic zeal'. The court duly recessed, and resumed the following morning.[66]

When the defendant addressed the court that day, he had benefited

---

[65] Ibid. p. 338; see also interruptions on pp. 352, 355, 361.   [66] *VG* 7 September 1945.

greatly from the stimulants Dr Leikvam had given him.[67] When he rose to resume, he began by confessing that the judge's interruption of the day before had reminded him of St Paul's defence before the governor, who had declared, 'Paul, thou art beside thyself; much learning doth make thee mad,' to which Paul had replied, 'I am not mad, most noble Festus; but speak forth the words of truth and soberness.' Turning to Solem he said, 'I also speak forth the words of truth and soberness in this case.' This latterday St Paul then went on to detail his journeys, beginning with his visit to Germany in 1939, including the ill-fated December talks in Berlin. He took his time, and supplied details which he had not mentioned before, allowing himself digressions into related subjects, all for the purpose of illustrating the background to the most serious charge he was facing: that it was pure coincidence, a simple twist of fate, which made it possible for these talks to be interpreted as his having intervened in the course of history by influencing Hitler to conquer Norway. However, he maintained that he had not said anything in Berlin beyond what he had always proposed openly in Norway, and had thus unexpectedly become involved in events as an instrument of fate. At the same time he had foreseen those very events: Norway's road to war in spring 1940 had indeed unfolded exactly as he had predicted, but he had not stepped in but simply left things to follow their own course, until he found that judgement day – 9 April – was upon him.

It was a very convincing speech, at least as an account of his own motives. He spoke freely and spontaneously with a sincerity his otherwise formal rhetoric could not convey. He even gave in to dramatic effects, mimicking some of the individuals in the drama, which provided some light relief. Perhaps Leikvam's injections had gone to his head but, be that as it may, it seemed as though Quisling was genuinely confiding both his innocence and his national despair to the court. But he stuck to his denial of the Copenhagen meeting on 3 April, and failed to give any satisfactory explanation of why it had been necessary to keep the Berlin meeting secret, without even mentioning it to any of his colleagues.

His account of April 1940 and his government was so prolix that Solem after a while urged him to come to the point. He did do so, after a fashion, but had little to add concerning Hansteen, Eilifsen or the Jews. However, when it came to the question of his resistance to German demands and requisitioning, he did have something new to say: his government had successfully blocked the Wehrmacht's plans for the confiscation of 100,000

---

[67] Tiedemann Olsen in *Fredrikstads Blad* 2 June 1990.

wool blankets, 10,000 rucksacks, all the bicycles in Oslo, cars and several properties. However, had he expected this to have had any bearing on his case he should certainly have mentioned it before.

Towards the end of four hours of unscripted speaking, he suddenly picked up the manuscript which lay in front of him, and began to read out a summarised account of his motives, and of how, in the past five years, he had acted as a 'buffer between the occupation power and the people'.[68] The account consisted of the opening and closing passages of his two written statements, and the effect of reading them out served this purpose well. In a loud, histrionic voice he delivered one well-turned sentence after another:

You Norwegians killed Saint Olav. During the Restoration the English dug up Cromwell's corpse and suspended it from chains in the gallows, having failed to catch him alive ... No prophet has ever been honoured in his own country. But on 9 April 1940, the warnings I had been making, and which had gone unheeded for the past ten years, proved justified.

Solem remained motionless throughout these outpourings, his face buried in his hands. 'If my work has really been treasonable, then I would pray to God for Norway's sake that a good many of Norway's sons would also become traitors like me, only that they be not thrown into prison!'

With these last words ringing in their ears the court withdrew to consider their verdict.

SENTENCING AND APPEAL

Solem and his colleagues did not waste time. After the court was adjourned on Friday 7 September following ten full days in session, only seventy-two hours elapsed before the voluminous verdict was reached; considerable parts of it must therefore have been written up while the trial was still in progress. On Monday 10 September at 2 o'clock the presiding judge read out the verdict: Vidkun Abraham Lauritz Quisling was to be sentenced to death under both the military penal code and the civilian criminal code paragraphs concerning treason, murder and theft. He was further ordered to pay 1,040,000 kroner in legal costs. The NRK recorded the occasion and the first filming of the trial took place that day, and later featured in the Norwegian Films weekly newsreel.[69] Quisling remained motionless during the reading of the verdict. He had come straight from an hour-long interrogation with the Danish police, who wanted information concerning his relationship with

---

[68] *VG* 8 September 1945.   [69] *Straffesak* pp. 336–82.

Frits Clausen. Nor did he move during Solem's hour-long reading of the judgement.[70] It appeared that the court had accepted all the prosecution's charges, with respect to both the facts and the application of the law. His explanations had hardly been taken into account at all. He was cleared only of some minor charges.

Above all, the court found him guilty of inciting the Norwegian army to mutiny and treachery on 9 April, of providing assistance to the enemy during the occupation, and of seeking to alter the Constitution by illegal means. He was also found guilty of murder: premeditated for his role in the Viggo Hansteen case; manslaughter in the case of the Jews; in the case of Eilifsen and the fourteen executions which followed the assassination of Marthinsen, he was found guilty of being an accessory to premeditated murder. The court concluded that these crimes were the result of an exaggerated belief in his own capabilities, and an inability to accept criticism or to tolerate opposition. In addition, he was declared guilty of embezzlement, receiving stolen property and theft on the grounds that he had appropriated items from the palace for personal enrichment, or, in certain cases, for party use.

To justify the death penalty the court on several points relied on testimonies which had in fact been rebutted by the defendant himself during the trial. For instance, the judgement bluntly stated that all his actions from the summer of 1939 onwards were guided by 'a plan' to co-operate with Nazi Germany – a plan consisting of occupation, coup and collaboration. He had succeeded in 'convincing the Germans and above all Hitler of the advantages to be gained from an occupation of Norway'. It further concluded that he had planned to smuggle German troops into the country and engineer the coup with their help. This wholly fictitious story was based on the memoranda from Rosenberg's office which gave a rather misleading account of what had actually happened. Besides inciting German action in Norway, the court also stated that it had been his aim to lead Norway into a 'Greater Germanic federation in which it would lose an essential part of its independence'. His

---

[70] There are varying press accounts of Quisling's reaction during the reading of the judgement. The version claiming that he almost collapsed in Trygve de Lange (*Quisling-Saken*, 1945, p. 177) does not tie in with NRK's version (NRK ho). After the reading of the verdict, the press reported that he collapsed and behaved in a pitiful manner once returned to his cell. This story was related by the Swedish tabloid *Expressen*, and was subsequently discredited by both the prison governor (the alleged source of *Expressen)* and the medical officer, Johan Scharffenberg (*Vårt Land* 2 October 1945), with a disclaimer and explanation on 3 October 1945. In fact Quisling showed his usual composure.

subsequent peace initiatives would at best have made Norway 'a vassal state under Germany'. This was certainly not what *he* had wanted, even if it might be said that this was the German aim. And with regard to the Jews, the court unanimously agreed to rely on the Gestapo officer Wagner's testimony that Quisling had pressured the Germans into persecuting the Jews, even if no such pressure had been presented to the court at all.

More surprisingly, the court also moved into areas which had not been considered in the trial at all. The verdict stated that Quisling had gone further than the Germans had wanted him to in his handling of the crises over the Church, the teachers and the labour effort; no evidence of this had been presented during the trial and, with the exception of his rage against Berggrav, the allegations were simply untrue. The NS Party was also said to have established a system of informers which had resulted in the imprisonment, torture and execution of several people. This had neither been mentioned in the indictment nor dealt with at all during the trial, and would indeed have been difficult to prove in such a sweeping, general form. On the other hand, nothing was said about the clemency system he had set up during the period of the Chancellery at the palace and his effort to free prisoners and hostages from German prisons.

When the reading finished, Solem asked the accused to rise, and to confirm that he had understood the judgement. The question of guilt, once established in this court, could not be appealed against. Should he wish to make an appeal, he would have to bring the case before the Supreme Court, on the grounds that either the sentence was too harsh or that the law had been wrongly applied. After a short conference with Bergh's assistant (Bergh was away from court because he was ill), Quisling replied that he did indeed wish to appeal to the Supreme Court.

He and Bergh had two weeks in which to draw up his appeal, a deadline which was later extended to 28 September. The appeal was mostly the result of Bergh's work, and followed the same general line of argument he had established in the High Court. It dealt exclusively with questions of legal technicalities, as the facts of the case had now been established.

When he appeared before the Supreme Court on 9 October 1945 both the guards and the journalists remarked on how physically reduced Quisling seemed after the trial, his clothes hanging loosely on him and his back looking much thinner than before. Curious members of the public had lined up outside the Court House in the hope of catching a glimpse of the condemned man; they were kept at sufficient distance to avoid volleys of abusive language.

Inside the Court House Paal Berg presided over the five judges on the podium. He and Quisling had met only once since the memorable episode in the NRK studio on 15 April 1940, when Berg communicated his unqualified appreciation for Quisling in his decision to resign as Prime Minister. This meeting took place when Berg was summoned to the palace in the spring of 1942 to explain himself regarding the circumstances surrounding the establishment of the Administrative Council. After 1942 Quisling had been informed by the state police that Berg was acting as some sort of head of the national civil resistance movement. In fact, Berg was entrusted with the formal leadership of the Home Front, secretly corresponding with the government in London and instructing the entire civil resistance on behalf of the Royal Norwegian Government, until the return of the King and his cabinet.

In front of this Supreme Court Quisling's defence counsel Bergh ran through the entire case in much the same way as he had done in the High Court in order to establish the grounds for his appeal, as did Schjødt on behalf of the prosecution to argue that the appeal should be thrown out of court.[71] Both lawyers were at least as thorough as they had been in the lower court, albeit in a more subdued and less agitated manner. After two and a half days in court, during which the psychiatrists Leikvam and Lofthus had also appeared to give a brief account of their findings, the judge who had been chosen as the first member of the panel to vote on the appeal took only half an hour to conclude that the appeal was groundless.

For Quisling, these two to three days in the Supreme Court were solemn ones, as they signalled the culmination of five months of battling through the country's legal system, a battle whose every phase had yielded results quite disproportionate to the enormous energy he had put into his defence. Now, he stated, he was meeting death 'face to face'.[72] He followed the proceedings from his seat next to a small table which had been placed behind Bergh's defence stand. It was not standard procedure for the appellant to be present in the Supreme Court, but Quisling insisted not only on being present but also on addressing the court. There was no precedent for this, but neither was there any formal ruling to prevent him from speaking. He was indeed anxious to address the select group of lawyers, psychiatrists and journalists who filled the forty spectator seats as this was his last chance to articulate the inner monologue which had dominated his thoughts for the past year, presenting the motives and higher aims behind

[71] *Straffesak* pp. 383ff.   [72] Quisling, ibid., p. 460.

his activity. He opened his address by thanking the court for listening to him, and continued, completely unscripted on this occasion, his statement, somewhat gentler in tone than was his wont, and a little less self-assertive than usual. He told the court that he realised that he had been 'objectively judged according to the law'; what he was asking for was to be judged for his good works too. 'My work, our effort, has never really come to light.' He made two references to Berg's speech of thanks in 1940, which was 'completely in keeping with the true and real circumstances', unlike the High Court judgement. He had also come up with an explanation for his ignorance of the cases of torture which were widely discussed: his colleagues had not dared tell him about them, a fact which he said he found 'most regrettable'. Otherwise, he did not have anything new to say.

Towards the end of his address, his tone changed as he went on to talk about the religious side of his work, the aspect that connected it to the course of history, 'the divine task': 'I have come to understand that there is a divine power in the universe, and that this power is connected to the development of those who live on this earth, and that what is happening here on earth during this important time is a watershed marking the beginning of God's kingdom here on earth.' He dared say so much, he said with a little smile, as he now had been formally certificated as not being insane. These had been the motives for all his efforts even though they did perhaps 'turn out negatively in some quarters'.[73]

Materialistic doctrines such as Russian Communism and German Nationalism were doomed to collapse – he had said as much to Hitler himself, that is that *Blut und Boden* was simply a form of materialism, which in its extreme forms would lead to total egoism. The new heavenly kingdom

---

[73] Subsequent psychiatric/psychoanalytical assessments of Quisling have not always been in agreement with Leikvam and Lofthus. The most significant contributions to the debate are as follows: Ernest Jones, 'The Psychology of Quislingism', *The International Journal of Psychoanalysis* 1940/22; Niels C. Brøgger, 'Bidrag til løsning av "gåten Quisling" ', *Kirke og Kultur* 1945 pp. 311–26; J. A. Selander, 'Varför andra gången', *Samtiden* 1947 pp. 430–8; Gabriel Langfeldt, *Gåten Vidkun Quisling* (1969); Langfeldt, 'The Mental State of the Norwegian Traitor Vidkun Quisling', *The Psychiatric Forum* 13 (1972) pp. 136–41; John Hoberman, 'Vidkun Quisling's Psychological Image', *Scandinavian Studies* 46 no. 3 (1974) pp. 242–64; Hoberman, 'The Psychopathy of an Abortive Leadership: The Case of Vidkun Quisling' in R. S. Robins (ed.), *Psychopathy and Political Leadership* (New Orleans 1977); Nils Retterstøl, *Sinnets labyrinter: Paranoide psykoser* (Oslo 1975), ch. 'Hitler og Quisling, Var de paranoiske?'; David Abrahamsen, *Men, Mind and Power* (New York 1982), ch. 'Abnormal Messiah'; Jørgen Ravn, 'Havde Quisling en paranoid skizofreni?', *Nordisk psykiatrisk Tidsskrift* 1982 pp. 33–7; Per Roar Anthi, 'Vidkun Quisling, Paranoid konspirasjon og apokalyptisk forestillingsverden', *NNT* 1991/1 pp. 12–27.

would not be like this, and it was to this end that he had been striving all these years.

QUISLING'S LAST DAYS

His last days, like most of his life over the previous fifty-eight years, were devoted to thought and reflection. During the busy war years he had had little time for meditation, and during his trial he had been completely taken up with constructing his defence. Now, as the end was approaching, the time had come to turn back, to close the circle of the rational universe which, ever since his youth, he had resolved to survey in its entirety.

His meditations took a more existential turn than before. Ever since his sentence had been passed in the High Court he had been preoccupied with religious questions concerning the meaning of life and the spiritual dimension of the task which he had to pay for with his life. He had always been a religious man, though Christianity in the usual sense does not adequately describe his thinking. Although he prayed a lot, and had several discussions with the prison pastor both at Akershus and in Møllergaten 19 concerning the power of prayer, he found himself unable to rediscover the pure and simple faith of his childhood.

In contrast to his father, the provost, he considered the Old Testament to be the Mosaic or Judaic holy book, closer in kind to the Koran than the New Testament, and lamented the fact that the Reformation had not done away with it: 'a fatal mistake'. Christ and Caesar had established a new era, a new religion and a new realm. He read and reread the New Testament in his cell, and there is much to suggest that he was particularly absorbed by Revelations. Its presentation of Christ made a deep impression on him, both as a witness to God and as the herald of God's kingdom on earth. On more than one occasion he made Christ's words his own, as though he himself was a new messenger.[74]

As divinity was a force that could be attained through philosophical and speculative activity, he continued working on Universism in the cell until the last. More strongly than before, he felt that human actions should serve the purpose of realising God on earth, the earth which he was about to leave

[74] Quisling, 'Den evige rettferdighet (Et testament)', RA LD 29 Q. The version printed in Maria Quisling, *Dagbok*, pp. 187f, is divided into two texts and is edited differently from the manuscript version used here. The question of Quisling's faith is given full treatment in Christopher Braw, 'Quislings tro', *Tidsskrift for Teologi og Kirke* 1989/1, although it does not take in 'Universistiske strøtanker'.

behind with a heavy heart. He cried quite often, especially during Maria's brief visits. He thought of St Olav constantly, and of the common ground between them. In both letters and conversations, and even in his statement to the Supreme Court, the comparisons came readily between himself and the king and saint who had shown his people the light only to be resisted at first by an angry mob.

Gradually he came to terms with his sentence, accepting it as part of his martyrdom in that it provided a faithful expression of the concept of justice which prevailed in society. 'I know that I have been judged according to the law,' he said, though insisting that the judgement contained several mis-understandings and not a few instances of downright injustice. During a nation's most fateful hour 'chaos must not be allowed to prevail', the wording of the Supreme Court judgement ran; 'for him who at such a crucial moment of his country sets himself above the country's constitu-tional authorities and thereby betrays his country, his country has no room'. These were words he could actually have spoken himself. Thus he had to accept that his efforts for a new Europe, or his interpretation of the world war as a move towards the unified growth of the world and towards the eventual advent of God's kingdom, could scarcely be appreciated in the contemporary situation.

But although his country had no room for him, this did not mean that there was no place for him in history. During the first week of October he finished a fifty-page manuscript entitled 'Universistic Aphorisms'.[75] His faith in God's kingdom as the decisive Universistic force, and the struggle against the materialism of National Socialism, its racism included, stand out as the most striking aspects of this document. It was understandably a time for reflection. During his trial he had confirmed that he believed the Jewish influence in history to be harmful or even damaging.[76] But when he was confronted with Leo Eitinger's testimony to Auschwitz, he had stated that he could not understand what the Germans wanted to achieve through their policy of extermination: 'It is completely incomprehensible to me, and I must confess, a very serious problem for me too.' The aphorisms from the last week of his life confirm that he considered the National Socialist racial policy to have been wrong, and that environmental factors seem to play a

---

[75] UBO MS fol. 3920 IV, 5. Shortened version in Maria Quisling, *Dagbok*, pp. 162–86; see also H. F. Dahl, 'Quisling i nytt lys', *NNT* 1984/4.

[76] *Straffesak* p. 130: '*The Chief Judge:* So you still consider the Jews responsible for a lot of those misfortunes that hit the world? *Quisling:* Absolutely, yes.'

more central role than he had thought, an admission which invalidated a great deal of what he himself had said in public, at least after 1941.[77]

He also offered a reappraisal of his political efforts. During the war he had set out his ideas for reorganising Europe into a free federal union in his 'Denkschrift über die russische Frage'. 'Why did Hitler want to wait like a blind man until the end of the war? ... Why was God allowing this to happen? Was Germany and its National Socialism unfit for this noble task?' However, the aphorisms bear no indication of a corresponding crisis of faith in himself. The text shows a confidence in logical structures which only he could understand, supported by an almost ecstatic revelation of truth and the light to come, which bore the mark of nothing less than a prophet. In fact, he saw a striking resemblance between himself and the prophet of Patmos. The author of the Revelations foretold the destruction of the Roman Empire in the stars as they moved across the night sky, much as the new prophet did now when glancing through the barred window of his prison cell: 'And I see a new heaven and a new earth, I see God's kingdom reaching forth, which Christ came to establish. And he that sits on the throne says to me: Write, for these are true and honest words.'

In a sermon text he simultaneously wrote, on 'Eternal Justice', he tried to achieve a synthesis of his religious and philosophical thinking in the space of a few pages. God's kingdom on earth was on its way, though at different stages of development in various parts of the world, where people were bringing the knowledge of God towards a reconciliation of the spiritual and the temporal, the goal which Ibsen's Julian had prophesied in *Emperor and Galilean*. Here on earth God's kingdom is only the beginnings of a colony, to be established fully by Christ at the Second Coming. Christ, sentenced to death as a blasphemer and a criminal.

Sacrificial death, the death of the best, is a tremendous thing. It is not simply a question of giving your life for your friends or for a cause, it is the sacrifice itself which is important. Blood is the symbol of the soul. For someone to spill his blood means that he is giving his entire soul as a testimony: Christ; St Olav.

With death all individual consciousness disappears, but the will lives on and affects all other wills, and sooner or later a rebirth will take place. He did not avoid the issue of reincarnation in his synthesis: 'Instinctively and magnetically, related souls are drawn together in existence after existence ... Death does not put an end to eternal life any more than a blink can cancel a gaze.

---

[77] Ibid. p. 363, UBO MS fol. 3920 IV, 5.

But when a person has completed his earthly task, his soul must be freed in order to be incarnated anew in a new existence.'

'Universistic Aphorisms' was dedicated to Maria, 'my beloved and loyal wife'. 'Eternal Justice' was written to her in letter form. Maria certainly deserved special gratitude during these days. Following her efforts when the case was at the High Court, she continued to campaign tirelessly for her husband. She wrote to all those who had stood witness for the defence and thanked them warmly. She expressed her prayer that Ruge would use his influence to save her husband's life: 'I beg you, put in a good word for him today and save him!' The reply Ruge sent expressed his sympathy for her as a wife, but he neither could nor would help. He had hoped, he said, that the doctors would declare his old colleague insane, as 'his development and his actions are inexplicable to me'. Maria did not stop at the General, and begged for an audience with the King. However, Bergh advised against that, suggesting she write instead. He helped her draft a petition of reprieve, both to King Haakon and to Prime Minister Gerhardsen. Her letter to the King read: 'And now I cry to Your Majesty: be merciful!', and to Gerhardsen: 'You, Prime Minister, who have suffered so many years in prison during the war and therefore know what suffering is, please show mercy.' She even considered writing to Stalin, her fellow countryman, thinking he might show appreciation for Quisling's work in the Ukraine, but her husband would not allow it. She also wrote to General Thorne, the Allied Commander-in-Chief in Norway, who had moved into Gimle.[78]

Her birthday was on 14 October. She visited Vidkun and as usual they met in the pastor's office. The previous day, the Supreme Court had rejected his appeal, and it was obvious that he would be shot. Neither of them held out any hope of clemency. Their conversation was recorded by a prison employee.[79]

Maria was magnificent. She urged him to be strong and not to think about her. Good friends would take care of her. She comforted him with the fact that he would soon be reunited with his beloved parents. Vidkun, tearful, was deeply moved and thought it hard on her to have to celebrate her birthday under such circumstances.

They discussed Paal Berg, and how inappropriate it was that he had been

[78] Maria Quisling's correspondence, cited in Maria Quisling, *Dagbok*, originals and answers in UBO MS fol. 3920 IX, 4.

[79] RA LD 29 Q, Div. 7. From Quisling's letter to the King 18 October 1945 (UBO MS fol. 3920 IX, 5), it appears that he only received official news of the Supreme Court judgement five days after it was made, and moreover did not receive written notice.

one of the judges. Quisling mentioned how he had spared him during the war although he had known that he was the leader of the Home Front. Maria then told him that Dr Scharffenberg wanted to see him. Scharffenberg had sat very close to him during the trial and was a good man. Quisling said he would be glad to see him, but even more he wanted to see Bishop Berggrav. Maria was against this as Berggrav had just published a hostile and implacable article 'Folkedommen over NS' (The People's Judgement on the NS) in his journal *Kirke og Kultur*, which terrified the movement's supporters in its harsh judgement on every single party member. Obviously there would be no mercy, no forgiveness, in the Church. Moreover, several Norwegian bishops had spoken out in favour of the death penalty although Berggrav was not among them. Maria told him once more that he had to be brave, and not worry about her, and that all his friends had the utmost admiration for him. Finally she cut off a lock of his hair.

The following day he wrote to her:

We should have shared a quiet peaceful life, but were thrown into an unsettled existence. By what? By whom? Neither you nor I wanted this. But the force of circumstances and an inner compulsion drove me, sometimes to the good, sometimes to the bad. I see God's government and will in everything, a deeper meaning. Therefore judge me not. Forgive everything.[80]

He would not ask for clemency, but he did write to the King and ask for lenience in the sentencing of NS members who were to stand trial. 'Do not allow the Norwegian legal community to become a whited sepulchre and the Norwegian people to harm their souls.' After that he wrote valedictory messages to Bergh, Vilhelm Ullmann, Halvor Hansson and his brother Jørgen, thanking them for everything, as well as several letters to Maria.[81]

Berggrav did in fact visit him on 16 October. The prison pastor, who had heard about the conversation between Quisling and Maria two days before, took the initiative and informed the Bishop of Quisling's wish to see him. Berggrav had no objection to visiting him as the judgement was now final and the facts of the case had been 'legally and irrefutably established'. In an atmosphere heavy with what was left unsaid, their conversation was, according to what Berggrav later related, throughout on a human and religious level; just as Quisling had wanted. Berggrav reminded him that nobody knows when the moment they will be judged by God will come. When confronted with death, he told Quisling that there was particular

---

[80] Vidkun to Maria 15 October 1945, UBO MS fol. 3920 IX, 6.
[81] UBO MS fol. 3920 IX, 5.

strength to be found in the Lord's Prayer: 'Forgive us our trespasses as we forgive those who trespass against us. Before God we can wipe away our bitterness and open the way to forgiveness.'

While Berggrav said what he had prepared, he gained the distinct impression that Quisling was taking his words in exactly the spirit they were intended; thus the two men had at last reached understanding, reconciliation and forgiveness. They did not discuss the past or the future, not even the forthcoming execution. Berggrav was an energetic opponent of the death penalty, even though he did not mention this to Quisling. After his visit, he wrote to Prime Minister Gerhardsen and asked for clemency on Quisling's behalf.[82]

Dr Scharffenberg, who visited him next, was also against the death penalty, although not prepared to sign any plea for clemency in this case. Their conversation dealt as much with personal matters as it did with the case, and for Scharffenberg it confirmed what he had always believed: that Quisling was a man who acted according to his lights. When he left he expressed his sympathy for what Quisling would have to face, to which Quisling sardonically replied that to his fellow Norwegians he would be at his most dangerous after his death.[83]

During the days that followed, he gave evidence in a whole series of cases brought against his former colleagues: Riisnæs and Hagelin on 17 and 18 October; Fuglesang, Stang and Hans S. Jacobsen immediately afterwards. Some found it in bad taste that someone who had been sentenced to death should assist the very legal apparatus which had condemned him. However, he wanted to do so. His testimonies were not particularly factual, but were, as was to be expected, sympathetic to the defendants.[84]

On 23 October towards 7 o'clock in the evening the prison pastor visited him in his cell, informing him that the sentence was to be carried out at midnight. He asked to see his wife for the last time. The request was turned down as contrary to the regulations. At around 8 o'clock a policeman arrived and announced the judgement and the execution. The government in Council with the King had been through the petitions for clemency earlier in the day and had rejected them. Vidkun sat down to write his last message to Maria, thanking her for her loyalty and love, and for what she had done for him during this difficult time: 'I submit to God's will. There must be a

[82] Interview with Berggrav in *Vårt Land* 18 October 1945; copy of letter from Berggrav's archives lent by Gunnar Heine.
[83] Olav Sundet, *Johan Scharffenberg* (1977) pp. 226f.
[84] Contemporary reports in the Oslo press and documents in RA LD.

deeper meaning to all this … I am so happy that we have been so completely open with each other and have forgiven everything!' Writing these words proved too much for him, and he suddenly broke down. By 11.30 he was calm again. In the meantime another prison pastor from Akershus had arrived. They were all expecting him to be fetched before midnight. Instead the pastor's wife offered coffee and cookies and there was a further wait. Quisling spoke quietly with the pastors, and there were readings from St John's gospel, interrupted only by the occasional silence.

Eventually, at around 2 o'clock the police returned. Everybody stood up. The Akershus pastor read John 6:40 for him for the last time: 'And this is the will of him that sent me, that everyone which seeth the Son, and believeth on him, may have everlasting life: and I will raise him up at the last day.' They went outside where the police cars were waiting, the cortege under heavy guard as they drove slowly through the night to Akershus Fortress, through the gate and up towards the gun tower.

He was led to an open wooden enclosure which had been built up against the tower wall, and under the glaring pencil rays of the searchlights was blindfolded. He protested at this, insisting that he wanted to look death straight in the face. At this point Bergh, who had been standing on the rampart in the group of about ten civilians which had already gathered, stepped down to explain that the blindfold was mandatory. Quisling acquiesced, and was placed with his back against the wall. His arms were tied. He asked Bergh to send his greetings to his wife. As the firing squad was taking up position he proclaimed his innocence for the last time.

At 2.40 in the morning the volley was fired. The police coroner declared Quisling dead.[85]

---

[85] The official police report, signed by chief of police K. Welhaven and police coroner Sten Florelius, records the persons present but neglects to mention the Danish chief of police Aage Seidenfaden, who had sought permission to attend. Seidenfaden's aircraft was due at Oslo airport well before the execution at midnight, but was re-routed due to fog problems. The chief of police decided to postpone the execution until 2 o'clock in honour of the Danish guest, which explains why Quisling had to wait in his cell. Aage Seidenfaden, *I politiets tjeneste* (Copenhagen: 1955), and his original report from 1945 printed in *Dagbladet* 23 October 1985. More details about the incident in Bratteli and Myhre, *Quislings siste dager*.

EPILOGUE

Dangerous?

To his fellow Norwegians, Quisling declared, 'I will be most dangerous after my death.' This, the very last of his political statements, turned out to be scarcely more realistic than most of his former judgements. A good fifty years after his execution it may be safely concluded that Quisling actually turned out to be of no danger whatsoever, either to the world in general or to Norway in particular. The main reason seems to be that the movement he created – the NS party in all its branches and divisions – was uprooted in a giant purge in the years 1945–50 in which altogether some 20,000 Norwegians were sent to gaol and another 30,000 punished by heavy fines or loss of civic rights for having been members, however passive, of the Quisling party.

In its transition to normal democracy from Quisling rule Norway actually penalised far more collaborators than most other countries. France and Denmark both punished some 300 per 100,000 inhabitants, Belgium close to a thousand, The Netherlands some 1,200 of their fellow countrymen. Thus the movements of both Anton Mussert and Frits Clausen came to an effective halt. The rate in Norway was 1,400, larger than in any of the other German-occupied countries during the Second World War.[1] True, the sentences handed out were milder than in many other countries. Executions ran to twenty-five Norwegians and twelve Germans only, about the same rate as in Denmark. Of the Quisling ministers, Hagelin and Skancke were both shot, but Fuglesang and Stang narrowly escaped with life sentences. Prisoners were also normally pardoned less than half-way through the sentence. By 1957 all, even Quisling's cabinet ministers, were free.[2]

The political annihilation of the NS movement turned out to be almost as final and complete as could ever have been envisaged of a movement which had penetrated society with such a thrust as this one. When the former NS members' were returning to society after having served their prison

---

[1] Data compiled by Professor Luc Huyse, University of Leuven.
[2] Stein Ugelvik Larsen, *Modern Europe after Fascism* (1998) II pp. 1777–1844.

sentences, the organisation for their rehabilitation and eventual revocation of the purge never attracted more than some 3,000 members. The organisation scarcely played any political role at all, at least not in spreading any form of 'Nazism' in Norwegian society again. Its newspaper still prints articles and speeches by Vidkun Quisling. Most of them date from the 1930s and scare nobody.

Still, the name Quisling did not die. In fact, his legacy in many ways increased with the intensity of the purge. With the possible exception of Ibsen, no other Norwegian ever became as famous as he did. More books, more newspaper articles have been written on Quisling than on any other of his countrymen, Knut Hamsun, Edvard Grieg and Fridtjof Nansen included. And no other single word from the Nordic languages ever acquired such ubiquity as his family name – a Latinised place-name from Jutland transplanted to the Telemark mountains and from there encompassing the whole world as an international synonym for traitor.

The verdict – the historic verdict – has been harsh, as his trial was, though the image of a monster, as maintained by the prosecution, soon gave way to more human images. Ten years after his trial it was established beyond doubt that he had never played that active role in Hitler's attack on Scandinavia, as the court believed in 1945.[3] Further evidence put forward in a prolific biographical literature suggests that he acted less in sinister vindictiveness and more in accordance with the stuffiness of his own intellectual system, than people believed at the time – precisely as his defence counsel stated. On the other hand, efforts to exculpate him altogether – which are put forward from time to time – have been rebutted as contrary to the very evidence of the case.

Even though his name has acquired world fame, in literal terms it is shrinking. The Telemark branch of the Quislings is by now defunct: no person of that name appears in the local telephone books. His only single descendant in direct parental line is living in the throng of New York city. In Madison, Wisconsin, where some of his cousins established a medical clinic in the inter-war years, the name lives on as a trademark for health and well-being.

Maria died in 1980, bequeathing the vast collection of manuscripts and letters from her husband to the University of Oslo library. The present biography is the first to have benefited in depth from this material, as well as

---

[3] Magne Skodvin, *Striden om okkupasjonsstyret* (1956).

from other collections belonging to the family; in addition to archives in Germany, Italy, Switzerland, the Ukraine, Denmark and the USA.

In her will Maria gave all her Russian antiques to a charity fund. Each year an advertisement carrying the names of 'Maria and Vidkun Quisling' is published in the Oslo press asking for applications from worthy senior citizens. Today, nobody seems worried by political overtones.

Archive sources

AAB Arbeiderbevegelsens Arkiv og Bibliotek, Oslo
ACS Archivo Centrale dello Stato, Roma
   MCP Ministero della Cultura Popolare 181, 386, 387, 388
Alfa Alfa Bibliotek, Oslo
BA Bundesarchiv, Koblenz
   NL 118, Nachlass Goebbels
   NS 6, Parteikanzlei d. NSDAP
   NS 8, Kanzlei Rosenberg
   NS 19, Reichsführer-SS Persönl. Stab
   NS 43, Aussenpolitisches Amt d. NSDAP
   R 2, Reichsfinanzministerium
   R 27, Prisenhof Hamburg
   R 43 II, Reichskanzlei
   R 58, Reichssicherheitshauptamt
   R 70, Pol. Dienststellen
   R 83, Reichskommissariat Norwegen
   58-Zsg, newspaper clippings (Abt. Potsdam)
BA-MA Bundesarchiv Militärarchiv, Freiburg
   N 172, Nachlass Boehm
   RH 2, OKW
   RH 24–21, Gruppe XXI
   RM 6, Ob. bef. Marine
   RM 7, Seekriegsleitung
   RM 11, Marineattachégruppe
   RM 12 II, Marineattaché Oslo
   RM 45 Norw, Komm. Adm. Norwegen
   RW 39, Wehrm. bef. h. Norwegen
CSASPI Central State Archive of the Supreme Power Institutions, Ukraine,
   Kiev

Fund 261, Central Representative ... in all Foreign Organisations of Aid.
   Photocopies of the files provided by Dr Alekseij Sottikov, Kiev
Fy ka Fyresdal kommunearkiv, Fyresdal
IfZ Institut für Zeitgeschichte, München
   ED 69, Huhnhäuser
   F 19/4, Terminkal. Hitler
   MA 107, Dr Hartmann
   MA 110, Hist. Institut
   ZS, Zeugenschrifttum
INO Institutt for Norsk Okkupasjonshistorie, Oslo
LAK Landsarkivet for Sjælland, Copenhagen
   Københavns Politi, Clausen-Sagen
MAE Ministero degli Affari Esteri, Roma: Archivo storico diplomatico
   Affari Politici, Norvegia 1930–40
MCP, Ministero della Cultura Popolare 166
NBA Norges Bondelags arkiv, Oslo
NFM Norges Forsvarsmuseum, Oslo
NHM Norges Hjemmefrontmuseum, Oslo
NRK Norsk rikskringkastning, Oslo programarkivet
   fa – fjernsynsarkivet
   ho – historisk opptaksarkiv
   pa – programarkivet
PAAA Politisches Archiv, Auswärtiges Amt, Bonn
   Bonn Inland II A/B
   Botschaft Rom (Qu) 1934–6
   Büro d. Staatssekretärs
   Dienstelle Ribbentrop
   Gesandtschaft Helsinki
   Gesandtschaft Oslo
   Handakten Etzdorf
   Handakten Luther
   Ha-Pol Wiehl
   Inland I D
   Nachlass Bräuer
RA Riksarkivet, Oslo
   FMK, Førerens og ministerpresidentens kansli
   GS IV 86–8, 147, 1373, generalstaben
   LD, LS landssvikdom, -sak.
   NS, Partirett

NSH, NS Hovedkontor 1933–40

NSP, Nasjonal Samling, partiarkiv 1933–40

NSRH, Nasjonal Samling, Riksledelsen, hovedkontoret 1933–40/1940–5

NSRG, NS Riksledelse, Generalsekretariat 1940–5

PA, Privatarkiv (Frederik Prytz, H. N. Østbye, H. H. Aall et al.)

PANS, Privatarkiv Nasjonal Samling – Generalsekretariat 1933–40

PAQ, Privatarkiv Vidkun Quisling

Statsrådssekretariat

UKA, Undersøkelseskommisjonens arkiv

RAK Rigsarkivet, Copenhagen

  BA, Boveruparkivet (DNSAPs arkiv)

  Rigsadvokaten, Frits Clausen-Sagen

  Privatarkiv 6332, Jørgen Sehested

UBO Universitetsbiblioteket i Oslo, håndskriftsamlingen

  MS fol. 154, Arnold Ræstad

  MS fol. 1988, Fridtjof Nansen

  MS fol. 2894, Jacob S. Worm-Müller

  MS fol. 3920, Vidkun og Maria Quisling

  MS fol. 4096, Quisling-papirene fra Nedre Slottsgt. 3

  brevsamling 1, 48, 337

UNL LNA United Nations Library, Geneva League of Nations Archives

  Int. Commission for Russian Relief, Archives and Info. Leaflets

  C 1321, C 1322, Archives de l'office Nansen

  12/ – / 46805, Armenian Refugee Settlement

  45/ – / 33944; 48/ – / 23458

Bibliography

Agøy, Nils Ivar, *Militæretaten og 'den indre fiende' fra 1905 til 1940*, Oslo 1997.

Akten zur deutschen auswärtigen Politik [ADAP] 1918–1945, Series D 1937–1941 VII–XIII, Frankfurt u. Göttingen, 1962–70; Series E 1941–1945 I–VII, Göttingen 1969–79.

Andenæs, Johs., *Statsforfatningen i Norge*, Oslo 1945.

    Det vanskelige oppgjøret. Rettsoppgjøret etter okkupasjonen, Oslo 1979.

    Et liv blant paragrafer. Juridiske spørsmål slik jeg så dem, Oslo 1987.

Andreyev, Catherine, *Vlasov and the Russian Liberation Movement. Soviet Reality and Emigré Theories*, Cambridge 1987.

Arneberg, Svein T. and Hosar, Kristian, *Vi dro mot nord. Felttoget i Norge i april 1940, skildret av tyske soldater og offiserer*, Oslo 1989.

Aspheim, Odd V. and Hjeltnes, Guri, *Tokt ved neste nymåne. Felttoget i 1940 – invasjon med kamera og panservogn*, Oslo 1990.

Backes, Uwe, Eckhard, Jesse and Zitelmann, Rainer (eds.), *Die Schatten der Vergangenheit. Impulse und Historisierung des Nationalsozialismus*, Frankfurt/a. M.–Berlin 1990.

Barth, Else M., *'Gud, det er meg'. Vidkun Quisling som politisk filosof*, Oslo 1996.

Benewick, Robert, *Political Violence and Public Order. A Study of British Fascism*, London 1969.

Berggrav, Eivind, *Da kampen kom. Noen blad fra startåret*, Oslo 1945.

    Staten og mennesket. Oppgjør og framblikk, Oslo 1945.

    Forgjeves for fred vinteren 1939–40. Forsøk og samtaler i Norden, Berlin og London, Oslo 1960.

    Front Fangenskap Flukt 1942–45, Oslo 1966.

Bergh, Trond and Eriksen, Knut E., *Den hemmelige krigen. Overvåking i Norge 1914–1997* vol. I, Oslo 1998.

Berntsen, Harald, *I malstrømmen. Johan Nygaardsvold 1879–1952*, Oslo 1991.

    To liv – en skjebne. Viggo Hansteen og Rolf Wicktrøm, Oslo 1995.

Birkenes, Jon, *Milorg i D17 (Nedre Telemark) 1940–45*, Skien 1982.

Birn, Ruth B., *Die höheren SS- und Polizeiführer*, Düsseldorf 1986.

Bjørnsen, Bjørn, *Det utrolige døgnet*, Oslo 1977.

    Narvik 1940, Oslo 1980.

Blindheim, Svein, *Nordmenn under Hitlers fane. Dei norske frontkjemparane*, Oslo 1977.

Blom, Ida, *Kampen om Eirik Raudes Land. Pressgruppepolitikk i grønlandsspørsmålet 1921–1931*, Oslo 1973.

Boehm, Hermann, *Norwegen zwischen England und Deutschland. Die Zeit vor und während des zweiten Weltkrieges*, Lippoldsberg 1956.

Bollmus, Reinhard, *Das Amt Rosenberg und seine Gegner. Studien zum Machtkampf im nationalsozialistischen Herrschaftsystem*, Stuttgart 1970.

Borge, Baard B., NS og makten. En studie av den norske førerstaten 1940–1945. Dissertation, UiB 1992.

Borgersrud, Lars, *Nødvendig innsat*, Oslo 1997.

Bowen, H., *German Theories of the Corporative State*, New York 1947.

Bramwell, Anna, *Blood and Soil. Richard Walther Darré and Hitler's 'Green Party'*, Abbotsbrook 1985.

Branner, Hans, *9. april 1940: Et politisk lærestykke?*, Copenhagen 1987.

Bratteli, Tone and Myhre, Hans B., *Quislings siste dager*, Oslo 1992.

Brevig, Hans Olav, *NS- fra parti til sekt 1933–1937*, Oslo [1970].

Brochmann, Caspar, *Mors hus. Hotel Continental gjennom 75 år*, Oslo 1984.

Brodersen, Arvid, *Mellom frontene*, Oslo 1979.

   Fra et nomadliv. Erindringer, Oslo 1982.

Bråtveit, Sigmund, Kornband og hakekors, Dissertation, NLH, 1990.

Bull, Trygve, *Mot Dag og Erling Falk*, Oslo 1955.

Bullock, Alan, *Hitler and Stalin. Parallel Lives*, London 1991.

Burleigh, Michael, *Germany Turns Eastwards. A Study of* Ostforschung *in the Third Reich*, Cambridge 1988.

Carlsen, Ingvald B., *Kirkefronten i Norge under okkupasjonen 1940–1945*, Oslo 1945.

Carr, Edward Hallett, *The Bolshevik Revolution 1917–1923* I–III, Harmondsworth 1966.

   Socialism in One Country 1924–1926 I–II, Harmondsworth 1970.

Castberg, Frede, *Minner om politikk og vitenskap fra årene 1900–1970*, Oslo 1971.

   Rett og Revolusjon i Norge, Oslo 1974.

Cecil, Robert, *The Myth of the Master Race: Alfred Rosenberg and Nazi Ideology*, London 1972.

Christensen, Christian, *Den andre siden*, Oslo 1988.

Christensen, Terje, *Gjerpen bygds historie* II, Skien 1978.

Christie, H. C., *Den norske kirke i kamp*, Oslo 1945.

Christophersen, Egil, *Vestfold i krig*, Sandefjord 1989.

Clausen, Frits, *Volk und Staat im Grenzland* (Internationale Arbeitsgemeinschaft der Nationalisten), Zurich 1936.

Conquest, Robert, *The Harvest of Sorrow*, New York 1989.

Curtis, Lionel, *Civitas Dei: The Commonwealth of God*, London 1938.

Dahl, Hans Fredrik, *Hva er fascisme? Et essay om fascismens historie og sosiologi*, Oslo 1972 (1974).

Dette er London. NRK i krig 1940–45, Oslo 1978.

Dahl, Hans Fredrik, with Hagtvet, Bernt and Hjeltnes, Guri, *Den norske nasjonalsosialismen*, Oslo 1982.

Dahlerus, Birger, *Sista försöket. London–Berlin sommaren 1939*, Stockholm 1945.

Dallin, Alexander, *German Rule in Russia 1941–1945: A Study of Occupation Policies*, London 1957.

Danielsen, Egil, *Norge–Sovjetunionen. Norges utenrikspolitikk overfor Sovjetunionen 1917–1940*, Oslo 1964.

Danielsen, Rolf, *Borgelig oppdemningspolitikk 1918–1940. Høyres historie* II, Oslo 1984.

Danielsen, Rolf and Larsen, Stein Ugelvik (eds.), *Fra idé til dom. Noen trekk fra utviklingen av Nasjonal Samling*, Bergen 1976.

Dawidowicz, Lucy S., *The War against the Jews 1933–1945*, New York 1975.

Debes, Jan, *Sentraladministrasjonens historie V: 1940–1945*, Oslo 1980.

Das deutsche Reich und der zweite Weltkrieg. Militärgeschichtliche Forschungsamt. Vol. II: *Organisation und Mobilisierung des deutschen Machtsbereichs. Erster Halbband*, eds. Bernhard Kroener, Rolf-Dieter Müller and Hans Umbreit, Stuttgart 1988.

Deutscher, Isaac, *The Prophet Outcast. Trotsky 1929–1940, Oxford 1963*.

Didriksen, Jan, *Industrien under hakekorset*, Oslo 1987.

Diesen, Einar, *Maidagene 1945*, Oslo 1982.

Domarus, Max, *Hitler. Reden und Proklamationen 1932–1945* I–II, Neustadt 1963.

Dorenfeldt, L. J., 'Tiden 1929–1979', in *Riksadvokater gjennom 100 år. Jubileumsskrift for riksadvokatembetet*, Oslo 1990.

Dyrhaug, Tore, *Norge okkupert! Tysk etteretning om Norge og nordmennene 1942–45*, Oslo 1985.

Eriksen, Knut Einar and Halvorsen, Terje, *Frigjøring. Norge i krig* VIII. Oslo 1987.

Eriksen, Knut Einar and Niemi, Einar, *Den finske fare. Sikkerhetsproblemer og minoritetspolitikk i nord 1860–1940*, Oslo 1981.

Espeseth, Karo, *Livet gikk videre*, Oslo 1983.

Felice, Renzo de and Goglia, Luigi, *Mussolini. Il mito*, Rome 1983.

Ferguson, Robert, *Gåten Knut Hamsun*, Oslo 1988.

Fest, Joachim C., *Hitler. En biografi*, Oslo 1973.

Feuerstein, Valentin, *Irrwege der Pflicht*, Munich 1963.

Findahl, Theo, *Undergang. Berlin 1939–45*, Oslo 1945.

Lange skygger, Oslo 1964.

Fjellbu, Arne, *Minder fra kamptiden*, Copenhagen 1945.

Fjørtoft, Kjell, *Mot stupet. Norge inn i krigen*, Oslo 1989.

Ulvetiden, Krig og sammenbrudd, Oslo 1990.

På feil side. Den andre krigen, Oslo 1991.

Foss, Gunnar Tønjum, *Den undertrykte presse. Bergenspressen og sensurapparater 1940–45*, Bergen 1990.

Fyrst, Walter, *Min sti*, Oslo 1981.

Gabrielsen, Bjørn, *Menn og politikk. Senterpartiet 1920–1970*, Oslo 1970.

Gilbert, Martin, *Finest Hour: Winston S. Churchill 1939–41. The Churchill Biography* VI, London (1983) 1989.

The Holocaust: The Jewish Tragedy, London 1986.

Second World War, London (1989) 1990.

Giverholt, Helge, *Nyhetsformidling i Norge. Norsk Telegrambyrå 1867–1967*, Oslo 1967.

Gjelsvik, Tore, *Hjemmefronten. Den sivile motstand under okkupasjonen 1940–45*, Oslo 1977.

Goebbels, Joseph, *Dagbok 1945 [28.2.-10.4.1945]. Med et forord av professor Dr philos. Magne Skodvin*, Oslo 1978.

Die Tagebücher von Joseph Goebbels. Sämtliche Fragmente, ed. Elke Fröhlich, Part 1: *Aufzeichnungen 1924–41*, vol. 4: *1.1.1940–8.7.1941*, Munich 1987. Part 2: *Diktate 1941–1945*, Munich 1993–6.

Gogstad, Anders Chr., *Helse og hakekors*, Bergen 1991.

Greve, Tim, *Det Norske Storting gjennom 150 år*, III: *Tidsrommet 1908–1964*, Oslo 1964.

Fridtjof Nansen II: *1905–1930*, Oslo 1974.

Bergen i krig I, Bergen 1978.

Spionjakt i Norge. Norsk overvåkningstjeneste i tiden før 1940, Oslo 1982.

Grimnes, Ole Kristian, *Hjemmefrontens ledelse*, Oslo 1977.

Overfall. Norge i krig I, Oslo 1984.

Veien inn i krigen. Regjeringen Nygaardsvolds krigsvedtak i 1940, Oslo 1987.

Günther, Hans Friedrich K., *Mein Eindruck von Adolf Hitler*, Pähl 1969.

Hambro, C. J., *De første måneder*, Oslo 1945.

Hamsun, Tore, *Efter år og dag. Selvbiografi*, Oslo 1990.

Hanisch, Ted, *Om sigøynerspørsmålet*, Oslo 1976.

Hannsson, Per and Jensen, Johan O., *Den farlige våren*, Oslo 1983.

Harrison, John R., *The Reactionaries*, London 1966.

Hartmann, Sverre, *Spillet om Norge*, Oslo 1958.

Fører uten folk. Quisling som politisk og psykologisk problem, Oslo 1959

Nytt lys over kritiske faser i Norges historie under annen verdenskrig, Oslo 1965.

Hartmann, Sverre and Vogt, Johan, *Aktstykker om den tyske finanspolitikk i Norge 1940–45*, Oslo 1958.

Hauner, Milan, *Hitler: A Chronology of his Life and Time*, London 1983.

Hayes, Paul M., *Quisling: The Career and Political Ideas of Vidkun Quisling 1887–1945*, Newton Abbot 1971.

Heger, Wanda, *Hver fredag foran porten*, Oslo 1984.

Heinrich, Walter, *Das Ständewesen*, Jena 1932.

Der Faschismus. Staat und Wirtschaft im neuen Italien, Munich 1932.

Hemming-Sjöberg, A., *Domen över Quisling*, Stockholm 1946.

Hewins, Ralph, *Quisling: Prophet without Honour*, London 1965 (*Profet uten ære*, Oslo 1966).

Hillgruber, Andreas (ed.), *Staatsmänner und Diplomaten bei Hitler* II, Frankfurt a. M. 1970.

Der 2. Weltkrieg. Kriegsziele und Strategie der grossen Mächte, Stuttgart 1989.

Hirschfield, Gerhard, *Nazi Rule and Dutch Collaboration: The Netherlands under German Occupation 1940–45*, Oxford 1988.

Hitler, Adolf, *Mein Kampf* I–II, Munich 1934.

Hjeltnes, Guri, *Hverdagsliv. Norge i krig* V, Oslo 1986.

Avisoppgjøret etter 1945, Oslo 1990.

Hjort, J. B., *Justismord*, Oslo 1952.

Hofer, Walther, *Nationalsocialismen. En dokumentarisk fremstilling*, Copenhagen 1963 (Frankfurt a. M. 1957).

Holtsmark, Sven G., (ed.), *Norge–Sovjetunionen 1917–1955. En utenrikspolitisk dokumentasjon*. Oslo 1995.

Hoprekstad, Olav, *Frå lærarstriden*, Bergen 1946.

Hubatsch, Walther, *Weserübung. Die deutsche Besetzung von Dänemark und Norwegen 1940*, 2nd edn, Berlin 1960.

Hughes, H. Stewart, *Oswald Spengler. A Critical Estimate*, New York 1952.

Huntford, Roland, *Nansen. The Explorer as Hero*, London 1997.

Høidal, Oddvar K., *Quisling. En studie i landssvik*, Oslo 1988. Also as *Quisling. A Study in Treason*, Oslo 1989.

Hølaas, Odd, *De talte dager. Kronikker og essays*, Oslo 1946.

Hæstrup, Jørgen, et al. (eds.), *Besættelsens Hvem Hvad Hvor*, Copenhagen 1985.

Irgens-Saken, Oslo 1948.

Irving, David, *Goebbels. Mastermind of the Third Reich*, London 1996.

Jensen, Johan O., *De nære årene. Norske kvinner og menn forteller om krigen*, Oslo 1986.

Jensen, Tom B., *Nasjonal Samlings periodiske skrifter 1933–1945. En bibliografi*, Oslo 1992.

Jerneck, Benkt, *Folket uten frykt. Norge 1942–43*, Oslo 1945.

Johansen, Per Ole, *Menstadskonflikten 1931*, Oslo 1977.

Oss selv nærmest. Norge og jødene 1914–1943, Oslo 1984.

Samfunnets pansrede neve, Oslo 1989.

Johnson, Thomas Frank, *International Tramps: From Chaos to Permanent World Peace*, London 1938.

de Jong, Louis, *Die deutsche Fünfte Kolonne im Zweiten Weltkrieg*, Stuttgart 1959.

Juritzen, Arve, *Privatmennesket Quisling og hans to kvinner*, Oslo 1988.

Kedward, H. R., *Occupied France: Collaboration and Resistance 1940–44*, Oxford 1985.

Keilhau, Wilhelm, *Det norske folks liv og historie i vår egen tid*, Oslo 1938.

Kersaudy, François, *Norway 1940*, London 1990.

Vi stoler på England. 1939–1949, Oslo 1991.

Kildal, Arne, *Presse- og litteraturfronten under okkupasjonen 1940–45*, Oslo 1945.

Kjeldstadli, Sverre, *Hjemmestyrkene. Hovedtrekk av den militære motstand under okkupasjonen I*, Oslo 1959.

Knudsen, Harald Franklin, *Jeg var Quislings sekretær*, Copenhagen 1951.

Koht, Halvdan, *Rikspolitisk dagbok 1933–40*, Norsk Historisk Kjeldeskrift-Institutt v/ Steinar Kjærheim, Oslo 1985.

Kolsrud, Ole, 'Kollaborasjon og imperialisme. Quisling-regjeringens "Austrveg"-drøm 1941–44', *Historisk Tidsskrift* 1988/3, pp. 241–70.

Kreyberg, Leiv, *Efter ordre – eller uten*, Oslo 1976.

Kristiansen, Laila, NS og nyordningen av arbeidslivet, Dissertation, UiO 1972.

Kroener, Bernhard R., Müller, Rolf-Dieter and Umbreit, Hans, *Das deutsche Reich und der Zweite Weltkrieg [DRZW]*, V: Stuttgart 1988.

Kuusisto, Seppo, *Alfred Rosenberg in der nationalsozialistischen Aussenpolitik 1933–1939*, Helsinki 1984.

Kweit, Konrad, *Reichskommissariat Niederlande. Versuch und Scheitern nationalsozialistischer Neuordnung*, Stuttgart 1968.

Lacoutre, Jean, *De Gaulle: The Rebel*, London 1990.

Lammers, Karl Christian, *Fascination og forbrydelse. De nazistiske tid 1919–1945*, Copenhagen 1992.

de Lange, Trygve, *Quisling-saken*, Oslo 1945.

Langfeldt, Gabriel, *Gåten Vidkun Quisling*, Oslo 1969.

Langholm, Sivert and Sejersted, Francis (eds.), *Vandringer, Festskrift til Ingrid Semmingsen*, Oslo 1980.

Lannung, Hermod, *Min russiske ungdom 1917–19 og 1922–24*, Copenhagen 1978.

Laquer, Walter, *The Terrible Secret*, London 1980 (*Det ufattelige var sant. Historien om hvordan Vesten fikk kjennskap til Endlösung*, Oslo 1991).

Larsen, Stein U., ed., *Modern Europe after Fascism 1943–1980*, Social Science Monograph, Boulder 1998.

Larsen, Stein U., Hagtvet, Bernt and Myklebust, Jan P. (eds.), *Who Were the Fascists? Social Roots of European Fascism*, Bergen 1980.

Lavik, Nils Johan, *Makt og galskap. En psykiater i konfrontasjon med nazismen*, Oslo 1990.

Ledeen, Michael, *Universal Fascism*, New York 1972.

Leggett, George, *The Cheka: Lenin's Political Police*, Oxford 1981.

Liddell Hart, B. H., *The Other Side of the Hill: Germany's Generals, their Rise and Fall, with their own Account of Military Events 1939–1945*, London 1948, (revised edn London 1951/1978).

Den annen Verdenskrig, Oslo 1971.

Lie, Haakon, *Martin Tranmæl. Et bål av vilje*, Oslo 1988.

Lied, Jonas, *Sidelights on the Economic Situation in Russia*, Moscow 1922.
  Over de høye fjelle, Oslo 1946.
Lindboe, Asbjørn, *Fra de urolige tredveårene. Dagboksnedtegnelser og kommentarer*, Oslo 1965.
Loock, Hans Dietrich, *Quisling, Rosenberg und Terboven. Zur Vorgeschichte und Geschichte der nationalsozialistischen Revolution in Norwegen*, Stuttgart 1970.
Lossberg, Bernhard von, *Im Wehrmachtsführungsstab*, Hamburg 1950.
Lukacs, John, *The Duel: Hitler vs. Churchill 10 May – 31 July 1940*, London 1990.
Lutzhöft, Hans-Jürgen, *Der nordische Gedanke in Deutschland 1920–1940*, Stuttgart 1971.
Lykke-Seest, Peter, *Omkring Quisling-prosessen. Iakttagelser og inntrykk*, Oslo 1945.
Lyng, John, *Brytningsår. Erindringer 1923–53*, Oslo 1972.
Lødrup, Hans, *Læreaksjonens sanne bakgrunn. Noen vitneprov*, Kristiansand 1948.
Manchester, William, *The Caged Lion: Winston Spencer Churchill 1932–40*, London (1989) 1990.
Matlock, Siegfried (ed.), *Danmark i Hitlers hånd. Rigsbefuldmegtiget Werner Bests beretning om sin besættelsespolitik i Danmark*, Åbenrå 1989.
Maurseth, Per, *Gjennom kriser til makt. Arbeiderbevegelsens historie i Norge* III, Oslo 1987.
Mayer, Arno J., *Why did the Heavens not Darken? The 'Final Solution' in History*, New York 1988.
Melsom, Odd, *På nasjonal uriaspost. Nødvendig supplement til okkupasjonshistorien*, Oslo 1975.
  Nasjonal Samling og fagorganisasjonen. Supplement til okkupasjonshistorien II, Oslo 1977.
  Fra kirke- og kulturkampen under okkupasjonen. Supplement til okkupasjonshistorien III, Oslo 1980.
Mendelsohn, Oskar, *Jødenes historie i Norge gjennom 300 år*, I–II, 1660–1940, Oslo 1989.
Meyer, Haakon, *Det norske Arbeiderparti. Samtlige landsmøtebeslutninger, resolusjoner, valg etc. 1912–1933*, Oslo 1934.
  Bak Moskvaprosessene, Oslo 1937.
  Et annet syn, Oslo 1952.
Michalka, Wolfgang (ed.), *Der Zweite Weltkrieg: Analysen, Grundzüge, Forschungsbilanz*, Munich 1989.
Milorg D 13 i kamp. Episoder fra det hemmelige militære motstandsarbeid i Oslo og omegn under okkupasjonen nedtegnet etter Milorg-rapporter og personlige beretninger, Oslo 1961.
Mjøen, Jon Alfred, *Germanen oder Slaven? Die Mongolisierung Europas*. Berlin 1917.
Mogens, Victor, *Tyskerne, Quisling, og vi andre*, Oslo 1945.
Mohler, Armin, *Die konservative Revolution in Deutschland 1918–1932. Ein Handbuch*, Darmstadt 1989.

Molland, Einar, *Norges Kirkehistorie i det 19. århundre*, II, Oslo 1979.

Montgomery, Ingun and Larsen, Stein (eds.), *Kirken, krisen og krigen*, Bergen 1982.

Mosley, Nicholas, *Beyond the Pale, Sir Oswald Mosley and Family 1933–80*, London 1983.

Mosley, Oswald, *My Life*, London 1968.

Myklebust, Jan Petter, Hvem var de norske nazistene? Sammenheng mellom sosial, økonomisk og politisk bakgrunn og medlemskap i Nasjonal Samling, Dissertation, UiB 1974.

Nag, Martin, *Kollontaj i Norge*, Oslo 1981.

Nansen, Fridtjof, *Gjennem Sibirien*, Oslo 1914

   Gjennem Armenia, Oslo 1927.

   Gjennem Kaukasus til Volga, Oslo 1927.

   Brev. Utgitt for Nansenfondet av Steinar Kjærheim IV, V, Oslo 1966, 1978.

Nansen, Odd, *Langs veien. Opplevelser, møter og samtaler*, Oslo 1970.

Nerbøvik, Jostein, *Bønder i kamp. Bygdefolkets krisehjelp 1924–1935*, Oslo 1991.

Neulen, Hans Werner, *An deutscher Seite. Internationale Freiwillige von Wehrmacht und Waffen-SS*, Munich 1985.

   Europa und das 3. Reich. Einigungsbestrebungen im deutschen Machtbereich 1939–1945, Munich 1987.

Nicosia, Francis R.,*The Third Reich and the Palestine Question*, Austin 1985.

Noack, Ulrich, *Norwegen zwischen Friedensvermittlung und Fremdherrschaft*, Krefeld 1952.

   Ein Leben aus freier Mitte. Festschrift zum 60. Geburtstag, Göttingen 1961.

Noakes, Jeremy and Pridham, Geoffrey (eds.), *Nazism: A History in Documents and Eyewitness Accounts* I–III, Exeter 1983–8.

Norge i krig. Fremmedåk og frihetskamp 1940–1945 I–VIII, ed. Magne Skodvin, Oslo 1983–7.

Norges Bank under okkupasjonen, Oslo 1945.

Norges krig 1940–1945, I–III, ed. Sverre Steen, Oslo 1947–50.

Norland, Andreas, *Hårde tider. Fedrelandslaget i norsk politikk*, Oslo 1973.

Norsk krigsleksikon 1940–45, ed. H. F. Dahl et al., Oslo 1995.

Nøkleby, Berit, *Nyordning. Norge i krig* II, Oslo 1985.

   Holdningskamp. Norge i krig IV, Oslo 1986.

   Josef Terboven – Hitlers mann i Norge, Oslo 1992.

   Skutt blir den. Tysk bruk av dødsstraff i Norge, Oslo 1996.

Næss, Hans Eyvind (ed.), *Partiet og politikken. Stavanger Høyre 1883–1983*, Stavanger 1983.

Næss, Hans Eyvind et al. (eds.), *Folkestyre i bygd og by. Norske kommuner gjennom 150 år.* Oslo 1987.

Ofte, Jon H., *Me ville vera med. Ei reise gjennom dei fem krigsår*, Tokke 1984.

Om landssviksoppgjøret. Innstilling fra et utvalg nedsatt for å skaffe tilvei materiale til en innberetning fra Justisdepartementet til Storting, Gjøvik 1962.

Oppenheim, Janet, *The Other World. Spiritualism and Psychical Research in England 1850–1914*, Cambridge 1985.

Ottmer, Hans-Martin, *'Weserübung'. Der deutsche Angriff auf Dänemark und Norwegen im April 1940*, Munich 1994.

Ottosen, Kristian, *I slik en natt. Historien om deportasjonen av jøder fra Norge*, Oslo 1994.

Paulsen, Helge (ed.), *1940 – fra nøytral til okkupert*, Oslo 1969.

   'Terboven i konflikt med Kriegsmarine', in Samtidshistorisk Forskningsgruppe (ed.), *Motstandskamp, strategi og marinepolitikk*, Oslo 1972.

Petersen, Hans Uwe, *Hitlerflüchtlinge im Norden. Asyl und politisches Exil 1933–1945*, Kiel 1991.

Petrick, Fritz, *Der 'Leichtmetallausbau Norwegen' 1940–1945. Eine Studie zur deutschen Expansions- und Okkupationspolitik in Nordeuropa*. Frankfurt 1992.

Pichler, J. Hanns, *Othmar Spann oder die Welt als Ganzes*, Böhlau 1988.

Picker, Henry (ed.), *Hitlers Tischgespräche im Führerhauptquartier*, Stuttgart 1976.

Pipes, Richard, *The Russian Revolution*, New York 1990.

Poulsen, Henning, *Besættelsesmagten og de danske nazister. Det politiske forhold mellem tyske myndigheder og nazistiske kredse i Danmark 1940–1943*, Copenhagen 1970.

Pryser, Tore, *Klassen og nasjonen 1935–1946. Arbeiderbevegelsens historie i Norge* IV, Oslo 1988.

   Arbeiderbevegelsen og Nasjonal Samling. Om venstrestrømninger i Quislings parti, Oslo 1991.

Quisling, Maria, *Dagbok og andre efterlatte papirer*, ed. Øystein Parmann, Oslo 1980.

Rees, Philip, *Fascism and Pre-Fascism in Europe 1890–1945. A Bibliography of the Extreme Right*, Brighton, Sussex 1984.

Regjeringen og hjemmefronten under krigen. Aktstykker utgitt av Stortinget, Oslo 1948.

Reitinger, Gerald, *The Final Solution*, London 1953.

   The SS: Alibi of a Nation (2nd edn), London 1981.

Reuth, Ralf Georg, *Goebbels*, Munich 1990.

Riisnæs, Sverre, *Den nye rettsstat på nasjonalsosialistisk grunn*, Oslo 1941.

Ringdal, Nils Johan, *Mellom barken og veden. Politiet under okkupasjonen*, Oslo 1987.

   Gal mann til rett tid. NS-minister Sverre Riisnæs. En psykobiografi, Oslo 1989.

Ringnes, Ellef, *Bak okkupasjonens kulisser*, Oslo [1950].

Riste, Olav, *'London-Regjeringa'. Norge i krigsalliansen 1940–45* I (1940–2): *Prøvetid*, Oslo 1973; II (1942–5): *Vegen heim*, Oslo 1978.

   Utefront, Oslo 1987.

Rudeng, Erik, *Sjokoladekongen. Johan Throne Holst – en biografi*, Oslo 1989.

Rødder, Sverre, *'Min ære er troskap'. Om politiminister Jonas Lie*, Oslo 1990.

Røed, Ole Torleif, *Fra krigens folkerett*, Oslo 1945.

Ræder, Gudrun, *De uunværlige flinke*, Oslo 1975.

Sandvik, Harald, *Krigsår. Med Kompani Linge i trening og kamp*, Oslo 1979.

Sars, Michael and Tranøy, Knut Erik, *Tysklandsstudentene*, Oslo 1946.

Schiøtz, Johannes, *Den militære Høiskoles historie 1817–1917*, Kristiania 1917.

Schjelderup, Ferdinand, *Fra Norges kamp for retten. 1940 i Høyesterett*, Oslo 1945.

På bred front, Oslo 1947.

Over bakkekammen. 1943–1944, Oslo 1949.

Schramm, P. E. (ed.), *Kriegstagebuch des Oberkommandos der Wehrmacht (Wehr-machtführungsstab) 1940–1945*, I: *1. August 1940 – 31. Dezember 1941*; II: *1. Januar 1942 – 31. Dezember 1942*; III: *1. Januar 1943 – 31. Dezember 1943*, Frankfurt a. M. 1965.

Schübeler, Ludwig, *Kirkekampen slik jeg så den*, Oslo 1956.

Seim, Jardar, *Hvordan Hovedavtalen av 1935 ble til*, Oslo 1972.

Seip, Didrik Arup, *Hjemme og fiendeland*, Oslo 1946.

Seraphim, Hans-Günther (ed.), *Das politische Tagebuch Alfred Rosenbergs aus den Jahren 1934/35 und 1939/40*, Göttingen 1956.

Short, K. R. M. and Dolezel, Stephan (eds.), *Hitler's Fall and the Newsreel Witness*, London 1988.

Skodvin, Magne, 'Det store fremstøt', in Sverre Steen (ed.), *Norges krig 1940–1945* II, Oslo 1948.

Striden om okkupasjonsstyret i Norge fram til 25. september 1940, Oslo 1956.

Samtid og historie. Utvalde artiklar og avhandlingar, Oslo 1975.

Norsk historie 1939–45. Krig og okkupasjon, Oslo 1991.

Skogen, Olav, *Ensom krig mot Gestapo*, Oslo 1992.

Smedal, Gustav, *Patriotisme og landssvik*, Oslo 1949.

Smelser, Ronald and Zitelmann, Rainer, *Die braune Elite. 22 biographische Skizzen*, Darmstadt 1989.

Smith, Bradley F. and Petersen, Agnes F. (eds.), *Heinrich Himmler: Geheimreden 1933 bis 1945*, Frankfurt a. M. 1974.

Smith, Denis Mack, *Mussolini's Roman Empire*, London 1976.

Snyder, Louis L., *Encyclopaedia of the Third Reich*, New York 1989.

Spann, Othmar, *Der wahre Staat*, 1921, 1931.

Speer, Albert, *Erindringer*, Oslo 1970.

Spengler, Oswald, *Untergang des Abendlandes* I–II, Munich 1920–2.

Preussentum und Sozialismus, Munich 1922.

Politische Schriften, Munich 1934.

Briefe, ed. Anton Koktanek, Munich 1963.

Sprenger, Heinrich, *Heinrich Sahm. Kommunalpolitiker und Staatsmann*, Cologne 1969.

Stangeland, Charles, *Amerikanisk Imperialisme*, Oslo 1942.

Steen, Sverre, *Rikrådsforhandlingene. Bilag 9 til Innnstilling fra Undersøkelseskommis-jonen av 1945*, Oslo 1947.

Steenstrup, Knut, *Dilemma. Opplevelser, minner og meninger*, Oslo 1989.

Stenersen, Sam and Stenersen, Sten, *Flyalarm. Luftkrigen i Norge 1939–45*, Oslo 1991.

Steltzer, Theodor, *Sechzig Jahre Zeitgenosse*, Munich 1966.

Sternhell, Zeev, *Neither Right nor Left. Fascist Ideology in France*, Berkeley 1986.

Strand, Tor, *Vår vei heter Nordveien, Norge. En bok om Erling Winsnes*, Oslo 1945.

Sundet, Olav, *Johan Scharffenberg. Samfunnslege og stridsmann*, Oslo 1977.

Sørensen, Jon, *Fridtjof Nansens saga*, Oslo 1931; 2nd edn, I–II, Oslo 1940.

Sørensen, Øystein, *Fra Marx til Quisling. Fem sosialisters vei til NS*, Oslo 1983.

   Hitler eller Quisling. Ideologiske brytninger i Nasjonal Samling 1940–45, Oslo 1989.

   Solkors og solidaritet. Høyreautoritær samfunnstenkning i Norge ca. 1930–1945, Oslo 1991.

Takala, Hannu and Tham, Henrik (eds.), *Krig og moral. Kriminalitet og kontroll i Norden under andre verdenskrig*, Oslo 1987.

Taylor, A. J. P., *English History 1914–1945*, London 1965.

Thowsen, Atle, *Den norske krigsforsikring for Skip-Gjensidig Forening – 1935–1985* I, Bergen 1988.

Thulstrup, Åke, *Med lock och pock. Tyska försök att påverka svensk opinion*, Stockholm 1962.

Tusa, Ann and Tusa, John, *The Nuremberg Trial*, New York 1985.

Ulateig, Egil, *Raud Kriger, raud spion*, Oslo 1989.

Ustvedt, Yngvar, *Verdensrevolusjonen på Hønefoss. En beretning om Leo Trotskijs opphold i Norge*, Oslo 1974.

Vogt, Benjamin, *Mennesket Vidkun og forræderen Quisling*, Oslo 1965.

Voksø, Per (ed.), *Krigens dagbok. Norge 1940–45*, Oslo 1984.

Walker, Christopher J., *Armenia. The Survival of a Nation* (2nd edn), London 1990.

Wasberg, Gunnar Christie, *Aftenposten i hundre år, 1860–1960*, Oslo 1960.

Weidling, Paul, *Health, Race and German Politics between National Unification and Nazism 1870–1945*, Cambridge 1989.

Weinberg, Gerhard L., *The Foreign Policy of Hitler's Germany. Diplomatic Revolution in Europe 1933–36*, Chicago 1970.

Weissman, Benjamin M., *Herbert Hoover and Famine Relief*, Princeton 1974.

Weizsäcker, Ernst von, *Die Weizsäcker-Papiere 1933–50*, ed. Leonidas E. Hill, Frankfurt a. M. 1974.

Wiesener, Albert, *Nordmenn for tysk krigsrett 1940–1942*, Oslo 1954.

   Seierherrens justis, Oslo 1964.

Wiskemann, Elisabeth, *The Rome–Berlin Axis. A Study of the Relations between Hitler and Mussolini*, London 1966.

Wyller, Thomas C., *Fra okkupasjonsårenes maktkamp. Nasjonal Samlings korporativ nyordningsforsøk 9. april 1940 – 1. februar 1942*, Oslo 1953.

   Nyordning og motstand. En framstilling og en analyse av organisasjonenes politiske funksjon under den tyske okkupasjon 25.9.1940–25.9.1942, Oslo 1958.

Wyller, Trygve, *Aprildagene 1940. Av Stavangers historie under okkupasjonen 1940–1945*, Stavanger 1959.

Wärenstam, Eric, *Fascismen och nazismen i Sverige 1920–1940*, Stockholm 1970.

Zitelmann, Rainer, *Hitler. Selbstverständnis eines Revolutionärs* (2nd edn), Stuttgart 1989.

Ørvik, Nils, *Norsk sikkerhetspolitikk*, Oslo 1962.

Sikkerhetspolitikken 1920–1939 I–II, Oslo 1960–1.

Østvedt, Einar, *På gamle tufter. Ti Telemarks-profiler*, Skien 1975.

Skien Gymnas gjennom halvannet sekel, Skien 1972.

BOOKS BY VIDKUN QUISLING

Om at bebodde verdner finnes utenom jorden, Oslo 1929.

Fra det daglige liv i Russland, Oslo [1930].

Russland og vi, Oslo 1930; 2nd edn 1941.

Russia and Ourselves, London 1931.

Politica de Oriente y Occidente, Madrid 1935.

Quisling har sagt I, Oslo 1940.

Quisling har sagt II, Oslo 1941.

Russland und wir, Oslo 1942.

Quisling ruft Norwegen! Reden und Aufsätze, Munich 1942.

For Norges frihet og selvstendighet [Quisling har sagt III], Oslo 1943.

Die nationale Revolution in Norwegen. Co-author Gulbrand Lunde, Oslo 1942.

Quisling har sagt IV, Oslo [1944].

Index

Hitler, Adolf (*cont.*)
Poland, 142; last diplomatic
appointment, 346; meeting with
Hagelin, 182, 300–4; meetings with
Quisling, 2, 150–6, 199–200, 214,
236, 251, 309, 340–5, 345–6, 349;
Mein Kampf, 36, 272; and Mussolini,
114; and NS coup, 175; and
occupation of Denmark, 174; and
peace settlement with Norway, 304,
310; plans for invasion of Norway,
157, 163–72; rejection of Quisling's
plans for conscription, 295; rejection
of Quisling's ultimatum, 270, 272;
removal of Quisling from office, 176,
183–6, 227; suicide, 360; view of
Quisling, 156–7, 205–35; war with
Russia, 226–7, 237, 263, 267–72,
290–4, 297, 300
Hjort, Johan B., 70, 74, 89–90, 95, 97,
101, 103, 105, 122, 124, 177, 181,
191–2, 197–8; arrested by SS, 240;
demand for shake-up in NS
leadership, 128; feud with Quisling,
128, 177, 198; head of Hird, 105; and
Jewish question, 121; Hjort–Mogens–
Jacobsen circle, 177, 181, 191–2;
negotiation with Terboven, 198
Hodann, Max, 119
Hodder and Stoughton, 130
Hohenstein, Prince von, 140, 147
Holdtfodt, General, 71
Holland, 73, 111, 114, 133, 156, 187,
196, 200, 203, 207, 219, 242, 246, 285,
298, 308, 361, 382
Holst, Anna, 89
Holst, Johan Throne, 74, 75, 89
Home Front, 206, 244–5, 357, 363–72,
380, 391, 407, 413; *see also* resistance
homosexuality, 119
Homvatn, 332
Hønefoss, 88, 122
Hoover, Herbert Clark, 44
Hordaland, 316
Horthy, Miklos, 301, 308, 316
Hotel Adlon, 25, 302
Hotel Astoria, 168
Hotel Bellevue, 302
Hotel Bristol, 143, 188
Hotel Britannia, 179

Hotel Continental, 161, 166, 170–2, 182,
184
Hotel d'Angleterre, 166
Hotel Frankfurter Hof, 223
Hotel Kaiserhof, 194, 302
Høyre, *see* Conservative Party
Hufudstadsbladet, 338
Hundseid, Jens, 84, 91–5, 98, 402
Hungary, 236, 301, 307
Husserl, Edmund, 8
Hustad, Anne-Margrethe, 103
Hustad, Tormod, 179, 194, 225
Hvide family, 331
Hvoslef, Ragnvald, 70, 153–4, 169, 179,
180, 356

Ibsen, Henrik, 22, 279, 354
Iceland, 186, 279, 304
IG Farben, 117
Independent Liberal Party (Frisinnede
Folkeparti), 93
independent ministers in Commissarial
Council, 209
Independent People's Party, 100
Industrial Protective Force, 345
Inner Mission (Indre Misjon), 14
intelligence, British, 166; Danish, 166;
French, 166; German, 145, 165–6
Internationale Arbeitsgemeinschaft, 125
Irgens, Kjeld Stub, 208–9
Iron Guard, 111
Istvestija, 322
Italy, 55, 80, 110, 114, 115, 116, 236,
252, 265, 301, 302, 306, 309, 315–17

Jacobsen, Hans S., 102, 114, 118, 159,
177, 189, 191, 197, 240, 291, 414
Jahr, Per, 341
Japan, 187, 235–6, 252, 265, 290, 309
Jessheim, 337
Jewish refugees in Norway, 119
Jews in Norway: and anti-Semitism,
118–19, 343; arrests of, 283–4; in
Berg, 284; and the Constitution, 120;
deportations of, 287–8, 289, 382;
executions of, 328, 386, 405;
expropriation of property of, 223–4,
286; identity cards, 283; marriage laws
concerning, 224, 284; Nuremberg
laws, 206; registration of, 283;